Principles of Financial Management

McGraw-Hill Series in Finance

Professor Charles A. D'Ambrosio, Consulting Editor

Curran: Principles of Financial Management

Sharpe: Portfolio Theory and Capital Markets

Principles of Financial Management

Ward S. Curran

Associate Professor of Economics and
George M. Ferris Lecturer in Corporation
Finance and Investments

Trinity College, Hartford, Connecticut

McGraw-Hill Book Company   New York, St. Louis, San Francisco, Düsseldorf, London, Mexico, Panama, Sydney, Toronto

TO

KATHLEEN

Principles of Financial Management

Library of Congress Catalog Card Number 79–99196

14923

1234567890 MAMM 79876543210

This book was set in Baskerville by European Printing Corp.
Ltd., and printed on permanent paper and bound by
The Maple Press Company.   The designer was Merill Haber;
the drawings were done by B. Handelman Associates, Inc.
The editors were Basil G. Davidson, Jr. and John M. Morriss.
Stuart Levine supervised the production.

Preface

This book is designed for use in a one-quarter or one-semester introductory course in business finance, whether the course is taught in a business school or in an economics curriculum of a liberal arts college.

In organizing the material I have tried to take into consideration both the similarities and the differences in approach to the subject within the two curricula. Thus, Chapters 1, 2, 3, 4, and 5 provide the necessary foundation for developing the principles of financial management in both curricula. At the same time, some students, particularly those in a business school curriculum, may have had considerable exposure to business law and are acquainted with the fundamentals of the income tax law. If so, the instructor may save time by omitting Chapter 2 and the appendix on tax reform in Chapter 24.

In Parts 2 and 3 of the book I have developed the principles of financial management, or what might be called microfinancial theory. The key chapters are 6, 7, 8, 11, and 12. In a systematic manner they deal with the principles of fixed-asset management, current-asset management, and the composition of financing. The analysis of business risk is contained in Chapter 7. It is applied to both fixed- and current-asset management, that is, to the material in Chapters 6 and 8. Those who prefer to emphasize the inventory approach to cash management will find the tools for doing so in Chapter 11.

In Chapter 12 I have developed the principles underlying the cost of capital. Here, of course, I have given consideration to the question of financial risk, relating it to the optimum capital structure.

Those wishing to place additional emphasis on working capital will find Chapters 9 and 10 on cash management and accounts receivable a useful extension of the principles developed. Similarly, further discussion of the composition of financing can be found in Chapters 13, 14, 15, and 16. Of these, perhaps Chapters 14, and 15 on long-term sources of funds are the most fundamental. Further, because of its importance, Chapter 16 on lease financing can provide the instructor with a useful addition to the discussion of long-term sources of funds.

In Chapter 17 I have related the material on the historical sources of funds to the cost-of-capital model developed in Chapter 12.

Part 4 of the book contains a discussion of the capital markets. The instructor can relate this material to the firm's supply curve of capital. He can also tie it to what might be called the principles of macrofinancial theory. Thus, in Chapter 18, I have developed a framework for viewing the capital markets and the role which financial intermediaries play. In Chapter 19 I have focused specifically on the new issues market for corporate securities and in Chapter 20 on the secondary or trading markets. In Chapter 21 I have treated at some length the impact of regulation of the securities markets on the supply of funds.

How much of the material in Part Four the instructor wishes to cover will depend on the time available and the extent to which the subjects are treated in other courses in the curriculum. In some schools, perhaps the material in Chapter 18 is covered in a money and banking course. The material in Chapter 19, of course, is traditionally a part of a business finance course. In Chapters 20 and 21 I am admittedly trying to break new ground in the teaching of the basic course in the subject. Yet the proposition developed in Chapter 20, that the current market price of the common stock can be viewed as an observation on a random variable, may be related to the cost-of-capital model developed in Chapter 12. The material in Chapter 21 reflects my own interest in the impact of regulation. Economists are just beginning to build models to explain the impact of regulation of the securities markets on the supply of capital and on financial flows.

Part 5 of this text consists of two chapters. Chapter 22 contains a discussion of corporate mergers and Chapter 23 a discussion of reorganizations in bankruptcy. I have related both to the principles of financial management. Each chapter can be viewed as an extension of the analysis.

Part 6 consists of one chapter. In it I have pointed out the limitations of the goal toward which I have directed the analysis, that is, maximization of the market value of the owners' equity. I have compared this goal with wealth maximization and with optimizing between two or more objectives. Moreover, I have given consideration to the conflicts in objectives which can arise when ownership is divorced from control.

With the exception of the first or introductory chapter, I have provided at the end of each a summary of the material presented, questions and problems, and selected references. Moreover, I have also supplied each chapter with a prefatory comment which I hope will be of benefit to those reading the text. Each prefatory comment will give the reader, particularly the student, an idea of what he should look for in the chapter and how to relate it to the treatment as a whole.

The book, of course, makes use of numerous ideas of authors who have contributed to the growing body of literature in business finance. I have endeavored to acknowledge these contributions where they appear.

I am also deeply indebted to several people for their helpful comments at various stages in preparing the manuscript. For their substantive criticisms of its contents, I wish to thank Professors Charles A. D'Ambrosio, University of Washington and consulting editor for McGraw-Hill; John J. Brosky, also of the University of Washington; Thomas C. Committee, University of West Florida; John S. Day, Purdue University; James A. Gentry, University of Illinois; John J. Klein, Georgia State College; James T. Murphy, Tulane University; Harold W. Stevenson, University of Minnesota; Henry C. Wallich, Yale University; and Chaucer F. Yang, State University of New York at Albany.

I wish to thank my father, Nathaniel B. Curran, John F. Butler, Trinity College, and David VanDyck, Kingswood School, for their helpful comments on style. I am also grateful to our department secretary, Carol L. Steiman, for typing the tables which appear in the Appendixes to this volume; to my student assistant, William A. Hastings, who checked the manuscript for computational accuracy; to Peter Anker and Robert Garrett, Smith Barney and Company, and Robert Perkins, Halsey Stuart and Company, for reading the initial draft of Chapter 19; and to my senior colleagues, Professors Lawrence W. Towle, Richard Scheuch, Robert A. Battis, LeRoy Dunn, and Randall W. Tucker, who helped confirm and sometimes caused me to qualify the presentation I have employed.

Finally, I wish to single out for special thanks three individuals. First, I am deeply grateful to Professor Robert Vandell of the University of Virginia whose page-by-page commentary on a large portion of the second draft of this manuscript proved very useful in tying together many of the points I have endeavored to make. Second, without the help of Priscilla A. Davis, who patiently typed the initial draft and subsequent revisions, this manuscript might never have been finished. Third, those who have written a book know that it is not only a considerable task but also requires one to be mentally and often physically removed from his family. Thus, I wish to thank my wife, Kathy, for her patience and understanding as I labored to complete the manuscript within a reasonable period of time.

While many have been of assistance to me in preparing this volume, I alone, of course, am responsible for the contents and apologize for any errors it may contain.

WARD S. CURRAN

Contents

Part Two
Principles of Asset Management

Six

Seven

Eight

Nine

Cash Management 163

Ten

Accounts Receivable 186

Eleven

Inventories 201

Part Three
Financial Principles

Twelve

Thirteen

Fourteen

Part Four
The Capital Markets — Principles and Practice

Twenty-one

Part Five
Mergers and Reorganizations

Twenty-two

Twenty-three

Part Six
The Goal of Financial Management—A Reconsideration

Financial Management—
The Environment
and Methodology

Introduction

chapter One

The Nature of Financial Decision Making

Let us assume that you have graduated from the hallowed halls of the college or university you now attend. With your degree of bachelor of business administration or your B.A. in economics clutched in your hands, you are now prepared to embark on a career which your father has been eagerly anticipating, namely, assistant manager of his firm.

Your father started a candy company 35 years ago. He began with a small shop and has turned it into a successful enterprise with numerous retail outlets scattered throughout the state. Now sixty and sole owner of the firm, he is looking forward to slowing down his activities and gradually turning over the operation of the enterprise to you. He knows that over the past few years the rate of growth in sales and profits has leveled off.   In spite of attempts to accelerate both, his efforts seem to have been in vain.   Always a progressive individual, he believes that perhaps he has begun to lose his resiliency and that the time has come for fresh ideas.   You have always been an eager person willing to learn and your education in business administration and economics has given you the appropriate background on which to make the decisions necessary to increase sales and profits.   What remains is to apply these principles to the particular situation in which you find yourself, that is, to the candy business.

Since your father is concerned with the slowing down of growth in sales and profits, you might begin your analysis with the financial statements of the enterprise.   You know from your training in accounting that the statement of financial position, or the balance sheet, depends in part on current and future sales.   If sales are growing rapidly, inventories and receivables will also be growing.   So too will current liabilities such as trade credit and loans payable designed to finance current assets.

On the other hand, because the rate of increase in sales is declining, your father has failed to reinvest profits in the operating assets of the firm and cash balances have begun to rise.   Thus the next question to ask is why sales and profits have leveled off.   The firm has a reputation for producing high-quality candy, particularly chocolates.   It does a good business at Christmas, Valentine's Day, and other times when candy is traditionally given as a gift.   But there has been no noticeable increase in demand at these particular seasons of the year.

As you search for reasons, you notice in perusing the trade journals and looking at the product lines of competitors that your rivals have begun to move into related areas.   For example, some are producing dietetic candy.   As you read further you begin to suspect that the reason for the slowing down in the rate of growth in sales and profits is that a weight-conscious public is spending its increases in income on other goods, including dietetic candy.   You also notice that some of the other candies your father's firm produces have done better than his main line. Chocolate bars and penny candy, which appeal to children, have enjoyed a good market. This you can attribute to the rise in the proportion of youth in the total population, a factor which has characterized the post-World War II period.   But you also take cognizance of the fact that the growth in birth rates has declined in the last few years.   Hence you can soon anticipate a slowing down in the rate of growth in this area of the market.

You conclude from your investigation that your father's firm has not done as well in the last few years as it had earlier because it has not kept pace with the changes in the market served.   Before sales and profits, which have begun to level off, actually start to decline, you make the decision to alter the firm's policy so as to meet the changing tastes of the public.

The Alternatives Open   Your researches indicate that at a minimum the firm must produce, in addition to its regular line of products, low-caloried dietetic candies which seem to have shown a relatively high rate of sales growth when compared with the rate for traditional lines. Now you face a new set of decisions.   First, you must offer a variety of palatable low-caloried candy products which, if possible, will be as tasty as the candy already produced.   Your father was fortunate in that he simply took some recipes handed down from your grandmother, experimented with them, found he was able to employ them in large-scale production, and then went into business.

You face a somewhat riskier decision in which specialized knowledge of the properties of certain artificial sweeteners may be useful.   If you do not have this knowledge yourself, you will have to hire a chemist who does.

Not only must you engage in product research, but you have to add specialized equipment if you are to manufacture dietetic candies.   Thus an additional capital outlay may have to be made in order to produce this line of products.

Let us assume that you estimate that it will require a $200,000 investment to carry out the necessary product research and pay for the new facilities to manufacture the product.   You now face the question of how to finance these investments.   Your father has $150,000 in cash and marketable securities in the asset structure of his business.   Current liabilities, that is, obligations due within a year, total $25,000. Both you and your father believe that liquid assets could be reduced without impairing the firm's ability to meet its obligations as they come due.

But by how much should they be reduced?   The answer to this question requires answers to a series of related questions.   For example, how much are you and your father willing to risk on the successful development of dietetic candies?   In part your answer will depend on the rate of return you expect on your investment.   It will also depend in part on how much you can borrow.   Moreover, since interest on debt as well as installments of principal must be paid at specific periods, borrowing will raise the firm's current liabilities and may therefore raise the risk of insolvency.   Yet if the project is a success, sales and ultimately cash and receivables will rise by more than the amount expended in the investment.   The difference between current assets and current liabilities may ultimately be greater than it is at present.   In short, both you and your father have to face two sets of risks. First, you each must decide whether to invest at all in expanding the firm's line of products. Second, assuming that you choose to go ahead with your plans, you must agree on the composition of the financing.

In the first instance you must weigh the expected return on the $200,000 investment against the return that might be anticipated if the funds you plan to employ were invested elsewhere, that is, in marketable securities such as government bonds, stocks of other companies, etc. Since the expected return is some function of the risk involved, you must make a subjective evaluation as to whether the differentials in return are compensating. For example, you may earn as much as 20 percent on the $200,000 investment in the production of dietetic candies or as little as 3 percent. If you invested the funds in government bonds you would virtually be assured of an income of, say, 5 percent. The risk involved in successfully producing and marketing a new line of products is much greater than the risk involved in receiving interest on government securities.

In the second instance you must decide whether to add to the business risk by assuming a degree of financial risk. For example, if you were to borrow $100,000 and use $100,000 of the firm's cash, you might be able to raise the return on the firm's portion of the investment to as much as 25 percent. But if the venture turns out to be unsuccessful, that is, if little or none of the dietetic product is sold, there may not be funds sufficient to pay principal and interest on the borrowed money. As a result your firm will go into bankruptcy. The assets may have to be sold in order to satisfy the claims of your creditors.

On the other hand, the threat of bankruptcy would be avoided if you and your father supplied all the funds, or you brought into the venture a third person who provided capital in exchange for an ownership interest in the business. You might, in other words, be able to use $100,000 of the firm's cash, and obtain from one or more persons the additional $100,000 in exchange for their right to share proportionately in the profits of the enterprise. In so doing you forego the opportunity to earn 25 rather than 20 percent on the investment, but at the same time you do not increase the risk of insolvency.

The essence of financial decision making is the trade-off between risk and return, or profits. Given the opportunity to earn more, you will ordinarily have to assume a greater risk in order to succeed. Moreover, it is evident from this brief discussion that the mode of financing is not necessarily independent of the nature of the investment. If it can be shown that financing a portion of the capital outlay out of debt will have little impact on the chances of bankruptcy, you and your father will be more apt to assume this risk. However, if the risk of bankruptcy rises substantially, you may be more likely to finance the investment out of ownership or equity funds, even if this means bringing new owners into the business.

You could, of course, after a thorough analysis of the alternatives, decide not to assume the risks involved in investing funds to expand the product line.   This may mean that you value more highly the relative certainty of a 5 percent return on government bonds to the possibility of earning as much as 20 percent, or the risk of earning as little as 3 percent, on an investment within the firm.   You may have also decided on a third alternative such as a portfolio of common stocks whose probable return might vary anywhere from 4 to 10 percent.   If you elect not to modernize your product lines, there is the implication that you and your father expect to terminate your investment in the business.   From your analysis of the potential market, you know that your sales and profits will grow at an even slower rate in the future than in the recent past. Recognizing this fact and yet deciding against expanding the firm's line of products, you may now begin to make plans to sell the business or gradually liquidate it by not replacing assets as they wear out, or by selling the land and buildings comprising the manufacturing and retail outlets.   One set of decisions, therefore, leads logically to another.

From the foregoing discussion it is apparent that the alternatives facing you and your father are numerous.   The effects of pursuing any set of decisions will be sufficiently far-reaching that you would both be advised to consider how each course of action would fit into your long-range goals or objectives.   For your father, preservation of the enterprise to which he has devoted much of his life may be the primary consideration.   Yet he may now be reluctant to assume the additional business risk necessary to modernize the product line, and even less desirous of threatening the firm's solvency by financing a considerable portion of the $200,000 investment out of debt.

On the other hand, you may have a less sentimental attachment to the enterprise, but see the opportunity to enhance its profits by assuming a certain amount of risk.   Being younger, with an opportunity to find employment elsewhere should this venture fail, you may be more likely than your father to assume the business risk and even the financial risk involved.

Developing a Framework   How the two of you can reconcile your differences is a point to which we shall return.   But even if there were no basis for reconciliation, we could still develop the principles on which the investment and financing decisions should be based.   In other words, we can develop a framework within which such decisions and their alternatives can be evaluated.   Since part of the framework consists of a subjective evaluation of risk, it is quite likely that two people will view the outcome of alternatives differently. If your father, for example, has a greater risk aversion than you, he will rank the alternative uses to which funds could be put and the alternative means of financing investments differently than you.

To admit that differences in evaluation exist, however, does not destroy the usefulness of the analytical framework; without it we would have no basis for recognizing and evaluating the opportunities available. If you had not been willing to use principles of financial management such as those developed in this text to calculate the return on investment opportunities, neither you nor your father would ever know what you were giving up or gaining by pursuing one course of action instead of another. Similarly, by not applying these principles of financial management in determining the composition of financing, you would have no way of knowing what the trade-offs between greater profits and increased risk of financial insolvency are expected to be. In other words, the analysis provides us with a systematic means of making investment and financial decisions.

But in this volume the principles of financial management are directed toward a single goal. Their validity or invalidity, as tools of decision making, depends on acceptance of the goal itself. Without further elaboration at this point we shall assume that management decisions should be oriented toward maximizing the market value of the owners' equity. In the case of your father's candy business, our principles will lead us to decisions which maximize the market value of his share in the business. Since he is the sole owner, this conclusion is the same as saying that the principles of financial management lead us to maximizing the market value of the firm itself.

Thus, suppose the return from the candy business can be improved by developing new product lines. Your father, however, is reluctant to assume this risk, while someone else is not. Then the market value of the equity would be at a maximum if he sold the enterprise. Presumably the person buying it (let us say it is you) would be willing to pay something in excess of its value based on current and projected earnings without additions to the product line. You would do so in anticipation of what the firm could earn if you made the appropriate investments.

A way to reconcile your differences with your father, therefore, may be to offer to purchase his business. Your resources, however, are limited. Moreover, the conflict has arisen because he is reluctant to assume additional risk, not because he is desirous of liquidating his interests in the firm. Thus you might be able to get him to agree to assume less of the risk involved in expanding the line of products. To illustrate, let us assume that your father had previously established a trust fund which became yours on graduation.   The present market value of the securities in the fund is $100,000.   You offer to liquidate these securities and invest the proceeds in the business.   In return your father will supply the additional $100,000 by reducing the level of cash and marketable securities of the firm.   These funds will be used to develop and market the dietetic chocolates.   In order to satisfy your father's desire for relative security, you agree to guarantee him annually not only 6 percent on the $100,000 he is contributing to the development of the new product line, but another 6 percent on the capital he has previously invested in the firm.   After this commitment has been made, the residual, if any, accrues to you.

Furthermore, should the venture fail to such an extent that total earnings are insufficient to satisfy the obligations of the firm presently outstanding, and the company is liquidated in order to meet these obligations, you will grant your father a prior claim to the proceeds from the sale of the assets less principal and interest owed to the firm's creditors. Before you can receive anything, his total investment must be repaid out of these proceeds.   In return for the preferred status accorded him, you are given complete control over the development and marketing of the dietetic chocolates as well as an equal role in formulating policy pertaining to producing, financing, and merchandising the standard lines of products.   Consequently, even though differences in evaluations of alternatives exist, there are means for reconciling them.

Financial Management — The Traditional View and the Contemporary Approach

The above example serves to illustrate what is involved in the decision-making process around which modern business finance is oriented. Profitability, liquidity, risk, and uncertainty are all factors with which management must contend when it makes decisions as to the composition of the firm's assets and its financial structure.   It helps in making these decisions to have an analytical framework.   The primary purpose of this volume is to develop the principles of such a framework.   As we indicated earlier, we have labeled the analysis the principles of financial management.

This modern approach to business finance stands in sharp contrast to the traditional view of the subject.   The latter approach was originally almost totally institutional.[1]   Primary emphasis centered

---

[1]For a brief but excellent discussion of the changing emphasis in finance, see J. Fred Weston, *The Scope and Methodology of Finance* (Englewood Cliffs, N.J.: Prentice-Hall, Inc., 1966), chap. 2.   See also Ezra Solomon, *The Theory of Financial Management* (New York: Columbia University Press, 1963), chap. 1.

initially on the acquisition of funds and only subsequently on their effective use. Episodic events such as the flotation of new securities were covered in great detail in the early textbooks and literature of the field. Moreover, given the fact that financial failure is always a possibility, authors placed particular emphasis on solvency. This trend was reinforced by the Great Depression. The capital structure was viewed more in terms of its impact on liquidity than its effect on the cost of capital and ultimately on profitability. Similarly, in administering funds, the primary concern of financial management was with working capital analysis. Until recently, little attention was paid to the principles underlying fixed-asset management and profitability. It is not that this topic was ignored.[2] Economists have discussed it in various contexts for years.[3] But it took a combination of events, including postwar prosperity, the slowing down of growth in profits among established enterprises, and a general discontent with the way investment decisions were handled, before businessmen took an active interest in the principles of fixed-asset management. Moreover, it required individuals with a knack for expressing this concern in such a way that management would recognize the problem as fundamental to the growth and development of the enterprise before the subject could receive widespread attention in the literature of business administration.[4]

Historically, therefore, finance has been concerned with the acquisition of funds, the administration of working capital so as to preserve the liquidity of the firm, and more recently the management of fixed or long-lived assets. Put these three topics together and we have a framework within which the decisions pertaining to the acquisition of funds can be related to the decisions pertaining to their effective use, that is, to the decisions required to enhance the profitability of the firm while preserving its liquidity. Within this context, institutional arrangements such as the tax laws and regulation of the securities markets can be viewed as having an impact on one or more aspects of the decision-making process. The income tax laws, for example, will affect the profitability of investments and therefore the total amount invested.

[2]See, for example, George Wing, "Capital Budgeting, circa 1915," *Journal of Finance*, vol. 20, no. 3 (September, 1965), pp. 472–479. See also Norman S. Buchanan, *The Economics of Corporate Enterprise* (New York: Henry Holt and Company, Inc., 1940), chaps. VI, VII, VIII, and IX, *passim*.

[3]See Ward S. Curran, "Depreciation in Economic Theory and Capital Budgeting," *Quarterly Review of Economics and Business*, vol. 8, no. 1 (Spring, 1968), pp. 61–63.

[4]Compare, for example, Joel Dean, *Capital Budgeting* (New York: Columbia University Press, 1951), with Friedrich and Vera Lutz, *The Theory of Investment of the Firm* (Princeton, N.J.: Princeton University Press, 1951). The former received fairly widespread attention while the latter did not. Dean's book did much to stimulate interest in developing techniques for managing fixed assets. The Lutzes' presentation, while more comprehensive, apparently was too formidable for the times.

Moreover, since the tax laws treat income from debt sources differently than income from equity sources, they will have an impact on the composition of financing, that is, on the capital structure.   Similarly, regulation of the securities markets will also affect the supply of capital to the firm and hence influence decisions pertaining to sources of funds.

Since financial decision making does not take place in a vacuum, these institutional arrangements are an important part of an introductory text.   What was lacking in the traditional approach to the field was an analytical discussion that lent substance to the institutional forces. Instead of viewing finance either as a staff function concerned primarily with making certain that bills can be paid as they come due, or as the preserve of those responsible for negotiating long-term sources of funds, we now see the subject as an integral part of the decision-making process.   The principles of financial management provide the tools for implementing the goals or objectives of management.   The institutional arrangements will affect the decisions designed to implement these objectives.

Thus, in reading the subsequent chapters, the student should note the role the material plays in explaining, affecting, or implementing the goal we have assumed — maximization of the market value of the owners' equity.   To assist the student, we have included in each chapter a prefatory comment, a summary, and questions and problems pertaining to the material presented.   There are also selected references at the end of each chapter, for those who wish to pursue these topics further.

SELECTED REFERENCES

"Developments in the Curriculum and Teaching of Finance — Discussion," *Journal of Finance*, vol. 21, no. 2 (May, 1966), pp. 423–434.

Robinson, Roland I. "What Should We Teach in a Money and Banking Course?" *Journal of Finance*, vol. 21, no. 2 (May, 1966), pp. 403–410.

Solomon, Ezra. *The Theory of Financing Management*. New York: Columbia University Press, 1963, chap. I.

———. "What Should We Teach in a Business Finance Course?" *Journal of Finance*, vol. 21, no. 2 (May, 1966), pp. 411–415.

Wendt, Paul F. "What Should We Teach in an Investments Course?" *Journal of Finance*, vol. 21, no. 2 (May, 1966), pp. 416–422.

Weston, J. Fred. *The Scope and Methodology of Finance*. Englewood Cliffs, N.J.: Prentice-Hall, Inc., 1966.

Types of Business Organizations

chapter Two

In choosing a legal form of business organization, management will want to consider the advantages and disadvantages of the options available. At some point it may even wish to change the present structure so as to realize the advantages inherent in an alternative. The student should view the information presented in this chapter from the perspective of a manager interested in selecting the form which will in the long run maximize the market value of the owners' equity.

Introduction

Agricultural, industrial, and commercial activity in the United States is carried on within three basic business units, the sole proprietorship, the partnership, and the corporation. Two other types, the joint-stock

12

company and the business or Massachusetts trust, are of limited importance.[1]

From Tables 2-1 and 2-2 it is evident that the sole proprietorship is by far the most numerous form of business organization. Yet it is the corporation which accounts each year for the bulk of our national income (i.e., wages, rents, interest, and profits).

This chapter has a twofold purpose: (1) to acquaint the student of business finance with the characteristics which distinguish different organizational units and (2) to explain why the corporation has become the major vehicle for producing goods and services in the United States.

Legal Setting — The Sole Proprietorship

In economics, the concepts of the firm and the entrepreneur are basic to the form if not the substance of price theory. In practice, the sole proprietorship comes closest to epitomizing these two concepts.

The theory of perfect competition functions on the proposition that there is ease of entry into the industry. In law, barriers to entry as a sole proprietor are nonexistent. There are neither fees to pay nor forms to file. If one can perform a service or acquire a product which is marketable, his proprietorship has begun. The law does not distinguish between the proprietor and his business. Statutes which govern him govern any individual. He is free to do business in each and every state in the Union. Barriers to entry could exist because of the type of good or service one wishes to sell — licensing to sell liquor and licensing to practice one of the learned professions are examples. But these restrictions have nothing to do with the form of business organization, merely with the product or service sold. The ease with which the sole proprietorship can be brought into existence is the basic reason for its widespread use in many areas of business.

Disadvantages   The sole proprietorship also has disadvantages. Since the proprietor is not legally distinct from the proprietorship,

---

[1]The cooperative, defined by Taylor as a "voluntary association organized for an economic purpose and distributing its surplus on the basis of owner participation," has been used in agriculture, wholesale and retail trade, and the service industries. See Bayard Taylor, *Financial Policies of Business Enterprise* (New York: Appleton-Century-Crofts, Inc., 1956), pp. 48–68. Savings and loan associations, mutual savings banks, and credit unions have been constructed along the lines of a cooperative. The growth of this type of organization is circumscribed when it sells to or buys from its members only. In addition, it might be, as in the case of producer cooperatives in agriculture, an association of sole proprietors selling their output as a unit in order to offset the real or imagined monopsony power of the buyer.

TABLE 2-1: SOLE PROPRIETORSHIPS, PARTNERSHIPS, AND CORPORATIONS— NUMBERS AND RECEIPTS BY INDUSTRY GROUP, 1965[a]

(Numbers in thousands; money figures in millions of dollars. Based on a sample of unaudited tax returns filed for accounting periods ending between July 1 of the year shown and June 30 of the following year.)

	1965					
	Number[b,f]			Business Receipts[c,d,f]		
Industry Group	Sole Proprietorships	Active Partnerships	Active Corporations	Sole Proprietorships	Active Partnerships	Active Corporations
Total	9,078	914	1,424	$199,385	$73,588	$1,120,382
Agriculture, Forestry, and Fisheries	3,225	128	28	32,160	5,024	7,186
Mining	36	15	13	943	866	11,903
Construction	705	58	113	19,308	7,003	55,696
Manufacturing	186	37	186	7,267	5,596	502,982
Transportation, Communications, Electricity, and Gas[e]	297	18	60	5,527	1,315	86,439
Wholesale and Retail Trade[b]	1,854	235	440	97,190	34,373	358,173
Wholesale	265	32	147	17,934	10,879	171,414
Retail	1,554	202	288	77,760	23,244	183,925
Finance, Insurance, and Real Estate	539	249	388	7,022	6,845	61,371
Services	2,208	169	188	29,789	12,442	36,547

[a]Source: Internal Revenue Service, *Statistics of Income, 1965, U.S. Business Tax Returns*, pp. 3–6.
[b]Includes business not allocable to individual industries.
[c]Individually owned businesses and farms.
[d]Receipts from sales and services less returns and allowances: (a) For sole proprietorships, excludes capital gains or losses and investment income not associated with the taxpayer's business; (b) For partnerships and corporations engaged in finance, insurance, and real estate, excludes a sizable part of income because reporting instructions prescribe separate entries for investment income.
[e]Includes sanitary services.
[f]Because of discrepancies in rounding, totals may not equal the sum of the components.

**TABLE 2-2:   NATIONAL INCOME BY SECTOR AND
LEGAL FORM OF ORGANIZATION, 1966, 1967, AND 1968**[a]
(In Millions of Dollars)

	Amount[b]			Percent of Total[b]		
	1966	1967	1968	1966	1967	1968
National Income	620,585	654,011	714,395	100.0	100.0	100.0
Income Originating in Business, Total	519,668	541,438	589,291	83.7	82.8	82.5
Corporate Business	347,737	367,487	403,458	57.0	56.2	56.5
Sole Proprietorships and Partnerships	117,518	122,202	130,557	18.9	18.7	18.3
Other Private Business	40,337	42,971	45,469	6.5	6.6	6.4
Government Enter- prises	8,076	8,778	9,807	1.3	1.3	1.4
Income Originating in General Government	76,607	85,346	95,171	12.3	13.0	13.3
Income Originating in Households and Institutions	20,206	22,716	25,188	3.3	3.5	3.5
Income Originating in Rest of World	4,104	4,511	4,745	0.7	0.7	0.7

[a]Source: *Survey of Current Business*, July, 1969, p. 21.
[b]Because of discrepancies in rounding, totals may not equal the sum of the components.

creditors have recourse to his personal assets.   If, for example, a proprietor were unable to meet debts incurred in the process of doing business, his home and other possessions, although not used by his firm,
might be sold to settle claims against his proprietorship.   To be sure,
the laws of some states provide for debtors' exemptions.   Thus if the
indebted proprietor cannot satisfy claims out of business assets, his
creditors may be unable to levy against his home, furniture, etc.[2]   Moreover, there is always the possibility of a proprietor putting personal
assets in his wife's name or purchasing insurance to protect himself
from business claims made against his personal assets.   Yet unlimited
liability is a feature of an unincorporated enterprise.   It is up to the
proprietor to take steps to mitigate its impact on his personal assets.

Perhaps an even greater disadvantage is the inherent difficulty in
obtaining capital.   For a proprietor the major sources of funds are his
own savings and those of relatives and close friends.   The supplier,
looking for a retail outlet for his goods, might finance the proprietor's
inventory.   The Small Business Administration, a federal agency,
could prove helpful if funds were unavailable on reasonable terms from

[2]Robert M. Davies and Melvyn H. Lawrence, *Choosing a Form of Business Organization* (Durham, N.C.: Duke University Law School, 1963), p. 18.

private outlets.   His most likely source, however, is the local banker. But a banker's enthusiasm varies in proportion to the collateral, i.e., personal and business assets, that can be used to secure the loan.   Because of these limitations, the sole proprietorship has had its greatest success in those industries where capital investment is relatively low, for example, in agriculture, wholesale and retail trade, and services.   As the optimum scale of enterprise grows, the initial capital required to enter the industry rises, and the sole proprietorship becomes a less suitable vehicle for organizing a firm.

Legal Setting—The Partnership

A logical extension of the proprietorship would be "an association of two or more persons to carry on as co-owners a business for profit,"[3] or more precisely a partnership.   A partnership can be set up almost as easily as a proprietorship.   An agreement between the partners can be verbal.   It is likely, particularly if there are several partners, that they will establish a formal arrangement or "articles of partnership" which among other things will spell out the terms by which they will share in the profits of the firm.

Disadvantages   While this agreement, by bringing together additional sources of funds, may enhance the capital of the business, the partnership does have drawbacks.   Two in particular stand out.   First, all partners are jointly and severally liable for the debts of the partnership. Second, death or withdrawal of a partner terminates the arrangement.

Since each and every partner can contract a debt in the name of the partnership, the feature of unlimited liability takes on added significance.   Care in selecting partners is of greatest urgency.   Partners can agree among themselves how they will share debts and liabilities, "but a contract of this kind has no effect on the rights of a . . . claimant."[4] The personal property of all partners, to the extent that it is not encumbered by personal liabilities, can be used to satisfy the debts of the partnership.[5]

---

[3]Uniform Partnership Act, Sec. 6(1).

[4]Davies and Lawrence, *op. cit.*, p. 19.

[5]Separating the personal assets and liabilities of the partnership from the liabilities and assets of each partner is subject to the rule of "marshaling of assets."   Personal creditors have primary claim to the personal assets of each partner and residual claim to the assets of the partnership.   Partnership creditors have primary claim to partnership assets and residual claim to the personal assets of each and every partner.   For a detailed example of "marshaling of assets," see Harry G. Guthmann and Herbert E. Dougall, *Corporate Financial Policy* (Englewood Cliffs, N.J.: Prentice-Hall, Inc., 1962), pp. 9–11.

In order to mitigate the burdens of unlimited liability, many states have authorized by statute a limited partnership. With this arrangement, one can provide capital as a limited partner, his liability circumscribed by the amount of capital contributed. Under the Uniform Limited Partnership Act adopted in many states, the limited partner or partners cannot actively participate in the management of the business. There must also be at least one general partner willing to assume unlimited liability. Finally, the limited partnership must be skillfully drafted in order to avoid full liability to the limited partners, and ordinarily copies of the agreement must be filed with a public official.[6]

Four states — Michigan, New Jersey, Ohio, and Pennsylvania — have enacted statutes which make it possible to create a partnership association in which all members have limited liability. This institution, unlike a general or limited partnership, is usually given a separate legal status but only in the state in which it is organized.[7]

Interests in a partnership association can be freely transferred. On the surface this feature would seem to eliminate the second major disadvantage of this form of organization: lack of continuity. In practice it does not. A partnership association usually has a fixed term of life without provisions for renewal. Furthermore, under the principle of delectus personae — the right of every partner to choose his associates — the interests are not always transferable.[8] If a buyer is not acceptable to the other partners, his only recourse is sale of his interest to the association.

The problem of partnership continuity has never been adequately solved under the law. A sole proprietorship terminates on the death or withdrawal of the proprietor. A carefully drawn will providing for an executor to continue the business until the estate is settled may preserve the proprietorship and successfully transfer it to the heirs. In a general partnership, complications arise because a general partner can terminate the partnership by withdrawing prior to the expiration of the partnership agreement. He is, however, responsible for the damages and losses sustained by his partners from breach of contract. On the other hand, withdrawal or death of a limited partner does not terminate a limited partnership although withdrawal or death of the general partner or one of the general partners would.

It has been suggested that one solution to the problem of continuity is a distant expiration date in the articles of partnership. Provisions

---

[6]Davies and Lawrence, *op. cit.*, p. 8.

[7]*Ibid.*, pp. 8–9. The partnership association can hold property and sue or be sued in the name of the association rather than in the name of the partners, which is the common law practice for general partnerships.

[8]*Ibid.*, p. 9.

for substantial damages from breach of contract by withdrawal would also be contained in the agreement. Since death as well as withdrawal would terminate the agreement, the articles could state that, in these circumstances, the "partners will have the option (1) to dissolve the partnership and liquidate it, (2) to purchase the interest of the deceased or withdrawing partner, or (3) to cause the firm to purchase it at a fixed price or at a price to be determined by formula."[9] Providing for these eventualities in the articles of agreement can save litigation because of disagreements and facilitate the transition to a new partnership if one is desired.

In spite of the possibilities of overcoming the problem of continuity, the partnership today is the least numerous of the three major forms of business organization. It is likely under present laws to remain so. While it does provide ways of obtaining new capital (limited partners, for example, are usually sought solely for their financial backing), care in selecting general partners and in drafting an acceptable agreement works against its proliferation. As in the case of an individual proprietorship, unlimited liability may be partially offset by insurance or the transfer of personal assets to the name of the partner's wife (a procedure not without risk should the marriage end in divorce). Lack of continuity can be provided for by a carefully drawn agreement, but partnership interests are not easily transferred even in the case of a partnership association. Verbal agreements are not likely, particularly if the partners are numerous. Under these conditions, flexibility becomes valuable and this characteristic, as we shall see, can be provided by the corporation.

As in the case of a proprietorship, therefore, the partnership is confined to those areas where the initial capital investment is small. Even then, in terms of business receipts, as Table 2-1 indicates, the corporation is dominant save in agriculture, forestry, and fisheries. Only in services, and to a lesser extent retail trade, does the proprietorship at least compare with the corporation, while the partnership is always the least important of the three.

Legal Setting — The Corporation

A corporation can be defined as an association of people who have come together for a common purpose and have been granted under the laws of the state or in some instances the federal government a charter which treats the association as a separate legal entity. This definition, how-

[9]*Ibid.*, p. 27.

ever, disregards the controversy which has surrounded the nature of the institution.   Is the corporation an artificial legal personality?   So Justice Marshall argued in the famous Dartmouth College decision in 1819.

> A corporation is an artificial being, invisible, intangible, and existing only in contemplation of the law. Being a mere creature of law, it possesses only those properties which the charter of its creation confers upon it, either expressly or as incidental to its very existence.[10]

Or is the corporation a contract between persons pursuing a common end?   In this case the government merely recognizes the corporation through a charter listing its rights and privileges.   Alternatively, the state can refuse to recognize the contract.   Marshall also provides support for this view.   The charter incorporating Dartmouth College

> . . . is plainly a contract to which the donors, the trustees and the crown (to whose rights and obligations New Hampshire succeeds) were the original parties . . . .   It is a contract for the security and disposition of property.   It is a contract on the faith of which real and personal estate has been conveyed to the corporation . . . .   It appears to me on the whole that . . . principles and authorities prove incontrovertibly that a charter of incorporation is a contract.[11]

A more philosophical view assigns to the corporation a role similar to that of a natural person capable of acting on its own behalf.[12]   For our purposes any or all of these views are acceptable.   Since it fails to shed light on the reasons why the corporation has come to dominate American business life, pursuit of the controversy is fruitless.

Unless the state dictates otherwise or the founders place a termination date in the charter, an indefinite life is one of the major features of a separate legal existence.   The corporation has a life of its own apart from the owners and does not terminate on the death of one or more of them.   "This conception of the life of the corporation, independent of the lives of the individual members, goes back to Roman law."[13]

As a separate legal entity, the corporation can own property and sue or be sued.   This feature is not necessarily unique.   For example, a partnership organized in a state which has adopted the Uniform

---

[10]*The Trustees of Dartmouth College v. Woodward*, 4 *Wheaton* 636 (1819).

[11]4 Wheaton 643, 644, and 659.

[12]Norman S. Buchanan, *The Economics of Corporate Enterprise* (New York: Henry Holt and Company, Inc., 1940), p. 41.   See also Arthur Stone Dewing, *The Financial Policy of Corporations*, 5th ed. (New York: The Ronald Press Company, 1953), vol. I, p. 18, ftnt.

[13]Dewing, *op. cit.*, vol. I, p. 14.

Partnership Act can hold property or sue and be sued in the name of the partnership.   With a corporation, however, this characteristic is inherent in the organization.   On the other hand, partnerships in some states operate under common law principles.   If so, property is held in the name of the general partners.   Lawsuits are also in their names and not in the name of the partnership.[14]

Limited Liability   A corporate feature frequently discussed is limited liability.   As a general principle, a person purchasing a share or shares of stock as an ownership interest in a corporation may forfeit his investment should the corporation find itself in bankruptcy.   He can lose what he has ventured but no more.   The creditors of the corporation must satisfy their claims from the corporate assets, and not from the personal assets of the stockholders.   There are exceptions. For example, some states hold shareholders personally liable for unpaid wage claims though not for claims of other creditors.   Since back wages receive preference to corporate assets over many other claims in bankruptcy, this provision is rarely invoked.   More important, should the stockholders participate in management either as officers or directors of the company, they may become personally liable for their actions. Paying illegal dividends, making loans to officers, directors, and share-holders, as well as negligent management are among the offenses for which those who oversee the corporation can be held responsible. Shareholders who are in control can abuse the corporate form to such a degree that "the courts will 'pierce the corporate veil', i.e., disregard the corporation's separate legal personality."[15]   For the majority of stockholders in the large corporation of today, a voice in management is the last thing in their minds.   Their shares represent an investment. While they risk the loss of all funds used to purchase the stock, their liability goes no further.   Other personal property cannot be seized to settle corporate debts.

This comforting thought, taken for granted by the average stock-holder, was not generally sanctioned by law in either the United States or England until well into the nineteenth century.   Limited liability was readily accessible in England after 1856.[16]   An exact date is more difficult to establish for the United States.   The Constitution contained no reference to corporations.   By implication the power to incorporate in this country was vested in the states.   The federal government was limited to chartering corporations to carry out the powers granted to it

[14]Davies and Lawrence, *op. cit.*, p. 32.
[15]*Ibid.*, p. 22.
[16]Bishop C. Hunt, *The Development of the Business Corporation in England 1800–1867* (Cambridge, Mass.: Harvard University Press, 1936), pp. 116–144.

under the Constitution.   Today, for example, since the Constitution gives the federal government control over the money supply, no one questions the right of the Comptroller of Currency to issue a federal charter to a commercial bank.   But the states can also grant bank charters.   Promoters of a new bank, therefore, have a choice of a national charter or one from the state in which they plan to establish the bank. In the early years of the Republic each state carefully nurtured its prerogative.   Charters were granted by the respective legislatures on an individual basis.   Their provisions followed the practice of English law. In that country a distinction had been drawn between purely profit-making enterprises and those of quasi-public status such as turnpikes, canals, and colonization corporations.   The latter group, because they were thought to advance the public welfare, were accorded special treatment.

Limited liability, a corporate feature recognized in English law in the seventeenth century,[17] could be specifically provided for or set aside by the charter.   In the United States, more often than not, charters specifically stated that liability of shareholders extended beyond their investment.   Creditors of the corporation could seize their personal assets.   Limited liability was reserved primarily for undertakings of a quasi-public nature.   After 1800 the distinction between an enterprise devoted primarily to the public welfare and one designed mainly for private gain became more nebulous.   Yet treatment, particularly of manufacturing concerns, continued to be severe and limited liability remained the exception.[18]

The first major break with tradition came in 1811 when New York enacted a law which permitted general incorporation.   No longer was political influence necessary to acquire a charter nor was the restraining hand of the legislature there to circumscribe it.   Nevertheless, unlimited liability was not completely abandoned upon enactment of the statute.[19]   Only in subsequent decades, as the major industrial states of the day, Massachusetts and Connecticut, passed general incorporation acts, in 1830 and 1832, respectively, did limited liability become less an exception.   The spirit of laissez faire which characterized Jacksonian Democracy manifested itself in the liberal incorporation laws enacted during the period.   Charters were freely granted and one of the inherent rights of the corporate form, limited liability, was restored.[20]

[17]Edward Jenks, *A Short History of English Law* (Boston: Little, Brown & Company, 1912), pp. 288–290.

[18]Shaw Livermore, "Unlimited Liability in Early American Corporations," *Journal of Political Economy*, vol. 43, no. 5 (October, 1935), pp. 675–679.

[19]*Ibid.*, pp. 684–685.

[20]Other rights often circumscribed by legislatures, notably perpetual life, were also restored under general incorporation laws. *Ibid.*, *passim.*

Although the foundation was laid, it was another 50 years before the corporation began its rise to prominence as the business unit through which the bulk of our nation's resources are allocated. "Big business" today is synonymous with the corporation. Prior to 1880, large corporations rarely existed outside the railroad industry.[21]   Two factors, the rise of a national market[22] and economies of scale, favored adoption of the corporate form by new enterprises.

Servicing the national market that rose for many products called for larger business units. The expansion of capital-intensive industries, where fixed costs were high and specialization and division of labor feasible, called for huge investment outlays to take advantage of decreasing average total costs. For many enterprises, particularly manufacturing concerns, the optimum scale of enterprise was beyond the resources of a few people. Thus businessmen turned to the corporation to amass the funds needed to take advantage of economies of scale.[23]

This trend, begun in the 1880s, has continued into the twentieth century. From the figures in Table 2-3 it appears that, by the year

TABLE 2-3:   PERCENTAGE DISTRIBUTION OF TOTAL NET TANGIBLE WEALTH FOR AGRICULTURE, UNINCORPORATED BUSINESS, AND CORPORATIONS FOR SELECTED YEARS [a,b]

End of Year	Agriculture	Unincorporated Business	Corporations
1900	27.88	8.24	24.89
1912	30.04	6.76	25.50
1922	20.77	7.43	28.09
1929	14.66	8.29	28.44
1933	12.41	7.57	28.67
1939	11.52	7.60	27.02
1946	14.05	7.04	26.26
1958	10.73	6.38	30.00

[a]SOURCE: Raymond W. Goldsmith, *The National Wealth of the United States in the Postwar Period* (Princeton, N.J.: Princeton University Press, 1962), table A-19, p. 145.   A study for the National Bureau of Economic Research, Inc.   Reprinted by permission of Princeton University Press.

[b]Net tangible wealth is the stock of tangible assets after allowances for depreciation.   The percentages are based on raw data converted to current prices, reflecting, therefore, replacement cost of the assets for each year.   *Ibid.*, p. 3.

[21]Alfred D. Chandler, Jr., "The Beginnings of 'Big Business' in American Industry," *Business History Review*, vol. 33, no. 1 (Spring, 1959), pp. 25–26.

[22]*Ibid.*, p. 31.

[23]The above discussion is not meant to imply that economies of scale continue indefinitely. For example, there is some evidence that the largest firms in the steel industry may be too big. See Joe Bain, *Industrial Organization* (New York: John Wiley &

1900, corporations, after allowance for depreciation, possessed nearly 25 percent of the nation's tangible assets. This figure increased to 30 percent by 1958. With the decline in the contribution of agriculture, a stronghold of unincorporated business, the relative importance of the corporation in the private sector has become even greater than its share in the national wealth would indicate.[24]

Advantages   In turning to the corporation, businessmen found it the ideal form for amassing the required capital. Because it is a separate legal entity, it can acquire funds in its own name. The indefinite life accorded it under the charter eliminates the problem of continuity. Securities reflecting a capital investment in the corporation can be transferred from person to person without legal obstruction. Ownership of the corporation, represented by shares, can be divided into any practical number of units. If $10,000,000 is needed, it can be raised with 1,000,000 shares priced at $10 each or 100,000 shares at $100 each or any other convenient combination. An investor can risk what he chooses, comforted by the fact that his liability will ordinarily be limited to the amount of his investment.

The corporation is also a convenient instrument for apportioning the elements of risk, income, and control inherent in any business venture.[25] Shareholders assume the greater risk in return for the bulk

---

Sons, Inc., 1959), p. 257. Nevertheless, the perfectly competitive model is concerned with economies of scale in reference only to production, not to marketing or finance or other dimensions which a firm must actually consider in selling a good or service. There may be economies of scale from multiplant operations not evident in the production function. It is also possible that vertical integration, i.e., a merger of separate companies one supplying raw materials to another which turns out the finished product, could add to the efficiency or inefficiency of the enterprise, depending upon the relative effectiveness of the market place over the firm in organizing the means of production. For an interesting theoretical treatment of this question, see R. H. Coase, "The Nature of the Firm," *Economica*, New Series 4 (November, 1937), pp. 386–405; reprinted in George J. Stigler and Kenneth E. Boulding, *Readings in Price Theory* (Homewood, Ill.: Richard D. Irwin, Inc. 1952), pp. 331–351 (vol. VI of republished articles on Economics).

[24]On the basis of shares in national income, the relative importance of the corporation seems to be a more recent phenomenon. Simon Kuznets found that, between 1919 and 1938, industries dominated by individual firms accounted for over half of the national income while corporations accounted for only a third. Simon Kuznets, *National Income: A Summary of Findings* (New York: National Bureau of Economic Research, Inc., 1946), table 2, p. 6. See also p. 8. He goes on to argue that the estimates are crude and the importance of individual firms probably exaggerated. But "even a finer allocation would attribute to individual firms at least as large a share of national income . . . [as] to corporations." *Ibid.*, p. 8. Longer-term changes in the distribution of income are available only by types, i.e., by wages, rents, interest, etc. There is, however, some evidence to indicate a long-term upward trend in the importance of the corporation from the point of view of relative increase in dividends and employee compensation, coupled with a decline in entrepreneurial income and perhaps rent. *Ibid.*, p. 49.

[25]W. H. Lyon, *Capitalization: A Book on Corporation Finance* (Boston: Houghton Mifflin Company, 1912), p. 2.

of the income from a successful venture, and, in theory at least, for the right to select the directors who in turn choose the officers to manage the corporation.   Creditors, on the other hand, seek no voice in the selection of management and do not participate in the profits of the enterprise.   They are instead guaranteed a fixed rate of interest on their loan, and the company is committed to return the principal within a specified period of time.   Failure to pay either interest or principal when due can cause the claimant to initiate bankruptcy.   If this happens, creditors, in order that the corporation's obligation to them may be satisfied, are granted prior claim to its assets.   Shareholders are left with only a residual claim on assets.   But the ingenuity of attorneys has resulted in a host of capital instruments which modify the basic relationship between creditors of the corporation and its owners. As a result, the divisions among the elements of risk, income, and control have been carried to a fine degree.

Disadvantages of the Corporation

Not all features of the corporate form encourage its adoption.   Indeed, as long as the technical conditions for producing and marketing the product or service require a relatively small initial capital investment, the institutional impediments still placed on the corporation may make the proprietorship or partnership the more practical means of initiating a new venture.

Even the simple matter of incorporation can be troublesome. The corporate charter, for example, must be carefully drawn so as to specify the scope of the firm's activities.   Unless specific laws dictate otherwise,[26] the founders will probably want to draft a broad charter to avoid lawsuits by stockholders or creditors objecting to a particular activity on the grounds that it was outside the scope of the corporation's charter.   It was, in a phrase, ultra vires.   Thus, assume that a manufacturing firm whose charter does not specify that it can engage in mining acquires such a concern; particularly if the purchase proves unprofitable, management has invited an ultra vires lawsuit.   Drafting the corporate charter and handling related matters entail additional legal fees not experienced when a proprietorship is formed.   Also, to incorporate is usually a more complex process than drafting articles of partnership agreement.

Another disadvantage of the corporate form stems from the legal

[26]Charters incorporating financial institutions often restrict the scope of their activities.

restrictions placed on it.   As a creature of the law, the corporation, unlike a natural person, can have its freedom curtailed.   When their business carries them from state to state, partners and proprietors are not encumbered by legal restrictions.   The activities of a corporation can be and often are restricted by law.   A firm incorporated in Connecticut is a foreign corporation in New York and in 48 other states.   Some of these states may curtail, deny, or charge for the privilege of doing business within their jurisdictions.   Others may not. The degree of severity will vary.   Laws may be more stringent for alien corporations, i.e., firms chartered outside the United States, than for domestic concerns, i.e., corporations chartered in one of the several states.

Differential Tax Treatment — The Most Important Disadvantage

In some instances, the single most important disadvantage of the corporation is the differential tax treatment accorded it.   This differential is manifested in at least three ways.   First, when applying for a charter of incorporation the organizers must pay a fee to incorporate and in most states an annual franchise tax.   Second, approximately 25 percent of the states impose taxes on corporate income, varying usually from 2 to 8 percent.   Third, the federal government taxes the income of corporations at special rates.

While one might legitimately question whether the burden or incidence of these taxes ultimately falls on the corporation and its owners,[27] each tax is initially placed on the institution.[28]   Proprietorships and partnerships do not pay annual franchise taxes.   For these forms of organization, income from the firm is treated as income to the owners and is subject to personal income taxes.   Net income after corporate taxes is subject to personal income taxes only if it is distributed as dividends.   There is an incentive, therefore, particularly where stockholders are in high personal income tax brackets, to retain funds within the firm.   But the Internal Revenue Service can and on occasion does make use of a provision in the revenue act taxing funds withheld

---

[27]The impact of any tax is to reallocate resources from the private to the public sector.   If firms are making "normal" profits before the income tax and these profits are taxed, then in the perfectly competitive model, firms will leave the industry until the price rises sufficiently for those remaining to earn normal profits.   Who bears the burden? Consumers who pay more?   Discharged employees who must now seek new work?   Those who supplied capital and must now find a new outlet for their funds?   Since mobility of resources is taken for granted, all we can say is that in long-run competitive equilibrium, output will fall and the market price will rise as a result of the tax.

[28]This is why sales and excise taxes were not included.   Presumably they are part of the price of the good or service so taxed.   Again economic analysis suggests in the long run a reallocation of resources away from the private sector.

to avoid taxes on dividends. These rates are 27.5 percent of the accumulated taxable income not in excess of $100,000 and 38.5 percent of income over $100,000.[29]

Compared with personal income taxes, the corporate income tax is relatively simple in structure. From Table 2-4 it is evident that, as the

TABLE 2-4:   CORPORATE INCOME TAX RATES
(In Percents)

Taxable Income	Initial Rate	Surtax	Total Tax Rate
First $25,000	22	0	22
More than $25,000	22	26	48

taxable income of a corporation grows, the average rate approximates 48 percent.

For personal income the rates vary, with application to a particular level of income depending on marital status and, for married persons, whether the husband and wife file joint or separate returns. From Table 2-5 it can be seen that these rates progress from 14 to 70 percent. For married taxpayers filing joint returns, the income bracket to which a given rate is applicable doubles. For example, single taxpayers or married persons filing separate returns pay 50 percent on taxable income between $22,000 and $26,000. For married persons filing joint returns, the same rate applies to taxable income between $44,000 and $52,000.[30]

The revenue code also distinguishes between ordinary income and capital gains. Capital gains or losses are derived from the sale of *capital assets*. Capital assets include, with a few exceptions, all property held by the taxpayer.[31] Gains on assets held 6 months or less are treated as ordinary income and taxed accordingly. If the gain is from sale of an asset held more than 6 months, only 50 percent of the gain is taxable. To illustrate, assume that an unmarried individual bought 100 shares of the XYZ Corporation at $10 per share. Five months later he sold them for $15 per share. Both transactions are calculated after allowances for brokerage commissions. He has, therefore, a net capital gain of $500. Now assume that his taxable income from other sources totaled $10,000 for the year. From Table 2-5 we see that his income tax

[29]Joint Economic Committee, U.S. Congress, *The Federal Tax System: Facts and Problems, 1964* (Washington: Government Printing Office), 1964(1), pp. 50–51.

[30]There is an intermediate schedule for unmarried or legally separated taxpayers who qualify as heads of households. Also certain widows and widowers can use the schedule for married taxpayers filing joint returns.

[31]Joint Economic Committee, *op. cit.*, p. 66.

TABLE 2-5: PERSONAL INCOME TAX RATES FOR SINGLE TAXPAYERS AND FOR MARRIED TAXPAYERS FILING SEPARATE RETURNS

Taxable Income Over	But Not Over	Calculate	Of Excess Over
$ 0	$ 500	$ 0, plus 14%	$ 0
500	1,000	70, plus 15%	500
1,000	1,500	145, plus 16%	1,000
1,500	2,000	225, plus 17%	1,500
2,000	4,000	310, plus 19%	2,000
4,000	6,000	690, plus 22%	4,000
6,000	8,000	1,130, plus 25%	6,000
8,000	10,000	1,630, plus 28%	8,000
10,000	12,000	2,190, plus 32%	10,000
12,000	14,000	2,830, plus 36%	12,000
14,000	16,000	3,550, plus 39%	14,000
16,000	18,000	4,330, plus 42%	16,000
18,000	20,000	5,170, plus 45%	18,000
20,000	22,000	6,070, plus 48%	20,000
22,000	26,000	7,030, plus 50%	22,000
26,000	32,000	9,030, plus 53%	26,000
32,000	38,000	12,210, plus 55%	32,000
38,000	44,000	15,510, plus 58%	38,000
44,000	50,000	18,990, plus 60%	44,000
50,000	60,000	22,590, plus 62%	50,000
60,000	70,000	28,790, plus 64%	60,000
70,000	80,000	35,190, plus 66%	70,000
80,000	90,000	41,790, plus 68%	80,000
90,000	100,000	48,590, plus 69%	90,000
100,000		55,490, plus 70%	100,000

would be $2,190 before the capital gains. Since he held the stock for less than 6 months, he must pay the marginal rate on taxable income in excess of $10,000 and therefore on the full amount of the gain. Thus

$$32\% \text{ of } \$500 = \$160$$
$$\text{Total tax} = \$2{,}190 + \$160 \quad \text{or } \$2{,}350$$

Suppose, however, that he had realized the same net gain of $500 but had held the stock in excess of 6 months before selling it. Then the rate of 32 percent would still be applicable but to only 50 percent of the gain, or $250. Thus the capital gain would be $80, or 16 percent of $500, and the total tax would be $2,270 instead of $2,350.

Moreover, for individuals, the maximum rate applicable to gains from assets held longer than 6 months, i.e., from long-term rather than short-term capital gains, is 25 percent. Thus, if our unmarried individual had a taxable income of $50,000 and a long-term gain of $500, the marginal rate of 60 percent applicable to the bracket would result in a tax of

$$60\% \text{ of } \$250 = \$150$$
$$\$150 = 30\% \text{ of } \$500$$

Since 30 percent exceeds the maximum rate of 25 percent, the latter is applicable to the total gain.   Thus

$$25\% \text{ of } \$500 = \$125$$

For a corporation, the 25 percent rate can in principle be substituted for either the normal rate or the surtax rate, depending on its taxable income exclusive of long-term capital gains.   Since the capital gains rate is greater than the normal rate, this procedure will not be applied unless taxable income before capital gains equals or exceeds $25,000.   To illustrate, suppose that the ABC Corporation had a taxable income of $25,000 and capital gains of $10,000.   Normally its tax would be

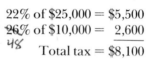

$$22\% \text{ of } \$25,000 = \$5,500$$
$$26\% \text{ of } \$10,000 = \ \ 2,600$$
$$\text{Total tax} = \$8,100$$

48

Alternatively, the corporation could apply the capital gains rate so that

$$22\% \text{ of } \$25,000 = \$5,500$$
$$25\% \text{ of } \$10,000 = \ \ 2,500$$
$$\text{Total tax} = \$8,000$$

Both individuals and corporations may compute their capital gains so that net capital gains equal long-term capital gains less the sum of long- and short-term capital losses.   Moreover, if capital losses exceed capital gains, individuals may offset them against ordinary income up to $1,000.   Capital losses in excess of amounts deductible may be carried over from one tax year to the next until they are exhausted. For corporations, however, capital losses cannot be set against ordinary income and can be carried over only as short-term losses for 5 years.[32]

What constitutes a sale or exchange of capital and, more important, what is considered to be taxable income are questions beyond the scope of an introductory text in finance.   Indeed, a thorough treatment of the subject would require at least a separate volume.[33]   Enough has been said to illustrate the point that differential tax treatment of corporations may be a serious impediment to adopting this form of organization.   In any given instance, whether it will be or not depends in large

[32]*Ibid.*, p. 67.

[33]For an introduction to the scope and complexities of the system, see *ibid.*, *passim*. See also Internal Revenue Service, U.S. Treasury, *Tax Guide for Small Business* and *Your Federal Income Tax* (Washington: Government Printing Office, published annually).

measure on the personal income of the owners. If their primary source of income is to be earnings from the firm, they would be better off not incorporating, thereby avoiding both the corporate income tax and the personal income tax on dividends received.

On the other hand, if the owners plan to participate actively in management, and the salaries they pay themselves would be viewed by the Internal Revenue Service as reasonable and hence a legitimate expense in computing corporate income taxes, there would be less reason for rejecting the corporate form because of separate tax treatment.

Assume that salaries are sufficient to meet personal needs. Then if dividends can legitimately be kept at a minimum or nonexistent (i.e., there appear to be ample investment opportunities within the firm, thus avoiding the specter of taxation on profits withheld to avoid personal income taxes), the disadvantages accorded to the corporate form in the revenue code may disappear altogether.

In closing this section we should note that Congress from time to time has not only altered the tax rates for both individuals and corporations but has also employed special and presumably temporary taxes on incomes, particularly corporate incomes. The excess profits taxes imposed during and after World War II are cases in point.

More recently, in May, 1968, Congress enacted legislation which imposed a temporary surcharge of 10 percent on the taxes of all individuals and corporations. Thus, if a person owed $10,000 in taxes on the basis of the rates applicable to him, the surtax of 10 percent would raise the amount owed from $10,000 to $11,000. Similarly, if a corporation owed $500,000 in taxes, the effect of the surcharge would be to raise the taxes payable from $500,000 to $550,000.

Since special taxes are not designed to be a permanent part of the structure, we shall ignore them in problems developed in this text. The student, however, should recognize that they are employed from time to time and will affect the profitability of the enterprise. When there are differences in the application of special taxes between individuals and corporations, they can have an effect, at least a temporary one, on the choice of business organization.

Other Legal Forms of Business Organization

At the beginning of this chapter, the joint-stock company and the business or Massachusetts trust were briefly mentioned. Neither is important today. Many states do not have statutes treating either as a separate form of business organization.

Joint-stock Company Historically the joint-stock company is the more important. Where specifically recognized under statute law, as in New York, the practice is to treat it as a corporation, except that the shareholders have unlimited liability. Prior to the enactment of liberal incorporation laws, the joint-stock company was not uncommon. It might be chartered, as in the case of some English colonization companies such as the East India and the Plymouth Companies. It can also be an unchartered private association. In either case, control is vested in the hands of the directors or trustees. Shares are freely transferable, but in practice the owners have no voice in management. The organization also has an existence independent of the lives of the shareowners.[34] Thus, the joint-stock company has not only the advantages of the corporation but the disadvantage of unlimited liability as well. It is therefore easy to see why, with the advent of liberal incorporation laws and limited liability, the joint-stock company declined in prominence.[35] In England, where all companies are joint-stock companies, the only distinction made is in the liability of the shareowners. Those with "Limited" after the company's name have limited liability and are similar to our corporations. They comprise the vast majority. Others, mostly old established firms, have chosen to retain the feature of unlimited liability. In the United States, Adam's Express Company is perhaps the best known joint-stock company.

Massachusetts Trust (or Business Trust) The business or Massachusetts trust is an organization in which trustees own the property of the enterprise and are responsible for management. Shares in the association are called certificates of beneficial interest and are freely transferable. Liability of the shareholders in states which recognize the business trust is limited, but certain measures must be taken in order to retain this feature. Creditors must be made aware of the fact that the assets of the business trust alone can be used to satisfy their claims and

[34]Livermore, *op. cit.*, pp. 674–676.

[35]The aftermath of speculation in the shares of the South Sea Company in 1720 tinged the joint-stock company with scandal. It was subsequently learned that the company had resorted to bribery in seducing Parliament into granting it a charter and giving the association among other things the right to trade in slaves in the West Indies. A grant of monopoly in a particular commodity was the usual reason for coveting a charter. The scandal precipitated the so-called Bubble Act of 1720. Unless chartered by Parliament, joint-stock companies could not organize, sell shares, or otherwise behave as corporations. The statute was not repealed until 1825. It applied, of course, to the American colonies until the Revolution. The Bubble Act was not always enforced; unchartered joint-stock companies existed in the colonies. These organizations, de facto corporations with unlimited liability, were the direct antecedents of the corporation as we know it today. See Hunt, *op. cit.*, pp. 3–55; Livermore, *op. cit.*, pp. 674–675, ftnt. 2; and Taylor, *op. cit.*, pp. 14–20.

the shareholders must give up the right to elect trustees.   Otherwise limited liability does not obtain.

The name Massachusetts trust comes from the state where it was popularized.   From 1827 to 1912, Massachusetts had a statute forbidding corporations to own real estate.   The formation of a business trust was a way around this restriction.   Public-utility holding companies, i.e., corporations specifically established to hold a controlling interest in the voting stock of an operating utility, have also used the Massachusetts trust device.   Under the laws of the Commonwealth, "any public utility will be dissolved if a foreign corporation . . . which controls a majority of the utility's stock issues certificates based upon this stock."[36]   Massachusetts trusts have been established to hold the utility's stock, thereby preventing it from becoming part of the assets of a foreign corporation.   Use of this form of organization, therefore, has been prompted more by restrictions placed on the corporation than by any advantages inherent in it.[37]   Among the more prominent business trusts are the New England Gas and Electric Association, the Eastern Gas and Fuel Associates, and the American Optical Company.

Both the Massachusetts trust and the joint-stock company are treated as corporations for federal income tax purposes.   Few states exempt them from the special taxes paid by corporations.

SUMMARY

The basic forms of business organization are the proprietorship, the partnership, and the corporation.   While the partnership form is the most numerous, the corporation form accounts for the bulk of our national income.   Other legal forms are of minor consequence.   The primary advantages of the corporation are continuity, limited liability,

---

[36] Elvin F. Donaldson and John K. Pfahl, *Corporation Finance, Policy and Management* (New York: The Ronald Press Company, 1963), p. 37.

[37] Beginning students of finance may confuse the business trust with the testamentary and voting trusts.   In the case of the former a will leaves property in the hands of the trustees, usually the trust department of a commercial bank.   The property is administered according to the terms of the will for the benefit of the heirs.

A voting trust is formed solely to exercise the voting privileges of the stock which is held in the trust.   The shareholders are given voting-trust certificates entitling them to the dividends on the shares, but the trustees have the power to vote the shares and hence have control over management of the corporation.   This was quite a popular device toward the end of the nineteenth century for controlling the stock of competing companies.   The Sherman Act, the first "antitrust" law, received its appellation because monopoly was associated with the voting trust.   Today, when used, the voting trust is confined to the shares of one company.   A corporation reorganized under the bankruptcy laws may become a voting trust for a temporary period.   The purpose may be to oversee management so that the mistakes which led to the previous failure will not be repeated.

and the ability to apportion to a fine degree the elements of risk, income, and control found in any business venture.   These features are not inherent in proprietorships or partnerships.   The primary disadvantages of the corporation are the ease with which its activities can be curtailed in foreign states and the separate tax treatment accorded it under the law.   Individuals cannot be restricted from carrying on business pursuits in various states.   Unincorporated enterprises are not automatically subject to separate tax treatment.   These advantages and disadvantages must be weighed by management when choosing its form of business organization or when considering a possible change in the legal status of the enterprise.

QUESTIONS

1.   "Although a proprietor or partners can take steps to lessen the burden or unlimited liability, only through incorporation can the owners guarantee limited liability."   Evaluate.

2.   "Economies of scale is the major reason for the importance of the corporation in the private economy."   Evaluate.

3.   Mr. Brown, Mr. Jones, and Mr. Smith have decided to go into the printing business.   It is estimated that it will cost $200,000 to put the firm into operation.   Each person is willing to contribute $50,000 and the bank will lend them an additional $50,000.   Discuss the factors they must consider before deciding whether to incorporate or form a partnership.

4.   "The corporate income tax has worked against proliferation of this form of organization in many areas of business enterprise."   Evaluate.

SELECTED REFERENCES

Chandler, Alfred D., Jr. "The Beginnings of 'Big Business' in American Industry," *Business History Review*, vol. 33, no. 1 (Spring, 1959), pp. 1–31.
Davies, Robert M., and Melvyn H. Lawrence. *Choosing a Form of Business Organization*. Durham, N.C.: Duke University Law School, 1963.
Hunt, Bishop C. *The Development of the Business Corporation in England 1800–1867*. Cambridge, Mass.: Harvard University Press, 1936.
Livermore, Shaw. "Unlimited Liability in Early American Corporations," *Journal of Political Economy*, vol. 43, no. 5 (October, 1935), pp. 674–687.
Joint Economic Committee, U.S. Congress. *The Federal Tax System: Facts and Problems, 1964*. Washington: Government Printing office, 1964.

Two Systems of Business Accounting

chapter Three

Financial managers must make decisions based on information supplied under generally accepted accounting principles. Yet the modern theory of financial management calls for information based on a different set of principles. Using the balance sheet, income statement, and sources of funds statement, we shall focus our attention in this chapter on the differences in information obtained from each set of principles. In particular, the student should note the effects on income and asset values of adhering to the accounting concept of original cost rather than the economic concept of replacement cost or market value.

Introduction

Throughout this volume the student of finance will encounter analytical tools calling for data to be used to measure such important concepts as net income, liquidity, flow of funds, and stocks of assets and liabilities. The raw data on which these measurements must be based are derived from a system of accounts established under "generally accepted principles of accounting."

While there is no single comprehensive list of principles binding the accounting profession, certain practices and procedures ordinarily used are important in interpreting the data on which financial decisions must be made, or in explaining the results of past decisions. There is a need, therefore, to bridge the gap between the data and the concepts applicable to an introductory analysis. To supply this bridge is the function of this chapter.

Income

To management and owners, actual or potential, perhaps the single most important statistic is the figure for net income or profit. In this measure lie the results of past decisions, the indicium of management's performance, the basis for valuing the owners' equity in the firm, and the guide to resource allocation in a market economy. Empirically, income is simply the difference between revenues and expenses. Conceptually, however, as John R. Hicks argues, income is what an individual "can consume during the week and still expect to be as well off at the end of the week as he was at the beginning."[1]

Net Income Applying this economic definition to the business firm, net income would be the maximum amount that could be distributed as cash payments to the owners during a period and still leave the value of their equity at the end of the period the same as it was at the beginning of the period. Empirically, therefore, if we are to implement this definition, income must be the difference between the revenue *earned* during a period and the cost of *replacing* the assets used up in obtaining the revenue. But generally accepted accounting procedures ordinarily result in a measure of income equal to *realized* revenue less the *historical*, or *original*, cost of the assets used up in obtaining this revenue.

The difference between earned and realized revenue can be illustrated by a simple example. Suppose that a manufacturing firm has, besides the usual investment in plant, equipment, and inventories, marketable securities, perhaps U.S. government bonds, whose original

[1]John R. Hicks, *Value and Capital*, 2d ed. (London: Oxford University Press, 1957), p. 176.

cost was $1,000,000. Their market value as of the end of the account-ing period is $1,100,000. If these securities were sold, an accountant would recognize the difference between the original cost and the sale price as realized revenue. Similarly, he would set off against these revenues the expenses involved in selling the securities, the difference being the income realized from the sale.[2] But Hicks, as well as other economists, would have the firm recognize the net proceeds as income earned during the accounting period, whether realized or not. Thus revenue earned would necessitate a periodic writing up, or if their value fell, a writing down, of the firm's assets. Accountants, however, deal in what is and not in what would be. In general they recognize revenue only when a sale is actually made.

A simple example can also illustrate the difference between cal-culating expenses based on the historical cost of assets and their re-placement cost. Many firms have funds invested in plant and equipment whose useful life is usually longer than the accounting period em-ployed in estimating profits.[3] The standard procedure is to estimate the useful life of the asset and its scrap value. Then, using a specific formula, the accountant will charge against revenues each year a portion of the original cost of the asset.

[2] The student with little or no training in accounting should bear in mind the fact that revenues and expenses can be realized either at the time the sale is made or when the money from the sale of the securities is received. The first procedure is called the accrual method of accounting. A sale has been made in good faith and payment is expected. The revenues as well as the expenses of marketing the securities are realized. Alterna-tively, if one keeps books on a cash basis, neither revenues nor expenses are recognized until the firm receives a check for the proceeds less commissions. The overwhelming majority of business firms establish their accounting system on an accrual rather than a cash basis.

[3] Fundamental to any set of accounting practices is the task of selecting which ex-penditures are assets and which are expenses assignable to revenues during a particular accounting period. Assume that this period is a calendar year. Then, in general, if an expenditure has a useful life in excess of a year, accountants will *capitalize* it, i.e., treat the expenditure as an asset. Thus a new machine with a useful life of 5 years is an asset. Accountants will depreciate the asset on the basis of its historical cost, its 5-year life, and its scrap value. The depreciation expense for each year is charged against revenues for that year. Alternatively, expenditures to repair a machine are usually not capitalized but treated as expenses in the year in which they occurred. This raises a fundamental question. Suppose the so-called maintenance expenditures lengthen the useful life of an asset. Should they be charged off against revenues? The answer is that to capitalize all repairs and maintenance associated with an asset may prove im-practical. Rather than depreciating the asset using the estimated useful life without maintenance and then capitalizing the maintenance expenditures, it is less complicated to write off the original cost of the machine using an estimated useful life with normal maintenance, and charging these expenditures as they occur to revenues for that period.

In passing, the student of finance should note the way the term capitalize is em-ployed. The standard accounting treatment is to equate the word with asset. The term has a different meaning, as we shall see, when applied to capital budgeting procedures. The nouns *capital* and *capitalization* also will be used in various contexts throughout this volume.

To illustrate, assume that the useful life of a machine is 5 years. Its original cost is $10,000. No scrap value is anticipated. Three of the many possible ways of depreciating the machine are illustrated in Table 3-1. Perhaps the most widely used is the *straight-line method*. We simply divide the original cost less the scrap value by the estimated useful life of the asset. Thus

$$\frac{\$10,000 - \$0}{5} = \$2,000$$

Assuming that the accounting period is a year, a depreciation expense of $2,000 is charged each year against revenues for that year. At the end of 5 years the asset is presumably replaced and the process begins all over again.

Accelerated Depreciation The other two procedures, the *sum of years' digits method* and the *double declining balance method*, are both techniques of accelerated depreciation. Each results in a larger depreciation expense in the earlier years of the asset's useful life than in the later years. To employ the first method we merely sum the years over which the asset is expected to be used. Thus

$$1 + 2 + 3 + 4 + 5 = 15$$

Depreciation for the first year can be calculated by taking the sum of years' digits as the denominator and the last year as the numerator, then applying the ratio to original cost. This gives

$$\frac{5}{15} \times \$10,000 = \$3,333.33$$

For the second year, the ratio is 4/15; for the third year, 3/15; and so on.

In using the double declining balance method to estimate depreciation, the procedure is to double the straight-line estimate and make it a percentage of original cost. This percentage is applied first to the original cost and then in subsequent years to the original cost less the accumulated depreciation. Thus depreciation for the first year is $4,000:

$$\$2,000 \times 2 = \$4,000 = 40\% \text{ of } \$10,000$$

The declining balance for the second year is $6,000, so that depreciation is

$$40\% \text{ of } \$6,000 = \$2,400$$

The impetus for employing techniques of accelerated depreciation comes more from the tax laws than from the belief that assets wear out in this way. As we shall see in the chapters on capital budgeting, a dollar today is worth more than a dollar a year from today. The

TABLE 3-1: THREE METHODS OF DEPRECIATING A MACHINE WHOSE ORIGINAL COST IS $10,000, WHOSE EXPECTED LIFE IS 5 YEARS, AND WHOSE SCRAP VALUE IS ZERO

Year	Straight-line Method		Sum of Years' Digits Method		Double Declining Balance Method	
	Book Value	Depreciation	Book Value	Depreciation	Book Value	Depreciation
First	$10,000 8,000	$2,000	$10,000.00 6,666.67	5/15 of $10,000 = $3,333.33	$10,000 6,000	40% of $10,000 = $4,000
Second	6,000	2,000	4,000.00	4/15 of $10,000 = $2,666.67	3,600	40% of $6,000 = $2,400
Third	4,000	2,000	2,000.00	3/15 of $10,000 = $2,000.00	2,160	40% of $3,600 = $1,440
Fourth	2,000	2,000	666.67	2/15 of $10,000 = $1,333.33	1,296	40% of $2,160 = $864
Fifth	0	2,000	0	1/15 of $10,000 = $666.67	0	$1,296

larger the depreciation expense, the lower the taxable income and hence the lower the corporate taxes. Even if the rate of asset expansion tapered off so that depreciation declined in later years and thus caused taxable income to rise, the earlier allowances and the tax savings could have been reinvested in income-producing assets.

Since the Internal Revenue Service recognizes for tax purposes both the sum of years' digits and the double declining balance methods — indeed, it recognizes any reasonable basis of depreciation — accountants have used these techniques in estimating taxable profits. They may, however, report profits on the basis of straight-line depreciation, reserving the accelerated techniques for income tax purposes. The result is to "normalize" reported profits, i.e., to prevent the figure from being affected by rates of change in the depreciation expense due to the procedures employed.

Regardless of the technique used, the outcome is depreciation based on original cost. To determine expenses on the basis of replacement cost, management would have to know the value of the present asset and the cost of replacing it with a new model. Thus, in the case of the machine, if at the end of the first year it could be sold for $8,000 and a duplicate purchased for $10,500, depreciation on the basis of replacement cost would be

$$\$10,500 - \$8,000 = \$2,500$$

In this way the calculation of expenses,[4] and therefore of profits, yields a figure which makes allowance for the fact that the original cost and the present value of assets are not necessarily the same. Since prices vary over time, to duplicate facilities[5] at current prices, there must be an appropriate allowance for depreciation equal to the funds needed to make up the difference between the market value of the existing assets and their replacement cost.

Calculation of Inventory Expenses   A similar problem arises in the calculation of inventory expenses. Accounting techniques do recognize changes in the prices of inventories used up in the production

---

[4]A complication arises because the Internal Revenue Service does not allow as a tax-deductible expense depreciation on the basis of replacement cost. Suppose that management elects to depreciate for tax purposes on a straight-line basis. The difference in depreciation would be $500 ($2,500 − $2,000). Since the additional $500 is not tax-deductible, the firm must earn $2,000 + $500 + tax rate($500). Using a rate of 48 percent, the firm must earn $2,000 + $500(1 + 0.48), or $2,740, before taxes to yield $2,500 after taxes.

[5]Note the emphasis on duplication. We are stressing change in prices due to shifts in demand or to increases in the costs and hence in the supply price of an asset. Excluded from consideration would be changes in price due to the substitution of a technologically different model. In practice, of course, it is difficult to separate the impact of technological advances from changes in price due to shifts in demand or inflation in costs.

or merchandising process.   But again the procedures employed simply allocate historical costs.   They do not give consideration to the costs of replacing these inventories.   To illustrate, suppose the ABC Corporation is a merchandising concern selling only one product.   It had the following record of inventory purchases for the accounting year.

Inventory at Beginning of Year	10,000 units × $10 = $ 100,000
Purchases, January 15th	200,000 units × 10 = 2,000,000
Purchases, June 15th	200,000 units × 15 = 3,000,000
Purchases, September 15th	90,000 units × 20 = 1,800,000

If we assume that inventory is used so that the first units purchased are the first units sold, and if at the end of the year there are 10,000 units in stock, then the value of the inventory on hand as of that date is 10,000 × $20, or $200,000.   This technique is known as the *first-in, first-out*, or *FIFO*, method of valuing inventories.

If, on the other hand, it had been assumed that the ABC Corporation depleted its inventory on a *last-in, first-out*, or *LIFO*, basis, each of the 10,000 units remaining would have been valued at $10, or a total of $100,000.   The two methods yield different values for inventories and hence for cost of goods sold.   In the first case, cost of inventory sold is $6,700,000.   In the second case, it is $6,800,000.   The LIFO method of inventory valuation would, in this instance, reduce reported income by $100,000 and income taxes by $48,000.

Similar difficulties arise when valuing raw materials for the purpose of arriving at the cost of finished goods for a manufacturing firm.   As long as there is an upward trend in the prices of the raw materials purchased, the LIFO method of valuation will raise the cost of goods sold and lower profits over what they would be if the FIFO technique had been adopted.   Should the prices of raw materials or inventories fall during the accounting period, the results would be reversed.   FIFO would give a higher cost of goods sold and lower profits than LIFO.

There are other methods of arriving at the cost of inventories,[6] but FIFO and LIFO are the most widely used.   Since FIFO is more likely to correspond to the physical flow of inventory, particularly where goods are perishable, it would seem to be the more logical of the two methods for allocating historical costs.   Until the postwar inflation

[6]Some firms rely on a weighted-average method in which all changes in the price of inventories purchased during the year are given consideration.   A few firms avoid the problem by charging inventory with the specific item as it is sold.   This method may prove quite costly for concerns whose inventories comprise numerous small items.   Hence most companies avoid this perpetual method of valuing inventories.   For a more complete discussion of these and related methods, see David A. Corbin, *Accounting and Economic Decisions* (New York: Dodd, Mead & Company, Inc., 1964), pp. 261–274.

occurred, it was the most popular method. But with rising prices swelling inventory costs and with the attempt to pass these costs on in higher retail prices, taxable profits were greater under FIFO than under LIFO. As a result there was an incentive to change. Many firms, with the approval of the Internal Revenue Service, did adopt, for tax purposes at least, the LIFO method.

In order to calculate inventory expense on the basis of replacement cost, we must allow for changes in the market value. Thus, in the above example, if it cost $25 per unit to replace the 10,000 units on hand at the end of the year, and assuming the 10,000 units at the beginning of the year cost $10 a unit to replace, then the cost of purchasing 10,000 units held at the end of the accounting period is $250,000 rather than $100,000 as the LIFO method indicates or $200,000 as the FIFO technique suggests. Moreover, as it is logical to assume that inventories are continuously being replaced at the current market price, we can approximate the replacement cost of inventory expense as follows:[7]

10,000 × January 15th purchase price of $10	= $ 100,000
200,000 × June 15th purchase price of $15	= 3,000,000
200,000 × September 15th purchase price of $20	= 4,000,000
90,000 × current purchase price of $25	= 225,000
Gross Inventory Purchases at Replacement Cost	$7,325,000
Less Closing Inventory Balance at Replacement Cost	− 250,000
Net Inventory Expense	$7,075,000

It will be instructive to illustrate the difference between the accounting and economic approaches to measuring net income by comparing an income statement based on realized revenues less historical cost with one estimated on the basis of revenues earned less replacement cost at current market values. Assume the XYZ Corporation, a manufacturing concern, writes off its assets using straight-line depreciation and estimates inventory expenses on a FIFO basis. This results in a depreciation expense of $1,000,000 and an inventory expense of $6,000,000. The book value of its fixed assets as of the beginning of the year was $21,000,000, while the replacement cost rose from $26,000,000 to $28,000,000. The cost of replacing inventory used up during the year

[7]Again the Internal Revenue Service would not allow inventory expense to be calculated on the basis of replacement costs. Assuming the FIFO method was employed, the difference in inventory expenses would be $7,075,000 less $6,700,000, or $375,000. In order to yield an inventory expense reflecting replacement costs after taxes, the firm would have to charge $6,700,000 + $375,000(1 + 0.48), or $7,255,000, before taxes.

was $8,000,000.   The XYZ Corporation also carried marketable securities whose original cost was $1,000,000.   None was sold during the year but the market value rose by $225,000.   To simplify computations, assume that the corporate income tax is a flat 48 percent of taxable income.   Assume further that gross sales for the year were $15,400,000. There were also finished goods on hand which when valued at retail totaled $400,000.   Finally, assume that for tax purposes the Internal Revenue Service will recognize both the economic and the accounting approaches to determining income.[8]   We then have the possibilities shown on the next page.

In comparing the two approaches to income determination, note first that the finished-goods inventory is included in the sales figure. We could have listed it among other income but orthodox economic analysis does not distinguish between the production of a good and its sale.[9]   Thus the market value of the finished-goods inventory can be recognized as sales revenue earned.   If we assume that the $100,000 allowance was for sales returns only, it follows that in employing the economic approach there would be no deduction from gross sales.   At the same time we would deduct the replacement cost of the finished-goods inventory, which we have assumed in this case to be 50 percent of the sales markup, or $200,000.

Similarly, when recognizing revenue earned but not realized from the sale of marketable securities, we should subtract the expenses associated with a sale should it take place.   Because the accounting approach to income determination recognizes only realized revenues, to be consistent it must also deduct only realized expenses.   Thus, in the accounting approach, accrued interest on marketable securities was $40,000 for the year but no other expenses were incurred.   When calculating income earned, in this instance an increase in the market value of $225,000, we must anticipate the expenses involved if the securities are sold.   This is assumed to be $25,000.

It would appear from a comparison of income statements that about all the two techniques have in common is identical calculations for wages, for selling, and for administrative expenses.   A more detailed analysis, however, would reveal that selling and administrative expenses also include depreciation on assets not directly associated with the

[8]Suppose that this were not the case.   Then on the basis of footnotes 4 and 7, compute the net income required before taxes to meet replacement cost criteria.   Also keep in mind the fact that the Internal Revenue Service, while not recognizing replacement cost, does not ordinarily tax unrealized income.

[9]The theories of imperfect or monopolistic competition do make the distinction but the more substantive models of pure competition and pure monopoly do not.   For a brief discussion of this point, see Donald Dewey, *Monopoly in Economics and Law* (Chicago: Rand McNally & Company, 1959), pp. 87–88.

XYZ CORPORATION

Statement of Income
Year Ending December 31, 19___

	Accounting Approach		Economic Approach	
Sales		$15,400,000		$15,800,000
Less Sales, Returns, Allowances, and Discounts		−100,000		
Net Sales		$15,300,000		
Deduct Cost of Goods Sold				
Inventory	−$6,000,000		−$8,000,000	
Replacement Cost of Finished-goods Inventory			−200,000	
Depreciation	−1,000,000		−2,000,000	
Manufacturing Wages	−500,000	−7,500,000	−500,000	−10,700,000
Gross Profit on Sales		**$ 7,800,000**		**$ 5,100,000**
Less Operating Expenses				
Selling Expenses	−$1,500,000		−$1,500,000	
Administrative Expenses	−900,000	−2,400,000	−900,000	−2,400,000
Net Operating Income		$ 5,400,000		$ 2,700,000
Add Other Income		40,000	265,000	
Deduct Other Expenses			−25,000	240,000
Income before Interest and Taxes		$ 5,440,000		$ 2,940,000
Less Interest		−300,000		−300,000
Income before Taxes		$ 5,140,000		$ 2,640,000
Less Income Taxes		−2,467,200		−1,267,200
Income after Taxes		$ 2,672,800		$ 1,372,800
Less Dividends		−1,000,000		−1,000,000
Net Income after Taxes and Dividends		**$ 1,672,800**		**$ 372,800**

manufacturing plant. In order to simplify the example, we have ignored these factors and the differences that would result.

More generally, these approaches to income determination overlap in two areas. Both approaches include revenues realized. The economic approach simply adds revenue earned to this figure. Each approach accepts the actual cost of services rendered, whether they are wages, salaries, or rentals paid for assets. Accountants always recognize explicit costs as they occur.   The economist also accepts them because they measure the market value of the services rendered.   The results diverge because of different techniques for valuing assets and liabilities and because the economic approach recognizes income earned and the expenses associated with it.[10]

Assets and Liabilities

At the end of the accounting period we can, with the aid of the balance sheets at the beginning and the end of the year together with the income statement, calculate the flow of funds over the period as a whole.   To illustrate, using both the accounting and economic approaches to valuing assets, suppose the XYZ Corporation issued the balance sheet at the beginning of the year as shown on the following page.

The marked divergence in valuation is readily apparent.   The book value of cash is, of course, the same as its market value or replacement cost but there was a difference in marketable securities because of an increase in their market value.   We have assumed that the original costs (or book and market value) of the accounts receivables, as well as the current liabilities, are the same.   While the receivables might be sold to a factor, that is, to one specializing in the purchase of receivables, with the savings in collection costs more than offsetting the difference between the proceeds from their sale and their face value, we shall ignore the possibility.

Similarly, we can assume that the current liabilities are not marketable and hence there is no opportunity to repurchase them at a figure which varies from their book value.   On the other hand, we have also assumed that the long-term debt can currently be repurchased by the firm at a discount from its face value.   Apparently the 4 percent rate of interest is low relative to the going yield on long-term debt of comparable quality.

We assumed earlier that inventory for the accounting approach was valued on a FIFO basis.   Here, however, generally accepted principles of accounting do recognize market value.   The valuation is cost or market, whichever is lower.   We can see from the economic valuation that inventory based on original cost under FIFO is lower.

Note also that, in calculating the replacement cost of fixed assets, there is no allowance for depreciation.   This is because the deprecia-

---

[10]To the extent that wages are implicit, e.g., the salary of a proprietor, the economic but not necessarily the accounting approach would recognize the salary as an expense before calculating net profit.   The basis of determination is the salary the proprietor could earn elsewhere, i.e., his opportunity cost.

tion expense equals the change in replacement cost for the year.   Hence it is added to, or if negative is subtracted from, the market value of the asset at the beginning of the period so as to equal the replacement cost at the end of the period.

XYZ CORPORATION
Balance Sheet
December 31, 19___
Beginning of Accounting Period

Assets	Accounting Valuation		Economic Valuation	
Current Assets				
Cash		$ 1,000,000		$ 1,000,000
Marketable Securities		1,000,000		1,100,000
Accounts Receivable		5,000,000		5,000,000
Inventory				
Raw Materials	$100,000		$200,000	
Work in Process				
Finished Goods	100,000	200,000	200,000	400,000
		$ 7,200,000		$ 7,500,000
Fixed Assets				
Land		1,000,000		2,000,000
Buildings (Plant)	25,000,000			
Less Accumulated Depreciation	−10,000,000	15,000,000		17,000,000
Equipment	10,000,000			
Less Accumulated Depreciation	−5,000,000	5,000,000		7,000,000
Total Fixed Assets		$21,000,000		$26,000,000
Total Assets		**$28,200,000**		**$33,500,000**
Liabilities and Owners' Equity (Capital)				
Current Liabilities				
Accounts Payable		500,000		500,000
Notes Payable		300,000		300,000
Interest Payable		120,000		120,000
Taxes Payable		480,000		480,000
		$ 1,400,000		$ 1,400,000
Long-term Liabilities				
4% Mortgage Bonds Mature July 1, 1977		6,000,000		5,800,000
Total Liabilities		$ 7,400,000		$ 7,200,000

Assets	Accounting Valuation	Economic Valuation
Owners' Equity (Capital)		
Common stock, par value $10; 2,000,000 shares authorized; issued and outstanding, 1,000,000 shares	10,000,000	26,300,000
Capital Surplus	1,000,000	
Earned Surplus	9,800,000	
Total Owners' Equity (Capital)	$20,800,000	$26,300,000
Total Liabilities and Owners' Equity	**$28,200,000**	**$33,500,000**

Finally, since the value of the assets equals their replacement cost or market value and since the liabilities are also valued at market, the residual or owners' equity equals the market value of the common stock. In the economic approach to constructing a balance sheet, changes in net income after taxes and dividends as well as changes in the market value of assets and liabilities are reflected in changes in the market value of the common stock or owners' equity.   Accountants, however, regard the common stock and paid-in surplus accounts as equivalent to the consideration received when the company was formed.   In the accounting approach, income after taxes and dividends is added to the earned surplus account.[11]

---

[11]In general, changes in the earned surplus accounts of consecutive balance sheets must always equal net profit after taxes and dividends.   Assets and liabilities will rise and fall as the firm earns revenues and incurs expenses, liquidating the liabilities that result. The system of double-entry bookkeeping which underlies accounting techniques ensures that an asset, say accounts receivable, will be increased (in accounting terminology, debited) along with the sales revenue account (which is credited).   When an expense is incurred, say, property taxes, then a liability account, property taxes payable, is increased (credited) along with the expense account, property taxes (which is debited).   At the end of the year the revenue and expense accounts are "cleared," i.e., expenses are charged to revenues (revenues are debited and expenses credited).   The residual—that is, net profits after taxes and dividends—is credited to earned surplus.   Until they are paid, taxes and dividends are liabilities.

Those familiar with accounting techniques will recognize some oversimplifications. First, the cost of goods sold has been excluded.   But the same result is reached with or without this step.   Second, earned surplus can be affected by transactions not cleared through the income and expense accounts.   Revaluation of assets and stock dividends are examples.   Among the other numerous possibilities is repayment of credit extended. Notes payable, a liability, is reduced (debited), along with an asset, cash (which is credited). Finally, there are numerous expense items which, because they are liquidated shortly after they are incurred, rarely appear as liabilities on a balance sheet.   Wages are a good example.   This expense reflects, instead of an increase in a liability, wages payable, a reduction in an asset, cash.

Suppose that the corporation issued the accompanying balance sheet for the end of the year. We shall subsequently employ this balance sheet in constructing a funds statement.

XYZ CORPORATION
Balance Sheet
December 31, 19___
End of Accounting Period

Assets		Accounting Valuation		Economic Valuation
Current Assets				
Cash		$ 1,167,800		$ 1,372,800
Marketable Securities		1,000,000		1,300,000
Accounts Receivable		7,000,000		7,000,000
Inventory				
Raw Materials	$ 75,000		$ 25,000	
Work in Process				
Finished Goods	150,000	225,000	400,000	425,000
		$ 9,392,800		$ 10,097,800
Fixed Assets				
Land		$ 1,000,000		$ 2,000,000
Buildings (Plant)	$ 25,000,000			
Less Accumulated				
Depreciation	− 10,750,000	14,250,000		18,000,000
Equipment	$ 10,000,000			
Less Accumulated				
Depreciation	− 5,250,000	4,750,000		8,000,000
Total Fixed Assets		$ 20,000,000		$ 28,000,000
Total Assets		**$ 29,392,800**		**$ 38,097,800**
Liabilities and Owners' Equity (Capital)				
Current Liabilities				
Accounts Payable		$ 100,000		$ 100,000
Notes Payable		100,000		100,000
Interest Payable		120,000		120,000
Taxes Payable		600,000		300,000
		$ 920,000		$ 620,000
Long-term Liabilities				
4% Mortgage Bonds				
Mature				
July 1, 1977		6,000,000		5,700,000
Total Liabilities		$ 6,920,000		$ 6,320,000

Assets	Accounting Valuation	Economic Valuation
Owners' Equity (Capital)		
Common Stock, par value $ 10; 2,000,000 shares authorized; issued and out- standing, 1,000,000 shares	$ 10,000,000	$ 31,777,800
Capital Surplus	1,000,000	
Earned Surplus	11,472,800	
Total Owners' Equity (Capital)	$ 22,472,800	$ 31,777,800
Total Liabilities and Owners' Equity	**$ 29,392,800**	**$ 38,097,800**

Flow of Funds   To understand the *flow of funds* concept, we must keep in mind that any decrease in an asset account or increase in a liability or owners' equity account is in the accounting approach to valuation a source of funds.   By floating new stock issues, incurring debt, or selling assets, a firm receives funds which are then available to increase assets, repay debt, and retire stock issues.   Similarly, changes in the earned surplus account result from changes in net income after taxes and dividends.   Thus net income is a source of funds.   Finally, depreciation, although an expense and hence a charge against income, does not involve, as do wages, taxes, etc., a corresponding outlay of cash or an increase in a current liability account.   Thus it can also be regarded as a source of funds.[12]

In employing the economic approach to valuation, depreciation and net income are also sources of funds, but the latter is used to restate assets on the basis of their replacement cost.[13]   Similarly, a portion of net profits is allocated to replace inventory at its current market value.   To

---

[12]In the accounting fraternity eyebrows are usually raised when one speaks of depreciation, or for that matter any noncash expense—depletion, for instance—as a source of funds.   If depreciation is increased, other things remaining the same, reported profits fall.   The sum of the two is unchanged.   See Robert K. Jaedicke and Robert T. Sprouse, *Accounting Flows: Income, Funds, and Cash* (Englewood Cliffs, N.J.: Prentice-Hall, Inc., 1965), pp. 85–86.   Pursuing a controversy of this nature can be sterile.   Of course, changes in depreciation have no effect on the total sources of funds except insofar as a larger depreciation expense reduces taxable profits.   Moreover, if a loss occurs after depreciation has been subtracted, then cash expenses will absorb some or perhaps all of the funds that would otherwise have been available.   To call depreciation a source of funds is merely to accept the accounting format in determining total sources.

[13]Alternatively, in the accounting approach, instead of saying depreciation is a source of funds we could argue that a decrease in assets, because they are depreciated and/ or sold, is a source of funds.

the extent that these assets are increased, they represent a use of these funds.   To the extent that original cost exceeds replacement cost, both depreciation and the adjustment for inventory valuation are negative, thereby raising net profits.   As a result, additional funds are available to increase other assets, decrease liabilities, and increase dividends.   If assets are increased and liabilities decreased, then, other things remaining the same, the market value of the common stock will rise.   On the other hand, if dividends are increased, the market price of the common stock will fall.

Finally, as in the case of the accounting approach, increases in liabilities and owners' equity through the issuance of new shares represent sources of funds.   Using the two balance sheets and the income statement, we can construct the accompanying sources and applications of funds statement employing both approaches.

XYZ CORPORATION
Statement of Sources and Applications of Funds
Year _____

	Accounting Valuation	Economic Valuation
Sources of Funds		
Net Income	$1,672,800	$ 372,800
Depreciation	1,000,000	2,000,000
Total Funds from Operation	$2,672,800	$2,372,800
Decrease in Assets		
Increase in Liabilities		
Increase in Taxes Payable	120,000	
Increase in Owners' Equity		3,105,000
Total Sources	**$2,792,800**	**$5,477,800**
Applications (Uses) of Funds		
Increase in Assets		
Increase in Cash	$ 167,800	$ 372,800
Increase in Marketable Securities		200,000
Increase in Accounts Receivable	2,000,000	2,000,000
Increase in Inventory	25,000	25,000
Increase in Fixed Assets		2,000,000
Decrease in Liabilities		
Decrease in Accounts Payable	400,000	400,000
Decrease in Notes Payable	200,000	200,000
Decrease in Taxes Payable		180,000
Decrease in Bonds Payable		100,000
Decrease in Owners' Equity		
Total Uses	**$2,792,800**	**$5,477,800**

From a comparison of the two approaches, it is apparent that a major source of divergence lies in the increase in owners' equity. No new stock was issued, yet in employing the economic approach to valuation there was an increase of $3,105,800. From the two balance sheets we observe that the market value of the stock rose from $26,300,000 at the beginning of the year to $31,777,800 at the end of the year, or an increase of $5,477,800, of which $2,372,800 was accounted for by net income and depreciation. The remainder was accounted for by an increase in the market value of the assets and a decrease in the market value of the liabilities. In fact, we can drop the accounting convention and rearrange the above statement so that all funds are accounted for by changes in assets, liabilities, and owners' equity. We get the following statement.

	Accounting Valuation	Economic Valuation
Sources of Funds		
Decrease in Assets		
Decrease in Fixed Assets	$1,000,000	
Increase in Liabilities		
Increase in Taxes Payable	120,000	
Increase in Owners' Equity	1,672,800	$5,477,800
Total Sources	**$2,792,800**	**$5,477,800**
Application (Uses) of Funds		
Increase in Assets		
Increase in Cash	$ 167,800	$ 372,800
Increase in Marketable Securities		200,000
Increase in Accounts Receivable	2,000,000	2,000,000
Increase in Inventory	25,000	25,000
Increase in Fixed Assets		2,000,000
Decrease in Liabilities		
Decrease in Accounts Payable	400,000	400,000
Decrease in Notes Payable	200,000	200,000
Decrease in Taxes Payable		180,000
Decrease in Bonds Payable		100,000
Decrease in Owners' Equity		
Total Uses	**$2,792,800**	**$5,477,800**

Owners' Equity By presenting the flow of funds as changes in assets, liabilities, and owners' equity, we can see that in the accounting approach variations in owners' equity are the direct result of an increase in retained earnings. Most accountants prefer to separate this source of funds from changes in owners' equity due to, perhaps, the purchase or sale of new securities. Moreover, instead of treating depreciation as a source of funds, we have chosen to recognize as the source the decrease in book value of the assets resulting from the depreciation charge. The treatment of liabilities remains unchanged.

In the economic approach, however, changes in owners' equity are the result of three factors: (1) the flow of net income after expenses based on the replacement cost of assets used in the production process; (2) the change in the market value of the assets, net of selling costs, or, in the case of producing assets, net of replacement costs; and (3) changes in the value of the liabilities. These are not the only factors relevant to the market value of the owners' equity. As we shall learn in subsequent chapters, the variability in the flow of net income resulting from the nature of the business will affect the market value of the owners' equity. The nature of the business will in turn determine the composition of the assets and liabilities which will also affect the market value of a share in the firm. Finally, if new shares are issued or retired, the subsequent increase or decrease in the market value of the owners' equity becomes a source or a use of funds.

Ratio Analysis — Measures of Profitability

Those using accounting information, whether they be management, security analysts, or the investing public, have placed some reliance on financial ratios as indicators of both the profitability and the liquidity of the enterprise. These ratios are numerous and there are widespread variations on the same measure.[14] All of them, however, are subject to the limitations inherent in the information system based on generally accepted accounting principles. Thus it will be useful to compare selected ratios for the XYZ Corporation based on both original cost and market values.

Rate of Return on Total Assets Turning first to measures of profitability, the most comprehensive ratio is the *rate of return on total assets*, or alternatively, on total capital where capital equals the sum of the liabilities and owners' equity. Because we want a measure of the profitability of the assets employed, the numerator of the ratio is income or earnings before interest and taxes. Since our stock of assets is for the beginning and the end of the period while the flow of income is over the entire period, we do not have sufficient information to calculate changes

---

[14]For a discussion of key ratios, see Benjamin Graham et al., *Security Analysis: Principles and Technique*, 4th ed. (New York: McGraw-Hill Book Company, 1962), pp. 224–249 and related chapters.

in the rate of return over the entire period. The ordinary procedure, therefore, is to compute the return based on end-of-year balance-sheet figures. This facilitates comparisons between end-of-year results. Thus

$$\text{Rate of return on assets} = \frac{\text{income before interest and taxes}}{\text{total assets}}$$

Accounting Valuation:

$$\text{Rate of return on assets} = \frac{\$5,440,000}{\$29,392,800} = 18.51\%$$

Economic Valuation:

$$\text{Rate of return on assets} = \frac{\$2,940,000}{\$38,097,800} = 7.72\%$$

This ratio assumes numerous forms. Some analysts exclude from the denominator such nonoperating assets as marketable securities and such intangibles as the value of patent rights. From the numerator they would exclude nonoperating or other income. We have chosen to do neither. Our reasoning is that the total assets and income are the results directly or indirectly of the operations of the firm. Perhaps because of fluctuations in the demand for the products, there are reasons for holding given amounts of marketable securities which can be conveniently liquidated to meet the firm's obligations as they come due. Rather than keep these funds as idle cash, it is more profitable to place them in interest-bearing securities. Whether there is too much or too little in nonoperating assets is another question, which we shall explore more fully in subsequent chapters.[15]

From the results it is apparent that, because of rising replacement costs, the rate of return on the book value of the assets is overstated. On the other hand, because allowance has been made for these costs, the market value of the assets and owners' equity has risen. As we have seen, however, all of the increase is in the market value of the stock. Thus the rise not only results from allowing for the replacement cost of fixed assets and inventory as well as for increases in the value of marketable securities and the amount of receivables outstanding, but also results from debt reductions. Given the new composition of assets, liabilities, and owners' equity, the market rate of return on total assets or total capital is 7.72 percent.

[15]If the concern is diversified, we may wish to divide income and assets among the products produced or services rendered in order to arrive at separate rates of return. In so doing, we must make the assumption that the whole is equal to the sum of its parts. If diversification results in economies of scale, the assumption is not valid.

Rate of Return on Sales   A second measure of profitability is the *rate of return on sales*, defined as follows:

$$\text{Rate of return on sales} = \frac{\text{income before interest and taxes}}{\text{net sales}}$$

Accounting Valuation:

$$\text{Rate of return on sales} = \frac{\$5,440,000}{\$15,300,000} = 35.56\%$$

Economic Valuation:

$$\text{Rate of return on sales} = \frac{\$2,940,000}{\$15,800,000} = 18.61\%$$

Again, some analysts prefer to use operating income. For reasons already discussed, we have chosen to use total income before interest and taxes. The significance of this ratio lies in the way in which it can be related to the rate of return on assets. Thus

$$\frac{\text{Income before interest and taxes}}{\text{Net sales}} \times \frac{\text{net sales}}{\text{total assets}}$$

$$= \frac{\text{income before interest and taxes}}{\text{total assets}}$$

Given the desired rate of return on assets and the ratio of sales to assets or, as it is more popularly called, the *sales-asset ratio*, we can calculate the profit margin on sales necessary to achieve our goal. Some firms can anticipate absolutely low sales-asset ratios — public utilities, for example. Others can expect absolutely high sales-asset ratios — many wholesale and retail trade stores, for example. Manufacturing firms tend to fall somewhere in between. In general, firms requiring relatively high levels of plant and equipment to produce their goods or services will have low sales-asset ratios. Those whose assets consist largely of inventory will ordinarily experience high sales-asset ratios.[16] To the extent that inventory is turned over rapidly into sales, large amounts can pass through the firm during the course of the year with relatively low balances at the beginning and the end of the period. There can be a small profit margin on each item sold without diluting the rate of return on total assets. A definition of the *inventory turnover ratio* is

$$\text{Inventory turnover ratio} = \frac{\text{cost of inventory sold}}{\text{average inventory balance}}$$

---

[16] It is not difficult to suggest exceptions. If the inventory consists of furs, jewelry, etc., the turnover is likely to be low. Why?

For the XYZ Corporation inventory turnover is
   Accounting Valuation:

$$\text{Inventory turnover ratio} = \frac{\$6,000,000}{\$212,500} = 28.24$$

   Economic Valuation:

$$\text{Inventory turnover ratio} = \frac{\$8,200,000}{\$412,500} = 19.88$$

Yet the sales-asset ratio is

   Accounting Valuation:

$$\text{Sales-asset ratio} = \frac{\$15,300,000}{\$29,392,800} = 52.05\%$$

   Economic Valuation:

$$\text{Sales-asset ratio} = \frac{\$15,800,000}{\$38,097,800} = 41.47\%$$

In our illustration, depending on the valuation procedures employed, inventory turns over 28 and 20 times, respectively, during the year, or about once every 13 and 18.2 days.[17] Yet total assets turn over about once every 2 to $2\frac{1}{2}$ years. The reason, of course, is that cost of inventory sold accounts for about 20 per cent of total assets. In this instance, the relatively high level of fixed assets together with their slow turnover serves to lower the sales-asset ratio over what might otherwise be expected.

   Since our primary interest is in the owners' equity, we can estimate the rate of return by using either dividends or income after interest and taxes as a percentage of the book or market value of owners' equity. If book value equals the sum of the common stock, capital, and earned surplus accounts, then, using the accounting approach for the XYZ Corporation, we get

   Accounting Valuation: Earnings

$$\text{Rate of return on owners' equity} = \frac{\$2,672,800}{\$22,472,800} = 11.89\%$$

   Accounting Valuation: Dividends

$$\text{Rate of return on owners' equity} = \frac{\$1,000,000}{\$22,472,800} = 4.45\%$$

[17]365/28 = 13.04 days
  365/20 = 18.25 days

Using the market value of the common stock as the denominator and the economic concept of income as the numerator, we get[18]

Economic Valuation: Earnings

$$\text{Rate of return on owners' equity} = \frac{\$1,372,800}{\$31,777,800} = 4.32\%$$

Economic Valuation: Dividends

$$\text{Rate of return on owners' equity} = \frac{\$1,000,000}{\$31,777,800} = 3.15\%$$

Debt-equity Ratios.   In the modern theory of business finance the ultimate goal of the firm is to maximize the market, not the book value of the owners' equity.   Moreover, as we shall learn in subsequent chapters, there is some controversy over whether earnings or dividends is the particular variable relevant to determining the market value of a share in the firm.   It is universally accepted, however, that debt will at some point affect the value of the owners' equity.   Thus the ratios of debt and equity to total capital — the so-called *debt-equity ratios* — are important concepts. Using first the accounting approach, debt-equity ratios for the beginning and the end of the year are

Beginning of Year:

$$\frac{\text{Debt}}{\text{Total capital}} = \frac{\$7,400,000}{\$28,200,000} = 26.24\%$$

$$\frac{\text{Equity}}{\text{Total capital}} = \frac{\$20,800,000}{\$28,200,000} = 73.76\%$$

End of Year:

$$\frac{\text{Debt}}{\text{Total capital}} = \frac{\$6,920,000}{\$29,392,800} = 23.54\%$$

$$\frac{\text{Equity}}{\text{Total capital}} = \frac{\$22,472,800}{\$29,392,800} = 76.46\%$$

---

[18]In each case we could divide the numerator and the denominator by the number of shares outstanding to get the earnings or dividends per share and the book or market value per share.

	Accounting Valuation	Economic Valuation
Earnings per Share	$\frac{\$2,672,800}{1,000,000} = \$2.6728$	$\frac{\$1,372,800}{1,000,000} = \$1.3728$
Dividends per Share	$\frac{\$1,000,000}{1,000,000} = \$1.00$	$\frac{\$1,000,000}{1,000,000} = \$1.00$
Book Value per Share	$\frac{\$22,482,800}{1,000,000} = \$22.4828$	
Market Value per Share		$\frac{\$31,777,800}{1,000,000} = \$31.7778$

On the basis of market value the ratios are

Beginning of Year:

$$\frac{\text{Debt}}{\text{Total capital}} = \frac{\$7,200,000}{\$33,500,000} = 21.49\%$$

$$\frac{\text{Equity}}{\text{Total capital}} = \frac{\$26,300,000}{\$33,500,000} = 78.51\%$$

End of Year:

$$\frac{\text{Debt}}{\text{Total capital}} = \frac{\$6,320,000}{\$38,097,800} = 16.59\%$$

$$\frac{\text{Equity}}{\text{Total capital}} = \frac{\$31,777,800}{\$38,097,800} = 83.41\%$$

It should be pointed out that many of those employing ratio analysis would exclude short-term debt from the capital structure of the firm.   Since we have assumed that all assets are directly or indirectly relevant to the production process, to be consistent we shall include in our capital structure both short- and long-term debt.

Ratio Analysis — Measures of Liquidity

Turning now to measures of liquidity, it should be intuitive even to the beginning student of business finance that a firm, no matter how profitable, cannot continue to exist unless it is able to meet its obligations as they come due.   Profits are the difference between revenues and expenses.   Sales revenues can be recognized without cash being received. A promise to pay or an account receivable is in most cases sufficient. Moreover, even when cash is received it is often reinvested in other assets.   Hence the day-to-day problem of financial management consists of the highly important task of finding sufficient cash to meet current obligations.

In terms of financial analysis, the task of maintaining liquidity falls under the heading of working capital management.   Assets that consist of cash or that can be conveniently converted into cash are called current assets.   Obligations due within the year are called current liabilities.   The difference between current assets and current liabilities is *net working capital.* For the XYZ Corporation the figures are as shown on the following page.

Accounting Valuation:

	Beginning of Year	End of Year
Current Assets	$7,200,000	$9,392,800
Less Current Liabilities	1,400,000	920,000
Net Working Capital	$5,800,000	$8,472,800

Economic Valuation:

	Beginning of Year	End of Year
Current Assets	$7,500,000	$10,097,800
Less Current Liabilities	1,400,000	620,000
Net Working Capital	$6,100,000	$9,477,800

These figures can also be expressed as the ratio of current assets to current liabilities, or the *current ratio*.   Thus

Accounting Valuation:

Beginning of Year

$$\frac{\text{Current assets}}{\text{Current liabilities}} = \frac{\$7,200,000}{\$1,400,000} = 5.14$$

End of Year

$$\frac{\$9,392,800}{\$920,000} = 10.14$$

Economic Valuation:

Beginning of Year

$$\frac{\text{Current assets}}{\text{Current liabilities}} = \frac{\$7,500,000}{\$1,400,000} = 5.36$$

End of Year

$$\frac{\$10,097,800}{\$620,000} = 16.29$$

If we total cash, marketable securities, and receivables, we have a measure of *quick assets* and can calculate a *quick asset ratio*.   Thus

Accounting Valuation:

Beginning of Year

$$\frac{\text{Quick assets}}{\text{Current liabilities}} = \frac{\$7,000,000}{\$1,400,000} = 5.00$$

End of Year

$$\frac{\$9,167,800}{\$920,000} = 9.97$$

Economic Valuation

Beginning of Year

$$\frac{\text{Quick assets}}{\text{Current liabilities}} = \frac{\$7,100,000}{\$1,400,000} = 5.07$$

End of Year

$$\frac{\$9,672,800}{\$620,000} = 15.60$$

From the figures it appears that there are sufficient current assets to liquidate the obligations as they come due.   However, it is important to note that these ratios as well as net working capital are based on a statement of financial position at a moment in time.   Were we to draw up a balance sheet at the end of each quarter, we might notice considerable variation in these ratios due to seasonal fluctuations.   In a more detailed analysis of working capital management presented in a later chapter, we consider this possibility.   For the present it is sufficient to note that since the day-to-day problem of financial management is liquidity, forces changing the composition of current assets and current liabilities during the course of the year also affect the ability of the firm to meet its obligations as they come due.   Therefore, what constitutes a sufficient level of net working capital may depend on the season of the year as well as the cyclical nature of the goods and services produced. A ratio or level of net working capital at the end of the year is the result of changes that have taken place over the year.   A relatively liquid position then may cover up a less liquid situation at some point during the accounting period.[19]

Valuation Procedures – The Conflict over Techniques

From the preceding discussion, it should be apparent that differences in valuation procedures can yield considerable variations in the empirical measures necessary to implement the analytical concepts which comprise the theory of business finance.   Thus the question remains as to which path we shall take—replacement cost (that is, market value), or original cost.   On this, even accountants disagree.[20]   The choice, however, is dependent on the purpose at hand.   The market value of an

---

[19]In concentrating on working capital we have ignored such common ratios as *times interest earned,* defined as earnings before interest and taxes divided by the annual interest charges.   Thus, for the XYZ Corporation,

$$\frac{\text{Earnings before interest and taxes}}{\text{Interest charges}} = \frac{\overset{\text{Accounting Valuation}}{\$5{,}440{,}000}}{\$300{,}000} = 18.13 \qquad \frac{\overset{\text{Economic Valuation}}{\$2{,}940{,}000}}{\$300{,}000} = 9.8$$

From the discussion in the text, it should be evident that what is relevant is the ability of management to meet interest and other contractual obligations of the firm as they come due.   Interest is paid out of cash, not out of earnings.   As we have argued, it does not necessarily follow that a high level of earnings results in a high level of cash.

[20]For contrasting views, see David A. Corbin, "The Revolution in Accounting," *Accounting Review* (October, 1963), pp. 626–635, and Felix P. Kollaritsch, "Future Service Potential Value," *Journal of Accountancy* (February, 1965), pp. 57–62.   Both articles have been reprinted in Louis Geller (ed.), *Accounting* (Boston: D. C. Heath and Company, 1967), pp. 24–41.   See also Morton Backer, "The Measurement of Business Income: Part I—The Matching Concept," and Philip W. Bell, "The Measurement of Business Income: Part 2—Price Changes and Income Measurement," in Morton Backer (ed.), *Modern Accounting Theory,* a revision of *Handbook of Modern Accounting Theory* (Englewood Cliffs, N.J.: Prentice-Hall, Inc., 1966), pp. 68–97.

asset may not be readily available. Even if it is, its value to the firm may be greater or less than its market value. Moreover, as we shall subsequently argue, the market value of the equity interests in a firm is largely a function of two factors: (1) total earnings and (2) management's and presumably the owners' attitude toward variability in total earnings. The question management must ask of a specific asset is what its addition will do to total earnings and/or to the variability in total earnings. The market value or replacement cost of a specific asset must be seen in the light of its effect on the market value of the ownership interests in the firm. If the market value of the owners' equity rises or at least does not fall as a result of adding the asset, its acquisition in terms of the models developed in this text will be worthwhile.

Even though the replacement cost or market value of a particular asset may be at variance with its value to the firm, this difference, as we shall see, will be important in determining whether adding the asset will raise its market value. Since the theory of business finance makes use of market value, the information on which financial decisions are based should reflect replacement cost. Financial statements, however, are ordinarily based on original cost. There is a good reason for this. The material is for public consumption. The techniques employed in arriving at balance-sheet and income figures are or should be explicit and the results objective. As a guide to financial decision making, however, it is the future not the past, and the market value not the book value, which is relevant. Internally, therefore, managerial accounting has begun to employ the economic concepts of valuation in preparing statements to guide those who make financial decisions.

Our emphasis, at least throughout the analytical portions of this book, is on the economic approach to valuation. As the discussion turns from the firm to the capital markets, our approach becomes more empirical and institutional. The data employed will consist of a mixture of material based on original cost, data modified to approximate replacement cost, as well as data based on market value. The student, as he progresses, should note these shifts together with any exceptions which may occasionally occur in various sections of the text.

SUMMARY

There are two systems of business accounting. The system employed by accountants recognizes revenues when realized and costs when incurred. Moreover, the accountant employs historical cost. The economist, however, recognizes revenues when earned. He uses market value or replacement cost in estimating expenses. As a result, there are differences in income and asset valuation.

The accountant's concepts of revenues and costs are more objective than the economist's concepts of these categories. The former are useful in making financial information available to the public; the latter are more relevant to financial decision making.

QUESTIONS AND PROBLEMS

1. "One would expect the book value of the common stock to approximate the market value for a firm whose assets consist largely of securities, i.e., a financial institution, but not for a firm whose assets are mostly plant and equipment."   Evaluate.

2. "Making an allowance for replacement costs of assets used up in the production process will lower reported earnings without affecting the cash position of the firm."   Evaluate.

3. Is the rate of return on capital the same as the rate of return on assets?   Discuss.

4. As a class project take the annual report of a large manufacturing firm whose outstanding securities have a ready market.   Now calculate the rate of return for the year on the book value of these securities using interest and dividend payments actually made.   Do the same using the average market value of these securities for the year. Where there is no ready market, as in the case of short-term debt, assume that the book and market values are the same.   Explain carefully the reasons for the differences in the results.

5. "In employing information based on generally accepted accounting principles, we sacrifice estimates of actual value for unambiguous results."   Explain.

SELECTED REFERENCES

Backer, Morton (ed.). *Modern Accounting Theory*, a revision of *Handbook of Modern Accounting Theory*. Englewood Cliffs, N.J.: Prentice-Hall, Inc., 1966.

Corbin, David A. *Accounting and Economic Decisions*. New York: Dodd, Mead & Company, Inc., 1964.

Geller, Louis (ed.). *Accounting*. Boston: D. C. Heath and Company, 1967.

Graham, Benjamin, et al. *Security Analysis: Principles and Technique*, 4th ed. New York: McGraw-Hill Book Company, 1962.

Jaedicke, Robert K., and Robert T. Sprouse. *Accounting Flows: Income, Funds, and Cash*.   Englewood Cliffs, N.J.: Prentice-Hall, Inc., 1965.

Economic Theory and Financial Management

chapter Four

In the last chapter we stressed the economic approach to valuation on the grounds that it was more relevant to the modern theory of business finance. In this chapter we shall rationalize our assumption that financial management should maximize the market value of the owners' equity. In so doing, we shall contrast this goal with the economist's goal of profit maximization. The chapter, therefore, ties the theory of finance to the principles of microeconomic analysis.

The Role of Economic Theory

The elementary principles of microeconomic analysis[1] tell us that, given sufficient competition, that is, given the fact that business enterprises

---

[1]For a more detailed treatment of the principles of microeconomics, see Paul A. Samuelson, *Economics: An Introductory Analysis* 7th ed. (New York: McGraw-Hill Book Company, 1967), pp. 57–70, 361–482. See also Richard A. Leftwich, *The Price System and Resource Allocation*, 3d ed. (New York: Holt, Rinehart and Winston, Inc., 1966).

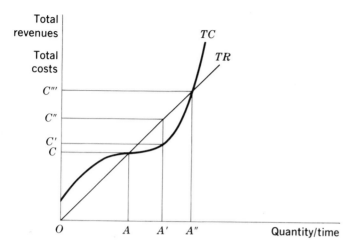

Figure 4-1 A perfectly competitive firm maximizing total profits.

have no control over the market price of the products or services they produce,[2] and assuming there is freedom of entry into the industry, firms will *maximize their total profits*. Total profits are defined as the difference between total costs and total revenues. Thus Figure 4-1 depicts the total revenue and total cost curves of a perfectly competitive firm. Since the enterprise has no control over market price, it can sell as much as it desires at the going price, say, $P. Each time it sells an additional unit, total revenue rises by the amount of the price. The rate at which total revenues change, that is, the slope of the total revenue function, or *marginal revenue*, is constant. Therefore the relationship between output and price is linear.[3]

Note, however, that the total cost function is curvilinear. It rises first at a decreasing, then at an increasing rate. This rate of change in total cost, or *marginal cost*, is the result of first increasing and then decreasing returns to scale.[4]   For example, if we construct an automobile plant and hire one worker to build automobiles, we would be able

[2]The firm, in short, faces an infinitely elastic demand curve for its product or service.

[3]$TR = PQ$, where $P = K$. Differentiating with respect to Q, $dr/dq = P$. Marginal revenue = price (or P).

[4]Those with a sufficient background in economic theory will recognize the oversimplification in the textual explanation. Total costs depend on both the prices of factors of production and the production function, with marginal cost a partial derivative. Thus

$$\text{Marginal cost} = \frac{\text{price of factor } a}{\text{marginal physical product of } a}$$

while other factors of production and their prices are held constant.

to go into production. But we might more than double the output in a given time period if we hire two workers. The reason for our optimism lies in the possibility of letting each worker specialize in certain aspects of producing the car. The opportunity to specialize may raise the productivity of every worker. If so, total costs will increase but at a decreasing rate.

Of course, specialization and division of labor can be carried just so far. There are only a finite number of parts on an automobile. Moreover, given the scale of enterprise, i.e., the size of the assembly line, beyond some point additional workers will get into one another's way. Their efficiency declines and the costs of production begin to increase sharply. When this happens, we have entered the area of diminishing returns where costs per unit of output and hence total costs rise at an increasing rate.

Midway between increasing and diminishing returns lies a third alternative: constant returns to scale. It is possible, for example, to carry specialization to the point where it does not raise the output of each worker. Yet we could still add more workers and raise the total output in proportion to the number hired. In so doing we recognize that we have not fully utilized the existing facilities. Our assembly line, in other words, is not being utilized to capacity. We can illustrate this situation by altering slightly the cost curves pictured in Figure 4-1. Figure 4-2 shows more realistically the production conditions which most firms actually face.

The difference between the two illustrations is the fact that in Figure 4-2 costs rise in proportion to output as production increases from OA' to OA''. Beyond OA'' costs rise rapidly as the firm approaches capacity, eventually reaching a point beyond which it is physically impossible to expand output without first increasing production facilities.

In both illustrations there are numerous levels of output at which the enterprise is profitable. In Figure 4-1 the total output can vary between OA and OA'' and the firm will still find that its total revenue exceeds its total cost. In Figure 4-2 the profitable range of output is between OA and OA''''.

To maximize total profits, however, the firm must produce at the greatest difference between total costs and total revenues. In Figure 4-1 this is shown as output OA', the distance $C'C''$ being at a maximum. Geometrically, if we drew a line parallel to the total revenue curve and tangent to the total cost curve, the distance between the two lines would be $C'C''$. Since the slopes of parallel lines are equal, where total profits are at a maximum, the rate of change in total costs, or marginal cost, must equal the rate of change in total revenues, or marginal revenue.

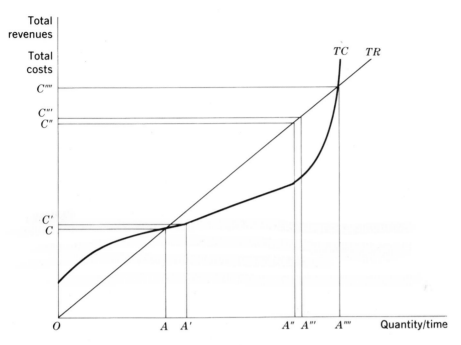

Figure 4-2 A perfectly competitive firm maximizing total profits.

The same reasoning holds for Figure 4-2.   At some point beyond
OA'' the change in total costs will equal the change in total revenues.
We have assumed this output to be OA'''.   Beyond this level, marginal
cost is greater than marginal revenue and total profits are less than a
maximum.   At any output less than OA''' the change in total revenues
is greater than the change in total costs.   Therefore, if the firm increases
total output, it will raise its profits.

**Economic Theory of the Firm as an Explanation of Market Be-
havior.** The economic theory of the firm, however, was developed
not as a means of explaining its actual behavior but as a tool for analyzing resource allocation in perfectly competitive markets.   Through
profit maximization, a firm producing in perfectly competitive markets
performs a social function.   Specifically, it is a channel through which
society efficiently allocates scarce resources to satisfy the alternative
and competing desires of consumers.[5]   A business enterprise, therefore,
is a means to an end, not the end itself.

[5]Similarly with the variety of theories of imperfect competition, particularly with
the theory of pure monopoly, economists have tried to show how resources are inefficiently
allocated in a market economy.

Thus a firm in a perfectly competitive industry not only will be forced by its competitors to produce as efficiently as possible (that is, given its demand to minimize its costs and hence maximize its total profits), but will also be prevented in the long run from earning profits in excess of what its owners could earn by investing their capital in some other line of activity. The condition which assures this outcome is freedom of entry. For example, the competitive producer referred to in Figures 4-1 and 4-2, although maximizing his total profits, is earning a return in excess of the amount necessary to keep the capital employed in the industry. This stems from the fact that economic costs, as we have seen in Chapter 3, reflect both the replacement costs of capital used up in the production process and the opportunity costs of those working for or supplying capital to the firm. Thus profit in economic theory consists of the owners' opportunity cost, which is included in the total cost curves, and the excess, which can be labeled pure profit. In competitive markets, any return above the owners' opportunity cost ensures the entry of new firms into the industry. Similarly, any return less than the opportunity cost will result in firms leaving the industry. The corresponding increases and decreases in supply will lower and raise the market price and hence the profits of all producers.

Profits, therefore, are a means of channeling resources into and out of various markets. In the long run the vehicle through which resources are allocated, that is, the business firm, earns only normal profits. This result is depicted in Figure 4-3. The total cost curve

Figure 4-3 A firm in long-run competitive equilibrium.

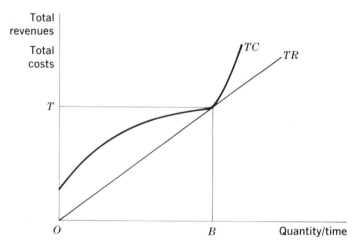

is tangent to the total revenue curve at one point only, represented by output *OB*. At this point, marginal cost equals marginal revenue. The competitive firm is maximizing total profits but its owners are earning a return only sufficient to keep them in the industry; that is, they are earning only normal profits. Thus there is no incentive for firms either to enter or to leave the industry.

From the above discussion[6] it should be evident that in economic theory the firm is a means to an end, the end being an optimum allocation of resources. Since economics is a market- not a firm-oriented discipline, it follows that a theory of the firm which is sufficient to explain market behavior may be lacking, if the purpose is to analyze more fully the operations of the enterprise itself.

Measuring Profits Let us return to the differences in the accounting and economic approaches to measuring profits. In Chapter 3 we developed particular measures of profitability using an accounting format, but comparing the accounting approach with the economic approach to valuation. Ultimately our purpose was to measure a rate of return on assets. The accounting format summarized in Figure 4-4, on the following page, shows the relationship between the income statement and the balance sheet. The economic diagrams depicted in Figures 4-1, 4-2, and 4-3 are related to the income statement. Costs and revenues are not broken down into their components. As we saw in Chapter 3, this presents no difficulties. What did prove to be a problem were the concepts of costs and revenues. This we resolved by arguing that the analytical tools of financial management articulated propositions that usually called for the economic definitions of replacement costs, oppostunity costs, and earned revenues rather than accounting measures couched in terms of historical costs and realized revenues. The market value of a firm's assets and hence of its owners' equity depends implicitly on the economic and not the accounting measures of costs and revenues. The rate of return on assets, for which there is no counterpart in Figures 4-1, 4-2, and 4-3, is the percentage earned on the market value of these assets. Thus far there is no conflict.

It is in taking the next logical step that we run into difficulties. When a firm maximizes total profits, we might expect that it would also maximize the market value of the owners' equity. Unfortunately, this

---

[6]In the various cases which comprise imperfect competition, the firm must lower its price in order to sell more. The addition to total revenue, or marginal revenue, therefore declines with price. Total revenue increases at a decreasing rate. Moreover, if there are sufficient barriers to entry into the industry, the firm can earn more than normal profits. Thus, in the long run, profits are at a maximum where marginal cost equals marginal revenue.

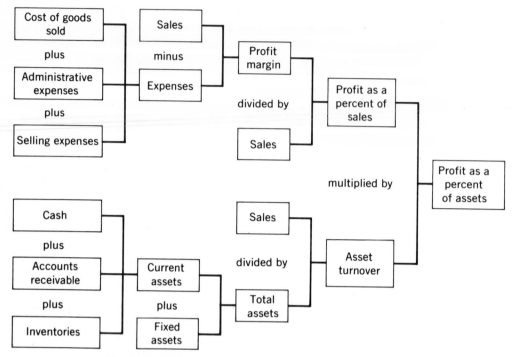

Figure 4-4 The relationships among the factors affecting rate of return on assets.

need not be the case. When developing the economic theory of the firm, at least on an elementary level, it is customary to abstract from uncertainty. It is assumed that a firm maximizes profits; indeed, under the pressures of competition it *must* maximize profits. There is no consideration given to the effect the composition of assets, liabilities, and owners' equity will have on the expected level of profits nor on their variability.

We saw in Chapter 1 how the use of fixed-income securities, largely debt, to finance assets may increase or decrease the per share earnings of owners over what might result if the firm had a capital structure consisting entirely of equity. Abstracting from the impact of corporate income taxes, it would appear that this difficulty might be overcome by treating profits as the sum of interest and earnings. But the enterprise in theory operates for the benefit of its owners, not its creditors.[7] Thus a theory of financial management must consider the

---

[7] How to treat fixed-income owners, that is, preferred stockholders, is another problem. For purposes of this volume we shall classify preferred stockholders as creditors. Failure to pay dividends does not precipitate bankruptcy, but preferred stock does add to the variability in earnings and dividends of the common stockholders.

impact of financial risk or leverage on the variability in the earnings of owners and subsequently on the market value of their equity.

Similarly, the composition of assets can also affect both the earnings accruing to owners and the variability in them. Two manufacturing firms producing the same line of products and financed by the same composition of liabilities and owners' equity may show differences in profitability which can be traced to the differences in the structures of their assets. The day-to-day task of financial management is to meet the obligations of the firm as they come due. We saw in Chapter 3 that liquidity ratios give us some insight into the ability of the firm to meet this objective. But the factors affecting the pool of cash are the result of changes in the various sources and uses of funds. The interrelationships among sources and uses are given in Figure 4-5.

Figure 4-5 Factors affecting cash flow.

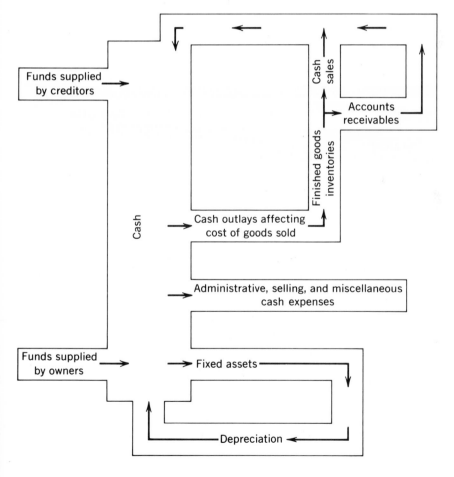

By holding constant the composition of liabilities and owners' equity, the differences in profitability of the two firms will be the direct result of differences in the allocation of these funds between cash and fixed assets. A dollar allocated to long-lived assets also entails outlays for wages, salaries, inventory, etc., all of which contribute to the manufacture of the product and hence to sales revenue. Direct sales, or indirect sales through accounts receivable, return cash to the firm. If revenues exceed expenses, the profits and depreciation, unless they are returned to the owners, add to the pool of cash. If cash expenses exceed revenues, the losses that result lower the pool of cash. On the other hand, a dollar not invested in operations neither raises nor lowers the cash pool. It could, of course, be invested in securities incidental to the operations of the firm. If so, then our pool of cash consists of cash and marketable securities or other liquid assets. The income from these investments less expenses associated with them would add to the total profits and hence to the cash pool.

However, the return expected on a dollar invested in marketable securities is ordinarily less than the return anticipated from a dollar invested in long-lived assets. At the same time the variability in the return is lower for marketable securities than for fixed assets. Thus the portfolio risk, that is, the variability in income earned on assets, as well as the expected rate of return, is a function of the composition of assets.

These two components of risk, the structure of assets and the structure of liabilities and owners' equity, affect both the level and variability of the return to the owners. There is no single profit figure based on differences in revenues and expenses; rather, we have a probability distribution of profits that results from the composition of assets and financing.

As we asserted earlier in the elementary economic theory of the firm, it is possible to abstract from an explanation of risk, even ignore it by assuming a world of certainty, and still reach useful conclusions concerning market behavior. As a simple example, consider the impact of imposing a specific tax of 10 cents on each pound of butter produced. Assuming perfect competition, we can see from Figure 4-6 that the market price of butter has increased[8] because, given the demand curve, the supply price has risen from OP to OP' while total industry output has declined from OA to OA'. The decline in output reflects a reallocation of resources away from the production of butter. Presumably they will be used to produce close substitutes such as oleomargarine[9] or allocated to areas in which the government spends the

---

[8] Although not by the amount of the tax. Why?
[9] A secondary effect of the tax would be to raise the demand curve for oleomargarine and hence lower the demand curve for butter.

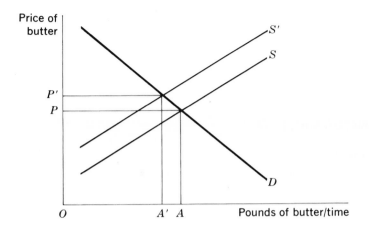

Figure 4-6   Impact of a specific tax on the market price and output of butter.

tax revenues. But if firms producing butter are maximizing total profits, and competitive pressures ensure that they will be, then they will be maximizing total profits after the tax increases.   What happens in the interim, that is, between the time the tax is imposed and the new equilibrium price OP' is established, is ignored in favor of showing the ultimate result.

In the simple model, therefore, no consideration is given to the impact of the tax increase on specific resources.   In the long run, we assume, they are employed elsewhere.   But if our primary interest lies in the effect of the tax not on the market price of butter but rather on the profitability of production and ultimately on the market value of the owners' shares, we must consider more fully the impact of the tax on the composition of assets, liabilities, and owners' equity and hence on the risk borne by the owners.

Just as a worker laid off because of the decline in production may be unable to find alternative employment at comparable wages, so the firm may not be able to allocate excess plant and equipment to other uses.   From management's and ultimately the owners' viewpoint, the tax is seen initially as an increase in costs to be passed on if possible to the consumers.   Since some of the burden of the tax will rest on the firm in the form of reduced output, to prevent profits from being adversely affected, management must reduce its variable costs, that is, labor and raw materials, while reallocating its plant and equipment to other uses. Hence the imposition of the tax means an increase in a liability account, taxes payable.   The risk involved is the ability of the firm to shift the burden of the tax to someone other than the owners.

The above analysis is not meant to imply that the burden of the tax is of no interest to the economist. On the contrary, just as the impact of the tax on the variability in earnings and ultimately on the market value of the owners' equity is important to the economist interested in business finance, the incidence of the tax on the pattern of resource allocation and the distribution of income is similarly of prime importance to the public finance specialist.

Nevertheless, when our primary interest is in the business enterprise, we must develop models of the firm which explain its reactions to changing and often uncertain market conditions and not models designed to emphasize the market changes themselves. Subtle though this point may be, to grasp it is to understand the difference between the theory of the firm as presented in treatises on the elements of microeconomic analysis and the financial theory of the firm with which much of this volume is concerned.

The Foundations of the Theory of Financial Management

Models are designed to analyze and implement goals or objectives. The ultimate aim of microeconomic analysis is an efficient allocation of scarce resources among the alternative and competing demands of consumers. We shall assume that the goal of financial management is to maximize the market value of the owners' equity. While both of these ends have been subject to considerable criticism,[10] each is a goal around which we can build a substantive analysis. More important, critics notwithstanding, our legal institutions are based on the assumption that business enterprises are run primarily if not entirely for the benefit of their owners.[11] Thus, in assuming for the purposes of analysis that business firms maximize the market value of their owners' equity, we are comfortably within the expectations accorded private enterprise under the law.

---

[10]For example, resources are scarce only if wants are unlimited. Moreover, business firms, particularly if they produce in imperfectly competitive markets, must usually keep in mind not only the interests of the owners but also those of labor as well as those of the community in general, particularly its educational and charitable institutions. For an analysis of these and related considerations, see the following works of John Kenneth Galbraith: *American Capitalism: The Concept of Countervailing Powers*, rev. ed. (Boston: Houghton Mifflin Company, 1956); *The Affluent Society*, college ed. (Boston: Houghton Mifflin Company, 1960); *The New Industrial State* (Boston: Houghton Mifflin Company, 1967).

[11]See Eugene V. Rostow, "To Whom and For What Ends Is Corporate Management Responsible?" in Edward S. Mason (ed.), *The Corporation in Modern Society* (Cambridge, Mass.: Harvard University Press, 1959), pp. 46–71. See also Wilber G. Katz, "Responsibility and the Modern Corporation," *Journal of Law and Economics*, vol. 3, (October, 1960), pp. 75–85.

In the final chapter of this book, we shall look more closely at the social implications of pursuing this goal.

Risk and Uncertainty From our discussion in the preceding section we have seen that to analyze more fully the relation of profits to the market value of the owners' equity, we must consider the implications of risk and uncertainty. More specifically, we must analyze the effect of the composition of assets and liabilities on the variability in earnings, and hence on the total and per share market value of the ownership interests.

When the market value of the owners' equity is at a maximum, the balance sheet of the enterprise will consist of an optimum combination of assets and liabilities. Unfortunately, developing a theoretical model which would take into consideration all the variables affecting this optimum is beyond the scope of an introductory analysis.[12]

We can establish certain principles of asset and liability selection, however, by holding particular factors constant. Thus we can discuss the techniques of capital budgeting, or principles of selecting fixed or long-lived assets, under the assumption that either the level of working capital and long-term liabilities and owners' equity is held constant or any changes will be of little consequence to the optimum combination. Similarly, we can discuss the principles of working capital management while assuming no change in long-term liabilities and fixed assets. In like fashion we can hold assets constant while discussing the principles underlying the optimum combination of liabilities and owners' equity. In all cases our objective is to develop tools of analysis designed to implement the ultimate goal: maximizing the market value of the ownership interests.

In reading the next several chapters, it will be useful to keep in mind the following points. First, the composition of long-lived assets and liabilities has a direct impact on profitability and ultimately on the market value of the owners' equity. But the level of working capital has a more indirect effect. The day-to-day task of financial management is to meet the firm's obligations as they come due. In the long run, profitability depends on liquidity. The direct function of working capital management is to keep the firm from bankruptcy. Within this context, of course, the firm can manage its current assets so as to add to the owners' profits. But management's decision to invest a dollar in nonoperating rather than operating assets is usually a choice in favor of lower profits. The implication is that by so doing it raises, or at least does not lower, the market value of the owners' equity.

[12]For an excellent advanced treatment see Eugene M. Lerner and Willard T. Carleton, *A Theory of Financial Analysis* (New York: Harcourt, Brace & World, Inc., 1966).

Second, when risk is incorporated into the analysis, we must take into consideration the owners' attitudes toward it. For example, how do they subjectively view the probability distribution of a stream of profits based on a change in the specific composition of assets and liabilities? Will the change raise or lower the market value of their interests? Where ownership is divorced from control, the financial decisions of management may not reflect the subjective risk preferences of the owners. Thus there will be a decline in the market value of their shares as those owners who disagree with management's policies choose to liquidate their interests. Over the long run, of course, one would expect in this situation that those continuing to hold shares in the enterprise would be individuals or representatives of individuals whose attitudes toward risk are similar to those of the managers of the firm.

Third, in the examples employed, emphasis will be placed on business enterprises producing real goods and services, that is, non-financial business firms such as manufacturing, public utility, and wholesale and retail trade establishments.[13] Another large group of business firms, including commercial banks and life insurance companies among others, hold assets consisting primarily of the liabilities of non-financial enterprises and households. These business firms are known as financial intermediaries. In initially ignoring them, we do not wish to leave the reader with the impression that we assume their primary responsibility is to some group other than their owners. On the contrary, we have no reason to assume that managements of these intermediaries have any less reason for maximizing the market value of their owners' equity than do managements of nonfinancial business firms. Institutional constraints aside, the principles of financial management with slight modifications apply to all private enterprise. We ignore financial intermediaries only initially; they play an important role in the channeling of funds from those supplying capital to those using it, that is, largely from households to nonfinancial business firms and government. Therefore, as our discussion shifts from financial management to the capital markets, we shall give greater consideration to financial intermediaries.

Finally, the principles of financial management, particularly the concepts relating to fixed assets and working capital, are independent of the type of business enterprise being analyzed. We saw in Chapter 2, however, that the primary reason for the rise of the corporation as the vehicle through which most of our goods and services are produced is its ability to raise funds by issuing instruments which make relatively

---

[13]While not explicitly excluding them from this category, we have implicitly excluded agricultural firms.

fine divisions among the elements of risk, income, and control. Thus, in analyzing the composition of liabilities and owners' equity, we shall want to discuss more fully the instruments employed in making these distinctions.

SUMMARY

Optimum allocation of resources has been the traditional concern of economists. To accomplish this optimum, firms must maximize their total profits within the framework of perfectly competitive markets. The goal of financial management is to maximize the market value of the owners' equity. To accomplish this, the financial manager must analyze the effect the composition of assets and liabilities has on variability in earnings and hence on the total and per share market value of the ownership interests. We must, therefore, as financial managers, go beyond the traditional principles of microeconomics and incorporate risk and uncertainty into our analysis.

QUESTIONS

1. "If a firm maximizes its total profits, it is maximizing the market value of the owners' equity." Evaluate.

2. Explain carefully the differences between the assumptions underlying the theory of the firm in microeconomics and those underlying the theory of financial management.

SELECTED REFERENCES

Leftwich, Richard A. *The Price System and Resource Allocation*, 3d ed. New York: Holt, Rinehart & Winston, Inc., 1966.
Lerner, Eugene M., and Willard T. Carleton. *A Theory of Financial Analysis.* New York: Harcourt, Brace & World, Inc., 1966.
Solomon, Ezra. *The Theory of Financial Management.* New York: Columbia University Press, 1963.
Weston, J. Fred. *The Scope and Methodology of Finance.* Englewood Cliffs, N.J.: Prentice-Hall, Inc., 1966.

The Mathematics of Finance

chapter Five

The student should view the material in this chapter as the mathematical foundation of some of the tools which a financial manager must use if he is to maximize the market value of the owners' equity.   In reading the material, the student should try to keep in mind that the techniques presented assume a regularity in the dependent variables rarely achieved by nonfinancial business firms.   Thus, whether he chooses to employ the method emphasized in the text or the techniques given in the Appendix to this chapter, the student should recognize the limitations which the regularity assumption imposes.

The Mathematics of Discounting

Much of the subject matter of financial management is future-oriented. By this we mean that the decisions made have ramifications extending beyond the period in which they were considered.   Management chooses to build a new plant the financial result of which is to tie up capital resources for a number of years in anticipation of earning income on this investment during its useful life. When the decision is made to raise $1,000,000 from a bond issue maturing in 20 years, the firm not only obligates itself to meet interest on the debt, at fixed intervals during this period but also must make provisions for repayment of the $1,000,000 when the bonds mature. Consequently, to understand a large portion of the material discussed in subsequent chapters, we must develop a pattern of thought which evaluates in present terms the expectations of future income and obligations arising from decisions made today.

To help in guiding our thinking, let us consider the following set of choices. Would the reader show no preference if offered the choice of receiving either $100 today, $100 a year from today, or $100 two years from today? Without hesitation you would say that among the three choices you would prefer $100 today. Your selection would be prompted by either or both of two considerations.

In the first place, you could argue correctly that $100 today would be worth more than $100 a year from today and still more than that two years from today. By allowing the funds to remain idle in a savings account for a year, you would be paid interest by the bank. If you let the interest earn interest, that is, *compound*, your original principal would be worth more at the end of the second than at the end of the first year. How much more depends on the interest rate and how often it is compounded. To illustrate, assume the bank pays you 4 percent compounded annually. At the end of the first year you will have credited to your savings passbook.

$$\$100 + (\$100 \times 0.04) = \$104$$

If you let the interest compound for a second year, you will have

$$\$104 + (\$104 \times 0.04) = \$108.16$$

We can generalize the arithmetic by letting the rate of interest r equal 4 percent, the original principal P equal $100, V_1 equal the value of the principal at the end of the first year, and V_2 equal the value of the principal at the end of the second year. Then

End of First Year:
$$P + Pr = V_1 \qquad \text{or} \qquad P(1+r) = V_1 \tag{1}$$

End of Second Year:
$$V_1 + V_1 r = V_2 \qquad \text{or} \qquad V_1(1+r) = V_2 \tag{2}$$

For the end of the second year, $V_1 = V_2/(1+r)$.

Since, for the end of the first year, $V_1 = P(1+r)$, then

$$P(1+r)(1+r) = V_2 \tag{3}$$

$$P = \frac{V_2}{(1+r)^2} \tag{4}$$

Generalizing for n years for V,

$$P = \frac{V_n}{(1+r)^n} \tag{5}$$

Alternatively,

$$P(1+r)^n = V_n \tag{6}$$

What Eq. (5) says is that the *present value*, or value today, of sum V_n payable n years in the future is equal to that sum divided by $(1+r)^n$. The sum is said to be *discounted* at a rate of interest r.   The reason for discounting can be seen from Eq. (6).   A sum P compounded at a rate of interest r for n years is equal to a greater sum V_n.   Consequently, $100 today is equivalent to $104 a year from today and $108.16 two years from today, assuming an annual compounding or discounting period and a 4 percent rate of interest.

Mathematically, compounding and discounting are two sides of the same coin.   Institutionally, these equations reflect the fact that as long as there is someone willing to pay a positive rate of interest to borrow the funds, then money has time value.   Even if a firm manufactured products in a world of certainty, management considering an investment of $1,000,000 of its retained earnings in plant and equipment would have to discount the difference between future revenues and expenses in order to compare the return on this investment with the return on alternatives to which the money could be put.   A dollar in the future is worth less than a dollar today because the latter can be reinvested at interest.   The student should keep this in mind for it is fundamental to understanding the analytical principles of financial management.

There is a second reason why the reader would not be indifferent if offered the choice of receiving $100 today, $100 a year from today, or $100 two years from today.   Individuals place greater value on present consumption than on future consumption.   Even if a person had no thought of saving $100, he would value $100 worth of consumption today over $100 worth of consumption in the future.   In short, an individual must be paid to abstain from consuming today.   Even when he abstains, a person does so because of the promise of a greater, not an equivalent, amount of future consumption.[1]

In order to test your understanding of these principles, let us probe more deeply into the mathematics of discounting.   Instead of being offered a choice of $100 at one of three alternative time periods, suppose that the reader is given the entire $300 but at the time intervals originally specified.   Although you might be considered ungrateful for saying so, you would nevertheless have to admit that the present value is not the face value of the gift or $300.   At 4 percent interest discounted annually, the present value P of the gift is

$$P = \$100 + \frac{\$100}{1.04} + \frac{\$100}{1.04^2}$$

$$= \$100 + \frac{\$100}{1.04} + \frac{\$100}{1.0816}$$

$$= \$100 + \$96.15 + \$92.46$$

$$= \$288.61$$

Under the terms of the grant the benefactor need only commit $288.61 to pay the reader a total of $300 at the various time intervals assumed in the problem:

Contributions of Benefactor		Annual Gift
$100	=	$100 today
$96.15(1.04)	=	$100 a year from today
$92.46(1.0816)	=	$100 two years from today

Finally, suppose that the gift had consisted of an annual grant of $100 to be paid in perpetuity to the reader or to anyone to whom he might sell the rights to the income.   What would be the value of the gift, assuming an interest rate of 4 percent?   Expressed mathematically,

$$P = \frac{\$100}{1+r} + \frac{\$100}{(1+r)^2} + \frac{\$100}{(1+r)^3} + \cdots + \frac{\$100}{(1+r)^n}$$

In order to solve the problem, let $D =$ the annual grant and $P =$ the present value of the grant.   Then, in general,

$$P = \frac{D}{1+r} + \frac{D}{(1+r)^2} + \frac{D}{(1+r)^3} + \cdots + \frac{D}{(1+r)^n} \tag{7}$$

[1]Those with training in economics will recognize that the first reason for discounting is the willingness of businessmen to pay a positive rate of interest to borrow money they can reinvest at higher rates.   This is the basis for the demand curve for capital funds. The second reason for discounting provides the rationale for the supply curve.

Multiply both sides of the equation by $1/(1+r)$:

$$\frac{P}{1+r} = \frac{D}{(1+r)^2} + \frac{D}{(1+r)^3} + \frac{D}{(1+r)^4} + \cdots + \frac{D}{(1+r)^{n+1}} \tag{8}$$

Subtracting Eq. (8) from Eq. (7), we get

$$P - \frac{P}{1+r} = \frac{D}{1+r} - \frac{D}{(1+r)^{n+1}}$$

Multiplying both sides by $(1+r)$, we get

$$P(1+r) - P = D - \frac{D}{(1+r)^n}$$

$$P + Pr - P = D - D(1+r)^{-n}$$

$$P = \frac{D - D(1+r)^{-n}}{r}$$

$$P = \frac{D[1 - (1+r)^{-n}]}{r} \tag{9}$$

As $n \to \infty$, $(1+r)^{-n} \to 0$. Hence, for a constant income stream received each year indefinitely,

$$P = \frac{D}{r} \tag{10}$$

In the example used,

$$P = \frac{\$100}{0.04}$$
$$= \$2,500$$

At a 4 percent rate of interest discounted annually the present value of a yearly income of $100 granted at the end of each year is $2,500.

If you have followed the presentation to this point, you have come away with three generalizations. First, in order to allow for the time value of money, all future returns from an investment must be discounted at some rate of interest. Second, the discounting procedure must be applied to each payment in the order in which it is to be received, that is, $100 received a year from today is discounted at $(1+r)$, $100 two years from today at $(1+r)^2$, etc. Third, the present value of a series of future payments is the sum of the discounted value of each payment unless the income is received indefinitely. In this instance the present value is simply the annual payment divided by the rate of interest. These concepts are summarized in Eqs. (9) and (10). Each is valid under the assumption that the payment received is a constant sum.

If you have not mastered these points you would do well to return to the rationale, including the mathematical proofs, out of which these generalizations have arisen. In subsequent chapters we shall use and extend these concepts in an attempt to solve the more complex issues that result from considering problems of optimum composition of long-lived assets, liabilities, and owners' equity.

In closing, it should be pointed out that all examples used in this text assume that the discounting or compounding period is annual with payments received either at the beginning or at the end of each year. Procedures for handling payments received semiannually, quarterly, or even continuously are developed in the Appendix to this chapter. The mathematically inclined student will find these concepts interesting and in some instances will find their application warranted.[2]   At an introductory level, however, it is the concept of discounting rather than the fine points of procedures which we shall emphasize.

SUMMARY

Since much of the subject matter of financial management is future-oriented, it is necessary to develop procedures for evaluating future income in terms of the present.   We can do this by discounting a series of receipts at some rate of interest, so that

$$P = \frac{D}{1+r} + \frac{D}{(1+r)^2} + \frac{D}{(1+r)^3} + \cdots + \frac{D}{(1+r)^n}$$

$$P = \frac{D[1 - (1+r)^{-n}]}{r}$$

The rationale for discounting is based on the observation that money has time value.   Depending on the interest rate, we can invest something less than a dollar today and it will be worth more than a dollar a year from today.   Consequently, the present value of a dollar received a year from today is less than a dollar.

QUESTIONS AND PROBLEMS

1.   "It is always true that a sum of money received in the future is worth less than that sum is worth today."   Explain carefully.

[2]Financial institutions such as life insurance companies, whose investments consist of securities, including mortgages, where interest is received at regular intervals of less than a year and where contractual payments can be estimated with reasonable accuracy, employ the more sophisticated techniques.   For nonfinancial firms whose receipts are both unequal and earned at irregular intervals, the assumption that they are received at the beginning or the end of the year does no serious injustice to the results and hence to the decisions based on them.

2. Find the present value of $100 a year received at the end of each year for the next 5 years.

3. Suppose you were given the rights to a perpetual income stream of $1,000 a year. If you choose to sell these rights, what would be their value?

4. "The present value of an income stream of $100, $200, and $300 is less than the present value of an income stream of $300, $200, and $100 even though the amount received in each case is the same ." Do you agree? Support your answer using calculations based on a 5 percent rate of interest.

5. "Discounting is the inverse of compounding." Explain. Illustrate your answer.

SELECTED REFERENCES

Merritt, A.J., and Allen Sykes. *The Finance and Analysis of Capital Projects.* New York: John Wiley & Sons, Inc., 1963, chap. 1.

Cissell, Robert, and Helen Cissell. *Mathematics of Finance*, 3d ed. Boston: Houghton Mifflin Company, 1968.

APPENDIX: Other Discounting Techniques

Suppose that we wanted to find the value of $100 at the end of a year using a nominal yearly rate of interest of 8 percent compounded semi-annually.   For a 6-month period, the rate of interest is 8 percent divided by 2, or 4 percent.   Under these conditions the value of $100 is

$100(1.04) = $104 at end of first 6 months

$104(1.04) = $108.16 at end of year

It is obvious that $100 at 8 percent compounded semiannually is equivalent, at the end of 1 year, to $100 compounded annually at 4 percent for 2 years.   Almost as obvious is the fact that the nominal annual rate of interest, 8 percent, is no longer the true rate of interest for the year; the true rate is 8.16 percent.   The discrepancy between the two can be traced to the fact that the interest for the first 6 months, or $4.00, earned interest at 4 percent, for a total of $0.16.

To generalize,

Let r = nominal yearly rate of interest

m = number of times per year invested sum is compounded or discounted

n = length in years of compounding or discounting period

Since $100 compounded semiannually at 8 percent is equivalent, at the end of 1 year, to $100 compounded annually at 4 percent for 2 years, then P dollars compounded m times per year at r percent becomes

$$P\left(1+\frac{r}{m}\right)^{mn}$$

Further, let $D =$ a sum due in n years.   Then

$$P\left(1+\frac{r}{m}\right)^{mn} = D$$

$$P = \frac{D}{(1+r/m)^{mn}}$$

$$P = D\left(1+\frac{r}{m}\right)^{-mn}$$

Recall from the text of this chapter the formula derived for an equal income stream received each year at the end of the year for n years.

$$P = \frac{D[1-(1+r)^{-n}]}{r}$$

Substituting for n years with the nominal rate of interest r discounted for m periods, we have

$$P = \frac{\dfrac{D}{m}\left[1-(1+r/m)^{-mn}\right]}{\dfrac{r}{m}}$$

Compounding a finite number of time periods per year implies that a dollar today can be reinvested at an interest rate which is compounded m times per year.   Given this as an alternative to which funds can be put, a dollar received n periods in the future must be discounted m times to allow for the time value of money.   By using m discounting periods per year, the present value of a future sum due in n years is smaller than if the sum were discounted annually, but the value of a sum invested today is greater in n years than if the interest were compounded annually.

To illustrate, assume that $100 is invested at 4 percent compounded annually for a year. Then

$$\$100(1.04) = \$104 \text{ at end of year}$$

But if the same sum is compounded semiannually with a nominal annual rate of interest of 4 percent, then

$$\$100(1.02) = \$102 \text{ at end of 6 months}$$
$$\$102(1.02) = \$104.04 \text{ at end of year}$$

Similarly, if the sum D is discounted at a nominal annual rate of interest of 4 percent for a year, its present value would be greater than if the discount period were semiannual. To illustrate,

$$P = \frac{\$100}{1.04} = \$96.15$$

but

$$P = \frac{\$100}{1.02^2} = \$96.12$$

As in the case of annual discounting or compounding, it is assumed that the sum is received or the interest is applied at the end of the period. Each time period, however, although shorter than a year, is still finite. Suppose that the number m of discounting periods approaches infinity (technically m increases beyond bounds), then the present value of a dollar for n periods is

$$P = \lim_{m \to \infty} \left(1 + \frac{r}{m}\right)^{-mn} = e^{-rn}$$

where

$$e = \lim_{m \to \infty} \left(1 + \frac{1}{m}\right)^m = 2.71828$$

This value of e is the base of the Naperian, or natural, system of logarithms. In general, the present value P of a sum D due in each of n years and discounted continuously is

$$P = De^{-rn}$$

Alternatively,

$$Pe^{rn} = D$$

Suppose now that a dollar is received each year for n years, but the payments are made in small installments throughout the year, i.e., they are received continuously. Under these conditions the present value of a dollar received each year is

$$P = \int_0^n de^{-rt} dt = \frac{1 - e^{-rn}}{r}$$

For those who find the calculus difficult, the verbal content of the above expressions is relatively easy to comprehend. To illustrate what we mean when we say that the number of discounting or compounding periods approaches infinity, we can imagine a savings bank paying interest first annually, then quarterly, then monthly, then weekly, etc., thereby dividing the nominal rate of interest into smaller and smaller portions. To approach the absurd from a realistic point of view, r/m would be small but still finite if the compounding or discounting period were every second.

Similarly, the import of the assumption that a dollar is received each year for n years but in small installments is simply that a change has been made in the assumptions under which the firm or individual receives the annual grant. Suppose you are told by a savings bank that you can withdraw your interest on $1,000 at the end of each quarter, the nominal or annual rate of interest being 4 percent. Under these conditions you would be paid in four $10 installments rather than in one $40 dollar payment at the end of the year. This annual payment could be divided into smaller and smaller units or until some small increment of the total is received continuously.

For many business problems, that is, in terms of the alternatives to which funds can be put, the relevant compound or discount period is nearly always finite. Moreover, while income on investments may be earned daily, it is usually received, particularly by nonfinancial enterprises, in irregular installments. For many purposes, therefore, it is no more realistic to assume a continuous income stream than to postulate receipt at the end of the year. But these observations are not meant to imply that continuous discounting is of no practical significance. If it can be shown that earnings from an investment are received continuously throughout the life of the project, and that the same conditions apply to the alternatives to which the funds can be put, then a case can be made for continuous compounding or discounting. If the data used in the calculations are based on knowledgeable but imperfect estimates, as they often are in the management of nonfinancial assets, then continuous compounding or discounting may not be worthwhile.

To illustrate, consider the present value of a dollar received at the end of the year discounted for 1 year at 4 percent.

$$P = \frac{1}{1+r} = \frac{1}{1.04} = \$0.9615$$

Now consider the present value of a dollar for a year under the assumption that it is received in small increments, i.e., continuously.

$$P = \frac{1 - e^{-rn}}{r} = \frac{1 - 2.71828^{-0.04}}{0.04}$$

$$\log 2.71828 = 0.434253$$
$$0.04 \times 0.434253 = 0.01737012 = 9.98262988 - 10$$

$$e^{-0.04} = 0.9608$$

$$P = \frac{1 - 0.9608}{0.04} = \$0.98$$

When one compares $0.98 with $0.9615, it is evident that it would require the discounting of a substantial sum to obtain an appreciable difference in present value using the two methods. If the sum to be discounted is $100, the difference in the two results is

$$\$98 - \$96.15 = \$1.85$$

On the other hand, when a million dollars is being considered, the difference is

$$\$980,000 - \$961,500 = \$18,500$$

Continuous discounting of a sum results in a higher present value than if annual discounting is used. Furthermore, if a dollar were paid in finite installments, say semiannually, the present value would also be higher than if annual discounting were employed. To illustrate, using a nominal annual rate of interest of 4 percent,

$$P = \frac{\$0.50}{1.02} + \frac{\$0.50}{1.02^2}$$
$$= 0.4902 + 0.4806$$
$$= \$0.9708$$

The student, by reflecting for a moment, should be able to see why these results are so. Under the assumption of annual discounting, a dollar or any sum is discounted for the full year. Under the assumption of continuous discounting, only an infinitesimal portion of the total is discounted for a year. Consequently, continuous discounting provides the upper limit and annual discounting the lower limit of the present value of a sum received at m intervals for n years.[1] Conversely, compounding continuously will result in a lower value for a sum at the end of n years than if the sum is compounded annually. The student should compare these generalizations with those following from earlier illustrations in which a dollar or any sum was received at the end of m discounting periods where m was an interval less than a year.

In employing annual discounting or compounding periods in subsequent chapters, the author can defend his treatment on grounds of expediency, that is, annual discounting is relatively easy to get across at the introductory level. But other arguments are more appropriate.

---

[1] The author has arbitrarily assumed that the upper limit is 1 year. It could be greater.

First, as indicated earlier, usually estimates as to the expected earnings on nonfinancial investments are at best educated guesses. Second, most sums are received in irregular amounts and at irregular intervals. Sophisticated techniques of discounting imply regularity in both.[2] Finally, for most problems the differences in results will not change the choices in the alternative investment opportunities under consideration. Nevertheless, to the extent that conditions favor it, there is no reason why compounding and discounting cannot be used on other than an annual basis.

SUMMARY TO APPENDIX

We can make various assumptions about the length of the intervals over which the payments are received as well as the appropriate compounding or discounting period. The intervals or periods can be finite or continuous. Different assumptions result, of course, in different formulas for finding the present value of future income streams. Ideally, we should use the formula which corresponds most closely to the pattern of expected receipts. Realistically, however, the future income from most nonfinancial investments is both uncertain and irregular. Moreover, since for most problems the differences in results will not affect the choice among alternatives, one technique may be just as useful as another.

QUESTIONS AND PROBLEMS FOR APPENDIX

1.   "It is no more realistic to assume that business firms receive income at the end of the discounting period than that they receive it at continuous intervals."   Evaluate.

2.   Assume that the rate of interest is 8 per cent and the stream of income is $100 each year for 3 years.   Find the present value of this income stream first for $m = 1$, then $m = 2$, and finally $m = 4$, given that income is received at the end of interval m.   Compare these results with those obtained assuming that $100 is received each year with the payments made continuously.

---

[2]The force of this argument is dissipated somewhat when one considers that annual discounting implies that receipts are earned in regular intervals, i.e., at the end of each year.

Principles of Asset Management

PART TWO

Capital Budgeting and the Management of Fixed Assets

chapter Six

The selection of fixed or long-lived assets is one of the major problems facing financial management. We say this because it is these assets which contribute directly to profitability. The techniques employed for selecting fixed assets are, therefore, among the most important principles of modern financial theory. Consequently, the student will want to pay particular attention to the analysis developed in this chapter. Since the material presented depends on the mathematics of finance, it may prove useful to refer back to Chapter 5.

Introduction

The purpose of developing the concept of discounting was to establish the principle by which a firm can rationally evaluate fixed or long-lived assets. Application of this principle has been the foundation on which the literature of *capital budgeting* has developed. Stated formally, capital budgeting is concerned with the criteria for the rational selection of those additions to assets whose contribution to earning power takes place over an extended period of time—for our purposes, at least a year.

Among the possibilities is an investment in which the dollar benefits resulting from dollar outlays at a particular moment in time materialize at one or more time periods in the future.[1] As an example, a public utility adds to its generating capacity (outlay), expecting to earn income (benefits) on this investment for each of several years in the future. When properly discounted, the firm can compare the dollar benefits with the dollar outlays and can select the most profitable investments from among the opportunities available. But the calculations are often based on information that is subject to a considerable degree of uncertainty. How to make adequate allowance for uncertainty is one of the most controversial topics in the literature of capital budgeting. Indeed, much of the debate over the techniques actually used to evaluate investment opportunities is really a disagreement over how to handle the risk involved in making decisions based on imperfect information.

In order to isolate the difficulties posed by uncertainty, let us first ignore the problem. By assuming that all the necessary estimates are not only available but certain, we can develop the capital budgeting techniques more easily. Moreover, in assuming a risk-free world, the economic goal of profit maximization is the same as the financial goal of maximizing the market value of the owners' equity. For the time being, at least, the two ends are the same. In a subsequent chapter we shall treat the question of uncertainty more fully, analyzing the attitudes of owners and management toward the risks involved in investing in long-lived assets, while at the same time developing techniques for handling the problem.

Cash Flows

We can define the periodic benefits from any given project as the cash flows of that project. *Gross cash flows* are the cash receipts associated with the project before allowance is made for cash expenses incurred in earning these receipts. *Net cash flows* are cash receipts associated with the project after cash expenses including taxes have been sub-

---

[1]This is one of the three main types of outlay-benefit—or in formal economics, input-output—relationships discussed in the esoteric body of literature that comprises the theory of capital. In a second type, inputs are applied at a single moment in time and the output emerges at one future time period. The time period elapsing between inputs and output, the investment period, is variable. In a third type, the investment period is variable but "the inputs contributing to any given output are applied continuously over time." See Friedrich and Vera Lutz, *The Theory of Investment of the Firm* (Princeton, N.J.:

tracted. For example, a firm invests $10,000 in a machine which is expected to wear out over the course of 5 years. By adding the machine to its stock of fixed assets, the company each year will receive $15,000 in additional sales revenue. Management knows that it must pay a worker $7,000 a year to operate the machine. Maintenance will entail another $1,000 a year. There will be taxes associated with the project, the most conspicuous of which is the federal income tax on the additional profits that result. There might also be a state income tax, and the local government may subject the new machine to the property tax.

Cash expenses directly associated with the project are not restricted to expenditures made to render the machine useful.[2] There are other expenses as well. First, there are the implicit opportunity costs. As an example, the space used up by the machine might also be employed in a profitable alternative. The cost of the foregone opportunity is properly chargeable to the cash expenses associated with the machine. Second, the elasticity of supply of factors of production can alter total costs. For example, to hire the additional worker at $7,000, the firm may also have to raise the salaries of present employees performing similar tasks. Again, the wage increase paid to other workers should be charged to expenses associated with the machine.

Similarly, the change in total revenue or marginal revenue from the sale of the machine's output depends on the elasticity of the demand for the product.[3] If we assume the enterprise produces in a perfectly competitive market, that is, its demand curve is infinitely elastic, the change in total revenue is simply the going market price times the additional quantity available for sale.[4] If the firm operates in an imperfectly competitive market so that any increase in output from the additional machine will cause the market price to fall, then marginal revenue is the price times the quantity produced by the machine less the revenue loss from all other sales. It is logical to reduce gross receipts by this amount since the market price would not have fallen if output had not

---

Princeton University Press, 1951), p. 5. This last type of investment opportunity refers to the ordinary production cycle, or "goods in process."

The serious student will find the Lutzes' book, one of the first attempts to apply economic principles to capital budgeting, among the best in the field. Their formidable presentation has unfortunately led to its neglect by many writers on the subject.

[2] We have not exhausted this category. The additional raw materials fed into the machine is another example.

[3] The output itself, of course, is the marginal physical product of the machine.

[4] Technically, of course, marginal revenue is the change in total revenue per unit change in output. In the above sentence, we are implicitly using an average of the change in total revenue from the sale of the machine's output, that is, the average marginal revenue.

expanded.[5] In forecasting gross cash flows, therefore, we must know the way in which total revenues change as output expands. In other words, we must know the shape and, therefore, the elasticity of demand.

Not only must we consider revenues and expenses associated with the machine, but we must also recognize that its purchase may entail increases in other assets such as additions to working capital. Perhaps the extra sales revenue will necessitate additional funds invested in receivables. Conceptually, the market value or replacement cost of these and related outlays results from purchasing the machine and should be added to its cost.

Although we can determine net cash flow by subtracting cash expenses from gross receipts associated with the project, there is one exception. The cost of the funds used to finance the project is not subtracted. Why we exclude the cost of funds from cash expenses will become clearer later in the chapter.

Besides cash expenses there are also noncash expenditures which must be given separate consideration. The most prominent of these is depreciation. We saw earlier that the estimate of depreciation depends on whether we are interested in the cost of replacing an asset, that is, its market value at the time of replacement, or simply in recouping its original cost. Conceptually, it is in replacement cost that our interest lies.

If we did not allow for replacement cost of the asset, we might ultimately overstate the profitability of a given investment opportunity, possibly leading us into projects which do not add to the total profits of the firm and hence to the market value of its owners' equity. For illustrative purposes we may assume that the replacement cost of the asset does not change, that is, the original cost equals the replacement cost. Moreover, to simplify calculations, we can also argue that once the machine is purchased its market value falls each year by $2,000. When it must be replaced at the end of 5 years, the old machine has no scrap value. Thus our annual depreciation allowance is $2,000 with a resale value at the end of the fifth year of zero.

Since depreciation is a noncash expense and the definition of net cash flows is gross cash flows less cash expenses, explicit or implicit and including taxes, then in determining net cash flow, we do not deduct the depreciation allowance. Moreover, to simplify the example still further, we shall restrict cash expenses[6] to wages, maintenance costs, and

[5]As students of economics know, if the firm can isolate its markets and charge two prices, one for the output of existing facilities and another (albeit lower) price for the output of the machine, then the change in total revenue is simply the lower price times the output of the machine.

[6]One factor affecting cash flows worthy of consideration is the investment tax credit. Under the present tax law, certain types of capital investments consisting of both

income taxes applicable to a corporation whose net taxable income before purchase of the new machine exceeds $25,000, thus making the 48 percent rate applicable. Furthermore, we shall exclude the possibility of implicit opportunity costs, additional outlays for working capital, and increases in expenses due to the elasticity of factor supply. Moreover, let us assume that the firm operates in a perfectly competitive market. Thus marginal revenue equals price. Hence, the addition to total revenue is simply price times quantity.

Finally, we shall also assume that depreciation is the only noncash expense. There are exceptions to this. A depletion allowance applicable to investments in wasting assets such as oil, natural gas, mineral property, and standing timber is a tax-deductible noncash expense, and therefore part of the after-tax cash flow.

How refined the analysis should be depends, of course, on the circumstances. The purpose of this chapter is to present a frame of reference for scrutinizing various investment proposals. Adaptation is an art requiring intimate knowledge of the institutional details of the industry and market environment for which the investments are relevant. The only generalization we can offer is that the cost of making some refinements is not worth the effort involved. Top management and the budgeting division also have an opportunity cost.

Since depreciation is a tax-deductible expense, the net taxable income from investing in the machine is

$$\$15,000 - (\$7,000 + \$1,000 + \$2,000) = \$5,000$$

---

new and used property can qualify for a deduction from the federal income tax liability. With the exception of public utilities, the rule applied is 7 percent but the basis for computation varies with the life of the asset. Moreover, the credit against income taxes is limited to $25,000 or the amount shown on the tax return, whichever is less. However, if the tax liability is more than $25,000 and the credit is also more than $25,000, then the credit is limited to $25,000 plus one-fourth of a firm's tax liability in excess of $25,000.

Ordinarily a new machine would qualify for the credit. Since its life is 5 years, only one-third of the original cost could be counted toward computing the tax credit. (No credit is given for eligible investments whose life is less than 4 years.) Two-thirds of the original cost can be counted if the asset has an estimated useful life of 6 or 7 years. All the original cost of assets having a life of 8 years or more can be used in computing the tax credit.

A $10,000 machine with a useful life of 5 years has an investment credit basis of $\frac{1}{3} \times \$10,000 = \$3,333.33$. Applying the 7 percent rate, $\$3,333.33 \times 0.07 = \$233.33$. For capital budgeting purposes this investment tax credit would ordinarily accrue at the end of the first year. It could then be added to the cash flows for that year.

As long as the total investment credit from a capital budget for a year is less than or equal to $25,000 plus one-fourth of the tax liability above $25,000 for that year, each project can be credited with its full tax savings. If the investment credit exceeds this upper limit, then, as a practical matter, a prorated decrease equal to the excess can be charged to each project. For further details see the annual editions of *Tax Guide for Small Business* (Washington: Government Printing Office).

Applying a tax rate of 48 percent to this figure, the after-tax profit per year on this machine is

$$\$5,000 - 48\% \text{ of } \$5,000$$

$$\$5,000 - \$2,400 = \$2,600$$

Adding back depreciation, the annual after-tax cash flow is

$$\$2,600 + \$2,000 = \$4,600$$

In general, whether we use the accounting or the economic approach to valuation,

Gross cash flow − cash expenses = net cash flow before taxes
Net cash flow before taxes − tax rate (taxable income)=

after-tax cash flow

Taxable income = (gross cash flow − cash and noncash expenses)

Rate of Return Method

In Chapter 5 it was shown that where

$$P = \frac{D}{1+r} + \frac{D}{(1+r)^2} + \frac{D}{(1+r)^3} + \cdots + \frac{D}{(1+r)^n}$$

and $D =$ a constant sum, then

$$P = \frac{D[1-(1+r)^{-n}]}{r}$$

Since the replacement cost of the outlay on the machine is $10,000 and the net cash flow is $4,600, then

$$\$10,000 = \frac{\$4,600}{1+r} + \frac{\$4,600}{(1+r)^2} + \frac{\$4,600}{(1+r)^3} + \frac{\$4,600}{(1+r)^4} + \frac{\$4,600}{(1+r)^5}$$
$$= \frac{\$4,600[1-(1+r)^{-n}]}{r}$$

The table in Appendix B of this volume gives values for $P = (D[1 - (1+r)^{-n}])/r$, where $D = 1$.   In order to solve for r, we can, by trial and error, find the number opposite 5 years in the table which when multiplied by $4,600 equals or approximates $10,000.

so that $P = (D[1-(1+r)^{-n}])/r$
For $r = 36\%$,
P for $n = 5$ years $= 2.18073 \times \$4,600 = \$10,031.36$
For $r = 37\%$,
P for $n = 5$ years $= 2.14269 \times \$4,600 = \$9,856.37$

Since r is some figure between 36 and 37 percent, we can interpolate on a linear basis as follows:

P for $r = 36\% = \$10,031.36$
P for $r = 37\% = 9,856.37$
_____

Difference $ 174.99

P for $r = 36\% = \$10,031.36$
Original cost $= 10,000.00$
_____

Difference $ 31.36

Let $x =$ a fraction of 1%; then

$$\frac{\$31.36}{\$174.99} = \frac{x}{0.01}$$

$$x = 0.18\%$$

For $P = \$10,000$, $r = 36.18\%$

While the interpolation above is a satisfactory approximation in most circumstances, the reader should note that the relationship between any two percentages based on discounted cash flows is not linear. Therefore, the assumption of proportionality on which the interpolation is based is not entirely accurate.

The figure 36.18 percent is a measure of the *rate of return on the investment*. This application of discounting, also called the *yield, marginal efficiency of investment*, or *internal rate of return*, results in a measure of profitability which can be compared with yields calculated in similar fashion on alternative investment opportunities.

Before making these comparisons, a simple rearrangement of the equation will prove useful in terms of understanding why depreciation, or for that matter any noncash expense representing a return of the outlay, is included in the cash flows.

$$0 = -\$10,000 + \frac{\$4,600}{1+r} + \frac{\$4,600}{(1+r)^2} + \frac{\$4,600}{(1+r)^3} + \frac{\$4,600}{(1+r)^4} + \frac{\$4,600}{(1+r)^5}$$

The replacement and, in this case, original cost of $10,000 is recouped over a 5-year period through annual depreciation allowances of $2,000. If depreciation is not counted among the future benefits, allowance for the outlay would have been made twice in the calculations—once when allowing for the replacement cost and again by failing to make provisions for return of the replacement cost in the cash flows. Thus, consistency demands that since the expenditure is included in the rate of return calculations, and since it is to be recouped from revenues, the dollars returned must be included in the future benefits.[7]

The Capital Budget

In order to compare projects on the basis of rate of return, we must first distinguish between two types of investment opportunities — those which are substitutes, called in the literature *mutually exclusive investments*, and those whose yields are independent of one another. As an example of the first type, consider a company interested in expanding its productive capacity. It has the opportunity of building additional facilities in either Chicago, New York, or San Francisco. Expansion in any of these cities would result in a 45 percent, 35 percent, and 20 percent yield, respectively. But the adoption of one site reduces the yield from building in other cities to zero. Consequently, the choice of Chicago as the site where it will build excludes the construction of other facilities in New York or San Francisco.[8]

Once the highest yield among alternative but substitute investment opportunities is found, it must be compared with the yields on other investments which are independent of one another. For example, as management considers expanding its production facilities, it may also be investigating the possibility of placing its bookkeeping, billing, and other clerical operations on computers. The yield on this "cost-saving"

---

[7]Although our concept of depreciation corresponds to the economic not the accounting definition, it is interesting to note that in economic theory it is ordinarily assumed that the amount deducted for depreciation goes back into the asset to maintain its productivity and hence its capitalized value indefinitely. This is why the value of an asset in economic theory is simply $P = D/r$, or the limit of the expression

$$P = \frac{D[1-(1+r)^{-n}]}{r} \qquad \text{as } n \to \infty$$

In this case, D is simply the net productivity of capital. If one assumes that the depreciation allowance of \$2,000 per year does indeed reflect the amount necessary to maintain indefinitely the productivity of the asset, then

$$\$10,000 = \frac{\$2,600}{r} = 26\%$$

In capital budgeting, the assumptions are more realistic. Not only does the asset wear out but the firm has the option of using depreciation allowances for purposes other than replacing the asset. The funds can be reinvested somewhere else, used to retire the debt which may have been used to purchase the asset, or for that matter paid out to stockholders.

[8]The differences in yields, we can imagine, results from the fact that the facilities to be built will all be used to service the same national market, but transportation costs are less when the plant is centrally located. Presumably, building three small plants at each of these locations is more costly than the savings in transportation costs.

investment can be considered independent of the rate of return on the expansion in productive facilities.[9]

Let us assume, therefore, that management is considering, along with the $10,000 investment in the machine, expansion in productive facilities and the installation of a computer. The yield on any of these investments is not affected by accepting or rejecting the others.[10] The rate of return for each has been calculated from discounted cash flows. The results are listed below, rounded to the nearest percentage.

Investment	Replacement Cost	Rate of Return, %
Machine	$ 10,000	36
Computer	500,000	40
Additional Production Facilities	1,000,000	45
Total Outlay	$1,510,000	

One can plot these results graphically as shown in Figure 6-1, on the next page. The smooth curve drawn through these points and labeled D_C is the company's demand curve for capital, or its capital budget, under the assumption that it has a total of $5,000,000 in investment opportunities at rates of return ranging continuously from 50 to 0 percent. Our firm, typical of most, would find that its investment opportunities are better likened to a flight of stairs, each step representing a capital outlay. The distances between steps—AB, BC, etc.,—represent the lack of investment opportunities at intermediate yields.

Although the rate of return, given adequate information, can be readily calculated for each project, there is no indication that a firm should cease investing short of a zero yield. On reflection, however, we would suspect that there is a positive rate of return below which the

[9]For purposes of analysis the extreme cases, in which there is complete independence or in which investment opportunities are perfect substitutes, are useful models. In practice, the rate of return on any capital outlay is usually affected by the adoption of another investment. But does it make any practical difference? The installation of computers can be expected to raise the yield on additional productive facilities in all three cities, but it is hard to visualize its adoption as altering the ranking and hence the choice among the three. On the other hand, if the 45-percent return for a Chicago location estimated without cost savings from the installation of a computer is too low (what too low means will be evident shortly), then its adoption may be a necessary prerequisite for expansion. To further complicate the problem, suppose also that the cost savings from eliminating clerical tasks under the assumption that there would be no expansion in plant did not justify purchase of the computer. Again the rate of return was too low. But if the additional facilities were built, the cost savings realized would result in an adequate yield. The investments are thus interdependent or complementary. In this case both must be accepted in order for either to have a satisfactory rate of return.

[10]The machine, let us assume, is a replacement for one that is technologically obsolete. The expansion in productive facilities and the installation of a computer are assumed to have a negligible effect on its yield. Thus the machine will yield 36 percent regardless of whether or not the other two investments are made.

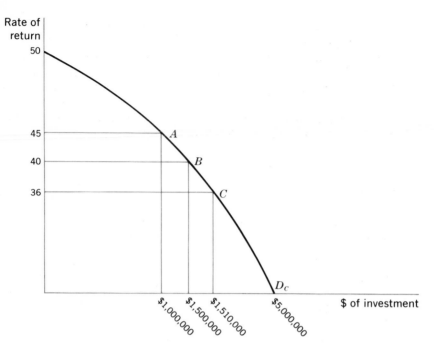

Figure 6-1

concern would add more to total costs than to total revenues, and hence fail to maximize total profits and with it the market value of the owners' interests. Recall from our earlier discussion that the one cash expense specifically excluded as a deduction from gross cash flows was the cost of the funds used to purchase the asset. This rate is called the *cost of capital.* If the cost of capital is 10 percent, then all investment opportunities with a yield in excess of 10 percent are profitable. Adopting them will contribute to the earnings of the company and therefore to the market value of the ownership interests. Projects whose yield is below the cost of capital should be rejected, for it costs more to use the funds than is received from their employment. Adopting these projects will therefore lower the market value of the owners' equity.

Since the cost of capital is the cutoff rate, if we included it in the cash expenses to be subtracted from the gross cash flows, we would be double counting. As a result we would reject projects which are otherwise profitable.

But what determines the cost of capital? To avoid subsequent confusion, we must admit at the outset that the answer is not clear-cut. Moreover, merely to begin an explanation we must explore several

98

complex issues.   However, in order to see what is in store for us, we recall from our earlier discussion of accounting that there are alternative sources of funds available.   Each of these sources has an explicit or implicit cost attached to it.   Thus there appears to be, not a cost of capital but the cost of each source of capital.   Yet we are assuming that, save for the source of funds to purchase the machine and the addition of the machine itself, the structure of assets, liabilities, and owners' equity remains unchanged.[11]   Consequently, when we are speaking of the cost of capital, we are by implication discussing the marginal cost of capital.

Since an introductory analysis must proceed step by step, for the present we shall beg the question of how the cost of capital is determined and take it as given.   Our capital budget, therefore, can be said to consist of three independent projects, each of which has a yield in excess of the assumed cost of capital of 10 percent.

Present Value Method

If the cost of capital is known, then an alternative and historically older method for comparing investment opportunities is available.   Instead of finding r, we can equate it with the cost of capital, in this case 10 percent.   Thus the equation

$$\$10,000 = \frac{\$4,600}{1+r} + \frac{\$4,600}{(1+r)^2} + \frac{\$4,600}{(1+r)^3} + \frac{\$4,600}{(1+r)^4} + \frac{\$4,600}{(1+r)^5}$$

becomes

$$\$10,000 = \frac{\$4,600}{1.10} + \frac{\$4,600}{1.21} + \frac{\$4,600}{1.331} + \frac{\$4,600}{1.4641} + \frac{\$4,600}{1.61051}$$

$$\neq \$4,181.818 + \$3,801.653 + \$3,456.048 + \$3,141.862 + \$2,856.238$$

$$\neq \$17,437.619$$

In the special case where the cash flows are equal,

$$\$10,000 = \frac{D[1-(1+r)^{-n}]}{r}$$

$$\neq \frac{\$4,600[1-(1+0.10)^{-5}]}{0.10}$$

[11]Recall our mentioning in footnote 2 of this chapter the possibility that the purchase of the machine may entail an addition to the stock of raw-materials inventory.   We also pointed out in the text that the firm may have to increase its level of receivables.   The cost of these current assets requires financing from some source.   Just as the market value of the outlays required should be included with the replacement cost of the machine, so the cost of these funds is included in the cost of capital.

Using the table in Appendix B for $r = 10$ per cent and $n = 5$ years we find

$$\$10,000 \neq 3.79078 \times \$4,600$$
$$< \$17,437.59$$

The substantive content of the present value method lies in the interpretation of the inequality that results. If the present value of the cash flows discounted at the cost of capital is greater than the replacement cost of the investment outlay — in this case, $10,000 — then the project is profitable. The difference between the present value of the cash flows and the replacement cost is the profit on the investment. In the above example,

Present Value of Cash Flows	$ 17,437.59
Replacement Cost	−10,000.00
Net Present Value	$ 7,437.59

The figure $7,437.59 is usually called the *net present value* of the investment. The return of the funds invested is accounted for by subtracting the replacement cost from the present value of the cash flows. The cost of using the funds each year is accounted for when the cash flows are discounted by the cost of capital. Hence the residual can be treated as a profit.

When comparing substitute methods of production, one chooses the process which results in the highest net present value. Investment under this method is carried out until the present value of the cash flows equals the replacement cost of the original investment, or the net present value is zero. The last increment of investment funds yields cash flows which, when discounted by the cost of capital, return the replacement cost of the investment and cover the cost of using the funds. The dollars invested in each independent investment project can be totaled. The result is a firm's demand curve for capital expressed in terms of net present value.

Assume that the net present value of the funds invested in the computer is $40,000 and the net present value of the funds invested in the additional production facilities is $70,000. Then Figure 6-2 depicts these results, i.e., the capital budget. D_C represents the demand curve for capital, expressed in terms of net present value. As in the case of Figure 6-1, this curve can be interpreted as a continuous function ranging from a net present value of $100,000 to a net present value of zero. Our firm views it, however, as a series of individual investment opportunities without alternatives in between the steps.

Just as a firm will not accept projects where the rate of return is less than the cost of capital, so too will it reject projects in which the net

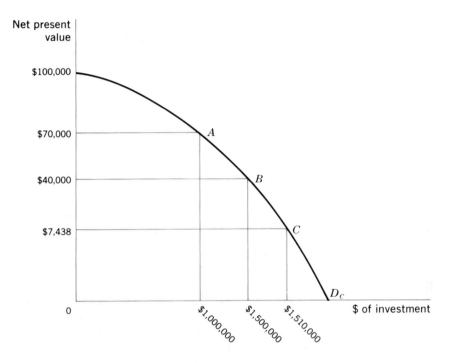

Figure 6-2

present value is negative. Otherwise it would be expending funds in areas where the cash flows fail to lower the replacement cost and the cost of using these funds.

When a firm must decide whether to accept or reject a project, either the rate of return or the present value method will give results consistent with the goal of maximizing the market value of the owners' interests. Investment in the additional production facilities will be more profitable than investment in the computer, while the machine is the least profitable of the three. All of these projects, however, add something to total profits and should be undertaken.

Rate of Return or Present Value — A Controversy over Techniques

Occasions do arise, however, when these two methods do not rank projects in the same order of preference. As a result there has been considerable debate as to which of the two techniques is better. While there are numerous aspects to the problem of choice (with each writer championing, often with modifications, one or the other of the two methods), for a large array of problems it makes little difference which technique is used.[12]   Many of the difficulties stem from the need to select from among mutually exclusive investment opportunities.

To illustrate, assume that Projects A and B below are mutually exclusive.   The cost of capital is 16 percent.

	Replacement Cost	Cash Flow, End of First Year	Cash Flow, End of Second Year
Project A	$1,000	$1,300	
Project B	$1,000	$ 100	$1,400

Project A terminates at the end of the first year, while Project B carries over into the second year at the end of which it ceases to be productive. For Project A the rate of return is

$$\$1,000 = \frac{\$1,300}{1+r}$$
$$r = 30\%$$

To find the yield on Project B, we can either solve the quadratic equation that results or use the table in Appendix A of this volume on a trial and error basis.   Here we can find the discounted value of a dollar received at the end of each year for n years at various rates of interest. Unlike the cash flows from the machine, the dollars received on Project B are in unequal increments.   Summation is therefore impossible. Using the table in Appendix A, we find through trial and error that for $r = 23$ percent,

$$\$1,000 = \frac{\$100}{1+r} + \frac{\$1,400}{(1+r)^2}$$
$$\neq \$100(0.81301) + \$1,400(0.66098)$$
$$< \$81.301 + \$925.372$$
$$< \$1,006.67$$

For $r = 24$ percent,

$$\$1,000 \neq \$100(0.80645) + \$1,400(0.65036)$$
$$> \$991.15$$

[12]Among the numerous pages devoted to the debate are those of Harold Bierman and Seymour Smidt, *The Capital Budgeting Decision*, 2d ed. (New York: The Macmillan Company, 1966), chap. 3; Pearson Hunt, *Financial Analysis in Capital Budgeting* (Boston: Harvard Graduate School of Business Administration, 1964), chap. 2; A. J. Merrett and Allen Sykes, *The Finance and Analysis of Capital Projects* (New York: John Wiley & Sons, Inc., 1963), chap. 5; James Lorie and Leonard J. Savage, "Three Problems in Capital Rationing," *Journal of Business*, vol. 28, no. 3 (October, 1955), pp. 229–239; Ezra Solomon, "The Arithmetic of Capital Budgeting Decisions," *Journal of Business*, vol. 29, no. 2 (April, 1956), pp. 124–129. See also Ezra Solomon (ed.), *The Management of Corporate Capital* (Glencoe, Ill.: The Free Press, 1959), *passim.*

Using linear interpolation,

$$r = 23.58\%$$

Substituting 16 percent or the cost capital into each equation and subtracting the replacement cost from the present value of the cash flows, the net present value of each is

	Net Present Value
Project A	$120.69
Project B	$126.63

Project A gives a higher rate of return than Project B, but the net present value of B is higher than the net present value of A.

Since the rate of return is in excess of the cost of capital and the net present value in both instances is positive, each, if it were not a mutually exclusive investment, would be acceptable. It is because both are substitutes for one another that the problem of ranking arises.

Leaving for the Appendix to this chapter a more complete explanation, the reason for the discrepancy can be most easily seen by calling attention to the different terminal dates. Project A has a 30-percent return on the basis of a single year. May we assume that if the funds are reinvested, this is the rate applicable during the second year? If so, then the *terminal value* of Project A would be

$$\$1,300(1.30) = \$1,690$$

Project B, on the other hand, has a rate of return of 23.58 percent on cash flows occurring in both the first and second years. Assuming that the cash flows for the first year are reinvested at that rate, the terminal value of Project B would be

$100(1.2358)	= $ 123.58
Cash flow, end of second year =	1,400.00
Terminal value	= $1,523.58

Suppose, however, that the cash flows from both projects can be reinvested only at the cost of capital, or 16 percent. The terminal value of Project A would be

$$\$1,300(1.16) = \$1,508$$

whereas the terminal value of Project B would be

$100(1.16)	= $ 116.00
Cash flow, end of second year =	1,400.00
Terminal value	= $1,516.00

Consequently, under the assumption that the funds are reinvested at their respective yields, Project A with a higher rate of return also has higher terminal value than Project B.   If it is assumed that the cost of capital is the relevant reinvestment rate, then Project B with the higher net present value also has the higher terminal value.

Generally speaking, the reinvestment rate on the shorter-lived of two mutually exclusive projects is implicitly assumed to be at least as great as the rate on the longer-lived project.[13]   In this case it could be even lower.   At a rate of 17 percent, the terminal value of Project A would be

$$\$1,300(1.17) = \$1,521$$

whereas the terminal value of Project B would be

$$
\begin{array}{lr}
\$100(1.17) & = \$ \ 117 \\
\text{Cash flow, end of second year} = & 1,400 \\
\hline
\text{Terminal value} & = \$1,517
\end{array}
$$

In order to render mutually exclusive investments strictly comparable, we must make assumptions as to the reinvestment rate.   The logical choice would seem to be the cost of capital at the time reinvestment is assumed to take place—in this example, at the end of the first year.   If Project B had terminated at the end of the third year, and if Project A remained unchanged, we would use, respectively, reinvestment rates equal to the cost of capital at the end of the first and second years.

Another problem which can yield conflicting results stems from differences in the replacement cost of cash outlays.   Assume that two projects, C and D, are mutually exclusive.   The pattern of cash outlays and cash flows are as follows:

	Replacement Cost	Cash Flow, End of First Year	Cash Flow, End of Second Year
Project C	$ 694.44		$\dfrac{\$1,000}{(1+r)^2}$
Project D	$7,181.84		$\dfrac{\$10,000}{(1+r)^2}$

[13]Solomon, "The Arithmetic of Capital Budgeting Decisions," *op. cit.*, p. 126. Assume there was a third alternative consisting of a $1,000 outlay valued at replacement cost and with a rate of return of 27 percent for three annual cash flows.   If Project A is selected, it is assumed that the funds from A are reinvested for two additional years at a rate equal to or exceeding 27 percent.

The cost of capital is 15 percent. Reinvestment is no problem since both projects have a common terminal date. For Project C, r equals 20 percent, and for Project D, r equals 18 percent, but the net present value of C is $61.70 as against $379.60 for D.

In this instance, the source of the disparity can be traced to the fact that the yield is independent of the absolute size of the cash outlay whereas the net present value is not. If we were to calculate the rate of return on the incremental cash flow, that is, on the difference between the replacement cost of the outlays and the cash flows of the two projects, we would find that

$$\$6,487.40 = \frac{\$9,000}{(1+r)^2}$$
$$r = 17.79\%$$

Since this yield is above the cost of capital, it would be worthwhile to undertake the project with the greater capital outlay. Total profits as measured by net present value would be larger by adopting Project D than by choosing Project C.

There is the further possibility that in some instances the cash flows from an investment consist of one or more negative values interspersed among periods of positive cash flows. Consider the following situation. A firm is given the opportunity of establishing a concession at a world's fair. It must build its facilities, use them for 2 years, and then dismantle them. It estimates that the cost of disassembling them is such that it will take a loss of $30,000 in the second year but will have a positive cash flow of $150,000 in the first year. The replacement cost of the outlay for establishing the concession is $90,000. The cost of capital is 10 percent. Hence

$$\$90,000 = \frac{\$150,000}{1+r} + \frac{(-\$30,000)}{(1+r)^2}$$
$$= \frac{\$150,000}{1+r} - \frac{\$30,000}{(1+r)^2}$$
$$r = 43.425\%$$
$$= -76.759\%$$

There are two unique solutions for r,[14] one appearing to suggest that the investment should be undertaken, the other indicating that it

[14]The equation reduces to the form $3r^2 + r - 1 = 0$. Using the quadratic formula

$$r = \frac{-b \pm \sqrt{b^2 - 4ac}}{2a}$$

where $a = 3, b = 1$, and $c = -1$, the values for r can be readily calculated.

should be rejected.[15]   In order to avoid this ambiguity, we can evaluate the project on the basis of net present value.

$$\$90,000 = \frac{\$150,000}{1.10} - \frac{\$30,000}{1.21}$$

$$= \$136,363.64 - \$24,793.39$$

$$\text{Net present value} = \$111,570.25$$

The investment at a cost of capital of 10 percent is profitable.

In the case of two mutually exclusive investments with different cash outlays, it is possible for negative cash flows to result when we calculate the incremental difference in outlays and cash flows.   The following example is illustrative.

	Cash Outlay at Replacement Cost	Cash Flow, End of First Year	Cash Flow, End of Second Year
Project E	$ 1,000	$ 300	$1,300
Project F	$10,000	$11,825	$1,000

Project E has a rate of return of 30 percent as against 25 percent for Project F.   However, assuming the cost of capital is 10 percent, Project E has a net present value of $247, but Project F has a net present value of $1,576, each estimate being rounded to the nearest dollar.

If we calculate the rate of return on the incremental cash outlays and cash flows, we find that

$$\$9,000 = \frac{\$11,825}{1+r} - \frac{\$300}{(1+r)^2}$$

$$r = 25.42\%$$

$$= -97.24\%$$

However, if the firm accepts Project F on the basis of its higher net present value, it will add $9,000 more to its capital budget but $1,329 more to its total profits ($1,576, the net present value of F, less $247, the net present value of E) than if Project F is adopted.

[15]For capital budgeting purposes a negative rate of return has no meaning unless it is equated to a negative cost of capital.   The latter concept implies that people are willing to pay business firms to invest their funds.   Discounting cash flows using a negative rate of return will make the present value of a dollar greater today than say a year from today.   For instance, the present value of $100 due a year from today discounted at −20 percent is

$$\text{Present value} = \frac{\$100}{(1-0.20)} = \$125$$

In summary, both the rate of return and the present value methods can be used to evaluate investment opportunities. All independent projects whose rate of return exceeds the cost of capital or whose net present value is greater than zero should be accepted. When negative cash flows are interspersed among positive cash flows the resulting equation can yield two or more solutions, or in some instances no solution. Under these conditions the present value method would be preferred in evaluating both an accept or a reject investment or for selecting from among mutually exclusive alternatives. When mutually exclusive investments have different terminal dates, it is necessary to introduce a rate at which intermediate cash flows can be reinvested. The project chosen will be the one with the highest terminal value.

Indeed, it is the terminal value approach which is the most complete technique for budgeting capital. But to carry it through consistently, we may have to use more than one reinvestment rate. Even in a world of certainty, we might expect the cost of capital to change from one period to the next. Moreover, when we incorporate uncertainty into our analysis, estimates of reinvestment rates, particularly for years further into the future, are virtually impossible to determine. Consequently, for pragmatic reasons, we must use either the rate of return or the present value approach for selecting from among independent projects and reserve the terminal value approach for reconciling conflicts among mutually exclusive investments.

As between the two, the present value approach appears to offer certain advantages over the rate of return approach. Not only does it avoid the problem of multiple and negative yields, but it is also easier to compute. More important, it is changes in total profits, not the percentage earned on a given project, which ultimately affects the market value of the owners' equity.[16] The net present value of a project is a measure of this change. The rate of return is not.

Yet there is a tendency among businessmen to think in terms of rate of return on investment rather than net present value. Accounting concepts couched in terms of ratio analysis are more familiar to many of them than the traditional economic concept of net present value.

But if ratios are needed, this can be accomplished by dividing the present value of the cash flows by the replacement cost. Thus in the case of our first example,

$$\$10,000 < \$17,437.63$$

---

[16]Of course, in the case of mutually exclusive investments considered in a world of uncertainty, there may be greater risk attached to a higher dollar outlay even though the net present value is greater. As we shall see, the only way to handle this problem is to evaluate mutually exclusive investments on a risk-adjusted basis.

could be replaced by

$$\frac{\$17{,}437.63}{\$10{,}000} = 1.743763$$

This *benefit-cost ratio* measures the rate by which the present value of the cash flows exceeds their replacement cost. We could rank independent projects on the basis of their benefit-cost ratios, accepting all investments where the ratio was one or greater.

Finally, there are those who object to the net present value technique on the grounds that it results in a "needless dispute about a firm's cost of capital."[17]   To this objection we can only argue that a firm must know its cost of capital in order to use either technique properly. Otherwise, management must resort to an arbitrary cutoff rate. While this is a possibility as a hedge against uncertainty, to do so not only avoids the issue of what constitutes the cost of capital but renders incomplete an analysis of how management can maximize the market value of its ownership interests.

There are, therefore, no weaknesses inherent in the net present value approach which are not also problems when projects are evaluated on the basis of rate of return. Since there are other advantages from using the present value technique, it is in this writer's view at least the more preferable of the two.

SUMMARY

Cash flows represent the future stream of benefits from a capital investment. Net cash flow is the difference between cash receipts and cash expenditures. When adjusted for taxes, the discounting techniques developed in the previous chapter can be used to equate the cash flows with the replacement cost—that is, the market value at the time of replacement—of the asset. In using these techniques we can either calculate the rate of return, that is, solve the equation for r, or substitute the cost of capital for r. For independent investment opportunities, if the rate of return is greater than the cost of capital, the project is acceptable. If the present value of the future cash flows is greater than the replacement cost of the investment, the project is also acceptable.

However, when we must make a choice among mutually exclusive investments, we find that the two procedures sometimes lead to a different ranking of projects. To reconcile these differences, we can

[17]See Merrett and Sykes, *op. cit.*, p. 150.

introduce a reinvestment assumption and make our selection on the basis of the highest terminal value of each project. Ideally, we should rank all projects on the basis of terminal values. In a world of uncertainty, however, future reinvestment rates would be difficult to estimate. Consequently, the present choice is between the two alternatives. While each has its advocates, the present value approach has several distinct advantages and none of the disadvantages inherent in the rate of return approach. It is, therefore, the author's preference.

QUESTIONS AND PROBLEMS

Where necessary, use the appropriate tables in the Appendixes of this volume for solving the following problems.

1. Find the rate of return on the following project:

	After-tax Cash Flows		
Replacement Cost	First Year	Second Year	Third Year
$10,000	$7000	$5,000	$1,000

2. Using the data in problem 1, find the net present value under the assumption that the cost of capital is 10 percent. On either basis, is the project acceptable? Explain.

3. Find the rate of return on the following project and explain your results.

	After-tax Cash Flows	
Replacement Cost	First Year	Second Year
$100,000	−$10,000	$200,000

4. Management is considering purchasing a computer. The original cost of the instrument is $400,000. It is estimated that it must be replaced within 5 years at a cost of $500,000. It is assumed that the annual economic depreciation represents 20 percent of the replacement cost. Management has made a detailed study of the annual savings in total costs which purchasing the computer would bring. It has concluded that these cost savings are $300,000 per year, before taxes. However, it expects to incur an additional $100,000 a year in new expenses associated with the operation of the computer. The firm is a corporation whose net taxable income without the computer exceeds $25,000. Its cost of capital is 10 percent. Should the firm purchase the computer? Explain.

5.   A firm is considering an investment with the following pattern of cash flows.

After-tax Cash Flows

Replacement Cost	First Year	Second Year	Third Year
$100,000	$50,000	$100,000	$10,000

The cost of capital is 10 percent and the reinvestment rate 5 percent.   Is the project worth undertaking?   Explain fully.

6.   Assume that a company with a cost of capital and reinvestment rate of 15 percent must make a choice between the following mutually exclusive investments. Which will it choose?   Why?

After-tax Cash Flows

	Replacement Cost	First Year	Second Year
Project X	$10,000	$5,500	$9,680
Project Y	$20,000	$24,200	

7.   Assume that a corporation with a 10 percent cost of capital must make a choice between the following mutually exclusive investments.   Which would it choose?   Why?

After-tax Cash Flows

	Replacement Cost	First Year	Second Year
Project A	$1,000	$1,300	
Project B	$1,000		$1,562.50

8.   Explain carefully why depreciation is included in cash flows when evaluating a project.   Would we treat all noncash expenses in the same way?   Explain.

9.   "The present value approach is inferior to the yield technique for selecting investments."   Evaluate.

SELECTED REFERENCES

Bierman, Harold, Jr., and Seymour Smidt.   *The Capital Budgeting Decision*, 2d ed.   New York: The Macmillan Company, 1966.

Dean, Joel.   *Capital Budgeting*.   New York: Columbia University Press, 1951.

Hunt, Pearson.   *Financial Analysis in Capital Budgeting*.   Boston: Harvard Graduate School of Business Administration, 1964.

Lorie, James, and Leonard J. Savage.   "Three Problems in Capital Rationing," *Journal of Business*, vol. 28, no. 3 (October, 1955), pp. 229–239.

Lutz, Friedrich, and Vera Lutz.   *The Theory of Investment of the Firm*.   Princeton, N.J.: Princeton University Press, 1951.

Merrett, A. J., and Allen Sykes. *The Finance and Analysis of Capital Projects.* New York: John Wiley & Sons, Inc., 1963.

Porterfield, James T. S. *Investment Decisions and Capital Costs.* Englewood Cliffs, N.J.: Prentice-Hall, Inc., 1965.

Quirin, C. David. *The Capital Expenditure Decision.* Homewood, Ill.: Richard D. Irwin, Inc., 1967.

Solomon, Ezra. "The Arithmetic of Capital Budgeting Decisions," *Journal of Business*, vol. 29, no. 2 (April, 1956), pp. 124–129.

—— (ed.). *The Management of Corporate Capital.* Glencoe, Ill.: The Free Press, 1959.

APPENDIX: Rate of Return and Present Value – The Reinvestment Assumptions

Both the rate of return and the present value techniques implicitly use reinvestment rates which result in the division of cash flows into depreciation and net profit figures which may not correspond to our original computations. To illustrate,[1] assume that both the original cost and the replacement cost of a capital outlay are $2,361.60, resulting in an annual net cash flow of $1,000 per year for 4 years consisting solely of net profits after taxes and depreciation. For the present we shall assume that we do not know the breakdown of this figure into its respective components.

The rate of return on this investment is[2]

$$\$2,361.60 = \frac{\$1,000}{1+r} + \frac{\$1,000}{(1+r)^2} + \frac{\$1,000}{(1+r)^3} + \frac{\$1,000}{(1+r)^4}$$

$$r = 25\%$$

Implicit in the discounting process, however, are the figures for net income and depreciation. The annual dollar income is $590.40,

---

[1]The above example is drawn from Ward S. Curran, "Depreciation in Economic Theory and Capital Budgeting," *Quarterly Review of Economics and Business*, vol. 8, no. 1 (Spring, 1968), pp. 61–68.   Reprinted by permission of the editor.

[2]Another way of interpreting the 25 percent return is as the yield on the capital remaining in the project at the end of any given period. For example, discount at 25 percent the $1,000 received at the end of the first year. Subtracting the result, or $800, from $2,361.60 leaves $1,561.60. Thus

$$\$1,561.60 = \frac{\$1,000}{(1+r)^2} + \frac{\$1,000}{(1+r)^3} + \frac{\$1,000}{(1+r)^4}$$

$$r = 25\%$$

This interpretation is not inconsistent with the one taken in the text. In order to earn 25 percent per annum on the replacement cost of the total capital invested and recover the funds at the end of the fourth year, $409.60 per year must be reinvested at 25 percent in the manner indicated above.

or 25 percent of $2,361.60. The depreciation is $1,000–$590.40, or $409.60. When reinvested at 25 percent,

End of Year	Depreciation	Amount
First	$409.60(1.25)^3$	$800
Second	$409.60(1.25)^2$	640
Third	$409.60(1.25)$	512
Fourth	$409.60	409.60
		$2,361.60

If we employ the present value technique, we can read into the figures on net cash flow still a different breakdown into depreciation and net profit. Assuming that the cost of capital is 10 percent, we get

$$\$2,361.60 = \frac{\$1,000}{1+0.10} + \frac{\$1,000}{(1+0.10)^2} + \frac{\$1,000}{(1+0.10)^3} + \frac{\$1,000}{(1+0.10)^4}$$

$$= \$909.09 + \$826.45 + \$751.31 + \$683.01$$
$$< \$3,169.86$$

The net present value of the cash flows is greater than the replacement cost of the outlay. The addition to total profits from adopting the project is $3,169.86 − $2,361.60 = $808.26.

In this example, instead of dealing with a rate which equates the cash flows with the replacement cost of the outlay, that is, with a rate of return *on* the investment, we are asking another question: What is the annual depreciation allowance which will recoup the replacement cost of the outlay on the assumption that these funds are supplied at a cost of 10 percent? A depreciation allowance of $745.01 will satisfy this condition. When discounted at 10 percent, it will recoup the replacement cost of $2,361.60. Similarly, the annual net income of $254.99 when discounted at 10 percent will equal the net present value of $808.26.[3]

Now let us drop the assumption that the breakdown between depreciation and net profits is unknown. Assume that there is an annual

[3]To calculate depreciation,

$$\$2,361.60 = x\left[\frac{1-(1.10)^{-4}}{0.10}\right]$$
$$= 3.16987x$$
$$x = \$745.01$$

To calculate profit,

$$\$1,000 - \$745.01 = \$254.99$$

$$\$254.99\left[\frac{1-(1.10)^{-4}}{0.10}\right] = \$254.99(3.16987) = \$808.28$$

The discrepancy of $0.02 is due to rounding in the table in Appendix B.

depreciation allowance of $590.40 and a profit of $409.60.   This is a return of 17.34 percent on the replacement cost of $2,361.60.   Note that the depreciation figure in this example equals the profit figure in the rate of return example.   Similarly, the profit figure in this example equals the depreciation figure in the rate of return example.   The reason for this discrepancy stems from the fact that, in estimating cash flows, we implicitly assumed a reinvestment rate of zero.

Thus we have three separate values for depreciation and three separate figures for net profit.   These can be summarized as follows:

Technique	Net Profit	Depreciation
Rate of Return	$590.40	$409.60
Zero Reinvestment Rate	409.60	590.40
Present Value Approach	254.99	745.01

Each has been derived under different assumptions.   In the rate of return approach the replacement cost of the asset is recovered by investing a sum at 25 percent.   Yet in estimating cash flows, we make no reinvestment assumption.   Under the present value technique, however, it is assumed that the replacement cost of the asset is recovered by reinvesting a sum at 10 percent.

Sinking Fund   Since the differences in figures result from the assumptions implied in the procedures employed, some analysts have felt that the assumptions under which depreciation is recouped should be made explicit.   One technique used in the nationalized industries in Great Britain is to set up a sinking fund.[4]   Thus if R is the replacement cost of the outlay, that is, the market value at the time of replacement, it can be recovered through sinking fund payments of $$a$ per annum, so that

$$R = a + a(1+r) + a(1+r)^2 + \cdots + a(1+r)^{n-1} \qquad \text{for } r > 0$$

$$= \frac{a}{r}\left[(1+r)^n - 1\right]$$

$$a = \frac{Rr}{(1-r)^n - 1}$$

The sinking fund payments can be reinvested at some rate r.   At the same time, they must be discounted to reflect the cost of committing them to a sinking fund rather than investing them elsewhere.   Let A equal the annual sum necessary to meet both of these requirements.

[4]Merrett and Sykes, *op. cit.*, pp. 39–42, 165–171.   See also Lutz and Lutz, *op. cit.*, pp. 228–230.

Assume that the opportunity cost, the reinvestment rate, and the cost of capital all equal 10 percent. Then

$$A = \frac{Rr}{(1+r)^n - 1} + Rr$$

$$= \frac{\$2,361.60 \times 0.10}{1.10^4 - 1} + \$2,361.60 \times 0.10$$

$$= \$745.01$$

Subtracting this amount from $1,000 gives an annual profit of $254.99.

Note that the profit and depreciation figures for the sinking fund method are the same as those for the present value approach. Given our assumption, the two methods yield the same result. To cover the cost of capital each year, we simply multiply the replacement cost of the outlay, or $2,361.60, by 10 percent. We get $236.16. Subtracting this from $1,000, we find the residual to be $1,000 − $236.16 = $763.84.

Compounding this amount at a reinvestment rate of 10 percent, we get

$$\$763.84(1.10)^3 + \$763.84(1.10)^2 + \$763.84(1.10) + \$763.84 = \text{terminal value}$$

$$\$1,016.67 + \$924.25 + \$840.22 + \$763.84 = \$3,544.98$$

Of the $745.01, $236.16 represents the amount set aside to cover the cost of capital. The residual, or $508.85 ($745.01 − $236.16), when compounded at 10 percent, equals $2,361.60. The annual profit of $254.99, when compounded at the same rate, equals $1,183.38. The sum of the two equals $3,544.98.

Thus the difference between the sinking fund and the present value methods is simply the fact that, in the former, cash flows are divided into three components — an amount to cover the cost of capital, an amount to cover the replacement cost of the asset, and the residual or profit. When we use the latter technique, there is no distinction made between the amount set aside to cover the cost of capital and the amount set aside to replace the asset. Therefore, given a 10 percent cost of capital, if we had assumed that depreciation could be reinvested at a figure which differed from 10 percent, the amount necessary to cover the cost of capital and replace the asset would have differed from $745.01. The residual or net profit would have varied accordingly.

Does the possibility that the reinvestment rate may differ from the cost of capital alter our earlier generalization that, for independent projects, either the rate of return or the present value techniques can be used to accept or reject proposals? To help us answer this question, let us look at the marginal project, that is, the project in which the rate of return just equals the cost of capital. In this case, there is the implicit assumption that the cash flows are either reinvested at the cost of capital (in this instance, equal to r) or used to repay those who supplied the capital.   Assuming a 10 percent cost of capital, the following pattern of cash flows exists for a project whose rate of return is also 10 percent:

$$\$100 = \frac{\$50}{1+r} + \frac{\$66}{(1+r)^2}$$

If the total amount extended by those who supplied the funds is not repaid until the end of the second year, but the cost of using the funds is due annually, then $10 of the $50 goes as payment for the use of the funds while the other $40 is assumed to be reinvested at the cost of capital.   That is,

$$\$40(1.10) = \$44 \text{ at end of second year}$$

This plus the $66 in cash flows for that year totals $110, the sum just sufficient to repay the proceeds — or the replacement cost of the amount supplied — and cover the cost of using $100 for the second year.

Had the $40 been applied to principal or replacement cost,[5] then the $66 in cash flows received at the end of the second year would have repaid the $60 due in principal plus the cost of 10 percent, or $6.00, for using these funds.

Problems may arise, of course, if the reinvestment rate for the cash flows falls below 10 percent or the current cost of capital.   In the case of the marginal project, if any portion of the cash flows were not reinvested at the cost of capital or used to repay those who supplied the funds, the result of adopting the marginal project would be a loss.   Ideally, therefore, we should know not merely the reinvestment rate or rates over the life of the project, but how much of the cash flows will be reinvested or returned to those who supplied the funds, whether they be owners or debtors.

Assuming that the firm must periodically pay the cost of using the funds while at the same time replacing those sources who have withdrawn their principal, we find that the firm can do only two things with the remainder: reinvest all or a portion of it in other projects or make a distribution to the owners.   Under what conditions the firm will do one or the other or both is a problem we cannot undertake at this stage in the analysis.   Once we have developed the cost of capital concepts, we shall be in a better position to solve this problem.

---

[5] If those who had supplied the capital had been debtors, the principal repaid would have represented the original cost of the asset.   If the replacement cost is greater than the original cost, the owners do not profit.   To replace the asset, management must find a new source of funds for the principal repaid, using this source and the difference between the replacement cost and the original cost to purchase a new asset.

SUMMARY TO APPENDIX

Implicit in the rate of return approach is the assumption that cash flows are reinvested at the rate of return. Implicit in the present value technique is the assumption that cash flows are reinvested at the cost of capital. As a consequence, the two procedures give different figures for profit and depreciation.

By making the reinvestment rate explicit, we can set aside an amount, A, which will recover the replacement cost of the asset in the terminal year of the project. When the annual cost of capital is subtracted from A and the residual is compounded at the reinvestment rate, the result equals the replacement cost of the asset. When A is subtracted from the annual cash flows, the residual is the annual profit. The terminal value of the project is the sum of the replacement cost and the annual profit figure compounded at the reinvestment rate.

The cost of capital may differ from the reinvestment rate. However, as long as the latter is greater than the former, the owners will benefit from what would otherwise be a marginal project. Only when the reinvestment rate falls below the cost of capital and the funds are not repaid to those who supplied them will the value of the owners' equity suffer from adopting a marginal project.

QUESTIONS AND PROBLEMS

1. The replacement cost of an asset with an expected life of 5 years is $33,521.40. The annual cash flows are $10,000 a year. The cost of capital and the reinvestment rates are both 15 percent. Find the rate of return and the net present value of the project. What is the profit and the depreciation figure for each? Using the sinking fund approach, calculate the depreciation allowance required to recover the replacement cost. Using this technique, what is the annual profit? Contrast these results with those obtained from using the rate of return approach and the present value approach. Do they differ? Why?

2. "When we speak of a rate of return on an investment, we are implicitly assuming that the replacement cost of the investment will be paid out of a sinking fund compounded at the rate of return." Evaluate.

3. Would the substitution of original cost for replacement cost in problem 1 change the substance of your answer? Explain.

4. "As long as the reinvestment rate stays above the current cost of capital, we need not use the terminal value approach to select from among investment alternatives." Evaluate.

Capital Budgeting: An Analysis of Risk

chapter Seven

All asset purchases contain elements of risk. Because they tie up funds for an extended period of time, the risk considerations inherent in fixed-asset management cannot be ignored. In this chapter, therefore, we shall present an approach to risk determination and develop techniques for incorporating risk into our procedures. We shall then compare our capital budgeting methods with those employed in practice. In reading the material, the student should note the limitations of what we call the "objective" approach to probability analysis. Moreover, he should be aware of the fact that, however we develop a probability distribution, it is management's and presumably the owners' attitude toward the probable outcomes which ultimately determines whether the rate of return approach or the present value approach will be used in practice.

Introduction

In order to concentrate on the development of rational techniques for budgeting capital, we have until now avoided the question of risk. Yet committing funds in the knowledge that the expected outcome may not materialize is the essence of capital budgeting. Thus any discussion which fails to incorporate risk into the analysis is incomplete. Nevertheless, making appropriate allowance for risk is a formidable task. A full discussion would require a separate volume.[1]

At the outset, therefore, we must be clear in our own minds as to the nature of the risks involved and the limitations of the approach presented here. In the first place, it has usually been customary to distinguish between *risk* and *uncertainty*.[2] If the possible outcomes of an investment decision are subject to a *probability distribution* known in advance, we can weigh the outcomes by these probabilities, giving us an *expected monetary value* as a result. If the probability distribution is unknown, we are uncertain as to the outcome. We shall assume for most of this chapter that the probability distribution is known or can be estimated.

Second, even if we can specify the appropriate probability distribution, we must still recognize that individuals differ as to their attitudes toward risk. The expected monetary value of a project can be greater than its replacement cost, yet management may reject it because it "does not like the odds." This is a subjective judgment based on how management feels about the probability distribution of the outcome. If we are to explain firm behavior adequately, we must consider the subjective risk preferences of management in our analysis. In so doing, of course, we are either implicitly assuming that the preferences of management are the same as those of the owners, or that the firm may not be maximizing the market value of the owners' equity. For the present, at least, we shall abide by our earlier assumption that over the long run, where ownership is divorced from control, the preferences of management will be the same as those of the owners.

Third, although we are going to concern ourselves with risk as it applies to specific projects, our ultimate concern is with the market value of the owners' equity. This in turn is a function of the variability in total income accruing to the owners. As we pointed out earlier, all other factors affecting variability—that is, capital structure and working capital—are fixed in our analysis. But we must also assume that the

[1]William Fellner, *Probability and Profit* (Homewood, Ill.: Richard D. Irwin, Inc., 1965).

[2]Frank H. Knight, *Risk, Uncertainty and Profit* (Boston: Houghton Mifflin Company, 1921). Republished in 1965 in the Harper Torchbook Series.

variability in income from adopting a capital budget is not affected by the interrelationship of projects within the budget. To demonstrate this point rigorously would take us beyond an introductory analysis.[3] We may note, however, that the probability distribution of two projects need not equal the average of the probability distributions of each.

To illustrate, consider the returns from the following set of independent investments, each with the same outlay.

Investment Y

Earnings		Probability	Expected Monetary Value
$1	×	.05	= $0.05
4	×	.75	= 3.00
6	×	.20	= 1.20
		1.00	$4.25

Investment Z

Earnings		Probability	Expected Monetary Value
$1	×	.20	= $0.20
4	×	.75	= 3.00
6	×	.05	= 0.30
		1.00	$3.50

Assuming these three outcomes are the only ones possible, the sum of the probabilities must equal one. Otherwise we would have left out a possible outcome. Note that while the earnings anticipated from each project are the same, the expected monetary value of Y is greater than the expected monetary value of Z. This is due to differences in the probability distribution. Investment Z has a higher chance of a lower return than Investment Y. Investment Y has a greater chance of a higher return than Investment Z.

Since the projects are not mutually exclusive, both may be considered for adoption. The variations in income are completely offsetting. But in order for the expected monetary values of both projects to equal the sum of the expected monetary values of each, the probability of both

[3]G. David Quirin, *The Capital Expenditure Decision* (Homewood, Ill.: Richard D. Irwin, Inc., 1967), chaps. 10 and 11.

outcomes would have to be the weighted average of the probability of each. In this case the weights, or expected earnings, are equal, so that

Investments X and Y

Earnings		Probability		Expected Monetary Value
$2	×	$\dfrac{.05 + .20}{2}$	=	$0.25
8	×	$\dfrac{.75 + .75}{2}$	=	6.00
12	×	$\dfrac{.20 + .05}{2}$	=	1.50
		1.00		$7.75

While this can be the case, we wish to point out that the probabilities of expected earnings from combined investments need not be proportional to the probabilities of expected earnings from their components. This assertion applies in the same way to a portfolio of securities as to a capital budget. The expected monetary value of the income on a combination of 100 shares of American Telephone and 100 shares of IBM need not be the same as the sum of the expected monetary value of the incomes on each stock.

In summary, in this chapter we are analyzing business risk as though it were the same as risk on individual projects. While this is an oversimplification, it is sufficient at an introductory level simply to recognize the limitations inherent in our approach. Moreover, by holding the capital structure constant we can put off until a later chapter the impact of the composition of financing on the variability in total income, thereby effectively separating for analytical purposes the business risk from the financial risk.

Probability and Capital Budgeting

Business investment decisions are sometimes likened to a game of chance in which one gambles on the expectation that the rate of return on the investment will exceed the cost of capital or the net present value will be greater than zero.[4] Toss a perfectly constructed coin and there

---

[4]The social implications are, of course, entirely different. The function of profit, at least in a competitive economy, is to allocate resources among the goods and services which people desire. Gambling, on the other hand, redistributes income. Nevertheless,

is a 50:50 chance of either heads or tails showing.   Spin a flawless roulette wheel[5] with 38 numbers on it and the odds are 37:1 against its stopping at the number selected.

If we tossed two coins into the air, both could come up heads or both could come up tails.   Alternatively, the first could come up heads and the second tails or the first tails and the second heads.   Assuming that we attach significance only to heads or only to tails, the odds that two heads would materialize are 1:4.   The odds that two tails would materialize are also 1:4.   But the chances of a mixture of heads and tails are 2:4.   In each case the sum of the probabilities is 1.   By letting $n =$ the number of *independent events*, in this case the number of coins tossed, we have the binomial

$$(p+q)^n = 1$$

For $n = 2$,

$$(p+q)^2 = p^2 + 2pq + q^2 = 1$$
$$(\tfrac{1}{2}+\tfrac{1}{2})^2 = \tfrac{1}{4}+\tfrac{1}{2}+\tfrac{1}{4} = 1$$

Similarly, if we spin two roulette wheels selecting in advance the number on which we wished to place our bet, the probability p of its materializing is 1:38.   The probability q of its not materializing is 37:38.   Thus

$$(1/38 + 37/38)^2 = (1/38)^2 + 2[1/38 \cdot 37/38] + (37/38)^2 = 1/1,444$$
$$+ 74/1,444 + 1,369/1,444 = 1$$

As n becomes larger,[6] the number of possible combinations increases. Moreover, if we repeat the game, that is, toss n coins N times or spin n roulette wheels N times, we can generate a frequency distribution representing the probable outcomes of desired results.   Thus, for $n = 2$ and $N = 100$ in the case of the coins and $n = 2$ and $N = 1,444$ in the case of

---

where games of chance are legal, as in Nevada, society through private enterprise is catering to a service which people rightly or wrongly desire.   Resources are being allocated accordingly.   Profits are earned by shading the mathematical odds.   If they are excessive, that is, if over time total revenues consistently exceed total costs including a normal profit, then the owners are reaping the rewards of monopoly power.

[5]Neither the coin nor the roulette wheel will be so perfectly balanced that for an infinite number of tosses or spins 50 percent will be heads or one out of every 38 will be the number selected.   But the mathematical odds are a close approximation to reality.

[6]The formula for the binomial expansion is

$$(p+q)^n = p^n + np^{n-1}q + \frac{n(n-1)}{1 \cdot 2}p^{n-2}q^2 + \frac{n(n-1)(n-2)}{1 \cdot 2 \cdot 3}p^{n-3}q^3$$
$$+ \frac{n(n-1)(n-2)(n-3)}{1 \cdot 2 \cdot 3 \cdot 4}p^{n-4}q^4 + \cdots + q^n$$

the roulette wheel, we have

$$\text{Coins} = 100$$
$$100\left[\tfrac{1}{4}+\tfrac{1}{2}+\tfrac{1}{4}\right] = 100$$
$$25 + 50 + 25 = 100$$

$$\text{Roulette wheel} = 1{,}444$$
$$1{,}444\left[1/1{,}444 + 37/722 + 1{,}369/1{,}444\right] = 1{,}444$$
$$1 + 74 + 1{,}369 = 1{,}444$$

These outcomes are portrayed graphically in Figure 7-1.

We can imagine that as the number of coins tossed (or the number of roulette wheels spun) increases, the range of probable outcomes will increase while the chances of all or none of the coins coming up heads (or all or none of the roulette wheels stopping at the number chosen) decreases.   Whether p and q are equal or unequal, as long as they do not vary with n, then as n approaches infinity, the frequency distribution generated is the normal curve widely used in statistical inference.[7]

If a business investment decision is analogous to a game of chance, then each outcome must be an independent event.   This means that just as n coins tossed or n roulette wheels spun are independent of one another, so too are the present values or rates of return on n streams of cash flows independent of one another.   Furthermore, just as we might toss n coins or spin n roulette wheels only once, so too might we make the investment only once.   Thus for $N = 1$, the ordinates in

[7]Frederick C. Mills, *Statistical Methods*, 3d ed. (New York: Henry Holt and Company, Inc., 1955), pp. 152–153.

Figure 7-1

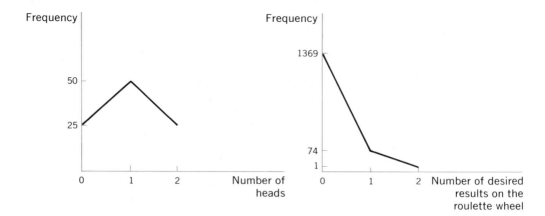

Frequency

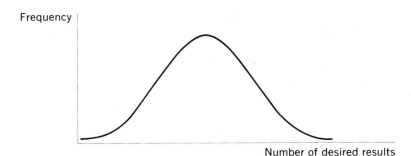

Number of desired results

Figure 7-2

Figure 7-2 would represent probabilities rather than frequencies.   The sum of the probabilities, of course, must equal one.

As for the abscissa, it would seem that the desired result p is a rate of return greater than or equal to the cost of capital, or is a net present value greater than or equal to zero.   The usual procedure, however, is to plot all probable rates of return or present values.   If we chose to do so, we could then note the point on the probability distribution at which the rate of return is less than the cost of capital or the net present value is less than zero.   Thus, in Figure 7-3, if the cost of capital is 10 percent and the replacement of the asset is $1,000, the area to the right of these amounts represents those outcomes which are desirable or acceptable while the area to their left represents undesirable or un-acceptable outcomes.

In each case OA measures the probability that the rate of return will equal the cost of capital or that the present value will equal the replacement cost of the asset.   The sum of the probabilities to the left of 10 percent or to the left of $1,000 measures the chances that the rate of return is less than the cost of capital or that the net present value is negative.   The sum of the probabilities to the right of each of these

Figure 7-3

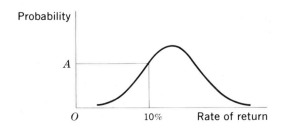

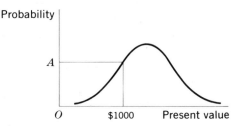

amounts indicates whether or not the rate of return exceeds the cost of capital or the net present value is positive.

Note the information we need. First, how many outcomes are there and what are their values; that is, what is the size of the present value or rate of return for each stream of cash flows and what is the number n of streams that can be estimated? Second, to make the investment decision strictly analogous to a game of chance, we need, in advance, values for p, q, and n.

We noted earlier that as long as n approaches infinity and p and q do not vary with n, then for any values of p and q the probability distribution is still the normal curve. However, once n is finite, then, as we saw in Figure 7-1, the probability distribution will vary with the values of p and q. As a result, there are as many probability distributions as there are values for p, q, and n.[8] What we have, therefore, are an unlimited number of models from which to choose, with the normal curve being but one.

Since it is independent of the size of p and q, the normal distribution is a highly useful model when, as in the case of an investment decision, we do not know the probabilities of p and q. There are, however, some difficulties attached in employing it. First, since the curve is asymptotic to the abscissa, it would appear that we must, for practical purposes, ignore the probabilities of rare events, say .5 of 1 percent at each end of the curve. These are very optimistic or pessimistic outcomes which, although possible, have a low chance of materializing.

Second, we must have numerous values for the rate of return or net present value. To accomplish this, we could employ discrete probability distributions with large values for n. Then, with electronic computers, we could make use of simulation techniques to allow us to approximate values associated with the normal curve or, for that matter, any other continuous probability distribution.[9]

While simulation techniques help to offset the first two difficulties, we can never be certain that the normal curve which underlies the frequency concept of probability, or any other probability distribution chosen, does indeed represent the probable pattern of discounted cash flows for a given investment opportunity. The implied assumption in statistical inference is that there is a limited amount of variation in natural phenomena. Events are not unique, whether they be the per-

---

[8] Once p and q vary with n, the range of distribution is further increased.

[9] D. B. Hertz, "Risk Analysis in Capital Investment," *Harvard Business Review*, vol. 42, no. 1 (January-February, 1964), pp. 95–106. See also Howard Raiffa, *Decision Analysis: Introductory Lectures on Choices under Uncertainty* (Reading, Mass.: Addison-Wesley Publishing Company, Inc., 1968).

centage of votes cast for a candidate in an election or the rate of return actually earned on an investment.   The student has probably noted the increasing accuracy of public opinion polls based on random samples. This has been particularly true of presidential contests.   Since correct predictions in other areas of human behavior have been based on probability estimates, we may assume, at the introductory level at least, that these same concepts can be applied to capital budgeting decisions.

Utility Analysis

But even if the various outcomes and their respective probabilities can be determined objectively, we still do not know whether or not the firm should accept the risk.   As we noted earlier, the decision is ultimately based on management's and presumably the owners' subjective evaluation of risk.

One approach to solving this problem is to develop a *utility function* which measures an individual's attitude toward varying amounts of gains and losses.[10]   This utility function differs from the ordinary concept of utility taught in courses on the principles of economics.   There we are concerned with a measure of an individual's preferences among consumer goods and services.   Here we want a measure of how he values changes in his income or wealth that result from accepting risks.

In order to develop the latter function, let us assign arbitrary figures of 0 and 1 to two outcomes, say \$0 and \$1,000,000.   Now let us select an outcome intermediate between these values, say \$400,000. We offer the individual either a chance p of receiving \$0 and a chance q of receiving \$1,000,000 or the alternative of receiving a certain sum equal to \$400,000.   Let us vary p until the individual is indifferent between the alternatives.   Suppose this is the case for $p = .3$.   Then the utility of a certain income of \$400,000 is

$$U(\$400,000) = .3(\$0) + .7(\$1,000,000)$$
$$= .3(0) + .7(1)$$
$$= .7$$

Having established the utility for \$400,000, we can use it to determine the utility of other points between \$0 and \$1,000,000.   Suppose this

[10]Milton Friedman and L. J. Savage, "The Utility Analysis of Choices Involving Risk," *Journal of Political Economy*, vol. 56, no. 4 (August, 1948), pp. 279–304; reprinted in George J. Stigler and Kenneth E. Boulding (eds.), *Readings in Price Theory* (Homewood, Ill.: Richard D. Irwin, Inc., 1952), pp. 57–96, and in Stephen H. Archer and Charles A. D'Ambrosio (eds.), *The Theory of Business Finance: A Book of Readings* (New York: The Macmillan Company, 1967), pp. 36–66.

person is offered either a chance p of receiving \$400,000 and a chance q of receiving \$1,000,000 or the alternative of a certainty equivalent of \$800,000.   If he is indifferent at $p = .1$, then

$$U(\$800,000) = .1U(\$400,000) + .9U(\$1,000,000)$$
$$= .1(.7) + .9(1)$$
$$U = .07 + .9$$
$$= .97$$

If we wish to measure the utility of amounts in excess of \$1,000,000, say \$10,000,000, we can offer the individual either a chance p of receiving \$0 and a chance q of receiving \$10,000,000 or a certainty equivalent of \$1,000,000.   If he is indifferent between the alternatives at $p = .2$, then

$$.2U(\$0) + .8U(\$10,000,000) = U(\$1,000,000)$$
$$.2(0) + .8U(\$10,000,000) = 1.00$$
$$U(\$10,000,000) = 1.25$$

By confining ourselves to very large amounts, we are, of course, beyond the horizons of the opportunities available to most individuals. Moreover, we observe that many people who insure themselves against loss of life, and their homes against fire and theft, etc., are also eager to play the roulette wheels, roll the dice, or feed coins into the "one-arm bandits" in a Las Vegas casino.   The explanation for this anomaly is the fact that they view "small" gains or losses in a different light than "large" gains or losses.

To a millionaire the risk of \$100 on the spin of a roulette wheel for a 37 to 1 chance of winning \$3,500 or losing the \$100 is not the same as risking the loss of his source of wealth, a manufacturing firm.   So he continues to pay premiums on a fire insurance policy while betting that the wheel will stop on the number he selected.   Similarly, a \$20,000-a-year college professor may place a dime in a "one-armed bandit" in hopes of winning more, although knowing that his chances of losing the dime are greater.   At the same time he continues to pay premiums on a life insurance policy to offset the loss of income to his wife and family in case of his untimely death.

In short, when offered opportunities of a gain in excess of the amount ventured as against the loss of this amount or the alternative of a certainty equivalent (that is, keeping the funds), individuals, depending on how they view the outcomes, will accept or reject the risk.   In the case of insurance, the certainty equivalent is the loss of a small amount of income, the risk premium, in order to prevent a more substantial loss.   In the case of gambling, the certainty equivalent is the amount that would be kept if the gamble were not taken.   In the case of the

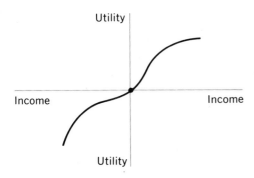

Figure 7-4

investment opportunity, the replacement cost[11] of the asset is the certainty equivalent.[12]

Graphically, an individual's utility function can be depicted as in Figure 7-4.

For "small" gains and losses (and what is small to one individual may be large to another), there is a tendency to accept risk. This can be reflected in the utility function by showing it to be increasing at an increasing rate on either side of the origin, that is, in situations where changes in income, both positive and negative, are near zero.

Presumably this affinity for accepting risk when changes in income are "small" and rejecting risk when changes are "large" would be manifested in the capital budget. To the extent that it is, the budget may reflect, in cases where ownership is divorced from control, the subjective risk preferences of those who manage rather than own the company. We have assumed away this problem by arguing earlier that in the long run those attracted to ownership will view risk in the same way as those who manage it. The behavioral characteristics of the firm, therefore, reflect the risk preferences of owners.

But managers as well as owners change over the years. As a result, there may be gradual or sudden alterations in firm behavior reflected in the composition of its long-lived assets. Consequently, any long-run

---

[11]While we shall continue to use replacement cost, technically, if the firm does not make the investment, it saves the present value of the cost of replacing the asset at some future date.

[12]Note that in each instance we appear to have shifted the available options. At best, the certainty equivalent is no loss, or in the case of insurance a small loss, of income. This is different from being offered a choice of a certain increase in income or the probability of an even greater increase or no increase at all. The nature of the options therefore will affect the utility function by affecting the probabilities at which the individual will be indifferent between receiving a sum with certainty and taking a chance on the alternatives.

adjustments toward similarity between managers' and owners' attitudes toward risk may never be complete. Moreover, where ownership is divorced from control, the professional manager tends to view decisions in terms of the continued financial health or liquidity of the individual firm with which he has presently cast his lot. The owner sees his interests as part of his, not the firm's, asset portfolio. This may lead to a permanent dichotomy in attitudes toward risk. We shall return to this point later. For the present, however, we note that the subjective risk preferences of management may be such that diminishing marginal utility of income may begin at levels nearer the origin than is the case for stockholders.

Over the long run, to the extent that these differences in attitude persist, they will be reflected in the composition of assets, liabilities, and owners' equity, with the market value of the owners' equity being consistently below the maximum.[13]

Allowing for Risk

In order to incorporate risk into the analysis of independent investment projects, we must have (1) the probability distribution of the rate of return or present value of the expected outcomes; (2) a utility function representing the subjective risk preferences of management and, it is hoped, of the owners. We noted earlier that, with the aid of electronic computers, it is possible to simulate a large but finite number of separate patterns of cash flows, calculating in each case either the rate of return or the present value, or both. Then we could locate either the cost of capital or the replacement cost of the outlay within the probability distribution and could readily calculate either the odds of the rate of return falling below or above the cost of capital or the odds of the present value being greater or less than the replacement cost.

Alternatively, we could weight each outcome by its probability, giving us the expected rate of return or the present monetary value of the investment opportunity. Each could be compared respectively with the cost of capital or the replacement cost of the asset. Even then, management must evaluate the outcome in terms of its own risk preferences.

---

[13]Owners, presumably common stockholders, will have to adjust as best they can by altering the composition of their own portfolios. Not only might this mean an increase in demand for stocks in which management will accept greater risk in the composition of the firm's assets and financing, but it might also mean that households will increase the amount of common stock held relative to other lower-risk instruments, such as bonds, savings accounts, etc.

But even if electronic computers are not available, it is possible to make certain assumptions concerning the outcome of a given investment opportunity, calculating the odds, say, on the most probable outcome,[14] the most pessimistic outcome, and the most optimistic outcome.

To do so, of course, we must estimate what will happen to revenues and expenses in each of these three instances. Perhaps on the basis of past experience, we can anticipate that revenues will fluctuate 10 percent above or below what would be considered normal. The factors affecting costs might lead to similar outcomes. To make the extreme possible assumptions, let us combine the lowest sales forecast with the highest estimate of costs to give us the most pessimistic pattern of cash flows. Similarly, let us combine the highest sales forecast with the lowest estimate of costs to give us the most optimistic outcome.

In such a simplified model, we are recognizing the possibility of three results and ignoring any outcomes in between. Furthermore, if we assume that the pessimistic result p is just as likely to occur as the optimistic result q, then each of the probabilities is .5. Although there are three outcomes, once two are determined, the third or most probable is simply one minus the sum of the probabilities of the other two. Thus, of the three outcomes, only two are independent. Consequently,

$$(p+q)^2 = p^2 + 2pq + q^2$$
$$(.5+.5)^2 = .25 + .50 + .25$$

Similarly, if we had chosen to make $p = .6$ and $q = .4$, then

$$(.6+.4)^2 = .36 + .48 + .16$$

In each instance we interpret the first figure, .25 or .36, as the probability attached to the most pessimistic outcome, the middle figure, .50 or .48, as the probability attached to the most probable outcome, and .25 or .16 as the probability attached to the most optimistic outcome.

However, since we are trying to be as objective as possible in predicting the probability distribution of outcomes, we shall assume that as n approaches infinity, the distribution of outcomes would approach the normal curve. Consequently, we shall approximate this outcome

[14]Those familiar with statistics will recall that the most probable outcome is the mode of the distribution. The median, a second measure of central tendency, is the value above and below which 50 percent of the values lie. The expected monetary value is the arithmetic mean of the distribution. If the outcomes are normally distributed, or for that matter fall into any symmetrical distribution, the mean, the median, and the mode coincide.

for small distributions by making $p = q$.   We could, of course, increase n by two by combining the lowest sales forecast with the lowest cost estimate, and the highest cost estimate with the highest sales forecast. This increases our number of independent outcomes to four and the total number of outcomes to five.   Each would have a probability attached to it.   In so doing, within a symmetrical distribution these two additional outcomes would lie on either side of the most probable outcome and have the same chance of materializing.   On the assumption that costs and revenues are more likely to vary directly than inversely, they have, of course, higher probabilities than those we have considered as the most pessimistic and optimistic forecasts.   To keep our illustrations simple, however, we shall confine our analysis to three probable outcomes.

With $p = q$ for a given investment opportunity, suppose that management arrives at the following estimates:

	(1) Present Value	(2) Proba- bility	(3) (1) × (2) Weighted Average	(4) Utility of Income	(5) (2) × (4) Weighted Utility
Most Pessimistic Outcome	$ 100,000	.25	$ 25,000	.40	.1000
Most Probable Outcome	600,000	.50	300,000	.80	.4000
Most Optimistic Outcome	1,100,000	.25	275,000	1.05	.2625
			$600,000		.7625

Assume that the replacement cost of the asset is $400,000, the utility of which is .7.   Note that the expected monetary value, that is, the sum of the present value of each series of cash flows weighted by their respective probabilities, is $600,000.   While this is greater than the replacement cost of the asset, it does not tell us whether the firm prefers this certainty equivalent whose utility is .7 to the investment opportunity. Thus we must weight the utility of the present value of each project by the probability of each outcome and sum the results.   In this case a weighted utility of .7625 is greater than .7.   The firm is willing to accept the investment opportunity.

We can employ the same technique to select from among mutually exclusive investments.   Suppose that the firm had a choice between the results shown above and the following alternative.

	(1) Present Value	(2) Proba- bility	(3) (1) × (2) Weighted Average	(4) Utility of Income	(5) (2) × (4) Weighted Utility
Most Pessimistic Outcome	$200,000	.25	$ 50,000	.50	.1250
Most Probable Outcome	450,000	.50	225,000	.70	.3500
Most Optimistic Outcome	700,000	.25	175,000	.85	.2125
			$450,000		.6875

Suppose that the replacement cost of the opportunity was $300,000. The utility of the amount is .6. By subtracting the replacement cost from the expected monetary value, we get the net present value; for this project it is $150,000, as against $200,000 for the alternative. Yet the utility of pursuing the second alternative (.6875 − .6) is greater than the utility of pursuing the first (.7625 − .7). Exercising its subjective risk preferences, management will select the second rather than the first alternative.

We could, of course, utilize probability distributions in calculating rates of return, obtaining a weighted average or expected rate of return. But subjective risk preferences are in terms of dollars, not rates of return. Thus we would still be required to consider the utility of income based on the present value of the cash flows or on the stream of cash flows before discounting.[15] Since it is more difficult to interpret management's attitude toward a probability distribution of rates of return, we can list this as one more reason for favoring the present value approach to capital budgeting.

In summary, therefore, if we cannot simulate a normal curve for each possible outcome, we can still estimate the probability distribution for a small number of possible outcomes. Unless we have good reasons for assuming otherwise, we shall be objective and use symmetrical distributions, that is, where $p = q$.

Whether simulation is employed or not, for each probable outcome we can multiply the anticipated present value by its probability. This gives us the expected monetary value of the outcome. The sum of the expected monetary values equals the expected present value of the investment. The expected present value less the replacement cost

[15]There is some question as to whether distributions of cash flows for successive periods are independent of one another. Through discounting we can avoid the problem by treating the rate of return or the present value as a random variable.

equals the expected net present value.   While we could choose from among alternative projects on the basis of differences in expected net present values, our analysis would be incomplete.   Thus we apply to the probability of the present value of each outcome a number representing the utility of this amount to management, and presumably to the stockholders, under conditions of risk.   On the basis of the sum of these risk-adjusted estimates, we choose from among mutually exclusive investments or decide whether or not to risk funds in an independent investment.   If the expected utility of the outcome is greater than the utility of a certain sum, that is, the utility of the replacement cost, the project is acceptable.   Among mutually exclusive alternatives, we choose the project in which the difference between the utility of the replacement cost and the expected utility is greater.

Once the project is selected, we can still rank it on the basis of rates of return, net present values, or cost-benefit ratios, using, if we choose, the expected outcomes, that is, the expected rates of return, expected net present values, or expected cost-benefit ratios.

Capital Budgeting in Practice

In this and the previous chapter we have presented procedures which the firm should follow if its composition of long-lived assets is to contribute to the ultimate goal of financial management, that is maximization of the market value of the owners' equity.   At this juncture it seems appropriate to inquire as to what extent these procedures are employed in practice.   Those who work in capital budgeting are, of course, aware of the procedures.[16]   But those who have had an opportunity to observe a broad range of management practices note that some classes of investments are undertaken without any estimate of the return.   Firms often fail to make a detailed analysis of projects designed to keep the company "competitive."   Such investments are considered to be in the normal course of business.   Other capital commitments, which may push the company into new areas unfamiliar to management are subjected to more thorough scrutiny.[17]   But how refined is the approach used?   One survey reported that out of 127 "well-managed" companies, 116 used some measure of return on capital but only 38 employed some variant of discounted cash flows.   It is doubtful that any of these employed risk-adjusted estimates similar

[16]See, for example, John M. Hackney, *Control and Management of Capital Projects* (New York: John Wiley & Sons, Inc., 1965), pp. 185–187, 190–191.
[17]Pearson Hunt, Charles M. Williams, and Gordon Donaldson, *Basic Business Finance: Text and Cases*, 3d ed. (Homewood, Ill: Richard D. Irwin, Inc., 1966), pp. 465–466.

to those we have developed.   The most widely used technique, relied on by 66 of the companies, was the *payback period*.[18]

Payback Period   The payback period is a deceptively simple technique for evaluating cash flows.   We simply estimate how long it takes to recover the original investment.   For example, consider two mutually exclusive investments, Projects G and H.   The following patterns of cash flows are assumed to reflect the most probable outcome.

	Outlay	Cash Flow, End of First Year	Cash Flow, End of Second Year	Cash Flow, End of Third Year
Project G	$10,000	$10,000	$1,000	$1,000
Project H	$10,000	$ 7,000	$3,000	$5,000

Project G has a payback period of 1 year as against 2 years for Project H. Without further analysis we would conclude that, since Project G repays the capital expended on it more rapidly, it is the preferred project.   But if the cost of capital is 10 percent, the most probable net present value of Project H would be $2,599.55 as against $668.66 for Project G.

The payback period therefore fails to consider the cash flows for the years following recoupment of the original capital.   Viewed in a different light, the payback period is a rule-of-thumb technique for handling uncertainty.   However, instead of mutliplying probability estimates by values calculated from a subjective utility function, analysts employing the payback period implicitly reject more-distant estimates of cash flows.   Perhaps they do so under the assumption that the further estimates are carried into the future the less they can be relied on.   Therefore, it is safer to conclude that they are zero.

Return on Book Value of Original Investment   Another technique often relied on to budget capital is the *return on the book value of the original investment*.[19]   There are two basic variations to this procedure.   In perhaps its more common form,

$$\text{Return} = \frac{\text{average annual profit after taxes}}{\text{average investment}}$$

[18]James H. Miller, "A Glimpse at Practice in Calculating and Using Return on Investment," NAA Bulletin (June, 1960), sec. 1, p. 73. Cited in Neil W. Chamberlain, *The Firm: Microeconomic Planning and Action* (New York: McGraw-Hill Book Company, 1962), p. 266.
   [19]*Ibid.*, p. 266.   Of the 116 companies who reported using some measure of return, 59 employed this method.

Depreciation is excluded from the numerator, while the denominator is one-half of the original cost plus scrap value. To illustrate the method, suppose that a project has the following pattern of cash flows:

Outlay	Cash Flow, End of First Year	Cash Flow, End of Second Year	Cash Flow, End of Third Year
$12,000	$7,000	$6,000	$5,000

Assuming that there is no scrap value and using straight-line depreciation,

$$\text{Return} = \frac{[(\$7,000 - \$4,000) + (\$6,000 - \$4,000) + (\$5,000 - \$4,000)]/3}{\$12,000/2}$$

$$= \frac{\$2,000}{\$6,000} = 33.33\%$$

If the rate of return on the original cost was calculated using discounted cash flows, then

$$\$12,000 = \frac{\$7,000}{1+r} + \frac{\$6,000}{(1+r)^2} + \frac{\$5,000}{(1+r)^3}$$

$$r = 25\%$$

As ordinarily employed, the return on the average investment fails to make allowance for either the time pattern of the profit portion of the cash flows or the replacement cost of the investment. Moreover, the problem of replacement cost aside, the assumption that one-half of the original cost is the average amount tied up in the project may be contrary to the manner in which the investment is actually recouped. Suppose that a method of accelerated depreciation — say the sum of years' digits — has been employed. There would have been an additional $2,000 in depreciation during the first year and $2,000 less in the third year of the project.[20] The internal rate of return, using discounted cash flows, would be

$$\$12,000 = \frac{\$9,000}{1+r} + \frac{\$6,000}{(1+r)^2} + \frac{\$3,000}{(1+r)^3}$$

$$r = 28.92\%$$

But the ratio of average profit to average investment remains unchanged.

$$\text{Return} = \frac{[(\$9,000 - \$6,000) + (\$6,000 - \$4,000) + (\$3,000 - \$2,000)]/3}{\$12,000/2}$$

$$= 33.33\%$$

---

[20]The depreciation would be 3/6 of $12,000, 2/6 of $12,000, and 1/6 of $12,000; or $6,000, $4,000, and $2,000, respectively.

Suppose that straight-line instead of accelerated depreciation had been used. If the pattern of net cash flows is negative for, say, the first year of the project, capital would not have been returned at a rate of $4,000 a year, and the average amount of funds actually employed is in excess of $6,000.[21]

In the second variation of this technique, there is no allowance at all for recoupment of the funds invested. The numerator is still the average profit, but the denominator is the original outlay, in this case $12,000. The return under this approach would be 16.67 percent.

Although other variations are possible,[22] there is enough available evidence to indicate that discounted cash flows are employed more infrequently than they should be in selecting long-lived assets. There are numerous reasons for this state of affairs. In the first place, the size of the capital budget relative to the size of the firm may be so small that it hardly seems justified to engage in a sophisticated analysis of projects. Second, as indicated earlier, some firms seem to know intuitively what is needed to keep them "competitive," that is, to keep their owners earning normal profits.

But suppose that the capital budget is large relative to the size of the firm. Suppose further that there are opportunities available which, if adopted, will augment rather than simply maintain the level of profits and therefore the market value of the owners' equity. There may still be reluctance to employ, or at least rely exclusively on, discounted cash flows. The reasons are twofold. First, the art of budgeting capital effectively requires skilled personnel. It also requires a management team willing to discard traditional accounting concepts in favor of the rate of return method, or, preferably, the present value method based on replacement rather than original cost of the assets. To overcome this difficulty may be largely a matter of time. Young men trained in capital budgeting techniques will not find the concept of discounting strange to them. They can be taught just as easily to think in terms of replacement cost as original cost. As some of these people succeed

---

[21]In other words, using one-half of the original investment less scrap value as the denominator implies that the funds employed for the first 18 months of a 3-year project exceed $6,000. Midway through the life of a project the funds are exactly $6,000 while they are less than $6,000 for the last 18 months. If straight-line depreciation is used, this is a good approximation. But if the cash flows will not cover depreciation for the early years so that the resulting profits are negative, then on the average more than half the original investment is tied up in the project. If cash flows in the later years of the project fail to cover depreciation, then profits in the early years were overstated and more than one-half of the original investment was recovered. In either of these cases, relying on the yield method will also lead to problems, since negative cash flows are the source of multiple rates of return.

[22]Harold Bierman, Jr., and Seymour Smidt, *The Capital Budgeting Decision*, 2d ed. (New York: The Macmillan Company, 1966), pp. 18–25.

to high levels of management, we can expect a more favorable reception for the sophisticated techniques they learned in colleges and universities.

The second problem, however, may be more difficult to overcome. While electronic computers have made it easier to simulate probability distributions which we might anticipate for a given investment opportunity, we must still evaluate these outcomes in terms of a subjective utility function. Moreover, we might find that the frequency concept of probability is incapable of explaining the actual outcome. It is possible, for example, that expected outcomes from individual investments are not independent events. Furthermore, even if they are independent, there is enough uncertainty over the estimates of cash flows, that is, over their revenue and cost components, to lead many to reject a finite probability distribution where $p = q$. Rather, the tendency is to overstate the odds favoring pessimistic outcomes and understate the odds favoring optimistic outcomes. This leads to the belief that the distribution is more like the one pictured in Figure 7-5 than to the bell-shaped normal curve.

With the distribution skewed toward the upper end of the scale, the probabilities of relatively optimistic outcomes are lowered, perhaps unduly. To the extent that management, in the face of evidence to the contrary, substitutes its own estimate of what it thinks the probabilities are, the whole approach to risk becomes subjective.

We hasten to add that this is not meant as a criticism of management. There may be good reason for suspecting a departure from symmetry. The point we wish to stress is that in spite of the progress made in handling risk, the approaches used to account for it still comprise the weak link in the operational techniques designed to provide a rational evaluation of long-lived assets. Therefore, while we can dismiss profitability estimates based on traditional accounting approaches, we cannot, save for questioning the use of original rather than replacement cost, reject the payback period out of hand.

Figure 7-5

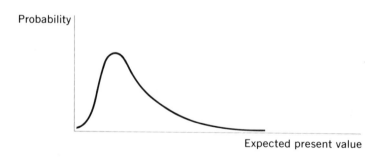

Though imperfect, this simple measure is a hedge against uncertainty. It may have a role to play, at least as a supplementary
measure, in determining whether or not a given investment opportunity is acceptable. Thus, if the expected net present value of a project is positive, and if at the same time it meets management's desire
for a low payout period, say three years, it may be acceptable without
the application of utility analysis to the probabilities of expected outcomes.

The problem, however, is to make certain that the payback period
remains a supplementary measure. Management tends to be pre-
occupied with the effect of its decisions on cash flows.[23] The longer
capital is tied up in a project, the longer is the effect of a given decision
on the amount of funds available for other purposes. We noted earlier
that in the case where ownership is divorced from control, stockholders
may be more willing than management to assume a greater risk. In the
final analysis, it might well be that management's concern with profitability is limited to what it considers adequate performance based on
past experience.[24] If a project meets this standard, then the overriding
issue is liquidity, or how long it takes to recoup the investment. If
the payback period is sufficiently low, management will adopt the
project.

This approach, of course, is not necessarily in the best interests of
the stockholders. As we have seen, the project should be evaluated in
terms of the cost of capital, not in terms of what has been earned on past
investment. Moreover, suppose that the payback period does not meet
management's standards. Then unless the amount involved is not worth
the cost of further analysis, it would appear that a subjective evaluation
of the probabilities of the expected outcomes is in order.

SUMMARY

On the assumption that the expected rate of return or the net present
value of a project is an independent event, we may conclude that the
probable outcomes are normally distributed. Although the assumption
of independence may not be accepted by all, it does provide us with an
objective approach to probability determination.

Using the binomial expansion, we can calculate the probabilities
of occurrence under the most pessimistic and the most optimistic
assumptions about costs and revenues. One minus the probabilities

[23]Gordon Donaldson, "Financial Goals: Management vs. Stockholders," *Harvard
Business Review*, vol. 41, no. 3 (May-June, 1963), pp. 116–129.
[24]*Ibid.*, pp. 121, 128–129.

of these two forecasts gives us the probability of the most likely outcome. We may increase the number of forecasts, that is, increase the number of observations, on a random variable.   With the binomial expansion or with simulation techniques, we can determine their respective probabilities.

To the probabilities, however, we must attach weights reflecting management's and presumably the owners' attitude toward risk.   To determine the weight applicable to a particular outcome, we need a function which will tell us how management values changes in wealth resulting from accepting risk.   To calculate this subjective utility function, we must assign arbitrary numbers to two outcomes and select a third alternative somewhere in between the two extremes.   The numbers reflect the utility of these extremes.   The third alternative is a certain amount whose utility we wish to determine.   The extremes represent probable outcomes.   We then vary the probable outcomes until we find the odds between the certain amount and the probable outcomes at which management will be indifferent.   The utility of this amount equals the sum of the utilities of the extreme outcomes times their respective probabilities.   Having determined the utility of a certain amount, we can use this figure as a probable outcome and repeat the process.

In applying this function to a project, we multiply the probability of each outcome by the utility of the present value of this outcome and total the results.   If the expected utility of the project is greater than the utility of the certainty equivalent, that is, the utility of the replacement cost of the asset, the project is acceptable.   If not, it should be rejected. Since the utility function is based on probable changes in the wealth or market value of the owners' equity, we have another reason for preferring the present value approach over the rate of return approach.

When we turn from the ideal to the actual, we find a considerable gap between theory and practice.   Variants of discounted cash flows are at times employed.   But the payback period is the most popular technique for budgeting capital.   However, it ignores the cash flows occurring beyond the payback period.   Nonetheless, since the techniques for handling risk are still the weak links in the principles of capital budgeting, the payback period, as a hedge against uncertainty, can be recommended as a supplementary measure.

QUESTIONS AND PROBLEMS

1.   Management is considering an expansion in facilities, the replacement cost of which is $3,000,000.   The following is a forecast

of the sales revenues and the after-tax cash expenses associated with the project.

First Year

	Pessimistic Forecast	Most Probable Forecast	Optimistic Forecast
Sales Revenue	$5,000,000	$6,000,000	$7,000,000
After-tax Cash Expenses	$4,900,000	$4,500,000	$4,000,000

Second Year

	Pessimistic Forecast	Most Probable Forecast	Optimistic Forecast
Sales Revenue	$4,000,000	$5,000,000	$6,000,000
After-tax Cash Expenses	$3,900,000	$3,500,000	$3,000,000

Third Year

	Pessimistic Forecast	Most Probable Forecast	Optimistic Forecast
Sales Revenue	$2,000,000	$3,000,000	$4,000,000
After-tax Cash Expenses	$1,900,000	$1,500,000	$1,000,000

Calculate the expected net present value under the assumption that $p = q$, first for $n = 2$, then for $n = 4$. How would you estimate the payback period? Should the project be adopted? Explain carefully. (*Hint:* Is all the necessary information available? Why or why not?)

2. The utility of $0 is 0 and the utility of $1,000 is 1. An individual is given a choice between this combination for $p = q = .5$ and a certainty equivalent of $400. What is the utility of $400?

3. In problem 2, if $p = .1$ and $q = .9$ for $0 and $1,200, respectively, what is the utility of $1,200 if the certainty equivalent is $1,000?

4. "Even if we can treat the outcomes from a given investment decision in the same way as we would treat the outcomes in a game of chance, there is a difference. In a game of chance we know all the possible outcomes and therefore the odds that any single event or combination of events will occur. For a business investment decision, we do not have this information." Do you agree? Explain fully.

5. "It is possible for an investment to meet payback criteria, yet fail to be acceptable under a rate of return or a cost of capital standard." Evaluate.

6. "If the outcomes of an investment decision fail to conform to the frequency concept of probability, then an objective evaluation of risk is impossible." Discuss.

7. "If management applies its own standards of risk evaluation to selecting investments, it may not be maximizing the market value of the owners' equity." Explain.

SELECTED REFERENCES

Bierman, Harold, Jr., and Seymour Smidt. *The Capital Budgeting Decision,* 2d ed. New York: The Macmillan Company, 1966, pp. 18–25.

Fellner, William. *Probability and Profit.* Homewood, Ill.: Richard D. Irwin, Inc., 1965.

Friedman, Milton, and L. J. Savage. "The Utility Analysis of Choices Involving Risk," *Journal of Political Economy,* vol. 56, no. 4 (August, 1948), pp. 279–304.

Hackney, John M. *Control and Management of Capital Projects.* New York: John Wiley & Sons, Inc., 1965.

Hertz, D. B. "Risk Analysis in Capital Investment," *Harvard Business Review,* vol. 42, no. 1 (January-February, 1964), pp. 95–106.

Knight, Frank H. *Risk, Uncertainty and Profit.* Boston: Houghton Mifflin Company, 1921.

Quirin, G. David. *The Capital Expenditure Decision.* Homewood, Ill.: Richard D. Irwin, Inc., 1967, chaps. 10 and 11.

Raiffa, Howard. *Decision Analysis: Introductory Lectures on Choices under Uncertainty.* Reading Mass.: Addison-Wesley Publishing Company, Inc., 1968.

Vandell, Robert F., and Richard F. Vancil. *Cases in Capital Budgeting.* Home-Wood, Ill.: Richard D. Irwin, Inc., 1962.

Principles of Working Capital Management

chapter Eight

In turning his attention to the principles which underlie working capital management, the student should contrast the analysis presented here with the analysis of the management of long-lived assets. What are the similarities and the differences? What is the role which working capital management plays in implementing our goal of maximizing the market value of the owners' equity?

Introduction

In the two previous chapters we concentrated on the principles underlying the additions to long-lived assets. In so doing we held constant the proportion[1] of liabilities and owners' equity, that is, the capital

---

[1]But not necessarily the absolute amounts of debt and equity. After all, the projects selected must be financed. Unless the sole source of funds is depreciation, we can anticipate some change in the amount of liabilities and owners' equity from adopting the budget.

structure, as well as the level and composition of current assets.[2]   We also assumed that the cost of capital was given.   From our analysis we concluded that if the risk-adjusted net present value was positive and if the expected utility of the probable outcomes was greater than the utility of the replacement cost of the asset, then adopting the project would raise the market value of the owners' equity.

In this chapter we shall hold the level of long-lived assets and the proportions of long-term debt and owners' equity constant, allowing current assets, and under certain conditions current liabilities, to vary. Our emphasis therefore is on the factors affecting the level of working capital.   Moreover, we shall also separate the factors responsible for permanent changes in working capital from those associated with temporary changes.

To begin, let us ask a fundamental set of questions.   First, why must the firm invest in current assets?   Assuming that there is a satisfactory explanation, then, second, what principles determine the optimum level of current assets and the optimum level of net working capital?

A firm invests in current assets not because it ordinarily anticipates a higher level of profits, but because it must face the reality that the timing of cash inflows from the sale of goods and services does not correspond to the timing of cash outflows representing expenses incurred in their production.   Indeed, if cash inflows were matched as to both amount and timing with cash outflows, there would be no need for management to consider investing in current assets.   For example, suppose a manufacturing firm could acquire raw materials, produce its product, and sell it all at the same moment in time.   Then unless it finds that tying up funds in cash, marketable securities, inventories, and receivables is more profitable than investing these funds in long-lived assets, it will never purchase current assets.

Ordinarily, therefore, we can regard current assets as a necessary evil.   There are exceptions.   A firm may find that investing funds in receivables, particularly through installment contracts, is a highly profitable outlet when compared with the alternatives available.   But as a general rule, we should look with disfavor on a firm whose ratio of current assets to long-lived assets shows a secular increase.[3]   If further analysis reveals the lack of profitable investments in long-lived assets, then management should be either investing in securities or assets of

---

[2]Again we must recognize the possibility that adoption of projects may necessitate a permanent increase in the level of working capital.

[3]It is possible for a few years for a firm, say a merchandising concern, to increase its inventories and hence its current assets relative to its fixed assets.   This is an indication of a more efficient use of existing facilities.   There will come a time, however, when it must expand its storage and perhaps its sales outlets, that is, its long-lived assets, to accommodate the increase in demand.

other firms, or liquidating the enterprise.   If it does none of these things, it could be pursuing policies which may ultimately result in failure to maximize the market value of the owners' equity.

OPERATING CYCLE

In order to understand what gives rise to differences in the amount and timing of cash flows, we must first know the length of time required to convert cash into the resources used by the firm, the resources into the final product, the final product into receivables, and receivables back into cash.   We must know, in other words, the *operating cycle* of the enterprise.

We can depict the operating cycle graphically as in Figure 8-1.

The length of the operating cycle is a function of the nature of the business.   For a vertically integrated manufacturing firm, the operating cycle consists of converting cash into raw materials, converting raw materials into finished goods, selling the product or products through its retail trade outlets, and converting the accounts receivables into cash. For an independent retail trade store, the manufacturing portion of the operating cycle is eliminated but the conversion of inventories into receivables and then into cash remains.   For those providing services, the inventory problem is usually eliminated but the collection of receivables remains.   Firms selling services on a strictly cash basis may be able to disregard working capital altogether, while cash-and-carry retail trade outlets eliminate the need to finance receivables.

Figure 8-1   The operating cycle of a business firm.

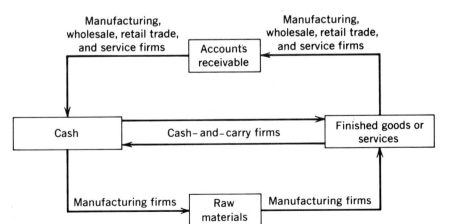

While the nature of the business determines the length of the operating cycle, management can within limits alter the time required to complete it.   Thus, in the above example, management of a manufacturing firm, say a steel producer, has little control over the time required to process iron ore into semifinished forms.   Given the state of technology, it must accept the time necessary to complete the production process.   Any hopes of altering it lie in technological breakthroughs such as continuous casting.   To this end, of course, and with the view of ultimately lowering costs, it may justify a capital expenditure on research and development.

On the other hand, by instituting aggressive selling techniques, management may immediately lower the time required to convert inventories into receivables.   An automobile dealer, for example, may offer a higher trade-in on old cars in order to move his stock of cars. Similarly, large service charges, say $1\frac{1}{2}$ percent, on the outstanding monthly balance may hasten the conversion of receivables into cash.[4] By making these and similar decisions, management can have an immediate and lasting impact on its operating cycle.

But competition imposes limits on the discretion of management. Indeed, changing the operating cycle may itself be a form of competition. The department store which allows customers to purchase home appliances or other consumer durables on a 90-day plan with no service charges is inviting an extension of its operating cycle.   In doing so, it may be competing with the discount house selling the same appliances on a cash-and-carry basis or on a limited credit plan with high monthly service charges.   The latter may compete by pricing the appliance lower than the former.   But it makes up the difference with a high turnover of inventories and with high credit charges on receivables, thereby lowering the inventory investment required to produce a given volume of sales.   The consumer is left to choose between the lower sales price with limited financing and the higher sales price with extended time payments and little or no service charges.[5]   Since competitive forces are naturally in a continuous state of flux, an efficient management will

[4]On the other hand, to the extent that it does not hasten conversion, the service charge ensures that the return on funds invested in receivables and in the facilities and personnel necessary to process them will cover the cost of capital.   Eighteen percent a year simple interest is in excess of the marginal cost of capital for most firms.

[5]The problem is further complicated by the fact that the department store may also pride itself on providing high-quality maintenance service whereas the discount house may not.   This additional overhead is reflected in the price differentials between the competing outlets.   The consumer is making the choice of buying the appliance alone in the case of the discount house or the appliance together with a series of other services in the case of the department store.   In perfect competition, the value of these additional services would be reflected in the differential on prices charged by competitors for the same appliance.

periodically review its operating cycle, revising it accordingly.   The decision to do so will affect not only the image it presents to the public but also its need for working capital.

The Permanent Level of Working Capital

The operating cycle provides us with a rationale for investing funds in current assets.   But it does not tell us at what level they should be maintained.   To determine the optimum level of permanent working capital, we must probe more deeply into the costs involved in investing funds in these assets.

We may distinguish between two types of costs.   The first, alluded to earlier, is the *opportunity cost*, or foregone earnings from allocating funds to current rather than long-lived assets.   Management can ordinarily anticipate a higher return from investing in plant and equipment than from holding cash or marketable securities.

The second type of cost stems from the consequences of having insufficient cash or other liquid assets to meet the firm's obligations as they come due.   This is the *cost of being caught short.*   The most severe consequence is bankruptcy.   Lesser penalties include a reputation for being delinquent in paying bills and a subsequent deterioration of the firm's credit rating.

As between the two types of costs, perhaps more emphasis has been given to the short cost.   This should not come as a surprise.   Bankruptcy may mean the liquidation of the company.   Managers in turn will lose their jobs and the owners all or most of their equity.   The traditional concern in working capital management, therefore, has been with a level of current assets sufficient to meet the firm's obligations as they come due, that is, a level sufficient to maintain liquidity.

Of course, management may be able to avert bankruptcy simply by financing all of the firm's assets out of equity.   Our goal, however, is to maximize the market value of the owners' equity.   While we have reserved until later the principles determining the composition of financing, we may note in passing that it is possible for owners to profit from the use of debt.   If, for instance, assets can be financed more cheaply out of debt than from the sale of stock, the market value of the owners' equity might rise from so doing.   Owners, in other words, are willing to accept some financial risk in addition to the business risk which they incur from investing in assets.

Even if it were in the owners' interests to finance assets entirely out of equity, management would still incur obligations which it would have to meet periodically—wages and taxes, for example.   Some of these cash expenses, however, unlike interest on debt, are a function of output or sales. If the firm produces nothing, management may lay off the production workers. If the firm fails to sell its product, there is no taxable income and hence no income taxes. Therefore, to the extent that management can lower cash expenses or current liabilities, it reduces the firm's need for current assets or at least the cash component.

But what of the opportunity costs? Besides the foregone earnings from investing in current rather than long-lived assets, we must consider the costs of not having sufficient inventory, that is, the loss of customers from not meeting their product demands. We must also consider the costs of not meeting their credit demands, that is, the loss of customers from failure to invest in receivables. Moreover, assuming that there are current liabilities, a low turnover of receivables or inventories may result in a cash deficiency which threatens the liquidity of the firm.

Consequently, each of the major categories of current assets — cash, receivables, and inventories — can be related to one or perhaps both of the costs involved in determining the permanent level of working capital. The principles of managing each category of assets are, however, of sufficient diversity to warrant treatment in separate chapters. This we shall do in the next three chapters.

Permanent and Temporary Levels of Working Capital — Fluctuations in Demand and Operating Expenses

While the principles determining the level of the components of working capital can be tied to both the short and the opportunity costs, these costs in turn ultimately depend on fluctuations in demand and operating costs or expenses. Moreover, these fluctuations can be subclassified into three categories: *secular*, *cyclical*, and *seasonal*.

By secular change we mean the long-term trend in demand and operating expenses. Both can be growing, declining, or showing no trend at all. Cyclical factors are those associated with fluctuations in the level of economic activity about the long-term trend. Figure 8-2 is a diagram portraying cyclical and secular changes in sales.

What is true of sales is also true of operating expenses. As output and sales rise, so do wages, taxes, and other cash outlays associated with increases in production and sales. We can, therefore, expect secular and cyclical trends in operating expenses similar to those in sales.

Indeed, cyclical factors may be viewed as forces affecting the timing of changes in the level of long-lived assets and the composition of permanent working capital. When there is excess productive capacity, management may be uncertain as to whether it is the result of a tem-

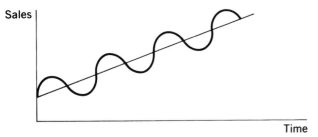

Figure 8-2 Secular and cyclical changes in sales for a hypothetical firm.

porary decline in the level of economic activity or the result of a slowing down in the secular growth in sales. It may, therefore, delay additions to long-lived assets. It may also build up the firm's cash balances, that is, alter the composition of the company's working capital. This management does in anticipation of expanding inventories and receivables should sales resume their secular growth. Similarly, if the firm is producing near capacity, management may accelerate additions to long-lived assets and reduce the cash component of its working capital.

Seasonal patterns are those with a duration of less than a year. Some companies may depend heavily on sales at a certain time of the year, a manufacturer of baseball bats, for example. The operating cycle of a firm in this position is such that it will have a large investment in inventories as it gears production to meet the seasonal peak. As inventories are liquidated, receivables build up. As receivables are liquidated, cash balances swell.

Consequently, one of the principle differences between the management of current assets and the management of long-lived assets is the distinction which must be made between permanent and temporary changes in working capital requirements. As we have seen, management adds to plant and equipment in anticipation of gains accruing to the firm over a period of years. These additions to plant and equipment represent the means by which secular increases in sales are accommodated. Management also adds to the firm's permanent level of working capital to accommodate an increase in sales. Clearly, a higher volume of sales usually means a higher level of cash balances.

Management, however, usually does not add to plant and equipment to meet seasonal needs.[6] But seasonal factors can radically affect

---

[6]A firm might rent equipment for a short time to meet seasonal needs. Additional delivery trucks employed during peak periods is an example. But the rental payments are current liabilities and the trucks are not purchased, nor are they leased on a long-term basis—a method which is tantamount to purchase, as we shall argue in a later chapter.

both the level and composition of current assets and liabilities. To illustrate this point we shall employ an arithmetic example, drawing together the factors affecting both temporary and permanent changes in working capital.

Projecting Working Capital — An Arithmetic Example

As the tool of analysis we shall employ *pro forma* financial statements representing projections for next year for the XYZ Corporation, a toy manufacturer. Using the economic approach to valuation, the accompanying tabulations represent the results of operations for the previous year.

XYZ CORPORATION
Statement of Income
Year Ending December 31, 19___

Sales		$8,100,000
Less Sales, Returns, Allowances, and Discounts		−100,000
Net Sales		$8,000,000
Deduct cost of Goods Sold		−4,000,000
Gross Profit		**$4,000,000**
Less Operating Expenses		
Selling Expenses	−$2,000,000	
Administrative Expenses	−1,250,000	−3,250,000
Net Operating Income		$ 750,000
Add Other Income	$75,000	
Deduct Other Expenses	−25,000	50,000
Income before Income Taxes		$ 800,000
Less Income Taxes (48% of $800,000)		−384,000
Net Income, or Profit		**$ 416,000**

XYZ CORPORATION
Balance Sheet
December 31, 19___

Current Assets	
Cash	$ 250,000
Marketable Securities	150,000
Receivables	500,000
Raw-materials Inventory	50,000
Work in Process	
Finished-goods Inventory	50,000
	$1,000,000

Long-term Assets

Land		100,000
Plant and Equipment	$1,400,000	
Less Accumulated Depreciation	−500,000	900,000

Total Assets	**$2,000,000**

Liabilities and Owners' Equity (Capital)

Current Liabilities

Accounts Payable	$ 50,000
Loans Payable	202,000
Interest Payable	19,000
Taxes Payable	300,000
Dividends Payable	29,000
	$ 600,000

Long-term Liabilities

6% Subordinated Debenture Bonds	
Maturing July 1, 1968	400,000
Total Liabilities	$1,000,000

Owners' Equity (Capital)

Common Stock, par value $5.00;	
200,000 shares authorized;	
issued and outstanding,	
100,000 shares	1,000,000

Total Liabilities and Owners' Equity	**$2,000,000**

The marketing division estimates that sales will rise by 10 percent in the coming year.[7] Assume that operating expenses or costs will rise in proportion to sales. There is sufficient capacity to handle the anticipated increase. While we are assuming that there are no additions to plant and equipment, in order to prevent a decline in the market value of these assets, we must further assume that the depreciation allow-

---

[7]If we assume that finance and marketing are separate areas of responsibility and that sales forecasts are in the hands of the latter division, we can take the results as given. This does not mean that the measures used to arrive at sales forecasts are unimportant—merely that they are outside the scope of an introductory text in finance. Models can be designed to take into account the level of demand, given the pricing policy for the year, the change in income, and the price and income elasticity of demand. If there is an anticipated change in sales due to factors which are not manifested in changes in income, this too can be incorporated into the model.

Furthermore, to assume that sales forecasting is in the hands of the marketing division may be an oversimplification. There could be a planning committee, concerned with both short- and long-range forecasts, staffed with marketing and financial experts and supervised by management personnel from both areas.

ance for the year is reinvested so as to maintain plant and equipment at its current value.[8]

We can project the income statement for the next year, so that we have the accompanying tabulations.

XYZ CORPORATION
Pro Forma Statement of Income
Year Ending December 31, 19___

Sales		$8,910,000
Less Sales, Returns, Allowances, and Discounts		−110,000
		$8,800,000
Deduct Cost of Goods Sold		−4,400,000
Gross Profit		**$4,400,000**
Less Operating Expenses		
Selling Expenses	−$2,200,000	
Administrative Expenses	− 1,375,000	3,575,000
Net Operating Income		$ 825,000
Add Other Income	82,500	
Deduct Other Expenses	−27,500	55,000
Income before Income Taxes		$ 880,000
Less Income Taxes (48% of $880,000)		−422,400
Net Income, or Profit		**$ 457,600**

If costs rise in proportion to sales, we can anticipate a 10 percent increase in liabilities to accommodate these cost increases and a 10 percent rise in current assets to handle the additional sales volume. Since we have assumed that the proportion of debt and equity to total capital remains unchanged, then debt must increase by 10 percent and the market value of the owners' equity by 10 percent.

While management anticipates that some of the increase in sales represents cyclical factors, it does not expect sales to fall below $8,800,000 the year after. Therefore, it will treat the increase as permanent. This leaves open the question of the composition of debt. Should the 10 percent increase in debt consist of short-term debt, long-term debt, or a mixture of both? To avoid at this time a prolonged discussion of the composition of financing, we shall assume that management is satisfied for the present to let current liabilities increase by 10 percent.

---

[8]We do this simply to stay strictly within our assumptions of holding the level of fixed assets constant. We could have let the value decline, showing a corresponding increase in one of the current assets, presumably cash or marketable securities.

It may be anticipating funding some of the short-term debt into long-term debt but feels that interest rates in the capital markets are above their long-term trend.   Thus it prefers to wait.[9]

In these circumstances, the projected balance sheet at the end of the year might appear as in the accompanying tabulations.

XYZ CORPORATION
Pro Forma Balance Sheet
December 31, 19___

Current Assets

Cash		$ 275,000
Marketable Securities		165,000
Receivables		550,000
Raw-materials Inventory		55,000
Work in Process		
Finished-goods Inventory		55,000
		$1,100,000

Long-term Assets

Land		100,000
Plant and Equipment	$1,400,000	
Less Accumulated Depreciation	−500,000	900,000
Total Assets		**$2,100,000**

Liabilities and Owners' Equity (Capital)

Current Liabilities

Accounts Payable		$ 50,000
Loans Payable		249,000
Interest Payable		22,000
Taxes Payable		300,000
Dividends Payable		29,000
		$ 650,000

Long-term Liabilities

6% Subordinated Debenture Bonds		
Maturing July 1, 1980		400,000
Total Liabilities		$1,050,000

Owners' Equity (Capital)

Common Stock, par value $5.00;		
200,000 shares authorized;		
issued and outstanding, 100,000 shares		$ 1,050,000
Total Liabilities and Owners' Equity		**$2,100,000**

[9]Realistically, management may be combining a funding operation with an investment in plant and equipment.   The proceeds from the sale of the bonds will be used to finance both.

Note that we have assumed that each component of current assets rises in proportion to the total.   We do this because there is no reason to assume a change in the operating cycle.   However, to simplify the arithmetic, we have assumed that the increase in debt represents an increase in bank loans and the interest on the loans.   Thus we have ignored the possibility that financing at least part of the increase out of accounts payable may be a cheaper, though certainly temporary, means of financing.

Moreover, the equity investment in the increase is only $50,000. If $29,000 reflects the quarterly dividend rate, then out of a projected net income of $457,600 only $166,000 ($29,000 $\times$ 4 + $50,000) is accounted for in the balance-sheet figures.   We can, of course, assume that the remainder will be paid out as dividends earlier in the year or as a year-end extra paid just prior to December 31 next year.   Any number of modifications are, of course, possible.   But the primary function in this case is to project permanent working capital requirements without varying the composition of financing and the level of long-lived assets. Thus we shall ignore these possible changes.

Besides anticipating the need for permanent increases, we must also recognize the fact that the toy business has a seasonal pattern with the major portion of the annual demand concentrated in the fourth quarter of the year.   On the basis of past experience, management knows that about 80 percent of output is for the Christmas market. Further, depending on the quarter in which Easter falls, 10 percent of sales are in the first or second quarter, with 5 percent in each of the remaining quarters.

This means that early in the year the bulk of the firm's working capital will be in cash and short-term government issues or other marketable securities.   Then, in preparation for the Christmas demand, there will be more invested in inventories.   Finally, as deliveries are made to various wholesale and retail outlets, finished-goods inventory will decline and receivables will dominate current assets.   Using replacement costs for raw materials and work in process and using market value for finished-goods inventory, quarterly results for working capital for the previous year are as shown in the accompanying tabulations on the next page.

	March 31	June 30	Sept. 30	Dec. 31
Current Assets				
Cash	$ 25,000	$ 20,000	$ 125,000	$ 250,000
Marketable Securities	700,000			150,000
Receivables	50,000	10,000	220,000	500,000
Raw-materials Inventory	60,000	2,250,000	455,000	50,000
Work in Process	5,000	220,000	110,000	
Finished-goods Inventory	60,000	50,000	6,400,000	50,000
Total Current Assets	**$900,000**	**$2,550,000**	**$7,310,000**	**$1,000,000**
Current Liabilities				
Accounts Payable		$ 1,500,000	$ 250,000	$ 50,000
Loans Payable	50,000		3,000,000	202,000
Interest Payable	700	12,000	35,000	19,000
Taxes Payable	42,300	21,000	21,000	300,000
Dividends Payable	29,000	29,000	29,000	29,000
Total Current Liabilities	**$122,000**	**$1,562,000**	**$3,335,000**	**$ 600,000**
Net Working Capital	**$778,000**	**$ 988,000**	**$3,975,000**	**$ 400,000**
Current Ratio	**7.4**	**1.6**	**2.2**	**1.7**

On the basis of a 10 percent increase in sales and costs but with no change in the seasonal pattern, management anticipates that its quarterly figures for working capital for the next year will be as shown in the accompanying tabulations.

	March 31	June 30	Sept. 30	Dec. 31
Current Assets				
Cash	$ 27,500	$ 22,000	$ 137,500	$ 275,000
Marketable Securities	770,000			165,000
Receivables	55,000	11,000	242,000	550,000
Raw-materials Inventory	66,000	2,475,000	500,500	55,000
Work in Process	5,500	242,000	121,000	
Finished-goods Inventory	66,000	55,000	7,040,000	55,000
Total Current Assets	**$990,000**	**$2,805,000**	**$8,041,000**	**$1,100,000**

	March 31	June 30	Sept. 30	Dec. 31
Current Liabilities				
Accounts Payable		$1,656,200	$ 250,000	$ 50,000
Loans Payable	$ 62,130		3,330,000	260,100
Interest Payable	770	12,000	38,500	20,900
Taxes Payable	42,300	21,000	21,000	300,000
Dividends Payable	29,000	29,000	29,000	29,000
Total Current Liabilities	**$134,200**	**$1,718,200**	**$3,668,500**	**$ 660,000**
Net Working Capital	**$885,800**	**$1,087,800**	**$1,072,500**	**$ 440,000**
Current Ratio	**7.4**	**1.6**	**2.2**	**1.7**

Problems Facing Management   Simplified though this example is, it serves to illustrate some of the problems management must face if it is to accommodate seasonal needs yet provide for permanent increases in working capital.

In our example, by the end of March the bulk of the investment in working capital is in short-term securities.   This means that the firm must have funds available for investing in raw materials, finished goods, and receivables so as to meet the seasonal peak.   While short-term sources are available, no lender would be willing to finance 100 percent of the replacement cost or market value of these assets.   Realistically, the firm could expect its suppliers to extend 100 percent credit on the purchase price of the raw materials.   This source of funds would be represented on the books of the toy manufacturer by accounts payable. But the terms are often 2/10, net 30, that is, 2 percent discount if paid within 10 days or the net amount in 30 days.   Thus, if the firm were purchasing $100,000 in raw materials, it would save $2,000 by paying the bill within 10 days.   Otherwise it is paying

$$\frac{\$2,000}{\$98,000} = 2.04\% \text{ per 20 days}$$

$$2.04\% \times \frac{365}{20} = 37.23\% \text{ per year}$$

Interest payments such as this will ordinarily encourage the manufacturer to substitute an alternative source of financing, perhaps a commercial bank loan with interest costs at, say, $6\frac{1}{2}$ percent.   But assuming that a bank is willing to make the loan, it will finance only a specified portion of the market value of the materials.   Moreover, if the market value or replacement cost is higher than the original cost, the bank may choose to use the latter as its base for making the loan.

Furthermore, when making loans, it is customary to ask for compensating balances.

Assume, for example, that the bank is willing to finance 80 percent of the original cost of the raw materials but demands a 10 percent compensating balance. Thus, if the firm is to take advantage of the 2 percent discount on the $100,000 purchase of raw materials, it will receive $80,000 from the bank. But it must let 10 percent, or $8,000, lie idle in the checking account. This frees $72,000 to repay the supplier.[10] The remainder, or $26,000, will come from liquidating other current assets, presumably marketable securities.

Since the firm's sales are concentrated in one quarter of the year, it will have to continue to rely on bank loans to finance most of the cost if not the market value of the finished-goods inventory. Because we have listed these goods at their market value, which may reflect as much as a 100 percent markup over cost, we notice an improvement in the current ratio and the net working capital from the end of the second to the end of the third quarter. If we had relied on original cost or had imputed to current liabilities certain anticipated costs such as selling commissions, the change would not have been so pronounced.

Sometime during the fourth quarter, the toy manufacturer will liquidate the inventory and build up receivables. The book value, of course, reflects the sales price. Again, the firm may rely on bank loans to finance as much as 80 percent of these receivables, with the proceeds being used to meet operating expenses as they come due. Once the receivables have been liquidated, the loan can be repaid. The result is a decline in working capital to the levels anticipated by December 31.

Now let us complicate the problem still further. Suppose, for instance, that the toy manufacturer experiences a seasonal pattern in sales similar to the one just described, but it finds that some of its overhead expenses continue to be incurred on a regular basis. For example, management may be able to hire production workers to meet seasonal needs, but conditions in the labor market force the firm to retain its white-collar employees on an annual basis.

Similarly, management may find that it can operate its production facilities more efficiently if it takes steps to even out its production cycle, building up finished-goods inventories early in the year in anticipation of the Christmas season. Ideally, perhaps it should produce 25 percent of its anticipated annual sales each quarter. Realistically, it will probably manufacture on this basis only those items representing lines for which demand over the years has been predictable. It will discontinue toys

---

[10]Although the interest charges are $6\frac{1}{2}$ percent of $80,000, or $5,200 per year, the effective annual rate of interest is now $5,200/$72,000 = 7.222$ percent. The firm, of course, will liquidate the loan within a few months.

which were poor sellers and introduce new lines, following intensive market research. These it may not produce until nearer the Christmas season. The result of the attempt to organize production more efficiently and yet manufacture so as to accommodate the demand for specific lines will lead management to alter its structure of current assets so that the stock of finished goods will increase more rapidly during the early part of the year. Production, in other words, will be somewhat less seasonal than the pattern of demand.

Moreover, to finance these inventories, management must know to what extent it can depend on current liabilities, primarily short-term bank loans, to finance, first, the raw materials and, ultimately, the finished goods and receivables.

Once it realizes that some cash costs need not follow the same seasonal pattern as demand and that it may be more efficient to smooth out the production process, then, to manage working capital effectively, the firm must recognize that its permanent needs depend on the interplay of these factors. What management must know is the maximum level of current assets required during the year and the maximum level of credit it can anticipate to finance these needs. Assume in the case of the toy manufacturer that this occurs during the first week in November. Suppose that the level, composition, and financing of working capital at this time for the previous year was as follows:

Current Assets	
Cash	$ 650,000
Marketable Securities	
Receivables	6,000,000
Raw-materials Inventory	50,000
Work in Process	50,000
Finished-goods Inventory	100,000
Total Current Assets	**$6,850,000**
Current Liabilities	
Wages Payable	$ 100,000
Accounts Payable	
Loans Payable	5,100,000
Interest Payable	40,000
Taxes Payable	
Dividends Payable	
Total Current Liabilities	**$5,240,000**
Net Working Capital	**$1,610,000**
Current Ratio	1.3

The receivables reflect the sales price. The bank will loan 85 percent of their face value but requires compensating balances of 10 percent of the loan, or $510,000. The additional $140,000 is sufficient to cover interest, some of it perhaps on long-term debt, and wages. Assume now that all costs and working capital requirements are expected to rise by 10 percent next year. Then management estimates that its peak working capital requirements will be as follows:

Current Assets

Cash	$ 715,000
Marketable Securities	
Receivables	6,600,000
Raw-materials Inventory	55,000
Work in Process	55,000
Finished-goods Inventory	110,000
Total Current Assets	**$7,535,000**

Current Liabilities

Wages Payable	$ 110,000
Accounts Payable	
Loans Payable	5,610,000
Interest Payable	44,000
Taxes Payable	
Dividends Payable	
Total Current Liabilities	**$5,764,000**
Net Working Capital	**$1,771,000**
Current Ratio	1.3

Viewing its situation in this light, management would estimate its permanent working capital requirements on the basis of the difference between the maximum level of current assets required during the year and the maximum level of current liabilities required to finance these assets. This figure, or net working capital, was $1,610,000 for the previous year. It is expected to rise 10 percent, that is, to $1,771,000. Since net working capital is the difference between current assets and current liabilities, this increase of $161,000 represents a permanent addition to working capital to be financed out of permanent sources of funds.

The Optimum Level of Permanent Working Capital

Assuming that the projected increases in sales, operating expenses, and hence net working capital are correct, the firm must allow for the permanent rise in working capital or face the prospect of being unable to accommodate the expected increase in demand.   Moreover, this rise in working capital may represent a minimum.   We noted earlier in our analysis that management expected sales to rise next year by 10 percent, that is, to $8,800,000.   We also noted that it did not anticipate a decline below $8,800,000 the year after next.   But we did not give an estimate of the probability which should be attached to this figure.   We may, however, infer from these facts that management is virtually certain that sales will hold at a level of $8,800,000 during the next 2 years.   They could rise further.   If they do, so would the need for an additional investment in permanent working capital.

In fact, if we assume that net working capital requirements, like net cash flows, are normally distributed, then the probability distribution of permanent working capital requirements would be as in Figure 8-3.

From our analysis, a net working capital requirement of $1,771,000 is associated with a sales volume of $8,800,000.   Since there is little likelihood that permanent working capital requirements, at least over the next 2 years, will be less than this figure, we have placed it near the lower end of the probability distribution.

But what of the probabilities that sales will rise by more than $8,800,000?   Should management raise the level of net working capital on the expectation that sales will grow by more than 10 percent next year and will remain the year after at this permanently higher level? Suppose that management allocates additional funds, say $3,000,000, to accommodate what is expected to be (excluding the outside chance represented by the upper extreme of the curve) the maximum level of

Figure 8-3

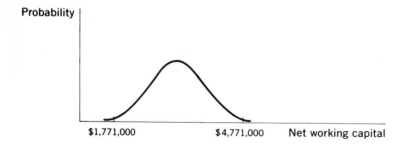

Probability

$1,771,000 $4,771,000   Net working capital

sales for next year. What are the trade-offs from pursuing this policy?

Reenter, now, the opportunity and short costs discussed earlier. Management must consider the effect on profit and hence on the market value of the owners' equity of allocating their funds to working capital rather than investing them in long-lived assets or distributing them as dividends. Suppose that management chooses to use the $3,000,000 together with a bank loan to purchase additional inventories in the hopes of satisfying the maximum possible demand. It then runs the risk of not selling the inventories, or selling them at such a low price that the proceeds will be insufficient to repay the bank loan. If so, management is caught short and the firm's liquidity is impaired. Bankruptcy ensues.

Management could have let the funds lay as idle cash balances, using them to help finance inventory only if it became apparent that sales were going to rise above $8,800,000. In this way, management avoids the extreme cost of being caught short. But if the sales volume does not increase beyond what was initially anticipated, the $3,000,000 earns nothing. It might then have been in the owners' interests to have distributed the funds as dividends.

Moreover, even if demand had risen and management had waited for the rise before committing the funds to inventories, the firm still runs the risk of not being able to satisfy customer demand in time. The delay, in other words, is too great, and customers will purchase their toys from other firms. Even if management were to rush the goods through the production and distribution processes, the additional costs in terms of overtime pay, the strain on facilities, and the deterioration in product quality might result in a lower level of total profits than if management had not attempted to satisfy the maximum possible demand.

It is apparent that the outcome depends on the policy pursued. Generalizations are therefore difficult to make. However, given our discussion of utility analysis, it would appear that the greater the extremes from following a particular policy, the less likely it is that the policy will lead to maximization of the market value of the owners' equity. Consider, for example, the following alternatives. Management retains the $3,000,000 as idle cash balances, or it invests the sum in inventory. Using an analysis similar to that employed in capital budgeting, the probable changes in total profit from investing the additional $3,000,000 in inventory are as shown on the following page.

	(1) Changes in Total Profits	(2) Proba- bility	(3) (1) × (2) Weighted Average	(4) Utility of Income	(5) (2) × (4) Weighted Utility
Most Pessimistic Outcome	− $2,000,000	.25	− $ 500,000	−.2	−.05
Most Probable Outcome	4,000,000	.50	2,000,000	.3	.1500
Most Optimistic Outcome	8,000,000	.25	2,000,000	.45	.1125
			$3,500,000		.2125

We may assume that changes in total profits resulting from invest-ing an additional $3,000,000 in inventories form a symmetrical distri-bution, where $p = q$. We shall also assume that under the most pessi-mistic alternative, a decline in total profits of $2,000,000 does not precipitate bankruptcy.[11] Assume that the utility of the certainty equivalent is .38. Then the utility of holding the funds as idle cash is greater than the utility of risking them in additional inventories.

These two alternatives, of course, are not the only ones. Perhaps we should compare the utility of holding the funds as cash with the utility of changes in total profits from accelerating production should management find sales rising above expectations. Similarly, we might compare the utility of holding the funds as cash with the utility of addi-tions to total wealth should the money be distributed as dividends. Given the various possibilities, we would choose the course of action which resulted in the highest expected utility. In this way we would arrive at the level of permanent working capital which maximized the market value of the owners' equity, that is, at the optimum level of permanent working capital.

SUMMARY

The fact that cash inflows are not matched in both timing and amount by cash outflows provides us with an operating cycle and rationale for investing in working capital. But it is the opportunity cost and the short cost which determine the optimum level of working capital.

Moreover, in any analysis of working capital, we must make a dis-

---

[11]If it did, we might expect the utility of the loss to approach −∞.

tinction between temporary and permanent working capital requirements. The latter are a function of secular and cyclical trends in sales and operating expenses. The former depend on seasonal factors. In a *pro forma* projection of working capital requirements, management must forecast the maximum level of current assets required to support an expected volume of sales and the maximum level of short-term credit it can anticipate to finance these assets.

If the sales volume represents minimal expectations, that is, sales may be considerably larger, then management must consider the opportunity and short costs of expanding the level of permanent working capital to meet a higher but less likely volume of sales. The numerous alternatives available will vary greatly in their impact on profits. As in the case of long-lived-asset management, however, the outcome with the highest expected utility will maximize the market value of the owners' equity.

QUESTIONS AND PROBLEMS

1. A small manufacturing firm found last year that its maximum level of working capital was $5,000,000, $4,000,000 of which could be financed out of short-term liabilities. The annual sales volume was $20,000,000. This year it anticipates a 7 percent increase in sales, only 5 percent of which is permanent. On the assumption that changes in working capital are proportional to changes in sales, what is the minimum increase in permanent working capital needs?

2. "A dollar invested in working capital is a dollar that might be adding more to total profits if allocated to long-lived assets." Discuss critically.

3. "The operating cycle is a function of the seasonal pattern of demand." Evaluate.

4. "The greater the proportion of current assets to long-lived assets, the smaller the business risk faced by the firm." Do you agree? Explain carefully.

5. What determines the optimum allocation of funds between current and long-lived assets?

6. Management of the ABC Corporation estimates that it will need $1,000,000 in additional net working capital to finance a 5 percent increase in sales. It expects the 5 percent increase to be a minimum

gain.   Sales could increase by as much as 20 percent.   If this happens, net working capital requirements will rise to $5,000,000.   Management is considering three possibilities.   First, it will not try to accommodate any increase in sales beyond the 5 percent which is now virtually certain. Second, it will set aside $4,000,000 to help finance additional inventory, but will not purchase the inventory until it is apparent that sales are increasing.   Third, it will purchase the inventory on the assumption that sales will rise by 20 percent rather than 5 percent.   Discuss the implications of pursuing each course of action.   What information must you have available in order to select from among the three options? How would you organize this information?

SELECTED REFERENCES

Beranek, William.   *Working Capital Management*.   Belmont, Calif.: Wadsworth Publishing Company, Inc., 1966.
Park, Colin, and John W. Gladson.   *Working Capital*.   New York: The Macmillan Company, 1963.

Cash Management

chapter Nine

In developing the principles of working capital management, we pointed out that the details of the primary categories of current assets were sufficiently diverse to warrant separate treatment. Thus we shall discuss in this chapter the principles of cash management. The student will find it useful to relate the material presented to the factors determining the optimum level of permanent working capital.

Introduction

In the previous chapter we discussed in a general way the problems posed in determining the optimum level of net working capital. We held constant the level and composition of fixed assets as well as the capital structure, save for increases resulting from current liabilities to finance seasonal needs. In this and the next two chapters we shall

163

discuss the problems involved in managing specific categories of current assets, beginning with the management of cash.

The Demand for Money

To a captain of industry whose memory is scarred by the Great Depression, the height of impudence must be the suggestion from a bright young controller that the firm's cash balance is above what is necessary to meet current and anticipated needs.   Yet the rising trend in interest rates has reached such a level that a firm whose cash is above what is required to meet bills as they come due, and assuage the bank's demand for compensating balances against loans, may be impairing growth in profits.   If so, management may be failing to maximize the market value of ownership interests.

When funds are temporarily idle because they are not needed to finance inventory and receivables or because they are soon to be utilized in expanding long-lived assets, they may be placed in marketable securities, used to reduce short-term debt more rapidly than anticipated, or else left as idle cash.   The first two uses of funds are revenue-producing or cost-saving and therefore contribute to the profitability of the firm.   The third does not.

But if idle cash is unproductive, would it not be better to lower the balance to zero and use the funds to reduce short-term debt and/or purchase marketable securities in such a way as to best contribute to the long-run goal of the firm?   In theory the answer is yes, but short-run contingencies may make it necessary to have some cash on hand. The famous British economist John Maynard Keynes argued that people hold cash for three reasons: the transactions motive, the precautionary motive, and the speculative motive.[1]   Applying these classifications to the firm, management has cash on hand in order to meet current cash obligations or those due within the very near future.   In other words, the firm holds cash to satisfy its transactions demand for resources used in the production process.

The firm also holds cash as a precaution against uncertainty. Here the subjective element bulks large.   The allusion to the young controller and his superior is a case in point.   Presumably the former views the future with considerably more optimism than the latter.   The controller, if he does not anticipate using the funds to increase inventory, receivables, or long-lived assets, may suggest that they be distributed as cash dividends or used to reduce debt.

[1]John Maynard Keynes, *The General Theory of Employment, Interest, and Money* (New York: Harcourt, Brace and Company, Inc., 1935), p. 170.

Making a decision of this nature, of course, involves us in the dividend and capital structure policy of the firm.   While we shall consider these topics later, we should note here that the decision as to whether to retain what in the eyes of the controller is an excessive cash balance or to reduce the debt ratio or raise dividends should be made on the basis of the impact of these policies on the market value of the owners' equity.   Presumably the controller's superior views the future with greater pessimism.   Perhaps anticipating a cyclical decline in demand, he may argue that the firm already has an excessive stock of finished goods on hand.   If the goods cannot be sold, then the additional cash is necessary to liquidate short-term liabilities which would normally be paid out of receivables.   If he believes that the sales forecast is overly optimistic, he will be unmoved by the argument that a portion of the cash balance is redundant.

In so doing, he is giving his view as to what should be the optimum level and composition of working capital.   We argued in the last chapter that the optimum level of working capital is a function of the expected utility of the outcome.   Moreover, we noted that the outcome itself is a function of the composition of working capital.   Do we hold funds as cash?   Invest them in inventory?   If we invest funds in inventory, when in the course of the operating cycle do we make the decision to alter the composition of working capital?   If we wait too long, we risk the loss of sales and hence profit.   If we move too early, we risk carrying a level of inventory much of which can be sold only at a substantial loss, if at all.

But are the controller and his superior debating the cash needs within a framework which ensures, whatever the choice, that the firm will remain solvent, or is the latter fearful that a reduction in cash not only will impair the profitability of the firm but will threaten its liquidity as well?   While we should have greater confidence in forecasts based on short-term rather than long-term projections, it still may be difficult to tell in any given instance whether a decision to distribute a particular amount of cash to the owners will threaten the firm's solvency.

The explanation for the uncertainty is relatively easy.   In the first place, while the firm may anticipate the maximum amount of bank loans available to finance its peak investment in working capital, there is always the possibility that a new source of funds can be found if the needs are underestimated.   Management may have to resort to a finance company or to some more unconventional lender, usually at higher costs. On the other hand, management might even be able to get an extension of terms from the firm supplying its inventory.   Second, even if management overestimates demand and inventories pile up, the merchandise can often be sold though not at the anticipated price.

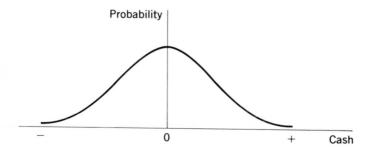

Figure 9-1 Probability distribution of cash outlays.

Thus additional financing may be had but often at higher costs, and excessive inventories may be liquidated but usually at lower than anticipated prices.   Liquidity is threatened only if one of these factors or a combination of the two results in a level of cash insufficient to meet obligations as they come due.

Assume that each year the factors affecting total revenues and total costs are such that the probability that total cash costs will exceed total cash revenues is the same as the probability that total cash revenues will exceed total cash costs. Then the probability distribution of cash outlays would be as in Figure 9-1.

As a practical matter, of course, we must exclude the area under the wings of the normal curve, that is, the outside chance that a very high cash figure, positive or negative, will occur.   Let us therefore assume that the chances are 1 out of 100 that either total cash costs will exceed total cash revenues by more than a given amount or total cash revenues will exceed total cash costs by more than the same figure.

We can graph the expected revenue and expense functions for the coming year as in Figure 9-2.

Between outputs *OB* and *OD*, the firm earns a profit, that is, its total revenues cover both cash and noncash costs.   At output *OC*, the firm maximizes total profit.   This is the point, you recall, where marginal cost equals marginal revenue.   Between outputs *OA* and *OE*, there is sufficient revenue to cover cash costs.[2]   Below output *OA*, there is insufficient revenue to cover cash costs.   Above output *OE*, costs rise so rapidly relative to sales that revenue is again insufficient to cover cash costs.   In terms of the probability distribution assumed in Figure 9-1, the odds are just as great that the outcome for the year will

[2]The student of economics should not confuse cash costs with variable costs. The latter are solely a function of output. Even if the firm produces nothing in the short run, it may experience cash costs such as maintenance as well as salaries of the staff and management personnel.

lie outside the range of output between *OA* and *OE* in Figure 9-2 as within it.

To use hypothetical figures, suppose the chances were 1 out of 100 that total cash costs could exceed total cash revenues by $100,000 or 1 out of 100 that total cash revenues could exceed total cash costs by $100,000. Ignoring the outside chance that cash outflows might be greater than $100,000, the firm might try to maintain at all times a cash balance equal to this amount.

But cash has an opportunity cost—that is, it can be invested in operating assets, marketable securities, or assets or securities of other firms; it can be used to reduce debt; or it can be returned to the owners to do with as they please. The greater the return on other investments, the greater the cost of debt, or the greater the satisfaction the owners attach to current income, the larger will be the incentive to reduce cash balances. If this is done, however, the firm increases its chances of being unable to meet obligations as they come due.

The differences of opinion between the controller and his superior may reflect differences as to the risk each is willing to incur. Alternatively, each may be viewing the outcomes in terms of a different probability distribution. The controller sees the odds against total cash

Figure 9-2

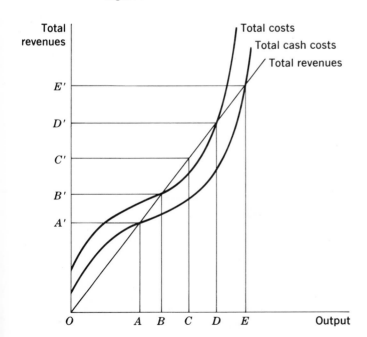

costs exceeding total cash revenues as so small relative to the existing cash balance that cash holdings could be reduced and not affect liquidity in a statistically significant way.[3]   His superior apparently does not share this view.

To the extent that the views of the owners are represented by the controller, the cash, if it cannot be profitably invested elsewhere or if the cost of debt is relatively low, should be returned to the shareholders. To the extent that the owners' views are represented by the controller's superior, the cash should be retained in the firm.

Investing in Marketable Securities

Besides holding cash for transaction and precautionary motives, individuals often retain cash as an alternative to investing these funds in securities.   As the yield rises, that is, as the market value of the securities falls, these individuals reduce their cash balances and increase their holdings of financial instruments.   As the yield falls, that is, as the market value of the securities rises, there is less incentive to purchase additional instruments and a greater incentive to liquidate investments on which one can realize capital gains.   Thus a portion of the cash balances is held to satisfy a speculative motive.

When applied to a business firm, however, we must modify the concept so as to distinguish between marketable securities and operating assets.   When applied to the latter, the speculative motive represents the trade-off between cash and the profits expected from investing in long-lived assets, inventory, or receivables.   Marketable securities should be viewed as an alternative to cash for funds temporarily un-employed because of seasonal or cyclical declines in demand.   The greater the yield, the greater the incentive to invest these funds rather than hold them as cash.

Nevertheless, marketable securities are not a risk-free alternative to cash.   Should costs suddenly rise, there would be an increase in the transactions demand for cash.   Should sales increase unexpectedly, management would have to use some of the firm's cash to purchase inventories and accommodate receivables.   In order to accommodate these needs, marketable securities may have to be sold prior to maturity and at a possible loss.   Yet to the extent that the yield on these instru-

---

[3]Statistically significant, in this context, should be interpreted to mean that there is a small chance, say 1 out of 200, that random forces will affect costs and revenues in such a way that the cash balance will be inadequate to meet current obligations.   The controller, however, accepts this risk.

ments rises, so does the incentive to accept a greater risk by reducing cash balances and investing more funds in short-term securities.

It is possible, of course, to find investments which are virtually risk-free. The 91-day Treasury bill is perhaps the best example. There are a sufficient number of these issues outstanding so that one issue matures every Thursday, save for holiday adjustments.[4] There is a well-developed secondary market in these instruments. Assuming that the return more than covers the cost of acquiring bills, a firm can keep its cash balance only as low as the projected needs for the next week permit. In these circumstances, even funds which would ordinarily be held as cash balances to satisfy the precautionary motive may be invested in risk-free alternatives.

In summary, therefore, while management may hold cash to satisfy its transactions, precautionary, and speculative motives, it will do so all the time to satisfy the transactions demand. To the extent that a risk-free alternative is available in income-earning marketable securities, management can reduce accordingly the balance it holds for precautionary motives. Finally, funds which would ordinarily be invested in operating assets,[5] but which are temporarily unemployed, should not be held as idle cash but invested in marketable securities.

In light of the above analysis, we are now ready to modify our earlier attempt to project permanent working capital needs for the coming year. Implicit in the discussion was the fact that cash was held for transactions purposes only. We must now recognize the possibility that there are insufficient risk-free alternatives or that those available do not provide sufficient income to cover the cost of purchasing them. Thus there will probably be some cash held as idle balances to satisfy precautionary motives. Moreover, when the long-term funds invested in working capital were temporarily unemployed, it was implicitly assumed that they would be invested in marketable securities. Finally, management would know when the outcome differed from expectations, because its cash balance would be different from its cash forecast. If the cash balance is lower than expected, then management will take appropriate steps to increase it. If the balance is greater than necessary to satisfy the transactions and precautionary motives, then management will reduce it accordingly.

---

[4]Edward J. Mock, "The Art of Investing Corporate Cash," in Edward J. Mock (ed.), *Readings in Financial Management* (Scranton, Pa.: International Textbook Company, 1964), p. 107.

[5]While we have in mind current assets associated with operations, that is, receivables and inventories, we do not in reality exclude long-lived assets. Thus, because of a cyclical decline in demand, a firm may not invest depreciation allowances immediately in replacing plant and equipment but will employ them in marketable securities.

	January	February	March
Receipts			
Cash Sales	$ 400,000	$ 300,000	$ 500,000
Collection of Receivables	1,100,000	300,000	200,000
Proceeds from Short-term Loans			
Total Receipts	**$1,500,000**	**$ 600,000**	**$ 700,000**
Disbursements			
Wages and Salaries	$ 500,000	$ 500,000	$ 500,000
Insurance	10,000		
Utilities	1,000	1,000	1,000
Taxes		50,000	200,000
Liquidation of Trade Credit			100,000
Liquidation of Short-term Loans	500,000		
Interest on Debt	4,000		
Dividends	25,000		
Total Disbursements	**$1,040,000**	**$ 551,000**	**$ 801,000**
Cash Available	$ 460,000	$ 49,000	–S 101,000
Cash Balance at Beginning of Month	150,000	610,000	659,000
Cash Balance at End of Month	$ 610,000	$ 659,000	$ 558,000
Less Precautionary Balance	−50,000	−50,000	−50,000
Funds Available for Investment in Marketable Securities or Held as Compensating Balances	**$ 560,000**	**$ 609,000**	**$ 508,000**

Cash Forecast

Projecting cash receipts and expenses can be done on any convenient basis.   We shall use a monthly forecast for next year of the cash budget for the ABC Corporation.   To keep cash receipts and disbursements manageable, we shall include only major receipts and expense items, assuming that these are the only sources and disbursements of cash anticipated for the year.   Moreover, we shall further assume that the differences between cash receipts and expenses represent funds not currently needed to satisfy the transactions demand for cash.   Finally, we shall continue to employ our earlier assumption that the level of fixed assets and the capital structure remain constant.   This still permits temporary changes in short-term loans to meet seasonal needs.

	April	May	June
Receipts			
Cash Sales	$ 300,000	$ 200,000	$ 300,000
Collection of Receivables	400,000	400,000	350,000
Proceeds from Short-term Loans			
Total Receipts	$ 700,000	$ 600,000	$ 650,000
Disbursements			
Wages and Salaries	$ 500,000	$ 500,000	$ 500,000
Insurance	10,000		
Utilities	1,000	1,000	1,000
Taxes			100,000
Liquidation of Trade Credit	50,000		
Liquidation of Short-term Loans			
Interest on Debt			
Dividends	25,000		
Total Disbursements	$ 586,000	$ 501,000	$ 601,000
Cash Available	$ 114,000	$ 99,000	$ 49,000
Cash Balance at Beginning of Month	558,000	672,000	771,000
Cash Balance at End of Month	$ 672,000	$ 771,000	$ 820,000
Less Precautionary Balance	−50,000	−50,000	−50,000
Funds Available for Investment in Marketable Securities or Held as Compensating Balances	$ 622,000	$ 721,000	$ 770,000

Given these assumptions, the ABC Corporation anticipates that its cash receipts and disbursements for each month during the coming year will be as in the accompanying tabulations.

As in the case of the toy manufacturer in the last chapter, the ABC Corporation has a seasonal pattern to its sales which is reflected in the rise and fall of its cash balances. Assume for the time being that $50,000 is needed to satisfy management's precautionary motives. Even then, early in the year, as receivables from the Christmas peak are liquidated, there are more than enough funds to meet the transactions demand for cash.

Cash balances are sufficient to purchase inventories and to satisfy demand during the next several months. There is no need to resort to short-term loans to cover cash expenses. By the end of September,

	July	August	September
Receipts			
Cash Sales	$ 100,000	$ 150,000	$ 375,000
Collection of Receivables	200,000	150,000	100,000
Proceeds from Short-term Loans			
Total Receipts	**$ 300,000**	**$ 300,000**	**$ 475,000**
Disbursements			
Wages and Salaries	$ 500,000	$ 500,000	$ 500,000
Insurance	20,000		
Utilities	1,000	1,000	1,000
Taxes		100,000	175,000
Liquidation of Trade Credit			
Liquidation of Short-term Loans			
Interest on Debt	2,000		
Dividends	25,000		
Total Disbursements	**$ 548,000**	**$ 601,000**	**$ 676,000**
Cash Available	−$ 248,000	−$ 301,000	−$ 201,000
Cash Balance at Beginning of Month	820,000	572,000	271,000
Cash Balance at End of Month	$ 572,000	$ 271,000	$ 70,000
Less Precautionary Balance	−50,000	−50,000	−50,000
Funds Available for Investment in Marketable Securities or Held as Compensating Balances	**$ 522,000**	**$ 221,000**	**$ 20,000**

however, the available cash balance has dipped to $20,000. Short-term loans are necessary to finance cash disbursements for the next two months. Although cash balances rise, they reflect the extension of bank credit. By December the firm is beginning to repay its loans.

Besides needing a sufficient amount of cash to help finance inventories and receivables, the ABC Corporation expects to pay $500,000 a month in wages and salaries to its regular employees. Seasonal help needed during November and December will raise this amount to $629,000 and $650,000, respectively. There are also periodic expenses such as quarterly insurance premiums of $10,000 and an additional annual premium of $10,000 due in July.[6] There are also quarterly tax

---

[6]Even if the premiums represent a prepaid expense, we are interested in the cash outlay, not the accounting treatment.

	October	November	December
Receipts			
Cash Sales	$ 300,000	$ 337,000	$ 850,000
Collection of Receivables	100,000	300,000	550,000
Proceeds from Short-term			
Loans	250,000	650,000	
Total Receipts	**$ 650,000**	**$1,287,000**	**$1,400,000**
Disbursements			
Wages and Salaries	$ 500,000	$ 629,000	$ 650,000
Insurance	10,000		
Utilities	1,500	1,500	1,500
Taxes			250,000
Liquidation of Trade Credit	100,000	600,000	300,000
Liquidation of Short-term			
Loans			210,000
Interest on Debt			2,500
Dividends	25,000		
Total Disbursements	**$ 636,500**	**$1,230,500**	**$1,414,000**
Cash Available	$ 13,500	$ 56,500	−$ 14,000
Cash Balance at Beginning			
of Month	70,000	83,500	140,000
Cash Balance at End			
of Month	$ 83,500	$ 140,000	$ 126,000
Less Precautionary Balance	−50,000	−50,000	−50,000
Funds Available for Investment in Marketable Securities or Held as Compensating Balances	**$ 33,500**	**$ 90,000**	**$ 76,000**

installments of varying amounts as well as semiannual interest payments of $2,000 on long-term debt payable in January and July. The remaining interest is on short term debt which is due when the loans are liquidated.

Management also expects to pay quarterly dividends of $25,000. Monthly expenses for utilities have been left constant except for a seasonal increase in the last quarter. We can assume that the seasonal pattern of sales requires that the firm be opened longer. As a result there is an increase in the electricity, heating, and telephone expenses.[7]

Since the minimum level of net working capital required was

[7]While heating expenses are seasonal, so are costs of using air conditioning. In our example, the implication is that one replaces the other in the outlays for utilities, with the increase in the total outlay due to the seasonal pattern of demand.

based on the seasonal peak, we might infer from the figures that it occurs sometime during November. By that time the ABC Corporation expects to have incurred $900,000 in short-term bank loans to finance inventories and receivables. If we assume that $510,000 in trade credit has not been liquidated and that wages and utility services are presently current liabilities, then the working capital figures at some point in November may appear as follows:

Current Assets	
Cash	$ 1,280,500
Marketable Securities	
Receivables	500,000
Total Inventories	900,000
Total Current Assets	**$2,680,500**
Current Liabilities	
Wages and Salaries Payable	$ 629,000
Utility Services Payable	1,500
Accounts Payable	510,000
Loans Payable	900,000
Total Current Liabilities	**$2,040,500**
Net Working Capital	**$ 640,000**

Suppose that $900,000 is the maximum the bank would lend on the projected balance of receivables and inventories. (The latter, of course, are listed at their replacement cost.) Then if all liabilities were liquidated except the $900,000 in loans, there would be $140,000 in cash. If $90,000 reflects compensating balances of, say, 10 percent, and $50,000 reflects precautionary balances, then at this time all cash is fully utilized. We shall assume that, from this moment, the ABC Corporation expects to experience an increase in cash sufficient to allow management to meet further expenses, including increases in accounts payable resulting from additions to inventories.

The projected monthly balances after allowances for the transactions and precautionary demands for cash are shown in Figure 9-3. The shaded areas for October and December represent the difference between the cash available for investment in marketable securities and the amount held for compensating balances. We shall assume that the bank finds it less costly in terms of its bookkeeping expenses and portfolio decisions to have the ABC Corporation borrow and repay its loans in multiples of $10,000. By the end of October, compensating balances

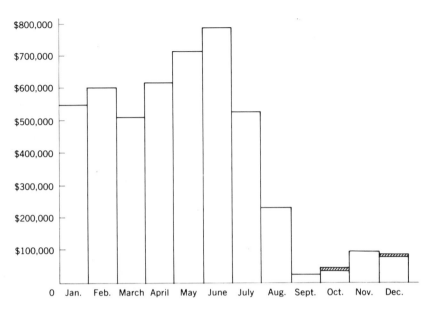

$800,000
$700,000
$600,000
$500,000
$400,000
$300,000
$200,000
$100,000
0   Jan.   Feb.   March   April   May   June   July   Aug.   Sept.   Oct.   Nov.   Dec.

Figure 9-3   Projected monthly cash balances of the ABC Corporation after allowances for the precautionary and transactions demands for cash.

are $25,000, i.e., 10 percent of $250,000. By the end of November, compensating balances have risen to $90,000, i.e., 10 per cent of $250,000 plus $650,000, or $900,000. However, during December, the company repays $210,000, thereby lowering its compensating balances to $69,000, i.e., 10 percent of $900,000 less $210,000 or $690,000. Thus, there are small amounts of unallocated cash for October and December. These amounts are, respectively, $8,500, i.e., $33,500 less $25,000 and $7,000, i.e., $76,000 less $69,000.

The chart reveals that from January through July the cash balance available to satisfy the firm's speculative motive does not fall below $500,000. These are, of course, end-of-month balances. The cash will begin to rise toward $500,000 during the month. Similarly, it will fall below $500,000 sometime during August. In the interim, the lowest level to which the supply of available cash will fall is $508,000 at the end March. Thus the ABC Corporation has this amount available for a period in excess of six months.

In fact, of this amount, $221,000 will still be available at the end of August and $20,000 at the end of September. This means that the latter figure could be invested in instruments with maturities of between 8 and 9 months, the difference (or $201,000) in maturities of 7 to 8 months, and the remainder (or $287,000) in maturities of 6 to 7 months. The actual pattern of maturities will depend on the time of the month the funds are received and the date at which they must be employed in the operations.

But the available cash balance in January is $560,000, not $508,000. Since the other $52,000 will not be needed until March, management can invest it in maturities of up to 2 months.   Between January and February the cash balance rises by another $49,000.   These funds are available for investment in securities maturing within a month or less.   These securities are liquidated during March to satisfy the rising transactions demand for cash.

By April there is a second and even longer upward trend in cash balances culminating in a decline in cash to $522,000 by the end of July. As the cash balance rises in April, $14,000 — that is, $522,000 less $508,000 — can be invested in maturities of up to 4 months.   The remainder of the $122,000 increase anticipated in April, or $108,000, can be allocated to maturities of up to 3 months.   From April to May and from May to June there are increases in cash balances of $99,000 and $49,000, respectively. These can be used to purchase, respectively, maturities of up to 2 and of 1 month.   The schedules are summarized in Table 9-1.

TABLE 9-1:   MATURITY SCHEDULE FOR MARKETABLE SECURITIES FOR ABC CORPORATION BASED ON PROJECTED CASH BALANCES AFTER ALLOWANCES FOR PRECAUTIONARY AND TRANSACTIONS MOTIVES

Months	Amount Available	Maximum Maturities
January to September	$ 20,000	9 months
January to August	201,000	6–8 months
January to July	287,000	6 months
January to March	52,000	2 months
January to February	49,000	1 month
April to July	14,000	4 months
April to June	108,000	3 months
May to June	99,000	2 months
June only	49,000	1 month

How close should the maturity date correspond to the date on which the funds are needed for transactions purposes?   In principle they should coincide; or at least the difference should be no greater than the time required to convert the securities into cash.   Yield is ordinarily a function of maturity.   The market risk in having to sell prior to maturity is, if the projections are reliable, nonexistent.   Moreover, to the extent that liquidation is forced, the closer the instrument is to maturity, the smaller will be the differential between the market price and the principal due.   Finally, there is, recall, a cash balance of

$50,000, the function of which is to protect the firm against changes in the transactions demand for cash resulting from unexpected increases in sales or costs. In light of these considerations, management would be failing to maximize the market value of the owners' equity if it did not plan its maturity dates in accordance with projected cash needs.

Let us now return to the rationale underlying the precautionary demand for cash. In the example employed, the primary purpose of this cash reserve, we must assume, is to provide management with a ready supply of funds during the peak period, that is, when marketable securities are at a minimum or nonexistent and cash is invested in inventories or receivables. It is at this point that errors in projecting sales and costs can have their greatest impact on the ability of the firm to finance these assets or to maintain its liquidity should the planned-for sales fail to materialize. For most of the year, the risks involved are not the same. It is possible therefore to argue that at least some of the funds set aside for precautionary motives might be invested in market-able securities at times when they are less likely to be needed. More-over, to the extent that the cash needs can be forecasted with certainty, say in 1- or 2-week intervals, management, if it finds it profitable, can invest the precautionary balances in Treasury bills maturing within this period.

Finally, we should note that we have ignored the small amounts of additional cash available in October and December. To the extent that the ABC Corporation can use these funds to repay loans, it should do so. The interest on the loan is ordinarily greater than the return on marketable securities. If management knows that the bank finds it no more convenient, that is, no more costly, to have the company borrow and repay loans in the amounts needed than in multiples of $10,000, then it will limit its cash deposits during this period to the sum of the compensating and uninvested precautionary balances. Otherwise it will invest the residual in short-term securities.

The Composition of Marketable Securities

From our analysis of the forces affecting the cash balances of most nonfinancial enterprises, we can conclude that the bulk of their port-folio of marketable securities consists of investments which mature within a year. There are in general three categories into which these instruments fall: obligations of the federal government, time deposits of commercial banks, and open-market paper. The changes in the relative importance of these instruments in relation to one another and to cash can be seen for selected years from the balance-sheet data for nonfinancial corporations given in Table 9-2.

TABLE 9-2: LIQUID ASSETS OF NONFINANCIAL CORPORATIONS FOR SELECTED YEARS
(Absolute Magnitudes in Billions of Dollars)

Asset	1953 Amount[a]	1953 Percent of Total	1960 Amount[a]	1960 Percent of Total	1966 Amount[a]	1966 Percent of Total	1967 Amount[a]	1967 Percent of Total
Currency and Demand Deposits	28.9	54.8	32.1	56.0	28.7	40.1	27.9	38.0
Time Deposits	.9	1.7	2.8	4.9	18.6	26.0	22.7	30.9
U.S. Government Securities	21.4	40.6	19.5	34.0	15.3	21.4	12.7	17.3
Open-market Paper	1.4	2.7	2.9	5.1	9.0	12.6	10.4	14.1
Total	52.7	100.0	57.3	100.0	71.5	100.0	73.5	100.0

SOURCE: Board of Governors of the Federal Reserve System, *Flow of Funds Accounts 1945–1967*, pp. 161–162.
[a]Because of errors in rounding, the total may not equal the sum of the parts.

Obligations of Federal Government Until recently, obligations of the federal government were the most popular instruments. Because of their relative safety and the fact that there are one or more issues maturing every week, they provide a convenient haven for short-term funds. The marketable portion of the government debt is divided into two components.[8] The first is composed of Treasury bills. Besides the 91-day instruments issued every Thursday, there are 181-day bills also issued regularly every Thursday. Each issue is sold at a discount from the par or face value. Thus it bears no interest rate, yet the holder in collecting the face amount at maturity earns a return on his investment. A 91-day Treasury bill, for example, might be selling at $98.75, that is, for every $98.75 invested, the holder will receive $100 at maturity. On an annual basis the bill is discounted at

$$1.25 \times \frac{360}{91} = 4.945\%$$

The reason for using 360 rather the 365 days is that commercial banks employ a 360-day year to determine discount, and Treasury bills are quoted at bank discount rates. To adjust the rate to an annual discount we would have to multiply the bank rate by the ratio of calendar year to the bank year, so that

$$4.945 \times \frac{365}{360} = 5.014\%$$

The yield to maturity on this Treasury bill would be the discount

[8]G. Walter Woodworth, *The Money Market and Monetary Management* (New York: Harper & Row, Publishers, Inc., 1965), pp. 74–78.

rate times face value, or 100 divided by the discounted price. Thus

$$5.014 \times \frac{100}{100 - 5.014} = 5.038\%$$

Besides regular Treasury bills, the Treasury employs tax-anticipation bills which are marketed so as to mature near the quarterly due dates, that is, the middle of March, June, September, and December. Corporations can purchase these bills as an offset against taxes payable. They will mature as the taxes are due and hence are acceptable to the Treasury in payment of taxes.

A second group of instruments is composed of Treasury certificates, notes, and bonds. Ordinarily, certificates are issued in maturities not exceeding 1 year, notes in maturities of 1 to 5 years, and bonds in maturities exceeding 5 years. These distinctions are conventional. However, notes and bonds may be and sometimes are issued in any desired maturity.[9]

Unlike Treasury bills, certificates, notes, and bonds are all interest-bearing instruments. The rate is a function of the face or par value. A 4 percent bond, for example, is 4 percent of $1,000, or $40. If this is below the going rate on government issues, then the bond will sell at a discount from par. To illustrate, suppose that a note due in one year had a stated interest rate of 5 percent with interest payable at maturity. But securities of the government maturing within a year were yielding $5\frac{1}{2}$ percent. The market price of the bond would be

$$\frac{\$1,050}{1.055} = \$995.26$$

Since bonds are quoted as though they are $100 denominations, the price would be $99.526. In Table 9-3 we show the Treasury selection available on Wednesday, March 27, 1968. For any corporation, besides the full selection of Treasury bills, there is also the selection of a few issues of notes and bonds which may mature within the time span during which funds are available. Within its projected schedule of maturities, the firm should select those issues which have the highest yield to maturity.

If it does this, however, management should note one complication. This can be illustrated by looking at two U.S. Treasury notes, the first maturing in August, 1968, the second in October. On the basis of face value, the interest rate on the first is 4.25 percent, but on the second only 1.5 percent. Yet the latter issue sells to yield a lower return than the first, that is, 4.65 as against 5.31. The reason for this

[9]*Ibid.*, p. 78.

is that a corporation buying the August maturity not only pays income taxes on the interest earned but, because it held the bond for less than 6 months, pays this tax at the same rate on the capital gains.   If it buys the October maturity, the difference between the purchase price and

TABLE 9-3:   TREASURY BILLS, NOTES, AND BONDS

Wednesday, March 27, 1968
Over-the-Counter Quotations: Source on request.
Decimals in bid-and-asked and bid change represent 32nds (101.1 means 101 1-32).   a-Plus 1-64.   b-Yield to call date.   c-Certificates of indebtedness.   d-Minus 1-64.

Treasury Bonds			Bid	Asked	Bid Chg.	Yld.
$3\frac{7}{8}$s,	1968	May.	99.26	99.28	...	4.78
$3\frac{3}{4}$s,	1968	Aug.	99.11	99.13	+.1	5.31
$3\frac{7}{8}$s,	1968	Nov.	99.3	99.5	+...	5.25
$2\frac{1}{2}$s,	1963–68	Dec.	98.12	98.14	...	4.75
4s,	1969	Feb.	98.26	98.30	+.1	5.25
$2\frac{1}{2}$s,	1964–69	June	96.30	97.2	...	5.02
4s,	1969	Oct.	97.24	97.28	+.1	5.49
$2\frac{1}{2}$s,	1964–69	Dec.	95.25	95.25	...	5.02
$2\frac{1}{2}$s,	1965–70	Mar.	95.2	95.6	...	5.11
4s,	1970	Feb.	97.5	97.9	+.1	5.54
4s,	1970	Aug.	96.13	96.17	+.3	5.57
$2\frac{1}{2}$s,	1966–71	Mar.	92.29	93.5	...	5.01
4s,	1971	Aug.	94.28	95.4	+.1	4.60
$3\frac{7}{8}$s,	1971	Nov.	93.31	94.7	...	5.66
4s,	1972	Feb.	94.4	94.12	+.2	5.63
$2\frac{1}{2}$s,	1967–72	June	89.20	89.28	+.2	5.21
4s,	1972	Aug.	93.18	93.26	+.2	5.61
$2\frac{1}{2}$s,	1967–72	Sept.	88.30	89.6	+.2	5.25
$2\frac{1}{2}$s,	1967–72	Dec.	88.12	88.20	+.2	5.26
4s,	1973	Aug.	92.8	92.16	+.0	5.63
$4\frac{1}{8}$s,	1973	Nov.	92.12	92.20	+.2	5.67
$4\frac{1}{8}$s,	1974	Feb.	92.8	92.16	...	5.64
$4\frac{1}{4}$s,	1974	May	92.14	92.22	...	5.68
$3\frac{7}{8}$s,	1974	Nov.	90.14	90.22	+.2	5.57
4s,	1980	Feb.	84.16	85.0	...	5.76
$3\frac{1}{2}$s,	1980	Nov.	80.8	80.24	...	5.65
$3\frac{1}{4}$s,	1978–83	June	76.14	76.30	−.2	5.51
$3\frac{1}{4}$s,	1985	May	76.8	76.24	−.2	5.34
$4\frac{1}{4}$s,	1975–85	May	84.0	84.16	...	5.68
$3\frac{1}{2}$s,	1990	Feb.	76.4	76.20	...	5.32
$4\frac{1}{4}$s,	1987–92	Aug.	81.22	82.6	+.2	4.60
4s,	1988–93	Feb.	79.6	79.22	...	5.51
$4\frac{1}{8}$s,	1989–94	May	79.22	80.6	+.2	5.57
3s,	1995	Feb.	75.28	76.12	...	4.53
$3\frac{1}{2}$s,	1998	Nov.	76.2	76.18	−.2	5.01

Table 9-3: (*Continued*)

U.S. Treas. Notes					U.S. Treas. Bills					
Rate	Mat	Bid	Asked	Yld	Mat	Bid	Ask	Mat	Bid	Ask
						Discount			Discount	
$1\frac{1}{2}$	4–68	99.27	99.31	5.28						
$4\frac{3}{4}$	5–68	99.30	100.0	4.67	3–31	6.75	5.45	7–18	5.23	5.07
$4\frac{1}{4}$	8–68	99.17	99.19	5.31	4–4	4.70	4.20	7–25	5.24	5.08
$1\frac{1}{2}$	10–68	98.10	98.14	4.65	4–11	4.75	4.25	7–31	5.23	5.08
$5\frac{1}{4}$	11–68	99.27	99.29	5.40	4–18	4.75	4.40	8–1	5.25	5.11
$5\frac{5}{8}$	2–69	99.30	100.0	5.63	4–22	4.75	4.50	8–8	5.25	5.11
$1\frac{1}{2}$	4–69	96.20	96.28	4.71	4–25	4.80	4.50	8–15	5.25	5.13
$5\frac{5}{8}$	5–69	99.28	99.30	5.68	4–30	4.77	4.50	8–22	5.26	5.12
$1\frac{1}{2}$	10–69	94.28	95.4	4.89	5–2	4.90	4.75	8–29	5.26	5.12
$1\frac{1}{2}$	4–70	93.4	93.16	4.94	5–9	4.95	4.80	8–31	5.26	5.13
$1\frac{1}{2}$	10–70	91.22	91.30	4.96	5–16	5.00	4.75	9–5	5.28	5.20
5	11–70	98.1	98.5	5.77	5–23	5.05	4.90	9–12	5.29	5.22
$5\frac{5}{8}$	2–71	98.28	99.4	5.71	5–31	5.05	4.90	9–19	5.31	5.26
$1\frac{1}{2}$	4–71	90.0	90.16	4.94	6–6	5.12	5.04	9–26	5.34	5.31
$5\frac{1}{4}$	5–71	98.10	98.18	5.76	6–13	5.12	5.05	9–30	5.30	5.12
$1\frac{1}{2}$	10–71	88.12	88.24	5.04	6–20	5.12	5.06	10–31	5.40	5.24
$5\frac{5}{8}$	11–71	98.20	98.28	5.72	6–24	5.14	5.10	11–30	5.39	5.32
$4\frac{3}{4}$	2–72	96.6	96.14	5.79	6–27	5.13	5.10	12–31	5.45	5.42
$1\frac{1}{2}$	4–72	86.28	87.28	4.87	6–30	5.17	5.03	1–31	5.42	5.28
$4\frac{3}{4}$	5–72	96.0	96.8	5.78	7–5	5.30	5.04	2–28	5.41	5.34
$1\frac{1}{2}$	10–72	85.26	86.26	4.79	7–11	5.20	5.05	3–31	5.53	5.49
$5\frac{3}{4}$	11–74	99.18	99.26	5.78						
$5\frac{3}{4}$	2–75	99.12	99.16	5.84						

SOURCE: *Wall Street Journal*, Mar. 28, 1968.   Reprinted by permission.

the principal received at maturity is subject to a capital gains tax.   It need pay only the regular rates on the interest income.

Time Deposits of Commercial Banks   Besides purchasing Treasury securities,[10] corporations have in recent years purchased an increasing proportion of negotiable certificates of deposit (CDs) which represent liabilities of commercial banks.   By the mid-1960s they had come to be the most important instrument in the portfolio of marketable securities held by nonfinancial corporations.   Although they existed for many years, certificates of deposit were infrequently employed prior to 1961.[11]   When used, they were rarely negotiable, that

[10]We can also include securities of agencies guaranteed by the federal government among the instruments purchased by nonfinancial corporations.   These include, among others, the Federal National Mortgage Association and the Federal Home Loan Banks.
[11]Richard Fieldhouse, "Certificates of Deposit," *Monthly Review*, Federal Reserve Bank of New York, vol. 45, no. 6 (June, 1963), pp. 82–87.   See also his *Certificates of Deposit* (Boston: The Bankers Publishing Company, 1962).

is, they were to be held by the purchaser to maturity or else redeemed by the bank.

However, as interest rates in the post-World War II period rose, financial managers began to find it profitable to reduce their cash balances to lower levels in relation to sales. In other words, the opportunity cost of funds was rising relative to the cost of having an insufficient volume of cash to accommodate unexpected increases in sales and costs. As commercial banks saw more of their customers' deposits being invested in United States government securities, they began to issue certificates of deposit, both negotiable and nonnegotiable, in large amounts. Although the CDs are of varying sizes, commercial banks have concentrated their attempts at attracting and holding business deposits by employing instruments of various maturities up to and in excess of a year. The CDs ordinarily issued to business firms have a face value in excess of $100,000. The most popular maturities are of 3 to 9 months. The fact that there is a well-developed secondary market adds to their attractiveness as does the yield of up to 6.25 percent permitted by the Federal Reserve Board in the late 1960s.[12]

Open-market Paper   Finally, nonfinancial corporations also invest in short-term open-market, or commercial, paper. Commerical paper "consists of short-term promissory notes issued by businesses and offered on the more or less impersonal open market."[13] Most of the issuers are nationally known concerns with prime credit ratings. Today the principal issuers are finance companies. The bulk of the maturities are within 30 to 270 days. Although they are sold in the same way as Treasury bills, i.e., at a discount from par, they yield a higher return and are therefore an attractive alternative to government issues.

In recent years it has not been unusual for short-term instruments, both government and private issues, to yield in excess of 7 percent, with the yields on federal securities, of course, in the lower end of the range.[14] While this is considerably above the bill rates in the early post-World War II period, it reflects a general increase in interest rates. It costs more to borrow funds. Moreover, business firms will usually find that the prime or lowest bank rate on short-term loans is above the

[12]Fieldhouse, "Certificates of Deposit," p. 83, table I; p. 85, table II; p. 86, table III; and Richard Fieldhouse, "Changes in Time and Savings Deposits, April–July 1967," *Federal Reserve Bulletin* (September, 1967), pp. 1488–1510. See also *Federal Reserve Bulletin*, August, 1969, p. A11.

[13]Richard T. Selden, *Trends and Cycles in the Commercial Paper Market* (New York: National Bureau of Economic Research, Inc., 1963), p. 1. See also Nevins D. Baxter, *The Commercial Paper Market* (Boston: The Bankers Publishing Company, 1966).

[14]*Federal Reserve Bulletin*, August, 1969, p. A33. During late 1969 both the rate on commercial paper and the prime rate on bank loans were in excess of 8 percent.

yield on short-term Treasury bills and commercial paper. If the latter is in the range of 6 to 6.75 percent, bank rates on short-term loans are usually in excess of 7 percent.

In closing we should note that nonfinancial corporations also invest in longer-term issues of government, particularly state and local governments. If, for example, a firm has funds which are cyclically unemployed or are being held for subsequent investment in long-lived assets, it may purchase maturities of a year or more. State and local governments issue longer-term instruments, and unlike the interest in federal issues, the interest on these is tax-exempt. Hence they provide an outlet for those funds which the company does not plan to use within the next year or longer.

SUMMARY

Keynes argued that individuals hold cash to satisfy transactions, precautionary, and speculative motives. To satisfy the first desire, management of a business firm holds cash to meet current obligations, including payment for resources used in the production process. The second motive reflects management's subjective attitude toward risk. It holds cash, in other words, to meet unforeseen contingencies.

The third motive reflects management's attitude toward alternative investments in operating assets as well as in marketable securities. The latter should be viewed as alternatives to cash for funds which are temporarily unemployed because of seasonal or cyclical declines in demand. The greater the yield, the greater is the incentive to invest these funds rather than hold them as cash.

To determine the optimum distribution of funds between cash and marketable securities, management must forecast its transactions and precautionary balances for the coming year and schedule the maturity dates accordingly.

While there are various short-term outlets for temporarily unemployed funds, U.S. Treasury obligations, certificates of deposit, and commercial paper are the most popular.

QUESTIONS AND PROBLEMS

1. After allowing for the transactions demand for cash, the LMN Corporation expects its cash balances for the next 12 months to be as follows.

	Cash Balance		Cash Balance
January	$1,000,000	July	$200,000
February	500,000	August	400,000
March	700,000	September	600,000
April	900,000	October	500,000
May	400,000	November	800,000
June	100,000	December	700,000

The precautionary demand for cash is $75,000. Establish a maturity schedule for investments in marketable securities. Is there any reason for assuming that cash balances are held for other than precautionary motives?

2. "The precautionary demand for cash is a function of the composition of current assets. Thus the level of cash held for this reason might change during the course of the year." Evaluate.

3. "If a firm experienced no seasonal pattern in sales, it would have no reason for investing in marketable securities." Do you agree? Explain fully.

4. "A high current-asset or quick-asset ratio is a sign of financial strength." Explain and evaluate.

5. "The demand for cash is a function of its opportunity cost." Evaluate.

SELECTED REFERENCES

Baxter, Nevins. *The Commercial Paper Market.* Boston: The Bankers Publishing Company, 1966.

Bierman, Harold, Jr., and Alan K. McAdams. *Management Decisions for Cash and Marketable Securities.* Ithaca, N.Y.: Cornell University, Graduate School of Business and Public Administration, 1962.

Bloch, Ernest. "Short Cycles in Corporate Demand for Government Securities and Cash," *American Economic Review,* vol. 53, no. 5 (December, 1963), pp. 1058–1077.

Fieldhouse, Richard. *Certificates of Deposit.* Boston: The Bankers Publishing Company, 1962.

Heston, Alan W. "An Empirical Study of Cash Securities and Other Current Accounts of Large Corporations," *Yale Economic Essays,* vol. 2, no. 1 (Spring, 1962), pp. 117–168.

Jacobs, Donald P. "The Marketable Security Portfolio of Nonfinancial Corporations: Investment Practices and Trends," *Journal of Finance,* vol. 15, no. 3 (September, 1960), pp. 341–352.

Law, Warren A., and M. Colyer Crum. "New Trends in Finance: The Negotiable C.D.," *Harvard Business Review,* vol. 41, no. 1 (January-February, 1963), pp. 115–126.

Mock, Edward J. "The Art of Investing Corporate Cash," in Edward J. Mock (ed.), *Readings in Financial Management*. Scranton, Pa.: International Textbook Company, 1964, pp. 101–116.

Pfloom, Norman E. *Managing Company Cash* (Studies in Business Policy No. 99). New York: National Industrial Conference Board, Inc., 1961.

Selden, Richard T. *Trends and Cycles in the Commercial Paper Market*. New York: National Bureau of Economic Research, Inc., 1963.

Accounts Receivable

chapter Ten

In dealing with receivables, the student should note the similarities as well as the differences in the principles of investing in consumer and trade credit as compared with long-lived assets. To what extent are receivables a working capital problem? To what extent are they a capital budgeting problem?

Introduction

The problem of receivables can be broken down into two elements. The first is the decision to extend credit. This is a capital budgeting problem. It can be viewed in three ways.

1. Management might assume that there is an outlay of funds equivalent to the replacement cost of the credit or collection facilities.

The net cash flow is the difference between the additional revenue anticipated and the periodic expenses associated with maintaining these facilities.

2. Alternatively, management might assume that an investment in receivables is a necessary condition for doing business at all. If it does assume this, and if it anticipates an increase in sales requiring an investment in long-lived assets, it will add to this outlay an amount representing additional investment in collection facilities and in working capital. The periodic expenses will be the sum of expenses associated with the investment in fixed assets as well as in receivables. The additional revenues will be equal to the sales volume expected from providing the goods or services and the privilege of charging them.

3. Again under the assumption that receivables are a necessary condition for doing business, management might assume, as we have, that long-lived assets, including the investment in credit facilities, can be held constant. In this case, the only additional outlay required is an increase in working capital.

Management in a given situation may find any of these alternatives relevant. Thus, if it has excess productive capacity relative to working capital, an increase in sales may necessitate an increase only in current assets. On the other hand, management may find that it must increase its investment in collection facilities as well as in working capital in order to finance an addition to the sales volume. If plant and equipment are at or near capacity, an anticipated increase in demand may require the need for additional capital outlay on production assets. It is also possible for the firm to have both excess capacity and excess working capital. In this case, an increase in sales would not involve a capital budgeting decision since the necessary capital to accommodate the rise is already available.

The second element in the problem of receivables is the question of their financing. Under our assumptions permanent increases in working capital to help finance receivables, as with additions to long-lived assets, are themselves financed out of proportional increases in debt and equity.[1] The permanent investment in current assets in turn allows management to use short-term loans to finance seasonal needs. The problem, therefore, is to determine the additional investment in

---

[1] Again we shall not tarry over the question of whether permanent increases in debt are short-term or long-term. As we shall learn in a subsequent chapter, so-called short-term sources may be relatively permanent. Some companies may be able to "roll over" their short-term bank loans by transferring them from one lender to another. The firm liquidates its loan from bank A by having it refinanced by bank B. When the loan matures the second time, perhaps bank C or even bank A will again refinance the firm. In this way, short-term debt is never completely liquidated. The balance rises and falls only with temporary needs.

working capital necessary to finance an increase in receivables expected from a rise in sales.

To illustrate, suppose that a company which makes only lawn mowers is considering expanding its product line to include snow-plows. From past experience, management knows that the firm's receivables reach their maximum in March. All of what would ordinarily be uninvested cash balances, save for those held for precautionary motives, are employed in financing this seasonal peak.[2] The firm's investment in receivables is 20 percent of their face value. The remaining 80 percent is financed through short-term loans from commercial banks.

If it also begins to produce snowplows, management anticipates a seasonal peak in this line of merchandise in October. Thus some of the working capital which would ordinarily be invested in marketable securities is now available for investing in receivables. In this case, the permanent addition to working capital is the sum of two components. First, is the increase, if any, in the funds needed to finance receivables in October over those required to finance receivables in March. Second, probably added to this amount is a sum representing an increase in precautionary balances.

There may be two reasons for an increase in precautionary balances. First, carrying additional receivables may entail a greater risk than when the funds were temporarily invested in marketable securities. If so, then in the eyes of management there is a greater probability that losses due to bad debts on a given sum invested in receivables would exceed losses due to market risks if the same sum were invested in short-term securities. Second, while we can assume that the permanent capital structure will remain the same, management must now rely on short-term loans of perhaps larger amounts and certainly over a longer period during the year.

Nevertheless, the permanent working capital needs in this case would probably be different and might possibly be smaller than if management had chosen to produce fertilizer spreaders for lawns. The reason, of course, is that the seasonal peak for fertilizer spreaders would overlap that for lawn mowers. Whether the needs would actually be smaller depends on factors other than their being complimentary items in production. We would have to compare the probability distribution of net cash flows from investing in snowplows with that from investing in fertilizer spreaders. There may be greater production risk in the former than in the latter. The savings in working capital

---

[2]Inventory, we shall assume, is at what management considers to be minimum levels. Otherwise some of the cash would be tied up in additional stock.

due to seasonal factors may be more than offset by an increase in precautionary balances held to compensate for the production of a riskier line of merchandise.

The Nature of Accounts Receivable

Receivables can be broken down into two classifications. The first consists of trade credit extended by one business firm to another, the manufacturer to the wholesaler or the wholesaler to the retailer, etc. While the firm extending credit recognizes it as a receivable, the recipient looks on it as a source of funds, that is, as an account payable. The second type of receivable consists of credit extended to consumers.

The reason for making the distinctions is that institutionally they can be treated differently. In the first place, the terms under which trade credit is granted usually differ from those under which consumer credit is granted. As we pointed out in an earlier chapter, trade credit is often extended so that there is a due date, a discount date, and a rate of discount. Thus the terms 2/10, net 30 give the recipient the option of a 2-percent discount if the bill for the goods or services rendered is paid within 10 days or no discount and the requirement that the entire amount be paid within 30 days.

While 2/10, net 30 is customary for many firms, some differences do exist. Those distributing perishable goods such as bakery products, fruits, meats, etc., often require cash on delivery. Also, the more competitive the industry, the larger the cash discounts and the longer the payment period. Various clothing manufacturers sometimes offer cash discounts as high as 8 percent. Some clothing manufacturers, as well as producers of furniture, paints, and electrical parts, are among those extending credit up to 60 days. Finally, the terms of trade vary with the size of the order. Large buyers receive greater discounts and perhaps a longer period before payment is due.[3]

The terms and conditions under which credit is extended to consumers are ordinarily different from those under which trade credit is granted. To be sure, there are similarities. As in the case of trade credit, for example, nonfinancial corporations may allow consumers 30 days and sometimes longer to pay the net amount. But here the similarity may end. Many stores, when they discount merchandise, often insist on cash payments. Others, of course, do extend the charge privilege to these items. For instance, a small men's clothing store may

[3]Martin H. Seiden, *The Quality of Trade Credit* (New York: National Bureau of Economic Research, Inc., 1964), p. 40.

hold semiannual cash sales in January and July.   The merchandise is
marked down perhaps 20 percent but the purchases cannot be charged.
At the same time, the men's clothing department of a large department
store may also be participating in such a sale.   Yet it allows its customers
to charge the items purchased even though they are marked down by
20 percent.   Thus the consumer may be getting both a cash discount
and the opportunity to charge, but rarely will he receive a discount on
bills paid within a certain period.

   More significant, perhaps, is the fact that there is usually some
form of service or finance charge attached to the unpaid balance.   This
is ordinarily not the case with trade credit.   On consumer debt, for
example,[4] a department store might attach a service charge of $1\frac{1}{2}$
percent a month on the unpaid balance of a customer's account; but
if the customer paid the amount due each month, there would be no
additional   charges.   Similarly,   nonfinancial   corporations   granting
longer-term credit in the form of loans on the consumer durables they
sell will "add on" a service charge.   Alternatively, the firm may quote
a cash price or propose a series of monthly payments the sum of which
is greater than the price of the goods.[5]

   For example, suppose that a person is considering buying a boat
from a large diversified retail outlet.   The company is willing to sell
him the boat for $1,057.53.   Alternatively it is willing to let him pay
for it under an installment contract calling for 12 equal monthly payments of $100.00.   If he chooses the latter plan, he is paying a total
of $1,200.   In other words, for the privilege of paying for the boat
over a 12-month period, the consumer must pay a service charge of
$142.47.   If we look at this as an interest payment, then the interest
rate on this loan is a function of the monthly payments.   Our formula

$$P = \frac{D[1 - (1 + r)^{-n}]}{r}$$

can be interpreted so that r is interest per month.   Hence $n = 12$. p is
the present value or purchase price of $1,057.53, while D is the monthly

   [4]Wallace P. Mors, *Consumer Credit Finance Charges: Rate Information and Quotation*
(New York: National Bureau of Economic Research, Inc., 1965), pp. 8–38.
   [5]The same applies to financial institutions such as finance companies and commercial
banks.   The rates stated may be dollars per hundred, percent of the cost, or, as in the example above, simply a monthly payment with the interest charges included.
   We should also note that while many nonfinancial corporations hold installment
contracts as receivables, they often sell them at a discount to banks or other institutions,
in some cases assuming and in other cases not assuming responsibility for deliquent
accounts.

payment of $100. Thus,

$$\$1,057.53 = \$100 \frac{[1-(1+r)^{-n}]}{r}$$

$$\frac{1-(1+r)^{-n}}{r} = \frac{\$1,057.53}{\$100} = 10.5753$$

From the table in Appendix B of this volume, we note that for $n = 12$, r for 10.5753 is 2 percent. On a per annum basis the interest rate is 12 times 2 percent, or 24 percent.

Installment contracts can, of course, be arranged in various ways. Repayments may be made in declining amounts. The entire service or finance charge may be included in the original payment. But whatever the terms, consumer loans often carry with them additional charges which, when reduced to simple interest payments, ordinarily result in rates substantially higher than interest rates on bank loans to help finance these receivables.

Periodically, these relatively high rates are called into question.[6] On the surface, therefore, receivables reflecting an extension of credit to consumers appear to be a relatively profitable outlet for working capital, while trade credit may be viewed as a necessary part of doing business. Perhaps this is indeed the case. However, before jumping to this conclusion, let us explore more fully the composition of the cash flows expected from extending credit to both business firms and consumers.

While there is no service charge attached to trade credit, it does not necessarily follow that there is no revenue gained from investing in receivables. Management may view a capital outlay to satisfy an anticipated increase in demand as consisting of an expansion in plant and equipment together with an increase in working capital to help finance receivables. Nevertheless, we can still conceptually separate the decisions by asking what the increase in sales would be if the firm did not extend trade credit. If the answer is that there would be some firms who would still purchase on a cash basis, then the problem is to determine the total revenues earned by the extension of credit and the amount expected by not granting this privilege. If the difference is positive, then, depending on the permanent working capital required,

[6]Mors, *op. cit.*, pp. 9–38. The assumption on which "truth in lending" legislation is postulated is that, from the way finance charges are quoted, such as 5 percent per $100 borrowed, consumers are led to believe that this is the effective rate of interest on the credit extended. But with the interest payments based on the original principal and not on the declining balance, the effective rate is much higher.

the costs associated with the receivables, and the cost of capital, the investment may be worthwhile.

To illustrate, assume that the QRS Corporation, a manufacturer, will increase its sales revenues by $1,000,000 each year for the next 3 years if it offers prospective purchasers terms of 2/10, net 30 on a new line of merchandise rather than insisting on cash sales. It is estimated that it will require $700,000 in additional working capital to help finance the increase in receivables. Although there is no need to expand the capital investment in the credit department, there will be cash costs of investigating the credit rating of a potential group of new customers who would be interested in the new line. Management also expects to hire additional personnel to process the receivables. Moreover, it must include in the periodic cash expenses the interest charges on short-term temporary loans used to finance the portion of receivables not covered by the permanent increase in working capital. The reason for this is that these loans are not a part of the permanent capital structure. Hence the interest on them is not included in the cost of capital. Let us assume that these and similar expenses amount to $500,000 per year. The cost of capital is 10 percent and there is no risk of bad debts. Then

$$\$700,000 = (\$1,000,000 - \$500,000)\left[\frac{1-(1+r)^{-3}}{r}\right]$$

$$\neq \$500,000\,(2.48685)$$

$$< \$1,243,425$$

Net present value $= \$543,425$

Since the present value is greater than the increase in working capital, management will find that granting the privilege of trade credit on a 2/10, net 30 basis will raise the market value of the owners' equity.

If management does not separate the investment in working capital and outlays for equipment to process receivables from the capital required to produce the goods or services, it is implicitly assuming that either or both cannot stand alone. For example, it may be that without the extension of credit, the net present value of the production facilities would be less than the replacement cost of these assets. Consequently, if the net present value of the combined investments is positive, then management would still sell, but only on open account.

However, suppose on the assumption that all sales are c.o.d., the net present value of an investment in production facilities is positive, while the net present value of an investment in receivables is negative. Under these conditions, the firm should refrain from extending credit and confine its activities to cash sales.

Trade and Consumer Credit—A Comparison of Differences

While the above analysis is applicable to both trade and consumer credit, there are differences in details. From our earlier discussion, we must include in the revenue earned on an investment in consumer credit not only the additional sales revenue from granting the privilege, but also the revenue representing service or finance charges.

From the revenue must be subtracted the cash costs associated with the investment. On a priori grounds these appear similar to the costs involved in trade credit. But there may be some subtle differences. For example, charge account privileges are ordinarily extended only after a thorough credit investigation. The four C's of credit—capacity, character, and capital of the borrower, together with conditions under which payment is made—provide the standard qualitative guides for determining the risk of incurring bad debts or delays in payments. In the case of trade credit, this can be accomplished with relative ease. Credit-rating services are readily available; Dun and Bradstreet, for example, provides detailed information in their *Reference Book* on about three million business firms. Subscribers to this service can obtain an estimate of the financial strength of most of the firms listed.

For individuals, however, credit references must be more informal. Other than the information given by the customer himself, probably the best source of information concerning a person's financial strength is his commercial bank. If he has charge accounts at other stores, they will provide an index of his ability to meet his obligations. So too will mortgage payments.

But even if the cost of a credit investigation is no greater for an individual than for a business firm, it usually takes many more such investigations for a given amount of consumer receivables than for the same volume of trade credit. Thus the cost per account receivable may be higher.

At the same time, the risk of a large loss due to the failure of a single account is smaller. This leads us to a second point. To what extent is the risk on consumer accounts similar to the risk on trade credit? One study indicated that during the 1947–1960 period, losses on trade credit may have been slightly greater than on credit extended to consumers by sales finance companies and commercial banks. On trade credit the average loss rate was 1.18 percent. For sales finance companies it averaged less than 1 percent and for commercial banks less than 0.17 percent.[7] However, the data on trade credit include retail and service corporations which sell to both businessmen and con-

[7]Seiden, *op. cit.*, p. 15 and p. 17, table 6, col. 3.

sumers. When these sectors are excluded from the data, the ratio of bad debts to total receivables for the same period averaged .94 percent.[8]

Moreover, as a rule, the closer the consumer is to the industry, the higher is the percentage of losses due to bad debts. The capital goods industries whose primary customers are manufacturers have the lowest loss experience. Manufacturers in turn have higher losses on receivables and their customers are largely wholesalers and retailers. Service industries have still larger bad-debt ratios, with retail trade having the highest of all. Thus, for the years 1947–1957, the ratio of bad-debt losses to outstanding receivables ranged from .53 to .65 percent for construction and mining corporations to 1.74 and 2.53 percent for services and retail trade concerns; for companies engaged in manufacturing and wholesale trade the range was between .81 and 1.32 percent, respectively.[9] In addition, credit losses are negatively correlated with the size of the firm; that is, the smaller the business corporation, the greater the ratio of bad debts to total receivables. For instance, a retail trade corporation with a relatively small sales volume might experience a bad-debt ratio of about 3.65 percent.[10]

On balance, therefore, the evidence seems to suggest that consumer credit granted by nonfinancial corporations may entail a greater risk than trade credit. Banks may experience a low loss ratio on their consumer loans because they skim off the best credit risks, offering them in many instances relatively low terms. Sales finance companies accept somewhat greater credit risks, while relatively small corporations under the pressures of competition sometimes assume even greater risks in order to sell goods and services.

Once the risk of bad debts or even delays in payments rises, so do the costs of servicing receivables. The rate at which receivables are turned into cash declines; that is, the length of time required to collect receivables increases. This in turn forces management to extend short-term loans to help finance receivables. As a result, interest payments on a given volume of receivables increase. In the interim, the credit department will take steps to collect these bills. This entails additional personnel or a fee paid to professional bill collectors. If unsuccessful, rather than incurring additional legal expenses, management may simply write off the debts as uncollectible.

Consequently, to the extent that there are greater risks as well as higher costs in investing in receivables representing consumer credit, even the additional revenue gained from the service charge may do no more than compensate for these risks and costs.

Besides considering the possibility that there are higher expenses

[8]*Ibid.*, p. 17, calculated from the data in table 17, col. 4.
[9]*Ibid.*, p. 19, table 7.
[10]*Ibid.*, p. 19.

associated with consumer credit, management must also question whether the volume of sales generated justifies a capital investment in collection facilities.   For many firms the answer is almost intuitively no.   For others the combination of the investment in credit facilities, the high unit costs of servicing relatively small accounts, the additional expenses involved in collecting these accounts, and the greater risk of loss results in management's refusal to invest in receivables.

Often the risk itself may be the factor leading to a negative decision. Suppose, for example, that for a small firm the most probable net present value from investing in receivables is $25,000 before an appropriate allowance for bad debts.[11]   It is also possible that the outcome could be as low as zero and as high as $50,000.   However, management expects bad debts to amount to as much as 3 percent of sales made on credit or as little as 1 percent, with the most probable outcome being 2 percent.   By subtracting the 2 percent from the most probable increase in sales resulting from investing in receivables, management finds that the expected net present value is $0.   Subtracting the most optimistic bad-debt allowance from the most optimistic sales forecast and the most pessimistic bad-debt allowance from the most pessimistic sales forecast, management finds that the net present value of an investment in receivables may be as high as $25,000 or as low as $-$35,000. The probability of occurrence in each case is .25.   The probability that the net present value will be zero is .5.   The utility of $0 is 0.   The utility of $25,000 is .15 while the utility of $-$35,000 is $-$.2.   Thus

$$
\begin{aligned}
\text{Expected utility} &= .25U(-\$35,000) + .5U(\$0) + .25(\$25,000) \\
&= .25(-.2) + .5(0) + .25(.15) \\
&= -.05 + 0 + .0375 \\
&= -.0125
\end{aligned}
$$

Since the expected utility of accepting the risk is negative, management will not invest in receivables but will confine its policy to cash sales, leaving consumers free to finance purchases through commercial banks or sales finance companies.[12]

---

[11]It is possible to reduce unusual or abnormal losses due to bad debts by using credit insurance.   For a full explanation, see Clyde William Phelps, *Commercial Credit Insurance as a Management Tool* (Baltimore: Commercial Credit Company, 1961).

[12]In between lies a void which commercial banks have tried to fill in recent years through charge cards issued to individuals.   Retailers honoring these cards, on presentation of the bills, will have their checking accounts credited with the face value of the sales.   The bank bills the purchasers directly.   The firm pays the prime rate, perhaps 6 percent on the funds lent to it.   This represents his customers' unpaid balances.   The bank in turn lets the consumer pay the bill in full within 30 days at no additional cost to him.   Otherwise he pays a monthly service charge on the unpaid balance.   Because small firms need no longer concern themselves with credit investigations, outlays, and expenses for collecting receivables, they might find that increases in sales justify the cost of the service.

On the other hand, if the retail trade or service establishment generates sufficient sales volume to realize economies of scale from an investment in facilities for collecting receivables, management may find that even after an allowance for bad debts, providing charge account privileges will add to the total profits of the firm and hence to the market value of its owners' equity.

As the sales volume expands relative to the size of the individual account, management is in a better position to accept higher-quality receivables and reject higher-risk applicants. Given a sufficiently high potential sales volume, the increase in revenues from granting the charge privilege to low-risk applicants will often offset the periodic costs associated with the investment. The offset may be so great that, when the resulting cash flows are discounted by the cost of capital, the net present value is positive. With relatively low risk of bad debts, perhaps 1 percent or less, the expected utility of the probable outcomes is also more likely to be positive.

Furthermore, relatively large merchandising and service concerns can use the receivables as a means of competing with their smaller rivals. This is particularly true in the case of consumer durables. Through aggressive selling techniques, management can lower the price on refrigerators, stoves, washing machines, air-conditioners, etc., to tempt the consumer. It can then offer him an installment contract with finance charges designed to make up the loss of revenue on the sales price. Of course, the consumer is always free to pay cash on such items and larger firms will ordinarily let him charge it. But if the sales price is high relative to his income, he still may have to pay for it over a period of months. The firm will earn a service charge on the outstanding balance.[13]

[13]A knowledgeable consumer with an excellent credit rating will finance the purchase through a commercial bank. Because of his rating, the interest payments on the personal loan will be several points below the payments on an installment contract or monthly service charge. Still, the payments may be on the order of 10 to 12 percent per annum. Consequently, if the purchaser has collateral such as high-grade common stocks, he can receive a low-cost short-term loan on perhaps as much as two-thirds of the market price of the stock. Suppose, for example, that an individual purchasing $1,000 of carpeting for his home had the choice of an installment contract with the retail outlet, a charge privilege, or a personal loan from the bank. The simple rates of interest on each of these loans are 14, 18, and 10 percent, respectively. He also had $2,000 in common stock on which the bank would loan him $1,000 for 6 months discounted at 6 percent per annum; that is, the bank would deduct 1/2 of 6% × $1,000, or $30, in advance. The interest on the loan would be

$$970 = \frac{\$1,000}{1+r}$$

$$r = 3.09\% \text{ per 6 months, or } 6.18\% \text{ per annum}$$

Because the interest is taken out in advance, the effective rate is above 6 percent. Yet it is still the cheapest way to finance the purchase. Moreover, most banks would let the customer renew his loan or some portion of it.

Consequently, once we look into the capital outlays, cost, and revenue factors affecting the decisions to invest in receivables, there may be instances where it will not be in the best interest of owners to extend credit. In the final analysis, concerning either consumer or trade credit, management must decide whether the firm is profitable without an investment in receivables. If the firm is not, then management may have to view investment in credit facilities and working capital as joint decisions. Expansion in production facilities will include an allowance for capital outlays to accommodate the receivables expected for an increase in sales.

If a firm is profitable without extending credit, then the decision to do so should be based on the fact that the net present value of an investment in receivables will, after allowances for risk, add to the total profits of the firm and hence to the market value of the owners' equity. If the investment does not result in this benefit, then management should refrain from offering the credit service.

THE IMPORTANCE OF RECEIVABLES

The attention which management must give to receivables is in part a function of their relative importance in the asset portfolio of the firm. From Table 10-1 it is evident that the importance varies with the nature

TABLE 10-1: PERCENTAGE OF NOTES AND RECEIVABLES TO TOTAL ASSETS AND BUSINESS RECEIPTS BY INDUSTRY GROUP FOR SELECTED NONFINANCIAL CORPORATIONS,[a] FISCAL YEAR 1961–1962

Industry Group	Notes and Receivables to Total Assets, %	Notes and Receivables to Business Receipts, %
All Corporations[b]	20.5	32.2
Agriculture, Forestry, and Fisheries	12.9	11.9
Mining	13.5	20.9
Construction	34.7	16.8
Manufacturing	18.1	13.5
Transportation and Utilities[c]	4.0	9.4
Wholesale Trade	36.3	12.3
Retail Trade	24.1	8.8
Services	17.8	16.5

SOURCE: U.S. Treasury, *Statistics of Income: U.S. Business Tax Returns 1961–62*, table 27.

[a]Percentages are calculated from raw data using receivables before allowances for bad debts. All figures are based on accounting valuation.

[b]Includes financial and real estate as well as miscellaneous corporations.

[c]Includes communications and sanitary services.

of the industry. For transportation and utilities firms, receivables, including notes, are a relatively minor proportion of total assets. They appear to be greatest within the construction and wholesale trade sectors of the economy. If we broke these classifications down still further, we might find considerable diversity among industries comprising a single subsector, such as manufacturing. Nevertheless, even on intuitive grounds, we would expect wholesalers, for example, to have a considerable portion of their assets representing trade credit. Their business consists in selling large lots of goods to retail outlets on a continuing basis. Part of the services they provide would be the inclusion of credit to their customers. They would combine an investment in receivables with an investment in the goods they sold. On the other hand, we would expect receivables for transportation and utility services to be small relative to total assets, simply because of the large proportion of long-lived assets required to generate a given sales volume, and the comparatively small amount spent by each customer on the services.

In the case of construction, the reason for the relatively high investment in notes and receivables is that a project is often begun with a down payment, the residual being financed out of short-term loans from commercial banks. The buyer pays the balance due when the construction is completed.

Retail trade outlets have a somewhat smaller investment in receivables than construction and wholesale trade firms primarily because they sell in relatively smaller amounts to consumers, and hence more often on a cash basis. Similar conditions hold true for many service industries.

Although trade credit is extended by both the manufacturing and the mining industries, when compared with trade and service firms, the former industries require a relatively high investment in long-lived assets to generate a given amount of sales. The same can be said of agriculture, forestry, and fisheries.

But whatever the relative importance of receivables, the more rapidly they are turned over into cash, the lower the periodic costs of maintaining the service. Management, therefore, will find that changes in the ratio of receivables to sales — or its reciprocal, the sales-receivables ratio — will help to explain the changes in costs associated with investment in receivables.

In Table 10-1 we have also shown the ratio of receivables to business receipts or sales for various industries. In retail trade, for example, the figure for 1961–1962 was 8.8 percent. The reciprocal is

$$100 \div 8.8\% = 11.36$$

To interpret this figure, we can say that receivables are turned over 11.36 times a year, or something less than once every month. The measure is, of course, crude.   In the first place, it implies that the ratio of the receivables balance at the end of the year to sales for the whole year is indicative of the ratio for the entire year.   This may not be the case, that is, the ratio of first-quarter sales to receivables at the end of the quarter may be different from the annual ratio.[14]   Nevertheless, to the extent that there are changes in the annual ratio, they may reflect changes in the costs of servicing receivables.   Thus, if a firm finds its sales-receivables ratio rising, the rate of collection is falling. Management will expect that more time and money will be spent collecting deliquent accounts.   Similarly, as short-term loans to help finance receivables must now be left outstanding for a longer period, interest costs rise.

A second problem with the ratio is the fact that business receipts, or sales, reflect cash sales as well as credit sales.   A firm can experience a greater volume in cash sales from one year to the next, which will tend to offset a deterioration in the collection of receivables.   Ideally, then, the business-receipts figure should exclude cash sales and include only sales on account.

But even with these qualifications, changes in the ratio, particularly increases in it, should alert management to the need to review its policy with respect to extending credit to its customers.

SUMMARY

Management may find it useful to view an investment in receivables as a problem in capital budgeting.   If it does so, it will decide whether an investment in receivables is profitable.   The present value of the cash flows is compared in the usual manner with the replacement cost of the investment outlay.   If the risk-adjusted net present value is positive, the firm will invest in receivables.

On the other hand, if it is assumed that to do business at all management must invest in receivables, the replacement cost of this investment may be added to the replacement cost of the outlay.   If there is excess capacity, that is, if the level of long-lived assets is held constant and sales rise, the investment in receivables is simply the amount of working capital necessary to finance the additional credit granted.

---

[14]Financial analysts will often calculate a sales-receivables ratio for a year using for receivables the average of the beginning-of-year and end-of-year balances.   This is to allow for changes in the level of receivables from the beginning of the year to the end of the year over which the sales were made.

There are two types of credit. One is credit granted by one business firm to another, that is, trade credit; the other is credit extended by business to customers, that is, consumer credit. While the details differ, the empirical evidence suggests that investment in consumer credit carries greater risk than investment in trade credit.

As a measure of efficiency in managing receivables, we can use the turnover ratio. Although we must be careful in interpreting the results, secular changes, particularly secular increases in the ratio, suggest a deterioration in the quality of credit extended.

QUESTIONS AND PROBLEMS

1. "The decision to invest in receivables is independent of the decision to invest in long-lived assets." Do you agree? Explain fully.

2. An automobile dealer is willing to sell a new car to a customer for his old car plus $2,000 in cash. Alternatively, he may pay for the car in 12 equal installments of $200 a month. What is the effective rate of interest on the installment loan?

3. A firm presently producing skis is considering the possibility of entering the market for either ice hockey equipment or baseball equipment. Discuss the differential impact on working capital required to finance each of these ventures.

4. "There are greater costs involved, including risk, in financing a given volume of trade credit as compared with an equal amount of consumer debt." Do you agree? Explain carefully.

SELECTED REFERENCES

Beckman, T. N., and R. S. Foster *Credits and Collections*, 8th ed. New York: McGraw-Hill Book Company, 1969.

Chapin, A. F., and G. E. Hassett, Jr. *Credit and Collection: Principles and Practice*, 7th ed. New York: McGraw-Hill Book Company, 1960.

Johnson, R. W. "More Scope for Credit Manager," *Harvard Business Review*, vol. 39, no. 6 (November-December, 1961), pp. 109–120.

Mors, Wallace P. *Consumer Credit Finance Charges: Rate Information and Quotation.* New York: National Bureau of Economic Research, Inc., 1965.

Phelps, Clyde William. *Commercial Credit Insurance as a Management Tool.* Baltimore: Commercial Credit Company, 1961.

Seiden, Martin H. *The Quality of Trade Credit.* New York: National Bureau of Economic Research, Inc., 1964.

Inventories

chapter Eleven

In dealing with inventories, the student should note the similarities between inventories and receivables as well as between inventories and long-lived assets. He should also pay particular attention to the model for determining what is called the economic order quantity. What role does it play in determining the optimum level of inventory? How can the same model be used to determine the optimum cash balance at the beginning of the operating cycle?

Introduction

There are numerous similarities between investing in receivables and investing in inventories. Both can be viewed separately as problems in capital budgeting. Alternatively, each can be seen as an integral part of the decision to produce or market a product.

To the extent that differences exist, they are in part due to differences in detail rather than in substance. Thus, just as the decision to invest in receivables entails a capital outlay for collection and credit facilities, so the decision to invest in inventories requires that management add warehouse facilities to its capital budget. Moreover, assuming that subsequent increases in either receivables or inventories do not alter the need for additional investment in long-lived assets, such increases will, nevertheless, require an expansion in permanent working capital.

At the same time, the decision to invest in inventories may be less independent than a decision to invest in receivables. For a manufacturing firm to produce at all, management may have to maintain minimum stocks of raw materials, or else accommodate the production process to stockouts of these materials. Frequent cessations of production due to lack of inventories will cause costs to rise and will therefore jeopardize profits. Management of a steel producer, for example, may bank the firm's blast furnaces because its stock of iron ore was depleted before being replenished. Yet to start them up again adds to the total cost of producing steel. If it left the furnaces running, but not utilized, there would also be an increase in costs.

One of the functions of carrying inventories, therefore, is to lower the costs resulting from stockouts. But since inventories in turn require an investment of funds, one of the primary problems of inventory control is to determine the amount required to keep the production costs at a minimum.

At the other end of the production portion of the operating cycle lie the costs involved in having insufficient quantities of finished goods to satisfy customer demand. How much business will be lost by delays in filling orders? A retail trade outlet, for example, may find that its customers prefer the convenience of being able to obtain an item when they purchase it rather than waiting for several weeks or months. Moreover, they are willing to pay for the service so that the costs of higher levels of inventory required to prevent stockouts are included in the price of the product.

But there is a limit to the price people are willing to pay. Thus a department store may stock air-conditioners which can be obtained when purchased or delivered shortly thereafter. Yet it will not stock large amounts of furniture. A customer purchasing a bedroom set may have to wait 6 weeks or longer before he receives it.[1] The depart-

---

[1] The manufacturer, when he receives the order, may not even have the furniture in stock. Because of the many specific items the firm produces, management will probably find it less costly to manufacture individual pieces in cycles. If the customer's order is out of phase, that is, bedroom sets are not being made at that time and the previous stock is depleted, the wait may extend much beyond 6 weeks.

ment store will probably find that the costs of having large inventories of a variety of furniture are relatively high when compared with the costs of stocking air-conditioners and other standard household appliances.   The nature of demand may be such that these costs cannot be passed on to the consumer without a substantial loss in sales volume.[2] Thus management will often confine the store's stock to floor samples, standard pieces with a relatively stable demand, and items which manufacturers, having overanticipated demand, are willing to sell at discounts.

Other retail trade outlets may accept a high incidence of stockouts on all of their merchandise but price their products relatively low. The consumer incurs longer delays but does not pay the price required to have sufficient inventories to satisfy his demand immediately.

Yet in considering inventories, the decision is less likely to be between investing in inventories or not investing in them than in deciding what is the necessary level of inventories required to keep the costs of production and distribution at a minimum.   Consequently, while some manufacturers and wholesalers may find that an investment in trade credit is unprofitable, they are less likely to view inventories in the same light.   Similarly, while retail trade outlets may be able to ignore frequent stockouts in particular items, it is doubtful that they can dispense with inventories altogether even though they might be selling their goods on a cash basis.   In the final analysis, only those who manage firms in service industries, or who manage firms in industries whose output is dependent primarily on investment in long-lived assets, are able to ignore or at least pay less attention to inventories associated with their business.   For others, establishing and reviewing inventory practices requires a considerable portion of management's time and energies.

Thus from the data presented in Table 11-1, on the next page, we can see that inventories comprise a substantial portion of the assets of wholesale and retail trade as well as manufacturing.   But they are of minor consequence to the service industries, transportation and utilities, and mining.   They are of intermediate importance in agriculture, forestry and fisheries, and construction.

As in the case of receivables, we would expect differences within the groups which comprise each subsector.   Yet services, by implication, are supplied without a substantial investment in inventories. Moreover, the combination of products and services provided by transportation and public-utility concerns are the result of an investment in long-lived assets.

Similarly in mining operations, from which raw materials are

---

[2]The market demand curve, in other words, is highly elastic.

TABLE 11-1:   PERCENTAGE OF INVENTORIES TO TOTAL ASSETS AND BUSI-
NESS RECEIPTS BY INDUSTRY GROUP FOR NONFINANCIAL
CORPORATIONS,[a] FISCAL YEAR 1961–1962

Industry Group	Inventories to Total Assets, %	Inventories to Business Receipts, %
All Corporations[b]	7.3	11.5
Agriculture, Forestry, and Fisheries	12.1	11.2
Mining	5.6	8.6
Construction	14.3	6.9
Manufacturing	20.8	15.6
Transportation and Utilities[c]	2.0	4.7
Wholesale Trade	28.5	9.7
Retail Trade	32.3	11.8
Services	4.8	4.5

SOURCE: U.S. Treasury, *Statistics of Income: U.S. Business Tax Returns 1961–62*, table 27.
[a]Percentages are calculated from raw data.   All figures are based on accounting valuation. Thus inventories include companies using FIFO, LIFO, or some other acceptable basis for allocating historical costs.
[b]Includes financial and real estate as well as miscellaneous corporations.
[c]Includes communications and sanitary services.

produced, inventories are relatively small when compared to the ore reserves and physical properties comprising the remainder of its assets. However, in the case of manufacturing, a firm often needs a substantial investment in long-lived assets as well as in inventory stocks, ranging from raw materials to work in process and finished goods.

For wholesale and retail trade establishments, on the other hand, long-lived assets are relatively unimportant. Hence, inventories as well as receivables bulk large in their asset structure. The construction industry must maintain levels of inventories representing the materials currently being used in fulfilling current and anticipated contract obligations. In agriculture, forestry, and fisheries, there is usually an inventory of products ready for sale to commercial and industrial users.

As in the case of receivables, the ratio of inventories to business receipts (also shown in Table 11-1)—or its reciprocal, the receipts- or sales-inventory ratio—provides a rough index of management's efficiency in utilizing inventories. Year-to-year changes, although they cover up seasonal fluctuations, do indicate that the costs of maintaining inventories are also changing.

Yet the ratio tells us nothing about the costs of stockouts. For example, management might work to lower its inventory-sales ratio (or raise its sales-inventory ratio) from 10 percent (or 10:1) to 5 percent (or 20:1). This will lower the costs of investing in inventory partly because, as the stocks are turned over more rapidly, less funds need be tied up in them.   But suppose management accomplishes this task by permanently lowering the level of inventory to accommodate a given volume of sales or by raising the sales without proportional increases in the stock of inventories.   In so doing it may be unable to accommodate unexpected increases in demand.   Thus, in lowering inventory costs, management runs the risk of not realizing its potential sales volume and therefore of not maximizing its total profits and ultimately the market value of the owners' equity.

Inventory Control

In the light of the above discussion, it is evident that being able to adjust to the vagaries of customer demand is a key element in the management of inventory.   Not only may too little an investment mean the loss of sales revenues, but too large an investment may raise the total costs of the product to such an extent that the profitability of the firm is threatened.   Moreover, as inventories increase relative to sales, management runs the counterrisk of being unable to sell them at the anticipated price.   Yet depending on the cash balances or their equivalent in marketable securities held for precautionary motives, management may have to lower the price in order to have sufficient funds to meet the firm's obligations as they come due.

Add to the fluctuations in customer demand, the technical difficulties of transporting inventory from one place to another (or of changing inventories of raw materials to finished goods) and we have the ingredients of the inventory problem.   Thus management of a manufacturing firm must have not only an estimate of the market demand for its goods but also knowledge of the time required to obtain raw materials.   It must know how long it takes to manufacture each line produced as well as the time required to transport finished goods to their destination.   Similarly, wholesalers and retailers must know the time required to fill an order for each of the many lines of goods they carry.   The stocks they hold, therefore, are in part a function of the time required to replenish them.

As a result of the nature of the inventory problem, there has grown up around it a body of literature whose contributors are often industrial engineers and production management specialists and to which an introductory text in finance cannot hope to do justice.[3]   It is possible, however, to indicate some of the procedures employed.   In

[3]See R. Stansbury Stockton, *Basic Inventory Systems: Concepts and Analysis* (Boston: Allyn and Bacon, Inc., 1965), for an introduction to the techniques employed.

doing so, it will be helpful to separate the technical problems of the production and distribution portions of the operating cycle from the uncertainties encountered because of unexpected variations in customer demand.

Classification of Costs   In ordering inventories, management must consider three classifications of costs: *acquisition costs, procurement costs*, and *carrying costs*.   Acquisition costs fall as a result of quantity discounts granted by most suppliers, manufacturers, and wholesalers. The larger the lot, the lower the price per unit.   Procurement costs, on the other hand, are independent of the size of the order.   Included are such items as processing, bookkeeping, and any other costs connected with making an order regardless of its size.

Carrying costs, however, rise with output.   They may include the opportunity cost of space, insurance, interest on loans or equity capital invested in inventory, and so forth.

The total cost of inventory is the algebraic sum of the procurement costs, the acquisition costs, and the carrying costs.   Under conditions of certainty, demand for a particular time period would be known. Suppose that the total demand is Y and the cost of acquiring each unit is A.   Then the total acquisition cost is AY.   The total procurement cost for the period is the number of orders times the cost of placing them. Since the total demand equals the number of orders times the size Z of the order, the number of orders made is Y/Z.   If P equals the procurement cost of each order, then $(Y/Z)P$ equals the total procurement cost.

The total carrying cost is a product of the average inventory held during the period times these charges.   Since demand is constant, the stocks will be at Z at the beginning of the period and at O or zero at the end of the period.   The average inventory is therefore $Z/2$.   The total carrying cost is $(Z/2)C$.

The pattern of inventory demand is shown in Figure 11-1.   This is the standard saw-tooth illustration of inventory changes from one period to the next under conditions of constant demand. OZ is the size of an individual order.   Midway through each period, inventory is at $Z/2$.   For half the period it is above that amount; for the other half it is below.

If T equals the total cost of the inventory, then

Total cost = acquisition cost + procurement cost + carrying cost

$$T = \qquad AY \qquad + \qquad \frac{Y}{Z}P \qquad + \qquad \frac{Z}{2}C$$

What management is seeking is the optimum, or least-cost, value for Z.   In the terminology of the inventory specialist, this value is called

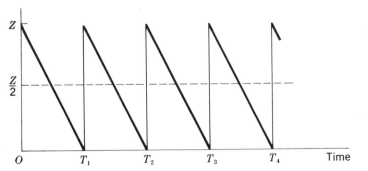

Figure 11-1 Sawtooth pattern of inventory demand.

the *economic order quantity*. In Figure 11-1 we assume that this amount is *OZ*.

Graphically,[4] *OZ* is the minimum point on the total inventory cost curve. This is shown in Figure 11-2.

[4]Using the calculus, we can differentiate the total inventory cost function with respect to Z, so that

$$\frac{dT}{dY} = -\frac{Y}{Z^2}P + \frac{C}{2}$$

The economic order quantity is the value for which the derivative of the total inventory cost curve with respect to Z equals zero. This is the case when

$$Z = \sqrt{\frac{2YP}{C}}$$

Figure 11-2

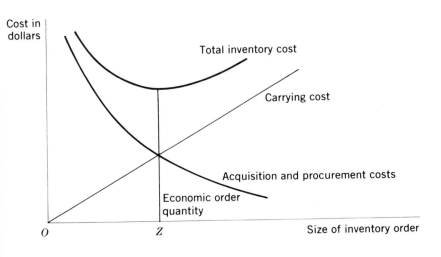

With demand known, the economic order quantity minimizes the total cost of inventory. Under these conditions, the firm should order in lots of OZ. Note also that since it was assumed that the time required to replenish the stock is known, the sawtooth diagram reproduced in Figure 11-3 tells the company the minimum stock level or reorder point. The diagonal ZT' shows the decline of inventories as a function of time. If r number of days are required to replenish the stock of inventory and r equals $T'T_1$ on the graph, then the economic order quantity OZ should be purchased when the stock of inventory declines to OZ'.

When the model is complicated by the vagaries of customer demand, two additional costs not easily quantified must be recognized. These are the costs of overstocking in order to accommodate unexpected increases in demand and the loss of sales revenue from understocking. When an enterprise has a seasonal pattern, it can adjust the reorder point accordingly. But fluctuations due to general business conditions or to random factors are more difficult to accommodate. Since management can be wrong in its expectations, judgment enters the picture. Sometimes attempts can be made to resolve the issue by retreating to a formula. *Standard-order-point* formulas, for example, contain a variable defining the *stockout acceptance factor* "based on the application of a formula known as the 'square root approximation of the Poisson distribution.'"[5] But the departures from this pattern require modifications[6] which may be at best educated guesses.

[5]Arthur Snyder, "Principles of Inventory Management," *Financial Executive*, vol. 32 (April, 1964), pp. 13–21; reprinted in James Van Horne (ed.), *Foundations for Financial Management: A Book of Readings* (Homewood, Ill.: Richard D. Irwin, Inc., 1966), pp. 70–90. The quotation is from p. 73.
[6]*Ibid.*, pp. 73–74.

Figure 11-3

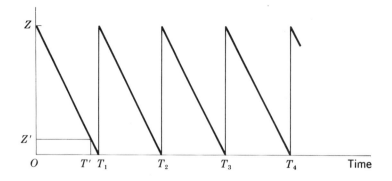

Moreover, the management of many concerns consists of a group of specialists whose values are related to their responsibilities. The treasurer or controller may be more willing to accept lower inventory levels than the sales manager. The former sees the funds invested in inventory as relatively unproductive when compared with their return elsewhere. The latter, however, has an easier time competing in the marketplace if he knows that he can fill an order without delays. The stockout acceptance factor therefore may in the last analysis be a matter of compromise with the result put into the formula.

Once agreed on, the additional stocks of inventory are held to provide a buffer against uncertainties. In Figure 11-4 it is assumed that the economic order quantity remains at OZ with the reorder point at OZ but with the $O'O$ level of inventories held as a buffer. Suppose that demand is overestimated at the reorder point. Then when the new stock arrives, the inventory levels will be at $O'Z''$ rather than at $O'O$. Similarly, if demand is underestimated at the reorder point, the stock will fall to $O'Z'''$ before being replenished. If demand is so great that it results in a stockout with $O''O'$ number of orders being unfilled, management is willing to accept the ill will of its customers and the revenue loss. In other words, it values the cost savings of not keeping inventories above $O'O$ more highly than losses from stockouts above this level.

Figure 11-4

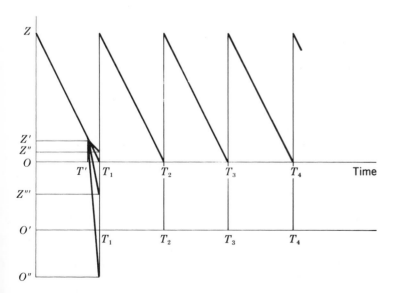

Determining the Level of Inventory – An Example

The introduction of electronic computers has further stimulated interest in the development of more-sophisticated tools of inventory control.[7] But any model, sophisticated or not, can provide information on which to base only an informed but subjective judgment. Thus management might estimate the economic order quantity on the basis of the most probable outcome, adjusting its buffer stocks so as to achieve the optimum trade-off between the costs of stockouts and the costs of maintaining excessive levels of inventory.

To illustrate, assume that management of a company distributing office equipment estimated that the firm's monthly demand for desks and chairs next year would most probably be 1,000 units of each. Based on past experience, management estimates that the chances are equal that sales could fluctuate 2 percent in either direction. Assume that there is no seasonal pattern to annual sales, so that the monthly sales volume will not rise or fall for this reason. Assume further that to replenish the stock requires 15 days from the time the order is placed. Finally, management estimates that the economic order quantity is 500 sets of desks and chairs.

Therefore, it if wants to be virtually certain that the firm will not face a stockout, management must provide the firm with a buffer of 20 sets. However, if demand falls by as much as 2 percent below the expected sales volume, the firm will have 40 sets of desks and chairs at the end of the month.

Suppose that the list price of each set is $300 and the replacement cost $190. The unit carrying cost is $15 per month. To hold a buffer of 20 units therefore requires a permanent investment of $3,800 and monthly carrying costs of $300. Assume that the cost of stockouts is the permanent loss of sales revenue, that is, $300 per unit or, if no buffer is kept, as much as $6,000. If demand is overestimated and sales are up to 2 percent below the anticipated monthly volume, then the carrying costs can again be as much as $15 a month times 20 units, or a total of $300. However, management, knowing that it takes but 15 days to receive a delivery, ordinarily orders 500 units near the middle and the end of each month. Consequently, it can lower the monthly carrying

---

[7]Even the simpler models are often misapplied. Strict adherence to the economic order quantity may not always be necessary. While there is only one minimum point on the total inventory cost curve, the quantity purchased may be so large that the difference in costs of several hundred or even a thousand units more or less than the optimum quantity is marginal. If examined in detail, the total inventory cost curve would appear relatively flat in the vicinity of the economic order quantity. Management then has more flexibility in raising or lowering the inventory order than would be indicated from strict adherence to the formula. See *ibid.*, pp. 75–83.

costs of an overinvestment in inventory by as much as one-half by adjusting its inventory order.   Thus, if for one month demand was 980 rather than 1,000 units, management could order 480 rather than 500 units in its next purchase.

The result is to reduce the carrying costs of overstocking from $300 to $150.   But what does a purchase below the economic order quantity do to the total inventory costs?   From Figure 11-2 it is evident that the total inventory costs are at a minimum when the economic order quantity is OZ, or in this case 500 units.   Hence, if management orders less or more than this amount, the total inventory cost and the cost per unit will rise.   If in reality the curve is relatively flat on either side of the economic order quantity,[8] then the additional cost of ordering less than 500 units may be small.   Let us assume that it is $10.

Putting all costs together, management can be virtually certain that with a permanent investment of $3,800 and carrying costs of $460 ($300 + $150 + $10), the firm will accommodate all unexpected increases in demand and yet allow for the cost of sales falling by as much as 2 percent below the anticipated volume.

The $460, of course, represents the maximum possible loss, based on the assumption that management carries a buffer of 20 units and that monthly demand falls 2 percent short of the anticipated volume of 1,000 units.   On the other hand, by carrying the buffer stock, the firm may receive as much as $6,000 in additional revenue during a particular month.   From this we can subtract the additional costs of purchasing more than the economic order quantity required to replenish the buffer. Let us assume that this cost is also $10.   The maximum net revenue per month from holding the buffer is $5,990.

The inventory decision, therefore, is a subjective evaluation of the odds of losing up to $460 per month in order to gain as much as $5,990 in additional revenue.   If the odds are .5 that the monthly demand will be 1,000 sets of desks and chairs, then the most probable outcome from holding a buffer of 20 units is the loss of $300 in carrying costs.   At the same time, we can assume that there are equal probabilities, that is, .25, that sales could be 2 percent above or below that figure.   The expected outcome is therefore

$$.25 \times (-\$460) \quad = -\$ \ \ 115.00$$
$$.5 \ \times (-\$300) \quad = -\$ \ \ 150.00$$
$$.25 \times \quad \$5,990 \quad = \quad \$1,497.50$$
$$\text{Expected outcome} = \quad \overline{\$1,232.50}$$

Yet it is on the basis of expected utility that a subjective evaluation

[8]See footnote 7.

must be made.   Suppose that the utility of a loss of $460 is −.2 and of $300, −.1.   The utility of the gain of $5,990 is 3.2.   Thus

$$.25U(-.2) + .5U(-.1) + .25U(3.2) = \text{utility of expected outcome}$$
$$(-.05) \quad + \quad (-.05) \quad + \quad (.8) \quad = .7$$

It would appear that since management finds the utility of the expected outcome positive, it will accept the costs of maintaining a buffer stock.   However, the costs and revenues expected are based on the assumption that management will carry 20 sets of desks and chairs.   Other alternatives are available, ranging from 19 sets down to zero.

In each instance the utility of the expected outcome must be set against the utility of the expected outcomes based on buffer stocks of other sizes.   The outcome with the highest utility determines the appropriate buffer stock.   Suppose, for example, that management is considering a buffer stock of 15 units.   The potential revenue gain is $4,500, that is, $300 times 15 units.   From this we must subtract the costs of purchasing in excess of the economic order quantity.   Assume that this is as much as $5.00.   The anticipated net revenues from holding a buffer of 15 sets of desks and chairs can be as much as $4,495.

In considering the carrying costs of the inventory, let us assume that they remain proportional to the size of the buffer stock, that is, $\frac{3}{4}$ of $300, or $225.   However, management may not sell up to 20 units, or 2 percent of the anticipated monthly demand.   As we assumed earlier, the cost of purchasing 20 units less than the economic order quantity is $10.   The carrying costs of overstocking are $\frac{3}{4}$ of $150, or $112.50.   By holding a buffer stock of 15 units, management can lose up to $347.50 ($225 + $112.50 + $10) per month or gain as much as $4,495.

As to the probabilities of these outcomes, we must remember that while management may experience sales increases or decreases of up to 2 percent of the anticipated demand, it is planning to accommodate only a $1\frac{1}{2}$ percent increase.   The fact that sales might go beyond that amount is irrelevant.   Consequently, while in the case of a decline in demand we are interested in the probability that sales will fall 2 percent below the expected level, in the case of an increase in demand we are interested only in the probability that they will be $1\frac{1}{2}$ percent above the amount anticipated.   Therefore, we might assume that the probabilities of the two extremes differ.   Suppose, for example, that the chance of a loss of $347.50 is .4 and of a gain of $4,495 is .6.   Then the probability distribution is

$$(.4 + .6)^2 = .16 + .48 + .36$$

Since the anticipated demand is 1,000 sets of desks and chairs, there is a probability of .48 that there will be $225 in carrying costs. The expected outcome is

$$.48 \times (-\$225) = -\$\ 108.00$$
$$.16 \times (-\$342.50) = -\$\ \ \ 54.80$$
$$.36 \times \$4,495 = \quad \$1,618.20$$
$$\text{Expected outcome} = \quad \$1,455.40$$

Suppose that the utility of the loss of $225 is −.08 and of $342.50, −.12. The utility of the gain of $4,495 is 2.0. Thus

$$.48(-.08) + .16(-.12) + .36(2.0) = \text{utility of expected outcome}$$
$$-.0384 + -.0192 + \quad .72 \quad = .6624$$

Since the utility of the expected outcome of holding 20 units as a buffer is greater than the utility of holding 15 units, management and presumably the owners would rather risk the costs of maintaining higher inventory levels than lose the revenue which might be earned if the stocks were available. Of course, further investigation might reveal that the utility of the expected outcome of carrying some intermediate level of inventories as a buffer stock, say 18 sets of desks and chairs, will be greater than the utility of holding 15 or 20 units.

An Inventory Model of Cash Balances

Just as it is possible to determine the economic order quantity for inventories under conditions of constant demand, so is it possible under the same conditions to determine the economic order quantity or optimum level of cash balances. For example, suppose we knew that in order to satisfy a given volume of sales for a particular period, we would need Y dollars to meet the firm's transactions demand for cash. Since we are postulating conditions of certainty, we need not consider carrying cash for precautionary motives. If we assume further that there is no seasonal or cyclical pattern to sales, we can eliminate the speculative trade-off between cash and marketable securities.

The cost of acquiring a cash balance, that is, A, could be a declining function of its size. Suppose, for example, that a firm employed long-term sources to finance its cash balances. The institutions or individuals supplying the funds might realize economies of scale in processing large orders. If so, they would be willing to lower the rate charged. Thus the acquisition cost AY could decline with the size of the cash balance.

But even if there were no "volume discounts" from increasing the cash balance, the procurement cost P would surely decline. As we shall see in our discussion of the sources of funds, the total flotation costs of long-term sources are virtually independent of the amount acquired. Hence they are a declining percentage of net proceeds.   As in the case of inventory, once management makes the decision to acquire funds, the costs of processing do not change substantially.

Unlike inventory, however, the funds, once acquired, would not have to be reordered.   The operating cycle does this automatically.   If Y is the total demand for a year and the operating cycle is 3 months, the number of "orders placed" is four.   In the case of inventory, we would actually have to order four times a year.   But in the case of cash the operating cycle would generate the amount Z four times a year. Since P equals the procurement cost of supplying Z initially, the total procurement cost is still $(Y/Z)P$.   Since P declines with Z, it is likely that the total cost of cash balances is a declining function of the acquisition and procurement costs, if not a declining function of the acquisition cost alone.

The carrying cost C, however, increases with the size of the cash balances.   The carrying cost represents the opportunity cost of funds. What could management be doing with the funds rather than leaving them as idle cash?   Under conditions of constant demand, the cash balance would be Z at the beginning of the operating cycle and zero at the end of the cycle.   As in the case of inventory, therefore, the total carrying cost is $(Z/2)C$.

Again combining the algebraic sum of the acquisition, procurement, the carrying costs, we can see from Figures 11-2 and 11-3 that the optimum size of the cash balance is $\$OZ$.   Since the operating cycle will automatically generate $\$OZ$ at the end of period OT, we need not concern ourselves with the time required to "reorder" the stock of cash.

However, as in the case of inventories, we must also consider the cost of understocking, that is, the short cost, as well as the cost of overstocking, that is, the long cost.   Recall from our discussion of cash management that cash held to satisfy the precautionary motive depends on management's and presumably the owners' subjective attitudes toward risk.   Just as the treasurer or controller may be willing to accept lower inventory levels than the sales manager, so may there be a difference in their attitudes toward cash balances.   The treasurer or controller, responsible for meeting obligations when they come due, is more alert than the sales manager to the consequences of an insufficient level of cash.   Thus he might choose to hold a higher precautionary balance than would the sales manager.   Yet, as we have seen, the treasurer and the controller can still differ between themselves.

Once a compromise has been reached, then, from Figure 11-4,

the amount OO' represents a "buffer" stock of cash held for precautionary reasons. Should the transactions demand for cash exceed the buffer stock OO', management is prepared to accept the consequences — that is, the cost of being caught short. In other words, it is prepared to accept such consequences as loss of profit from inability to accommodate unexpected sales increases, additional borrowing at a higher rate, a decline in the firm's credit standing, and perhaps even bankruptcy. These short costs are apparently outweighed by the long costs, that is, the opportunity costs of a buffer fund larger than OO', say OO''. In other words, the expected utility of the outcome of holding a buffer stock OO' is greater than the expected utility of the outcome of holding a larger buffer stock OO'', or for that matter of holding a buffer stock smaller than OO'.

Added to the buffer stock at particular times of the year can be an amount reflecting a seasonal pattern in the transactions demand for cash. Funds would be moved in and out of marketable securities as the seasonal needs for cash expanded and contracted. For the same reason, funds could move from cash into and out of inventory, thereby adding to or subtracting from the buffer stock at seasonal peaks.

Consequently, the optimum stock of cash and the optimum stock of inventories can be viewed in terms of the same model. The economic order quantity in the case of the latter is the optimum cash balance at the beginning of the operating cycle. The buffer stock reflects the precautionary motive for holding cash and can be altered to meet the seasonal pattern of demand.[9]

Inventories and Long-Lived Assets — Some Similarities

While we have treated inventories as part of the firm's investment in working capital, we have done so primarily because of the length of time during which funds are tied up in a specific stock of goods. For most firms, the stock of inventories is turned over several times during the year. In the case of long-lived assets, however, by definition, it takes several years to recoup the replacement or even the original cost of the investment. To be sure, we have also noted similarities. There is usually a buffer stock representing a permanent investment of funds.

[9]For a more detailed explanation, see William J. Baumol, "The Transactions Demand for Cash: An Inventory Theoretic Approach," *Quarterly Journal of Economics*, vol. 66, no. 4 (November, 1952), pp. 545–556; Stephen H. Archer, "A Model for the Determination of Firm Cash Balances," *Journal of Financial and Quantitative Analysis*, vol. 1, no. 1 (March, 1966), pp. 1–11. Both are reprinted in Stephen H. Archer and Charles A. D'Ambrosio (eds.), *The Theory of Business Finance: A Book of Readings* (New York: The Macmillan Company, 1967), pp. 569–586.

Moreover, there is likely to be a capital outlay reflecting an investment in long-lived assets to store and perhaps process inventories. But the same can be said of an investment in the credit and collection facilities required to process receivables. Furthermore, just as there may be a permanent investment in receivables even though individual accounts are cleared, so may there be a permanent investment in inventory while the original stocks are liquidated.

However, what makes inventories unique among current assets is that they represent real rather than financial assets. Cash, marketable securities, and receivables are all financial claims. Inventories, as well as plant and equipment, represent tangible wealth. In economic terminology, they are part of the nation's stock of capital. Each year, changes in the level of business inventories are one determinant of a nation's gross private domestic investment. In Table 11-2 the investment figures for the years 1946–1968 are broken down into three components: nonresidential investment which includes both plant and equipment, residential housing comprising farm and nonfarm structures, and changes in business inventories.

Of the three components, nonresidential investment — consisting of outlays representing additions to plant and equipment as well as costs for replacement of those long-lived assets used up in the production of current goods — often constitutes 60 percent of gross private domestic investment. Residential construction usually represents about 30 percent of the total, while changes in business inventories fill out the remainder.

Although the figures are gross rather than net of depreciation, since the end of World War II, the only year-to-year changes which have taken place in the three components that reflect disinvestment are changes in inventories. For the most part, business investment in plant and equipment has trended upward.

Residential construction, however, has shown sporadic movements. Shortly after World War II, there was a large increase in this component as veterans returning home took advantage of special mortgage rates and low down payments to purchase their first homes. With the exception of a few years, housing starts leveled off in the 1950s. This was due in part to the relatively low number of births in the Great Depression. These people were now beginning to seek homes but their numbers were insufficient to stimulate a new boom.

By the early 1960s, however, relatively stable interest rates and easy money resulting in low down payments helped to bring about an upward trend in the construction of new houses. But by the mid-1960s a surge of inflation stimulated by the war in Vietnam forced the Federal Reserve Board to tighten credit. The result was a drain of

TABLE 11-2: COMPOSITION AND RELATIVE IMPORTANCE OF COMPONENTS OF GROSS PRIVATE DOMESTIC INVESTMENT, 1946–1968

(Absolute Magnitudes in Billions of Dollars)

Year	Total Gross Private Domestic Investment[a]	Percent[a]	Total Non-residential Investment[b]	Percent	Residential Investment[c]	Percent	Change in Business Inventories[d]	Percent
1946	30.6	100.0	17.0	55.6	7.2	23.5	6.4	20.9
1947	34.0	100.0	23.4	68.8	11.1	32.6	-0.5	-1.5
1948	46.0	100.0	26.9	58.5	14.4	31.3	4.7	10.2
1949	35.7	100.0	25.1	70.3	13.7	38.4	-3.1	-8.7
1950	54.1	100.0	27.9	51.6	19.4	35.9	6.8	12.6
1951	59.3	100.0	31.8	53.6	17.2	29.0	10.3	17.4
1952	51.9	100.0	31.6	60.9	17.2	33.1	3.1	6.0
1953	52.6	100.0	34.2	65.0	18.0	34.2	0.4	0.8
1954	51.7	100.0	33.6	65.0	19.7	38.1	-1.5	-2.9
1955	67.4	100.0	38.1	56.5	23.3	34.6	6.0	8.9
1956	70.0	100.0	43.7	62.4	21.6	30.9	4.7	6.7
1957	67.8	100.0	46.4	68.4	20.2	29.8	1.3	1.9
1958	60.9	100.0	41.6	68.3	20.8	34.2	-1.5	-2.5
1959	75.3	100.0	45.1	59.9	25.5	33.9	4.8	6.4
1960	74.8	100.0	48.4	64.7	22.8	30.5	3.6	4.8
1961	71.7	100.0	47.0	65.6	22.6	31.5	2.0	2.8
1962	83.0	100.0	51.7	62.3	25.3	30.5	6.0	7.2
1963	87.1	100.0	54.3	62.3	27.0	31.0	5.9	6.8
1964	94.0	100.0	61.1	65.0	27.1	28.8	5.8	6.2
1965	108.1	100.0	71.3	66.0	27.2	25.2	9.6	8.9
1966	120.8	100.0	81.3	67.3	24.8	20.5	14.7	12.2
1967	114.3	100.0	83.6	73.1	24.6	21.5	6.1	5.3
1968	127.5	100.0	90.0	70.6	30.0	23.5	7.6	6.1

SOURCE: *1969 Economic Report of the President*, p. 240.

[a]Due to errors in rounding the totals may not comprise the sum of their parts.
[b]Includes producers' durable equipment as well as structures.
[c]Includes both farm and nonfarm residential structures.
[d]Includes both farm and nonfarm changes in business inventories.

funds away from institutions specializing in home mortgages. The reason for the drain lay in the fact that these institutions, particularly savings banks and savings and loan associations, could not raise interest on their existing deposits because they could not ordinarily raise rates on outstanding mortgages in which the depositors' funds were invested. A concomitant of tight money is usually higher interest rates on new loans, including new mortgages. Other institutions, particularly commercial banks, had a large proportion of short-term loans in their portfolios. As these loans came due, the banks were able to renew them at higher rates. In the meantime they could, within the interest ceilings set by the Federal Reserve Board, use certificates of deposits to bid for new funds. A large portion of these funds would be made available as business loans rather than as residential mortgages. As a result of the drain of funds away from institutions specializing primarily in mortgages, new housing starts declined.[10]

Investment in plant and equipment and changes in business inventories have not shown the same degree of sensitivity to tight money.[11] But all the components have to some degree affected or been affected by changes in the level of economic activity. Time series for each element of gross private domestic investment represent leading indicators of changes in the business cycle, that is, they tend to rise or fall before the level of economic activity does.[12] They in turn respond to cyclical changes.

While this pattern is more evident when monthly or quarterly values are used, even in our annual data in Table 11-2 we can sometimes discern this pattern. In particular, the data on nonresidential investment display conformity to the business cycle. For instance, October

[10]As we shall see in a subsequent chapter, life insurance companies also participate in mortgages. However, the nature of the contract they make with the insuree calls for periodic premiums. No one has to add periodically to his savings account, although certain higher-interest investment accounts stipulate that advance notice of withdrawal must be given.

The difficulty experienced by life insurance companies is that the contract also requires the company, if asked, to loan the cash surrender value of the policy to the policyholder, often at relatively low rates of interest, usually 5 percent.

[11]This does not mean that management has not had to alter its plans to finance plant and equipment and inventory because of tight money. From the credit squeeze which took place in the latter part of 1966, some firms learned that commercial banks must sometimes fail to accommodate their loan demand in order to meet reserve requirements and preserve their liquidity. As a result, there was a rash of long-term-debt financing, partly to increase the level of permanent working capital and to decrease management's dependence on commercial banks. See Carol J. Loomis, "That Epic Corporate Bond Binge," *Fortune* (February, 1968), pp. 120–125, 180–181, 184.

[12]See the leading indicators in the monthly issue of *Business Cycle Developments* published by the U.S. Department of Commerce for the Bureau of the Census. See also Geoffrey H. Moore and Jules Shiskin, *Indicators of Business Expansions and Contractions* (New York: National Bureau of Economic Research, Inc., 1967).

1945 through March 1948 marked a period of economic expansion.[13] Nonresidential investment expanded as well. A recession occurred between November, 1948, and October, 1949. With it came a decline in this component of gross private domestic investment. Economic activity rose again between October, 1949, and July, 1953, between August, 1954, and July, 1957, between April, 1958, and May, 1960, and again in February, 1961. In between were recessions, that is, July, 1953, to August, 1954, July, 1957, to April, 1958, and May, 1960, to February, 1961. In general, the annual data on nonresidential investment conformed to the level of economic activity. Note, for example, the year-to-year declines not only from 1948 to 1949, but from 1953 to 1954, from 1957 to 1958, and from 1960 to 1961.

This same conformity is not present in the annual data on residential construction. In fact, with the exception of 1948 to 1949, there were usually year-to-year increases in this component during the recession years. Moreover, the very tight money policies of the mid-1960s are reflected in the decline in residential construction from 1965 to 1967. Similarly, during the Korean War, when restrictions were placed on mortgage loans, there was also a decline in this component. This can be seen in the change from 1950 to 1951.

As with expenditures on plant and equipment, rates at which inventories have been accumulated have also declined in years reflecting a downturn in economic activity. In some cases there has even been disinvestment in inventories. In 1948, for example, business firms, including agriculture, raised their investment in inventories by $4.7 billion above the 1947 level. Yet in 1949 stocks were reduced by $3.1 billion. There were also disinvestments in 1954 and 1957, both years of recession. Stocks, however, increased at a slower rate from 1960 to 1961. Nevertheless, there were also years which were not marked by general declines in the level of economic activity, but during which inventories increased at a decreasing rate. 1951 to 1952 and 1952 to 1953 are examples. So too are 1955 to 1956, 1956 to 1957, as well as 1966 to 1967.

We can sometimes attribute these year-to-year decreases in nonrecession years to overestimating the level of demand. In other cases, stocks are increased in anticipation of shortages due perhaps to the threat of a strike. For instance, manufacturers who require steel often stockpile larger than usual quantities in years during which contract negotiations take place. If an agreement is reached without a strike or with a relatively short stoppage, the immediate result is often

---

[13]The business cycle reference dates are those of the National Bureau of Economic Research and can be found, for example, in *Business Cycle Developments*, March, 1968, p. 65.

a decline in new steel orders and a reduction in the stocks of inventories purchased as a hedge against the strike.

In the final analysis, therefore, an investment in inventories is an investment in real capital. Yet by nature it is a relatively more-flexible outlet for funds than long-lived assets. While it is logical for purposes of financial management that we treat it as part of working capital, we should keep in mind that inventories have a larger role to play in the level of economic activity.

SUMMARY

There are numerous similarities between investing in inventories and receivables. Both require capital outlays and can therefore be viewed as problems in capital budgeting. Yet management may have less independence in its decision to invest in inventories than in receivables. This is because the need for inventories often depends on technological conditions, that is, on the production portion of the operating cycle.

In inventory control, the central problem which management faces is the determination of the economic order quantity. Under conditions of constant demand, the total inventory cost is the algebraic sum of the acquisition costs, the procurement costs, and the carrying costs. The economic order quantity is the minimum point on the total inventory cost curve.

To the economic order quantity, management can add a buffer stock which is a function of the cost of understocking (or the short costs) and the cost of overstocking (or the long costs). Given the economic order quantity, we can calculate the expected utility of the outcomes based on different buffer stocks, choosing the one with the highest utility.

The inventory model can also be applied to determining the optimum level of cash balances at the beginning of the operating cycle. The optimum reflects the transactions demand for cash balances over the course of the cycle. To the optimum we must add a buffer stock representing the precautionary motive. The optimum buffer stock is again the one where the expected utility of the outcome is the greatest. In the case of both inventories and cash, we can add to or subtract from the buffer stock to meet the seasonal pattern of demand.

Finally, we can note that inventories are unique among current assets. This is because they represent real rather than financial assets. Inventories are part of the nation's gross private domestic investment. Changes in the level of inventories reflect changes in the level of investment.

QUESTIONS AND PROBLEMS

1. "The economic order quantity is a function of the anticipated level of demand. The buffer stocks are a function of the variability in demand." Discuss critically.

2. A distributor of confectionary goods estimates that the firm's economic order quantity for cookies for the next quarter is 50,000 boxes. From past experience it expects sales to fluctuate in either direction by as much as 5 percent. Under such conditions the economic order quantity is the most probable outcome. The probabilities of these extreme outcomes are each .5. Assume management is considering a policy of ignoring these fluctuations. If it does, it runs the risk of losing $1,500 in revenues should the optimistic sales forecast materialize. The carrying cost is $0.25 per unit. But the economic order quantity can vary 3,000 units in either direction without altering the acquisition cost. Suppose that the utility of the expected outcome under the most pessimistic conditions is $-.2$. The utility of the expected outcome under the most probable conditions is $-.1$. The utility of the outcome under the most optimistic assumptions is .2. Should management ignore the fluctuations in sales? Why or why not?

3. "Inventory has characteristics which make it more akin to long-lived assets than to current assets." Evaluate critically.

4. "Not in every industry must management concern itself with inventory control." Comment.

5. "The inventory turnover ratio is a reflection of management's efficiency in utilizing inventory stocks." Do you agree? Explain fully why or why not.

6. Management anticipates that under conditions of stable demand the firm's optimum level of cash balances over the operating cycle is $1,000,000. Depending, however, on the trend in sales, its demand for cash may be 10 percent more or 10 percent less than this amount. Assume, therefore, that the $1,000,000 represents the most probable outcome. Management estimates that the probabilities of these extreme outcomes occurring are each .25. However, if the firm does keep a cash balance which is 10 percent above the optimum, it could, if the optimistic sales forecast materializes, increase its profits by $200,000. The opportunity cost of the funds retained as cash is 20 percent. Calculate the expected outcome. Suppose the expected utility of the outcome under the most pessimistic conditions is $-.1$. Under the most probable conditions the expected utility is $-.1$. Under

the most optimistic conditions it is .4.   Should management maintain a buffer stock of 10 percent above the optimum cash balance?   Why or why not?

SELECTED REFERENCES

Baumol, William J.   "The Transactions Demand for Cash: An Inventory Theoretic Approach," *Quarterly Journal of Economics*, vol. 66, no. 4 (November, 1952), pp. 545–556.

Magee, John F.   "Guides to Inventory Policy," *Harvard Business Review*, vol. 34, no. 1 (January-February, 1956), pp. 49–60.

Snyder, Arthur.   "Principles of Inventory Management," *Financial Executive*, vol. 32 (April, 1964), pp. 13–21.

Stockton, R. Stansbury.   *Basic Inventory Systems: Concepts and Analysis*.   Boston: Allyn and Bacon, Inc., 1965.

Whitin, T. M.   *The Theory of Inventory Management*.   Princeton, N.J.: Princeton University Press, 1953.

Financial Principles

PART THREE

The Cost of Capital

chapter Twelve

In dealing with the cost of capital, we shall place considerable emphasis on the optimum capital structure. To do this, however, we must first discuss the cost of individual sources of funds. We shall then question whether there is an optimum combination of sources. If there is, it is the combination of sources which both minimizes the average cost of capital and maximizes the market value of the owners' equity.

Introduction

In the previous chapters our emphasis has been on management of both current and long-lived assets. While we did discuss the possibility of increasing both types of assets simultaneously, in general we were able to separate the management of working capital from the management of fixed assets. We also abided by the assumption that the composition of financing, except for changes due to temporary increases in short-term loans to finance seasonal needs, was constant. Moreover, we took the cost of capital as given.

In this chapter our primary purpose is to develop the principles determining the cost of capital and the effect, if any, which the composition of financing has on it. To do so, we shall have to hold the composition (if not the level) of assets constant; that is, we shall abstract from the *business risk* and concentrate on the *financial risk*. Even under these simplifying assumptions, to posit the problem of determining the cost of capital is one thing. To solve it is another. Perhaps no other aspect of business finance is so complex, so resistant to solution, yet so demanding of one. There are at least three important factors which contribute to the difficulties involved in determining the cost of capital: imperfect capital markets, risk differentials, and differences in tax treatment.

In neoclassical theory a firm's cost of capital was constant[1] at the market rate of interest. The market rate of interest in turn resulted from the intersection of the savings and investment schedules. As befitted a market-oriented discipline, emphasis in the literature of economics centered on the factors determining these schedules, and therefore on the question of why interest exists.[2] The tools developed in this volume in the chapters on managing long-lived assets are adaptations of techniques employed by economists in constructing the investment schedule. Perhaps similar alterations in the theory of interest can lead to a workable if not theoretically complete concept of the cost of capital.

To achieve this end, we must start with the fact that there are numerous sources of capital and that a firm often has choices among alternatives. Other than depreciation and retained earnings, there is a variety of financial instruments available, particularly to an established corporation. Each of these instruments has its own particular cost. Part of this cost differential stems from the fact that the capital markets are not perfectly competitive. In other words, the price

---

[1]The supply curve, in other words, was infinitely elastic at the market rate of interest.

[2]This at least is the central problem which occupied the writers of the nonmonetary school including Eugen von Böhm Bawerk, Irving Fisher, and Frank Knight. Derivative to this basic question are explanations of the structure of interest rates and fluctuations about the equilibrium. These, together with the effect of changes in interest rates on the level of employment, also concerned economists, particularly the so-called monetary school of writers. Ideally, a theory of interest should answer all these questions. At present, of course, no universally accepted comprehensive theory exists. For an excellent modern treatise on interest, see Joseph W. Conrad, *An Introduction to the Theory of Interest* (Berkeley: University of California Press, 1959).

competition among individuals and institutions supplying the funds is often imperfect.[3] But even if perfect competition prevailed, various degrees of financial risk would account for differences in the costs of alternative sources of funds. We can anticipate, for example, that interest on a short-term loan would ordinarily be lower than on a long-term loan. In the first place, the longer funds are tied up, the greater the risk of not having them returned. Thus, conditions which might force the firm into bankruptcy are easier to discern in the short run than over the long run.

Second, if interest rates are expected to rise over time, then the rate negotiated today will be insufficient a few years from today. The person lending the funds must be compensated with a higher interest rate; for once the rate is established, it cannot be altered until maturity, which is several years away. On the other hand, a short-term note matures within a few months. If renewed, rates can be renegotiated to reflect the conditions existing at the time.

In reality, we must recognize risk differentials for various sources of funds. Analytically, for the time being at least, we need distinguish only between debt and equity. Better still, we can develop principles of the cost of capital under the assumption that there are two types of sources: those for which income and principal are specified, and those for which they are not. This latter category includes most types of ownership interests. An exception consists of funds acquired through the sale of what is called straight preferred stock. As with debt, the income on this type of preferred stock is specified. Yet unlike debt, this stock does not mature but can, in principle, remain outstanding as long as the corporation continues to exist.

For purposes of this chapter, with the exception of straight preferred stock, we shall usually ignore contractual differences in the various

[3]More technically, the demand curve of capital to those providing funds is less than infinitely elastic, that is, it is downward sloping. The statement also implies that the degree of competition among institutions supplying alternative sources varies. For example, it is conceivable that competition is greater among firms providing long-term debt than among those supplying short-term debt, or vice-versa. Competition, moreover, can vary from one time period to the next. The rise of private placement may have made the investment banking industry more competitive today than it was in, say, the 1920s. We can also question whether competition is perfect among those demanding the funds. Is the supply curve of funds, even after the allowance for risk and uncertainty, infinitely elastic for all firms, or do some corporations possess monopsony power? Finally, does the broad array of legislation—from restrictions on the nature of the securities which a life insurance company can purchase for its portfolio to regulation of the securities markets—and implementation of the monetary policy of the Federal Reserve Board raise or lower the degree of competition and hence the cost differential among sources?

sources of funds. This is not because these details are unimportant. Indeed, this information is properly part of an introductory text in finance, and in subsequent chapters we shall consider these details more fully. To do so now, however, would unnecessarily complicate an already difficult task without seriously modifying our conclusions.

Finally, differences in tax treatment will affect the cost of various sources. To be specific, interest charges are deductible before arriving at profits subject to corporate or, in the case of unincorporated enterprises, personal income taxes. In order to simplify the discussion, we shall first ignore, with one exception, the income tax laws and incorporate the relevant provisions later into the analysis.

The Market Value of Ownership Interests

Since our goal is maximization of the market value of the owners' equity, it is well to begin the discussion by developing a measure which will implement this goal. Once this formula has been determined, we shall argue that it is the basis for measuring the cost of equity capital.

As a starting point we can assume that a person buys a share or interest in a business because of the dollar returns he anticipates receiving. The price he is willing to pay for the share is the present value of this income stream discounted at some rate r. The rate of discount is logically the rate of return he could earn by investing in the shares of another enterprise subject to the same risk as the shares under consideration. In other words, r is the opportunity cost of equity capital. The concepts of expected dollar returns and the rate at which they are discounted provide the means for arriving at a valuation of an interest in a business venture.

But this is only the beginning. It is also useful to have a market price for the shares in the enterprise. In this way we can compare his valuation with that of the market. Unfortunately, for the vast majority of business enterprises, there is no ready market price with which to make comparisons. Transfer of interests in unincorporated enterprises is difficult. While the corporate form of business organization surmounts this obstacle, many corporations are closely held. Hence shares exchange hands infrequently. When they do, the price at which the transaction takes place is usually a compromise between the maximum the purchaser is willing to pay and the minimum the seller is willing to take. Each has arrived at a range of values based on his respective maximum and minimum estimates of r and the dollar returns. Since they are based on imperfect knowledge and different attitudes toward risk and uncertainty, the estimates will rarely coincide.[4] But there must be some overlap, for a transaction will take place only if the maximum price the prospective purchaser is willing to pay equals or exceeds the minimum price the prospective seller is willing to accept.

For the shares of many publicly held corporations, there is a ready market price. But now a different complication arises. Ownership in these companies is usually divorced from control. Do those who purchase shares in the corporation value them for the dividends they receive or for the earnings which accrue to them whether paid out as dividends or retained in the company? This question has been one of the most hotly debated issues in the literature of finance,[5] with those favoring earnings apparently in the minority. It is the view of the author, however, that for purposes of an introductory analysis the debate has little relevance. However, in order to rationalize this assertion, we must first develop the techniques under the assumption that one or the other of the variables is controlling.

Since dividends ultimately depend on earnings, let us proceed as though no debate existed and argue that investors value an anticipated stream of earnings of E_a dollars per year. If P is the investment value of a share in the company, then

$$P = \frac{E_a}{1+r} + \frac{E_a}{(1+r)^2} + \frac{E_a}{(1+r)^3} + \cdots + \frac{E_a}{(1+r)^n}$$

$$P = \frac{E_a[1 - (1+r)^{-n}]}{r}$$

[4]Institutional factors will also prevent identical estimates. The prospective seller may be near the end of his life and wishes to dispose of his holdings, placing the receipts in trust or in a foundation in order to minimize or avoid inheritance taxes. The discounted value of the dollar returns are for him lower than they would be otherwise.

[5]For a sample of the literature pertaining to the controversy, see M. J. Gordon, "Optimal Investment and Financing Policy," *Journal of Finance*, vol. 18, no. 2 (May, 1963), pp. 264–272; John Lintner, "Dividends, Earnings, Leverage, Stock Prices and the Supply of Capital to Corporations," *Review of Economics and Statistics*, vol. 44, no. 3 (August, 1962), pp. 243–269; B. G. Malkiel, "Equity Yields, Growth, and the Structure of Share Prices," *American Economic Review*, vol. 53, no. 5 (December, 1963), pp. 1004–1031; Franco Modigliani and Merton H. Miller, "Dividend Policy, Growth, and Valuation of Shares," *Journal of Business*, vol. 34, no. 4 (October, 1961), pp. 411–433; Ezra Solomon, *The Theory of Financial Management* (New York: Columbia University Press, 1963), pp. 37–68; and J. E. Walter, "Dividend Policy: Its Influence on the Value of the Enterprise," *Journal of Finance*, vol. 18, no. 2 (May, 1963), pp. 280–291. For some of the difficulties involved in testing cost of capital models, see Eugene F. Brigham and Myron J. Gordon, "Leverage, Dividend Policy, and the Cost of Capital," *Journal of Finance*, vol. 23, no. 1 (March, 1968), pp. 85–103. For a criticism based on the proposition that a single equation analysis as used in the text is an inadequate representation of the factors determining the market price of the ownership interests, see Eugene M. Lerner and Willard T. Carleton, "The Integration of Capital Budgeting and Stock Valuation," *American Economic Review*, vol. 54, no. 5 (September, 1964), pp. 683–702.

For an infinite income stream,

$$P = \frac{E_a}{r}$$

In the more general case, however, E_a will grow or decline at some rate g, so that

$$P = \frac{E_a}{1+r} + \frac{E_a(1+g)}{(1+r)^2} + \frac{E_a(1+g)^2}{(1+r)^3} + \cdots + \frac{E_a(1+g)^{n-1}}{(1+r)^n}$$

It is possible to simplify this expression; the proof is in the Appendix to this chapter.   We get

$$P = \frac{E_a\{1 - [(1+g)/(1+r)]^n\}}{r - g}$$

In the above equation, when $r = g$, there is no solution.   But it is evident from the original expression that the equation for $r = g$ reduces to

$$P = \frac{E_a}{1+r} + \frac{E_a}{1+r} + \frac{E_a}{1+r} + \frac{E_a}{1+r} + \cdots + \frac{E_a}{1+r}$$

$$P = \frac{E_a}{1+r} \cdot N$$

where N is the number of terms in the series.   As $N \to \infty$, so does P.   Hence there is no finite solution.

When g is negative, that is, when earnings are expected to decline, $r - g$ becomes $r + g$ and the market price P is smaller than it would be if E_a remained constant and g was zero.

When $r < g$, the rate of growth exceeds the discount rate, so that

$$\frac{1+g}{1+r} = (1+r_1)^n$$

where r_1 is the net rate at which earnings are compounded.   Hence

$$P = \frac{E_a[1 - (1+r_1)^n]}{r - g}$$

As $n \to \infty$, the market price of a share will also approach infinity.   A finite value for the market price of the common stock is again impossible.

However, if $r > g$, the discount rate is higher than the rate at which earnings are compounded.   Consequently, we can let the expression

$$\frac{1+g}{1+r} = \frac{1}{1+r_2}$$

where r_2 is the net rate at which earnings are compounded.   Hence

$$P = \frac{E_a\{1 - [1/(1 + r_2)]^n\}}{r - g}$$

As $n \to \infty$, the expression $[1/(1 + r_2)]^n \to 0$.   As a result,

$$P = \frac{E_a}{r - g}$$

Economic analysis suggests that in the long run (that is, as $n \to \infty$), $r > g$, or alternatively, $g < r$.   The reasoning runs as follows: First, if g is forever $> r$ for a particular firm A, it would imply that investors can always expect earnings to grow more rapidly for this firm than for the highest-yielding alternative.   In such circumstances there would be a rush by those holding securities in lower-yielding companies to liquidate them, and offer to purchase the stock of firm A.   The result would be a decline in the market price of the stock of the other firms. Since their earnings have not changed, the yield on the shares of these firms rises, which in turn raises the opportunity cost r for firm A.

Second, the fact that $g > r$ implies that the productivity of physical capital, that is, plant and equipment, is greater in firm A than it is elsewhere.   Otherwise these firms would also experience $g > r$.   Hence there is an incentive for firm A to expand its investment in plant, equipment, and working capital.   If such an investment is made, the well-known principle of diminishing returns (in economic theory, the diminishing marginal physical productivity of capital) sets in. The result is a decline in the productivity of capital and hence a retardation in the rate of growth in earnings — in other words, a fall in g.   These two forces, one working to raise r, the other to lower g, will in the long run make $r > g$.[6]   The value for g can, of course, be positive or negative, thus encompassing the case of a declining as well as a growing industry.

Will the investment value P calculated in this manner equal the current market price of the stock?   Or should we consider, as some do, that the price today is a random variable?[7]   Appealing to the assumption

[6]Those familiar with the economic theory of the firm would point out that in long-run equilibrium analysis certain relevant factors such as technology and the market demand curve are held constant. It is quite possible that diminishing productivity of capital could be offset by technological progress and/or a rising demand curve for the product.   But can this go on indefinitely?   Implied in our analysis is the assumption that these factors serve only to lengthen the period during which $r < g$.

[7]The theory of random walks implies that "successive price changes in individual securities are independent random variables."   See Eugene F. Fama and Marshall E. Blume, "Filter Rules and Stock Market Trading," *Journal of Business*, vol. 39, no. 1 (January, 1966), part II, p. 226.   These authors question the applicability of the theory. See also pp. 226–241.   For a more detailed discussion, see Paul Cootner (ed.), *The Random Character of Stock Market Prices*, rev. ed. (Cambridge, Mass.: The M.I.T. Press, 1964).

of perfectly competitive markets, the values for E_a, r, and g would be known. The investment value and the current market price would coincide. Realistically, market imperfections would virtually ensure a divergence in results. But if our estimates of E_a, r, and g are reasonably accurate, then the trend in the market price should be toward the long-run investment value of the stock.

The calculations for E_a and g are, of course, educated guesses. Estimates of each may be either the most likely outcome or the expected value of the probability distribution of outcomes. But what about the discount rate r? Realistically, it too is an educated guess. Analytically, however, we can grasp its significance by pursuing the implications of the assumption of perfectly competitive markets. The equation

$$P = \frac{E_a}{r - g}$$

can be rearranged so that

$$r = \frac{E_a}{P} + g$$

P is now an independent variable—the current market price of the common stock. Seen in this light, r is the rate of return which investors expect to earn on their capital, given the risks inherent in this and other enterprises in which they might have placed their funds. In short, as asserted earlier, r is the opportunity cost of capital.

As a measure of the risks inherent in other enterprises, r reflects the subjective evaluation of the probability distribution of E_a and g. Suppose, for example, that the most likely outcome for the expected earnings of two firms was $2.00 per share. The expected growth rate was 10 percent per annum. Yet the variability in E_a and g was greater for the first firm than for the second. Depending on how the market views this difference, we would expect different values for r. If the subjective utility functions of investors were such that they placed a premium on stability, then r would be lower and the market price higher for the shares of the second firm than for the shares of the first.

The Controlling Variable—Dividends or Earnings?

Let us now return to the issue of whether earnings or dividends are the controlling variable. It is possible to conceive of r in terms of expected dividends D_a, so that

$$P = \frac{D_a}{r - g}$$

or

$$r = \frac{D_a}{P} + g$$

Except in the case of a declining firm where a company liquidating itself may pay dividends in excess of 100 percent of earnings, we can ordinarily expect $D_a < E_a$. Similarly, since r reflects the opportunity cost to the stockholder, it would be correspondingly lower when alternative investments are compared on the basis of expected dividends rather than expected earnings. With a tendency toward compensating differences in D_a and r, the long-run market value of a common stock may be approximately the same whether we use expected dividends or expected earnings as the variable which investors value. This is why the author asserted previously that the debate over whether dividends or earnings are the controlling variable has little relevance to an introductory analysis.

Yet if we were to pursue the analysis further, we might have reason to suspect that dividends can make a difference. To do so, however, would carry us far beyond an introductory analysis. We can, however, discuss some of the implications that dividend policy might have on the market price of the shares. Consider the following illustration. Management of the ABC Corporation has over the years maintained a policy of paying 50 percent of the firm's earnings as dividends. It is now considering raising the ratio to 60 percent.

Suppose that the current earnings are \$2.00 per share a year. Expected earnings E_a are \$2.20. The growth rate g is 10 percent. If dividends are maintained at 50 percent of earnings, the dividend this year is \$1.00. Next year it would rise to \$1.10. If dividends are increased to 60 percent of current and anticipated earnings, they would total \$1.20 this year and \$1.32 next year. But what would happen to g? If the payout ratio rises, other things the same, g must fall. The reason for this is that with a higher payout ratio there is a lower retention ratio. Less funds are available for reinvestment in current and long-lived assets. Growth in earnings reflects both the future return on existing assets and the earnings on additions to them. As E_a grows at a slower rate, there will be some point in the future where dividends will be lower because earnings will be lower due to the lower value for g. Thus if g falls to 6 percent because the payout ratio rises to 60 percent, earnings will compound at 6 percent, not 10 percent. At the end of 5 years, if dividends had not been increased, earnings and dividends would have reached

$$\$2.00(1.10)^5 = \$2.00(1.61051) = \$3.22102 \text{ in earnings}$$
$$50\% \text{ of } \$3.22102 = \$1.61051 \text{ in dividends}$$

If dividends had been increased, earnings and dividends would have reached

$$\$2.00(1.06)^5 = \$2.00(1.33823) = \$2.67646 \text{ in earnings}$$
$$60\% \text{ of } \$2.67646 = \$1.605876 \text{ in dividends}$$

From this point forward, dividends at 50 percent of earnings will exceed dividends at 60 percent of earnings.

As a result, when management alters its dividend policy, it changes the future stream of both earnings and dividends because it changes the growth rate g.   We must ask ourselves to what extent investors value higher current dividends over lower future dividends.   The answer depends on how they view the probability distribution of a stream of dividends based on a new payout ratio when compared with the stream based on the old payout ratio.   In a world of uncertainty, will the discount rate fall as the payout ratio rises, even though dividends at some point in the future will be forever greater because of a lower payout ratio today?   Alternatively, will the discount rate rise or remain unchanged?   There is no satisfactory answer to this question, for we are not dividing, say, $300 over 3 years into different annual installments. If we were, on the basis of time value of money alone, we would prefer the option which gave us the largest portion of the $300 in the first year.

By altering the payout ratio, we alter not only the stream of dividends but the size of the total amount available to pay dividends. Moreover, the further g is lowered by an increase in the payout ratio, the sooner will the dividend payments resulting from the increase fall below the payments that would have been made if the payout ratio had remained unchanged.

Since we do not know how investors will react to this situation, the simplest solution is to hold the payout ratio constant.   Owners, therefore, know that, in an anticipated stream of earnings, there will be an anticipated stream of dividends proportional to it.   With the payout ratio constant, the growth rate g[8] will not be affected because of changes in the proportion of earnings retained in the firm.

Our formulas therefore will be stated in terms of earnings rather

---

[8] We should note here that a change in the growth rate g due to a dividend increase could be offset by floating new equity issues or debt to replace the funds paid out to the owners.   If they are to avoid a decrease in dividends per share and hence in total dividends, then, taxes on dividends and costs of floating new shares aside, the present owners would have to buy the new shares with their dividend payments.   If debt is used, there is no change in the number of shares outstanding, but the increase in leverage raises the financial risk and hence may raise r.

The student should also remember that in keeping other things the same, the marginal productivity of capital is unchanged. Hence each dollar of earnings paid out as dividends would, if retained, have been invested at a constant, not a declining, rate.

than dividends.   However, since the controversy over whether dividends or earnings are the controlling variable has not been resolved, we cannot be adamant on the matter.   Hence the student should feel free to substitute D_a for E_a in the models which follow.

The Cost of Equity Capital

By employing the assumption of perfect competition, we were able in the previous section to use the current market price as an independent variable, rearranging our original equation so that

$$r = \frac{E_a}{P} + g$$

This rearrangement provides the basis for measuring three of the four components of equity capital: depreciation, retained earnings, and common stock.   Only straight preferred stock requires special treatment.

While stockholders may anticipate a growth in earnings at rate g, they need not expect depreciation to be reinvested at a rate higher than the E_a/P ratio.   In other words, we can assume that, for depreciation, g is zero.   The rationale for this assertion lies in the nature of the allowance.   It is designed to replace the capital invested in the enterprise, not to augment it.   Therefore, the cost of each dollar of depreciation, E_a, is simply the ratio E_a/P.

However, given the payout ratio for say a year, each dollar of earnings reinvested in the company is expected to grow so that the total amount invested averages g percent.[9]   Thus, the cost of the first unit of retained earnings is $E_{a'}/P$, which is greater than E_a/P because of the anticipated growth in E_a.   The cost of the second unit of retained earnings is $E_{a''}/P$, which is greater than $E_{a'}/P$.   The cost of the third unit is $E_{a'''}/P$, which is greater than $E_{a''}/P$; and so on.   In other words, suppose that r was originally 15 percent.   If an investment whose rate of return equals 20 percent is undertaken, then this additional investment raises r on the total invested capital to a figure in excess of 15 percent, say 15.6 percent.   The cost of the next unit of retained earnings therefore rises to this level.   As further investments are undertaken, the cost of additional units of retained earnings continues to rise.

But what about the market price of the stock?   Does it rise to

---

[9]We must keep in mind that it is the adoption of projects whose return is greater that E_a/P which causes E_a to grow at an average rate of g.   Each unit of retained earnings does not have to grow at this rate, but the total must at least average this percentage unless earnings on existing investments are greater than previously anticipated for the year.   Otherwise P will decline.

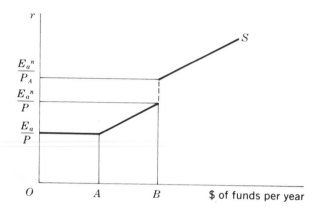

Fig. 12-1

offset the higher level of earnings, thereby maintaining r at 15 percent? The answer to this question is yes, it should. But our purpose is to develop the techniques which explain why the market price should rise to its new level at the end of the budgeting period. Assuming that its value is at a maximum, we can start with the old level for P because we do not want to accept investments which will lower P. At the same time we wish to accept projects which will ensure that the new level for P is also at a maximum.

Until all retained earnings after allowances for dividends are profitably reinvested, there is no logical reason for issuing new shares of common stock. To do so would involve the additional expenses of investment banking services, the printing of new certificates, and the costs of filing the information required under the provision of the Securities Act of 1933 governing offerings of new issues. P must be reduced by the amount of these costs. We can call this adjusted value P_A. If E_a^n/P is the cost of the last dollar of retained earnings, then E_a^n/P_A is the cost of the first dollar of common stock capital. The outcome of this reasoning is shown graphically[10] in Figure 12-1.

OA is the volume of depreciation expected during the budgeting year. AB is the amount of earnings anticipated after an allowance for dividends. All funds secured beyond amount OB would come from the sale of common stock. The discontinuity at B reflects the flotation costs, as measured by the difference between P_A and P.

This schedule represents the incremental or marginal cost of three sources of equity capital: depreciation, retained earnings, and common stock. Suppose that these were the only three sources of

[10]Ezra Solomon, "Measuring a Company's Cost of Capital," *Journal of Business*, vol. 28, no. 4 (October, 1955), pp. 240–252.

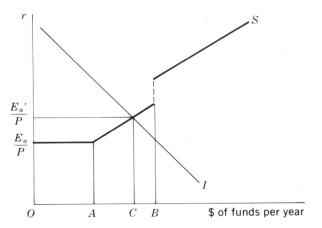

Fig. 12-2

funds, that is, there is no debt or preferred stock in the capital structure. Then, if we employ the rate of return approach to capital budgeting, the solution to the problem of budgeting funds to maximize the market value of the owners' equity is to invest sums up to the point where the rate of return on the marginal investment equals the cost of making that investment. This is shown in Figure 12-2.[11]

Over this budgeting period, management should invest all of the firm's depreciation allowances. Of the available earnings after regular dividend payments, management should invest AC dollars, paying CB dollars as an extra dividend to stockholders. To reinvest these funds within the firm would result in E_a growing at a rate lower than g. Thus the market price of the owners' equity would decline. To stop short of reinvesting AC dollars in the enterprise would also be a disservice to the stockholders. This is because the rate of return on each project is greater than the cost of these funds. Unless the investments are undertaken, the market price of the common stock will not be at a maximum at the end of the budgeting period.

The application of the marginal cost of capital principle to the rate of return method is straightforward. To employ this same approach using the present value technique is more difficult. There is no single cost of capital save an average which can be determined only

---

[11]To remain strictly within our frame of analysis, we must assume that the investment schedule contains an amount invested in current assets sufficient to maintain the present division between current and long-lived assets. As we have pointed out before, additions to working capital may be included in the outlays representing additions to long-lived assets.

after the total volume of investment is known.   In order to use the present value method, we must first determine the marginal cost of capital under the assumption that all the proposed projects are acceptable investments.   For example, assume that the total is $10,000,000 and the marginal cost of capital at that point is 20 percent.   Of this total, $8,000,000 would be depreciation and retained earnings, $2,000,000 would be common stock.

The second step is to discount the cash flows of all projects at 20 percent.   Let us assume that we find that projects equaling $6,000,000 of the total are acceptable at this rate; that is, they have a positive net present value.   The marginal cost of capital at $6,000,000 is 14 percent.

The third and successive steps consist in lowering the discount rate in stages from 20 percent for the previously unacceptable projects. Those with the lowest negative net present values at 20 percent are the ones most likely to become positive as the discount rate is reduced. With each successive reduction, the number of acceptable projects rises along with the marginal cost of an additional investment.   When the discount rate equals the marginal cost of capital, investment ceases at that point.   In our illustration, assume that this stage is reached where the marginal cost is 16 percent and the volume of investment is $7,000,000.   Under these conditions there would be no new common stock flotation and $1,000,000 of earnings could be paid out as extra dividends.

Although we shall find it more difficult to employ, conceptually at least, we can arrive at a discount rate which implements the present value technique.   Because of the advantages discussed in earlier chapters, we can continue to argue that it is in principle the preferred technique for budgeting capital.   Nevertheless, under the assumption that there is no debt in the capital structure, we can adapt the marginal cost of capital schedules to either the rate of return or the present value technique and in so doing continue to maximize the long-run market value of the owners' equity.[12]

---

[12]Those who choose to measure the cost of capital in terms of dividends will use D_a/P rather than E_a/P.   Suppose that in Figure 12-2, for example, $E_{a'}/P$ was $D_{a'}/P$. Dividends would grow at rate g, that is, in proportion to earnings.   Since the payout ratio is ordinarily lower than earnings, the value for $D_{a'}/P$ would also be lower than the value for $E_{a'}/P$, say 8 percent instead of 16 percent. AB would still represent earnings available for reinvestment.

Consistency, however, would also require that cash flows on the demand side be stated in terms of dividends.   With dividends ordinarily lower than earnings, the outcome would be a decline in the demand schedule.   Otherwise we should arrive at the same conclusions, that is, there should be OC or $7,000,000 in investment and $1,000,000 in extra dividends.   The marginal cost of capital as well as the marginal rate of return is now 8 percent rather than 16 percent.

The Cost of Debt Capital and Straight Preferred Stock

Because owners ordinarily receive an unspecified income on their investment, there may always be disagreement over whether dividends or earnings are the appropriate variable in determining the cost of equity capital. However, no such controversy rages with respect to debt. Whatever its form—bonds, notes, or trade payables—the principal and interest payments are contractual. The cost of capital in each instance is simply the rate of interest which equates these payments with the proceeds from the loan. If the funds received are equivalent to the principal amount of the loan, then the cost of capital is the contractual rate of interest. If the proceeds exceed the principal, the cost of capital is lower than the contractual rate. If the principal exceeds the proceeds, then the reverse is true.

To illustrate, assume a corporation floats an issue of $1,000 bonds with a nominal rate of interest of $4\frac{1}{4}$ percent paid semiannually. The bonds mature in 20 years. The corporation receives the equivalent of $980.20 per bond from the proceeds. The cost of this issue to the company is the rate of discount which equates 40 semiannual payments of $21.25 and $1,000 at the end of 20 years with $980.20 today.

We can find this rate from specially prepared bond tables, a portion of one page of which is reproduced in Table 12-1. Since the values are in units of $100, we must shift the decimal point to the right. For a $4\frac{1}{4}$ percent bond which sells for $980.20, the yield to maturity is 4.40 percent. Since the company views the $980.20 as proceeds from a loan, the 4.40 percent is the cost to maturity of the issue.

Similar tables are available for bank loans using a 360- rather than a 365-day year. In fact, given the nominal rate of interest, the principal

TABLE 12-1:   YIELD TO MATURITY ON BONDS
4¼% Interest Coupon

Yield to Maturity	20 Years	20½ Years	21 Years	21½ Years	22 Years
4.10	102.03	102.07	102.10	102.13	102.16
4.20	100.67	100.68	100.69	100.70	100.71
4.25	100.00	100.00	100.00	100.00	100.00
4.30	99.33	99.32	99.31	99.30	99.29
4.40	98.02	97.99	97.96	97.93	97.90
4.50	96.73	96.68	96.63	96.58	96.53
4.60	95.46	95.39	95.32	95.25	95.19

SOURCE: *Comprehensive Bond Value Tables*, 4th ed. (Boston: Financial Publishing Company 1958).   Reprinted by permission of the publisher.

on which the interest is paid, the maturity date, the number of interest payments, and, if it differs from the principal, the proceeds of the loan, we can always calculate the cost of debt capital. Published tables are merely a convenient reference for what are repetitious and tedious computations similar to those required to find the rate of return on an investment in long-lived assets.

The principles used to determine the cost of debt capital are applicable to straight preferred stock as well. With no maturity date and with a stated dividend, its cost is the rate of interest which equates the dividend with the net proceeds from the sale of stock. For example, suppose that a company expects to receive from the sale of an issue of $6.00 straight preferred stock the equivalent of $95 per share. Then the cost of the stock is simply

$$\$95 = \frac{\$6.00}{r}$$
$$r = 6.316\%$$

Leverage

Because holders of debt capital and preferred stock do not ordinarily participate beyond the terms of their contracts, the marginal cost of additional increments of this type of capital is independent of increases in expected earnings from adopting new investments. Thus, should earnings rise above the cost of these funds, the difference accrues to the residual owners, that is, to the common stockholders. However, should the earnings fall below the cost of these sources, they must be paid for out of earnings which would otherwise accrue to the common stockholders. In other words, holders of securities whose contractual obligation is fixed have prior claim to earnings. These *senior securities* participate ahead of common stock.

As a result, fixed prior claims can act as a lever on the per share earnings of common stock. To illustrate, using the accounting approach to valuation, suppose that a company has $1,000,000 in bonds and $1,000,000 in common stock and surplus. There are no other sources of capital on the liabilities and owners' equity side of the balance sheet. The interest rate on the bonds is 4 percent and there are 100,000 shares of stock outstanding. During the previous year earnings before interest in taxes were $200,000. For the current year they are $400,000. The income tax rate is 48 percent. Therefore

	Previous Year	Current Year
Earnings before Interest and Taxes	$200,000	$400,000
Interest on $1,000,000	−40,000	−40,000
Earnings after Interest	$160,000	$360,000
Income Taxes	−76,800	−172,800
Earnings after Taxes	$ 83,200	$187,200
Earnings per Share on 100,000 Shares	$ 0.832	$ 1.872

Suppose that instead of $1,000,000 in bonds the company could have sold 50,000 shares of stock at $20 a share at the time they were issued. The change that would have taken place would have been

	Previous Year	Current Year
Earnings before Taxes	$200,000	$400,000
Income Taxes	−96,000	−192,000
Earnings after Taxes	$104,000	$208,000
Earnings per Share on 150,000 Shares	$ 0.693	$ 1.387

In both cases earnings per share were higher when assets were financed out of both bonds and common stock. Moreover, as earnings per share rose, they increased by only $0.694, or approximately 100 percent, when financing took place only out of common stock. With 50 percent of the assets financed out of debt, earnings per share rose by $1.04, or 125 percent.

If earnings had declined, however, the effect would have been just the opposite. Suppose that in the current year earnings had been $100,000 instead of $400,000. All other conditions obtain.

	Current Year with Debt	Current Year without Debt
Earnings before Interest and Taxes	$100,000	$100,000
Interest on $1,000,000	−40,000	
Earnings after Interest	$ 60,000	$100,000
Income Taxes	−28,800	−48,000
Earnings after Taxes	$ 31,200	$ 52,000
Earnings per Share on 100,000 Shares	$ 0.312	
Earnings per Share on 150,000 Shares		$ 0.347

With 50 percent of the assets financed by debt, earnings would fall by $1.56, or approximately 83 percent. If debt had not been used, earnings per share would have fallen by $1.04, or approximately 75 percent.

If we had employed the economic approach to valuation, the results would have been similar. In either case, use of debt increases the variability in total earnings and hence earnings per share. Debt acts as a lever raising and lowering earnings above and below what they would be otherwise. In financial parlance this variability is referred to as the *leverage* effect of debt or senior securities.

We can apply the same argument to straight preferred stock. The consequences of failing to meet the contractual payments as they come due will, however, differ. Suppose that earnings fall to such a level that the cash balance is insufficient to meet interest on bonds. If there are no other sources of cash, such as sale of other assets or additional borrowings, then failure to pay interest usually precipitates bankruptcy. Failure to pay preferred dividends, however, does not precipitate bankruptcy. Ordinarily the dividends cumulate. No dividends on common stock can be paid until all back dividends on preferred have been paid.

Whether the risk is bankruptcy or an interruption in the current dividend policy, the use of senior securities increases the financial risk to common stockholders. Moreover, the marginal cost of senior securities may rise because the proportion of capital derived from them rises relative to the proportion supplied by common stockholders. The greater the dependence of earnings before interest and preferred dividends on investments financed out of senior securities, the greater the risk that the contractual obligations of these senior-security holders will not be met. The firm, making use of leverage, can at some point anticipate a rise in the cost of senior securities to compensate prospective purchasers for the greater risk they assume.

Similarly, since the increase in leverage raises the financial risk to stockholders, it will affect the market price of the stock. At some point the impact of this additional financial risk will make itself felt in a reduction in the market price of the common stock.

Thus there are two costs to senior securities. The first is contractual and relatively straightforward. The second is the impact of leverage on the long-run market price of the common stock. As long as the market price of the stock is unaffected by leverage, the cost of senior securities is lower than the cost of a new issue of common stock. How much lower depends on the nature of the instrument employed. The greater the risk to the senior-security holder, the higher the cost of capital to the company. The risk, however, is never as great as that

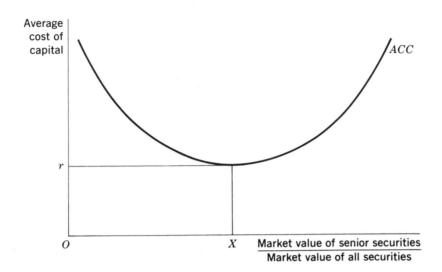

Average
cost of
capital

ACC

r

O   X   Market value of senior securities
                          ─────────────────────────────
                          Market value of all securities

Fig. 12-3

faced by the common stockholder. Hence, in perfectly competitive markets, we can expect a differential reflecting this risk.

The crucial question, which many students of finance would consider at least as controversial as the disagreement over dividends or earnings in the valuation of common stock, is the amount of leverage necessary before there is a decline in the market value of the owners' equity. In short, is there an optimum capital structure for a firm? If so, what are the principles which determine it? It is to this problem that we must now turn our attention.

The Optimum Capital Structure—the Traditional View

In 1958, as a result of the publication of an article by Modigliani and Miller,[13] there was a renewed interest in the concept of the cost of capital. Until that time it had been assumed, although never proved, that a firm did indeed have an optimum capital structure: a ratio of senior securities to total capital which minimized the average cost of capital. This belief is illustrated in Figure 12-3.

[13]Franco Modigliani and Merton H. Miller, "The Cost of Capital, Corporation Finance, and the Theory of Investment," *American Economic Review*, vol. 48, no. 3 (June, 1958), pp. 261–297.

It is assumed in this figure that as long as no more than OX percent of the market value of a firm's capital structure is in senior securities, the average cost of capital will be at a minimum.   Implied in this illustration is the assumption that up to that point the cost of senior securities is lower than the cost of equity.   Moreover, the use of leverage raises the per share earnings of the common stock without causing an offsetting decline in its market price.   The result is a lower weighted-average cost of capital, the additional earnings accruing to the shareholders.   Beyond this point, further leverage would depress the market price of the stock more than it would raise the per share earnings, thereby increasing the $(E_a/P) + g$ ratio.   Even if the cost of debt remained the same, the weighted-average (and hence the average) cost of capital would rise with additional leverage.

To use an arithmetic illustration, suppose that a firm has an all-equity capital structure.   The growth rate g is zero.   The E_a/P ratio is 10 percent.   The total expected earnings are $100,000.   The market value of the stock is, therefore, $1,000,000.   There are 100,000 shares outstanding.   Hence the price per share is $10.

Now suppose that management issues $400,000 in senior securities, in this case long-term debt.   The cost to maturity is $6\frac{1}{4}$ percent.   The proceeds are used to retire $400,000 in stock.   Assume that management is able to repurchase the stock at $10 per share.

To simplify, let us further assume that there is no difference in tax treatment between debt and equity.   The effect of the leverage on earnings per share is summarized below.

	All-equity Capital Structure	Capital Structure with Leverage
Earnings before Interest	$ 100,000	$ 100,000
Interest on $400,000 in Debt at 6¼%		−25,000
Earnings after Interest	$ 100,000	$ 75,000
Earnings per Share on 100,000 Shares	$ 1.00	
Earnings per Share on 60,000 Shares		$ 1.25

Earnings per share have risen from $1.00 to $1.25.   Since an element of financial risk has been introduced, let us assume that these earnings are now capitalized at 11 rather than 10 percent.   Thus

$$\frac{E_a}{P} = 11\%$$

$$\frac{\$1.25}{P} = 11\%$$

$$P = \$11.36$$

The market price of the common stock has risen from \$10 to \$11.36 as a result of using leverage.   With 60,000 shares outstanding, the total market value of the stock is now \$681,600.   Using the new cost of equity capital, the weighted-average cost of capital is

$$\text{Average cost of capital} = \text{Cost of debt} \left(\frac{\text{market value of debt}}{\text{market value of all securities}} \right)$$

$$+ \text{New cost of equity} \left(\frac{\text{market value of equity}}{\text{market value of all securities}} \right)$$

$$\begin{aligned} \text{Average cost of capital} &= 6.25\% \left(\frac{\$400,000}{\$1,081,600} \right) + 11\% \left(\frac{\$681,600}{\$1,081,600} \right) \\ &= 6.25\%(0.37) + 11\%(0.63) \\ &= 2.31\% + 6.93\% \\ &= 9.24\% \end{aligned}$$

Under our simplifying assumptions, management is able to retire 40,000 shares of stock at \$10 per share.   The use of leverage has raised both the earnings per share and the rate at which they are capitalized. The result in this instance is a rise in the market price of the stock and a decline in the average cost of capital.   But suppose the use of \$400,000 in leverage had raised the capitalization on equity from 10 percent to 15 percent. Then

$$\frac{E_a}{P} = 15\%$$

$$\frac{\$1.25}{P} = 15\%$$

$$P = \$8.33$$

The market price of the stock would have fallen from \$10 to \$8.33. With 60,000 shares outstanding, the total market value is now \$499,800. Using the new cost of equity capital, the weighed-average cost of capital is

$$\begin{aligned} \text{Average cost of capital} &= 6.25\% \left(\frac{\$400,000}{\$899,800} \right) + 15\% \left(\frac{\$499,800}{\$899,800} \right) \\ &= 6.25\%(0.445) + 15\%(0.555) \\ &= 2.781\% + 8.325\% \\ &= 11.106\% \end{aligned}$$

In this case, leverage has raised the cost of equity capital to such an extent that it has lowered the market price of the common stock and raised the average cost of capital.

Finally, suppose that the capitalization rate had risen from 10 percent to 12.5 percent.   In this instance,

$$\frac{E_a}{P} = 12.5\%$$

$$\frac{\$1.25}{P} = 12.5\%$$

$$P = \$10.00$$

The capitalization rate has risen in proportion to earnings, so that the market price of the stock is unchanged.   Thus the average cost of capital is

$$\text{Average cost of capital} = 6.25\%\left(\frac{\$400,000}{\$1,000,000}\right) + 12.5\%\left(\frac{\$600,000}{\$1,000,000}\right)$$

$$= 6.25\%(0.4) + 12.5\%(0.6)$$

$$= 2.5\% + 7.5\%$$

$$= 10\%$$

In summary, in our example, if the capitalization rate rises by less than 2.5 percent, the market price of the stock will rise and the average cost of capital will fall.   If the capitalization rate rises by more than 2.5 percent, the market price of the stock will fall and the average cost of capital will rise.   If the capitalization rate rises by 2.5 percent, the market price of the stock and the average cost of capital will remain the same.

In general, when leverage causes earnings per share to rise, the effect on the market price of the stock and the average cost of capital will depend on the change in the capitalization ratio.   If the change is compensating, that is, the capitalization rate rises in proportion to the rise in earnings, the market price of the stock and the average cost of capital remain the same.   In the illustration employed, earnings per share rose from $1.00 to $1.25, that is, by 25 percent.   A compensating rise in the capitalization ratio would be 10 to 12.5 percent, that is, 25 percent.   If the capitalization ratio rises less than in proportion to earnings, the market price of the stock will rise and the average cost of capital will fall.   If the capitalization ratio rises more than in proportion to earnings, the market price of the stock will fall and the average cost of capital will rise.

We can infer from this analysis and from Figure 12-3 that as the capital structure changes, so do earnings per share and the capitalization ratio.   Moreover, the percentage difference between the increase in earnings and the increase in the capitalization ratio is greater at capital structure OX than at any other ratio.   At this point the market value of the owners' equity is at a maximum and the average cost of capital is at a minimum.

If we accept the traditional approach, it follows that senior securities should be employed in a given capital budget so as to maintain this optimum. Suppose, for example, that OX represented a ratio of senior securities to total capital of 0.5. While there are various types of senior securities, as we noted earlier, we can treat their individual costs as reflecting compensating differences. Preferred stock, for instance, being riskier than debt, has a higher cost. We can therefore speak of a supply curve of senior securities as though all sources had but one cost. Assume this is 7 percent. Assume also that the cost of equity for capital structure OX is 11 percent. The average cost of capital is

$$\text{Average cost of capital} = 7\%(0.5) + 11\%(0.5)$$
$$= 9\%$$

The 7 percent represents the marginal cost of senior securities for a ratio of senior securities to total capital of 0.5. The 11 percent represents the marginal cost of equity for a ratio of senior securities to total capital of 0.5. Using the traditional approach to the capital structure, the marginal cost of capital is the weighted average of the marginal cost of individual sources. This cost is at a minimum at OX, or 9 percent. Thus, given the capital budget for a particular year, the cutoff point in Figure 12-4 is 9 percent. Alternatively, to be acceptable, the net present value of projects discounted at 9 percent must be zero

Fig. 12-4

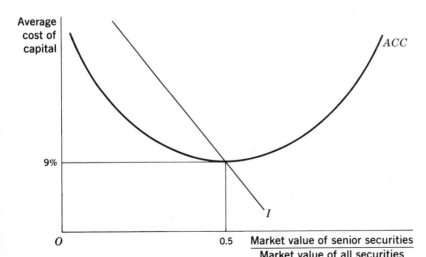

or greater. The capital budget may be $1,000,000 or $100,000,000. However, for the capital structure to be at an optimum, half of the budget must be financed out of senior securities and the remainder out of equity.

The Optimum Capital Structure — the Modigliani and Miller Hypothesis

But is there an optimum capital structure? The Modigliani and Miller thesis is that the capital structure makes no difference. In short, "the market value of any firm is independent of its capital structure and is given by capitalizing its expected return at the rate . . . appropriate to its [risk] class."[14] Moreover, "the average cost of capital to any firm is completely independent of its capital structure and is equal to the capitalization rate of a pure equity stream of its [risk] class."[15]

Stated briefly, Modigliani and Miller argue that firms in different industries face different risks. An electric utility, for example, may be subject to less variability in earnings than an oil company. Hence it is appropriate in perfectly competitive markets for earnings of the former to be capitalized at a lower rate than earnings of the latter. If the E_a/P ratio were 8 percent for a utility and 12 percent for a manufacturing firm, these differences would be compensating.

What Modigliani and Miller deny is that either company can raise the market price, or at least prevent it from falling, by using leverage. If, for instance, the utility issues a series of bonds at 5 percent or a series of preferred stock at 6 percent, there would be an immediate and compensating impact on the market price of the common stock. Investors would adjust their portfolios by selling shares of this utility, replacing them with some of the bonds issued. This process will raise the E_a/P ratio of the common stock as shown in Figure 12-5.

In general, if we let

x = average cost of capital

r' = cost of equity capital for a firm with leverage in the capital structure

d = market value of senior securities divided by market value of all securities

r = interest rate on senior securites

[14]*Ibid.*, p. 268.
[15]*Ibid.*, pp. 268–269.

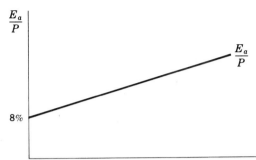

$$\frac{E_a}{P}$$

$$\frac{E_a}{P}$$

8%

Market value of senior securities
─────────────────────────────
Market value of all securities

Fig. 12-5

then

$$x = rd + r'(1-d)$$

The value of d is zero for an unlevered capital structure. The upper limit theoretically is 1. Institutionally, of course, there will always be some equity in the capital structure.

Thus it is Modigliani's and Miller's proposition that the average cost of capital of a firm is the same as the E_a/P ratio for its risk class. This ratio remains unchanged because the cost of cheaper debt is offset by the increase in the cost of equity due to a rise in the capitalization ratio. Recall our earlier illustration where earnings rose by 25 percent, that is, from $1.00 to $1.25. The capitalization ratio also rose by 25 percent, that is, from 10 to 12.5 percent.

To generalize this thesis, let r'' equal the cost of capital for an all-equity capital structure. In this case the marginal and average cost are the same. Therefore,

$$x = r''$$

But

$$x = rd + r'(1-d)$$

In the Modigliani and Miller hypothesis the two are equated, so that

$$r'' = rd + r'(1-d)$$
$$r'(1-d) = r'' - rd$$
$$r' = \frac{r'' - rd}{1-d}$$

249

In our example,

$$r' = \frac{10\% - 6.25\%(0.4)}{0.6}$$

$$= \frac{7.5\%}{0.6}$$

$$= 12.5\%$$

If the cost of an all-equity capital structure was 19 percent, the cost of debt 8 percent, and the ratio of senior securities to total capital 0.5, then

$$r' = \frac{19\% - 8\%(0.5)}{0.5}$$

$$= \frac{15\%}{0.5}$$

$$= 30\%$$

Again the average cost of capital would be

$$x = rd + r'(1 - d)$$
$$= 8\%(0.5) + 30\%(1 - 0.5)$$
$$= 4\% + 15\%$$
$$= 19\%$$

Once more we should emphasize that no distinction is made in the type of securities employed.   If 10 percent preferred had been used rather than 8 percent debt, the E_a/P ratio would not have risen as much, because common stockholders would have incurred less risk.   In the Modigliani and Miller thesis we always come back to this argument: In perfectly competitive markets the yields on securities reflect compensating differences in risk to holders of those securities.

Moreover, it is the assumption of perfectly competitive markets which allows Modigliani and Miller to conclude that the average cost of capital is independent of the capital structure.   To illustrate, suppose in our earlier example that when earnings rose from $1.00 to $1.25, there was no change in the capitalization ratio.   It continued to be 10 percent. In this case the market price of the stock would rise from $10 to $12.50.

The company has increased its financial risk, yet its shares sell at a 25 percent premium over the shares of another company facing the same business risk but with no leverage in the capital structure.   The earnings of this company, we shall assume, are also $1.00 per share. Since it faces the same business risk, the capitalization ratio is also 10 percent.   Hence the market price is $10.00 per share.

In perfectly competitive markets a stockholder owning 100 shares of the levered company could sell them for $12,500. He could then borrow $10,000 at the going rate of interest—in this case, 6.25 percent. With the proceeds from the sale of the stock and the loan, that is, with $22,500, he could buy 225 shares of stock in the unlevered company facing the same business risk. In so doing the shareholder has a net return of:

$$225 \times \$1.00 = \$225.00 \text{ earnings}$$
$$\$10,000 \times 6.25 = - 62.50 \text{ interest on loan}$$

$$\text{Net return} = \$152.50$$

This compares with $125 on the shares in the unlevered company. As long as the shares of the levered company sell at a premium over the shares of an unlevered company facing the same business risk, it will be profitable for the shareholder to substitute his own personal leverage for the corporate leverage.

The sale of shares in the levered company will cause its price to decline. When it reaches the price per share of the unlevered company, there is no further incentive to switch. This is why Modigliani and Miller conclude that the average cost of capital for a firm always equals the cost of capital without senior securities in the capital structure.

As we might imagine, the Modigliani and Miller argument has been attacked from many angles.[16] It is, of course, easy to question the assumption of perfect competition. We have already discussed at suitable length the question of whether stockholders are indifferent as between earnings and dividends. To Modigliani and Miller, cost of capital is not a function of dividends.

There is also some doubt as to whether the stockholder can borrow at the same rate as the company employing leverage. Moreover, the price of the stock of the levered company falls as shares are sold, but the price of the stock of the unlevered company does not change. For this to happen we must assume that there are numerous firms facing the same business risk. Shareholders in the levered company can buy stock in any of them. As a result, their purchases are such a small percentage of the total that they have no effect on the market price of the shares of unlevered concerns. Again, the assumption of numerous companies in the same risk class is consistent with the assumption of perfect competition.

[16]See, for example, David Durand, "The Cost of Capital, Corporation Finance, and the Theory of Investment: Comment," *American Economic Review*, vol. 49, no. 4 (September, 1959), pp. 639–655; J. Fred Weston, "A Test of Cost of Capital Propositions," *Southern Economic Journal*, vol. 30, no. 2 (October, 1963), pp. 105–112; and Ezra Solomon, "Leverage and the Cost of Capital," *Journal of Finance*, vol. 18, no. 2 (May, 1963), pp. 273–279.

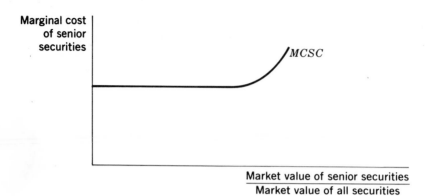

Fig. 12-6

Other assumptions have been criticized, including the assumption that the cost of capital is solely a function of leverage. It may depend on the size of the firm, the composition of assets, as well as the growth in earnings. There have also been charges that there is no empirical evidence supporting the Modigliani and Miller argument.

One of the more substantive criticisms of their analysis[17] is directed at their failure to explain satisfactorily why the average cost of capital remains constant at very high levels of leverage. As we noted earlier, at some point it would seem that the cost of additional increments of senior securities would rise as the return on these securities becomes a larger share of expected earnings. In other words, we would expect that at some point the marginal cost of these securities will rise as the ratio of debt to total capital approaches 1. Thus, in Figure 12-6, the marginal cost of debt is constant for a wide range of ratios of debt to total capital while rising thereafter. In order for the average cost of capital to remain constant, the market price of the stock, which has been falling because of leverage, must now rise. There is no logical reason for this to happen. Nor do Modigliani and Miller offer a satisfactory explanation.[18] Whether this point is of practical importance is another matter. It is quite possible that firms stop far short of a levered capital structure in which the marginal cost of senior securities is rising.

Of greater urgency is the question: Does the average cost of capital fall with modest increases of senior securities in the capital structure? The answer to this as well as to the previous question must ultimately

[17]Solomon, *ibid.*

[18]Modigliani and Miller, "The Cost of Capital, Corporation Finance, and the Theory of Investment," pp. 275–276.

depend on empirical analysis. Yet there are two primary difficulties in testing the model. First, how do we identify firms which are in the same risk class? Oil companies, for example, are heterogeneous with respect to the regions served, products produced, etc. In short, they do not face the same business risk.

Second, the empirical data available are current E/P ratios, not E_a/P ratios. Moreover, our analysis goes one step further, as we are concerned with the impact of the growth rate g on the cost of capital. As we emphasized before, many factors can affect current market prices. Our models are projected toward the future trend in the value of these shares. Current market prices may not fully reflect these variables. On the contrary, the price today may be more influenced by short-run occurrences such as illness or death of the President.

Bearing these points in mind, one empirical study of electric utilities found, among other things, that the average cost of capital rose with increases in leverage.[19] This was due in part to the year selected, 1959. Stock prices were high, reflecting anticipated growth in earnings and resulting in relatively low current E/P ratios. At the same time, debt was relatively expensive when compared with earlier years. The weighted average rose slightly with increases in leverage.

Modigliani and Miller,[20] drawing on a study of electric utilities using 1947–1948 data, found that the average cost of capital was independent of the capital structure. In these years the current E/P ratio was relatively high, reflecting less optimism about the future. Debt, on the other hand, was comparatively cheap. These tendencies were apparently offsetting, giving rise to an average cost of capital unaffected by leverage.

To the extent that optimism about the future results in a high value for g, there will be a relatively low E/P ratio. At the same time, if the cost of debt is relatively high, the weighted-average cost of capital could rise, as it apparently did in 1959. In these circumstances the empirical evidence fails to uphold the Modigliani and Miller hypothesis. On the other hand, during one or more years, there may be offsetting tendencies in the capital markets which yield empirical results that support the thesis.

Under the assumption of perfectly competitive markets, where g is zero, it is difficult to quarrel with their analysis save for doubts concerning its validity where leverage is very great, that is, where d

---

[19]Weston, *op. cit.*, pp. 107–109.

[20]Modigliani and Miller, "The Cost of Capital, Corporation Finance, and the Theory of Investment," pp. 281–284. They reached similar conclusions from a study based on oil companies. Weston did not pursue his analysis in this area for the reason indicated in the text.

approaches one. Thus the question remains: Of what use is the Modigliani and Miller model in implementing our goal?

Capital Budgeting and the Cost of Capital

The answer is that the Modigliani and Miller hypothesis not only was a brilliant piece of abstract analysis but also provides a point of departure from which soundings into the real world can be made. Even if the average cost of capital is independent of leverage, we must relax the rigorous assumptions imposed in order to develop a workable model for budgeting capital. For example, when we consider the impact of federal income taxes, the average cost of capital does fall with modest amounts of leverage.[21]

There are three areas in which an impact is made by corporate and personal income taxes. First, by making interest tax-deductible, the direct cost of corporate debt is reduced. Let 6 percent equal the cost to maturity on debt. Using a 48 percent tax rate, management saves 48 cents on each dollar of interest paid. In other words, net income subject to taxes is reduced by 48 percent of that amount. Thus

$$6\% - 48\%(6\%) = 3.12\%$$

If we let x equal the cost to maturity before taxes and x' equal the after-tax cost to maturity, then

$$x - \text{tax rate}(x) = x'$$
$$x(1 - \text{tax rate}) = x'$$

With a tax shield of approximately 50 percent of the interest costs, many corporations find that leverage in the capital structure lowers the average cost of capital and thus works to the long-run advantage of the common stockholders.

But taxes also discourage the use of straight preferred stock. Dividends on preferred are not deductible in arriving at taxable net income. Taxes are paid before preferred dividends are deducted. Thus the cost of an issue of preferred whose dividends amount to 7 percent of the net proceeds is

$$7\% + 0.48(7\%) = 10.36\%$$

If y equals the pretax cost of preferred and y' equals the after-tax cost of preferred, then

$$y + \text{tax rate}(y) = y'$$

[21]Weston, *op. cit.*, pp. 107–109.

A company which under the Modigliani and Miller hypothesis is indifferent as to the type of securities it will hold in its capital structure, is by virtue of the tax laws no longer indifferent to 7 percent preferred and 6 percent debt, nor indifferent to a levered and an unlevered capital structure.   As our data on the sources of funds will show later, what were largely compensating differences between senior securities are distorted to such an extent that the use of straight preferred has all but vanished from the corporate scene.

Finally, personal income taxes raise the discontinuity between the marginal cost curve of retained earnings and the marginal cost curve of common stock encouraging the retention of earnings. Because of flotation costs a corporation with profitable projects will always find it cheaper to retain earnings than to raise the dividend rate, replacing these funds with a new issue of common stock.

Add to this the fact that dividends are subject to income taxes, while profit on the sale of stock held 6 months or more is taxed at a capital gains rate. Thus the cost of retained earnings relative to new common stock is lowered still further. Considering first the impact of personal income taxes, the rate would depend on the marginal tax rate of the stockholders. This can vary, as we saw in Chapter 2, from 14 to 70 percent, depending on the personal income tax bracket of most shareholders. But even if we use the average of the marginal rates applicable to each owner, the cost of each dollar of retained earnings is now

$$\frac{E_a}{P}\,(1-\text{average of marginal tax rates})$$

Moreover, to the extent that the market price of the stock rises because earnings are retained within the company, stockholders can delay indefinitely any tax on the gains. Only when these gains are realized will they be taxed, and then, as we have seen, at rates not exceeding 25 percent. Thus, if an individual envisions not selling his shares, then, under the present law, he can avoid the capital gains tax altogether. At the date of his death the shares become part of his estate, with their market value at the time providing the basis on which estate taxes are levied. Furthermore, it is the present value of the anticipated capital gains or estate tax which provides the relevant basis for comparison with the tax on dividends today. Thus we can say that the cost of retained earnings adjusted for taxes is

$$\frac{E_t}{P_{AT}}\,(1-\text{average of marginal tax rates})$$

where P_{AT} is the market price of the share adjusted for the present value of the average capital gains tax.

Statistically, the impact of income taxes on retained earnings can be seen by comparing a period of relatively low taxes, say 1922–1924, with a period of relatively high taxes, say 1952–1960. One observer has noted that the retention ratio was lower and hence the payout ratio higher in the first than in the second period.[22] Thus even in assuming that our supply curve of equity capital consists of retained earnings after dividend requirements, we can infer that the impact of the tax laws has served to lower the proportion of earnings available for dividends.[23]

Corporate and personal income taxes, therefore, favor a sequence of financing which encourages the use of depreciation and retained earnings together with a limited amount of leverage in the form of debt rather than preferred stock. New issues of common stock will be used only when cheaper sources are exhausted.

Besides proper allowance for taxes, those responsible for budgeting capital so as to maximize the long-run market value of the owners' equity must assess realistically the imperfections in the capital markets. Not only is it possible that the current market price of a company's common stock may be overpriced or underpriced relative to its long-run market value,[24] but the level of interest rates on senior securities may be temporarily above or below their long-term trend. Moreover, it is possible that the structure of yields may not reflect, at least for a short period, the risk differentials we would expect in perfectly competitive capital markets. In any given year, what should be the marginal cost of various sources must be compared with what their costs are at the time the decision is made. This must be followed by careful scrutiny of the assumptions underlying the calculations of what should be, together with an analysis of what is, happening in the capital markets.

Suppose, for instance, that a tight money policy has caused the

---

[22]Arnold W. Sametz, "Trend in the Volume and Composition of Equity Finance," *Journal of Finance*, vol. 19, no. 3 (September, 1964), p. 465. Sametz states his data as retention ratios of .28 and .38, respectively.

[23]Assuming that there was a ready market for the stock, it would appear from our analysis that dividend policy should result in irregular payments consisting only of those funds which cannot be profitably retained in the business. Shareholders who find the income inadequate for consumption purposes would sell a portion of their holdings.

Yet managements of many concerns continue to stress stable dividends even though they may have to replace these funds with more expensive sources. Individual, if not always institutional, investors continue to separate the dividend from market appreciation, not realizing that in many instances their after-tax income might be greater if the corporation discontinued regular dividends and plowed most and sometimes all of the earnings back into the company, leaving each stockholder to adjust his holdings to meet his current income requirements.

[24]One of the arguments against the suggestion made in footnote 23 that dividends be a residual is the fact that investors are ill-equipped to judge the right moment at which to sell shares to meet their current income requirements. They are willing, therefore, to pay a premium for a stable dividend policy.

level of interest rates to rise drastically above their apparent long-term trend. Yet there are enough profitable projects to exhaust the available supply of retained earnings and warrant an issue of senior securities. Policy might dictate in this instance that the bond issue, if possible, be postponed and the projects financed out of short-term debt, with the debt funded into long-term securities at a later date when the interest rates have fallen.

Consider a more complex case where an issue of new common stock is in order, but, because of factors which are difficult to pinpoint, the current market price of the common stock is considerably below its long-run investment value. To issue new stock now, even to the old stockholders, would not be in the long-run interests of the common stockholders. In essence, what should be the marginal cost of common stock does not correspond to what *is* the marginal cost. The firm may readjust its investment plans, arguing that the projects are not profitable at current costs. On the other hand, it may well be that the opportunities available to finance these investments may not have been fully explored. Could management, for example, combine both the debt and equity features into one instrument, issuing what are called convertible bonds? If the stock is underpriced today, these bondholders might be content to earn interest on their investment while waiting for the opportunity for the market price of the stock to rise sufficiently to make it profitable to convert it into common stock.

Suppose, for example, that if the interest rate is $6\frac{1}{2}$ percent and the bonds can be converted into common stock on the basis of 10 shares of stock for each bond issued, management of a company can receive, after flotation costs, the face value of $1,000 from the sale of 10,000 bonds, or a total of $10,000,000. The current market price of the common stock is $85 per share. Assume that to acquire the same amount of funds from the sale of new stock, the company would incur flotation costs of $5.00 per share. The net proceeds per share would be $80. To receive $10,000,000, therefore, the company must issue 125,000 shares. If the investment value of the stock is greater than the market price today—say it is $120—then when the price goes above $100 it becomes profitable to convert the bonds into stock.

Suppose, for example, that the price of the stock rises to $110. A bond is now worth $1,100 because it can be converted into 10 shares of common. Since this is greater than the $1,000 the bondholder will receive at maturity, he may be encouraged to convert. If the dividends on the stock, after appropriate allowances for risk differentials, exceed the interest payments on bonds, the bondholder will definitely find it profitable to convert. Assume that this is the case. Then when the bondholders receive stock, the 10,000 bonds are the equivalent of

100,000, not 125,000, shares.   The firm has raised the same amount of money, $10,000,000, but has ultimately issued 25,000 less shares than if it had used an issue of common stock in the beginning.   Expected earnings per share and the market price are therefore greater than they would have been otherwise.   While in the period prior to conversion, stockholders saw an increase in financial risk due to leverage, they also enjoyed the tax savings resulting from the use of debt.

Thus even though we can develop a working model for maximizing the market value of the owners' equity by differentiating between debt, including preferred and common stock, realistically we must recognize the implications of market imperfections.   Management adjusts to these imperfections by making use of various sources, the details of which will concern us in the next few chapters.

SUMMARY

While there are numerous individual sources of funds, for analytical purposes we need only distinguish between two: those which specify principal and/or return and those which do not.   The former includes all debt; the latter includes common stock but not straight preferred.   Although straight preferred stock has no maturity date, the return on it is fixed.   It can, therefore, be included with the former.

The investment value of a share of common stock depends on expected earnings E_a or expected dividends D_a, the growth rate g, and the discount or capitalization rate r.   If P equals the investment value of the stock, then

$$P = \frac{E_a}{r-g}$$

or

$$P = \frac{D_a}{r-g}$$

In perfectly competitive markets the investment value equals the market price of the common stock and the market value of the owners' equity.   We can, therefore, let P be the independent variable.   Rearranging the equation we have

$$r = \frac{E_a}{P} + g$$

or

$$r = \frac{D_a}{P} + g$$

We can ordinarily expect D_a to be less than E_a. Consequently, the opportunity cost to the stockholder would be correspondingly lower when alternative investments are compared on the basis of expected dividends rather than expected earnings. Since the differences in D_a and r are compensating, the long-run market value of a common stock may be approximately the same whether we use expected earnings or expected dividends as the variable which investors value. However, since we do not know how investors will react to changes in the dividend policy, we have chosen to hold the payout ratio constant. The growth rate g is therefore unaffected by the proportion of earnings retained in the firm. Using a constant payout ratio, we have employed

$$r = \frac{E_a}{P} + g$$

as our basic model of the cost of equity capital.

When applying the model to depreciation, we can assume that g is zero. Depreciation is designed to replace, not to augment, the capital invested in the enterprise. Therefore, the cost of each dollar of depreciation E_a is simply the ratio E_a/P.

For retained earnings, however, the total amount invested must average g percent. Because of the anticipated growth in earnings, each unit of retained earnings must be reinvested at a higher rate. The ratio E_a'/P for the second unit is higher than the ratio E_a/P for the first, etc. The same principles apply to common stock except that flotation costs make it more costly than retained earnings. Thus the cost of the last dollar of retained earnings reinvested at E_a''/P is less than the cost of the first dollar of common stock capital E_a'/P_A, where P_A is the market price of the stock adjusted for flotation costs.

With a capital structure consisting entirely of common stock, management will maximize the market value of the owners' equity by investing in assets up to the point where the cost of the last dollar employed equals the rate of return on the last project considered. In other words, the return on the marginal investment equals the marginal cost of capital.

Although it is more difficult to employ, we can use the marginal cost of capital in determining the net present value of projects in the capital budget. To do so, we must begin with the assumption that all projects are acceptable. We then find the net present value of each project using the marginal cost of capital for the figure representing the total budget. As some projects are eliminated, the total budget is reduced. We now move down in successive stages along the marginal-cost-of-capital schedule. Projects with the lowest negative net present values are the ones most likely to become positive as the discount rate is reduced. With each successive reduction, the number of acceptable projects rises along with the marginal cost of an additional investment. When the discount rate equals the marginal cost of capital, further investment ceases.

In contrast to the principles determining equity, those determining the cost of debt are relatively straightforward. Whatever the nature of the obligation, the cost of capital in each instance is simply the rate of interest which equates the contractual payments with the proceeds from the loan. We can call this rate the yield or cost to maturity on debt. Similarly, the cost of straight preferred stock is simply the rate of interest which equates the dividend with the net proceeds from the sale of the preferred stock.

Since the return on debt and straight preferred stock is fixed, it can cause earnings per share to rise or fall more than they would if the capital structure consisted entirely of equity. In financial parlance, this increase in variability in earnings per share is known as the leverage effect from employing senior securities.

Can the use of leverage raise the market price of the common stock? Although it increases the potential earnings per share, leverage also raises the financial risk. In the traditional view of the capital structure it is assumed that there is an optimum combination of financing. Up to some ratio of senior securities to total securities, the percentage increase in earnings per share from the use of leverage is greater than the percentage increase in the capitalization rate. The market price of the stock rises and the average cost of capital falls. Beyond this point the percentage increase in earnings per share is more than offset by the rise in the capitalization rate. The market price of the stock falls and the average cost of capital rises.

According to the Modigliani and Miller hypothesis, the average cost of capital for a firm is independent of the capital structure. It is equal to the cost of a pure equity stream for a firm in its risk class. Thus, regardless of the capital structure, earnings per share rise in proportion to the capitalization rate. The market price of the stock remains the same and the average cost of capital is constant.

There has been considerable debate about the Modigliani and Miller hypothesis. Can we accept the assumption of perfect competition on which their thesis depends as a satisfactory explanation of reality? Must we assume that the average cost of capital is solely a function of leverage? Could it not also depend on growth in earnings and composition of assets?

In reality, when we consider such factors as the income tax laws, we find that financial management is encouraged to use leverage. Moreover, because interest is tax-deductible and dividends are not, financial management is encouraged to use debt and not preferred stock. Thus, the Modigliani and Miller hypothesis may be consistent with the assumption of perfect competition and a growth rate of zero. But since either of these assumptions rarely holds in practice, financial management must consider the impact of senior securities on the average cost of capital and hence on the market price of the common stock.

QUESTIONS AND PROBLEMS

1. Assume that Corporations X, Y, and Z are engaged in similar operations, that is, they have the same asset structures and growth rates. The earnings per share given below differ solely because of differences in leverage. Which firm, if any, is "overlevered"? Explain carefully.

	X	Y	Z
Earnings per Share	$ 4.00	$ 2.50	$ 3.00
Market Price	$24.00	$25.00	$24.00

2. Company X is presently earning a total of $500,000 on its common stock, the aggregate market value of which is $5,000,000. There are presently 100,000 shares outstanding. There is no debt in the capital structure and the growth rate g is zero. What is the cost of equity capital? Suppose that for the coming year the capital budget of $500,000, which is acceptable at the current cost of capital, can be financed out of bonds whose cost to maturity is 5 percent. Using the Modigliani and Miller hypothesis, what will happen to the cost of capital if the budget for next year is financed entirely out of debt?

3. "Corporate and personal income taxes serve to lower the cost of retained earnings and raise the cost of common stock." Do you agree? Explain fully.

4. Compare the current E/P ratio of IBM with the current E/P ratio of Commonwealth Edison. How do you account for the difference?

5. "The cost of equity capital is the same whether expressed in terms of dividends or in terms of earnings." Do you agree? Explain carefully.

6. "One of the difficulties with the Modigliani and Miller hypothesis is its assumption that the average cost of capital is solely a linear function of leverage." Evaluate critically.

7.   If expected earnings are $2.00 per share, the growth rate g is 5 percent, and the market price of the stock is $30.00, what is the cost of depreciation and the cost of the first dollar of retained earnings reinvested in the company?

8.   "There is little confusion over what constitutes the cost of debt capital.   There are, however, considerable difficulties both in the concept and in the measurement of the cost of equity capital."   Do you agree?   Explain fully.

9.   "The fundamental difficulty in determining the cost of equity capital stems from the fact that unlike debt or straight preferred stock, the contractual obligation to the common stockholder is unspecified." Evaluate critically.

10.   "If the growth rate g was greater than the opportunity cost r, the market price of a share in a company would tend toward infinity." Substantiate or refute this statement.

11.   Suppose that the cost of equity capital is 15 percent for a firm with no debt in the capital structure.   Management issues a series of bonds whose cost to maturity is 6 percent.   The proceeds are used to retire a portion of the stock outstanding.   As a result, earnings per share rise from $2.00 to $2.50.   The ratio of senior securities to total capital rises from 0 to .30.   The capitalization rate on equity rises to 18 percent.   What was the market price of the stock when there was no leverage in the capital structure?   What is the market price now? What is the average cost of capital?   Are the results consistent with the Modigliani and Miller hypothesis or with the traditional view of the capital structure?

SELECTED REFERENCES

Archer, Stephen H., and Charles A. D'Ambrosio (eds.).   *The Theory of Business Finance: A Book of Readings.* New York: The Macmillan Company, 1967, pp. 91–373.

Bodenhorn, Diran.   "On the Problem of Capital Budgeting," *Journal of Finance*, vol. 14, no. 4 (December, 1959), pp. 473–492.

Brigham, Eugene F., and Myron J. Gordon.   "Leverage, Dividend Policy and the Cost of Capital," *Journal of Finance*, vol. 23, no. 1 (March, 1968), pp. 85–103.

Donaldson, Gordon.   *Corporate Debt Capacity.*   Boston: Harvard Business School, Division of Research, 1961.

Durand, David.   "The Cost of Capital, Corporation Finance, and the Theory of Investment: Comment," *American Economic Review*, vol. 49, no. 4 (September, 1959), pp. 639–655.

Gordon, Myron J. "Optimal Investment and Financing Policy," *Journal of Finance*, vol. 18, no. 2 (May, 1963), pp. 264–272.

————. *The Investment, Financing and Valuation of the Corporation.* Homewood, Ill.: Richard D. Irwin, Inc., 1962.

Lerner, Eugene M., and Willard T. Carleton. "The Integration of Capital Budgeting and Stock Valuation," *American Economic Review*, vol. 54, no. 5 (September, 1964), pp. 683–702.

Lewellen, Wilbur G. *The Cost of Capital.* Belmont, Cal.: Wadsworth Publishing Company, Inc., 1969.

Lintner, John. "Dividends, Earnings, Leverage, Stock Prices and the Supply of Capital to Corporations," *Review of Economics and Statistics*, vol. 44, no. 3 (August, 1962), pp. 243–269.

————. "The Cost of Capital and Optimal Financing of Corporate Growth," *Journal of Finance*, vol. 18, no. 2 (May, 1963), pp. 292–310.

Malkiel, B. G. "Equity Yields, Growth, and the Structure of Share Prices," *American Economic Review*, vol. 53, no. 5 (December, 1963), pp. 1004–1031.

Modigliani, Franco, and Merton H. Miller. "The Cost of Capital, Corporation Finance, and the Theory of Investment," *American Economic Review*, vol. 48, no. 3 (June, 1958), pp. 261–297.

———— and ————. "Dividend Policy, Growth, and Valuation of Shares," *Journal of Business*, vol. 34, no. 4 (October, 1961), pp. 411–433.

Robichek, Alexander, and Stewart C. Myers. *Optimal Financing Decisions.* Englewood Cliffs, N.J.: Prentice-Hall, Inc., 1965.

Schwartz, Eli. "Theory of the Capital Structure of the Firm," *Journal of Finance*, vol. 14, no. 1 (March, 1959), pp. 18–39.

Solomon, Ezra. "Leverage and the Cost of Capital," *Journal of Finance*, vol. 18, no. 2 (May, 1963), pp. 273–279.

————. "Measuring a Company's Cost of Capital," *Journal of Business*, vol. 28, no. 4 October, 1955), pp. 240–252.

————. *The Theory of Financial Management.* New York: Columbia University Press, 1963.

APPENDIX: Derivation of a formula for determining the investment value of a stock

The expression

$$P = \frac{E_a}{1+r} + \frac{E_a(1+g)}{(1+r)^2} + \frac{E_a(1+g)^2}{(1+r)^3} + \frac{E_a(1+g)^3}{(1+r)^4}$$
$$+ \frac{E_a(1+g)^4}{(1+r)^5} + \cdots + \frac{E_a(1+g)^{n-1}}{(1+r)^n} \tag{1}$$

can be simplif ed by recognizing that it is a geometric progression. It is, in other words, a sequence of numbers such that each number after the first is the preceding number multiplied by the "common ratio" of the progression. In short, Eq. (1) can be rewritten as

$$P = \frac{E_a}{1+r}\left[1 + \frac{1+g}{1+r} + \left(\frac{1+g}{1+r}\right)^2 + \left(\frac{1+g}{1+r}\right)^3 + \left(\frac{1+g}{1+r}\right)^4 + \cdots + \left(\frac{1+g}{1+r}\right)^{n-1}\right] \tag{2}$$

The expression within the brackets is a geometric progression whose common ratio is $(1+g)/(1+r)$. If the first number in the progression is a (or in this case 1) and if the common ratio is p, then a general expression for the geometric progression is

$$a + ap + ap^2 + ap^3 + \cdots + ap^{n-1}$$

where $a \neq 0$ and $p \neq 1$.

Let S equal the sum of this geometric progression:

$$a + ap + ap^2 + ap^3 + \cdots + ap^{n-1} = S$$

Multiply both sides of the equation by $(p-1)$.

$$(p-1)[a + ap + ap^2 + ap^3 + \cdots + ap^{n-1}] = (p-1)S$$
$$ap - a + ap^2 - ap + ap^3 - ap^2 + ap^4 - ap^3 + \cdots + ap^n - ap^{n-1} = (p-1)S$$
$$\frac{ap^n - a}{p-1} = S$$

Therefore

$$a + ap + ap^2 + ap^3 + \cdots + ap^{n-1} = \frac{ap^n - a}{p-1}$$

Substituting these terms in Eq. (2), we get

$$P = \frac{E_a}{1+r}\left[1 + \frac{1+g}{1+r} + \left(\frac{1+g}{1+r}\right)^2 + \cdots + \left(\frac{1+g}{1+r}\right)^{n-1}\right]$$

$$= \frac{E_a}{1+r}\frac{[(1+g)/(1+r)]^n - 1}{(1+g)/(1+r) - 1}$$

$$= \frac{E_a(1+r)^{-1}\{1 - [(1+g)/(1+r)]^n\}}{1 - [(1+g)/(1+r)]}$$

$$= \frac{E_a(1+r)^{-1}\{1 - [(1+g)/(1+r)]^n\}}{(r-g)/(1+r)}$$

$$= \frac{E_a\{1 - [(1+g)/(1+r)]^n\}}{r-g}$$

Short-term Sources of Funds

chapter Thirteen

In this chapter the student should contrast the costs of the major sources of short- and intermediate-term funds. What are the likely alternatives open to most firms? What are their costs to maturity?

Introduction

As we saw in the last chapter, a model which distinguishes simply between debt (including preferred stock) and equity as sources of funds is a useful tool in implementing the ultimate goal of maximizing the market value of the owners' equity. Yet we also pointed out that, realistically, management must have some knowledge of the relevant characteristics of various sources if it is to seek out in imperfect capital markets the cheapest source or sources available at the time a decision to finance assets is made. Thus in this and the next three chapters we shall discuss more fully the characteristics of the alternatives which might possibly be available to an individual concern. In this chapter we shall concentrate primarily on short-term sources of funds. While the emphasis will be placed on credit extended for periods of a year or less, we shall also include intermediate-term loans of banks and insurance companies.

Commercial Bank Credit

Although a subsequent chapter on the flow of funds will show that it is less important than some other short-term sources, credit extended by commercial banks is, nevertheless, unique among all sources. As students of the principles of economics know, the uniqueness of commercial bank credit is the method by which it is extended. When a commercial bank agrees to lend to an individual or to a business firm, it ordinarily adds the proceeds of the loan to the borrower's checking account or demand deposit. Demand deposits are the major component of the money supply. This ability to add to or create a deposit, if the borrower does not already have one, is the process by which the nation's money supply is expanded.

If, for example, a commercial bank receives a deposit of $1,000 in cash from a customer, it credits the customer's demand deposit for $1,000 and either retains the $1,000 in cash in its vault or ships it to the Federal Reserve Bank in the district in which it is located. Thus if the bank were located in Hartford, Connecticut, it would send the cash to the Federal Reserve Bank of Boston. This Federal Reserve Bank is one of 12 such banks located in principal cities throughout the United States. Together they represent the central banking system in the United States. Each commercial bank, if it has a federal charter of incorporation, must belong to the Federal Reserve System. Those incorporated under state laws can belong. Most of the state-chartered banks do belong.

Each bank must abide by the rules of the system. One of these rules is the requirement that a minimum amount of cash representing a specified percentage of deposits be kept either in the bank's vault or on deposit at the Federal Reserve.

Suppose that in our example the reserve requirements are 16 percent. Then the commercial bank must maintain a $160 balance against the $1,000 deposit of its customer. Statistically, cash of $1,000 is traded for a checking account of $1,000. Since the cash component of the money supply includes only coins and currency in circulation, the total amount of money outstanding remains the same; only its composition has changed. There is now $1,000 less in cash but $1,000 more in demand deposits.

But a commercial bank is a profit-making institution. Within the constraints imposed on it, the management of the bank will seek to maximize the market value of its owners' equity. Thus it will not want to let the $840 in excess reserves lay idle. It will seek to lend out these funds at interest. If successful, it will add to or create a demand deposit representing that amount less interest if deducted in advance. Note that if the borrower wanted cash, the bank could have given it to him. The bank would still have $160 remaining as reserves against the original $1,000 deposit. In either instance the money supply increases by $840.[1]

Whether the funds received by commercial banks are derived from the deposit of cash in checking accounts or savings accounts,[2] they are relatively liquid and hence easily convertible into cash. The bulk of the assets of commercial banks, therefore, consist of short-term loans and investments. In fact, the traditional theory of commercial banking has paid homage to the principle that all loans should

---

[1] If the money is withdrawn and spent, with the recipient depositing the funds in another bank, there may be a further increase in the money supply. The bank receiving the funds holds 16 percent of $840, or $134.40, as required reserves. The residual, or $705.60, is available for additional loans. This process can be continued until

$$\$1,000[1 - (0.84) - (0.84)^2 - \cdots - (0.84)^n] = \$1,000 \times \frac{1}{1 - 0.84}$$

$$\$1,000 \times \frac{1}{0.16} = \$6,250$$

Although the desire for profits will encourage it to do so, the bank need not lend its excess reserves. Furthermore, there may be no one willing to borrow them and customers might withdraw the funds and hold them as cash. For any of these reasons the expansion in the money supply could stop before it reached the maximum permissible under the reserve requirement. See Paul A. Samuelson, *Economics: An Introductory Analysis*, 7th ed. (New York: McGraw-Hill Book Company, 1967), chap. 16; and Federal Reserve Bank of Chicago, *Modern Money Mechanics: A Workbook on Deposits Currency and Bank Reserves*.

[2] While the money supply is ordinarily defined as demand deposits and coins and currency in circulation, time deposits including savings accounts as well as negotiable and nonnegotiable certificates of deposit are considered by some to be part of the money supply. This is because many time deposits, even though they are not technically payable on demand, are in practice treated as if they were. Statistics on the money supply are published monthly in the *Federal Reserve Bulletin*. If time deposits are excluded, checking accounts comprise about 80 percent of the nation's money supply.

For the student who finds the distinction between savings accounts and time deposits confusing, we can note that under the regulations of the Board of Governors of the Federal Reserve System, only individuals and nonprofit organizations may own savings deposits. These must be "evidenced by a passbook." Time deposits "evidenced by a negotiable or a nonnegotiable instrument" and payable at a fixed date in the future "not less than 30 days after the date of deposit," may be owned by depositors of any type.

be short-term and *self-liquidating*.[3]　In practice, some types of commercial bank credit are rarely liquidated.　As an illustration, consider lines of credit.　A *line of credit* consists of an "informal understanding between the borrower and the bank as to the maximum amount of credit which the bank will provide the borrower at any one time."[4]　Because the arrangement is informal, the maximum line of credit can change from year to year.　The interest rate may also change, as well as the amount stipulated by another requirement often accompanying this type of loan: the borrower must have on deposit at all times an amount varying from 10 to 20 percent of the line of credit.　The commercial bank, eager to maintain satisfactory relations with a good customer, will always try to accommodate such a firm.　Because it is expected that the bank will require the company to "clean up" its loan once a year, one method of accommodation is to provide for transfer of the line of credit from one bank to another.　While the author is not suggesting that all companies do "clean up" their lines of credit in this fashion, to the extent that a firm does, it has acquired a relatively permanent source of funds even though it is technically labeled short-term financing.

While a bank can preserve its own liquidity by providing for transfers of lines of credit, the argument that a loan will be self-liquidating is, if the concept is interpreted narrowly, largely a fiction.　The granting of a loan and the possibility of transferring credit from one bank to another are dependent on the firm's ability to repay, that is, on its projected working capital position.　Yet it does not necessarily follow that the proceeds from a particular loan will, when invested, actually generate funds sufficient to liquidate the loan on or before the date of its maturity.　A manufacturer, for example, may produce a variety of products, one of which requires a heavy investment in raw materials in the spring.　In order to help finance these inventories, the firm has a maximum line of credit of $100,000.　Each year, early in April, the manufacturer borrows this amount with the intention of repaying it by October 1.　Sales of the goods produced from these raw materials can ordinarily be expected to generate cash sufficient to liquidate the loan on schedule.　But suppose that because of delays in liquidating the firm's accounts receivables from distributors, there are times when management requires more than 6 months to obtain the proceeds from the sale of these particular products.　The firm may still be able to repay the loan out of funds generated from other facets of its opera-

---

[3]The theory that banks should confine themselves to short-term, self-liquidating loans dates to 1776.　See Adam Smith, *An Inquiry into the Nature and Causes of the Wealth of Nations*, (New York: Random House, Inc., 1937), pp. 288–292.

[4]Caroline H. Cagel, "Credit Lines and Minimum Balance Requirements," *Federal Reserve Bulletin*, vol. 42, no. 6 (June, 1956), p. 573.

tions or from funds held for precautionary motives. The pivotal question is: Can the firm repay the loan at maturity out of current assets even though it may not wish to do so at the time? If in projecting its working capital management finds that it will have sufficient cash to repay the loan at maturity, then it should be immaterial to the bank whether the funds generated actually came from investing the proceeds.

From the point of view of the bank, therefore, it is not of primary importance that the loan be short-term and self-liquidating. Customers worthy of lines of credit are those whose asset structures, relative to the size of their borrowing and the composition of their other liabilities and owners' equity, virtually ensures repayment. Under such conditions the loans can usually be transferred or, if necessary, liquidated at maturity.

But what does the management of the borrowing firm gain from structuring its assets and financing so as to meet, in the eyes of the bank, the necessary standards of creditworthiness? The primary advantage is a ready source of funds to meet unexpected needs. Suppose, for example, that a wholesale concern with a $200,000 line of credit uses $100,000 of it to finance normal inventory needs. However, an unexpected increase in demand forces management to increase its inventory levels. Since the line of credit is available, management is prepared to take advantage of trade discounts granted by suppliers.

Having made the commitment, the commercial bank will do everything in its power to honor it. Thus, in a period of tight money, banks will sell government securities from their portfolios to accommodate the customers' demands for credit. Yet, for the privilege of having a ready line of credit, the management of the borrowing firm may be paying a relatively high price. Other than the interest rate on the loan, the most obvious costs are the compensating balances. For example, suppose that a manufacturing concern has met what the bank considers satisfactory standards for an extension of a line of credit of $200,000 on demand. In other words, appropriate company officials can sign at any time an unsecured promissory note or notes[5] maturing within

---

[5]The note will be signed by a designated officer or officers of a corporation, by the proprietor, or by one or more general partners in an unincorporated enterprise. Procedures are more formal in the United States than in the United Kingdom and Western Europe. There lines of credit are extended through overdrafts on the customers' checking account. The bank honors the overdrafts by providing the funds up to the line of credit, less compensating balances if any. Commercial banks in this country have begun to approximate overdrafts for individuals by guaranteeing personal loans up to a specified amount. The customer can count on the funds being deposited in his account should they be needed. Yet technically the funds advanced are a loan, not an overdraft on a checking account. In this country, in other words, a loan account of a customer is separated from his checking account.

a specified period, say a year from the date the line of credit is extended, for amounts up to $200,000. Interest is $6\frac{1}{2}$ percent per annum paid in advance. There are compensating balances of 10 percent.

Suppose that management chooses to take advantage of the entire line of credit at one time; that is, it borrows $200,000. Then the proceeds available for investment are $200,000 less 10 percent of $200,000, or $180,000. Since the note is discounted, that is, interest is deducted in advance, the proceeds are reduced still further to $180,000 less $6\frac{1}{2}$ percent of $200,000, or $167,000. With the compensating balances accounting for $20,000 of the loan, the repayment is reduced to $180,000. Thus the effective annual rate of interest[6] is

$$\$167,000 = \frac{\$180,000}{1+r}$$
$$r = 7.78\%$$

If management was not forced to maintain compensating balances, it could have actually borrowed $180,000 rather than $200,000. In other words, management had to borrow $20,000 more than it needed in order to satisfy the bank's demand for compensating balances. Thus it must pay an additional $1,300 in interest. To put it another way, if management had borrowed $180,000 rather than $200,000, it would have paid $11,700 in interest rather than $13,000. The effective rate of interest would have been

$$\$168,300 = \frac{\$180,000}{1+r}$$
$$r = 6.95\%$$

Maintaining a line of credit, therefore, is more costly than it appears, once full consideration is given to compensating balances and the fact that the loan is often discounted. Moreover, the credit department of the commercial bank may require liquidity ratios and net working capital positions at all times to be in excess of what management and presumably the owners feel are sufficiently prudent levels. To put it differently, cash or the equivalent in marketable securities held to satisfy the precautionary motive may be insufficient to meet the bank's requirements for extending an unsecured line of credit. If so, then to acquire this credit privilege, management must invest more funds in

---

[6]Since banks used 360-day years, as we saw in an earlier chapter, the effective rate of interest is somewhat higher. In this instance the loan would have to be repaid 5 days prior to the corresponding date on the next calendar year. Thus we could simply multiply

$$7.78\% \times \frac{365}{360} = 7.89\%$$

working capital than it had originally planned. As a result the market value of the owners' equity may decline.

The bank's ability to impose standards depends, of course, on the competition it faces from other sources available to the firm, as well as the demand for loans relative to the existing supply of funds. Some companies, for example, may find better terms at a different bank or by flotating their own promissory notes in the market for short-term paper. On the other hand, a small company whose business is primarily local may find the impersonal capital markets unaccessible. Its only source of borrowed funds may be a single local bank.

But even if management finds too costly the terms under which an unsecured line of credit is extended, it may be able to arrange more favorable terms by pledging collateral. In fact, unsecured lines of credit, particularly those for which a reasonably firm commitment is made, are not commonplace. Banks are more likely to make commitments conditional on the availability of funds and on the firm's meeting its standards of profitability and liquidity at the time the loan is made. Moreover, the loans, particularly if they are for relatively large amounts, are usually secured.

The nature of the collateral will vary. So too will the loan as a percentage of the value of the security. U.S. government bonds, for instance, may be used to secure a loan whose principal amount may equal 90 percent of the market value of the bonds. Common stocks may also be acceptable as collateral but only for a loan equivalent perhaps to 50 percent of the market value of the stock.

While business firms may pledge security that is unrelated to its operations—a proprietor, for instance, may use the cash surrender value of a life insurance policy as security for a business loan—it is more likely that commercial loans will be secured by the real assets which play a major role in the operations of a nonfinancial enterprise. Management of a firm may pledge its marketable securities, but since these are usually liquidated to meet seasonal needs, management is more apt to pledge the inventory it wishes to finance. If the commodity enjoys a ready market—for example, coffee, cotton, lead, wheat, etc.—a commercial bank is often receptive to making a loan equal to at least a substantial portion, perhaps 75 percent, of its value.

In fact, inventory loans are among the most common types of short-term bank loans. As in the case of an unsecured line of credit, a promissory note agreeing to repay the loan at maturity is signed by the borrower, or the appropriate officers if the firm is incorporated. But there is an additional document common to all secured loans signed by the borrower, giving the lender lien or title to the inventory in the event of default. The inventory, however, may remain in the hands of the borrower or be transferred to a third party.

If the goods remain in the hands of the borrower, they may be released through a *trust receipt*, a document showing that the lender, who has been given title to the goods, has in turn released them in trust to the borrower.   Floor plans of automobile dealers are often financed in this manner.   Alternatively, the lender may obtain a general or factor's lien on all the firm's inventory.   In each case the bank must depend on the integrity of management reinforced by periodic and costly inspections.   Because of this problem, and because the legal status of factor liens and trust receipts is shaky in some states, the bank is likely, where feasible to prefer placing control of the inventory in the hands of a third party.   This third party, a professional warehouseman storing goods for a profit, takes title to the merchandise and issues in return a *warehouse receipt.*   The borrower cannot withdraw any of the inventory unless he has permission from the lending bank.   Only if he repays a portion of the loan or pledges additional security is he likely to receive permission.

The warehouse receipts may be *negotiable*, that is, freely transferable from hand to hand, or *nonnegotiable*.   If negotiable, title is likely to be vested in the hands of the lender, although it might be made out to the borrower who in turn endorses it over to the bank. Nonnegotiable warehouse receipts are issued in favor of the lender. The latter are more widely used because, with a negotiable receipt, the document must be presented each time a withdrawal is made.   With a nonnegotiable receipt the lender can simply, through a written order, instruct the warehouseman to release a certain amount of the inventory in the hands of the borrower.   Again, unless a pro rata share of the loan is repaid, the borrower is not likely to receive this permission.

Since management will usually have need for frequent access to the inventory, it may prove inconvenient to transfer the merchandise to the warehouse of the third party.   As a result, a method known as field warehousing has become popular over the last 40 years.   The storage facilities containing the inventory of the borrower are fenced off by the warehouseman.   When the borrower gets permission to remove some of the inventory, he is spared the expense of having to transfer it from the warehouse of the third party.[7]

The merchandise of some firms — the output of a novelty manufacturer, for example — might be considered too risky as collateral for bank loans.   But once the items are sold, the accounts receivables, or

---

[7]In spite of efforts to improve the efficiency of inventory financing, the fact that the collateral cannot be kept in the bank's vault adds to the risk involved in relying on it as security for loans.   This fact was brought home in 1963 as a result of the salad oil scandal.   See "Lessons from the Haupt Affair," an editorial in *Fortune*, vol. 69, no. 1 (January, 1964), pp. 74–78.

a portion of them, may be satisfactory collateral for a receivables loan. Depending on their quality, a commercial bank may be willing to lend 80 to 90 percent of the face value of the accounts receivables which the firm is willing to pledge and the bank is willing to accept.   As the lender collects these accounts, it either endorses the proceeds over to the bank, thereby reducing the loans, or retains the funds but replaces the accounts liquidated with new ones of comparable quality.

Other collateral may be used to secure loans.   Notes payable to the borrowing firm are one example.   The notes are discounted, say at $3 per $100 of notes payable.   The actual loan is $97 per $100 of notes payable.   However, except for a few industries, it is common practice for American business to make sales on open account.   Accounts receivable rather than notes payable are apt to appear in the balance sheet.   Many companies often resort to notes only for slow-paying customers who are continually in arrears.   It may be a step prior to cutting off their credit completely.   To the extent that this is the case, these notes will not be acceptable for loans.

While notes receivable are not frequently used as security, installment contracts for consumer durables such as automobiles, stereos, refrigerators, etc., are pledged.   Under the terms of an installment contract, the dealer or supplier selling the goods receives a down payment on the purchase price.   The consumer agrees to pay the balance in monthly installments.   The dealer obtains a *chattel mortgage*[8] on the commodity sold.   If the consumer does not live up to his obligations—he fails to meet the monthly installments—the dealer can repossess the merchandise.   Because the consumer has ordinarily made a down payment on the item, the probable market value of the commodity is in excess of the credit extended to him.   Hence the collateral is readily accepted by a commercial bank as collateral for a loan to the dealer.   In some instances the bank may even assume the contracts with or without recourse to the dealer or supplier.   The purchaser then makes his payments directly to the bank.

There are other arrangements and types of collateral which can be used to obtain or secure loans made by commercial banks.[9]

[8]A chattel mortgage is a mortgage on movable property such as an automobile as distinct from a mortgage on real estate.

[9]A trade acceptance is a substitute for a note receivable.   It differs from the ordinary promise to pay in that a trade acceptance is drawn by the seller on the customer but made payable to the seller.   A note receivable, consisting of a simple promise to pay, is drawn by the customer and made payable to the seller.   While this distinction can be important legally, it is of little financial significance.   Trade acceptances are not widely used in this country and hence are not a major source of collateral for bank loans.

Accommodation paper is also a rare form of security.   It is a type of two-name paper in which the one seeking the loan must, as a condition of having credit extended to him, have a third party who for no, or at most nominal, consideration is willing to

However, it can be said that most of these are of minor significance.[10]

For financial management, however, the question must be asked: What concessions, if any, will the use of collateral bring in the cost of short-term loans? For some firms the answer is none. Without security, the company would receive no credit at all. For others, the use of collateral, particularly if there is a ready market price for the goods pledged, may lower the cost of bank loans. The most likely concession will be in the rate charged, say $6\frac{1}{4}$ percent instead of $6\frac{1}{2}$ percent. Management may, however, also be able to pay interest at maturity rather than in advance, thereby lowering the effective cost of the loan. If it can be arranged, of course, a reduction or even the elimination of compensating balances may be the greatest factor in lowering the cost of the loan.

------

add his signature to the note, thereby becoming liable along with the borrower in case of default. Since American business firms try to avoid notes receivables from one individual in favor of open accounts, we cannot expect them to use accommodation paper in order to sell goods. A bank loan made because a dealer has discounted his customer's installment note is in effect a type of accommodation paper. Without the endorsement of the seller the bank may not have been willing to lend the buyer the funds to purchase the automobile, television set, etc.

[10]A bank acceptance (or banker's acceptance) is quite important in international trade. Suppose that a British exporter of men's wear is desirous of selling $10,000 worth of jackets and slacks to an American importer equally as anxious to buy them. The American importer obtains a letter of credit from his New York bank stating that the bank is willing to lend the importer or anyone the importer designates the sum of $10,000 subject to terms and conditions stated in the letter. The bank is willing, in short, to accept drafts, that is, demands for payment, drawn on the importer. The importer sends the letter of credit along with the order for $10,000 worth of goods to the British exporter in London. He in turn will prepare a draft and send it along with the letter to his local bank. In return he will receive the pound equivalent of $10,000 less fees charged for the service rendered. The British bank will forward the draft and all necessary papers to its New York correspondent or, if it has one, its New York office. Assuming that everything is in order, the draft will be presented and accepted by the New York bank. At maturity, which may be 30, 60, or 90 days after the date the exporter has drawn the draft, the New York bank will honor it. In the meantime, the British bank may keep its funds invested in the acceptance or, since there is a ready market for bankers' acceptances, it may sell it.

What does the accepting bank receive for its troubles? First, it acquires a fee for lending the importer its name. Second, if everything goes well the importer will pay the bank $10,000 before or at the time the acceptance matures. If so, the New York bank will have avoided tying up its own funds. In the meantime it has the bill of lading issued by the shipper who has the goods consigned to him. If the goods have been shipped, the bank has the warehouse receipts. In either instance these documents must be presented in order to receive the merchandise. If the importer fails to live up to his obligation, the New York bank takes title to the goods and can sell them to compensate itself for honoring the acceptance.

Since checking credit internationally can be difficult and costly, bank acceptances are ready substitutes for this process. This is why they have been used extensively in foreign trade. Alternatively, for domestic purposes, a credit check may be relatively inexpensive as against the fee charged for the bank's name. Consequently, bank acceptances are not an important means of financing the sale of goods domestically.

As in the case of an unsecured line of credit, management must consider the costs of conforming to the bank's requirements in light of the alternatives available. We pointed out earlier that banks will place a heavy premium on liquidity. A good earnings record and a large equity investment in the assets of the concern will be major factors in satisfying this demand.[11] Yet if the structure of assets and the composition of financing are more conservative than is suggested by the subjective risk preferences of the owners, then management may find other sources less costly.

Trade Credit

For many firms the alternatives available may be very few indeed. If its operations are sufficiently large to justify accounts in more than one bank, then management may be able to shop among banks for the best terms. But bankers do not ordinarily favor loan applicants unwilling to open and maintain balances in a checking account.[12]

For the small firm with only one banking connection and with no access to the impersonal capital markets, the only other major source of short-term financing is trade credit. We have already had occasion to deal analytically with the cost of trade credit and with the conditions under which firms should invest in receivables. Usually, when goods, destined for ultimate resale, are received from a manufacturer or supplier, the wholesaler, dealer, or retailer acknowledges receipt of these goods as an account payable. More technically, an invoice describing the merchandise is used as evidence of an open-account purchase by the firm receiving the goods and an open-account sale by the

---

[11]We should note that commercial banks may reject applications for reasons other than the firm's earnings record and its proportion of equity in the financing of total assets. The collateral could be of insufficient quality. The bank may question management's ability to operate the enterprise profitably. The concern may be requesting a loan whose maturity is too long, or it does not have a deposit relationship with the bank. It may also be requesting loans which the bank does not handle. The possible specific reasons, therefore, are numerous. We have simply singled out the more important ones.

[12]A notable exception will be situations where the amount lent would be in excess of the legal limits placed on loans to a single customer. The limits vary, but for banks with a national charter, loans may not be in excess of 10 percent of the book value of the bank's capital and surplus. The loan limits are generally somewhat higher for state-chartered banks. See Thomas G. Gies, Thomas Mayer, and Edward C. Ettin, "Portfolio Regulations and Policies of Financial Intermediaries," in The Commission on Money and Credit, *Private Financial Institutions* (Englewood Cliffs, N.J.: Prentice-Hall, Inc., 1963), p. 164. In these circumstances, other banks will participate with the primary lender even though the firm borrowing the funds does not have an account. Such firms, however, are often relatively large, with access to the impersonal money and capital markets. Hence there are many financing alternatives available to them.

company sending the merchandise. For the receiving company the amount of the invoice is charged to accounts payable while the shipping company debits accounts receivable on its own ledger.

As in the case of credit extensions to consumers, business firms in the United States find it easier to rely on open-account transactions with one another than to depend extensively on either trade acceptances or notes payable. When employed these instruments are similar to those used for retail transactions. The result, as we shall see in a later chapter, is that trade credit is quantitatively the most important financial asset of nonfinancial corporations. For many firms it ranks behind retained earnings and depreciation as a source of funds and is therefore the most important external source of funds, whether short-term or long-term.

The reader will also recall from an earlier chapter that, because of trade discounts, the cost of trade credit in terms of simple interest can be very high; that is, the standard terms of 2/10, net 30 represent a loan whose simple rate of interest approximates 37 percent.

In practice there is some flexibility. For example, if an invoice is paid within 12 days, the supplier may grant a discount. If the firm receiving the merchandise fails to meet the 30-day payment but liquidates his obligation 10 days later, the supplier may ignore the late payment and not impose more-stringent credit conditions on the next shipment. The manufacturer or wholesaler, if he values his sales outlet, will ignore minor infractions. There are limits, of course, but management of the firm receiving the credit has an incentive to meet its obligations to trade creditors faithfully. To do so will usually require bank loans to finance the stocks beyond the discount period, or cash and liquid assets sufficient to take advantage of the discount. In either case the funds should come from the cheapest source. For many firms, the sole alternative to bank loans is additional equity in the firm.

Taxes Payable

Other than trade credit, perhaps the most widespread, if not quantitatively the most important, source of short-term funds has in the past been taxes payable, particularly income taxes. For corporations, however, the fact that taxes could be paid 6 months or longer in arrears is no longer the case. As with unincorporated enterprises subject to personal income taxes, the trend is toward a pay-as-you-go basis. For example, suppose that a corporation's income taxes based on profits for the last quarter of the current year were $1,000,000. In the past this amount could be carried as a current liability due at the end of the second or the beginning of the third quarter. It becomes, therefore, a source of funds. When paid, it will be in part replaced or exceeded by taxes due at the end of the second quarter of the following year.

With a corporation making quarterly tax payments based on taxes due 6 months ago, the company has a permanent source of funds whose total varies solely with the taxes due at the end of a particular quarter and the tax liability for that quarter. Suppose, in our example, that taxes for the first quarter of the current year were $1,500,000, for the second quarter, $2,000,000, and for the third quarter, $1,500,000. The taxes payable account at the beginning of the year was $2,500,000, consisting of $1,000,000 in taxes on profits on the third quarter of the previous year and $1,500,000 in taxes on the profits of the fourth quarter of that year. As taxes are paid, the tax-liability account for each quarter of the year is the taxes payable at the beginning of the quarter less the amount due at the end of the quarter plus the taxes payable on profits earned during the quarter. Thus, at the end of each quarter of the current year, taxes payable for our hypothetical firm were

	Balance at Beginning of Quarter	Less Taxes Due	Plus Taxes Incurred	Balance at End of Quarter
First Quarter	$2,500,000	$1,000,000	$1,500,000	$3,000,000
Second Quarter	3,000,000	1,500,000	2,000,000	3,500,000
Third Quarter	3,500,000	1,500,000	1,500,000	3,500,000
Fourth Quarter	3,500,000	2,000,000	1,000,000	2,500,000

In practice, the year-to-year percentage of taxes that could be paid in arrears has varied. But as long as the taxes remained in arrears and as long as the corporation was profitable, management had an interest-free source of funds. Since 1951, however, the trend in the percentage which could be paid in arrears has been downward. By the late 1960s, taxes were close to a pay-as-you-go basis, with 25 percent of the taxes on estimated income due each quarter. This means that if taxes for a given year are underestimated, the firm will have to liquidate assets at the end of the year, or finance the tax payments from another source. Of course if taxes are overpaid, the firm will receive a refund and the source from which the tax payments ultimately come, earnings, will be increased.

Factors and Commercial Finance Companies

There are other, less well-known sources of funds which in some instances can serve as substitutes for commercial bank financing. Accounts receivable, for example, may be sold directly to *factors*.[13] Simply put, factoring is a form of lending in which the factor buys the accounts receivables. The factor assumes the risk and expenses of collection. Notice is usually given to customers that their accounts have been purchased. Thereafter they are to be paid directly to the factors. Once the factor accepts the accounts receivable, he has no recourse to the firm for bad debts.

For the services rendered the factor charges from $\frac{3}{4}$ of 1 percent to $1\frac{1}{4}$ percent of the net amount of receivables purchased. In addition the factor charges a rate of interest, traditionally 6 percent, although somewhat higher in periods of tight money, on advances against uncollected accounts. The interest is typically paid in advance. To illustrate, suppose that a manufacturing firm makes extensive use of trade credit. Its customers are other business firms with good credit ratings. Management of the manufacturing firm, in light of its present financing arrangements (that is, an equity investment of 20 percent in receivables and a discounted bank loan for the additional 80 percent), is considering the possibility of selling its accounts on a nonrecourse basis to a factor. For a given volume of receivables, say $1,000,000, the cost of equity invested in them is 16 percent per annum. The full cost of the bank loan to finance the remainder is 12 percent per annum. The cost of financing this amount of receivables is

$$0.2 \times 16\% + 0.8 \times 12\% = 12.8\%$$

A factor investigating the creditworthiness of the manufacturer's clients agrees to accept on a nonrecourse basis all sales to the accounts of the manufacturer's current clients. The fee charged is $1\frac{1}{2}$ percent of the amount signed. In addition, management of the manufacturing firm will receive funds as soon as a copy of the invoice acknowledging receipt of the goods is forwarded to the factor. The charge for these funds is 6 percent, with the interest paid in advance. Assume that by eliminating the collection and credit costs and the risk of bad debts, the manufacturing firm saves $50,000 for each $1,000,000 in receivables. Thus the effective service charge is $150,000 less $50,000, or $100,000. The manufacturer can expect to pay an annual charge of $60,000. If a factor is employed, the total expenses would be $160,000 for each

[13]Clyde W. Phelps, *The Role of Factoring in Modern Business Finance* (Baltimore: Commercial Credit Company, 1956). See also Carrol G. Moore, "Factoring—A Unique and Important Form of Financing and Service," *Business Lawyer*, vol. 14, no. 3 (April, 1959), pp. 703–727; reprinted in John L. O'Donnell and Milton S. Goldberg, *Elements of Financial Administration* (Columbus, Ohio: Charles E. Merrill Books, Inc., 1962), pp. 100–126.

$1,000,000 in receivables.   The effective cost of the total package offered by the factor is

$$\$840,000 = \frac{\$1,000,000}{1+r}$$
$$r = 19.05\%$$

In this instance, the cost of the factor's services would be much greater than the cost of financing the receivables out of a combination of bank loans and equity investment.   But even if the cost of the factor's sources had been lower, management would still have to consider the possible loss of business which might result if its clients resented the fact that they would be billed by a third party.   The risk may be more imaginary than real.   Yet it is possible to lose business because clients prefer an arrangement solely between themselves and their supplier. Their feelings may be motivated by the belief that they have a more flexible arrangement with those extending trade credit than with third parties with whom they have little or no contact.

In similar fashion, management might compare the costs of borrowing against receivables or selling receivables to a bank or factor with the costs of using receivables as collateral for a loan from a commercial finance company.   A commercial finance company is one of a group of firms specializing in financing credit purchases.   Many confine their activities to consumer installment credit, others to personal finance or personal loans.   The commercial finance company specializes in loans to business mostly on the basis of accounts receivable but occasionally on the basis of inventory and even equipment.   Unlike factors and like commercial banks, business finance companies extend credit; they do not make a commitment to purchase the receivables.

While these alternatives do exist for many firms, we must ask the question: Can management realistically expect that the cost of finance company credit and the purchase of accounts receivables by factors, after due allowance for the value of the services performed, will be lower than if the credit had been extended by a commercial bank? Although management in each instance must determine the answer for itself, there is reason to suspect that in many instances the cost of borrowing will not be lower.

We say this because both factors and finance companies make extensive use of bank credit themselves, often at the prime or lowest rate.. Most of these firms are incorporated, with a capital structure consisting primarily of equity and debt which can, in the event of bankruptcy, be subordinated to other loans.   The remainder of their funds can be secured through bank loans and commercial paper floated in the open market or placed privately with other institutions.

Given the structure of financing, we must assume that if a finance company or factor is intent on maximizing the market value of its shareholders' equity, it would be charging rates on loans which exceed the rates at which it can borrow funds. If the nonfinancial business firm seeking financing of its receivables (or even of its inventory or equipment, for which these financial firms occasionally make loans)[14] can obtain the prime rate on a bank loan of its own, where is the incentive to finance these assets through the use of these other intermediaries? The answer in many cases is that there is none.

In fact, one of the reasons why finance companies and factors[15] specialized in accounts receivable was because commercial banks for years did little with respect to financing them. This was particularly true of consumer credit, but it was also the case with trade credit. The reason ostensibly was that the costs involved in maintaining records associated with particular accounts did not justify the return on the loan. Since the end of World War II, however, commercial banks have found that if their dollar volume is sufficiently large, receivables can be financed profitably.

Thus it is quite possible that commercial banks may have skimmed off the best credit risks, leaving finance companies if not factors with lower-quality risks. Given the equity investment of finance companies, commercial banks can still safely lend them funds or purchase their paper in the open market. Factors, of course, by assuming the costs of collecting the receivables without recourse to the company's assets, do provide an additional service, the fee for which, in any given instance, may be less than the cost to a nonfinancial business firm of maintaining its own credit and collection facilities. As a result, some finance companies also provide factoring services.

Commercial Paper

While credit from factoring and commercial finance companies is a possible alternative to bank loans, open-market paper is a less common source of funds. To float commercial paper today requires a credit rating sufficiently high to warrant its purchase by banks and non-

---

[14]While factors purchase receivables, they will make loans on inventory, and even on fixed assets. See Phelps, *op. cit.*, p. 9.

[15]Factors were originally more heavily involved in transferring and storing merchandise shipped from the mother countries such as England to the colonies. Collection and credit facilities were only part of their operations. By 1900, the development of manufacturing firms in closer proximity to their customers eliminated the role that factors played in merchandising. But they continued to be useful in collecting accounts. See Moore, *op. cit.*, pp. 101–102.

financial corporations who may have no business connection with the issuer. As a result, there are today only about 430 firms issuing commercial paper, with the bulk of the dollar volume coming from finance companies, some of which (such as General Motors Acceptance Corporation, General Electric Credit Corporation, the Sears and Roebuck Acceptance Corporation) are wholly owned subsidiaries of nationally known nonfinancial corporations.[16]

Of the nonfinancial corporations issuing commercial paper to finance their own assets, most do so to meet seasonal borrowing needs. A food canner, for example,[17] may have to purchase raw materials as they come onto the market, but must store the canned goods to meet a demand which exhibits little or no seasonal pattern. This requires considerable equity investment in working capital—as was the case with our toy manufacturer—in order to take advantage of the maximum line of credit needed to finance the seasonal volume of sales. Suppose that the commercial bank is willing to finance a substantial portion of the inventory of canned goods but is less willing to have a loan secured by perishable raw materials. Yet the credit rating of the firm is sufficiently high to warrant purchase of its open-market paper by nonbank investors with less-liquid liabilities.

The canning company will then issue a series of notes maturing so that they can be replaced with a bank loan. To illustrate, assume that the company will have to maintain a minimum equity investment of $3,000,000 if it is to finance the perishable food while processing it into inventory acceptable for commercial bank loans. Yet its credit rating is such that it can float $1,000,000 in commercial paper at an effective cost of 6 percent per annum, reducing its equity investment to $2,000,000.

The flotation of commercial paper to finance a portion of these seasonal needs frees equity capital for investment in long-lived assets. Moreover, even if the commercial bank relented and agreed, because of the firm's high credit rating, to extend its loan policy to include a substantial portion of the funds invested in perishable foods, its likely demand for compensating balances may raise the cost of the loan above what it would be if commercial paper were employed. Indeed, in principle, assuming a firm had the option, it should employ commercial paper, commercial bank credit, and equity capital up to the point where the marginal costs of each source are equal.[18]

---

[16]Nevins D. Baxter, *The Commercial Paper Market* (Boston: The Bankers Publishing Company, 1966), pp. 32–34. *The New York Times*, April 28, 1968, sec. 3, pp. 1, 12.

[17]Baxter, *op. cit.*, p. 32.

[18]It is often pointed out that the interest rate on commercial paper, the total volume of which has grown from over $4 billion in 1961 to over $18 billion in 1968, is usually a full 1 percent below the prime bank rate. Yet few companies substitute it for bank

Other Short-term Sources

The only other nonbank source of some importance comes from the appropriations of a federal agency such as the Small Business Administration (SBA).   When credit is not otherwise available on reasonable terms, the SBA as a lender of last resort may make loans to small business[19] enterprises.   Alternatively, the agency may guarantee loans made by commercial banks to small businesses or participate in loans to small businesses.   Yet many of these applications, often in excess of 20 percent, are denied.[20]   The reasons for denial may be similar to those offered by commercial banks: inadequate working capital and an insufficient record of earnings — in short, the loans are too risky even for a government agency.

On the other hand, when loan demand exceeds the available appropriations, the SBA may ration credit by stressing assistance to "those small firms which did the most to help meet national goals and community needs."[21]   This includes loans to those engaged in defense procurement, control of air and water pollution, etc.   In other words, a loan application may be rejected for the same reasons as those a bank might use to reject the application as well as for reasons which would ordinarily be of little concern to the commercial bank.

Other minor sources of short-term funds are available, including money from private lenders and advances from customers such as down payments on orders for equipment to be manufactured or delivered at some future date.   For most firms, however, the primary external sources of short-term capital are bank loans and trade credit.[22]   The remainder constitutes equity investment, the primary source of which is retained earnings, rather than new equity issues.

To the extent that a firm can tap the external capital markets, it may be able to lower its cost of external capital by increasing the financing alternatives available.   To do so may require a relatively large volume of sales or assets.   Production economies may also be an incentive to management to increase its scale of enterprise and hence its

---

loans.   Dealers in commercial paper stress that it is designed to supplement, not replace, bank loans.   This is particularly true of firms whose short-term credit needs exceed the statutory limits placed on loans which a commercial bank can make to a single company. See *The New York Times, ibid.*

[19]What is small in any given instance is difficult to define.   In some industries a firm may be small if its assets exceed several million dollars.   In other industries a firm is large if its assets exceed $50,000.   See Roland I. Robinson, *Financing the Dynamic Small Firm* (Belmont, Calif.:   Wadsworth Publishing Company, Inc., 1966), p. 2.

[20]The 1966 *Annual Report of the Small Business Administration*, p. 13.

[21]*Ibid.*, p. 10.

[22]Robinson, *op. cit.*, p. 27.

investment in long-lived assets. But the economies of finance, that is, the reduction in the marginal cost of capital, may be an equally important factor in expanding the size of the firm as it seeks to maximize the market value of the owner's equity.

Intermediate-term Debt

Commercial banks for years confined the bulk of their loan portfolio to short-term loans which, if not always self-liquidating, were at least of sufficiently high quality that they could be repaid out of assets at maturity. Recently, however, they have shown considerable interest in maturities extending beyond a year. The principal of these term loans, as they are called, is usually repaid in periodic installments over a number of years. While the maturities vary, most term loans are written for a period of 2 to 5 years. Indeed there are commercial banks which restrict their portfolios to 5-year maturities. It is not impossible however, to find commercial banks extending credit on term loans for 5 to 10 years or longer.

The demand for term loans comes from the need of many firms to finance assets with a relatively short life expectancy—assets, for example, which must be replaced every few years. Certain types of equipment fall into this category. To finance new machinery, say every 5 years, out of a series of bonds publicly offered through investment bankers may be more costly than renewing an intermediate-term loan. To illustrate, suppose that a commercial bank grants a freight handler a $100,000 term loan to purchase trucks whose life expectancy is 5 years. The loan must be repaid in semiannual installments beginning 6 months (or, in the banker's calendar, 180 days) after the date the agreement is signed. Interest is 7 percent per annum on the outstanding balance, payable semiannually beginning with the first installment. The schedule of payments together with the interest charges are listed in Table 13-1 on the next page.

Note that the first eight installments are each $9,000. The interest paid is based on the balance outstanding when each installment is due. The sum of each installment plus the interest for the period equals the semiannual payment. The last two installments are each $14,000 plus interest. Having a "balloon," as it is called, on the end of a term loan is not uncommon. Because of the greater risk involved, interest rates are usually higher on this type of loan than on short-term credit. The lender receives the higher rate on a substantial portion of the loan for the entire period during which it is outstanding. Of course, the proportion paid at maturity might well have been higher.

TABLE 13-1: SCHEDULE OF SEMIANNUAL PAYMENTS ON A TERM LOAN OF $100,000 MATURING IN 5 YEARS WITH AN INTEREST CHARGE OF 7 PERCENT PER ANNUM ON THE OUTSTANDING BALANCE

Time Period	Balance of Loan	Interest		Semiannual Payments
Date of agreement	$ 100,000			
6 months later	91,000	$\frac{1}{2}$ of 7% × $ 100,000 = $	3,500	$ 12,500
1 year later	82,000	$\frac{1}{2}$ of 7% × 91,000 =	3,185	12,185
18 months later	73,000	$\frac{1}{2}$ of 7% × 82,000 =	2,870	11,870
2 years later	64,000	$\frac{1}{2}$ of 7% × 73,000 =	2,555	11,555
30 months later	55,000	$\frac{1}{2}$ of 7% × 64,000 =	2,240	11,240
3 years later	46,000	$\frac{1}{2}$ of 7% × 55,000 =	1,925	10,925
42 months later	37,000	$\frac{1}{2}$ of 7% × 46,000 =	1,610	10,610
4 years later	28,000	$\frac{1}{2}$ of 7% × 37,000 =	1,295	10,295
54 months later	14,000	$\frac{1}{2}$ of 7% × 28,000 =	980	14,980
5 years later	0	$\frac{1}{2}$ of 7% × 14,000 =	490	14,490
Total			$20,650	$ 120,650

To reduce the risk to the bank, the provisions of the loan agreement may contain clauses which allow the interest rate to vary proportionally to the general level of interest rates in the capital markets. If the prime rate, for example, was $6\frac{1}{2}$ percent and rose to $6\frac{3}{4}$ percent, the rate charged on the term loan might rise to $7\frac{1}{4}$ percent. Similarly, the bank may require net working capital or the current ratio to be maintained at a particular level at all times. The firm may be prohibited from using cash to repurchase its own stock or increase the dividend rate. In addition, a term loan may contain a provision requiring compensating balances equal to a specific percentage of the portion of the principal still outstanding. Finally, there may be a provision in the agreement to the effect that if principal and interest payments are not met when due, the balance of the loan including unpaid interest is accelerated, that is, due immediately. The result, of course, is usually bankruptcy.

As with many external sources of capital, the conditions under which term loans are granted depend in part on the alternatives available to the borrower. For a small firm requiring specialized equipment or other durable assets and with insufficient equity capital to finance them, the term loan from a commercial bank may be the only source of funds available. If management can, within its risk constraints, add to total profits and to the market value of the shares in the business by borrowing under the conditions offered by the bank, it will do so.

Assuming that the firm is not sufficiently well known to float debt in the impersonal capital markets, it might attempt to acquire term loans from a life insurance company. Given the long-term nature and fixed-income provisions of many life insurance contracts and the periodic premium payments available for investment, term debt of maturities up to 10, 15, or 20 years are ideal investments. In some cases, what would otherwise have been a public offering of bonds to finance long-lived assets is a series of notes with maturities up to 20 years placed privately with an insurance company.

However, management of a relatively small firm may have little or no connection with the insurance company to which it applies. Before granting the loan, a thorough credit investigation would be required. Because of these costs, together with the costs of administering it, a loan the size of the amount which the freight handler required might be too small to justify its acceptance. Alternatively, the insurance company might charge a rate sufficient to cover these costs which, even after allowances for compensating balances, is higher than the cost of the loan made by the bank where the freight handler has an established relationship.

In fact, rather than viewing the insurance company as an alternative, the freight handler, if he needed credit in excess of 5 years, say 15 years, might find that a commercial bank has a working relationship with the life insurance company whereby the bank handles the credit investigation and administers the loan. However, the bank has its own funds invested for a period of, say, 2 to 5 years, with the insurance company committing itself to financing the loan for the remainder of its life.

Besides the possibility of using a commercial bank or an insurance company, management may be able to finance certain assets on an installment basis through a commercial finance company. As is the case of short-term loans, it is possible for a firm to receive term credit from federal agencies such as the Small Business Administration.[23]

Finally, since trade credit is an indispensable source of funds for many small business firms, it is possible that suppliers who may have access to alternative sources of funds would consider loans as a way to finance the long-lived assets of their wholesale or retail outlets. An oil company, for instance, might finance a service station, setting the owner up in business while extending trade credit on the gasoline and supplies he buys.

Once the maturity on intermediate-term loans exceeds 5 to 10 years or at most 15 years, then, in the traditional parlance of the financial community, the loan becomes long-term debt. But in practice the distinction is often blurred. Therefore, in dealing with long-term debt

---

[23]Stewart Johnson, "Statistics on Federal Lending and Loan Insurance Programs in the United States, 1929–1958," Commission on Money and Credit, *Federal Credit Programs* (Englewood Cliffs, N.J.: Prentice-Hall, Inc., 1963), pp. 1–245.

in the next chapter, we shall have occasion to mention instruments whose maturities might just as easily have classified them as intermediate-term debt.

Summary

Although there are numerous sources of short-term funds, most non-financial corporations rely primarily on commercial bank loans and trade credit. Commercial bank loans, whether secured or not, usually require compensating balances. Moreover, interest is ordinarily deducted in advance; the cost of the loan is therefore greater than the stated rate of interest.

Trade credit often provides management with an interest-free loan during the discount period but an expensive source of funds if the discount is not taken.

Other short-term sources of funds, such as loans from a commercial finance company or sale of receivables to a factor, are usually more expensive than either a bank loan or trade credit. However, some companies, that is, those with the highest credit ratings, are able to float commercial paper at the prime rate. By eliminating compensating balances and interest paid in advance, commercial paper may be cheaper than a bank loan.

When credit is extended beyond a year, perhaps for 2 to 5 and even for 10 years or more, it is usually known as a term loan. Commercial banks grant many term loans. But once the maturity extends beyond 5 years, the lender is more likely to be a life insurance company. Sometimes a commercial bank will provide the funds for the first 2 or 3 years with the balance of the loan taken by a life insurance company.

QUESTIONS AND PROBLEMS

1. "In light of the discussion in this chapter, it is highly probable that the Modigliani and Miller hypothesis would have to be amended to allow for the size of the firm as a factor determining the cost of capital." Evaluate.

2. A commercial bank will finance 80 percent of the dollar volume of a company's receivables. For this service it requires compensating balances of 10 percent. The cost of bank credit is 7 percent per annum discounted. A factor will also finance the receivables of the firm

charging 6 percent discounted for the credit extended and 1 percent of the dollar volume for assuming the collection and credit risk. For this firm the cost of equity capital is 16 percent and the cost of collecting the receivables is $\frac{1}{2}$ percent of the dollar volume. Assuming that the average amount of receivables is always $1,000,000, should management borrow from the bank or sell its receivables to a factor?

3. "The firm's cost of short-term debt will be unduly high without a banking connection." Do you agree? Explain carefully.

SELECTED REFERENCES

American Bankers Association. *The Commercial Banking Industry* (a monograph prepared for the Commission on Money and Credit). Englewood Cliffs, N.J.: Prentice-Hall, Inc., 1962.

Baxter, Nevins D. *The Commercial Paper Market.* Boston: The Bankers Publishing Company, 1966.

Bogen, Jules (ed.). *Financial Handbook*, 4th ed. New York: The Ronald Press Company, 1964, sec. 2, 5, and 24.

Johnson, Stewart. "Statistics on Federal Lending and Loan Insurance Programs in the United States, 1929–1958," Commission on Money and Credit, *Federal Credit Programs.* Englewood Cliffs, N.J.: Prentice-Hall, Inc., 1963, pp. 1–245.

Moore, Carrol G. "Factoring—A Unique and Important Form of Financing and Service," *Business Lawyer*, vol. 14, no. 3 (April, 1959), pp. 703–727.

Phelps, Clyde W. *The Role of Factoring in Modern Business Finance.* Baltimore: Commercial Credit Company, 1956.

Robinson, Roland I. *Financing the Dynamic Small Firm.* Belmont, Calif.: Wadsworth Publishing Company, Inc., 1966.

Long-term Debt

chapter Fourteen

In this chapter the student should familiarize himself with the major features of the primary sources of long-term debt. What are their common characteristics? What are their unique characteristics? What are the advantages and disadvantages to management and presumably to the owners of using one instrument rather than another?

Introduction

When management of an enterprise, incorporated or unincorporated, negotiates a 15-year loan, it is largely a matter of semantics whether the loan is a form of intermediate- or long-term debt. Yet the student should be aware of the fact that the loan is evidenced by a *promissory note.* If, however, the company was incorporated, management might be able to employ the further option of raising the same amount of capital through an issue of *bonds* or debentures offered to the general public.

The primary distinction between a bond and a promissory note is the existence in the case of a bond of a third party, an independent trustee, often a commercial bank, which represents the bondholders. The *bond contract, deed of trust,* or *indenture* is signed by the appropriate officers of the corporation and the trustees. The bond itself is merely an instrument containing a promise to pay a specific amount of money at a fixed date in the future together with periodic interest payments to compensate the bondholder for use of the funds. The *bond certificate* will summarize the conditions under which principal and interest will be paid, but the bondholder must turn to the indenture for full details.

The primary distinction between bonds and debentures is that the former usually have a lien on property while the latter are simply general obligations of the corporation. For example, in 1966 the General Telephone Company of California had 18 different issues of first-mortgage bonds with due dates varying from 1969 to 1996. The principal amount outstanding was in excess of $346,000,000. The total book value of the liabilities and owners' equity was in excess of $851,000,000. At the same time, $13,350,000 in principal amount of debentures were outstanding. Moreover, in March, 1967, the company issued an additional $50,000,000 in debentures.[1] The first two paragraphs of the indenture are reproduced here.[2]

> INDENTURE, dated as of the first day of March, 1967, between GENERAL TELEPHONE COMPANY OF CALIFORNIA, a California corporation (hereinafter referred to as the "Company"), and UNITED CALIFORNIA BANK, a California corporation (hereinafter referred to as the "Trustee").
>
> WHEREAS, the Company desires to provide funds for its lawful corporate purposes and to that end, pursuant to resolutions adopted by its Board of Directors at meetings duly and regularly called and held for the purpose, has duly determined to borrow money and for that purpose to issue its debentures (hereinafter referred to as the "debentures") under this indenture (hereinafter referred to as the "Indenture"), as hereinafter provided, said debentures to be issued from time to time in one or more series commencing with the Series Due 1992, but subject to the restrictions and provisions contained in this Indenture with respect thereto, the debentures of each series to be in coupon form with interest coupons attached (hereinafter referred to as "coupon debentures"), or in fully registered form without coupons (hereinafter referred to as

[1]*Public Utility Manual* (New York: Moody's Investors Service, 1967), pp. 293–298.
[2]A copy of the indenture from which this and subsequent references are made is by courtesy of the investment banking firm of Halsey, Stuart and Company. The material is reprinted by permission of both Halsey, Stuart and Company and the issuer.

"registered debentures"), or in part as coupon debentures and in part as resistered debentures, and (except the Series Due 1992, which shall be substantially as hereinafter provided) to bear such date, to be payable on such date or, in case of serial maturities, on such dates, and at such place or places, to bear interest at such rate, payable at such time or times and at such place or places, to bear such designation or title herein provided for, and to contain such provisions, if any, with respect to tax exemptions, tax reimbursements, redemptions, sinking fund, conversion into stock or other securities of the Company, limitations as to aggregate principal amount of debentures of such series issuable and other characteristics not in conflict with the terms of this Indenture as the Board of Directors shall determine with respect to each successive series prior to the authentication of any debentures thereof . . . .

The next 89 pages lay out in detail the terms and provisions under which this series is issued.   It is the function of the Trustee, in this case the United California Bank, to see that the General Telephone Company adheres to these provisions.

Note first that the borrower is given the option of issuing "coupon debentures," "registered debentures," or both.   If registered, the name and address of the owner is recorded with the trustee.   The owner has legal title to the certificate.   Interest is paid when due, by check, to the registered owner.   A coupon debenture is payable to the bearer.   Attached to the bonds are coupons representing the periodic interest payments.   Each coupon, when presented to the trustee, is paid from corporate funds designed to meet the interest payments.   When the principal is due, the bearer presents the bond for payment.   In between these two types lies a hybrid in which the bond is registered as to principal but the interest payments are in the form of coupons payable to the bearer.

In the case of the General Telephone Company, management issued bonds which were fully registered.   Interest is $5\frac{3}{4}$ percent per annum.   The face value of each bond is $1,000 or specified multiples of $1,000.   Interest is paid semiannually on September 1 and March 1.[3] Thus each interest payment is $\frac{1}{2}$ or $5\frac{3}{4}$ percent of $1,000, or $28.75. Semiannual interest payments and denominations of $1,000 are common among bonds and debentures.   On rare occasions, however, if management feels that it can acquire more favorable terms by offering a debt issue to a broad range of investors, it will issue bonds or debentures in denominations of $100.   These, of course, are designed to appeal to small individual accounts rather than institutional investors.

The restrictive covenants of an indenture vary with the nature of the debt obligation and the creditworthiness of the corporation.   In the

[3] *Public Utility Manual, op. cit.,* pp. 297–298.

case of the General Telephone Company, management can issue additional debentures subject to the restrictive convenants contained in the indenture. In order to do so, management must satisfy two conditions. First, before the debentures can be issued, net earnings for the preceding 12 out of 15 months must equal at least twice the annual interest charges on debt outstanding. Second, no additional debentures can be issued if the total *junior funded indebtedness*, including the proposed debentures, exceeds at the time of issue 25 percent of the *net tangible assets* of the company.[4]

The relevant terms are also defined in the indenture. In this case, costs subtracted from revenues to determine net earnings include among other things provisions for depreciation, interest, and taxes. Moreover, the figure must be arrived at in accordance with "such system of accounts as may be prescribed by governmental authorities having jurisdiction in the premises."[5] Had the company been a nonregulated enterprise rather than a public utility, the calculations for net earnings may have been spelled out more fully, but probably in accordance with "generally accepted accounting principles."

Similarly, net tangible assets of the company comprise the book value of all its property at the date the proposed debentures are to be issued. The property included is real (for example, the plant and equipment and inventories) and personal (for example, the stocks or bonds of a subsidiary). In this case it is tangible, that is, it includes both real and personal property together with certain intangibles, including accounts receivable, but exclusive of patents, goodwill, trademarks, etc. Moreover, in calculating assets, there must be adequate provision for depreciation, depletion, and obsolescence. From assets are subtracted current liabilities, including special reserves to meet liabilities that will be incurred within one year of the date from which the debentures are to be issued.[6] The result is net tangible assets for purposes of the indenture provisions.

Finally, in defining junior funded indebtedness, the indenture makes the traditional distinction between short-term debt and debt whose maturity extends beyond a year. The latter is funded debt. Furthermore, junior funded debt includes all funded indebtedness of the company save those issues which are secured by mortgages and those whose principal and interest payments are specifically subordinated to this series of debentures.[7]

[4]*Indenture*, p. 28.
[5]*Ibid.*, p. 9.
[6]*Ibid.*, p. 10.
[7]*Ibid.*, p. 6.

Thus, while the details will differ from one indenture to another, the purpose of the restrictive clauses is to protect payment of principal and interest on the debt outstanding. Additional requirements may include restrictions on dividends and payments into a sinking fund designed to retire a certain portion of the debt each year.[8] Since it is the responsibility of the trustees to see to it that management adheres to the terms of the indenture, they can take legal steps to prevent management from making decisions contrary to the provisions of the indenture.

Perhaps the most important function of the trustee is to see to it that interest payments are met when due. Failure to pay interest, and in some instances installments on sinking funds, will after a 30-day period of grace usually cause the principal amount of the issue to be due immediately. Since interest cannot be paid, it is not likely that the company can meet the payment of principal either. The trustee, sometimes with the approval of a specified percentage of the bond-holders, will initiate bankruptcy proceedings in an effort to collect the amount due from the sale of the firm's assets.

Secured Debt—Mortgage Bonds

In the previous section, in distinguishing between bonds and debentures, we noted that a bond ordinarily has a lien on property whereas a debenture does not. If collateral is pledged, then, in the event of bankruptcy and subsequent liquidation, these assets can be sold to satisfy the claims of the bondholders. If the collateral fails to provide sufficient revenues to pay principal and accrued interest, the bond-holders have a claim equal to that of unsecured creditors for the residual due them. To illustrate, suppose that $2,000,000 in principal and interest is due to the bondholders of a corporation that is liquidated following bankruptcy proceedings. Collateral pledged by the company yields $1,700,000 when sold. The bondholders have a general claim of $300,000 against the remaining assets of the company. They participate equally with the remaining unsecured creditors. In this instance, assume that the only other debt is trade credit of $3,700,000. If the remaining assets of the corporation yield $4,000,000, all creditors will be satisfied.

If sale of the assets results in less than $4,000,000, the amount received is distributed in proportion to the value of the claims outstanding. For example, should the assets sell for $3,000,000, then the

[8]*Ibid.*, pp. 37, 40–42.

trade creditors would receive $0.75 on each dollar of debt outstanding and the bondholders $0.75 on each dollar of their unsatisfied claim of $300,000.   Under no conditions will creditors receive more than the value of their unpaid claims.   If the assets sold for more than $4,000,000, the residual would be distributed to the owners.   Because secured creditors, to the extent that their collateral has value,[9] participate ahead of unsecured creditors, secured instruments are referred to as senior securities and unsecured instruments as junior securities.

In the case of the General Telephone Company, senior securities consisted solely of bonds with a mortgage on the utility plant.   Bonds secured by real property of this nature are called *mortgage bonds*. Depending on the law in the state in which the company is incorporated, the mortgagor (or in this case, the trustee acting on behalf of the bondholders) either has a lien on the property or has title conveyed to him.[10]   In either case, the company issuing the bonds or the mortgagee continues to use the property.

In the past, particularly in financing railroads, liens have been quite complicated.   Second or junior mortgages have at times been superimposed on the first or underlying mortgage against the property. Even third mortgages were not unknown.   Priority as to proceeds from the sale of the property varied accordingly.

With a tendency in recent years toward simplified capital structures, efforts have been made to avoid complex liens.   As an alternative, corporations may use an *open-end mortgage*. A public utility, for example, could in this manner finance its plant and subsequent additions to it.   It would issue Series A bonds for perhaps $25,000,000; five years later it would issue Series B bonds for $20,000,000; etc.   The entire issue, consisting of several series, has a first mortgage on the utility plant.   To prevent the corporation from diluting the bondholders' interest in the value of the property mortgaged, the amount of bonds outstanding is often restricted to a specific percentage, perhaps 60 percent, of the cost of the plant and subsequent additions.   Thus the 18 different series of first-mortgage bonds of the General Telephone Company were issued under an open-end mortgage which in certain cases could limit the par value of bonds to 60 percent of the cost of the plant.[11]

[9] Two or more sets of secured creditors have prior claim to the assets specifically pledged for their satisfaction as well as a general claim on the remaining assets for the residual due them.

[10] If title is conveyed, then as long as the company continues to meet interest payments when due, a defeasance clause in the contract keeps the title "dead."   It becomes "alive" only in the event of default in these payments.   When the bonds are retired, the mortgagor's title is forever "defeated."

[11] *Public Utility Manual, op. cit.*, pp. 295–297.

A logical concomitant of an open-end mortgage is an *after-acquired clause*. Under it, any property acquired after the date of financing is part of the security of the bonds outstanding. As long as there is no upper limit on the size of the issue or little prospect of reaching the limit, then the after-acquired clause should present no difficulties. If the limit is reached and the mortgage closed, then all real property subsequently acquired is part of the security of the mortgage bonds outstanding.

In certain instances, personal property of the corporation will be subject to the after-acquired clause. The technical distinction between real and personal property hinges on whether it is movable. Equipment can often be transferred from place to place as can securities, but not land and plant. When personal property is purchased under a chattel mortgage, it could become part of the security of an outstanding series of mortgage bonds whose indenture contains an after-acquired clause. But the terms of the indenture may restrict the clause to real property, including equipment attached to the plant but not movable equipment such as trucks.

Secured Debt — Equipment Trust Certificates

An industry which has a heavy investment in both real and movable property will find an unrestricted after-acquired clause particularly burdensome. Railroads are in this position. As a consequence they must engage in legal maneuvers to circumvent its effects when making additions to the rolling stock of the line. In such circumstances the railroad is precluded from issuing a series of bonds using the equipment as collateral. Since the after-acquired clause pertains only to property the corporation owns, a method must be devised to avoid taking title to the equipment until the funds borrowed to purchase it have been repaid.

In order to achieve this end, two techniques of financing have been employed. One is a *conditional sales contract*. Under its terms a railroad makes a down payment to the manufacturer, who transfers title to the trustee or the lending institution that provides the balance of the purchase price. The railroad issues bonds or notes for the balance.[12]

---

[12]Since the trustee is eliminated when the conditional sales contract is negotiated directly with the lending institutions, in accordance with our earlier explanation the securities issued are technically notes, not bonds. If a trustee is employed and the obligations marketed publicly, the securities issued would be bonds. As subsequently explained in the text, when conditional sales contracts are employed, notes are ordinarily issued to private lenders, not bonds to the public. The first method of financing railroad equipment is therefore tantamount to an intermediate-term loan.

These securities must be redeemed in installments, with a portion of them maturing at various intervals over a 15- to 20-year period. Until these installments and the interest on them are paid, the trustee or lending institution retains title to the equipment. Once the obligation has been liquidated, title is transferred to the railroad.

A second method involves leasing the equipment. Under this arrangement, known as the *Philadelphia Plan,* the manufacturer, after receiving a down payment of 20 to 25 percent of the purchase price, builds the equipment and transfers title to a trustee. The trustee, not the railroad, issues a series of *equipment trust certificates* marketed publicly through investment bankers for the balance of the purchase price. The down payment is an advance rental. The railroad leases the equipment, paying a rental sufficient to cover periodic interest, often called dividend payments, and installments of principal as they come due. As part of the lease agreement, the railroad when it has paid all rentals, receives title to the equipment. A specimen of an equipment trust certificate for the Western Maryland Railway is shown in Figure 14-1[13] on page 296.

Since the certificates as well as the securities issued under a conditional sales contract are retired more rapidly than the equipment depreciates, the value of the collateral should always be greater than the balance of the certificates or notes outstanding. Enhancing the security of both types of instruments is the fact that in the event of bankruptcy the court cannot tie up the equipment so purchased, as it can the property owned by the railroad. In effect, the trustee can seize the property and sell it to another railroad if the rentals are not continued. Needless to say, since major railroads are reorganized and not liquidated, and since the equipment is vital to their operations, payments on equipment trust certificates or on instruments representing conditional sales contracts are rarely delayed during bankruptcy proceedings.

Nevertheless, when railroad equipment is financed out of a series of publicly issued securities, the instruments used are almost invariably equipment trust certificates. For years a troublesome legal issue plagued securities issued under a conditional sales contract. Since the equipment was not leased but was financed out of notes issued by the railroad, some jurisdictions into which the rolling stock moved would not recognize the title vested in the trustees. As a result, the after-acquired clause would become effective. Today "it is believed that all states now give as satisfactory protection to the conditional sales contract as to the lease agreement for railroad equipment, if indeed any dif-

[13]The certificate is by courtesy of the investment banking firm of Halsey, Stuart and Company. It is reproduced with their permission and with permission of the issuer.

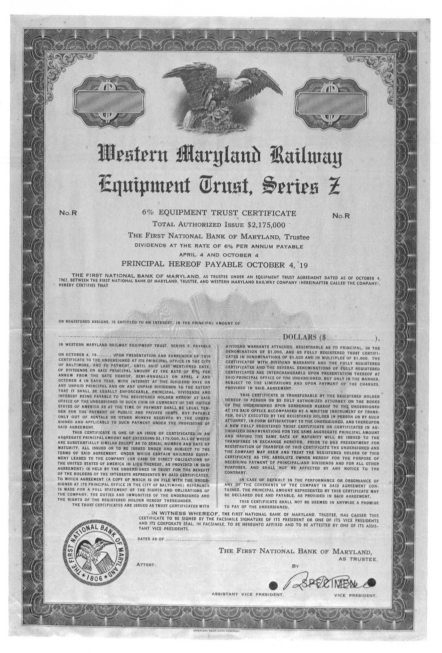

Fig. 14-1 Specimen of equipment trust certificate for Western Maryland Railway.

ference exists."[14]   Since leasing arrangements financed out of equipment trust certificates have never been subjected to this uncertainty, the Philadelphia Plan is preferred by investment bankers offering these securities for resale to the general public.   On the other hand, if a direct loan can be negotiated with a few institutional investors, the trustee can be eliminated.   The railroad will purchase the equipment on a conditional sales contract and issue installment notes, similar to those representing a term loan, for the balance.

To forestall any wild generalizations based on inferences from the above discussion,[15] the student should take cognizance of the fact that the after-acquired clause may not be relevant to the financial decisions of many companies, nor of all railroads.   Moreover, he should not assume that equipment trust certificates relied on by railroads are used extensively by other transportation companies.   Bus, marine, and airline corporations have issued them on occasion, but the equipment of each of these types of enterprises may have a more uncertain resale value because of either depreciation, obsolescence, or lack of standardization than is true of the rolling stock of railroads.   Consequently, the quality of the collateral may be relatively inferior.

This is not to imply that the credit standing of the companies involved is poor.   On the contrary, some railroads may finance out of equipment trust certificates simply because there is no alternative available.[16]   Thus even if the after-acquired clause on real property is lacking or cannot be construed to include chattel mortgages, a railroad's own credit rating may be so low that bankruptcy is a distinct possibility.   For other concerns, equipment trust certificates may be only one of a number of alternatives.

In general, like manufacturers, transportation companies other than railroads are apt to rely on chattel mortgages under conditional sales contracts, repaying the funds borrowed within a relatively few years.   Banks and insurance companies, for instance, helped to finance the transition of airlines from piston to jet aircraft and subsequently to even larger and more expensive jet planes.   Term loans secured by chattel mortgages repaid within 5 years was the method through which funds were secured.[17]

[14]Harry G. Guthman and Herbert E. Dougall, *Corporate Financial Policy*, 4th ed. (Englewood Cliffs, N.J.: Prentice-Hall, Inc., 1962), p. 197, footnote 16.

[15]We can, however, note that leasing is a technique generally employed to circumvent an after-acquired clause.   Establishing a subsidiary to issue bonds is another alternative.   For a discussion of the various possibilities, see Jules Bogen (ed.), *Financial Handbook*, 4th ed. (New York: The Ronald Press Company, 1964), sec. 14, p. 20.

[16]Donald M. Street, "The Role of Equipment Obligations in Postwar Railroad Financing," *Journal of Finance*, vol. 15, no. 3 (September, 1960), pp. 333–340.

[17]We might argue that an additional reason for the limited use of equipment trust certificates in financing of airplanes and marine vessels is the substantial cost differential

Secured Debt — Collateral Trust Bonds

Many corporations, of course, have little or no equipment needs. They may not even possess substantial amounts of real property. The bulk of the assets of a holding company, for example, consist largely of common stocks of the corporation whose operations it controls. If the holding company uses these stocks as security for a series of bonds, the instruments issued are known as *collateral trust bonds*. Under a collateral trust indenture the securities pledged are deposited with a trustee. As long as the issue is not in default, the holding company or pledgor continues to receive dividends paid on the stocks pledged.[18] Management of the holding company can also vote the stocks pledged, thereby retaining control over the operating companies.

To an investor, the securities pledged may not be very valuable in the event of default. If the holding company has no other operating assets, the interest it pays to the bondholders is dependent on the dividends it receives on the stocks. If the companies it owns have insufficient earnings to pay dividends, then the market value of the stocks will suffer accordingly. In the event of default, the holders of collateral trust bonds may be left with securities which, when sold, will not adequately compensate for the principal and accrued interest due them.

Perhaps collateral trust bonds best dramatize the problem inherent in any secured instrument. In the event of default, what will be the value of the security pledged? If the collateral has value to some other firm, that is, if it has an opportunity cost, then the obligations based on it (assuming they are drafted so that the claim to the collateral is valid) are high-quality investments. As implied earlier, standardized equipment, such as the rolling stock of railroads, is valuable to other lines. Highly specialized tools designed for an individual manufacturer may not be very useful to another firm. It is, therefore, poor collateral for debt obligations. Any obligations issued with such equipment for security are apt to be low-quality investments. If they are not, then the nature of the collateral does not explain their investment status.

In looking for explanations, we can go beyond the type of collateral to limitations placed on the principal amount of bonds issued as a

_____

between this equipment and a freight or passenger car of a railroad. Equipment trust agreements require the lessee to replace equipment destroyed. But if there is adequate property insurance, it would seem that this factor does not (unless, of course, the cost of the insurance is prohibitive) contribute to the explanation.

[18]The securities pledged can be bonds or other debt obligations as well as stocks. If bonds are used, the pledgor has the right to receive interest subject to the condition stated in the text.

percentage of the cost of the security.   If the figure is relatively small, then the low opportunity cost of the collateral was considered when the indenture was drafted.   Severe restrictions may also be placed on the total amount of debt, secured or unsecured, which the corporation may undertake.

If limitations such as these are part of the bond contract — and in many instances they are — then it is fair to ask why a corporation goes to the trouble of issuing a series of secured bonds in which the value of the collateral pledged is so uncertain.   The answer is that many companies do try to avoid mortgage and collateral trust bonds in favor of unsecured obligations or debentures.

If the bulk of a firm's assets are of little value to other concerns but are highly profitable when employed in the specialized type of work for which they were designed, then the value of a series of bonds issued by the corporation lies in its ability to pay interest and principal out of the income generated from operations and nonoperating assets.   Restricting claims on income by limiting the total amount of debt outstanding is the best guarantee of safety for the bondholder.   Even if the assets do have value elsewhere, bondholders expect to receive their interest payments out of earnings before interest and taxes.   To the extent that it has an opportunity cost, any collateral pledged should be viewed simply as enhancing the quality of the bonds by reducing the risk involved in the event of bankruptcy.

The nature of the industry, as well as the likelihood of liquidation in the event of failure, will also influence the type and amount of debt securities issued.   Regulated industries, particularly public utilities, have profit limitations placed on them.   A basic source of capital, retained earnings, is severely limited.[19]   Nevertheless, the rate of return is reasonably assured, although never guaranteed, with the risk of loss at a minimum among privately owned enterprises.[20]   Hence bonds and other debt often comprise as much as 50 percent of the total capital of a public utility.   Much of this debt, as in the case of the General Telephone Company, is secured by a lien on the plant.   These mortgage bonds are issued not because the facilities are useful to another concern but because they are vital to the utility itself.   If bankruptcy should occur, the utility, as a public-service corporation, would be reorganized rather than liquidated.   Since the plant is necessary to the continuation

---

[19]In regulating profits by adjusting rate levels, commissions often lag behind changing conditions.   During a period of falling prices or costs to utilities, profit levels at existing rates will expand, thereby potentially increasing internal sources of funds.

[20]Yet over the long run, utilities face (as the railroads have faced) the risk of a secular decline in demand.   See Burton A. Kolb, "The Rise and Fall of Public Utilities: An Appraisal of Risk," *Journal of Business*, vol. 37, no. 4 (October, 1964), pp. 329–345.

of operations, bondholders with a lien on it have security of value. They will be treated accordingly in the reorganization of the company receiving new securities, presumably equal in value to the principal and accrued interest on the bonds they have surrendered. Debtors with unsecured claims will not fare as well in bankruptcy proceedings.[21]

Most manufacturing concerns, particularly small companies in highly competitive markets, face a different environment. Unlike the earnings of electric-light, gas, telephone, or water companies, theirs are apt to fluctuate. Substantial profits and losses are not uncommon. Because they are under no obligation to provide service in the event of bankruptcy, liquidation is a possibility. Moreover, most of the assets are often highly specialized and hence of little value to other concerns. Consequently, long-term debt not only would be kept at a relatively low percentage of invested capital, it would also consist primarily of debentures.

Subordinated Debentures and Income Debentures

Recall from our earlier discussion of the indenture of the General Telephone Company that "junior funded indebtedness" was distinguished from secured debt and debt subordinated to it. In other words, besides debt secured by real or personal property or unsecured debentures, there is a third type of long-term obligation which, in the event of bankruptcy, is subordinated to both. In fact, in the terms of the indenture under which it is issued, it will usually be subordinated to all debt, short-term or long-term, secured or unsecured.

Subordinated debentures have maturity dates, and failure to pay interest and principal when due ordinarily precipitates bankruptcy. But in the event of failure the assets purchased from the proceeds of the sale of these bonds can first be used by other creditors of the corporation to satisfy their own claims. Thus, as might the assets purchased out of equity, those financed out of the sale of subordinated debentures add to the protection afforded others supplying debt capital. Firms that make extensive use of bank credit will have a series of subordinated debentures in their capital structure. In this way they are able to finance working capital needs at a lower cost. Whether the average cost

[21]In railroad reorganizations, secured creditors who have a lien on a branch line whose value to the railroad is negligible may be treated as unsecured creditors. This is what happened in the 1946 reorganization of the Sea Board Air Line. In this instance, unsecured creditors were eliminated from participation in the reorganized company. See Arthur Stone Dewing, *Financial Policy of Corporations*, 5th ed. (New York: The Ronald Press Company, 1953), vol. 2, p. 1470. See also pp. 1462–1481.

of capital is lower is a moot point. As greater risk is borne by these debenture holders, they, in turn, may have to be compensated with higher interest rates than if the securities were straight debentures. In perfectly competitive markets, of course, the differences in interest costs (that is, the lower rate on bank loans and the higher rate on subordinated debentures) would be compensating. However, in imperfectly competitive markets or where there is a desire on the part of long-term debt holders to accept greater risk, the average cost of capital might be lowered by using a series of subordinated rather than straight debentures.

Whatever the reason, the instrument, initially confined largely to finance companies,[22] has in recent years been widely adopted by industrial firms,[23] whose bonds are often made convertible into common stock. In fact, as we shall argue shortly, it may be the conversion feature which has encouraged the more widespread use of subordinated debentures.

Another distinctive debt instrument is the income debenture, or as it is sometimes called, the *adjustment debenture*.[24] As with all debt instruments, income debentures have a maturity date. The unique feature of the instrument lies in the fact that interest need be paid only if earned. Income debentures, therefore, present an exception to the general rule that interest on debt must be paid when due. To the extent that interest is not earned, failure to pay it will not, as it will in the case of other types of debt, render the principal due as of that date and hence precipitate bankruptcy. In order to prevent any misunderstanding over what constitutes a profit figure which shows that interest has indeed been earned, the methods for calculating costs and revenues must be spelled out in the indenture.

The use of the income debenture has been confined largely to railroads which have undergone reorganization as a result of bankruptcy proceedings. When the reorganized company emerged, its capital structure was often altered so as to eliminate most of the interest payments which brought about the failure. By using income debentures, the company would avoid subsequent default if earnings generated cash payments insufficient to meet the interest when due. At the same time, interest payments on this debt, as well as on all types of debt, are tax

[22]Robert W. Johnson, "Subordinated Debentures: Debt that Serves as Equity," *Journal of Finance*, vol. 10, no. 1 (March, 1955), pp. 1–16.

[23]Keith L. Broman, "The Use of Convertible Subordinated Debentures by Industrial Firms, 1949–1959," *Quarterly Review of Economics and Business*, vol. 3, no. 1 (Spring, 1963), pp. 65–75. Reprinted in James W. VanHorne (ed.), *Foundations for Financial Management: A Book of Readings* (Homewood, Ill.: Richard D. Irwin, Inc., 1966), pp. 219–233.

[24]Sidney M. Robbins, "A Bigger Role for Income Bonds," *Harvard Business Review*, vol. 33, no. 6 (November-December, 1955), pp. 100–114.

deductible.   Thus management reduces the risk of bankruptcy by using income debentures while realizing the tax savings inherent in the payment of interest.   Nevertheless, since the risk borne by the income-debenture holder is greater[25] than if he held some other form of debt, we would expect him to be compensated with a correspondingly higher rate of interest.

Combine a subordinated feature with an interest-payable-only-if-earned clause and we have a subordinated income debenture.   Attach a mortgage clause to an income debenture and we have a mortgage income bond.   Clearly these and other similar arrangements can be made in the bond contract, creating numerous variations on the straight debenture or secured bond.

While we can multiply the various types of bonds almost indefinitely, to do so would involve describing instruments whose importance in modern business finance is negligible.   Most of the complex instruments employed in the past were the result of attempts to raise funds for, or to reorganize the capital structure of, railroads.   Moreover, as our statistics in a subsequent chapter will reveal, the market for these securities consisted largely of individuals, whereas today bonds as well as other forms of debt are held largely by financial institutions. The terms of bond indentures are established so as to meet the needs of life insurance companies, savings banks, and others.   These needs in turn are partly the result of regulation of their portfolios.   The tendency therefore is toward straight debentures or mortgage bonds whose contract provisions are fairly standard.

Convertible Debentures

Subordinated debentures, income bonds, and variations on them may be employed.   But if so, they as well as straight debentures are often convertible[26] into common stock.   Although the use of convertibles has varied over time, in recent years they have represented between

[25]The risk can be mitigated somewhat by making the interest payments cumulative; that is, if interest is not earned in one year, it is carried over to the second year.   Management pays that portion of current and cumulated interest earned during the year.   In order to lower the risk still further dividends may be restricted or, if interest has cumulated, curtailed altogether.

[26]For a detailed background on the use of convertibles from 1933–1952, see C. James Pilcher, *Raising Capital with Convertible Securities* (Ann Arbor: Bureau of Business Research, School of Business Administration, The University of Michigan, 1955), pp. 5–23.   For an analytical treatment of the conversion option, see Eugene F. Brigham, "An Analysis of Convertible Debentures: Theory and Some Empirical Evidence," *Journal of Finance*, vol. 21, no. 1 (March, 1966), pp. 35–54.

9 and 20 percent of long-term debt.[27]   Moreover, even when management seeks out long-term loans or places debt securities directly with institutional investors, the subsequent agreement often includes a provision allowing the investor to purchase common stock at a stated price over a designated period of time.   The option is usually evidenced by *warrants* stating the price at which the shares can be purchased and the period over which the warrants can be exercised.[28]

The post-World War II experience has been conducive to the use of convertibles.   The combination of full employment and for the most part a rising price level has made the debt instrument a less satisfactory outlet for those supplying funds.   Under these conditions the purchasing power of fixed-income payments will decline while the relative safety afforded the bondholder in the widespread business bankruptcies which usually accompany an economic depression becomes less valuable.   Yet the legal restrictions placed on the portfolios of many institutional investors, together with the fact that substantial portions of their own sources of funds consist of liabilities in fixed dollar amounts, severely limit the equity participation of these investors.

However, if we assume that the legal restrictions are such that the investment portfolio of financial intermediaries consists of more debt than would be required to satisfy the subjective risk preferences of management and presumably of the owners of these institutions, then the purchase of convertibles or other debt instruments, with detachable warrants will help to assuage the desires of management and the owners for greater equity participation.   Given the conversion ratio, the market price of the bond will never fall below its investment value, that is, the discounted value of the principal and future interest payments.   If the market price of the stock into which the bonds are convertible rises above the investment value, then management can sell these bonds at a capital gain.

For example, suppose that a life insurance company purchases debentures which are convertible into common stock.   The conversion ratio is 20:1.   For each $50 of the face value of a $1,000 bond, the insurance company will receive one share of stock in the enterprise.   The current market price of the stock is $35.   The bond has an interest rate of 6 percent of the face value, or $60 per year, paid semiannually.

---

[27]In 1965, 1966, and 1967, convertibles were 9.2%, 12.0%, and 20.4%, respectively, of long-term debt. Calculated from data in Securities and Exchange Commission, *Statistical Bulletin*, March, 1968, p. 16. In 1968, convertibles were 14.9% of long-term-debt. See *Statistical Bulletin*, March, 1969, p. 16.

[28]Charles M. Williams and Howard A. Williams, "Incentive Financing—A New Opportunity," *Harvard Business Review*, vol. 38, no. 2 (March-April, 1960), pp. 123–134.

Assume that the investment value of a bond of this quality[29] is also 6 percent.   The market price of the bond is, therefore, $1,000 (or 100, as it would be quoted in the market).   Since the market value of the stock into which it can be converted is only $700 ($35 × 20), the bond will sell at its investment value.   But if the price of the stock times the conversion ratio rises above the investment value of the bond (that is, $50 a share, or $1,000), the market price of the bond will rise in proportion.   Suppose that after a year the market price of the stock has risen to $60 a share.   The price of a bond, excluding the costs of conversion or the brokerage fees in selling it, will also have risen, in this instance to $1,200.   The investment value of the bond will be the floor below which the market price will not fall.   Otherwise the price of the bond is determined by the market price of the stock times the conversion ratio.

The institutional investor, in this instance the insurance company, need never convert the bond into stock.   It can stay within its portfolio restrictions by selling each bond at $1,200, realizing a capital gain of $200 per bond less brokerage fees.

Similarly, suppose that the insurance company agrees to an intermediate- or long-term loan.   One of the provisions of the contract is the issuance of warrants which can be used to purchase stock at a given price or sold to a third party in the open market.   If each warrant issued allowed the institution to purchase a share at $45 and the market price of the stock was $40, then the warrants could at best be sold at a nominal figure reflecting the present value of the anticipated increase in the price of the stock less the option price.   Once the market price of a share exceeds $45, the price of the warrant will vary accordingly.   If the price of the stock rose to $55, the value of each warrant is $10 less the costs of exercising or selling the option.   Again, the institutional investor can realize a gain from the sale of the warrants without ever owning the stock.   Management, therefore, is able to let its owners participate in the benefits of capital appreciation which can come from

---

[29]Bonds are rated by independent investor service organizations.   One of the best known is Moody's.   Their ratings are Aaa, Aa, A, Baa, Ba, B, Caa, Ca, and C.   The Aaa rating is for bonds carrying the "smallest degree of investment risk."   Bonds rated C have "extremely poor prospects of ever attaining any real investment standing."   See the annual issues of Moody's Manuals for various industries for full explanation of the intermediate ratings for bonds, for example, Moody's *Transportation Manual*, 1966, pp. v–vii.

Institutional investors are often restricted as to the quality of bonds they may purchase.   Many, for instance, may not be able to go below Baa.   Moreover, since judgment is a part of any rating, two services may see the bond differently.   One may call a high-quality investment Aaa while another service rates it as Aa.

the ownership of stock while at the same time enjoying the relative security of an investment in a debt instrument.

From the point of view of the issuer, that is, a nonfinancial business firm, the major advantage, as we pointed out in an earlier chapter, is the delayed sale of equity securities. This is particularly true of convertibles. The current market price of the common stock is, in management's eyes, below its long-run investment value. It anticipates a favorable trend in earnings and dividends which will eventually be capitalized in the market price of the shares. By raising perhaps $10,000,000 through the sale of convertibles at 20:1, it will eventually issue 200,000 shares of stock. With the market price of the stock currently at $35, it would necessitate at least 285,715 shares to realize $10,000,000. In fact, it would probably require more shares. A common stock offering, in order to be successful, would have to be floated at several points below the current market price—perhaps $30 to $32, instead of $35. This is to allow for the temporary decline in price which may accompany a large increase in the number of shares outstanding. Of course, if the funds are to be invested at an expected rate of return higher than the marginal cost of new shares, the decline should be only temporary, not permanent.

Management of the issuing company might also find that institutional investors anxious to enjoy the equity features of convertibles or warrants will be willing to accept a lower interest rate on the funds they provide. If the going rate of interest on a straight debenture of a firm with a superior credit rating is $6\frac{1}{2}$ percent, management of the firm might be able to market the debt at 6 percent by making the debentures convertible. Similarly, if its subordinated debentures would carry a 7 percent interest rate, by making them convertible management might be able to issue them at a yield to maturity of $6\frac{1}{2}$ percent.

Furthermore, as we shall see in a subsequent chapter, the costs of floating debt, whether the bonds are offered to the general public or placed privately in the hands of institutional investors, are lower than if the same amount of funds were raised through an issue of common stock.

There are, therefore, reasons why the supply of funds might increase at each rate of interest if the lenders are given some chance to participate in the gains accruing to those owning common stock. Management of the borrowing firm can respond by raising capital with convertibles or issuing warrants to those granting intermediate- and long-term loans. In so doing, it is accepting on behalf of its stockholders additional financial risk in the short run. Over the long run, in the case of convertibles, it is acquiring equity on more favorable terms than if more of the current capital budget had been financed out of new stock issues.[30]   In the case of warrants granted to institutional investors, it is also acquiring equity although the warrants are in addition to rather than a substitute for the debt.

In some cases, of course, management of the issuing firm may be doing more than anticipating the substitution of common stock for debt. It could also be paving the way for increasing its use of, say, bank credit by issuing subordinated debentures.   As a "sweetener," it offers the option of converting these securities into equity.   In so doing, it may be anticipating the need for short-term funds to expand working capital, which in turn is the result of investing the proceeds of the debentures into long-lived assets.   In other words, management is anticipating the profitable employment of these funds and the subsequent increase in the market value of the shares.   In the interim it will require additional financial leverage in the form of short-term loans.   In order not to jeopardize its ability to acquire the funds needed, management will subordinate the debentures to senior debt.   To ensure their marketability to those who would prefer to hold or at least profit by the equity features, the debentures are made convertible.

The Call Premium

While warrants have an expiration date, it is common practice not to place a time limit on the option to convert debentures into stock. Instead, in the bond indenture is a *call price* or *premium* over the stated value of the bond which can be exercised by management of the issuer in order to force conversion.[31]

To illustrate using our earlier example, suppose that when the debentures were sold at par there was a call premium of 105, that is, management could call in or redeem the debentures at a price of $1,050 each.   This is $50 above what management would have to pay if it redeemed them at maturity.   As we argued earlier, once the price of

[30]We might also note that convertible debentures, unlike straight debentures, are purchased by individuals as well as institutions.   Traders have preferred them because in the past they could borrow perhaps 80 percent of the market price of the bond, whereas if they purchased the stock into which it was convertible, then, depending on the margin requirements, they might have to put up as much as 70 percent of the purchase price, that is, borrow as little as 30 percent.   However, effective March 11, 1968, the ability to use large amounts of leverage in the purchase of convertibles was lessened following the adoption by the Federal Reserve Board of a 50 percent margin requirement for convertibles.   See *Federal Reserve Bulletin*, February, 1968, p. 168.   The requirement was subsequently raised to 60 percent and is altered, as are the margin requirements in general, in accordance with Federal Reserve policy.

[31]Willis J. Winn and Arleigh Hess, Jr., "The Value of the Call Privilege," *Journal of Finance*, vol. 14, no. 2 (May, 1959), pp. 182–195; reprinted in VanHorne, *op. cit.*, pp. 234–246.

the stock times the conversion ratio exceeds the investment value of the debenture, the market value of the debenture will vary according to the fluctuations in the price of the stock. When the price of the stock reaches $52.50, the market price of the debenture, brokerage commissions aside, equals $1,050, or the call price. Beyond that point management could conceivably exercise the call privilege, thereby forcing conversion.

To allow for short-run declines in the market price of the stock resulting from an increase in the number of shares accompanying a conversion, management may wait until the market price of the stock, and therefore of the debenture, is sufficiently high to ensure conversion and complete elimination of the debentures from the capital structure. Assume that the price of the stock continues to rise to $55 a share. The market price of the bond is then $1,100. Suppose that there are presently 10,000,000 shares outstanding. The increase resulting from the conversion ratio is 200,000 shares, or 2 percent of the number presently outstanding. While the current market price should reflect the impending increase in the number of shares as well as the reduction in the leverage resulting from the conversion, management might assume that, random factors aside, the price in the short run could fall by the full amount of the increase. Thus the market price could decline to $53.92 a share ($550,000,000 divided by 10,200,000 shares). Even if it did, there is still a sufficient buffer to ensure conversion if the bonds are called at $1,050. The holders have the choice of receiving $1,050 from the company or as much as $1,100 in common stock, depending on what happens to the market price as a result of the announcement to call in the securities. Even if the debenture holders do not want to convert, they will sell their securities at a price in excess of the call premium. Those purchasing the bonds will then convert them into common stock.

While the call premium is a technique employed in forcing conversion of debentures into stock,[32] we should also note that the call price is an integral part of most indentures whether the instruments are convertible or not. Indeed, perhaps the most controversial areas in drafting a bond indenture are the determination of the call price and the length of time from the date of issue before management of the borrowing firm can exercise the call option. If interest rates are near

[32]Some firms raise the dividend on the common stock to the point where it exceeds the income on the debenture, thereby encouraging conversion. See Brigham, *op. cit.*, pp. 52–53. Of course, the variability of the income on a bond is less than the variability of the income on stock. The amount paid would have to be sufficient to compensate the debenture holder for the additional risk. Since what is adequate might vary among the debenture holders, an increase in dividends need not eliminate all the convertibles in the capital structure.

historic peaks, the prospective purchaser or purchasers, again institutional investors, will want a provision in the indenture preventing management from exercising a call option for some time. For instance, suppose that, in order to float a series of straight debentures, a public utility with a high credit rating must, due to tight money markets, pay 6¾ percent if it is to market the instruments at par. Management expects credit conditions to ease somewhat in the next year or two. It anticipates that it could sell the same issue under more normal conditions at an interest rate of 6 percent. It would therefore be anxious to have the option of calling in the bonds and refunding them with a new issue at a lower rate.[33]

Management of the institutional investor, on the other hand, is anxious to limit the call option so that its owners can enjoy the higher yield for as long as possible. Moreover, if interest rates do fall, the market price of the bond will rise above the par or face value. The bond will therefore sell at a premium. This will give the institution a chance to realize a capital gain from the sale. Whether it will sell or not depends on the opportunity cost of the funds. If it sells, it must find a new outlet for the proceeds. If 6¾ percent bonds are now selling at a premium, those of comparable quality selling at par must yield less than 6¾ percent. Unless the capital gain after taxes more than offsets the present value of the loss of interest after taxes, management of the institutional investor will want to continue to hold the bond. Thus it will seek in tight money markets issues with high call premiums and/or relatively long periods before the call option can be exercised.

Suppose, for example, that management of the public utility wishes to float at par a 20-year bond issue yielding 6¾ percent; it finds that in competitive capital markets, it must include in the indenture a clause preventing it from exercising the call option for 2 years. After that it can repurchase the securities at 105 (or $1,050 a bond) for the next 5 years, at 104 (or $1,040 a bond) for the next 3 years, at 102 (or $1,020 a bond) for the next 5 years, and finally at 101 (or $1,010 a bond) for the final 5 years.[34]

---

[33]The problem here is not that the funds cannot be profitably employed at 6¾ percent. Were this the case, management would not even float the bonds. What it is trying to do is minimize the cost of capital by lowering the overall cost of the bond issue through the use of a call premium. Whether it will exercise the option will depend on the cost of refunding less the present value of savings in interest.

[34]Presumably management might be able to shorten the call period still further by raising the call premium and hence making it more expensive to refund the issue. Similarly, for more liberal call terms, the utility might have to pay a higher rate of interest. Yet once the date at which the call option can be exercised has been determined, it is not uncommon to lower the price as the bonds get closer to maturity. For the 5¾ percent debentures of the General Telephone Company of California, a call price of 105.75, or $1,057.50, was effective with minor exceptions during the first year in which the bonds were outstanding. It drops each year until the year in which the bonds mature; the call price is now the par value, or $1,000. See *Indenture*, pp. 24–25.

At the end of 2 years, management finds that it can refund the series with a new 18-year issue with identical features: that is, marketed at par, or at $1,000, and carrying an interest rate of 6 percent. Assume that the principal amount of the bond issue is $10,000,000. The incidental costs of retiring the outstanding bonds and issuing and floating the new bonds are $200,000. The annual savings in interest before income taxes are $75,000 ($\frac{3}{4}$ of 1 percent of $10,000,000). Since interest is tax-deductible, the savings are reduced by 48 percent. The total savings in interest are therefore $75,000 $(1 - 0.48)$, or $39,000. Assume further that the expenses associated with retiring the old issue and floating the new series are, for federal income tax purposes, deductible in the year in which the debentures are called. The after-tax cost of these expenses is therefore $200,000 $(1 - 0.48)$, or $104,000. Finally, since the debentures would be called at a premium of 105, or 5 percent of the face value of the debentures, this is a loss of $500,000 and is fully deductible in the year the bonds are called.[35] Thus the effective cost of exercising the call premium is $500,000 $(1 - 0.48)$, or $260,000. The total expense after taxes associated with calling in the old series and replacing the bonds with a new issue is $104,000 plus $260,000, or $364,000. The savings in interest after taxes are $39,000 a year. Therefore

$$\$364,000 = \$39,000\frac{1 - (1+r)^{-18}}{r}$$

[35]The tax features of recalling any given issue are sufficiently complex to warrant the generalization that management should check with the Internal Revenue Service or its own legal counsel before assuming that certain expenses are deductible. In the above example, for instance, expenses of issuing the original series are usually amortized over the life of the bonds. If the bonds are called before the issue matures, the unamortized portion of these expenses together with the call premium are ordinarily deductible in the year in which the bonds are recalled. Expenses associated with the new issue, however, should be amortized over the life of the new issue.

If the original issue had sold at a premium, say 102 (or $1,020), then under the tax laws the premium would be amortized that is, $20 divided by 20 years, or $1.00 a year — and reported as income over the life of the series. If the bonds are recalled and there is unamortized premium, this must be used as an offset against retirement costs. If the new bonds are issued at a premium, the premium must be amortized and written off as income over the life of the new series.

Similarly, if the bonds were originally sold at a discount, the discount is amortized over the life of the bond. Thus, if the original issue sold at $980 rather than $1,000, there would be $1.00 a year per bond in bond discount which can be treated, as can interest, as a tax-deductible expense. If the issue is recalled, the unamortized discount is included in the expenses associated with recalling the bonds. It is deductible in the year the bonds are recalled. If the new bonds are issued at a discount, the amount of the discount must be amortized over the life of the issue.

For an interesting example of the calculations involved in recalling an issue of bonds, see Robert F. Vandell and Alan B. Coleman, *Case Problems in Finance*, 4th ed. (Homewood, Ill.: Richard D. Irwin, Inc., 1962), pp. 598–611. The same case, that of the Merrimack-Essex Electric Company, can also be found in Robert L. Masson, Pearson Hunt, and Robert N. Anthony, *Cases in Financial Management* (Homewood, Ill.: Richard D. Irwin, Inc., 1960), pp. 173–185.

Since the savings as well as the expenses will accrue to the owners, we can assume that r should reflect the marginal cost of equity capital. Suppose this is 10 percent. Then from the table in Appendix B of this volume, we get

$$\$364,000 \neq \$39,000 \times 8.20141$$
$$\$364,000 > \$319,854.99$$

Under these conditions the present value of the savings in interest is less than the expenses associated with exercising the call option. It would be in the interests of the owners not to issue a series to replace the debenture presently outstanding.

Thus a substantial call premium and a delay in allowing the option to be exercised work in favor of the holder of the bond or debenture. For management of the issuing corporation, the terms of the call option can be very important in a period of relatively tight money. Management might even be willing to grant a slightly higher current rate in order to lower the call premium and shorten the time period over which the premium is to become effective.

However, in a period of relatively easy credit, or when it is apparent that the long-term trend in interest rates is upward, management may be less concerned about calling the issue. Suppose that the going rate on highest-quality unsecured debentures is 6 percent but is expected to rise toward 7 percent within the next few years. If this does indeed occur, management will no longer be interested in exercising the option. Only if the current yield falls below the stated rate of interest is there a chance for realizing cost savings through exercising the call option. The opportunity to do so, however, is still important if the issue is convertible. Under these conditions the sole purpose of the option is to force conversion of debt into equity, not to replace one series of bonds with another.

The Sinking Fund

We noted earlier that in addition to making interest payments, management of the borrowing corporation may have to make periodic payments into a *sinking fund.* Suppose, for example, that a company floats $20,000,000 in debentures. The securities are marketed at par and carry a $6\frac{1}{2}$ percent interest rate. As part of the terms of the issue, management agrees to make annual payments of $1,000,000 into a sinking fund administered by the trustee. The amount placed in the sinking fund will be used to repurchase bonds, thereby gradually retiring the issue over the 20-year period rather than at the end of it.

Those purchasing the debentures know from the provisions of their contract that their instruments could be redeemed at the end of each year following the date on which the debentures were issued. If the series was floated on March 1, 1969, $1,000,000 par value, or 5 percent of the original issue, would be redeemed on March 1, 1970. This process would continue until the entire series was retired. Unlike the call option, sinking fund purchases are usually made at par, not at a premium. Since the series was not issued in serial maturities, that is, 5 percent of the debentures would mature each year, we shall assume that the instruments selected for redemption are chosen at random.

From the viewpoint of the borrower, the chief burden of the sinking fund is the question of the availability of cash to meet the sinking fund payments as they come due. For the first year, therefore, in addition to $130,000 in interest payments, management must raise $1,000,000 in cash to meet its obligations under the terms of the indenture. Moreover, unlike interest, sinking fund payments provide no tax shield except in the case of a capital loss for bonds or debentures sold at a discount but redeemed at par.

But suppose that the firm is unable to generate income sufficient to meet the sinking fund payments. Will bankruptcy result? In most instances it will not. While sinking fund payments are an obligation which management should meet, unless specifically stated in the indenture, failure to make the payments, unlike failure to pay interest, usually does not accelerate the maturity of the issue. The liquidity of the firm, therefore, is rarely threatened by the inability to meet sinking fund payments.

Yet since management views the terms of the indenture as obligations to which it must adhere if it is to maintain the firm's credit standing, it should consider these payments in determining the appropriate level and structure of the firm's working capital. In planning on an additional $1,000,000 in cash payments to meet sinking fund requirements, management may raise the level of cash and/or marketable securities by the same amount. When management considers the opportunity cost of capital (that is, the funds could be reinvested more profitably elsewhere), the burden of the sinking fund can appear to be great indeed.

On the other hand, there are situations in which a sinking fund can work if not to the advantage of the owners, at least not to their disadvantage. For example, suppose that the instruments had been mortgage bonds with a lien on the production facilities. Instead of redeeming bonds each year, management is given the option of using $1,000,000 to add to the facilities which are the underlying security. Assuming that at least $1,000,000 could be profitably invested each year in these long-lived assets, the terms of the sinking fund cannot be considered restrictive.

Suppose further that the bonds were issued in a period of relatively high interest rates. In subsequent years these rates decline. Management has an opportunity to redeem a portion of the original issue at par rather than at a premium. Moreover, in taking advantage of lower interest rates, it may be able to refinance the sinking fund payments from an alternative source, say a term loan, rather than out of cash. Of course, if the bonds were sold during a period of relatively low rates of interest, refinancing would have to take place at a higher cost.

In considering sinking fund payments, therefore, we must take into account several relevant factors, including the opportunity cost of funds set aside to meet these payments, alternative uses to which the sinking fund can be put, and other means of financing them. The total burden may not be as great as would appear from the terms of the indenture.

SUMMARY

When long-term debt is publicly offered, it is evidenced by a three-party contract. The parties are the issuer, the purchaser, and the trustee. The last of these represents the purchaser or bondholder. He sees to it that the issuer honors the terms of the indenture. When the debt is placed privately in the hands of an institutional investor, it is evidenced by a promissory note to which only the issuer and the purchaser are parties.

Long-term debt can be secured or unsecured. When the debt is secured, the collateral may consist of land and plant, equipment, or securities. In the case of real property, the instruments issued are mortgage bonds. There may also be a mortgage on equipment. In some instances, however, notably the rolling stock of railroads, equipment is technically leased. Ownership rests in the hands of the railroad only after the principal on the equipment trust obligations has been paid in full. When the lien is on securities, the bonds issued are called collateral trust obligations. Long-term debt contracts may be open- or closed-end. Moreover, secured obligations, particularly mortgage bonds, may be issued with an after-acquired clause. Although secured obligations represent senior debt, their safety, in the event of default, may be only as great as the value of the collateral pledged to protect their principal and interest.

Unsecured debt offered publicly is evidenced by a debenture; the debenture may be subordinated. If so, in the event of bankruptcy, its claims are subordinated to the claims of all debt, secured or un-secured. If the interest on the debenture is paid only when earned, the instrument is known as an income or adjustment debenture.

Today, one of the most popular features in a debenture contract is the conversion option. By making the issue convertible into common stock, at a figure higher than the going market value of the stock, management avoids issuing stock at a price which, for one reason or another, is below its long-run investment value. As the market price of the stock rises, so does the price of the debenture. Reflecting the conversion ratio, the price of the debenture will eventually exceed the call price. When this happens, management can then force conversion by exercising the call option.

There will ordinarily be a call price in the contract of a bond or debenture whether it is convertible or not. This call feature will allow management to replace an issue of debt floated in a period of relatively high interest rates with one reflecting a lower cost to maturity. The costs of replacing the debt issue must be compared with the present value of savings in interest. If the latter is greater than the former, the issue should be replaced.

Finally, many indentures contain provisions for sinking funds. How much of a burden the sinking fund entails depends on the extent to which monies must actually be set aside and on the uses to which they can be put.

QUESTIONS AND PROBLEMS

1. "Both the issuer and the purchaser will benefit from the use of debentures which are convertible into common stock." Evaluate critically.

2. "Considering the asset structure of most companies and the market for corporate debt, a capital structure consisting of mortgage bonds with various liens and debentures with payment of principal and interest subordinated to all debt and/or contingent on earnings is unnecessarily complex." Do you agree? Explain fully.

3. Assume that a principal amount of a straight debenture issue is $20,000,000. When the issue was sold at par, the interest cost was 7 percent. The call premium is 104. The issue matures in 25 years. The call option can be exercised within a year after the bonds are issued. Next year management finds that it can recall the issue, replacing it with a series of bonds maturing in 24 years, selling at par

with a 6 percent interest rate. The expenses associated with floating a new bond issue and recalling the old one are $200,000. Should the company exercise the call option? Explain carefully.

4. A firm issues a series of subordinated debentures whose par value is $50,000,000. They are convertible into common stock at a 10:1 ratio. The par value of each bond is $1,000. The market price of the stock is $65 a share. There are presently 50,000,000 shares outstanding. If the call premium is 104, to what price should the stock rise before management tries to force conversion?

5. "Security enhances the quality of a bond or equipment trust certificate only if the property pledged has an opportunity cost." Evaluate.

SELECTED REFERENCES

Bogen, Jules (ed.). *Financial Handbook*, 4th ed. New York: The Ronald Press Company, 1964, sec. 14.

Bowlin, Oswald D. "The Refunding Decision: Another Special Case in Capital Budgeting," *Journal of Finance*, vol. 21, no. 1 (March, 1966), pp. 55–68.

Broman, Keith L. "The Use of Convertible Subordinated Debentures by Industrial Firms, 1949–1959," *Quarterly Review of Economics and Business*, vol. 3, no. 1 (Spring, 1963), pp. 65–75.

Johnson, Robert W. "Subordinated Debentures: Debt that Serves as Equity," *Journal of Finance*, vol. 10, no. 1 (March, 1955), pp. 1–16.

C. James Pilcher. *Raising Capital with Convertible Securities*. Ann Arbor: Bureau of Business Research, School of Business Administration, The University of Michigan, 1955.

Robbins, Sidney M. "A Bigger Role for Income Bonds," *Harvard Business Review*, vol. 33, no. 6 (November-December, 1955), pp. 100–114.

Street, Donald M. "The Role of Equipment Obligations in Postwar Railroad Financing," *Journal of Finance*, vol. 15, no. 3 (September, 1960), pp. 333–340.

Williams, Charles M., and Howard A. Williams. "Incentive Financing—A New Opportunity," *Harvard Business Review*, vol. 38, no. 2 (March-April, 1960), pp. 123–134.

Winn, Willis J., and Arleigh Hess, Jr. "The Value of the Call Privilege," *Journal of Finance*, vol. 14, no. 2 (May, 1959), pp. 182–195.

Corporate Stock

chapter Fifteen

In familiarizing himself with the details of corporate equity, the student should contrast the features of preferred stock with those of debt. When reading the material on common stock, he should critically analyze the various "rights" which stockholders enjoy. Which are of lasting value? Which are of value under particular circumstances?

Preferred Stock — Equity That Serves as Debt

In our discussion of the cost of capital we chose to include preferred stock, at least straight preferred stock, in the debt component of the capital structure. Our rationale for doing so was the fact that the dividends, like bond interest, were fixed in amount. We were interested at that time in developing an elementary model of the cost of capital. It simplified matters to take advantage of the similarities in the contractual obligations of bondholders and preferred stockholders.

Legally, however, preferred stock represents ownership interest in and not a liability of the corporation. Failure to meet commitments to a preferred stockholder is not grounds for bankruptcy. And what are these commitments? Foremost among them is the fact that the owner of preferred stock has the right to receive dividends before they are paid to the common stockholder. Indeed it is preference as to dividends which best distinguishes preferred from common stock. A dividend need not be paid on either type of stock. But if the board of directors elects to distribute a cash dividend to the common stockholders, the full dividend due to the preferred stockholders must also be paid.

Preferred dividends are stated either in dollars or as a percentage of the par value of the stock. Par value is a minimum figure at which a share can be sold by the corporation. It has little significance save at the date of issue. To illustrate, suppose that the par value of a share of preferred stock is $100. As long as the issuing corporation receives at least $100 for each new share marketed, the stock is "fully paid and non-assessable." If the company receives cash or other assets worth less than $100, say $90, the stockholder is theoretically liable for the additional $10.[1] If the stock sold for $105, the extra $5 represents paid-in or capital surplus. In determining the accounting or book value of the stock, the paid-in surplus is listed as such on the balance sheet of the corporation. Otherwise the preferred stockholder's liability, like the liability of the common stockholder, is limited to the amount of his investment.

A preferred stock whose par value is $100 may have a dividend rate stated as a specific percentage, say 6 percent. Alternatively, it may be known as the $6.00 preferred of the company. Using the above example, suppose that the board of directors does pass the dividend on the preferred stock for 1 year and the common stockholders also receive nothing. Must the directors pay $12.00 the following year before a dividend may be paid to the common stockholders? If the preferred stock contract states that the dividends are *cumulative*, then dividends that have been passed in previous years must be paid before any cash distributions can be made to the common stockholders. Alternatively, the dividends may be noncumulative. Under this feature, if management fails to pay dividends during one year, the corporation is not obliged to meet the past commitments during the next year. Dividends on common stock can be paid if the directors also pay

---

[1] If the assets received by the corporation are valued on its books as though it had received $100 and the preferred stock account is credited with the full $100, the stock is said to be watered. Similar techniques have been used in the sale of common stock, of which there are numerous historical examples.

the dividend due to the preferred stockholders for the current year.

While there may be limitations placed on the number of years for which dividends can accumulate, at present most preferred stock outstanding is cumulative. At times, arrears have built up to such an amount that payment would entail a severe drain on the cash position of the corporation. Consequently, if a company decides that it is ready to meet its commitments, it may choose to satisfy its preferred stockholders by issuing shares of common stock whose market value equals the dollar value of the cumulated dividends. As long as they are fully compensated, preferred stockholders have no recourse in the courts as to the form of payment.[2]

Preferred stock is also likely to be *nonparticipating.* Its dividend is set. Having paid the dividend, the corporation has no further income obligation. However, even if we admit that dividends rather than earnings are the relevant variable controlling the market price of common stock, the value of the stock usually reflects a growing rather than a constant stream of dividends. In other words, for most common stocks (or at least for those selling at high multiples of dividends or earnings), the growth rate g is positive, not zero or negative. Nevertheless, common stockholders may receive nothing at a time when preferred stockholders are fully compensated. At another time they may receive considerably more. In those rare instances when preferred stock is participating, a possible formula consists in paying dividends on common stock equal to those paid to preferred stockholders, then distributing any additional dividends to both groups on the basis of an agreed-to formula varying from equal to proportional participation weighted in favor of the common stockholders.

Preferred stock also has features similar to those of bonds. For example, unless the practice is prohibited by state law, preferred stock can be denied voting rights[3] except on matters expressly concerning it,

[2]Other factors remaining the same, the market price of the common stock will fall because of the increase in shares outstanding. A cumulative dividend commitment of $24 per share may be met by giving a share of common stock for each share of preferred stock owned, the market price of the common being $24 at the time the announcement is made. If there are 700,000 shares of common outstanding at the time and an additional 100,000 shares must be issued to the preferred stockholders, the common stock equity is said to be diluted. Preferred dividends have not changed. A past commitment is merely being observed. Total earnings on the common stock have not changed as a result of this action but earnings per share have fallen. Unless this cumulative commitment had been discounted in the market price of the common—that is, the stock was priced lower than it would be if there were no cumulative dividends due—then the additional shares issued will depress the market price. Preferred stockholders will get a stock valued at $24 at the time the announcement is made but which will subsequently fall in price because of the additional shares issued.

[3]Illinois does not allow nonvoting stock issues. See Jules Bogen (ed.), *Financial Handbook*, 4th ed. (New York: The Ronald Press Company, 1964), sec. 13, p. 21.

such as changes in the contract under which it is issued.   Bondholders never vote save on proposals changing covenants in the indenture. Moreover, the more junior the debt, the closer it resembles preferred stock.   For instance, in the event of liquidation, subordinated debentures are similar to preferred stock in that they participate after other debt claims have been satisfied.   While preferred stock is junior to subordinated debentures, one may be a substitute for the other.   Hence both are rarely part of the capital structure of the same corporation. Interest on income bonds is perhaps more akin to preferred dividends than to ordinary bond interest.   Yet the preferred dividends can be passed even if earned, whereas interest on an income bond cannot be passed, thereby threatening the financial solvency of the corporation.

While preferred stock does not mature and a bond does, both types of securities can have a call price and each may be convertible into common stock.   As in the case of a bond or debenture, the function of the call premium is to allow management to replace a high-cost preferred stock with a cheaper issue — or if the stock is convertible, to force conversion.

For instance, assume that a firm issued $10,000,000 in straight (that is, nonparticipating) preferred at its par value, or $100.   The dividend rate is $7\frac{1}{2}$ percent of par, or $7.50.   The preferred is callable any time at $110 per share.   The following year management anticipates that it could replace the preferred with a new issue selling at par and carrying a dividend rate of $6\frac{1}{2}$ percent.

Theoretically, just as it would if it were an issue of bonds or debentures, the preferred stock will sell at its investment value.   If a $6\frac{1}{2}$ percent preferred can now sell at $100 a share, then a $7\frac{1}{2}$ percent preferred of comparable quality should sell, commissions aside, at

$$\frac{\$7.50}{0.065} = \$115.38$$

However, because the company can exercise the call option, the market price will not rise to that amount.   If an investor bought shares at, say, $115, he would run the risk of losing $5.00 per share should management exercise the call option.

In recalling the $7\frac{1}{2}$ percent preferred at $110 and issuing a $6\frac{1}{2}$ percent preferred at par, or $100, management could make up the difference or $10 per share by paying cash.   Alternatively, it might issue additional preferred.   The original series consisted of 100,000 shares marketed at par, or a total of $10,000,000.   To recall the issue and replace it with a new series, management will either sell an additional 10,000 shares or pay $1,000,000 to the old preferred shareholders.

If the stock is to be recalled, the simplest procedure is to issue the additional shares.   Moreover, management will probably offer the new shares to the old stockholders.   Doing so will make it relatively easy for both the corporation and the shareholders to comply with the tax law. An exchange of shares of a corporation for the same type of shares in the same corporation is tax-free.   In addition, under the *preemptive* right, management may have to offer the shares to the stockholders. Under common law a stockholder has the right to subscribe to a new issue of stock before it can be offered to others.   This right can be circumscribed by statute and in some states it is.   It is also more likely to be waived in the case of preferred, particularly nonvoting preferred, than in the case of common stock.

If there is some uncertainty as to whether the preemptive right applies in a given instance, or if management feels that the existing preferred stockholders should be offered the chance to subscribe to the new issue, it will in this case offer 11 shares of new preferred stock for every 10 shares of the original issue.   Ignoring the incidental expenses of recalling the old and issuing a new series, redemption is in the interests of the common stockholders if the result is to lower the annual dividend payments.   Since preferred dividends are not tax-deductible, there is no loss in tax savings as a result of a lower dividend payment. Thus

$$100,000 \text{ old shares } \times \$7.50 = \$750,000$$
$$110,000 \text{ new shares } \times \$6.50 = \underline{715,000}$$

$$\text{Annual savings in preferred dividends } = \$ \ 35,000$$

Management would find that a tax-free exchange of shares would lower the preferred dividend payments and raise the income accruing to common stockholders.

If the preferred stock is not only callable but convertible into common stock, then, as in the case of a bond or debenture, it will sell at its investment value or call price, whichever is lower, until the conversion value exceeds this price.   Suppose that the series just employed was not only callable at $110 but convertible into common stock with the exchange ratio being a share of common for each share of preferred. At the time the preferred is issued, a price of a share of common is $85.   The stock will, therefore, sell at a figure no higher than $110. However, once the market price of the common exceeds $110, the market price of the preferred will rise with it.   Management can then force conversion by exercising the call option.

The preferred stock contract, particularly if the issue is not convertible, may also include provisions for a sinking fund.   The fund may consist of cash to be used to retire the stock or it may merely represent a bookkeeping transaction transferring funds (in accounting terminology) from earned surplus to a reserve for retirement of preferred stock. For example, suppose the contract specified that a reserve equivalent to 5 percent of earnings after taxes be set aside to retire preferred stock. Assume further that after-tax earnings for the year totaled $1,000,000. Then earned surplus would be charged (in accounting terminology debited) and a reserve for retirement of preferred stock increased (in accounting terminology credited) in the amount of $50,000. There need be no steps taken to retire the stock.

However, if the contract specified that 1 percent of the original issue is to be retired each year, then cash would have to be set aside to meet this obligation. The shares would ordinarily be retired at the call price. Using our earlier example, this price would be $110 with 1,000 shares retired each year. However, management usually has the option of buying the shares in the open market. If, after allowance for brokerage commissions, the stock is selling below $110 per share, management will try to meet its commitment by purchasing the shares in the open market.

Adherence to sinking fund provisions may be less formal in the case of preferred stock than in the case of bonds. In either instance, management will feel obliged to honor the commitment. But where inability to meet cash payments on a bond sinking fund may or may not precipitate bankruptcy, failure will never occur for inability to meet sinking fund payments on preferred stock. If the payments are not met, however, what is ordinarily nonvoting preferred stock may be able to vote on the same matters and on the same basis as common stock.

To complete the distinction between preferred and common stock, the contract issued often states that in the event of dissolution, the former is preferred as to assets up to perhaps its par or some stated value. Suppose that a firm is liquidated and the sale of its assets brings $10,000,000. There is $8,000,000 in debt outstanding. There are also 100,000 shares of preferred stock with prior claim on assets of up to $25 a share. Since the preferred stock is junior to the debt but senior to common stock in the event of liquidation, it will divide $2,000,000 equally among 100,000 shares. It receives, therefore, $20 per share, or 80 percent of its claims. Since there are no further assets out of which to pay the additional $5.00, the remainder of the claim goes unsatisfied. The common stockholders receive nothing.

Unless preference as to assets in the event of liquidation is specified in the preferred stock contract, preferred stock participates on an equal basis with common stock. Assume in the above example that there were also 100,000 shares of common stock. Then each share of preferred and common would receive $10. How much value preferred stockholders should attach to the right to preference in the event of liquidation is debatable.   As indicated in a subsequent chapter on corporate reorganization, the market value of the assets of many firms in bankruptcy is less than the principal and interest due on the outstanding debt.   When this is the case, then under the law neither preferred nor common stock will receive compensation.

While preferred stock has features which resemble debt, particularly subordinated and income debentures, we should note that treating junior debt as a substitute for preferred stock may not always be in the interests of common stockholders.[4]

It is conventional wisdom today to accept the proposition that a series of subordinated debentures, or perhaps a series of income bonds, is more satisfactory because interest is tax-deductible whereas preferred dividends are not.   Indeed, our cost-of-capital models indicated that preferred stock is the most expensive source of funds.   If management is to maximize the long-run market value of the owners' equity, then rarely if ever will it rely on preferred stock.   Moreover, as our subsequent discussion of the historical importance of various sources of funds indicates, the issuance of preferred stock has declined to perhaps 1 percent or less of total sources of funds utilized by corporations.

But "rarely if ever" suggests that there might be situations in which the employment of preferred stock would add to the market value of the ownership interests.   What are these conditions?   If we extend our cost-of-capital model to include preferred stock in the supply of funds, the most obvious situation in which preferred stock would be employed exists when the investment schedule in a particular year is so large that the marginal cost of common stock exceeds the marginal cost of preferred stock.

Assume, for example, that the potential capital budget for the XYZ Corporation consists of $100,000,000 in investment opportunities. Assume further that even if the marginal cost of capital were 20 percent, each of the projects would have a net present value greater than or equal to zero.   Finally, suppose that the market price of the common stock is at a maximum when the debt ratio is 30 percent.   The firm is now at this level.   Management anticipates that there will be, after dividend requirements are met, $20,000,000 in retained earnings and depreciation.   This will allow management to raise $30,000,000 in debt if the other $50,000,000 can be obtained through equity.

But can it still raise the entire amount through the sale of common

---

[4]What follows has been prompted by Gordon Donaldson, "In Defense of Preferred Stock," *Harvard Business Review*, vol. 40, no. 4 (July-August, 1962), pp. 123–136.   The conclusions reached, however, as well as the analysis employed, do not always parallel Donaldson's.

stock yet hold the marginal cost—that is, the cost of raising $50,000,000 below 25 percent?   Suppose that in order to sell this amount, whether to existing stockholders or to outsiders, management must price the issue so far below the current market price that in adjusting P for this, the ratio $E_a/P_F + g$ exceeds 20 percent.   However, if the size of the issue of common stock is reduced to $30,000,000, the adjustment in P is less and the ratio will not exceed 20 percent.

Turning to preferred stock, management finds that it can also float a $20,000,000 issue of straight preferred so that D/P_F, after adjustment for taxes on the profits required to earn the dividend, is also less than 20 percent.   Management will therefore float a series of preferred stock.   Thus, while it is rare for demand to reach such levels that preferred stock can be profitably issued, it is a possibility.

But what of the argument that preferred stock is a substitute for debt, and that given the tax advantage the latter should be employed first?   In the above example, both debt and preferred stock were used. What if the capital budget, when each project was discounted by 20 percent, totaled $60,000,000 rather than $100,000,000?   Then our analysis suggests that there would be no preferred stock issued.   Thirty percent, or $18,000,000, would come from debt, $20,000,000 from retained earnings and depreciation, while the remainder of $22,000,000, would be financed out of an issue of common stock.

But the critic might respond by saying that in recognizing the tax advantage accorded bond interest, we are assuming that these savings more than offset the additional financial risk borne by the stockholders. While management should treat bond interest and sinking fund payments as obligations to be met, the fact that failure to meet the latter cannot ordinarily precipitate bankruptcy is a point to consider.   In a more sophisticated analysis, therefore, we must ask this question: Is there some combination of debt and preferred stock whose total market value is K which would result in a higher market price for the common stock than if the K in senior securities consisted entirely of debt?   If so, then the preferred stock should be used probably in lieu of subordinated or income debentures to the point where the market price of the common stock is a maximum.

The answer to the question depends on a subjective appraisal of the marginal increase in earnings resulting from the substitution of bond interest for preferred dividends as compared with the cost of the steps required to offset the increase in the risk of bankruptcy due to failure to meet contractual obligations on the debt employed.   Nor is there a simple answer, for we are in effect comparing small gains or losses in income with small changes in the probabilities that there will be insufficient cash to meet financial requirements as they come due.

To illustrate, management is considering replacing 50,000 shares of $8.00 preferred stock whose market value is $5,000,000 with 25-year debentures which are subordinated to senior debt and whose interest payments are contingent on earnings. To issue this series at par, management must pay 7 percent interest. If unearned, the interest payments accumulate and are payable out of earnings next year. Moreover, if earnings are available after interest has been paid, an accounting reserve of $200,000 a year must be established for periodic retirement of the debentures. While management is not required to retire $200,000 of debentures each year, it is expected to do so to the extent that cash is available. Therefore, the only financial risk assumed is the threat of bankruptcy if cash flow is insufficient to pay interest when earned.

Suppose that management feels virtually certain that earnings before taxes will be sufficient to cover interest on the debentures. Then the increase in profits accruing to the common stockholder is

50,000 shares of preferred stock × $8.00	= $400,000
5,000 debentures × $70(1 − 0.48)	= 182,000
Annual increase in earnings available to common stockholders	= $218,000

Since management is confident that the firm will generate sufficient earnings to pay $350,000 in interest, this payment will be partially offset by a decline in income taxes payable, leaving a net increase in current liabilities of $182,000. But this is less than the preferred dividends of $400,000. Thus current liabilities, which include dividends payable, will fall by $218,000 and net profits will rise by $218,000.

A firm, of course, can report a profit and still have insufficient cash to meet liabilities as they come due. But what is management doing in replacing the preferred stock with subordinated income debentures? It is substituting a net figure of $182,000 in liabilities which it must honor (assuming that interest is earned), whether cash is available or not. This results in a $400,000 liability which it can pass if funds are insufficient.

The problem to resolve, therefore, is how much of the net increase of $218,000 in profits should be set aside in cash or marketable securities to offset the $182,000 in liabilities which must be paid when due. Clearly, in this instance, management could set aside the full amount and still have $36,000 a year available for investment in long-lived assets or disbursement as dividends. Unless the expenses associated with replacing the preferred stock with debentures more than offsets the present value of this amount plus the income on the marketable securities, management should refinance the preferred stock with the debentures.

Changing the indenture to make interest payable, whether earned or not, would alter the details somewhat. The debentures might be sold to yield 6¾ rather than 7 percent. If management is confident that interest will always be earned, the firm will gain from this cost savings. What could be a problem is the sinking fund requirement. In our example, there is no burden. If management sets aside an accounting reserve, it may still invest $200,000 in long-lived assets without violating the terms of the indenture. But suppose the worst possibility: that interest and sinking fund payments must be paid when due. Failure to do so will precipitate bankruptcy. In this instance, management is substituting a $382,000 liability for the next 25 years for an indefinite commitment of $400,000 which it can pass. But the net increase in earnings is less than the cash commitments. Therefore, if cash or marketable securities are to be increased by the amount of the liability, the difference of $164,000 ($382,000 less $218,000) must come from liquidation of long-lived assets or from earnings before the increase.

We can assume, of course, that management will have considered preferred dividends in determining its level of working capital, so that any increase in current assets need reflect only the marginal difference in the risk assumed. Yet the imposition of a sinking fund with mandatory cash payments does add to the debt burden and therefore to the desire to increase the level of cash and marketable securities. It may well be that when management considers the impact of the interest and sinking fund payments on the structure of assets (and ultimately on the profitability of the firm), it might conclude that the market price of the common stock will be greater if the preferred stock is retained in the capital structure.

Between the stringent clause that failure to meet sinking fund payments will precipitate bankruptcy and the decision to eliminate the sinking fund altogether lie numerous alternatives. One is a restriction placed on dividends if sinking fund payments are not met. Management must therefore consider the impact of this clause on the market value of the common stock.

In essence, while much of the literature (including our model of the cost of capital) assumes that the tax advantage is sufficiently large to justify replacing preferred stock with debentures, in any given situation not only must we compare the interest with the preferred stock dividends but we must also compare the total burden posed by the indenture with that anticipated under the preferred stock contract. In many cases the tax advantage is sufficient to justify the use of debentures. In other instances the market price of the common stock might fall due to offsetting features, particularly the need to meet sinking fund payments.

We should also note in passing that when preferred stock of non-financial firms is retired, it is not unusual to attach a sinking fund to the debentures used to retire the issue.   Not only are these sinking fund payments a part of the burden of the debt, but it is often the objective of financial management to replace the preferred stock with retained earnings.   This adds another dimension to our capital budget.   Presumably management has weighed the alternatives, that is, investment in long-lived assets, and found that retiring preferred stock and ultimately debt is a more profitable use of the common stockholders' funds. Since the personal income tax laws tend to work in favor of retaining earnings, it should come as no surprise that management may ultimately prefer to finance a large proportion of the firm's assets out of profits. Nevertheless, management may find that by committing the concern to sinking fund payments, it can be forced in future years to issue additional debt in order to finance the prospective capital budget.   Instead of replacing debt with retained earnings, it will be using retained earnings to retire one series of debt while issuing a new series to help finance the capital budget for that year.[5]

Common Stock

In a corporation the common stock represents the owners' equity toward which the modern theory of financial management is directed.   Under the law, the number of shares a company is authorized to issue is spelled out in the charter of incorporation.   The number of shares actually issued either are outstanding in the hands of the investor or have been repurchased by the company.   If outstanding, whether common or preferred, the shares will be evidenced by certificates similar to the one shown in Figure 15-1[6] on page 326.   If preferred, the certificate will state this.   Otherwise we can assume that the term capital stock employed in the illustration is synonymous with common stock.

When shares have been repurchased by the company, they are called *treasury stock*.   Corporations will repurchase stock for a variety

---

[5]Implied above is the fact that the major constraint on management is financial; that is, the marginal cost of capital determines the last project acceptable.   Suppose, as it has been argued, that the critical factor limiting expansion is management's ability to carry out all the possible projects.   See F. K. Wright, "Project Evaluation and the Managerial Limit," *Journal of Business*, vol. 37, no. 2 (April, 1964), pp. 179–185.   Then we might admit that the debt could ultimately be retired.   But in a financial sense, depending on how leverage affects the market price of the common stock, the firm may be undercapitalized.   In retiring both preferred stock and debt, management has failed to maximize the market value of the ownership interests.

[6]This certificate is reproduced with permission of the issuer.

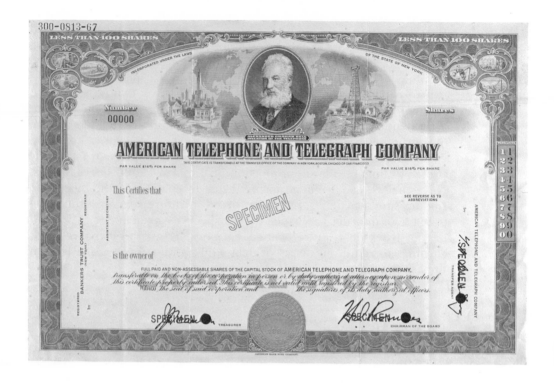

Fig. 15-1 Specimen of stock certificate for American Telephone and Telegraph Company.

of reasons, and since management has been doing so more frequently in recent years, we shall want to look more closely at the implications of this practice later in the chapter.

Once the number of shares authorized equals the number of shares issued, whether they be outstanding or in the treasury, new stock can be issued only by amending with stockholder approval the authorization limits in the corporate charter.

As in the case of preferred stock, common stock may also have a par value. As long as the common stock initially sells for at least par value, then like the preferred stock it is "fully paid and non-assessable." The par value of the share shown in Figure 15-1 is $16\frac{2}{3}$. "Full(y) paid and non-assessable" is clearly printed on the certificate.

Since corporations pay franchise taxes in the states in which they are incorporated, and since these taxes are usually based on par value, companies have tended to issue both common and preferred stocks with low or nominal par values. Par value stocks in denominations of $1, $5, and $10 are not uncommon. There are also issues of common

326

stock with no par value.   Such stock is merely listed on the books of the corporation at its stated value, that is, at the price at which the shares were originally sold.   Because some states, for franchise tax purposes, treat no-par-value stocks as though they were $100-par-value stocks, they are not as popular as low- or nominal-par-value shares.

Since common stock has a residual claim on income, its holders assume more risk than the owners of debt instruments or preference shares.   In return for accepting the risk, they have the opportunity to realize a considerably larger gain than that which accrues to alternative sources of funds.   Moreover, in principal, common stockholders have the right to elect the directors of the enterprise who in turn appoint the officers to conduct the business in the interest of the owners.   In practice, the right to control corporate policy may have been delegated to a team of professional managers who in turn select the directors who are then dutifully elected by the stockholders.

The voting right, therefore, is important only if ownership is not divorced from control, or, in the case where ownership is so divorced, there is enough widespread discontent among owners that it can be channeled into a stockholder revolt culminating in the replacement of top management with a new group.   The fact that this does occur on occasion will help to keep the stockholders' interests foremost in the mind of management.

To mount a challenge to those presently in control of a company is not an easy task.   Under common law the right to vote is vested in the stockholder.   He has one vote regardless of the number of shares owned.   Moreover, he cannot delegate his vote through power of attorney, that is, by proxy.   He must be present at stockholder meetings in order to vote on policy issues.   In the United States, however, state statutes have modified the common law privilege by granting votes based on the number of shares held, each share having one vote.   Furthermore, it is common to grant the power of attorney on those issues which affect corporate policy and which must be approved by stockholders.   Management will often solicit proxies for the election of directors and other matters to be voted on.   If a dissident group with its own slate of directors is desirous of electing people representing its own point of view, it will also have to solicit proxies from stock-holders.   Under the system of one vote for one share, in order to ensure selection of its slate, those opposed to the present management must obtain proxies from at least 50 percent of the shares voting.

Their task is not necessarily easier if *cumulative voting* is permitted or, as in the case of the statutes in some states, is mandatory.   Under cumulative voting, each stockholder continues to receive one vote per share. However, he also gets as many votes as he has shares times the number of directors to be elected. If there are four directors to be elected and there are 400,000 shares outstanding, there are 1,600,000 potential votes. Unlike noncumulative voting, however, cumulative voting does not require that the shareholder cast his votes for the entire slate of directors. Thus, if a person owns 100 shares, he has 400 votes, all of which may be cast in favor of one director. Suppose that a dissident minority is dissatisfied with management's financial policy. It cannot muster enough votes to elect a majority of the board but through cumulative voting it might be able to have its views represented through the election of one director. There are 500,000 shares outstanding and there are to be four directors elected this year at the annual stockholders' meeting. Assuming that all shares outstanding vote, the dissident group of stockholders can elect one director if it acquires votes according to the following formula:

Minimum number of shares required to elect one director

$$= \frac{\text{total number of shares outstanding} \times \text{number of directors desired}}{\text{total number of directors to be elected} + 1} + 1$$

$$100,001 = \frac{500,000 \times 1}{4 + 1} + 1$$

If the group can collect the votes on 100,001 shares, it can cumulate 400,004 votes for one director. Assuming that the present management solicits proxies for the remaining 399,999 shares, it will cast the votes equally among its share of four directors, giving each of them 399,999 votes. By a margin of five votes the minority group of stockholders will elect a director of its own choosing.

In spite of the fact that cumulative voting will allow at least minority representation, it will still require 300,001 shares to ensure the election of all four directors, whereas under the system of noncumulative voting the number of shares required to control the election of the entire slate of directors is a simple majority. Under cumulative voting, controlling a majority of shares ensures the election of only a majority of the directors. Thus, while it is easier under cumulative voting for a minority group to gain representation on the board of directors, it is also more difficult for them to unseat the entire board.

The nuances flowing from the right to vote, even if the voting is cumulative, are ordinarily of little concern to the stockholder who purchases shares in a corporation where ownership is divorced from control.[7]   He may evidence interest when asked by the directors to approve the terms of a merger in which he gives up his shares in exchange for the shares of the acquiring corporation.   This is because the outcome will affect both his income and wealth.   But ordinarily he could not care less when asked to approve management's selection of an independent public accounting firm to audit the books or when asked to vote on any other procedural matter which might necessitate stockholder action.   Other than in making proposals which affect the income and market price of the stock, management need concern itself with adverse shareholder reaction only if earnings or dividends, together with the market value of the shares, do not show gains comparable to the alternatives available to the stockholders.

Dividend Policy

We pointed out in the chapter on the cost of capital – Chapter 12 – that dividends might have some influence on the market price of the stock. Yet we assumed that we had minimized the impact by holding the payout ratio constant.   Dividends would therefore fluctuate with earnings. Each would be subject to the same probability distribution.

However, for the moment at least, let us suppose that dividend policy did not affect the market price of the stock.   Then our simple model clearly implies that as long as there are profitable investment opportunities, all earnings should be used for investing in assets before outside financing, particularly equity financing, is employed.   Dividends should therefore be a residual fluctuating with the level of investment demand.   Since the investment schedule reflects the opportunity cost of capital, earnings which cannot be profitably invested within the firm should (according to our model) be distributed to the stockholders. They in turn could reinvest these funds in the stocks of other corporations.

Unfortunately, our analysis runs up against the reluctance of management, particularly management of a corporation where ownership is divorced from control, to allow the absolute level of dividends to fluctuate, in particular to allow them to fall.   Even though it may want to maintain a constant payout ratio, once the dividend rate is es-

---

[7]The rights range from inspecting the books of the corporation to protecting the corporation against wrongful acts of management. See Bogen, *op. cit.*, sec. 13, p. 1. These rights can be circumscribed if the state laws under which the firm is incorporated permit the organizers to do so. We have already seen that the voting rights of preference shares can be circumscribed or eliminated. This cannot be done with common stock unless it is divided into two groups, one voting and the other nonvoting.

tablished, management would rather curtail investments or seek more expensive outside financing than let dividends decline because of insufficient earnings. In the short run at least, the payout ratio may rise in order to preserve the level of dividends.

To illustrate, Figures 15-2, 15-3, and 15-4 show the hypothetical demand and supply curves of funds for a firm. In each graph the sum *AC* represents retained earnings available each year, and *OA* the depreciation allowances. The size of a specific source of funds can vary each year, as will the cost of capital. Demand is such that management does not have to resort to outside financing. However, unlike our earlier model, the figure for retained earnings does not allow for dividend requirements.

Assume that dividends for each year equal *AB* dollars, a constant amount equivalent to $1.00 per share per year. If management adheres to the principle of a constant dividend, only in the second year (Figure 15-3) will demand be such as to absorb *BC* dollars in retained earnings and pay *AB* dollars in dividends. In the first year (Figure 15-2), if any dividends are paid, the firm will have to resort to outside financing, possibly debt rather than equity, or abandon what would otherwise be profitable projects. In the third year (Figure 15-4), management should pay all the firm's earnings as dividends, for to retain them within the firm would lower the market value of the shares.

But assuming that it is in the stockholders' interests to let the dividend fluctuate with investment needs, why should management desire to maintain a stable dividend? The answer lies in the fact that some investors may be willing to pay a premium for stability in dividend payments. They are attracted to shares of companies in which the dividend, once set, is not likely to be cut. They do expect it to grow over time, but they are confident that management will not raise the dividend unless it is certain that there will be a sufficient amount of cash generated to ensure that the new level will be maintained. When there are additional funds available, as shown in Figure 15-4, and when management is uncertain that it can maintain an increase in dividends, one solution is to declare an extra dividend, thereby placing the shareholders on notice that the same payment may not be made again next year.

The major source of conflict is usually the situation in which it may be in the stockholders' interest to cut or eliminate the dividend in order to take advantage of profitable investment opportunities within the firm. This is the situation illustrated in Figure 15-2. As a result of suddenly cutting dividends to invest the proceeds within the firm, there would be an adjustment in the market price of the common stock. Those attracted to the stock because of its stable dividend policy will begin

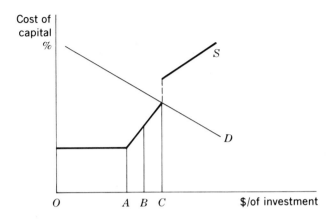

Fig. 15-2

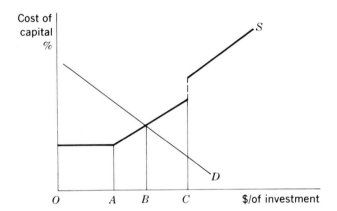

Fig. 15-3

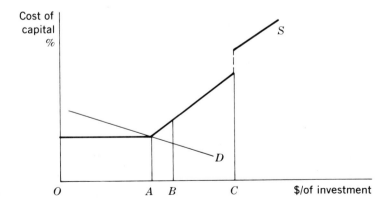

Fig. 15-4

to liquidate their investment. But presumably others less interested in dividends will not buy the shares.

Whether the market price of the stock will, on balance, rise or fall is a moot point. Dollars which were certain today are reinvested in projects whose cash flows are subject to a probability distribution. As a result, depending on the outcome of these investments, dividends a year from today or 5 years from today could, as we saw earlier, be greater or less than they might have been if the decision to replace a stable dividend policy with a residual dividend policy had not been taken. To the extent that investors are willing, on balance, to accept this risk, the market price of the common stock will rise and the cost of equity capital fall. To the extent that they are not, the market price of the stock will fall and the cost of equity capital rise.

If management feels that investors prefer, on balance, a stable dividend rate which grows steadily and which may on occasion be supplemented with extra dividends, it will make every effort to pursue this policy. Dividends may therefore be paid even if they are not earned.[8] Moreover, as earnings show a secular rise, there may be a tendency to delay an increase in dividends until management is confident that the new level can be maintained. Thus, even if management over the long run has in mind a constant payout ratio, it will in the short run be more concerned about maintaining the current level of dividends. It will therefore let the payout ratio fluctuate from year to year with changes in the level of earnings after taxes.

Indeed, there is evidence that the payout ratio, at least the aggregate ratio for all corporations, has varied over the years. In 1920 it was 64.1 percent. In 1929 it was 71.2 percent. In 1947 it was 35.6 percent. In 1960 the payout ratio was 61.8 percent.[9] But aggregate figures can cover up diverse trends among firms and industries. Moreover, these years provide benchmarks for trends. The payout ratio rose in the 1920s, fell during the 1930s, continued falling until 1947, and has been rising since that time.[10]

---

[8]Management always had the opportunity to pay a dividend or not pay it as it chose. Once declared, however, it becomes a liability subject to certain legal constraints. Some states, for example, will permit dividends to be paid only out of accounting profits. This may include both current earnings and past earnings, that is, earned surplus. If management cannot charge a dividend payment to current earnings or earned surplus, it may not be able to pay it. Some states forbid writing down the par value or paid-in surplus to accommodate a dividend payment on the grounds that it would impair the legal capital of the corporation. Finally, if payment of a dividend would precipitate bankruptcy, or if the firm was already in bankruptcy, management might not be allowed to declare a dividend, or if declared, to pay it. If the dividend were paid under these conditions, the stockholders would be liable for its return.

[9]John A. Brittain, *Corporate Dividend Policy* (Washington: The Brookings Institution, 1966), table 1, p. 3.

[10]*Ibid.*, p. 2.

Even though we may assume that management bases its dividend policy primarily on income after taxes and depreciation,[11] there may be other variables which "explain," at least in a statistical way, the variations in dividends over time. For example, in the period since 1947, the rise in the payout ratio is more closely associated with changes in cash flows, that is, profits after taxes and depreciation, than with the former alone.[12] Liberalization of depreciation for tax purposes, a product of the post-World War II period, has had the effect of lowering reported profits and with it income taxes payable. A firm, once allowed to write off the original cost of its assets in 10 years, is now given the opportunity to do so in, say, 5 years. Thus, on a straight-line basis, the annual depreciation allowance of an asset whose original cost was $1,000,000 is now $200,000 — assuming no scrap value — rather than $100,000. Reported profits fall by $100,000 and income taxes payable by $48,000. Other things remaining the same, the cash flow generated for the year is now $148,000 greater than before.

But what of the impact of personal income tax rates? We have noted before than on analytical grounds the higher the personal income tax bracket of stockholders, the greater is the incentive to retain earnings within the firm. Changes in tax rates do help to explain changes in the payout ratio. In particular, the rise in taxes between 1929 and 1947 is the dominant factor in explaining the decline in the payout ratio. Cuts in taxes between 1947 and 1960 played a role in the rise in payout ratio over this period, but liberalized depreciation allowances appeared to be a more dominant factor.[13]

While these as well as other factors help to explain the trend in dividends,[14] the results are not inconsistent with the hypothesis that management, interested in preserving a dividend once established, will raise it only if it is confident that it can be maintained. If the source of this confidence is the increased cash flow generated by liberalized depreciation allowances and the tax savings inherent in them, then we can expect the payout ratio as a percentage of earnings after taxes to rise.

Stock Dividends and Splits

Although we can never be certain of the effect the dividend policy will have on the market value of the stock, we can confidently predict that

[11]John Lintner, "Distribution of Incomes of Corporations Among Dividends, Retained Earnings, and Taxes," *American Economic Review*, vol. 46, no. 2 (May, 1956), pp. 97–113.

[12]Brittain, *op. cit.*, chap. III.

[13]*Ibid.*, Chapter IV, particularly pp. 98–99.

[14]*Ibid.*, Chapters V–IX.

unless the dividend is paid in cash or other assets of the firm, say securities of another company held as an investment, there will be no lasting impact on the market price.[15]   A stock dividend composed of shares of the firm paying the dividend does not represent a decline in the assets of the company.   Rather, the capital structure is rearranged. For example, assume that the ABC Corporation declares a 10 percent stock dividend.   Prior to the declaration its ownership equity accounts appear as follows:

Common stock, par value $ 10;	
5,000,000 shares authorized; issued	
and outstanding, 1,000,000 shares	$ 10,000,000
Capital Surplus	8,000,000
Earned Surplus	50,000,000
Total Owners' equity	$68,000,000

The book value per share is $68; the par value is $10.   Assume that the market value prior to the dividend was $75.   The stock dividend will increase the number of shares outstanding to 1,100,000 and reduce the book value per share to about $62 ($68,000,000 divided by 1,100,000 equals $61.82).   The market value will fall to about $68 ($75,000,000 divided by 1,100,000 equals $68.18).

The accounting procedure for handling stock dividends varies, but one possibility is to charge the difference between par value and book value per share to capital surplus, reducing the earned surplus account by $68 per share.   Following this procedure, the owners' equity account would be rearranged as follows:

Common stock, par value $ 10;	
5,000,000 shares authorized; issued	
and outstanding, 1,100,000 shares	$ 11,000,000
Capital Surplus	13,800,000
Earned Surplus	43,200,000
Total Owners' Equity	$68,000,000

Regardless of how the transaction is treated, a stock dividend is merely a rearrangement of the accounts comprising owners' equity.   A person who owns 100 shares of stock gets 10 new shares.   The total

[15]C. Austin Barker, "Evaluation of Stock Dividends," *Harvard Business Review*, vol. 36, no. 4 (July-August, 1958), pp. 99–114.

market value of his holdings after the stock dividend is the same as before, but the price per share has fallen accordingly.

If the stockholder had received the equivalent in cash, the market price, at least in the short run, might have fallen by the amount of the dividend, thereby reflecting the decline in assets used to pay the dividend. If this had occurred, then the shareholder could have sold the stock dividend. The market value of his holdings would be the same as if he had received cash. The gain, if any, would be due to the lower capital gains tax paid on the profit from the sale of the shares as distinct from regular rates paid on dividends.

Suppose, for example, that a shareholder received the equivalent of $50 in stock which he sold immediately. The stock represented 10 percent of his holdings. He bought the original shares at $30. Since his per share equity has been reduced 10 percent, for tax purposes his equity is now $27.27 ($30 divided by 110 percent). Brokerage commissions aside, the profit on the sale of the stock is $22.73. The shareholder pays a maximum of 25 percent on the capital gains. If the personal income tax rate at the margin was 30 percent, the capital gains rate would be 15 percent. On the other hand, if he had received $50 in cash, it would have been subject to the 30 percent personal tax rate.

Tax considerations aside, however, a stock dividend by itself can have, for the reasons cited, no lasting impact on the market value of the owners' equity. In fact, a 10 percent stock dividend has the same effect on the value of an owners' holdings as a stock split of one for ten. In either instance, the shareowner would receive a single new share for each 10 shares he presently owned. Similarly, a 100 percent stock dividend would be the same as a stock split of one for one. A two-for-one split would be equivalent to a 200 percent stock dividend.

Privileged Subscriptions

While most beginning students easily grasp the substantive difference between a cash and a stock dividend, they sometimes fail to see that when a shareholder is given rights to purchase additional shares at a subscription price he is also receiving nothing of value.[16] If the preemptive right applies, as it does in many states, existing shareholders are entitled to purchase additional stock before it can be offered to outsiders. The procedure is known as a *privileged subscription*.[17]

---

[16]J. Russell Nelson, "Price Effects in Rights Offerings," *Journal of Finance*, vol. 20, no. 4 (December, 1965), pp. 647–650.

[17]In recent years as much as two-thirds of the stock sold has been marketed through privileged subscriptions. See *ibid.*, p. 647.

In order to understand the mechanics of privileged subscription, assume that the per share market price of the common stock of a company is $100. There are 1,000,000 shares outstanding. The officers have made a decision to raise an additional $8,000,000 through the sale of common stock. Under the laws of the state in which the company is incorporated, if they float the issue publicly, the directors must seek stockholder approval to waive the preemptive right. Moreover, a public offering would entail selling the stock to a group of investment bankers. These underwriters would offer the company a figure somewhat lower than the price at which they would market the stock, the difference being the commission or spread for accepting the risk of marketing the securities.

Assume that the company has a ready market for its stock, with widespread ownership. Warrants representing rights to purchase shares can be issued to these shareowners, allowing them to buy stock at a subscription price below the current market price but above what the corporation would receive from investment bankers. Management can therefore avoid the underwriting spread. If the stockholder does not wish to participate in the privileged subscription, he may sell his warrants through brokerage channels designated by the corporation.

The market value of these warrants will depend on the difference between the subscription price and the market price of the stock, the number of warrants per share, and whether the stock is selling cum rights or ex rights.

While each share has a single right, the number of warrants required to purchase one share is dependent on the number of shares outstanding, the subscription price, and the amount the corporation desires to raise. Assume that the company chooses to offer the stock at $80 per share, or $20 below the current market price, to shareholders who purchase the stock within 60 days.[18] As long as the investor buys the stock prior to the end of the subscription period, he purchases his shares *cum rights*, that is, with rights. Those purchasing stock after this date are not eligible to buy the stock at $80 per share. The stock under these circumstances sells *ex rights*, that is, without rights.

In order to raise $8,000,000, the company must issue 100,000 shares or 1 new share for each of the 10 old shares outstanding. It follows that the number of rights required to purchase 1 share is 10. When the

---

[18]The details of determining the stockholders of record are often left to the transfer agent, usually a commercial bank and trust company. The agent also distributes dividends, notices of shareholder meetings, etc. A second trust company is often engaged as a registrar. Its function is to serve as a check on the transfer agent and to see to it that the number of shares issued does not exceed the amount authorized in the charter of incorporation. Similar arrangements are used for bonds, but the transfer agent is in this case a trustee for the bondholders.

stock sells cum rights the theoretical value of each right is determined as follows:

$$\text{Value of a right} = \frac{\text{market price of old stock} - \text{subscription price}}{\text{number of rights required to purchase one share} + 1}$$

$$= \frac{\$100 - \$80}{11}$$

$$= \$1.818$$

When the stock sells ex rights, then

$$\text{Value of a right} = \frac{\text{market price of old stock} - \text{subscription price}}{\text{number of rights required to purchase one share}}$$

No longer will there be 1 new share issued for each 10 shares of stock presently outstanding. When the stock sells ex rights, the warrants are available to the shareholder only through purchase in the open market. He must therefore assume that he is buying stock in a company which will have 1,100,000 shares outstanding. When the stock sold cum rights, he could protect himself from the dilution in market value by exercising his privilege to purchase at the subscription price. This accounts for the difference in the denominators in the two formulas. To reflect the subsequent dilution in equity, the market price in the numerator will also change as the stock goes ex rights. An additional $8,000,000 is added to the total market value of $100,000,000 and the number of shares increases to 1,100,000. When the stock goes ex rights, the market price falls to $98.1818 ($108,000,000 divided by 1,100,000).[19]   But the theoretical value of a right remains unchanged.

$$\text{Value of a right} = \frac{\$98.1818 - \$80}{10}$$

$$= \$1.818$$

Since earnings prospects are being constantly reevaluated and since there are numerous random variables affecting the market in the short run, we would not expect the market price of the stock to remain unchanged during the 60-day subscription period. Nevertheless, when the stock goes ex rights, the market price will fall by the amount of the dilution.[20]   Meanwhile, the price of the rights will fluctuate in accordance with changes in the market price of the common stock. Except

[19]Since stocks are ordinarily traded at minimum intervals of an eighth of a point, the price would fall to either $98⅛ or $98¼.
[20]When a stock goes ex dividend, the price at the opening on the following day will be lower by the amount of the dividend. Of course, it can rise or fall even further before the end of the trading session.

for brokerage costs involved, arbitrage will prevent a right from falling below or exceeding its theoretical value for any length of time. To the extent that these departures are observed, they reflect imperfections in the market place, more specifically, insufficient arbitrage transactions.

That the shareholder receives nothing directly is evidenced by the fact that what he gains by the subscription price, he loses in the subsequent decline in the market value of the stock. For every new share purchased at $80, he loses approximately $20 on the 10 shares that he presently holds. The total market value of his holdings, as in the case of the stock split or stock dividend, does not go up as a result of the privileged subscription. If he sells his rights, he is in effect selling part of his equity in the corporation.

Indirectly, of course, the privileged subscription has saved the underwriting costs. If investment bankers had charged $5 per share to underwrite the issue then at a price of $80 per share, the corporation would have received only $75. Additional shares would have been required to raise $8,000,000, and the value of the stockholders' equity would have fallen accordingly.

Even if the underwriting syndicate had marketed the stock at $85, giving the company a net of $80 per share, there is no reason why the corporation could not have also used a privileged subscription at $85, thereby reducing the number of shares required to raise $8,000,000 and lowering the per share decline in the market value. As in the case of a stock dividend or split, there will be no increase in the market value of the shareholder's interests as a result of the exercise of his privileged subscription.[21]

Share Repurchases

In recent years, there has been a tendency for management of some of the nation's largest corporations to repurchase shares of their own stock. By the mid-1960s, stock repurchases represented as much as

---

[21]He can, of course, lose by not exercising this right through either purchase of the shares offered or sale of the warrants. Because as much as 2 to 5 percent of the rights offered may expire without the stockholder exercising them, the corporation can fall short of its capital goal. In anticipation of this occurrence and in spite of warnings to stockholders to either sell or exercise their rights, management often finds it necessary to engage the services of an investment banker on a standby arrangement to purchase the unsubscribed securities at the subscription price. Moreover, should the market price fall below the subscription price and the stockholders not exercise their rights, the investment banker is obliged to purchase the unsubscribed allotment. The further removed the offering price is from the current market price, the less is the risk of a privileged subscription failing for this reason.

$2\frac{1}{2}$ percent of the total volume of shares traded on the New York Stock Exchange.[22]

Ostensibly, management can have various motives for repurchasing its own shares. A major reason often cited is the acquisition of shares to use as payment for the stock or assets of another company which management is intent on buying. In addition, management may be purchasing shares to employ in stock option programs for officers of the company. But each of these motives can be satisfied by having stockholders vote to increase, if necessary, the number of shares authorized under the corporate charter. Thus, if management is repurchasing shares for any of these purposes, it must want to avoid increasing its equity base.

Similarly, if management is buying the shares of its own company without any intention of reissuing them later, it must be doing so in order to shrink the equity base.

But why should management wish to shrink or avoid expanding its equity base? If we reflect for a moment, we can only conclude that repurchasing shares for either of these reasons implies that there are more funds available than management can profitably invest. Otherwise it would have no reason to lower or avoid expanding the firm's equity. On the contrary, it would be adding to equity through retained earnings, using this broader base to support additional debt issued to help finance new assets.

But if there are more funds available than can be profitably invested, why not distribute the cash as an extra dividend? If truly redundant, the extra dividend will not depress and might even raise the market price of the shares. The logical answer is that share repurchases will place a lighter tax burden on many stockholders. Assuming that the shares repurchased are owned by individuals who have held them 6 months or more, the difference between the purchase and the sale price will be taxed at one-half of the personal income tax rate applicable, or a maximum of 25 percent. Dividends, on the other hand, will be taxed at the full rate. If the stockholder would ordinarily pay 40 percent on the dividends, he will pay 20 percent on its equivalent in capital gains.

Furthermore, since the corporation is repurchasing the shares, the Internal Revenue Service in certain instances may treat all or a sub-

[22]Leo A. Guthart, "Why Companies Are Buying Back Their Own Stock," *Financial Analysts Journal*, vol. 23, no. 2 (March-April, 1967), p. 105. See also pp. 106–110. For further discussion, see Donald H. Woods and Eugene F. Brigham, "Stockholder Distribution Decisions: Share Repurchases or Dividends?" *Journal of Financial and Quantitative Analysis*, vol. I, no. 1 (March, 1966), pp. 15–26; and Charles D. Ellis, "Repurchase Stock to Revitalize Equity," *Harvard Business Review*, vol. 43, no. 4 (July-August, 1965), pp. 119–128.

stantial part of the repurchase price as a "return of capital" rather than as a capital gain. If this occurs, then the shareholder will pay taxes only on the difference between the purchase price and the amount the Internal Revenue Service allows as a return of capital. To illustrate, suppose that a corporation buys stock from a stockholder at the current market price of $100 per share. On the books of the corporation the par value and paid-in surplus accounts show the stock to be "worth" $80 a share. The corporation, when it purchases and retires the stock, informs the shareholder that he has received a distribution of capital of $80 a share. The shareholder purchased the stock 2 years ago at $60 a share. His capital gain would ordinarily be $40 a share but because of the "return of capital" of $80, his taxable base is only $100 − $80, or $20, per share.

Some stockholders, however, would have been better off if they had received cash dividends. Individuals owning stock can receive up to $100 in dividends tax-free. If a small shareholder had received $90 a year in dividends from the company, and if the funds used to repurchase shares had been equivalent to an additional $10 in dividends on his investment, then he would have received a tax-free distribution.

Had the stockholder been another corporation, then 85 percent of the dividends received would have been excluded from the corporate income tax. Taxes at the regular rate, that is, 48 percent on net income in excess of $25,000, would have been applied to the remaining 15 percent. Thus, on dividends of $10,000, only $1,500 would be subject to the 48 percent rate. This is equivalent to $720, or 7.2 percent of the total dividend payment, which is less than one-third of the capital gains applicable if the shares had been sold.

Whatever management's reason for repurchasing shares,[23] if the funds had instead been distributed as dividends, it is evident that some shareholders would have benefited more from the dividend increase than from the share repurchases. Furthermore, while the dividends would have gone to all, the share repurchases, if conducted in the open market, would have been at the expense or for the benefit of only a portion of shareholders. To be equitable, therefore, management should at the very least announce its intention to repurchase a

---

[23]Sometimes shares are repurchased to raise the number of votes controlled by management. The shares outside the hands of management, for example, may represent a majority interest. If the votes came under the control of one person, he could take steps to discharge the present officers and hire new ones. By purchasing shares from stockholders who are not part of the present management team, management raises the number of shares it holds relative to the total number of shares outstanding. This is not, however, a common reason for share repurchases, and certainly not among management of some of the nation's largest corporations. Their combined holdings are often a minute fraction of the total number of shares outstanding.

specified percentage of the shares outstanding. Shareholders would then be forewarned of the impending reduction in the equity base and the possible per share increase in the market price of the stock resulting from the added, that is, the corporation's, demand for the stock.

If the shares repurchased represent something more than, say, 1 percent of the total number of shares outstanding, management might find it not only equitable but, in terms of costs, feasible to issue repurchase warrants distributable to stockholders in proportion to their holdings. Suppose that a company had 1,000,000 shares outstanding and management, in order to encourage the shareholders to sell the stock, was willing to purchase 20,000 shares at, say, $50 a share or at a premium of $5.00 per share. A person owning 100 shares would receive the right to sell 2 shares at the offer or tender price. Moreover, the warrants, including fractions earned for lots of less than 50 shares, would be marketable. The price of the warrant would equal the difference between the tender price and the current market price less the costs of transfer. In this way, those who found it to their advantage to do so could have the company repurchase more or less than their proportional number of shares in the company.

For extremely small amounts of shares repurchased, however, the costs of handling the warrants may be excessive in relation to the amount spent to repurchase the shares. Management will, therefore, confine its efforts to an announcement that it plans to buy in the open market a specified number of shares during a particular time period.

Owners' Equity — Other Types of Securities

As with other components of the capital structure, the owners' equity — or in traditional accounting and legal parlance, the capital accounts — have become more simplified. The ownership interests of many corporations, as with their unincorporated counterparts, consist of the funds initially invested in the enterprise. Preferred stock is rarely employed in most industries. When it is, the shares are often convertible.

Unusual types of equity arrangements, such as common stock divided into voting and nonvoting issues or into classes A and B, can be found, but one may have different dividend arrangements than the other or the nonvoting common is issued for a special purpose. For example, the Ford Motor Company has class A and class B common stock in its capital structure. The former, however, is owned by the Ford Foundation and except in special situations has no voting rights.[24]

[24]Moody's *Industrial Manual* (New York: Moody's Investors Service, 1966), p. 2742.

Similarly, Citizens Utilities has an equity structure consisting of a common stock of series A and common stock of series B. They are the same except that when dividends are declared, holders of series A receive stock and holders of series B receive the same amount in cash.[25]

While these as well as other departures from standard equity instruments are sometimes employed, they do represent arrangements which are not always in the mainstream of modern business finance. Yet, since the primary advantage of the corporation is the ability to use the vehicle to effect fine divisions among the elements of risk, income, and control, when they are found to be useful, modifications in the equity contract as well as in standard debt instruments will be employed.

SUMMARY

Traditionally, corporate equity has been broken down into two broad classifications: preferred stock and common stock. Preferred stock, however, has features similar to those of bonds or debentures. For example, the income or dividend is fixed. Moreover, while the issue does not mature, it is often callable. It is usually nonvoting. There may also be a sinking fund formed to retire the issue. Yet in the eyes of the law, preferred shareholders are owners, not creditors, of the corporation. As a result, the dividends are not tax-deductible. Thus, in most cases, it is cheaper to substitute junior debt such as subordinated or income debentures for preferred stock.

The common stock of the corporation represents the owners' equity toward which the modern theory of financial management is directed. Since common stockholders are the residual claimants to corporate income, they assume the major portion of the business risk. As a result, common stockholders in principle control the affairs of the corporation through their right to vote. As a practical matter, however, whether the vote be cumulative or noncumulative, it is important, only in cases where ownership is not divorced from control.

The important right of the common stockholder, therefore, is usually the right to income. Again we run up against the problem of whether earnings or dividends are the variable which investors

[25]Moody's *Public Utility Manual* (New York: Moody's Investors Service, 1966), p. 1083. Series A can be converted into series B, share for share, at any time save for a period between the declaration of a cash dividend on series B and the date at which ownership must be recorded in order to receive the dividend. Until April 14, 1956, series B could also be exchanged into series A. For a discussion of the background leading to the decision to reclassify stock in this manner and the reaction of the Internal Revenue Service, see Robert L. Masson, Pearson Hunt, and Robert N. Anthony, *Cases in Financial Management* (Homewood, Ill.: Richard D. Irwin, Inc., 1960), pp. 433–450.

value.   The evidence indicates that the payout ratio, while varying, has declined over time.   This trend has in part been prompted by the tax treatment of dividends and the rise in cash flows due to liberalized depreciation allowances.   Yet management is reluctant to let the absolute level of dividends fluctuate with earnings.   There seems to be a preference toward stable dividends.   Management apparently prefers not to raise dividends until it is sure that it can maintain the new level.

While we may disagree over the relative merits of cash dividends and earnings in valuing the stock, it is evident that in the absence of tax considerations, stockholders receive nothing of lasting value from stock dividends, stock splits, or privileged subscriptions.   In each instance, the market price of the stock will ultimately adjust to the additional number of shares outstanding.

In recent years, the managements of many nonfinancial corporations have used funds to repurchase shares in their respective enterprises.   While there are ostensibly many reasons for repurchasing the company's stock, they all imply that there are more funds available than management can profitably invest.   Whether an individual stockholder fares better from repurchase than through cash dividends depends on how these alternatives are taxed in his particular case.

Finally, if voting is important and a group of stockholders wishes to maintain control of a corporation, it can issue two or more classes of common stock, one with voting rights, the other without.   Similarly, it may be able to issue two classes of stock, one paying cash dividends and the other paying stock dividends.

QUESTIONS AND PROBLEMS

1.   The going yield on preferred stock is currently 6 percent. Management of a corporation issues $5.50 convertible preferred stock callable at 110.   It can be converted into common stock, share for share, at $120.   The current market price of the common stock is $100.   At what price will the preferred stock sell?   What will determine the maximum price of the preferred stock?   Explain.

2.   Management of a corporation offers its stockholders the right to purchase five new shares for each old share owned.   The rights are evidenced by warrants.   The subscription price of the stock is $40.   The market price is $50.   What is the theoretical value of a right during the subscription period?   What is this value after the stock has gone ex rights?   Would you expect the warrants to sell at their theoretical value?   Explain.

3. "The market price of a share of participating preferred stock in which the preferred and common stockholders shared dividends equally would be the same as the market price of the common stock." Do you agree? Explain carefully.

4. "Share repurchase is a more equitable way of using redundant funds than distributing them as dividends." Evaluate.

5. "The market value of the stock of a shareholder will be unaffected by a stock dividend or split or by exercise of his rights under a privileged subscription." Evaluate.

SELECTED REFERENCES

Brittain, John A. *Corporate Dividend Policy.* Washington: The Brookings Institution, 1966.

Bogen, Jules (ed.). *Financial Handbook*, 4th ed. New York: The Ronald Press Company, 1964, sec. 13.

Donaldson, Gordon. "In Defense of Preferred Stock," *Harvard Business Review*, vol. 40, no. 4 (July-August, 1962), pp. 123–136.

Ellis, Charles D. "Repurchase Stock to Revitalize Equity," *Harvard Business Review*, vol. 43, no. 4 (July-August, 1965), pp. 119–128.

Fischer, Donald E., and Glenn A. Wilt, Jr., "Non-convertible Preferred Stock as a Financing Instrument, 1950–1965," *Journal of Finance*, vol. 23, no. 4 (September, 1968), pp. 611–624.

Guthart, Leo A. "Why Companies Are Buying Back Their Own Stock," *Financial Analysts Journal*, vol. 23, no. 2 (March-April, 1967), pp. 105–110.

Lintner, John. "Distribution of Incomes of Corporations Among Dividends, Retained Earnings, and Taxes," *American Economic Review*, vol. 46, no. 2 (May, 1956), pp. 97–113.

Nelson, J. Russell. "Price Effects in Rights Offerings," *Journal of Finance*, vol. 20, no. 4 (December, 1965), pp. 647–650.

Sussman, Richard A. *The Stock Dividend.* Ann Arbor: Bureau of Business Research, School of Business Administration, The University of Michigan, 1962.

Woods, Donald H., and Eugene F. Brigham. "Stockholder Distribution Decisions: Share Repurchases or Dividends?" *Journal of Financial and Quantitative Analysis*, vol. I, no. 1 (March, 1966), pp. 15–26.

Lease Financing

chapter Sixteen

Leases are a relatively popular means of financing assets. In reading this chapter, therefore, the student should note the unique aspects of lease financing. Moreover, he should contrast the costs of leasing with alternative means of financing assets. If cost differences do exist, to what can we attribute them?

Introduction

Up to this point in our analysis we have implicitly assumed that the assets of a firm are financed out of liabilities or equity. Whether we employ the accounting or economic approach to valuation, the balance-sheet identity holds. The total book or market value of a firm's assets equals the total book or market value of its liabilities and owners' equity. However, under standard accounting treatment, nowhere on a balance sheet of a business enterprise will we find evidence of assets acquired through leases or the liabilities incurred in financing them.   Information on leases is sometimes included in footnotes of annual reports, and the rental payments are part of the expenses listed in the income statement.   But unless the item leased is really being purchased on the installment plan and a series of supplemental obligations used to pay for it are issued, the lease itself is never a liability of the company and the item is never included among its assets.   When the item is in effect purchased on an installment basis, as in the case of railroad equipment, equipment obligations are issued, and the lease itself is a technicality.

The reason leases are not ordinarily capitalized—that is, in the accounting sense of the term, listed as assets—is because the item leased is owned by another party.   While the *lessee* may eventually purchase it, or even (as part of the contract) have an option to purchase it, title will not automatically vest in the hands of the lessee once the agreement is terminated.   If the item is leased with the rental payments representing periodic installments of principal and interest, once the terms of the contract have been fulfilled, the *lessor* turns title to the asset over to the lessee.   This is the case with railroad or other equipment purchased with the proceeds of equipment obligations issued under the Philadelphia Plan.

Under an ordinary lease arrangement, however, in return for the use of the asset, the lessee pays a periodic rental.   Under standard accounting practice, these payments are charged to income.   When the lease expires, the lessee may have the option of renewing it, purchasing the property, or returning it to the owner.   But there is no clause in the agreement giving the lessor title to the property at the expiration of the lease, and the rental payments do not include installments on the purchase price.

There has been considerable debate among practitioners and students of finance as to whether or not the accounting treatment of leases is misleading.[1]   Suppose, for example, that management of a large retail trade chain leases the land and buildings comprising the company's outlets.   Under terms of the lease the firm can use the facilities for 30 years with the option to renew for an additional 30 years.   The firm does not own the land or the buildings.   Its only contractual obligation is the periodic rental payment.   Hence, under standard accounting practice,

[1]For opposing arguments, see Donald R. Gant, "Illusion in Lease Financing," *Harvard Business Review*, vol. 37, no. 2 (March-April, 1959), pp. 121–142, and Donald C. Cook, "The Case Against Capitalizing Leases," *Harvard Business Review*, vol. 41, no. 1 (January-February, 1963), pp. 145–155.   See also "Re: 'Illusion in Lease Financing' by Donald R. Gant," in columns of "From the Thoughtful Businessman," *Harvard Business Review*, vol. 37, nos. 3 and 4 (May-June and July-August, 1959), pp. 19–26, 172–174, and 178.

the land and buildings are not recognized as assets. The sole liability is the periodic rental payment which, though a current liability, is ordinarily liquidated prior to the compilation of the balance sheet.

But is not the lease arrangement an alternative to purchasing the property out of the proceeds of a sale of debt obligations? If so, should not the property be capitalized at a price reflecting its value to the firm? As an offset, should there not be a liability equal to this amount reflecting the indebtedness which would have been incurred had the property been purchased out of a series of long-term obligations? Thus, if the land and buildings are worth $10,000,000 to the firm, then even though it leases these facilities, perhaps it should include this figure in its assets and add a like amount to its long-term liabilities.

The problem with doing so, of course, is that in capitalizing a lease we run up against the cherished principle of accounting that assets be listed at cost. Since there is no purchase price, there is no basis for determining the cost of the asset. The value to the company would be an estimate, not an actual price, and at best would be an informed judgment. Moreover, even if everyone agreed as to the value of the land and buildings to the firm, it does not follow that if purchased, they would be financed solely out of debt. Instead, management may employ some equity as well as debt, or finance them entirely out of equity.

Because there is no cost basis for determining the value of the assets leased nor certain knowledge of the mode of financing that would be employed if the assets were purchased rather than leased, the accountant prefers to treat a lease more or less in accordance with the legal status it enjoys. The sole obligation is the rental payment. If the lessee fails to meet it when due, the lessor can see to it, through court action if necessary, that the property is returned.

The Nature of Lease Financing

Even if we admit that accountants, in presenting financial statements for public consumption, have a valid reason for wanting to avoid the controversy and misunderstanding inherent in imputing values, we must nevertheless recognize that for purposes of financial management, the leasing arrangement can be a substitute for purchase of assets. When this is the case, management is presented with an alternative means of financing. If it is to maximize the market value of the ownership interests, management should compare the costs of leasing with the costs of other modes of finance.

In many instances, of course, leasing is for practical purposes the sole means of acquiring the asset or the service it renders. Suppose that the nature of the service requires the firm providing it to locate in a particular place.   For example, a commercial printing firm may find it necessary to locate near its customers, that is, in the center of the business district of a large city.   Yet the size of its operations demands a relatively small amount of space as compared with the space available in the building.   Unless it is considering diversification into real estate, management will enter into an agreement which we shall call an *operating lease*.[2]   Under its terms the lease can be canceled with due notice by the lessor.   The lessee commits himself at most to a short-term contract, perhaps paying some rent in advance.   But he is not obligated to make fixed payments over any extended period of time.   As long as management of the lessee is in agreement with management of the lessor as to the rent paid, the obligation is simply to pay the rent as long as the lessee cares to use the office space or the lessor cares to rent it to the firm.

On the other hand, if management signs a long-term lease—for example, management of the retail trade chain mentioned earlier—it will probably make a series of payments to the lessor which over the life of the lease will exceed the purchase price if not the replacement cost of the asset leased.   Once signed by both parties, the contract is irrevocable.   Such an arrangement can be called a *financial lease*.[3] In accepting it, management is leasing property which it might otherwise have purchased.   In other words, it is employing a leasing arrangement to finance assets.

While there are exceptions,[4] most leases fall into one of these two categories.   The primary difference between an operating and a financial lease lies in the fact that when management employs the latter, it has implicitly decided that the asset would be worth purchasing and that leasing is the cheapest or perhaps the only means of financing it.[5]

Lease or Borrow—A Comparison of Alternatives[6]

As a method of finance, what makes leasing so difficult to analyze is the fact that the benefits accruing to the firm and the costs incurred by it under a lease must be made comparable with the benefits and costs

[2]Richard F. Vancil, "Lease or Borrow—New Method of Analysis," *Harvard Business Review*, vol. 39, no. 5 (September-October, 1961), p. 122.

[3]*Ibid.*, p. 122.

[4]*Ibid.*, p. 123.

[5]*Ibid.*, pp. 127–128.

[6]See *Ibid.*, pp. 128–136, for a somewhat different comparison between leasing and alternative modes of finance.   For further discussion, see Richard F. Vancil, "Lease or Borrow—Steps in Negotiation," *Harvard Business Review*, vol. 39, no. 6 (November-December, 1961), pp. 138–159.

of purchasing an asset. For example, when management enters into a lease it loses the depreciation allowances on the asset, a tax-deductible expense. In return, however, it is able to deduct the full amount of the lease payments. Moreover, the risk of obsolescence, a problem of particular consequence in the case of certain types of equipment such as computers, may be shifted to the lessor. This is more likely to be the case, however, when the contract is an operating lease. If a computer becomes obsolete in, say 3 years, the lessee may return it to the owner. Under a financial lease, however, management may still have several more years of payments for which it has contracted. Even if it returns the computer, it may still have to fulfill these contractual obligations.

If the asset leased is a combination of land and buildings, obsolescence may be less of a problem. The lease payments, however, cover both the land and the buildings. If the firm owns them, only the latter can be depreciated for tax purposes. But what is an advantage to the lessee is a disadvantage to the lessor. In establishing the lease payments, therefore, the lessee will take into consideration the fact that since the firm owns the land, management cannot depreciate it for tax purposes. Furthermore, if the lessee is assuming the risk of obsolescence, then its management expects to be compensated for doing so.

Looking at the outlay side of the analysis, the lease payments are scheduled so as to return to the lessor the cost of the asset together with compensation for risks assumed and services performed, if any, over the life of the lease. This would or would not be the case if some other form of debt financing were employed. For example, if the land and buildings were purchased out of a series of mortgage bonds, management might be able to sell them without provisions for a sinking fund. Only the interest payments would be due periodically. When the bonds matured, the company could perhaps refund them with a new series, thereby extending the maturity of the loan indefinitely. Moreover, if the assets had been purchased solely out of equity, there would have been no maturity date. Had they been purchased out of a combination of debt and equity, such as a 25 percent down payment and a 75 percent mortgage, part of the financing would have had no maturity date while the remainder might have been extended indefinitely.

But can lease financing really be compared with equity financing? We think not. As with debt, but unlike equity, the lease carries with it financial obligations which must be met periodically if the lessee is to continue to enjoy use of the asset. Failure to meet the contractual obligations may not lead to bankruptcy, but might result in repossession of the land, buildings, or equipment leased. If the item plays a key role in the production process, repossession would make it difficult to continue operations and hence generate cash flows sufficient to meet other obligations as they come due. This in turn could precipitate bankruptcy. It seems more appropriate, therefore, to treat a lease arrangement as a substitute for debt financing. In the final analysis, the risk involved depends on the terms of the contract and the importance in the production process of the asset or assets leased. Since a financial lease obligates the firm to payments in excess of the purchase price and perhaps the replacement cost of the asset, the risk is greater than if the asset had been procured under an operating lease. If the asset plays a key role in the operations, failure to meet the contractual obligations as they come due increases the risk still further.

Finally, we should recognize that when an asset is leased, the firm avoids paying directly certain costs which might accompany other forms of debt financing. These range from compensating balances, if the asset had been purchased out of the proceeds of a bank loan, to investment banking fees if the funds employed had come from proceeds of bonds issued to the general public. Part of the payments made to the lessor reflects compensation for these services, for the firm leasing the asset may have had to finance it out of bank loans requiring compensating balances, or bonds floated through an investment banking syndicate.

Let us proceed, therefore, as though financial leasing is simply an alternative form of debt financing. If the method is to be employed in the stockholders' interests, management must make the lease payments comparable with other forms of debt financing. To illustrate the analysis involved, assume that management of a manufacturing concern is considering additions to equipment whose original and replacement costs are both $10,000,000. The anticipated useful life is 10 years. The expected net present value, the probabilities, and the utilities attached to the probabilities are as follows.

Net Present Value	Probability	Utility	Expected Utility
−$1,000,000	.25	−.2	−.050
8,000,000	.5	.7	.35
5,000,000	.25	.5	.125
			.425

The utility of the outcome is positive. Thus management is willing to accept the risk involved in adding to the equipment. The next step in the analysis is to determine the cheapest means of financing the asset.

Recall from our model of the cost of capital (Chapter 12) that the discount rate used in determining net present value is the marginal cost of capital. In perfect capital markets, which Modigliani and Miller postulate, the cost of capital is independent of the capital structure. The marginal cost equals the average cost regardless of the mode of financing. We have seen, however, that the rigorous assumptions under which the Modigliani and Miller hypothesis is predicated must be altered considerably. Market imperfections, the impact of the tax laws, and the fact that debt and equity can be combined in one source of financing all affect the cost of capital. This makes it possible for management to assume that cost variations in alternative sources of funds are not due entirely to compensating differences reflecting the degree of risk borne by those supplying funds. Thus, if we can make the alternatives comparable, adopting the cheapest source of debt financing will add more to earnings and ultimately to the market value of the owners' equity.

Suppose, for example, that in adding to its equipment, management can either obtain a 10-year term loan or lease the equipment for the same length of time. Under the first alternative, an insurance company is willing to lend 80 percent of the $10,000,000 at an interest rate of 6 percent, with repayments at the end of each year equaling 10 per cent of the principal amount of the loan. The schedule of payments are shown in Table 16-1.

If the firm leases the equipment, management will pay $1,400,000 annually, or a total of $14,000,000.

There are adjustments which must be made in the data before the alternatives are comparable. In the first place, under the term loan

TABLE 16-1: SCHEDULE OF PRINCIPAL AND INTEREST PAYMENTS ON TERM LOANS

End of Year	Principal Outstanding	Interest Payments at 6 Percent	Total Payments of Principal and Interest
First	$8,000,000	$ 480,000	$ 1,280,000
Second	7,200,000	432,000	1,232,000
Third	6,400,000	384,000	1,184,000
Fourth	5,600,000	336,000	1,136,000
Fifth	4,800,000	288,000	1,088,000
Sixth	4,000,000	240,000	1,040,000
Seventh	3,200,000	192,000	992,000
Eighth	2,400,000	144,000	944,000
Ninth	1,600,000	96,000	896,000
Tenth	800,000	48,000	848,000
		$2,640,000	$ 10,640,000

management is borrowing only 80 percent of the purchase price or replacement cost of the asset. Under the leasing arrangement it is, in effect, borrowing the full $10,000,000. To make the alternatives comparable, we could add to the cost of borrowing the return expected on the equity invested in the equipment. Let us assume that the marginal cost of equity capital is 10 percent. We can therefore add 10 percent of $2,000,000, or $200,000, to the cost of financing the equipment out of a term loan. Whether this is the only or even the best way of making the two modes of financing comparable is a point to which we shall return later.[7]

Second, if the firm purchases the asset, management can realize savings in taxes through depreciation of the equipment. Moreover, management can also deduct the interest payments. On the other hand, if the firm leases the asset, there are no separate deductions for depreciation or interest; the entire lease payment can be subtracted before calculating taxable income.

Let us assume that the asset has no scrap value and that the straight-line method of depreciation is employed. The annual tax saving from owning the equipment is 0.48 of $1,000,000, or $480,000. Thus the effective annual outlay for the return of the principal on both the debt and equity is $1,000,000 ($800,000 plus $200,000) less $480,000, or $520,000. The annual tax saving due to interest is 0.48 of the annual interest payment. Using the information in Table 16-1, the effective interest for the first year is $480,000(1 − 0.48), or $249,600. Since the annual cost of equity capital is $200,000, the first-year expenditures — including the cost of equity capital and under the assumption that the equipment is purchased — are $969,600. The results for subsequent years are listed in Table 16-2.

If the firm chooses to lease the equipment, then the effective annual expenditure is $1,400,000(1 − 0.48), or $728,000. Since the cost of purchase using a term loan is greater for each of the ten years, without further analysis we can conclude that in this instance leasing is the cheaper of the two alternatives.

Yet the student might argue that the conclusion reached may be due entirely to the provisions made for the return of the equity invested as well as the cost of equity required as a condition for obtaining the term loan. Since leasing is assumed to be an alternative to debt financing,

---

[7]Implicitly, we have assumed that the use of equity in acquiring the equipment does not change the debt-equity ratio. This asset is one of many which comprise the capital budget of the firm. We can merely assume that if the term loan is preferable, management will use $200,000 more in debt to finance additional assets. Alternatively, if leasing is the cheaper mode of financing, management will use $200,000 more in equity to finance the remainder of the firm's budget.

TABLE 16-2: TAX-ADJUSTED ANNUAL EXPENDITURES, INCLUDING
COST OF EQUITY CAPITAL ASSOCIATED WITH PURCHASE
OF EQUIPMENT

End of Year	Return of Principal	Interest	Cost of Equity	Annual Expenditures
First	$520,000	$249,600	$200,000	$969,600
Second	520,000	224,640	200,000	944,640
Third	520,000	199,680	200,000	919,680
Fourth	520,000	174,720	200,000	894,720
Fifth	520,000	149,760	200,000	869,760
Sixth	520,000	124,800	200,000	844,800
Seventh	520,000	99,840	200,000	819,840
Eighth	520,000	74,880	200,000	794,880
Ninth	520,000	49,920	200,000	769,920
Tenth	520,000	24,960	200,000	744,960

would it not be more consistent to compare the costs under the assumption that the firm either leased the asset or borrowed the amount necessary to finance its purchase? The answer, of course, is yes, assuming that management can borrow the entire amount. Our analysis to this point was based on the assumption that the firm had two specific alternatives available, one of which required some equity.

Ordinarily, if management is willing to pay a high enough rate of interest, it may be able to finance the entire purchase price of a particular asset out of debt. It may in some cases have to resort to a more unconventional lender such as a commercial finance company, but the possibility of finding this source of funds usually exists.

Suppose, therefore, that management can acquire the equipment under a conditional sales contract through a finance company. The stated interest is 7 percent, but, unlike the case of a term loan, interest payments on this loan do not decline as the principal is reduced. Thus the annual interest payments are a constant amount equal to 7 percent of $1,000,000, or $700,000. Principal is repaid in 10 annual installments of $1,000,000. Assuming no scrap value, the annual depreciation allowance on a straight-line basis is again $1,000,000. The annual interest payment after taxes is $700,000(1 − 0.48), or $364,000. The annual repayment of principal after allowance for the tax deductibility of depreciation is again $1,000,000(1 − 0.48), or $520,000. If the asset is purchased, the annual expenditures after taxes are $884,000—as compared with $728,000 if it is leased. Once more, leasing appears to be the cheaper mode of financing.

When the expenditures associated with leasing can be reduced to a constant yearly amount, then all we need do is compare the annual outlay for the lease with the outlay if the asset is purchased. Suppose, however, that the interest payments decline with repayment of principal, as in the case of the term loan used in the first example. Can we always conclude by inspection which is the preferred alternative? As an illustration, assume that management can borrow the entire $10,000,000 at 7 percent. Again, each year the principal will be reduced by $1,000,000. This time, however, interest is a function of the declining balance. Otherwise there is no change in the underlying assumptions. The annual outlay associated with the loan after adjustment for income taxes is shown in Table 16-3.

TABLE 16-3: TAX-ADJUSTED ANNUAL EXPENDITURES ASSOCIATED WITH PURCHASE OF EQUIPMENT, WITH INTEREST EQUAL TO 7 PERCENT OF DECLINING BALANCE

End of Year	Return of Principal	Interest	Annual Expenditures
First	$520,000	$364,000	$884,000
Second	520,000	327,600	847,600
Third	520,000	291,200	811,200
Fourth	520,000	254,800	774,800
Fifth	520,000	218,400	738,400
Sixth	520,000	182,000	702,000
Seventh	520,000	145,600	665,600
Eighth	520,000	109,200	629,200
Ninth	520,000	72,800	592,800
Tenth	520,000	36,400	556,400

The annual expenditures associated with purchase of the equipment are now less than the lease payments in 5 out of the 10 years. Although we might suspect from the pattern of the data that leasing is still preferred, it will be useful to develop a general procedure for making the choice.

To do so, let us assume that management tentatively chooses to lease the asset. Then the difference between the annual expenditures associated with purchasing the equipment and leasing it can be discounted at the marginal cost of equity capital. The difference will, of course, be positive for some years and negative for others. But if the present value of the differences in annual expenditures is positive, leasing is the preferred alternative.

To illustrate, let us use the data in Table 16-4. Under the assumption that the marginal cost of equity capital is 10 per cent, we can find from the table in Appendix A of this volume the present value of a dollar for each of the ten years. When this is multiplied by the difference

TABLE 16-4: A COMPARISON OF TAX-ADJUSTED ALTERNATIVES FOR FINANCING EQUIPMENT

End of Year	Lease Payments	Expenditures If Asset Is Purchased	Difference between Expenditures and Lease Payments	Discount Factor When Marginal Cost of Equity Capital Is 10 Percent	Present Value of Difference If Positive	Present Value of Difference If Negative
First	$728,000	$884,000	$156,000	.90909	$141,818.04	
Second	728,000	847,600	119,600	.82645	98,843.42	
Third	728,000	811,200	83,200	.75131	62,508.99	
Fourth	728,000	774,800	46,800	.68301	31,964.87	
Fifth	728,000	738,400	10,400	.62092	6,457.57	
Sixth	728,000	702,000	−26,000	.56447		−$ 14,676.22
Seventh	728,000	665,600	−62,400	.51316		−32,021.18
Eighth	728,000	629,200	−98,800	.46651		−46,091.19
Ninth	728,000	592,800	−135,200	.42410		−57,338.32
Tenth	728,000	556,400	−171,600	.38554		−66,158.66
Total					$341,592.89	−$216,285.57
Net Present Value					$125,307.32	

between the expenditures and the lease payments, the result is the present value of the additional funds, or, if negative, the present value of the loss of funds should management adopt the leasing alternative. At the end of the first year, for example, the present value of the difference is $141,818.04 ($156,000 × 0.90909). At the end of the eighth year it is −$46,091.19 (−$98,800 × 0.46651). The net present value, that is, the sum of the present value of the positive differences less the sum of the present value of the negative differences, is greater than zero. The additional funds retained in the company during the first 5 years, when discounted by the marginal cost of equity capital, more than compensate for the loss of funds in the last 5 years. Management should, therefore, lease rather than purchase the equipment.

In summary, we have used three arithmetic examples, treating the lease in each instance as though it were an alternative means of debt financing. As we generalized our analysis, it became evident that if we are to make a lease arrangement strictly comparable with purchasing, we must assume that the asset, if bought, will be financed out of debt. In practice, the alternatives available may require equity funds. If so, we must include both their return and cost in the outlay for the asset.

In principal, however, management can usually estimate the interest cost under the assumption that the asset can be financed entirely out of debt. When comparing the options, we must be careful to make the outlays associated with purchase of the asset comparable with those associated with leasing.   With the former, therefore, we must allow for tax savings which come from owning the asset, that is, depreciation, as well as the savings due to interest.   With the latter, the tax savings are applicable to the entire lease payment.

If the annual outlays adjusted for taxes are constant, then the alternative with the lower annual expenditure is preferred.   On the other hand, the outlays associated with purchase of the asset, or for that matter associated even with the lease, may vary in such a way that in some years the outlay for one exceeds the outlay for the other, while in other years it does not.   We can tentatively conclude from inspection that one is preferred over the other.   In our example, we assumed that leasing was preferable to purchase.   In order to see whether our guess was correct, we discounted the annual difference in expenditures under the two alternatives by the marginal cost of equity capital.   The choice of the cost of equity funds is appropriate since the difference in expenditures, whether positive or negative, accrues to the owners.   If the net present value of these differences is positive, leasing is preferred.   If the net present value is negative, management should purchase the asset.

Leasing in Practice

There is considerable evidence that many companies employ long-term leases to finance assets.   In one study it was found that about 50 percent of the industrial corporations included in the survey were parties to long-term leases.   This figure rises to 88 percent for wholesale and retail merchandising concerns and 93 percent for integrated oil companies.[8]

There are even cases where firms owning assets sell them and then lease them back again.   A chain of retail trade stores, for example, may contract to sell all its land and buildings to a group of life insurance companies.   The insurance companies in turn lease them back for a period of, say, 25 years with the option that the chain can repurchase the stores and the land on which they sit at the end of that period.   The retail chain will probably agree to assume the responsibility for care and maintenance of the property.

Perhaps one of the primary gains to the retail trade chain comes from the fact that the rental for the land is now tax-deductible.   When the firm owned the land it could not depreciate it.   Moreover, under the Internal Revenue code the income of life insurance companies is taxed

---

[8]Richard F. Vancil and Robert N. Anthony, "The Financial Community Looks at Leasing," *Harvard Business Review*, vol. 37, no. 6 (November-December, 1959), p. 125. See also pp. 123–124.

at rates which are considerably lower than the 48 percent paid by nonfinancial corporations. Hence the life insurance companies have less incentive to reduce taxable income. Thus they need not be compensated as heavily in the lease payments for purchasing a nondepreciable asset.

Leasing may also be employed to circumvent features in the loan contracts of many corporations. Often, though by no means always, a bond indenture restricting the amount of long-term debt that can be issued by a corporation contains no effective provision restricting leases. The lease itself, however, may contain a clause restricting further leases. A common provision is a limitation placed on the total dollar payments that can be made each year under a lease agreement.[9]

When loan contracts do restrict leases, it is not unusual to capitalize them by discounting the future rentals at some specified rate of interest, and including the capitalized value in the restrictions placed on the issuance of debt under the terms of the contract.[10] To illustrate, suppose that a corporation has a series of debentures the principal amount of which is $30,000,000. Under the terms of the indenture the corporation can issue additional debt equal to only two-thirds of the principal amount of the bonds outstanding. Included in the restriction are obligations incurred through leasing. The company presently has outstanding annual payments of $100,000 on long-term leases. For purposes of the bond indenture, these and any subsequent additions to lease payments are to be treated as though they will continue indefinitely. Also, according to the provisions of the bond indenture, the lease payments are to be capitalized at 5 percent. Thus the total value of the lease for purposes of complying with the restriction placed on the subsequent issuance of new debt is $100,000 divided by 5 percent, or $2,000,000.

Some firms will go so far as to establish "dummy corporations" to own the assets of the parent company. These in turn are leased to the parent. The lessor is thinly capitalized, with only a nominal amount of equity. Most of its funds for purchasing the assets are acquired from financial institutions, particularly life insurance companies and commercial banks. The lending institutions are, of course, aware of the relatively low levels of equity in the capital structure of the dummy corporation. In return, most or perhaps all of the lease payments are assigned to the lenders. Thus the lessor borrows most of the purchase price of the assets from third parties, the rentals on the equipment leased being used to cover principal and interest on the amount borrowed.

[9]*Ibid.*, pp. 124–125.
[10]*Ibid.*

Since the lessor is merely an intermediary between the lending institutions, the loans granted are made entirely on the basis of the financial strength of the lessee, that is, the parent company.[11]   In this way the lessee retains ownership over the assets of the corporation by owning the stock of the lessor.   Since this company has only a nominal amount of equity, it is the lending institution which is, in an economic if not a legal sense, the lessor.

But why would management of a corporation owning assets go to the trouble and expense of establishing an intermediary to purchase them, when it might deal directly with the financial institutions involved?   Most of the tax advantages accruing to the company from leasing the assets can be obtained through a sale-leaseback agreement. To be sure, by owning the stock in the subsidiary, the company is taxed on dividends received at a low rate of 15 percent rather than 48 percent. But the dummy corporation will at most earn a nominal income.   Its sole source of revenue is in the form of rentals on the assets, most if not all of which have been assigned to the lending institutions to cover principal and interest on the loans.[12]

If there is an advantage in establishing a dummy corporation, it lies in the fact that it may be in the stockholders' interests to enjoy the benefits both from leasing and from ownership.   The chief advantage of owning the asset lies in the residual value it might have when the lease expires.[13]   In the example employed earlier, we assumed that the equipment leased had no scrap value.   More often than not it can be sold.   A computer, for example, may become technologically obsolete as far as the company is concerned, yet may serve the purposes of another concern.   Its resale value, though a fraction of original or replacement cost, accrues to the owner, not the lessee.

This is true not only of personal but also of real property. Management of a corporation with a fully depreciated plant might find that the plant is no longer serviceable.   But the land on which it sits may have appreciated several times in value over its original cost.   To be sure, the value of the land may decline and the resale value of the equipment may be less than the difference between its original and replacement cost.   The possibility both of loss and of gain from the sale of assets therefore, accrues to the owners.   When management chooses to lease, it can expect the lessor to incorporate these risks in the rental payments.

---

[11]*Ibid.*

[12]Management could, of course, turn the dummy corporation into a commercial leasing company purchasing assets of other firms and leasing them back to the selling companies.   In this way it might turn the subsidiary into a profit-making institution which pays dividends to the parent.

[13]Gant, *op. cit.*, p. 126.

But the valuation is essentially subjective.   While the lessee might be able to purchase the asset on expiration of the lease, unless the purchase price is agreed to in advance, the firm leasing the assets may not be able to reap the rewards of ownership.   Moreover, even if there is agreement on the purchase price at the time the lease is signed, it is at best an estimate of the value of the asset at the time the lease expires. Apparently the arrangement is satisfactory to both parties or else a purchase price would not have been agreed to in advance.   Nevertheless, when the option is exercised, it is possible that the gain could accrue to either the lessor or the lessee.   Suppose, for example, that management of a firm agreed to repurchase land and buildings for $1,000,000 at the expiration of the lease.   When the lease expires, the market value of these assets is $2,000,000.   The lessee will realize $1,000,000 from the purchase. On the other hand, if the value had fallen to $600,000, the lessor would have realized a $400,000 gain from the sale.

We should note that ordinarily the agreement to purchase the asset at the expiration of the lease is an option.   Rarely is it mandatory. Moreover, the terms of purchase are likely to be agreed upon near the expiration date, not when the lease is signed.   This leaves the lessor with the opportunity to realize the market value of the asset as of the expiration date.   If it is in excess of what was expected when the lease was drawn, that is, $2,000,000 instead of $1,000,000, the lessor will realize the gain.   On the other hand, if it has fallen, that is, the value is $600,000 instead of $1,000,000, the lessee will exercise his option only at that price. The firm leasing the asset has realized less than was anticipated when management negotiated the terms of the lease.   The loss therefore accrues to the firm's owners.

Bearing in mind that ownership carries with it both the opportunity for gain as well as the chance for loss, management may still conclude that it wants to lease particular assets for the tax advantages the firm can realize, but it does not want to lose ultimate control over the assets. Establishing a dummy corporation gives the firm the opportunity to lease plant and equipment while at the same time it enjoys the rewards as well as assumes the risks of ownership.

Yet, regardless of the techniques which management might employ in seeking to lower the cost of capital through leases, when the costs of leasing are set against the costs of other forms of debt financing, the savings, if any, may be small.   To the extent that savings exist, they stem, as we have noted, from market imperfections and institutional factors, particularly the income tax laws.   But as we also observed earlier, what the lessee gains is often at the expense of the lessor.   Thus, if management wants to avoid compensating balances on an equipment loan from a commercial bank, it might lease the equipment. Yet the lessor, in financing the asset, might borrow the funds from a commercial bank. If it does so, then it will have to maintain compensating balances. Consequently, if the costs of financing the asset are not borne directly by the lessee, they will accrue to him indirectly through the rental payments. When these costs differ—that is, the lessor for various reasons may be able to obtain better terms on a loan to purchase the asset than if the lessee were to borrow for the same purpose—then there may be a cost advantage to leasing.

Finding these and similar differences and bargaining over how they should be shared are integral parts of negotiating a lease agreement.[14] Therefore, if in the final analysis management finds that differences in the costs of leasing and borrowing to purchase a particular asset are small, it should not be surprised. Yet these differences, small though they may be, could result in dollar savings sufficiently large to justify the time and effort required to make the comparison.

SUMMARY

Ordinarily, when a firm leases an asset for a period of time, it does not take possession of the asset when the lease expires. Since there is no purchase price and hence no evidence of ownership, accountants do not capitalize the assets leased. However valid the procedure for financial reporting, it fails to recognize that leases are often used as a substitute for asset purchase. Rather than purchasing plant or equipment out of debt or equity, management leases it. Since a lease represents a series of contractual payments over an extended period of time, it is a substitute more properly for debt financing than for equity financing. In practice, however, the alternative means of financing, such as a term loan or a series of bonds, ordinarily represent something less than 100 percent of the purchase price or replacement cost. The remainder is supplied out of equity. Of course, if management is willing to pay a high enough rate of interest, it may be able to finance the entire purchase price out of debt.

To contrast the cost of lease financing with the alternatives available, we may compare the tax-adjusted annual lease payments with the tax-adjusted annual expenditures associated with other means of financing. If annual payments are unequal, we can find the present value of the difference between the annual lease payments and the annual expenditures if the assets were purchased. Since the annual differences

[14]Vancil, "Lease or Borrow—Steps in Negotiation," *ibid.*

represent gains or losses to the owners, they should be discounted at the marginal cost of equity capital. If the net present value of the difference is positive, leasing is preferred. If the net present value is negative, management should purchase the asset.

Although in practice lease financing is widespread, we should note that the advantages may appear to be illusory. What is the lessee's gain may be the lessor's loss, or vice versa. If, for example, the lessor assumes the burden of obsolescence, he would be compensated with higher annual rentals. If the lessee assumes the risk, his rentals would be correspondingly lower. Thus, while market imperfections and differences in tax treatment may lead to variations in the costs of borrowing and leasing, these differences may be small.

QUESTIONS AND PROBLEMS

1. "Leasing is always an alternative to financing an asset out of long-term debt." Do you agree? Explain carefully.

2. Management of a corporation has a choice of purchasing land and buildings for $20,000,000 or leasing them for 20 years and paying an annual rental of $1,500,000. Both the original cost and the replacement cost of the building are $10,000,000. It is estimated that the value of the land will rise from $10,000,000 to $15,000,000 by the time the lease expires. The building, however, has no scrap value. Assume that the cost of borrowing $20,000,000 is 7 percent, with principal being repaid in equal installments over the 20-year period. The marginal cost of equity capital is 10 percent. Should management lease or borrow to finance these assets?

3. "We can ordinarily expect the cost of leasing to be considerably lower than the cost of borrowing to finance assets." Evaluate.

4. "The sale-leaseback arrangement has no advantages over establishing a dummy corporation to purchase a firm's assets." Do you agree? Explain carefully.

SELECTED REFERENCES

Cook, Donald C. "The Case Against Capitalizing Leases," *Harvard Business Review*, vol. 41, no. 1 (January-February, 1963),pp. 145–155.
Gant, Donald R. "A Critical Look at Lease Financing," *Controller*, vol. 29, no. 6 (June, 1961), pp. 274–277, 311–312.

———— "Illusion in Lease Financing," *Harvard Business Review*, vol. 37, no. 2 (March-April, 1959), pp. 121–142.

Vancil, Richard F. "Lease or Borrow—New Method of Analysis," *Harvard Business Review*, vol. 39, no. 5 (September-October, 1961), pp. 122–136.

————. "Lease or Borrow—Steps in Negotiation," *Harvard Business Review*, vol. 39, no. 6 (November-December, 1961), pp. 138–159.

Vancil, Richard F., and Robert N. Anthony. "The Financial Community Looks at Leasing," *Harvard Business Review*, vol. 37, no. 6 (November-December, 1959), pp. 113–130.

Sources of Funds

chapter Seventeen

In studying this chapter, the student may first want to read the introduction and then the summary.   He can then return to the body of the
chapter to fill in the details.   In so doing, he should relate the underlying
trends in the data to the cost-of-capital model developed earlier.   Is there
anything unique in the results, that is, are the results inconsistent with our
model?   Moreover, how can the empirical evidence be used to explain the
behavior of business firms with respect to financing assets?   What are the
limitations of generalizations based on the data?

Introduction

Having developed the principles on which the decisions of financial
management should be based and having further discussed the specific
details of the major instruments of finance, it seems appropriate now to

look at the actual record in determining the historical importance of the various sources of funds.   We do so for two reasons.   First, we want to acquaint ourselves with the trends or lack of trends in the major com-ponents of the capital structure of American business firms.   Second, and more important, we want to relate these trends to the analysis presented in the previous chapters.   Are the results consistent with our cost-of-capital model?   Must we alter the conclusions reached earlier?   If so, how?   In this chapter we shall try to shed light on these and related questions.

Sources of Funds — The Historical Record

The widespread use of computers has greatly facilitated the task of collecting, organizing, and interpreting statistical data.   As a result there has been an outpouring of material on the sources and uses of funds[1] designed to show the interrelationships among various sectors of the economy.   Of the data pertaining to the private sector, the most reliable figures are for the largest sector of the business community — nonfarm, nonfinancial corporations.   Concentrating on this sector allows us to separate nonfinancial from financial firms.   Financial in-stitutions are of importance, but they are intermediaries in the process of capital formation.   Their significance lies in their effect on the capital

[1]Perhaps the most comprehensive work has been done under the direction of the National Bureau of Economic Research.   Of the several volumes constituting its studies in capital formation and financing, the author has relied heavily on Simon Kuznets, *Capital in the American Economy: Its Formation and Financing* (Princeton, N.J.: Princeton University Press, 1961); Raymond W. Goldsmith, *The Flow of Capital Funds in the Postwar Economy* (New York: National Bureau of Economic Research, Inc., 1965); and his *Financial Intermediaries in the American Economy Since 1900* (Princeton, N.J.: Princeton University Press, 1958).   See also his *A Study of Saving in the United States*, 3 vols. (Princeton, N.J.: Princeton University Press, 1955 and 1956).   This last work was sponsored by the Life Insurance Association of America.

Among other important works are David Meiselman and Eli Shapiro, *The Measurement of Corporate Sources and Uses of Funds* (New York: National Bureau of Economic Research, Inc., 1964); John Lintner, "The Financing of Corporations," in Edward S. Mason (ed.), *The Corporation in Modern Society* (Cambridge, Mass.: Harvard University Press, 1959), pp. 166–201; Merton H. Miller, "The Corporation Income Tax and Corporate Financial Policies," in Commission on Money and Credit, *Stabilization Policies* (Englewood Cliffs, N.J.: Prentice-Hall, Inc., 1963), pp. 381–470; Arnold W. Sametz, "Trends in the Volume and Composition of Equity Finance," *Journal of Finance*, vol. 19, no. 3 (September, 1964), pp. 450–469; Eli Shapiro and William L. White, "Patterns of Business Financing: Some Comments," *Journal of Finance*, vol. 20, no. 4 (December, 1965), pp. 693–707; Arnold W. Sametz, "Patterns of Business Financing: Reply," *Journal of Finance*, vol. 20, no. 4 (December, 1965), pp. 708–718.

The student of business finance and the financial manager seeking raw data on sources and uses of funds will find publications by the Department of Commerce, and more recently the Federal Reserve particularly useful.

markets. We shall develop their role in a subsequent chapter. While nonfarm unincorporated business could be included to complete the picture, the historical data are less reliable, and the importance of unincorporated business in the money and capital markets is insignificant in comparison with nonfinancial corporations.[2] Thus we shall confine our analysis to data based on this last category.

Tables 17-1 through 17-3 contain data on sources and uses of funds for nonfarm, nonfinancial corporations prepared by the Department of Commerce and subsequently extended by the Federal Reserve Board. Table 17-1 contains absolute magnitudes while the relative importance of each source and use can be found in Tables 17-2 and 17-3. In each case the data reflect annual changes in assets and liabilities, with owners' equity included in the latter. Since financing through leases is not included in accounting data, we shall not consider this form of financing in the discussion which follows.

The categories are largely, but not entirely, self-explanatory. Capital consumption allowances, for example, include not only depreciation but also accidental damage to fixed capital as well as capital outlays charged to current expenses.[3] Bank loans, however, refer to all loans made by banks. Recall from our earlier discussion that bank loans cover numerous classifications including term loans and lines of credit. Thus by including term loans, the figures for bank loans contain an item which might be more appropriately labeled long-term debt.

One of the most important items in the list is *inventory valuation adjustment*. This is an estimate of the contributions, positive or negative, to total profits that are the result of gains or losses on the inventory account resulting from changes in the price level. As we have argued before, the book value of inventories may differ from their replacement cost. Since inventories are a part of the cost of goods sold, then depending on the accounting technique employed, that is, FIFO or LIFO, inventory expense may be understated or overstated. Reported profits vary accordingly. For the time being, the estimate has been left as it stands and expressed as a percentage of total sources. Nevertheless, depending on whether it is a positive or negative figure for the year in question, inventory valuation adjustment has the effect of raising or lowering internal, and hence total, sources.

[2]Goldsmith, *The Flow of Capital Funds in the Postwar Economy*, pp. 140–145. In particular compare the absolute magnitudes in Table 37 with those in Table 39.

[3]The composition of the gross-national-product accounts from which these data are ultimately derived is periodically revised. Thus the figures for any given year can change. They can also change because of revisions in the definitions of categories. For the latest revision in the gross-national-product accounts, see "The National Income and Product Accounts of the United States, Revised Estimates, 1924–1964," *Survey of Current Business*, vol. 45, no. 8 (August, 1965), pp. 6–22.

TABLE 17-1: **SOURCES AND USES OF FUNDS FOR NONFARM, NONFINANCIAL CORPORATE BUSINESS, 1946–1968** (In Billions of Dollars)

Source or Use of Funds	1946	1947	1948	1949	1950	1951	1952	1953	1954	1955
Sources, Total	16.9	27.2	27.1	18.7	41.5	38.7	31.5	29.4	29.1	53.6
Internal Sources	7.8	12.6	18.7	19.1	17.9	19.9	21.2	21.1	23.3	29.2
Undistributed Profits	8.5	12.8	14.0	9.5	14.3	11.1	9.0	9.3	9.0	13.9
Corporate Inventory Valuation Adjustment	−5.3	−5.9	−2.2	1.9	−5.0	−1.2	1.0	−1.0	−0.3	−1.7
Capital Consumption Allowances	4.6	5.7	6.8	7.8	8.6	10.0	11.2	12.9	14.6	17.0
External Sources	9.1	14.6	8.5	−0.4	23.6	18.8	10.4	8.3	5.8	24.5
Stocks	1.1	1.2	1.0	1.3	1.4	1.9	2.3	1.8	1.6	1.9
Bonds	1.0	2.8	4.3	2.9	1.6	3.3	4.7	3.4	3.5	2.8
Mortgages	0.8	0.9	0.3	0.5	1.0	0.2	0.5	0.3	0.7	0.7
Bank Loans, n.e.c.†	2.9	2.3	0.5	−1.6	2.8	3.8	1.7	−0.4	−1.0	3.2
Other Loans	*	0.1	0.3	0.5	0.9	1.2	*	*	−0.2	*
Trade Debt	3.1	3.7	0.8	−2.2	7.6	2.2	2.0	0.6	2.3	8.7
Profits Tax Liability	−1.9	2.3	0.9	−2.4	7.5	4.7	−3.3	0.3	−3.0	4.1
Other Liabilities	2.1	1.3	0.3	0.6	0.8	1.5	2.5	2.2	1.8	3.0
Uses, Total	21.7	30.7	26.1	14.3	43.4	35.9	27.6	26.3	26.9	51.4
Purchases of Physical Assets	17.6	16.7	19.8	14.0	22.2	28.9	23.4	23.6	20.5	31.5
Nonresidential Fixed Investment	10.9	14.6	17.2	14.8	15.8	20.1	20.6	22.3	21.4	25.8
Residential Structures	0.7	0.8	0.5	0.9	1.5	0.2	0.6	0.5	1.1	0.8
Change in Business Inventories	6.0	1.2	2.1	−1.7	4.8	8.6	2.2	0.8	−1.9	4.9
Increase in Financial Assets	4.1	14.0	6.3	0.4	21.2	7.0	4.1	2.7	6.3	19.9
Liquid Assets	−4.6	1.1	1.1	3.2	4.4	3.0	0.3	1.9	−0.2	5.2
Demand Deposits and Currency	1.1	2.2	0.2	1.1	1.5	1.8	0.8	0.1	2.1	1.0
Time Deposits	*	*	*	*	*	*	*	*	0.2	−0.1
U.S. Government Securities	−5.8	−1.2	0.7	2.0	2.9	0.9	−0.7	1.6	−2.3	4.2
Finance Company Paper	0.1	0.1	0.2	0.2	*	0.3	0.3	0.2	−0.2	0.1
Consumer Credit	0.6	0.6	0.5	0.4	0.8	0.5	0.8	0.2	0.3	0.7
Trade Credit	3.4	5.9	2.1	−1.8	10.2	1.8	3.5	−0.7	4.7	11.4
Other Financial Assets	4.7	6.3	2.6	−1.5	5.7	1.7	−0.5	1.2	1.4	2.3
Discrepancy (Uses Less Sources)	4.8	3.5	−1.0	−4.4	1.9	−2.8	−4.0	−3.1	−2.2	−2.2

SOURCES: For the years 1946–1953, *Survey of Current Business*, November, 1965, p. 10, table 1; for the years 1954–1968, see the 1966, 1967, 1968, and 1969 issues of *Economic Report of the President*, statistical tables entitled Sources and Uses of Funds, Nonfarm, Nonfinancial Corporate Business. The ultimate source for the later period is the Board of Governors of the Federal Reserve System. In 1965, the Department of Commerce, the source for the earlier period, ceased to publish its series. There are some discrepancies between the data published by the Department of Commerce and those published by the Federal Reserve Board. Compare, for example, the tables cited above for overlapping years. See also *Survey of Current Business*, November, 1965, "Note on Revised Statistics on the Sources and Uses of Corporate Funds," pp. 13, 24. The reader will also find discrepancies in the Federal Reserve data published in various issues of the *Economic Report of the President.* This is due to revisions in the data.

†N.e.c. means not elsewhere counted.

*Less than 0.1 billion dollars.

Because of rounding, totals may not equal the sum of their components.

TABLE 17-1 (*Continued*)

1956	1957	1958	1959	1960	1961	1962	1963	1964	1965	1966	1967	1968
47.2	42.0	42.2	55.5	47.3	54.7	63.3	65.9	70.2	89.3	99.1	94.0	109.9
28.9	30.6	29.5	35.0	34.4	35.6	41.8	43.9	50.5	56.6	61.1	61.5	63.8
13.2	11.8	8.3	12.6	10.0	10.2	12.4	13.6	18.3	23.1	24.4	20.7	21.3
−2.7	−1.5	−0.3	−0.5	0.2	−0.1	0.3	−0.5	−0.5	−1.7	−1.7	−1.2	−3.1
18.4	20.3	21.4	22.9	24.2	25.4	29.2	30.8	32.8	35.2	38.4	42.0	45.6
18.3	11.4	12.7	20.5	12.9	19.1	21.5	22.0	19.7	32.7	38.0	32.5	45.3
2.3	2.4	2.1	2.2	1.6	2.5	0.6	−0.3	1.4	*	1.2	2.3	0.2
3.6	6.3	5.7	3.0	3.5	4.6	4.6	3.9	4.0	5.4	10.2	15.1	13.4
0.4	0.4	1.2	1.2	0.7	1.8	2.9	3.5	3.3	3.1	2.7	3.8	2.9
4.4	1.1	−0.6	3.0	1.3	0.1	2.5	2.9	3.6	9.2	6.9	5.2	5.5
*	0.7	0.2	0.3	1.0	0.3	0.7	0.5	1.3	1.3	2.5	1.7	4.3
5.7	0.5	4.3	4.9	3.1	6.6	4.5	6.0	3.4	7.4	7.8	3.1	11.1
−2.0	−2.1	−2.6	2.4	−2.2	1.2	1.1	1.5	0.9	1.9	0.2	−3.8	2.1
3.9	2.2	2.4	3.6	4.0	1.9	4.7	4.0	1.8	4.3	6.6	5.1	5.8
43.1	40.0	42.1	54.3	45.3	55.0	61.6	65.8	66.9	88.2	96.7	90.6	106.2
35.9	34.7	27.3	36.9	39.2	37.0	44.7	46.7	53.5	64.9	79.8	74.1	81.3
30.7	33.4	28.4	31.1	34.9	33.2	37.0	38.6	44.0	53.2	63.0	64.9	70.1
0.4	0.7	1.4	1.7	1.3	2.2	3.0	3.7	3.6	3.8	2.8	3.7	3.9
4.9	0.6	−2.5	4.1	3.0	1.5	4.7	4.3	5.9	7.9	14.1	5.5	7.4
7.2	5.3	14.8	17.4	6.1	18.0	16.9	19.1	13.4	23.3	16.9	16.5	24.9
−4.2	−0.1	2.5	5.6	−3.9	3.5	4.1	4.3	0.6	0.8	1.0	0.9	7.4
0.1	*	1.5	−1.0	−0.5	1.7	−0.9	−0.8	−2.5	−1.8	0.7	−1.7	0.3
*	*	0.9	−0.4	1.3	1.9	3.7	3.9	3.2	3.9	−0.7	4.1	2.0
−4.5	−0.4	*	6.6	−5.4	−0.2	0.5	0.5	−1.4	−2.1	−1.2	−3.0	0.8
0.1	0.3	0.1	0.4	0.7	0.1	0.9	0.7	1.4	0.8	2.3	1.4	3.6
0.4	0.2	0.5	0.8	0.2	0.1	0.9	0.7	1.0	1.2	1.1	1.0	1.6
7.5	2.6	7.9	7.2	6.3	10.0	8.2	8.5	9.1	12.8	10.8	8.7	13.8
3.4	2.5	3.5	3.3	3.7	4.6	4.1	4.8	2.5	7.9	3.3	5.3	2.2
−4.1	−2.0	−0.1	−1.1	−2.0	0.3	−1.6	−0.1	−3.3	−1.1	−2.3	−3.4	−2.9

TABLE 17-2: PERCENTAGES OF TOTAL SOURCES ACCOUNTED FOR BY SPECIFIC SOURCES OF FUNDS FOR NONFARM, NONFINANCIAL CORPORATE BUSINESS, 1946–1968

Source	1946	1947	1948	1949	1950	1951	1952	1953	1954	1955
Internal Sources	46.2	46.3	69.0	102.0	43.1	51.4	67.3	71.8	80.1	54.5
Undistributed Profits	50.3	47.0	51.7	50.8	34.5	28.7	28.6	31.6	30.9	25.9
Corporate Inventory Valuation Adjustment	−31.4	−21.7	−8.1	10.2	−12.0	−3.1	3.2	−3.4	−1.0	−3.2
Capital Consumption Allowances	27.2	21.0	25.1	41.7	20.7	25.8	35.6	43.9	50.2	31.7
External Sources	53.8	53.7	31.3	−2.1	56.9	48.6	33.0	28.2	19.9	45.7
Stocks	6.5	4.4	3.7	7.0	3.4	4.9	7.3	6.1	5.5	3.5
Bonds	5.9	10.3	15.9	15.5	3.9	8.5	14.9	11.6	12.0	5.2
Mortgages	4.7	3.3	1.1	2.7	2.4	0.5	1.6	1.0	2.4	1.3
Bank and Other Loans	17.2	8.8	3.0	−5.9	8.9	12.9	5.4	−1.4	−4.1	6.0
Trade Debt	18.3	13.6	3.0	−11.8	18.3	5.7	6.3	2.0	7.9	16.2
Profits Tax Liability	−11.2	8.5	3.3	−12.8	18.0	12.1	−10.5	1.0	−10.3	7.6
Other Liabilities	12.4	4.8	1.1	3.2	1.9	3.9	7.9	7.5	6.2	5.6

SOURCES: Same as for Table 17-1.
For any given year the sum of the percentages for internal and external sources may not equal 100 because of rounding. Similarly, the percentages for internal and external sources may not equal the sum of the percentages for their respective components.
*Less than 0.1 billion dollars.

TABLE 17-3: PERCENTAGES OF TOTAL USES ACCOUNTED FOR BY SPECIFIC USES OF FUNDS FOR NONFARM, NONFINANCIAL CORPORATE BUSINESS, 1946–1968

Use	1946	1947	1948	1949	1950	1951	1952	1953	1954	1955
Purchase of Physical Assets	81.1	54.4	75.9	97.9	51.3	80.5	84.8	89.7	76.2	61.3
Nonresidential Fixed Investment	50.2	47.6	65.9	103.5	36.4	56.0	74.6	84.8	79.5	50.2
Residential Structures	3.2	2.6	1.9	6.3	3.5	0.6	2.2	1.9	4.1	1.6
Change in Business Inventories	27.6	3.9	8.0	−11.9	11.1	24.0	8.0	3.0	−7.1	9.5
Increases in Financial Assets	18.9	45.6	24.1	2.7	48.8	19.5	14.9	10.2	23.4	38.7
Liquid Assets	−21.2	3.6	4.2	22.4	10.1	8.4	1.1	7.2	−0.7	10.1
Consumer Credit	2.8	2.0	1.9	2.8	1.8	1.4	2.9	0.8	1.1	1.4
Trade Credit	15.7	19.2	8.0	−12.5	23.5	5.0	12.7	−2.7	17.8	22.2
Other Financial Assets	21.7	20.5	10.0	−10.4	13.1	4.7	−1.8	4.6	5.2	4.5

SOURCES: Same as for Table 17-1.
For any given year the sum of the percentages for the purchase of physical assets and the increases in financial assets may not equal 100 because of rounding. Similarly, the percentages for the purchase of physical assets and the increases in financial assets may not equal the sum of the percentages for their respective components.

TABLE 17-2 (*Continued*)

1956	1957	1958	1959	1960	1961	1962	1963	1964	1965	1966	1967	1968
61.2	72.9	69.9	63.1	72.7	65.1	66.0	66.6	71.9	63.4	61.7	65.4	58.1
27.7	28.1	19.7	22.7	21.1	18.6	19.6	20.6	26.1	25.9	24.6	22.0	19.4
−5.7	−3.6	−0.7	−0.9	0.4	−0.2	0.5	−0.8	−0.7	−1.9	−1.7	−1.3	−2.8
39.0	48.1	41.3	41.3	51.2	46.4	46.1	46.7	46.7	39.4	38.7	44.7	41.5
38.8	27.1	30.1	36.9	27.3	34.9	34.0	33.4	28.1	36.6	38.3	34.6	41.2
4.9	5.7	5.0	4.0	3.4	4.6	1.0	−0.5	2.0	*	1.2	2.4	0.2
7.6	15.0	13.5	5.4	7.4	8.4	7.3	5.9	5.7	6.0	10.3	16.1	12.2
0.8	1.0	2.8	2.2	1.5	3.4	4.6	5.3	4.7	3.5	2.7	4.0	2.6
9.3	4.3	−1.0	5.9	4.9	0.7	5.1	5.2	7.0	11.8	9.5	7.3	8.9
12.1	1.2	10.2	8.8	6.6	12.1	7.1	9.1	4.8	8.3	7.9	3.3	10.1
4.2	−5.0	−6.2	4.3	−4.7	2.2	1.7	2.3	1.3	2.1	0.2	−4.0	1.9
8.3	5.2	5.7	6.5	8.5	3.5	7.4	6.1	2.6	4.8	6.7	5.4	5.3

TABLE 17-3 (*Continued*)

1956	1957	1958	1959	1960	1961	1962	1963	1964	1965	1966	1967	1968
83.3	86.8	64.8	68.0	86.5	67.3	72.6	71.0	80.0	73.6	82.5	81.8	76.6
71.2	83.5	67.5	57.3	77.0	60.4	60.1	58.7	65.8	60.3	65.1	71.6	66.0
0.9	1.8	3.3	3.1	2.9	4.0	4.9	5.6	5.4	4.3	2.9	4.1	3.7
11.3	1.5	−5.9	7.6	6.6	2.7	7.6	6.5	5.8	9.0	14.6	6.1	7.0
16.7	13.2	35.2	32.0	13.5	32.7	27.4	29.0	20.0	26.4	17.5	18.2	23.4
−9.7	−0.2	5.9	10.3	−8.6	6.5	6.7	6.5	0.9	0.9	1.0	1.0	7.0
0.9	0.5	1.2	1.5	0.4	0.2	1.5	1.1	1.5	1.4	1.1	1.1	1.5
17.4	6.5	18.8	13.3	13.9	18.2	13.3	12.4	13.6	14.5	11.2	9.6	13.0
7.9	6.3	8.3	6.1	8.2	8.4	6.7	7.3	3.7	9.0	3.4	5.8	2.1

As we might expect, the chief uses to which nonfinancial corporations put the funds are nonresidential fixed investment, inventories, and trade credit. Thus, changes in these categories usually dominate the year-to-year changes in assets. Furthermore, the fact that the absolute magnitudes of sources and uses have shown an upward trend is consistent with the post-World War II growth in the American economy.

Internal sources have been the chief means by which these corporations have financed their assets. To be sure, year-to-year fluctuations are considerable. Internal sources as a percentage of total sources reached a low of 43.1 percent in 1950 after a high of 102 percent the previous year.

The fact that internal sources of funds have been relatively more important than external sources should not be surprising. The result is consistent with our cost-of-capital model developed earlier. There we argued that, given the dividend policy, the firm would employ depreciation and retained earnings before entering the capital markets for outside debt or equity funds. Ordinarily we would expect the demand curve for capital to intersect the supply curve so that internal sources of funds would be the primary component of total sources. However, during periods of rapid expansion in assets when demand for capital is relatively high, heavier reliance may be placed on external sources. Due to changes in demand,[4] therefore, we might expect year-to-year changes in the composition of funds. Nevertheless, it is relatively rare that shifts in demand are such that external sources become more important than internal sources for any given year.[5] Since 1951, for example, internal sources each year have accounted for more than 50 percent of total sources.

Since the corporation has for this century been the dominant form through which the private sector of the American economy has organized its resources, it would be appropriate to survey the trends in the relative importance of various sources over this entire period. This can be done, but the results must be interpreted carefully for the sources

[4]In the conceptual framework developed earlier, recall that the demand curve was the demand for long-lived assets. The figures presented in this chapter pertain to total uses, including financial assets whose primary function may be to maintain the firm's liquidity. This fact does not alter the conclusions advanced in the text. It merely adds to the demand curve, expenditures, the amount of which is not primarily a function of the rate of return or cost of capital.

[5]To emphasize the demand curve is not to minimize the importance of supply in determining the composition of funds. Suppose, for example, that demand remained constant but the profitability on existing assets rose. This would, if the payout ratio is held constant, raise the proportion of internal sources to total sources of funds. Similarly, suppose that the useful life of assets declines over time. Then depreciation as a source of funds for any given year rises. In practice, therefore, changes in both demand and supply may account for fluctuations in the percentages of external and internal sources to total sources.

of information often contain definitional differences which make comparisons difficult. To help alleviate this problem, it is useful to have time series which overlap. One author, Raymond W. Goldsmith, having provided extensive coverage[6] of the period 1901–1945, has extended his data to 1958.[7] This allows us to compare differences in his data and those of the Department of Commerce and the Federal Reserve Board and, where possible, to extrapolate trends.

In making historical comparisons, there is also a set of problems concerning the calculation of depreciation and the handling of the inventory valuation adjustment. Since the purpose of this chapter is to develop and analyze historically trends in the flow of funds, it is not necessary to estimate depreciation on the basis of the cost of replacing assets. Nor is it necessary to make a similar adjustment to undistributed profits to allow for the cost of replacing inventories. Such adjustments are more appropriate for measuring the corporate contribution to gross national product.

Unfortunately, as we shall see, in one critical area of comparison, in the post-World War II period, Goldsmith has estimated depreciation on the basis of replacement rather than original cost. Moreover, throughout his series, inventories are based on current rather than book value. For the sake of comparison we shall treat the Commerce–Federal Reserve inventory valuation adjustment as a contribution, positive or negative, to total profits and hence to total sources. Thus our data will reflect adjustments for the replacement cost of inventory but not for long-lived assets.

A final problem in making historical comparisons is to combine the series into meaningful periods. To draw valid conclusions from the data, it is necessary to organize the figures so that the forces affecting the composition of funds are similar. As Simon Kuznets observes, it is possible to do so by eliminating "the periods of war and distortion due to cyclical depressions, and observe the ratios over the periods marked by substantial capital formation under relatively prosperous conditions."[8] Alternatively, it is possible to establish long-term trends

[6]See particularly his *A Study of Saving in the United States, Financial Intermediaries in the American Economy Since 1900, The Flow of Capital Funds in the Postwar Economy* (all previously cited), and, with Robert E. Lipsey and Morris Mendelson, *Studies in the National Balance Sheet of the United States*, 2 vols. (Princeton, N.J.: Princeton University Press, 1963). A study by the National Bureau of Economic Research, Inc.

[7]The data even when extended from sources by the same author, are not completely comparable. Note, for example, his figures on sources of funds for nonfinancial corporations for the years 1946–1949 in table 53, pp. 222–223, in *Financial Intermediaries in the American Economy Since 1900*. Compare these with the sum of the figures for nonfinancial corporations for the same years in table VII-4 of *Studies in the National Balance Sheet of the United States*, vol. II, pp. 408–409.

[8]Kuznets, *op. cit.*, p. 242.

by including all periods, even the exceptional ones of war or other unusual conditions. On the theory that those exceptional periods were the product of antecedent years—which were consequently also exceptional because they gave rise to exceptional effects—and that those exceptional spans were in turn followed by periods that represent reactions and thus were also in some way unusual, we should include all periods.[9]

Since it might prove fruitful to employ both categories, the data in Tables 17-4 through 17-8 use both classifications. Periods which exclude wars and the Great Depression but which are otherwise cyclically comparable are labeled "Short periods," while those including these distortions are labeled "Longer periods." In the case of the post–World War II period, the data are divided so as to facilitate comparison between the Goldsmith and the Commerce–Federal Reserve estimates. The terminal year is 1958, which also marks the end of the sharpest recession since World War II. The Commerce–Federal Reserve data are then extended from 1959 to the present and totaled from 1946 to the present to bring them up to date.

Turning first to Table 17-4, we note that the Goldsmith data for the periods 1901–1912, 1923–1929, and 1946–1958 show internal sources to be 55.2, 54.7, and 55.9 percent of total sources, respectively. The

TABLE 17-4:   INTERNAL SOURCES OF FUNDS AS A PERCENT OF TOTAL SOURCES FOR NONFINANCIAL CORPORATIONS FOR SELECTED YEARS, 1901–1968

Short Periods	Internal Sources as a Percent of Total Sources	Longer Periods	Internal Sources as a Percent of Total Sources
1901–1912[a,b]	55.2	1901–1922[b]	58.7
1923–1929[a,b]	54.7	1913–1939[b]	65.8
1946–1958[a,c]	55.9	1940–1958[a,b,c]	59.4
1946–1958[d]	62.9	1946–1968[d]	64.0
1959–1968[d]	64.6		

SOURCES: [a]Raymond W. Goldsmith, *The Flow of Capital Funds in the Postwar Economy* (New York: National Bureau of Economic Research, Inc., 1965), table 37, p. 142. Reprinted by permission of the National Bureau of Economic Research, Inc.

[b]Calculated from data in Raymond W. Goldsmith, *Financial Intermediaries in the American Economy Since 1900* (Princeton, N.J.: Princeton University Press, 1958), table 53, p. 222. A study by the National Bureau of Economic Research, Inc. Reprinted by permission of the National Bureau of Economic Research, Inc.

[c]Raymond W. Goldsmith, Robert E. Lipsey, and Morris Mendelson, *Studies in the National Balance Sheet of the United States* (Princeton, N.J.: Princeton University Press, 1963), vol. II, table VII-4, pp. 408–409. A study by the National Bureau of Economic Research, Inc. Reprinted by permission of Princeton University Press. (Internal sources are equivalent to "saving." Total sources as well as "saving" reflect inventory valuation adjustment.)

[d]See Table 17-1.

[9]*Ibid.*, p. 244. Reprinted by permission of Princeton University Press.

Commerce–Federal Reserve data for the last period indicate that internal sources were 62.9 percent of total sources with an upward trend continuing to the present.   When the two world wars and the Great Depression are included, the Goldsmith data show an upward trend through 1939, then a decline in the importance of internal sources from 1940 to 1958.   The Commerce–Federal Reserve data show internal sources for the post World War II period to approximate the levels in the Goldsmith data for the 1913–1939 period.

The fact that internal sources are relatively less important in the short periods than in the longer periods is not surprising.   During periods of peacetime prosperity containing relatively minor recessions, an expansion in demand for goods and services is often followed by an expansion in the demand for capital.   The demand curve for funds intersects the supply curve at a relatively high level, reflecting an expansion in external sources.   In a depression the opposite occurs.   In fact, between 1930 and 1933, there was a net decline in sources of funds, with an internally generated figure of $4.1 billion more than offset by the decline of $4.8 billion in external sources.   From 1934 to 1939 total sources increased, but almost 98 percent came from internal sources.[10]

During war periods a nation's capital resources are fully utilized. Restrictions are often placed on the supply of funds, with the war effort taking precedence.   The government dominates the capital markets and corporations are forced to rely heavily on internally generated funds. This does not mean that external funds cannot be obtained.   For the 1940–1945 period, for example, external sources accounted for nearly 20 percent of total sources.[11]   But even this figure indicates that there were severe restraints in the capital markets at a time of expanding military demand for goods and services.

From the data presented, it is apparent that wars and depressions, particularly World War II and the Great Depression, have generated forces raising the proportion of internal sources to total sources which in Goldsmith's estimates were not apparent in more normal or short periods.   Within the latter category, the Goldsmith estimates show little change in the ratio of internal sources to total sources.   Kuznets, however, extrapolating the Goldsmith estimates for the period 1946–1956, found that internal sources had risen to 61 percent of total sources.[12] Moreover, if we extrapolate the Goldsmith data under the assumption that the ratio of his figures on the Commerce–Federal Reserve estimates

---

[10]Percentages are calculated from raw data in Goldsmith, *Financial Intermediaries in the American Economy Since 1960*, table 53, p. 222.

[11]*Ibid.*

[12]Kuznets, *op. cit.*, table 39, p. 248.

for the 1946–1958 period persists into the later period, then internal sources would be 57.4 percent of total sources from 1959 to the present.[13] There is, therefore, a possibility of a slight upward trend in the importance of internal sources to total sources in the post-World War II period, when the figures are compared with those of the two earlier periods, also marked by "substantial capital formation under relatively prosperous conditions."

Turning from internal sources to their components, we find that generalizations are even more difficult. Table 17-5 contains data on retained earnings and capital consumption allowances. Goldsmith's estimates for capital consumption allowances for the years 1901–1949 are based on original cost.[14] However, in his subsequent analysis of the flow of funds in the post-World War II economy, capital consumption allowances are based on replacement cost.[15] For the 1946–1958

TABLE 17-5: RETAINED EARNINGS AND CAPITAL CONSUMPTION ALLOWANCES AS A PERCENT OF TOTAL SOURCES FOR SELECTED YEARS, 1901–1968

Percent of Total Sources			Percent of Total Sources		
Short Periods	Retained Earnings	Capital Comsumption Allowances	Longer Periods	Retained Earnings	Capital Consumption Allowances
1901–1912[a]	21.7	33.5	1901–1922[a]	25.1	33.6
1923–1929[a]	17.4	37.3	1913–1939[a]	8.1	57.7
1946–1949[a]	34.0	30.5	1940–1949[a]	33.1	37.8
1946–1949[b]	37.0	27.7	1946–1968[b]	23.3	40.7
1946–1958[c]	14.8	41.2			
1946–1958[b]	27.1	35.8			
1959–1968[b]	21.1	43.5			

SOURCES : [a]See footnote b of Table 17-4.
[b]See Table 17-1.
[c]See footnotes a and c of Table 17-4. The values reflect the replacement cost, not the cost of the original cost, of depreciation.

[13]$\dfrac{55.9}{62.9} = \dfrac{x}{64.6}$

$x = 57.4\%$

[14]Kuznets, *op. cit.*, p. 247.

[15]Goldsmith, *The Flow of Capital Funds in the Postwar Economy*, p. 81 and table 37, p. 142. Goldsmith also lists capital consumption allowances on a replacement cost basis for the years 1901–1912, 1923–1929, 1934–1939 but not for the intervening years. Capital consumption allowances for each of these periods were respectively 37.9, 39.8, and 124.8 percent of total sources. Profits, or net savings, were 17.3, 14.9, and −27.3 percent, respectively. Excluding 1934–1939 as an unusual period on the basis of replacement cost, it appears that capital consumption allowances have increased somewhat relative to retained earnings.

period, capital consumption allowances are 41.2 percent and retained earnings are 14.8 percent. This compares with the Commerce–Federal Reserve estimates of 35.8 and 27.1 percent, respectively, based on original cost. Since the price level was rising throughout this period, Goldsmith has arrived at a higher value for capital consumption allowances and a correspondingly lower value for retained profits than if his estimates had been based on original cost.

Thus we are left with a relatively short 3-year span during which the data overlap. This means that the conclusions drawn are even more tenuous than those based on internal sources as a percent of total sources. Turning first to the longer periods, capital consumption allowances in the 1913–1939 period were nearly twice total sources for those years.[16] Given the fact that new capital formation did not accelerate until the post-World War II period, it becomes evident why capital consumption allowances were so important in the 1913–1939 period as compared with the 1940–1949 period. The Great Depression dominated the earlier series to such an extent that it distorted the long-term trend in both capital consumption allowances and retained earnings. World War I did not produce the same effects as either the Great Depression or World War II. Hence the series for 1901–1922 does not show the same distortion. Recognizing the limitations in generalizations based on extrapolating different series, it would appear that capital consumption allowances have been a relatively more important source of funds in the post-World War II period than in the years from 1901 to 1922. Retained profits, however, while perhaps rising slightly, seem not to have increased as much in relative importance.

When looking at the short periods—particularly 1901–1912, 1923–1929, 1946–1958, and 1959 to the present—we can reach similar conclusions. The importance of capital consumption allowances as a percentage of total sources seems to have increased; whereas retained earnings exhibit little or no trend in either direction.

The conclusions differ slightly from those reached by Kuznets. In extrapolating the Goldsmith data from 1946–1956, he found capital consumption allowances to be 38 percent of total sources, and retained earnings 37 percent of total net uses.[17] Since the estimates in Table 17-5 are based only on total sources, his figures for retained earnings are not comparable with Goldsmith's. However, in making similar calculations for the periods 1901–1912 and 1923–1929, Kuznets finds retained earnings to be 33 and 28 percent, respectively. For short comparable periods, therefore, his data show that there might be a

---

[16]Goldsmith, *Financial Intermediaries in the American Economy since 1900*, pp. 222–223.
[17]Kuznets, *op. cit.*, table 39, p. 248.

slight upward trend in both retained earnings and capital consumption allowances.[18]

Turning to external sources of funds, the data in Table 17-6 are

TABLE 17-6: LONG-TERM DEBT* AS A PERCENT OF TOTAL SOURCES FOR NONFINANCIAL CORPORATIONS FOR SELECTED YEARS, 1901–1968

Short Periods	Long-term Debt as a Percent of Total Sources	Longer Periods	Long-term Debt as a Percent of Total Sources
1901–1912[a]	22.5	1901–1922[a]	15.6
1923–1929[a]	21.6	1913–1939[a]	13.9
1946–1958[b]	17.3	1940–1958[c]	12.1
1946–1958[d]	12.1	1946–1968[d]	12.3
1959–1968[d]	12.5		

SOURCES: [a]See footnotes a and b of Table 17-4.
[b]See footnotes a and c of Table 17-4.
[c]See footnotes b and c of Table 17-4.
[d]See Table 17-1.
*Long-term debt is the sum of bonds and mortgage liabilities of nonfinancial corporations.

for long-term debt, that is, for bonds and mortgages. A downward trend is evident in both the short and longer periods in the Goldsmith data as well as the Commerce–Federal Reserve series. To be sure, the trend becomes less pronounced as we break down the post-World War II period. Moreover, if we extrapolate the Goldsmith estimate again on the assumption that the 1946–1958 proportions would persist in the period from 1959 to the present, these proportions would

[18]*Ibid.* Based on extrapolations of Goldsmith's estimates to 1956, the trend for both short and longer periods is

Short Periods	Internal Sources to Total Sources, %	Capital Consumption Allowances to Total Sources, %	Retained Earnings to Net Uses, %
1901–1912	55	34	33
1923–1929	55	37	28
1946–1956	61	38	37

Longer Periods	Internal Sources to Total Sources, %	Capital Consumption Allowances to Total Sources, %	Retained Earnings to Total Sources, %
1901–1922	59	34	38
1913–1939	66	58	19
1940–1956	64	40	40

SOURCE: Simon Kuznets, *Capital in the American Economy: Its Formation and Financing* (Princeton, N.J.: Princeton University Press, 1961), table 39, p. 248. A study by the National Bureau of Economic Research, Inc. Reprinted by permission of Princeton University Press.

be 17.9 percent of total sources for these later years.[19]   What would have been a continuation of a downward trend was forestalled somewhat by the heavy debt financing during the late 1960s.

On the other hand, it is clearly evident from Table 17-7 that the reliance on short-term debt has increased considerably in both the

TABLE 17-7: SHORT-TERM DEBT* AS A PERCENT OF TOTAL SOURCES FOR NONFINANCIAL CORPORATIONS FOR SELECTED YEARS, 1901–1968

Short Periods	Short-term Debt as a percent of Total Sources	Longer Periods	Short-term Debt as a percent of Total Sources
1901–1912[a]	8.0	1901–1922[a]	13.6
1923–1929[a]	4.3	1913–1939[a]	4.3
1946–1958[b]	20.0	1940–1958[c]	22.0
1946–1958[d]	20.1	1946–1968[d]	20.8
1959–1968[d]	21.2		

SOURCES: [a]See footnotes a and b of Table 17-4.
[b]See footnotes a and c of Table 17-4.
[c]See footnotes b and c of Table 17-4.
[d]See Table 17-1.
*All debt other than mortgages and bonds.

short and the longer periods.   Moreover, there is a remarkable degree of agreement between the Goldsmith and the Commerce–Federal Reserve data.

These opposite trends in the pattern of debt financing deserve some explanation.   In the final section of this chapter we shall attempt to do this in an overall analysis of the role of the various sources of funds in business finance.

For the time being we need only point out to the student that these trends may be somewhat overstated.   As we noted earlier, term loans are part of bank loans.   But bank loans are included in short-term debt. Therefore part but by no means all of the decline in importance of long-term debt and rise in importance of short-term debt is due to the classifications employed rather than to changes in the term structure of debt.

Finally, turning to Table 17-8, it is also evident that stock as a percent of total sources has declined in importance over the years. Again, this trend is apparent in the Goldsmith data and is reinforced by the Commerce–Federal Reserve estimates, whether we use the short or the longer periods.   When extrapolating the Goldsmith figures on

[19] $\frac{17.3}{12.1} = \frac{x}{12.5}$
$x = 17.9\%$

TABLE 17-8: STOCK AS A PERCENT OF TOTAL SOURCES FOR NONFINANCIAL CORPORATIONS FOR SELECTED YEARS, 1901–1968

Short Periods	Stock as a Percent of Total Sources			Longer Periods	Stock as a Percent of Total Sources		
	Total	Preferred	Common		Total	Preferred	Common
1901–1912	14.0[a]	2.5[b]	11.5[e]	1901–1922	12.1[a]	2.9[b]	9.2[e]
1923–1929	19.4[a]	6.5[b]	12.9[e]	1913–1939	16.1[a]	4.2[b]	11.9[e]
1946–1958	6.8[c]		5.8[e]	1940–1958	6.5[d]	0.9[b]	5.6[e]
1946–1958	5.0[f]	*	*	1946–1968	2.8	*	*
1959–1968	1.6[f]	*	*				

SOURCES: [a]See footnotes a and b of Table 17-4.
[b]Calculated using preferred stock data in Raymond W. Goldsmith, *A Study of Saving in the United States* (Princeton, N.J.: Princeton University Press, 1955), vol. I, table V-9, p. 482. Reprinted by permission of Princeton University Press.
[c]See footnotes a and c of Table 17-4.
[d]See footnotes b and c of Table 17-4.
[e]Total less preferred.
[f]See Table 17-1.
*Data are unavailable.

the assumption that the proportions between these figures and the Commerce–Federal Reserve data remain the same in the later period, the proportion of stock to total sources from 1959 to the present would be 2.2 percent.[20]

Unfortunately, the Commerce–Federal Reserve data do not contain a breakdown as to common and preferred stock. The ultimate source of this information is the Securities and Exchange Commission. It releases gross figures on the sale of preferred stock in relation to total issues. But our interest at this stage is in the net increase in preferred stock, that is, new issues less retirements in relation to total sources of funds. There is, however, no evidence to indicate a marked increase in the sale of preferred stock since 1959. Thus we can accept the Goldsmith estimate of 1 percent of total sources for 1946–1958 as the maximum contribution which preferred stock has made since then.

Drawing together the trends in financing, we can conclude that, save for short-term debt, external finance as a percent of total sources for nonfinancial corporations has declined over the years. The trend in internal sources is unclear. However, to the extent that a slight upward trend has occurred, it appears from the calculations presented in this chapter to be the result of an increase in capital consumption allowances.

$$[20] \frac{6.8}{5.0} = \frac{x}{1.6}$$
$$x = 2.2\%$$

Finally, it should be reemphasized that undistributed profits have been altered because of the allowance for inventory valuation adjustment. Depreciation, however, except in the case of Goldsmith's 1946–1958 data, has been estimated on an original cost basis, thus preventing further changes in reported profits which reproduction cost would necessitate.

Historical Trends – Disaggregation of the Data

Before attempting to explain the trends in the sources of funds, it would be useful to have the data broken down into industry components. Perhaps some of the aggregate results are due to movements in one or more industrial subclassifications. More important, lack of trends in the aggregate data could be the result of offsetting tendencies in the component parts. Unfortunately, no such comprehensive breakdown exists. Some work has been done in mining and manufacturing and in the regulated industries.[21] The data on sources of funds are spotty; however, they are the best available for the pre-World War II period.

Beginning in 1947, the Department of Commerce published a series on sources and uses of funds by individual industries but abandoned it together with the aggregate series in 1964. The Federal Reserve Board now publishes the latter but has not put out a series breaking the data down into its industrial components.

Thus we are forced to rely on the Department of Commerce series for data on the post-World War II period. Although there is considerable room for improving the definitional classification on which the data are based,[22] the figures in Table 17-9 on the next page do indicate that there is a considerable degree of diversity among industries in the relative importance placed on various categories of funds. Communications and public utilities, for example, appear to rely much more heavily on external sources than do any of the other subclassifications. Yet in the period 1959–1963 the importance of internal sources seems to have increased for all groups for which data are available.

[21]Daniel Creamer, Sergei Dobrovolsky, and Israel Borenstein, *Capital in Manufacturing and Mining: Its Formation and Financing* (Princeton, N.J.: Princeton University Press, 1960). A study for the National Bureau of Economic Research, Inc. Melville J. Ulmer, *Capital in Transportation, Communications, and Public Utilities: Its Formation and Financing* (Princeton, N.J.: Princeton University Press, 1960). A study for the National Bureau of Economic Research, Inc.

[22]For a critical analysis of the Commerce data and a more detailed breakdown of the data for the years 1950–1955, see David Meiselman and Eli Shapiro, *The Measurement of Corporate Sources and Uses of Funds* (New York: National Bureau of Economic Research, Inc., 1964).

TABLE 17-9: RELATIVE DISTRIBUTION OF SOURCES OF CORPORATE FUNDS BY INDUSTRY, 1947–1958 AND 1959–1963 (In Percentages)

Sources of funds	Manufacturing and Mining[a]	Railroads[a]	Nonrailroad Transportation[a]	Public Utilities and Communications[a]	Trade[b]
Internal Sources					
1947–1958	67.0	87.9	66.9	32.9	71.6
1959–1963	74.9	109.1	71.7	53.4	†
Retained Earnings					
1947–1958	32.9	33.1	9.5	3.3	40.1
1959–1963	25.3	−27.3	−0.9	7.8	†
Depreciation					
1947–1958	34.1	54.8	57.4	29.6	31.5
1959–1963	49.6	136.4	72.6	45.6	†
External Sources					
1947–1958	33.0	12.1	33.1	67.1	28.4
1959–1963	25.1	−9.1	28.3	46.8	†
Short-term Debt					
1947–1958	16.5	4.0	13.5	7.8	23.2
1959–1963	16.6	12.1	14.2	8.2	†
Long-term Debt					
1947–1958	14.3	10.5	19.6	35.1	5.2
1959–1963	9.3	−21.2	14.2	23.8	†
Stock					
1947–1958	2.2	−2.4	*	24.2	*
1959–1963	−0.7	*	*	14.8	†

SOURCES: [a]Calculated from data in *Survey of Current Business*, September, 1957, table 2, p. 10, November, 1964, table 2, p. 9. Short-term debt includes all debt that is not bonds, mortgages, and long-term bank loans.

[b]Calculated from data in *Survey of Current Business*, September, 1957, table 2, p. 10; October, 1959, table 2, p. 15. Data for 1957 and 1958 are for fiscal years. There is some unavoidable double counting of minor significance.

*Aggregate amounts were less than $50 million.

†Data are unavailable.

Internal and external sources may not equal 100 percent because of rounding.

In terms of external sources, retail trade seems to rely heavily on short-term debt but requires relatively little long-term financing. For public utilities the opposite is true. Given the nature of the assets of both industries, these results merely confirm what the student of finance would expect on a priori grounds.

Mining and manufacturing firms use the money and capital markets for somewhere between a quarter and a third of all their sources, but the reliance on long-term external sources seems to have declined since 1959. There is a similar pattern in nonrailroad transportation corporations, whereas railroads appear to have abandoned the long-term capital markets altogether. Indeed, the issuance of equipment obligations recorded in long-term debt was, for the 1959–1963 period, more than offset by the retirement of these and other long-term-debt obligations.

Finally, it appears that only manufacturing and mining, public utilities, and communications have tapped the equity markets for new issues of stock during the post-World War II period. In relative terms, public utilities have placed heavier reliance on equities while for mining and manufacturing there seems to have been a net retirement of equity issues during the 1959–1963 period.

From the relatively spotty data available on the pre-World War II period, there seems to be no trend in the reliance manufacturing and mining corporations have placed on internal sources. According to Kuznets, the ratio of internal financing to total uses was "0.70 in 1900–1910, 0.97 in 1920–1929, and 0.67 in 1946–1953."[23] Moreover, "the ratios of the two components of gross retention—capital consumption allowances and undistributed earnings—to total uses were also relatively constant."[24]

On the other hand, there has been a marked upward trend in the reliance on internal funds in the regulated industries. Data go back to the 1880s for steam railroads and electric light and power, and to the 1890s for telephones. The terminal point of a comparable series is, however, the period 1941–1950. Containing, as it does, the war years, the period shows a heavy reliance on internal financing. Nevertheless, Kuznets estimates that between 1901 and 1910, internal sources for all regulated industries would have accounted for at most 20 percent of total uses. In the 1941–1950 period, the proportion was about 62 percent.[25] Even allowing for the heavy reliance placed on internal sources during World War II, there is no indication that the post-World War II percentages have fallen to the 1901–1910 estimates.

But if the ratio of internal financing to total sources increased in the regulated industries while the ratio for manufacturing and mining corporations remained relatively constant, then why was there at best only a slight rise in this ratio for all nonfinancial corporations? Apart from discrepancies in the data, the answer seems to lie in the decline in the importance in total financing of regulated industries as compared with nonregulated industries. As the proportion of internal financing rose in the former, its contribution to total sources or uses declined.

[23]Kuznets, *op. cit.*, p. 253.
[24]*Ibid.*, p. 254.
[25]*Ibid.*, p. 256.

With apparently no change in internal financing on the part of the non-regulated industries—at least in their major component, manufacturing and mining—and with the relative contribution of this sector rising, the result was little or no change in the importance of internal funds for non-financial corporations.   The lack of a marked upward trend in the ratio was therefore due to a shift in weights between the regulated and non-regulated sectors, "not by offsetting movements in the ratio [of internal financing] within the nonregulated industry corporations."[26]

Historical Trends—An Analysis

In order to analyze the trends in total sources, it will be useful to have an equation based on the respective components of the sources.   Thus

$$\frac{\text{Total sources}}{\text{Total sources}} = \frac{\text{retentions}}{\text{total sources}} + \frac{\text{debt}}{\text{total sources}} + \frac{\text{external equity}}{\text{total sources}}$$

Retentions are equal to the sum of capital consumption allowances and undistributed profits, while debt includes both short- and long-term obligations.   External equity equals the sum of both common and preferred stocks.

From the discussion in the previous section, it is evident that there has been a decline in the importance of long-term debt and stock but a rise in the importance of short-term debt.   The trend in internal finance is less clear but there is at most a slight increase.   From these facts and from the above equation it is apparent that the important question which remains concerns the trend in the ratio of debt to total sources.   Has the upward trend in short-term debt offset the downward movement in long-term debt?   In other words, have the debt-to-total-sources and equity-to-total-sources ratios, the so called debt-equity ratios, remained unchanged?

According to Arnold Sametz, there is considerable evidence that these ratios are indeed secularly constant.   Using Goldsmith's data, he found that for the period 1901–1929, the ratio of equity, exclusive of preferred stock, to total sources was 68.2 percent.   The ratio of debt to total sources would therefore be 31.8 percent.   For the period 1930–1958 the ratios were 69.7 and 30.3 percent, respectively.   Even when preferred stock is treated as equity, the ratios remain relatively constant: 72.2 and 27.8 percent for the 1901–1929 period and 70.6 and 29.4 percent for the 1930–1958 period.[27]   Citing other authorities, Sametz argues that

---

[26]*Ibid.*, p. 257.
[27]Sametz, *Trends in the Volume and Composition of Equity Finance,*" table 8, p. 463.

the debt-equity ratios are apparently constant whether calculations are based on totals, that is, on balance-sheet figures, or on changes in these totals, that is, on data on sources or uses, as they were in our calculations.[28]

If the debt-equity ratios are indeed secularly constant, there are some interesting implications. From our model of the cost of capital, there is the implication that once management and presumably the owners have decided on the appropriate level of debt, the sequence in financing is determined in the following way. First, internal sources are exhausted. Then debt is utilized, its term structure being a function of the marginal cost of various sources. As the cost of long-term debt rises relative to the cost of short-term debt, the latter is substituted for the former. Should there be a sufficient backlog of profitable projects, then, rather than increasing the debt ratio and therefore the financial risk, management resorts to what would otherwise be the most expensive source of funds: external equity finance.

There are, of course, numerous weaknesses in generalizations based on empirically observed constants. In the first place, to show that the debt-equity ratios are secularly constant does not explain why they are unchanged. Second, would disaggregation of the data reveal offsetting tendencies among industrial groups? Even more fundamental to an analysis of firm behavior is the possibility that a secularly constant aggregate figure is covering up diverse attitudes on the part of individual managements. Nevertheless, to the extent that the debt-equity ratios are constant, they are useful in providing explanations — although, as we shall see, less than optimal explanations — of the patterns of financial behavior.

The difficulty is that the debt-equity ratios vary somewhat more than Sametz's calculations would indicate. Using the format employed previously, it is clear from Table 17-10 on page 384 that the Goldsmith data show the debt ratio to be higher and the equity ratio to be lower for the 1946–1958 period than for the 1901–1912 period. Extrapolating the Goldsmith data to the present would not materially alter this conclusion.[29] The upward trend is more pronounced when preferred stock is excluded from the debt ratio. This is due to the declining importance of preferred stock, its peak use having occurred in the 1920s. Turning to the longer periods, the upward trend in the debt ratio is still apparent although the substitution of equity for debt during the Great Depression, together with the high levels of equity flotation in the

[28]*Ibid.*, pp. 462–463.

[29]$\dfrac{62.7}{67.9} = \dfrac{x}{66.2}$

$x = 61.1\%$

$1 - 61.1\% = 38.9\%$

TABLE 17-10:   DEBT-EQUITY RATIOS FOR NONFINANCIAL COR-
PORATIONS FOR SELECTED YEARS, 1901–1968

Short Periods	Equity Ratio Excluding Preferred	Debt Ratio Including Preferred[a]	Equity Ratio Including Preferred	Debt Ratio Excluding Preferred[a]
1901–1912[b]	66.8	33.2	69.3	30.7
1923–1929[b]	67.6	32.4	74.1	25.9
1946–1958[c]	61.7	38.3	62.7	37.3
1946–1958[e]	*	*	67.9	32.1
1959–1968[e]	*	*	66.2	33.8

Longer Periods	Equity Ratio Excluding Preferred Stock	Debt Ratio Including Preferred Stock[a]	Equity Ratio Including Preferred Stock	Debt Ratio Excluding Preferred Stock[a]
1901–1912[b]	67.9	32.1	70.8	29.2
1913–1939[b]	77.6	22.4	81.9	18.1
1940–1958[d]	65.0	35.0	65.9	34.1
1946–1968[e]	*	*	66.8	33.2

[a]Debt ratio equals 1 – equity ratio.
[b]See footnote b of Table 17-4 and footnote b of Table 17-8.
[c]See footnote c of Table 17-4.
[d]See footnotes b and c of Tables 17-4 and footnote b of Table 17-8.
[e]See Table 17-1.
*Data are unavailable.

1920s,[30] served to push the debt ratio for the period 1913–1939 to an un-precedented low.   Compensating tendencies from 1940 to at least 1958 resulted in a higher debt ratio than occurred during the 1901–1922 period. As a result the debt-equity ratios are seen to be relatively con-stant when the years 1901–1929 are compared with 1930–1958.

While others have also viewed the debt-equity ratios as being secu-larly constant, one authority, John Lintner, has combined this point with the additional fact that "outside equity issues in most years are small relative to the total amount of new outside financing."[31]   If they are small relative to total new outside financing, then outside equity issues are even smaller in relation to total sources.   By ignoring them altogether, Lintner argues that there must be relative stability in the ratio of internal sources to total sources.   Lintner goes on to argue that this secular stability is the result of invariant target payout ratios.   Dividends rise, albeit with some lag, as earnings rise.   The result is a tendency

[30]Goldsmith, *Financial Intermediaries in the American Economy Since 1900*, table 53, p. 222, data for the years 1923–1929, 1930–1933, and 1934–1939.
[31]Lintner, *op. cit.*, p. 179.

for retained earnings to be secularly stable.[32]   As Sametz points out, however, the retention ratio over time seems to have risen.   For the years 1922–1929, it was 0.28.   During the period 1950–1956, it was 0.46. Even allowing for a payout lag because "of unusually high but erratic profits" in the post-World War II period, Sametz finds that the retention ratio was 0.38 for the years 1952–1960.[33]

Because Goldsmith had used reproduction costs to estimate profits for the period 1946–1958, we cannot easily arrive at trends in retention and payout ratios.   Thus we shall accept Sametz's calculations and reject the assumption that a constant payout ratio helps to explain secular stability in internal finance.   Nor is there sufficient evidence to indicate that a lag in the payout ratio explains what might be a slight rise in the importance of internal finance relative to total finance.   The result could just as easily be due to increases in capital consumption allowances caused perhaps by a decline in the useful life of depreciable assets.

What the Goldsmith and Commerce–Federal Reserve data appear to indicate is that there has been a substitution of debt and perhaps internal sources for external equity finance.   In part this is a reflection of the income tax laws.   With interest on debt tax-deductible and with dividends on preferred stock subject to corporate income taxes, the increased financial risk of the higher debt ratios in the post-World War II period is partially offset by the tax shield.   Moreover, the personal income tax laws encourage the increased use of retained earnings rather than external financing.   In view of the relatively high level of personal income taxes in the later years, it seems strange that there is not a more pronounced upward trend in the importance of internal sources. Finally, the tax laws have until recently provided for lags between the incurrence of corporate income tax liability and payment of it, thus creating a means of short-term financing.   In fact, until the late 1960s, a large part of the secular increase in short-term debt was due to tax accruals.[34]

The student of finance should not infer from the above that the income tax laws alone have been responsible for the patterns of business finance.   These laws are but one of the many factors that must be considered.   Developing a comprehensive model to encompass all variables explaining financial behavior and ultimately the market value of the

[32]*Ibid.*, pp. 177–180.

[33]Sametz, *"Trends in the Volume and Composition of Equity Finance,"* p. 465.   See also Miller, *op. cit.*, table V-A8, pp. 457–458.

[34]Sametz, *"Trends in the Volume and Composition of Equity Finance,"* pp. 456–458, and his *"Patterns of Business Financing: Reply,"* pp. 712–714.   See also Goldsmith, *The Flow of Capital Funds in the Postwar Economy,* p. 142.

owners' equity not only is beyond the scope of an introductory text, as we noted in an earlier chapter, but is on the very frontiers of knowledge in the discipline.[35] Yet, tax and other institutional factors aside, a simple model will illustrate not only the problems involved but the usefulness of empirical models such as those of Sametz and Lintner.

Recall from our discussion of the cost of capital that the market price of a share in the firm is a function of both the expected earnings and the degree of leverage in the capital structure. This relationship can be expressed as

Market price = F (expected earnings, expected dividends, debt ratio)

But what determines expected earnings and dividends and the appropriate debt ratio? Intuitively the relationship is

Expected earnings = F (expected rate of return on assets, retention ratio)

Debt ratio = F (business risk)

These relationships in turn suggest

Rate of return on assets = F (composition of assets, debt ratio)

Retention ratio = F (expected rate of return on assets, business risk, debt ratio)

Business risk = F (composition of assets)

While additional variables could be included (the absolute size of the firm, for example), these functions illustrate the complex interrelationships among the variables ultimately determining the market value of the owners' equity. If we could establish specific equations for each function, we could reach an optimal solution to the goal of modern financial theory. Since the interrelationships have yet to be articulated, we must content ourselves with less than optimal solutions. Thus we developed a maximizing model, first holding the composition of financing constant, then varying the capital structure while holding the composition of assets constant.

In observing secularly constant debt-equity ratios, Sametz can justify holding the debt ratio constant in the equation

Market price = F (expected earnings, debt ratio)

The contribution of the capital structure to maximizing the market value

---

[35]See Eugene M. Lerner and Willard T. Carleton, *A Theory of Financial Analysis* (New York: Harcourt, Brace & World, Inc., 1966); also their paper "The Integration of Capital Budgeting and Stock Valuation," *American Economic Review*, vol. 54, no. 5 (Sept., 1964), pp. 683–702.

of the owners' equity is reduced to one of minimizing the cost of funds within a constant debt-equity framework.

Lintner's observations can be used to attack the same problem. In this case, however, the payout ratio as well as debt-equity ratios are held constant. Thus there is one less variable affecting the anticipated stream of earnings and hence the per share price of the owners' equity.

In short, an explanation of the trends in the empirical data requires a comprehensive model which is as yet unavailable. In the interim, if it can be shown that certain relevant variables are secularly constant, this fact in turn can be employed in generating working or suboptimal models to help explain the historical pattern of financing and predict future trends. While it would appear that there is greater evidence that the debt-equity ratios, not the payout-retention ratios, are secularly stable,[36] neither group is invariant. A constant debt ratio, however, is not necessarily inconsistent with the cost-of-capital model developed in this volume. Furthermore, we should remember that by holding the payout ratio constant, we abstracted from the problem of whether dividends or earnings was the controlling variable in determining the cost of capital. In a subsequent chapter, however, we made the assumption that dividends had no effect on the market price of the stock. As a result dividends were viewed as a residual. The payout ratio varied accordingly. Those who object on the grounds that payout ratios are determined in advance and once set remain relatively stable are not without their supporters. Since the issue is unsettled, we leave the student free to draw his own conclusions.

SUMMARY

As a percentage of total sources of nonfinancial corporations, long-term debt and external equity finance have declined over time. On the other hand, there has been an upward trend in short-term debt. Internal sources, however, have shown at best a slight upward trend, with depreciation probably accounting for most of the increase that exists.

Since the trends are based on aggregates, they could cover up underlying trends in the components. From the spotty evidence available, it appears that manufacturing and mining concerns have shown no upward trend in their reliance on internal sources. On the other hand, there has been a marked upward trend in the use of internal sources among public utility companies. The latter industry, however,

[36]To the extent that disaggregation of the data shows pronounced fluctuations in the debt-equity ratio, our confidence in holding the ratio constant for analytical purposes is correspondingly diminished.

has declined in importance relative to manufacturing and mining.   As a result, the aggregate data on internal sources have not reflected the upward trend noted in public utilities.

In analyzing the historical trends, an intriguing question that arises is whether the debt-equity ratios are secularly constant.   Has the upward movement in short-term debt largely offset the downward trend in long-term debt?   The evidence indicates that there is considerable stability in the aggregate ratio.   Again the aggregate data may cover up differences in individual industries or firms.   However, to the extent that the debt-equity ratios are secularly constant, management is holding constant one variable which affects the market price of the common stock, that is, the capital structure.

It has also been argued that external equity sources are small relative to total sources.   They can, therefore, be ignored.   If the ratio of debt to total sources is constant, then the ratio of internal sources to total sources must also be constant.   To the extent that this latter ratio is constant, it might be due to a secularly constant payout ratio. The evidence, however, indicates that the payout ratio seems to have declined over time.   Alternatively, the retention ratio seems to have risen.

But whether the payout ratio and the debt-equity ratios vary or not, the purpose in holding them constant is to develop suboptimal models for predicting the market price of the stock.   Until the interrelationships among the various factors affecting the price of the stock are articulated, the assumptions we've made will help in developing working models for predicting the market value of the owners' equity.

QUESTIONS

1.   "The empirical data clearly indicate that there has been, over time, an increase in debt financing on the part of nonfinancial corporations."   Evaluate.

2.   "Internal equity has been substituted for external equity in the financing of American business firms."   Do you agree?   Explain fully.

3.   "To observe meaningful trends in the data on sources of funds, we must relate cyclically comparable periods."   Evaluate.

4.   "The trends in the pattern of financing are consistent with the cost-of-capital model developed in this volume."   Do you agree? Explain fully.

5. "Disaggregation of the data reveals considerable differences in the pattern of financing among the various industries which make up the category of nonfinancial corporations." Evaluate.

SELECTED REFERENCES

Goldsmith, Raymond W., *The Flow of Capital Funds in the Postwar Economy.* New York: National Bureau of Economic Research, Inc., 1965, chap. 4.

Kuznets, Simon., *Capital in the American Economy: Its Formation and Financing.* Princeton, N.J.: Princeton University Press, 1961, chaps. 5 and 6.

Lintner, John., "The Financing of Corporations," in Edward S. Mason (ed)., *The Corporation in Modern Society.* Cambridge, Mass.: Harvard University Press, 1959, pp. 166–201.

Meiselman, David, and Eli Shapiro., *The Measurement of Corporate Sources and Uses of Funds.* New York: National Bureau of Economic Research, Inc., 1964.

Miller, Merton H., "The Corporation Income Tax and Corporate Financial Policies," in Commission on Money and Credit, *Stabilization Policies.* Englewood Cliffs, N.J.: Prentice-Hall, Inc., 1963, pp. 381–470.

Sametz, Arnold W., "Trends in the Volume and Composition of Equity Finance," *Journal of Finance*, vol. 19, no. 3 (September, 1964), pp. 450–469.

The Capital Markets—Principles and Practice

PART
FOUR

The Capital Markets and the Role of Financial Intermediaries

chapter Eighteen

Up to this point in our analysis we have viewed the cost of capital as though the various sources of funds were independent of the structure of the capital markets. In the next several chapters, however, we shall discuss more fully the impact of the capital markets on the supply curve of particular sources and ultimately on the market value of the owners' equity. In this chapter the student should familiarize himself with the analysis underlying the rationale for financial intermediaries. What role have they played in corporate financing? What future role will they play in supplying corporate funds? As in the case of the previous chapter, the student may wish first to read the initial section and the summary and then to turn to the historical trends to fill in the details.

The Appendix to this chapter provides a matrix of the interrelationship between the savings and investing sectors of the economy.

A Rationale for Financial Intermediaries

We have now reached the point in our survey where we can deal with the structure of the capital markets and the impact of these markets on the supply of capital.   In so doing we shall shift our analytical perspective from the firm to the economy as a whole.   Whereas the principles of capital budgeting are extensions of the economic theory of the firm, or microeconomics, the appropriate touchstone for an analysis of the capital markets is the theory of income determination, or macroeconomics.

A fundamental proposition developed in the principles of macroeconomics is the equality between *realized savings* and *realized investment*. *Ex post* savings always equal investment. *Ex ante* desired savings may be greater or less than desired investment.   If the latter is the case, there will be a shift in the level of gross national product together with a new equilibrium between realized savings and realized investment.[1]   It is customary in developing the principles of macroeconomics to point out that the savings units in a highly developed capitalistic economy differ from the investing units.   Households, for example, are a major source of savings while nonfinancial corporations are a primary source of investment.   Moreover, the reasons why households save need not correspond to the reasons why businessmen invest.[2]   In this dichotomy lies the rationale for differences in desired savings and desired investment and therefore the basis for developing an explanation of changes in the level of gross national product.   But in elementary macroeconomic theory there is no discussion of the capital markets and the financial intermediaries whose function is to bridge the gap between those who save and those who invest.

The reason for ignoring these institutions is that on the surface they appear to have no effect on the total amount of savings and investment or on the aggregate amount of real wealth.   A simple example will

---

[1]For a widely used standard treatment of the elementary principles of macroeconomics, see Paul A. Samuelson, *Economics: An Introductory Analysis,* 7th ed. (New York: McGraw-Hill Book Company, 1967), pp. 170–237.   In his analysis, net savings equal net investment.   Equilibrium is in terms of net national product, not gross national product.   Conceptually this can be remedied by simply adding capital consumption allowances to both savings and investment.

[2]More technically, we might assume that Investment $= F$ (interest rate, gross national product, uncertainty); Savings $= F$ (interest rate, disposable income, uncertainty).

In an econometric model we might postulate specific functions.   While in macroeconomics it is usually the practice to concentrate on the interest rate, gross national product, and disposable income, it is the question of uncertainty, as we shall see, which provides the foundation for explaining the role of the capital markets and of financial intermediaries.

illustrate the point.   Let us assume that all production in an economy can be accounted for by two sectors: households and nonfinancial corporations.   To be somewhat realistic with respect to their actual contribution, assume that households account for all the residential construction component of investment and nonfinancial corporations are responsible for the rest, that is, plant and equipment and inventories.[3]   Each sector subtracts from income an allowance to cover the replacement cost of the three components of investment spending.   The residual, or net, income accrues to households that ultimately own the corporations.   However, again to approximate reality, corporations retain a portion of their net income to expand plant, equipment, and inventories.

Assume that the balance sheet for the economy as a whole is as follows.

Assets		Owners' Equity	
(In Billions of Dollars)			
Residential Construction	$ 10		
Plant and Equipment	14		
Inventories	1	Owners' Equity	$25
Total Assets	$25	Total owners' Equity	$25

Let us further assume that households have a net savings balance and nonfinancial corporations a net investment balance.   In short, households are net lenders and nonfinancial corporations are net borrowers. To facilitate the transfer of funds between the two sectors, we shall introduce debt instruments and draw up a balance sheet for both.   Thus

NONFINANCIAL CORPORATIONS

Assets		Liabilities and Owners' Equity	
(In Billions of Dollars)			
Plant and Equipment	$ 14	Liabilities	$ 0
Inventories	1	Debt to Households	$ 5
		Owners' Equity	10
		Total Liabilities and	
Total Assets	$ 15	Owners' Equity	$ 15

[3]We shall follow the practice of national income accountants and list durables such as automobiles with personal consumption expenditures.

HOUSEHOLDS

Assets		Liabilities and Owners' Equity	
(In Billions of Dollars)			
Financial Assets		Liabilities	$ 0
Debt of Nonfinancial Corporations	$ 5		
Stock of Nonfinancial Corporations	10	Owners' Equity	25
Fixed Assets			
Residential Construction	10		
		Total Liabilities and	
Total Assets	25	Owners' Equity	$25

What we observe from these relationships is that the real wealth of the society remains unchanged. Households ultimately own all of it. The financial liabilities of corporations, including stock, are merely financial assets of households. The use of these instruments has facilitated the transfer of funds from the sector with a positive savings balance to the sector with a negative savings balance without a change, it appears, in the total of real wealth.

We could reach the same conclusion if we introduce the third sector represented by the most fundamental of the several financial intermediaries: the commercial banking system. Suppose further that there is a fixed supply of money consisting of coins and currency and demand deposits. The reserve requirements are $16\frac{2}{3}$ percent. Banks invest these funds in short-term obligations of nonfinancial corporations and households. Since the banks are incorporated, their stock is publicly owned, all of it by households. The equity funds are used to purchase mortgages and other debt obligations representing investment in plant, equipment, and residential construction. Assume further that banks have no real investment of their own. Their asset structure, in other words, consists solely of financial obligations of others. We can draw up a balance sheet for each of the three sectors as follows.

NONFINANCIAL CORPORATIONS

Assets		Liabilities and Owners' Equity	
(In Billions of Dollars)			
Current Assets		Liabilities	
Cash	$ 2	Debt to Households	$ 5
Demand Deposits	8	Debt to Commercial	
		Banks	10
Fixed Assets			
Plant and Equipment	14	Owners' Equity	10
Inventories	1		
Total Assets	$25	Total Liabilities and	
		Owners' Equity	$25

HOUSEHOLDS

Assets		Liabilities and Owners' Equity	
(In Billions of Dollars)			
Financial Assets		Liabilities	
Cash	$ 1	Debt to Commercial Banks	$ 5
Demand Deposits	4		
Debt of Nonfinancial			
Corporations	5		
Stock of Nonfinancial			
Corporations and Banks	15		
Fixed Assets		Owners' Equity	30
Residential Construction	10	Total Liabilities and	
Total Assets	$35	Owners' Equity	$35

COMMERCIAL BANKS

Assets		Liabilities and Owners' Equity	
(In Billions of Dollars)			
Financial Assets		Liabilities	
Reserves	$ 2	Demand deposits	$ 12
Loans	10		
Mortgages, etc.	5		
Fixed Assets		Owners' Equity	5
Total Assets	$ 17	Total Liabilities and	
		Owners' Equity	$ 17

Again real wealth is unchanged. Of the $25 billion, $10 billion remains directly in the hands of households. Since households have ownership claims equal to the sum of the owners' equity of commercial banks and nonfinancial corporations, or $15 billion, they continue to own directly or indirectly the entire amount of real tangible wealth. All other assets and liabilities represent offsetting financial claims. The function of the commercial bank is to act as an intermediary between the savings and investing sectors. It does so by providing a service: checking accounts. The producing sectors exchange most of their cash for these demand deposits and the banks invest the funds. The financial interrelationships have, of course, become more complicated because some households now borrow and some nonfinancial corporations, by keeping demand deposits, are now, indirectly at least, lenders.

But are the real variables unaffected by the issuance and exchange of financial assets among sectors and through intermediaries within the framework of a capital market? As in our discussion of the principles by which a firm maximizes the market value of the owners' equity, a complete answer to this question would take us beyond what might be regarded as an introductory analysis.[4]   But we can discuss briefly some of the factors considered important in explaining the impact of these institutions on savings and investment and hence on the aggregate amount of real wealth.

Let us start with an assumption that, on balance, households display a relative aversion to risk when compared with nonfinancial corporations.   For verification we can appeal to empirical evidence.   In 1965, for example, financial assets of households totaled $1,438.8 billion as against $342.5 billion in liabilities.   During the same year nonfinancial corporations held financial assets of $287.4 billion.   Their total liabilities, including owners' equity, was $351.9 billion.[5]   While the magnitudes will differ, we can observe similar results in the data for other years. Because their proportion of financial or liquid assets relative to total liabilities is greater when compared with that of nonfinancial corporations, households show a tendency toward risk aversion.[6]

Once we recognize sector differences in attitudes toward risk, it follows that a capital market and the most elementary of financial assets, money, together provide the mechanism through which the net-savings and risk-aversion sector (households) can transfer its funds to the net-investment and risk-accepting sector (nonfinancial business enterprises).

Money provides the standard of deferred payments on which all financial obligations are based.   From here it is but a short step to the multiplicity of types of financial obligations designed to accommodate the diverse attitudes of individuals with respect to risk and uncertainty. Efficient capital markets can accommodate such diversity.

But efficient capital markets do more than merely transfer savings to the investing sectors in return for financial assets.   It is also their function to accommodate the consumption and savings patterns of households over time by giving these instruments the quality of liquidity. For various reasons those holding financial assets may desire to sell or transfer them for cash so as to increase their personal consumption expenditures.   They choose in effect to dissave, that is, to spend more than current income.   Therefore, to accommodate this desire, in efficient capital markets there would materialize secondary markets or markets for existing securities.

[4]For a lucid commentary on this question, see Basil J. Moore, *An Introduction to the Theory of Finance: Assetholder Behavior under Uncertainty* (New York: The Free Press, 1968), *passim.*   The beginning student will find Chaps. 1 and 4 particularly useful.
[5]Board of Governors of the Federal Reserve System, Division of Research and Statistics, *Flow of Funds Accounts, 1945–1967* (Washington: Board of Governors of the Federal Reserve System, 1968), pp. 160, 162.
[6]From the figures quoted we cannot exclude the equity component.   But even if we did, the results would still show households to be more liquid.

To illustrate these properties of transferral and liquidity, suppose that a nonfinancial corporation desired to issue long-term debt to finance an investment in long-lived assets. But households do not wish to purchase such obligations if they must be held to maturity. Under these conditions if the debt is to be sold, a secondary market in this issue must evolve. If this is actually the attitude toward corporate debt, then we can anticipate that trading markets will indeed develop.

There is, however, another alternative. Enter, now, a financial intermediary, that is, an insurance company marketing its own debt: life insurance policies. Households appear to lack the desire to hold long-term corporate bonds to maturity, but they do demand protection against financial loss in the event of death of the head of the household. Since this is a long-term proposition, and since the insurance company can objectively evaluate its risk with probability distributions based on mortality tables, the nonfinancial corporation may be indirectly financed by households. The latter purchase insurance policies and the premiums are invested in the long-term debt of nonfinancial corporations. Management of the insurance company, within its own risk constraint, maximizes the market value of its owners' equity,[7] selling policies tailored to meet the needs of the individual household and altering its composition of financial assets accordingly.

Whether the secondary market is the mechanism through which liquidity is achieved or whether the financial intermediary is a substitute for it depends, in competitive markets, on the relative cost of each institution. It is always possible for both to exist. A secondary market in certain types of instruments — common stock, for instance — may exist along with large institutional investors such as owners of pension funds and investment companies purchasing shares in corporations. But with respect to corporate debt, at least, there is today relatively little trading activity. In 1965, for example, households held about 3.8 percent of the corporate debt.[8] Most of the rest was in the hands of financial institutions.[9] To ascribe the outcome in this case to the relative efficiency of institutional investors might be misleading. Favorable tax treatment of some financial intermediaries and, as we shall see, regulation of new security offerings have been factors accelerating, if not by themselves causing, the institutionalization of corporate debt.

[7]Even a company which is owned by the policyholders, that is, a mutual company, has the incentive to minimize costs and therefore the premiums paid.

[8]Board of Governors of the Federal Reserve System, *op. cit.*, p. 174A. Of the $124.7 billion in corporate and foreign bonds, $4.6 billion were held by households. The results are similar for the more recent years although the high interest rates of the late 1960s have attracted more individuals into the bond market. See *Wall Street Journal*, October 17, 1969, p. 1.

[9]State and local governments presumably held $24.8 billion in their pension funds.

Since capital markets provide the means for transferring funds from the savings to the investing sector, the more efficient they are in performing this function, the greater will be their impact on the stock of real wealth.   Furthermore, to the extent that the desire to save and invest out of current income is a function of accumulated wealth, the capital markets have a role to play in determining the current and future levels of gross national product.

The Capital Markets and Financial Intermediaries — The Historical Record

Over time, the definition of capital markets has varied.   Traditional writings in the field of business finance have made a distinction between the money market and the capital market.   The former consists of the market or markets for instruments which mature in less than a year, the latter for instruments whose maturity extends beyond a year.[10] For some purposes, this definition can be useful.   In the next two chapters, for example, we shall concentrate on the primary and secondary markets for corporate bonds and stocks, that is, the markets for long-term liabilities and equity.   We shall do so because shaping the supply curve of these sources are institutional factors which are not particularly relevant to the supply of short-term funds such as trade credit and bank loans.

Nevertheless, for many purposes, this distinction is arbitrary.   For instance, it would be a mistake to argue that because the Federal Reserve sold $500 million in 90-day Treasury bills, the only impact would be a decline in the price of short-term government securities and a corresponding rise in their yields.   As any student familiar with the mechanics of deposit creation knows, the primary effect of the sale of Treasury bills by the Federal Reserve is a decline in the reserves of commercial banks and, depending on the level of excess reserves, a potential contraction in the money supply, or at least a contraction in the rate of increase in the money supply.   There could be repercussions in the long-term capital markets as well.   A reduction in loans made to carry new or existing securities could affect the supply price and yield on corporate bonds and stocks.   In competing for available deposits, commercial banks might be able to bid away savings accounts from savings and loan associations and mutual savings banks.   These latter institutions are a major source of funds for residential mortgages.   As a result there could be a decline in new mortgages and in residential construction.   Similarly, given the demand for new mortgages and a

[10]Sidney Robbins, *The Securities Markets, Operations and Issues* (New York: The Free Press, 1966), pp. 4–20.

decline in the available supply of funds, there is a tendency for the cost of, or the yield on, new instruments to rise.

Many economists, therefore, have tended to eschew distinctions between money markets and capital markets, preferring instead to concentrate on the interrelationships among the instruments used and the sectors of the economy issuing or holding them. For the rest of this chapter we shall employ this aggregate approach to the capital markets, for it will provide us with a frame of reference which we can subsequently narrow to encompass in greater detail the traditional areas of business finance, that is, the markets for long-term securities.

Broadly speaking, the capital markets "cover all financial assets and liabilities and all transactions in such assets except those which involve the exchange of money for a nonfinancial consideration, i.e., except monetary payments in exchange for commodities and for labor and capital services."[11]

Statistically, the task of implementing this definition is formidable. It requires a catalog of all instruments exchanged together with a list of the sectors issuing and holding them. Fortunately, a small group of these instruments constitute the bulk of the market value of all financial assets outstanding.[12] Moreover, the vast majority are held by either households, nonfinancial corporations, or financial institutions. We can therefore concentrate on these assets and the sectors of the economy holding them, paying particular attention to the role of financial institutions. From this survey we can gain an insight into the changing structure and magnitude of the American capital markets.[13]

To do so, we must use balance-sheet rather than flow-of-funds data (that is, changes in balance-sheet data). Moreover, to obtain some idea of the structural changes that have taken place over time, we need data going back to the emergence of nationwide capital markets, that is, at least to 1900. Again Raymond Goldsmith, with the help of others, has provided a series of statistics which gives us a satisfactory idea of the way in which the American capital markets developed from 1900 to 1958. For the period prior to World War II there is no comparable set of figures from another source. From 1945 to the present, however, the Federal Reserve has issued both balance-sheet and flow-of-funds data. Although similar to the Goldsmith series from 1945 through 1958, there are differences in the Federal Reserve classification of both

[11]Raymond W. Goldsmith, *The Flow of Capital Funds in the Posswar Economy* (New York: National Bureau of Economic Research, Inc., 1965), p. 30.

[12]*Ibid.*, pp. 149–164.

[13]See the Appendix to this chapter for a matrix showing in greater detail the breakdown of financial assets and the relationships between the sectors issuing and holding them. Also included is a more detailed explanation of the problems involved in constructing such a matrix.

instruments and sectors of the economy. To make the student more aware of the discrepancies, we have used both the Goldsmith and the Federal Reserve data for 1958.

Table 18-1 shows eight financial instruments, each of which accounts for a substantial share of the market or face value of all financial assets. Of the eight, only three — corporate bonds, corporate

TABLE 18-1: MAJOR CAPITAL MARKET INSTRUMENTS, ABSOLUTE MAGNITUDES AND PERCENTAGES, SELECTED YEARS, 1900–1968

Instrument	Absolute Magnitudes (In Billions of Dollars)									
	1900	1912	1922	1929	1939	1945	1958[a]	1958[b]	1965	1968
Total[c]	35.6	82.3	180.3	331.7	248.4	536.7	1,207.7	1,093.8	1,831.3	2,317.7
U S. Treasury Securities	1.2	1.2	23.0	16.3	47.1	275.8	274.4	233.8	272.2	307.9
State and Local Government Securities	2.1	4.4	10.3	16.8	19.8	21.2	61.0	58.7	101.0	123.7
1–4 Family Nonfarm Residential Mortgages	2.7	4.1	8.6	18.9	16.3	18.6	117.8	117.6	213.8	251.2
Corporate Bonds[d]	5.1	14.6	23.6	38.1	32.6	27.5	88.7	80.0	124.5	158.6
Corporate Stock	13.9	37.9	76.1	186.8	100.2	146.6	465.5	418.2	778.2	1,035.8
Bank Loans (n.e.c.)*	3.9	9.0	18.2	20.5	9.8	13.3	53.8	51.5	103.8	136.5
Consumer Credit	1.0	2.9	5.6	8.6	7.8	5.7	46.1	45.2	87.9	113.2
Trade Credit	5.7	8.1	14.9	25.7	14.7	28.0	100.4	88.8	149.9	190.8
	Percentages									
Total[c]	100.0	100.0	100.0	100.0	100.0	100.0	100.0	100.0	100.0	100.0
U.S. Treasury Securities	3.4	1.5	12.8	4.9	19.0	51.4	22.7	21.4	14.8	13.3
State and Local Government Securities	5.6	5.3	5.7	5.1	8.0	3.9	5.1	5.4	5.5	5.3
1–4 Family Nonfarm Residential Mortgages	7.6	5.0	4.8	5.7	6.6	3.5	9.8	10.8	11.7	10.8
Corporate Bonds[d]	14.3	17.7	13.1	11.5	13.1	5.1	7.3	7.3	6.8	6.8
Corporate Stock	39.0	46.1	42.2	56.3	40.3	27.3	38.5	38.2	42.5	44.7
Bank Loans (n.e.c.)*	11.0	10.9	10.1	6.2	3.9	2.5	4.5	4.7	5.7	5.9
Consumer Credit	2.8	3.6	3.1	2.6	3.2	1.1	3.8	4.1	4.8	4.9
Trade Credit	16.0	9.8	8.3	7.7	5.9	5.2	8.3	8.1	8.2	8.2

SOURCES: Raymond W. Goldsmith, Robert E. Lipsey, and Morris Mendelson, *Studies in the National Balance Sheet of the United States* (Princeton, N.J.: Princeton University Press, 1963), vol. II. A study for the National Bureau of Economic Research, Inc. Reprinted by permission of Princeton University Press. For the years 1900, 1912, 1922, 1929, and 1939, see Tables IV-b-13d, 14a, 11c-2, 15a, 17b, 1-a, IV-b-6a, and 7a. For the years 1945 and 1958, see Tables IV-b-13, 14, 11a-2, 15, 16, 17, 9, 6, and 7. For the remaining years, except 1968, the data were taken from Board of Governors of the Federal Reserve System, Division of Research and Statistics, *Flow of Funds Accounts, 1945–1967*. For 1968 the data are courtesy of the Federal Reserve System.

[a]Goldsmith, Lipsey, and Mendelson data.

[b]Federal Reserve data.

[c]Because of rounding, absolute magnitudes may differ slightly from the totals listed in the sources. For the same reason, the sum of the individual percentages may not equal 100.0.

[d]In the Goldsmith data, government corporations fully guaranteed by the United States government are included in corporate bonds for the prewar years and in the Treasury securities for 1945 and 1958. Moreover, the classifications are mixed in other ways. The Federal Reserve data are labeled "corporate and foreign bonds"; the Goldsmith data for 1945 and 1958 are labeled "other bonds and notes," and for earlier years merely "corporate bonds."

*N.e.c. means not elsewhere counted.

stock, and trade credit—are instruments associated completely with business finance.

Bank loans, not elsewhere counted, represent loans made to various sectors of the economy but not included in other classifications. Some of these classifications are part of this table, others are not. For example, bank loans made to finance 1–4 family nonfarm residential mortgages are included in that category. So too is the credit extended on commercial paper. Yet the aggregate amount of commercial paper outstanding is small enough to exclude from our table. The remainder of the bank loans are then liabilities of various sectors of the economy. Thus in the Federal Reserve data for 1965, bank loans (n.e.c.) are $103.9 billion. They are liabilities of the following sectors.[14]

Total Bank Loans (n.e.c.)	$ 103.9
Households	11.8
Farm Business	7.7
Nonfarm Unincorporated Business	16.5
Corporate Business	48.4
Savings and Loan Associations	.5
Finance Companies	11.6
Rest of World	7.5

Most of the total, of course, does represent loans to business firms, both financial and nonfinancial, but loans to the household sector are also included.

In the case of mortgages, we have confined ourselves to 1–4 family nonfarm residential mortgages. There are two reasons for this. First, as the 1958 figures illustrate, the Goldsmith and Federal Reserve data are comparable. In other subclassifications they are not. Second, this group constitutes the bulk of mortgages issued. We again illustrate using the Federal Reserve data for 1965[15] (figures in billions of dollars):

1–4 Family Nonfarm Residential Mortgages	**$213.7**
Incurred by	
Households	$204.0
Nonfarm Unincorporated Business	5.5
Corporate Business	1.9
In Process at Savings and Loan Associations	2.2

[14]Board of Governors of the Federal Reserve System, *op. cit.*, p. 179.

[15]*Ibid.*, p. 176A. Because of rounding, the totals do not necessarily equal the sums of the components.

Other Mortgages	**85.6**
Incurred by	
Households	13.6
Farm Business	21.2
Nonfarm Unincorporated Business	25.4
Corporate Business	25.4
Total	**$299.2**

Thus, while business firms have mortgage debt in their capital structure, theirs is a relatively small portion of the mortgage debt outstanding.

Turning now to the trends in these instruments, we should recognize that 1939 and 1945 are unusual in that the impact of the Great Depression dominated the asset structure in 1939 and World War II the asset structure in 1945. Thus a more relevant comparison would be the periods after World War II with 1929 and earlier years. The years 1939 and 1945 provide a sharp contrast. But in spite of the dominance of war finance in 1945, there is still a discernible upward trend in the relative importance of the federal sector in the capital markets. In fact, the Federal Reserve data probably underestimate the importance of this sector because they exclude (whereas the Goldsmith data include) United States government securities held in government pension funds. In 1958 the gross public debt of the federal government was $283.0 billion.[16] Consequently, the Goldsmith figures are a better approximation of the relative importance of United States government securities in the capital markets.

On the other hand, state and local government securities have displayed remarkable stability over the years. As a percentage of the value of these seven instruments, their relative importance in recent years is similar to what it was early in the century. The category of 1–4 family nonfarm residential mortgages, however, has shown a slight upward trend over the years.

With respect to the major instruments of business finance trade credit in the selected years since 1945 has been as important as it was in 1922 and 1929, although down somewhat in importance from earlier years. In spite of a general upward trend in market value since the end of World War II, common stock has not reached the level of relative importance that it held in 1929. Discrepancies in the coverage of the series aside, we can reach similar conclusions concerning corporate

[16]*The 1967 Economic Report of the President* (Washington: Government Printing Office, 1967), p 279. This includes—as do Goldsmith's figures for 1958—securities of government corporations fully guaranteed by the federal government.

TABLE 18-2:   DISTRIBUTION OF HOLDINGS OF MAJOR CAPITAL MARKET INSTRUMENTS, SELECTED YEARS, 1900–1968

Holder	Absolute Magnitudes (In Billions of Dollars)									
	1900	1912	1922	1929	1939	1945	1958[a]	1958[b]	1965	1968
Total[c]	35.6	82.3	180.3	331.7	248.4	536.7	1207.7	1093.8	1831.3	2317.7
Nonfarm Households	16.6	43.2	90.7	181.3	111.7	197.7	448.5	479.8	797.4	1027.0
Nonfarm Unincorporated Business	2.0	2.4	3.6	4.2	3.8	5.5	16.3	4.8	7.1	8.8
Agriculture[d]	*	*	0.5	*	0.2	4.2	5.2	*	*	*
Nonfinancial Corporations	7.4	15.4	39.1	72.5	38.4	73.3	192.5	114.0	177.2	217.3
State and Local Governments[e]	0.6	1.1	2.4	3.9	3.1	6.8	15.0	31.1	57.5	65.8
Federal Government	*	*	0.2	0.1	6.1	6.8	13.1	6.4	9.5	19.6
Rest of World[f]								15.8	28.8	32.8
Financial Institutions	9.0	20.2	43.8	69.7	85.1	242.4	517.1	441.9	753.8	946.4
	Percentages									
Total[c]	100.0	100.0	100.0	100.0	100.0	100.0	100.0	100.0	100.0	100.0
Nonfarm Households	46.7	52.5	50.3	54.7	45.0	36.8	37.1	43.9	43.5	44.3
Nonfarm Unincorporated Business	5.6	2.9	2.0	1.3	1.5	1.0	1.3	0.4	0.4	0.4
Agriculture[d]	*	*	0.3	*	*	0.8	0.4	*	*	*
Nonfinancial Corporations	20.8	18.8	21.7	21.9	15.5	13.7	15.9	10.4	9.7	9.4
State and Local Governments[e]	1.7	1.3	1.3	1.2	1.2	1.3	1.2	2.8	3.1	2.8
Federal Government	*	*	0.1	*	1.6	1.3	1.1	0.6	0.5	0.8
Rest of World[f]								1.4	1.7	1.4
Financial Institutions	25.3	24.6	24.2	21.0	34.3	45.2	42.8	40.3	41.1	40.8

SOURCES : Same as for Table 18-1.   Reprinted by permission of Princeton University Press.
[a]See Table 18-1, footnote a.
[b]See Table 18-1, footnote b.
[c]See Table 18-1, footnote c.
[d]Represents United States government securities held in the agricultural sector. Federal Reserve data do not make this distinction.
[e]In the Federal Reserve data assets of state and local governments include state and local retirement funds.
[f]As presented, the Goldsmith data do not include foreign holdings of the major instruments constituting the United States capital markets.
Less than $0.05 billion or less than 0.05 percent.

bonds.   Bank loans, not elsewhere counted, seem to have declined over the years.

When compared with the 1920s and earlier years, consumer loans are the only other series showing an increase.   The data therefore lead us to the conclusion that the instruments which are liabilities of the sectors representing private enterprise have become subordinate in importance to instruments which are liabilities of consumers and of the federal government, particularly the latter.

More revealing than changes in the relative importance of the major capital market instruments is the trend in their distribution among various sectors of the economy.   From Table 18-2 it is apparent that there is a downward trend in the percentage of capital market

TABLE 18-3:   HOLDINGS OF MAJOR CAPITAL MARKET INSTRUMENTS BY HOUSEHOLDS,[a] SELECTED YEARS, 1900–1968

Security	Absolute Magnitudes (In Billions of Dollars)									
	1900	1912	1922	1929	1939	1945	1958[b]	1958[c]	1965	1968
Total[d]	16.6	43.2	90.2	181.3	111.7	197.7	448.5	479.8	797.4	1027.0
U S. Treasury Securities	0.6	0.4	10.8	5.1	9.1	59.7	58.6	65.3	77.6	92.2
State and Local Government Securities	0.5	1.5	5.0	7.6	8.3	11.9	24.8	23.8	38.4	37.8
1–4 Family Nonfarm Residential Mortgages	1.5	1.7	3.5	6.2	4.3	5.2	11.0	11.5	10.3	13.1
Corporate Bonds	3.3	9.5	15.9	24.1	16.8	9.3	11.1	6.9	4.6	10.7
Corporate Stock	10.7	30.1	55.5	138.3	73.2	111.6	343.0	372.3	666.5	873.2
	Percent of Total Holdings by Household									
Total[d]	100.0	100.0	100.0	100.0	100.0	100.0	100.0	100.0	100.0	100.0
U.S. Treasury Securities	3.6	0.9	11.9	2.8	9.0	30.2	13.1	13.6	9.7	9.0
State and Local Government Securities	3.0	3.5	5.5	4.2	7.4	6.0	5.5	5.0	4.8	3.7
1–4 Family Nonfarm Residential Mortgages	9.0	3.9	3.9	3.4	3.8	2.6	2.5	2.4	1.3	1.3
Corporate Bonds	19.8	22.0	17.5	13.3	15.0	4.7	2.5	1.4	0.6	1.0
Corporate Stock	64.5	69.7	61.2	76.3	65.5	56.4	76.5	77.6	83.6	85.0

SOURCES : Same as for Table 18-1.   Reprinted by permission of Princeton University Press.
[a]Households exclude agriculture.   See Table 18-2, footnote d.
[b]See Table 18-1, footnote a.
[c]See Table 18-1, footnote b.
[d]See Table 18-1, footnote c.

instruments held by nonfinancial corporations. Only financial institutions exhibit a definite percentage rise in their holdings of these instruments.

From our earlier analysis, this is precisely what we would expect from developing capital markets. To the extent that nonfinancial corporations and many unincorporated businesses hold financial assets, they do so, as we have seen, to preserve their liquidity. Financial institutions specialize in these assets. They are intermediaries between the ultimate source of savings (households) and the final users of funds (government and nonfinancial private enterprises).[17] To the extent that they can perform more efficiently both the functions of transferring savings to the investing sector and the liquidity function, financial institutions will continue to grow in importance.

If we look more closely at both households and nonfinancial corporations (see Tables 18-3 and 18-4, respectively), we gain further insight

[17]To the extent that government and nonfinancial private enterprise save (that is, government runs budget surpluses, and private enterprise retains profits), they merely avoid the capital markets and perhaps financial intermediaries. The income ultimately accrues to the household sector.

TABLE 18-4: HOLDINGS OF MAJOR CAPITAL MARKET INSTRUMENTS BY NONFINANCIAL CORPORATIONS, SELECTED YEARS, 1900–1968

Security	Absolute Magnitudes (In Billions of Dollars)									
	1900	1912	1922	1929	1939	1945	1958[a]	1958[b]	1965	1968
Total[c]	7.4	15.4	39.1	72.5	38.4	73.3	192.5	114.0	177.2	217.3
U S. Treasury Securities	*	*	3.6	3.2	1.8	20.7	17.6	18.4	16.5	14.5
State and Local Government Securities	0.1	0.1	0.3	0.6	0.4	0.3	1.6	2.0	3.6	4.0
Corporate Bonds	*	*	*	0.5	0.1	0.2	2.7			
Corporate Stock	2.8	7.1	19.2	42.3	22.0	27.7	79.0			
Consumer Credit	0.6	2.0	4.0	4.0	3.0	1.7	8.2	8.1	12.9	17.9
Trade Credit	3.9	6.2	12.0	21.9	11.1	22.7	83.4	85.5	144.2	180.9
	Percent of Total Holdings by Nonfinancial Corporations									
Total[c]	100.0	100.0	100.0	100.0	100.0	100.0	100.0	100.0	100.0	100.0
U.S. Treasury Securities	*	*	9.2	4.4	4.7	28.2	9.1	16.1	9.3	6.7
State and Local Government Securities	1.4	0.6	0.8	0.8	1.0	0.4	0.8	1.8	2.0	1.8
Corporate Bonds	*	*	*	0.7	0.3	0.3	1.4			
Corporate Stock	37.8	46.1	49.1	58.3	57.3	37.8	41.0			
Consumer Credit	8.1	13.0	10.2	5.5	7.8	2.3	4.3	7.1	7.3	8.2
Trade Credit	52.7	40.3	30.7	30.2	28.9	31.0	43.3	75.0	81.4	83.2

SOURCES: Same as for Table 18-1.   Reprinted by permission of Princeton University Press.
[a]See Table 18-1, footnote a.
[b]See Table 18-1, footnote b.
[c]See Table 18-1, footnote c.
*Less than $0.05 billion, or less than 0.05 percent.

into the change in their relative roles in the capital markets. In terms of the total value of the portfolio of households, common stock has always figured prominently But because of the post-World War II rise in the market value of this security, corporate stock has surpassed even the 1929 high of 76.3 percent. In fact, of the eight capital market instruments chosen other than common stock, only government securities, particularly those of the federal government, can be said to play an important role in the portfolio of households.

Turning to nonfinancial corporations, the long-term trend is more difficult to portray. This is because the corporate stock and bond holdings of this sector are excluded from the Federal Reserve data. Exclusion can be justified on the grounds that nonfinancial corporations purchase stock of similar concerns in order to exert control over their operations. If the subsidiary, although technically not merged, is truly an integral part of the parent company, statistically their assets can be combined, the stock eliminated, and the debt of the subsidiary included with that of the parent. The combined concern is then treated as a single unit. If we eliminate stocks and bonds from the Goldsmith data, we can restructure the series as in the accompanying table.

Security	Absolute Magnitudes (In Billions of Dollars)									
	1900	1912	1922	1929	1939	1945	1958	1958	1965	1968
Total	4.6	8.3	19.9	29.7	16.3	45.4	110.8	114.0	177.2	217.3
U.S. Treasury Securities	*	*	3.6	3.2	1.8	20.7	17.6	18.4	16.5	14.5
State and Local Government Securities	0.1	0.1	0.3	0.6	0.4	0.3	1.6	2.0	3.6	4.0
Consumer Credit	0.6	2.0	4.0	4.0	3.0	1.7	8.2	8.1	12.9	17.9
Trade Credit	3.9	6.2	12.0	21.9	11.1	22.7	83.4	85.5	144.2	180.9
	Percent of Total Holdings by Nonfinancial Corporations									
Total	100.0	100.0	100.0	100.0	100.0	100.0	100.0	100.0	100.0	100.0
U.S. Treasury Securities	*	*	18.1	10.8	11.0	45.6	15.9	16.1	9.3	6.7
State and Local Government Securities	2.2	1.2	1.5	2.0	2.5	0.7	1.4	1.8	2.0	1.8
Consumer Credit	13.0	24.1	20.1	13.5	18.4	3.7	7.4	7.1	7.3	8.2
Trade Credit	84.8	74.7	60.3	73.7	68.1	50.0	75.3	75.0	81.4	83.2

* Less than 0.05 billion, or less than 0.05 percent.

Among the remaining instruments, the role of nonfinancial corporations seems to have declined perceptibly in the extension of consumer loans. This sector's major contribution to the capital markets continues to be, as we might expect, the extension of trade credit. Since most of the credit extended by one nonfinancial corporation is a liability of another, the bulk of the transactions in trade credit tends to take place within rather than between sectors.

State and local government securities are a minor part of the portfolios of nonfinancial corporations. Since there are larger amounts of shorter maturities and a wider secondary market in U.S. Treasury securities, the latter are more liquid and therefore, as we have seen, play a more important role in the financial assets of this sector. The primary advantage in holding securities of state and local governments is that the interest earned is tax-exempt.

Apart from the abnormal proportions of government debt resulting from war finance, there appears to have been somewhat less reliance on Treasury securities in recent years than in the 1920s. Part of the explanation for the downward trend, as we noted in an earlier chapter, is the rise in the importance of commercial time deposits, particularly negotiable CDs. The upward trend in interest rates since the end of World War II had by 1958 reached the point where it became profitable for nonfinancial corporations to consider the yield on assets held

TABLE 18-5: HOLDINGS OF MAJOR CAPITAL MARKET INSTRUMENTS BY FINANCIAL INSTITUTIONS, SELECTED YEARS, 1900–1968

Security	**Absolute Magnitudes** (In Billions of Dollars)									
	1900	1912	1922	1929	1939	1945	1958[a]	1958[b]	1965	1968
Total[c]	9.0	20.2	43.8	69.7	85.1	242.4	517.1	441.9	753.8	946.4
U.S. Treasury Securities	0.6	0.8	7.7	7.6	33.6	181.7	176.1	126.2	140.4	162.1
State and Local Government Securities	0.9	1.7	2.8	5.0	8.0	7.0	31.2	26.3	54.2	77.4
1–4 Family Nonfarm Residential Mortgages	1.2	2.4	5.1	12.7	9.8	12.5	101.4	100.9	193.6	222.6
Corporate Bonds	1.8	5.1	7.7	13.5	14.8	17.7	74.2	65.5	94.2	114.7
Corporate Stock	0.4	0.7	1.4	6.2	4.4	7.3	43.5	37.6	97.1	143.1
Bank Loans (n.e.c.)[†]	3.9	9.0	18.2	20.5	9.8	13.3	53.8	51.5	103.8	136.5
Consumer Credit	0.2	0.5	0.9	3.3	3.7	2.5	33.2	32.3	67.9	86.5
Trade Credit	*	*	*	0.9	1.0	0.4	3.7	1.6	2.6	3.5
	Percent of Total Holdings by Financial Institutions									
Total[c]	100.0	100.0	100.0	100.0	100.0	100.0	100.0	100.0	100.0	100.0
U.S. Treasury Securities	6.7	4.0	17.6	10.9	39.5	75.0	34.0	28.6	18.6	17.1
State and Local Government Securities	10.0	8.4	6.4	7.2	9.4	2.9	6.0	6.0	7.2	8.2
1–4 Family Nonfarm Residential Mortgages	13.3	11.9	11.6	18.2	11.5	5.2	19.6	22.8	25.7	23.5
Corporate Bonds	20.0	25.2	17.6	19.4	17.4	7.3	14.4	14.8	12.5	12.1
Corporate Stock	4.4	3.5	3.2	8.9	5.2	3.0	8.4	8.5	12.9	15.1
Bank Loans (n.e.c.)[†]	43.3	44.6	41.6	29.4	11.5	5.5	10.4	11.7	13.8	14.4
Consumer Credit	2.2	2.5	2.1	4.7	4.3	1.0	6.4	7.3	9.0	9.1
Trade Credit	*	*	*	1.3	1.2	0.2	0.7	0.4	0.3	0.4

SOURCES: Same as for Table 18-1.   Reprinted by permission of Princeton University Press.
[a]See Table 18-1, footnote a.
[b]See Table 18-1, footnote b.
[c]See Table 18-1, footnote c.
*Less than $0.05 billion, or less than 0.05 percent.
[†]N.e.c. means not elsewhere counted.

primarily for liquidity purposes.   A return of 2 percent on government securities as against no interest on demand deposits may not be worth the costs involved in managing a portfolio, while a 5 percent return might.   We pointed out earlier that commercial banks, feeling the strain of dwindling demand deposits, instituted a form of time deposit or negotiable CD to compete with other interest-bearing instruments.[18] An indeterminable proportion of funds of nonfinancial corporations which might have gone from demand deposits into Treasury securities were instead channeled into certificates of deposit of commercial banks.   As a result, nonfinancial corporations in recent years have become less of a participant in the major capital market instruments.

[18]Warren A. Law and M. Colyer Crum, "New Trends in Finance, The Negotiable C.D.," *Harvard Business Review* vol. 41, no. 1 (January-February, 1963), pp. 115–126.

TABLE 18-6: DISTRIBUTION OF HOLDINGS OF MAJOR CAPITAL MARKET INSTRUMENTS AMONG SPECIFIC FINANCIAL INSTITUTIONS, SELECTED YEARS, 1900–1968

	Absolute Magnitudes (In Billions of Dollars)									
	1900	**1912**	**1922**	**1929**	**1939**	**1945**	**1958**[a]	**1958**[b]	**1965**	**1968**
Total[c]	9.0	20.2	43.8	69.7	85.1	242.4	517.1	441.9	753.8	946.4
Commercial Banks	5.6	13.0	28.5	35.4	35.7	115.2	174.2	172.8	276.0	355.8
Life Insurance Companies	0.9	2.2	4.1	7.6	17.6	35.9	80.8	80.8	108.7	120.8
Non-life Insurance Companies	0.2	0.8	2.0	4.4	4.5	8.1	25.5	23.2	38.6	46.1
Savings Banks and Savings and Loan Associations	1.9	3.4	6.7	12.0	11.1	21.4	76.1	76.7	145.7	172.5
Investment Companies	*	*	0.1	2.3	1.4	3.4	20.0	13.0	34.3	50.6
Pension Funds	*	*	0.1	0.5	1.1	2.6	26.4	27.7	69.2	92.9
Other[d]	0.4	0.8	2.3	7.5	13.8	55.8	114.1	47.7	81.3	107.7
	Percent of Total Holdings by Financial Institutions									
Total[c]	100.0	100.0	100.0	100.0	100.0	100.0	100.0	100.0	100.0	100.0
Commercial Banks	62.2	64.4	65.1	50.8	42.0	47.5	33.7	39.1	36.6	37.6
Life Insurance Companies	10.0	10.9	9.4	10.9	20.7	14.8	15.6	18.3	14.4	12.8
Non-life Insurance Companies	2.2	4.0	4.6	6.3	5.3	3.3	4.9	5.3	5.1	4.9
Savings Banks and Savings and Loan Associations	21.1	16.8	15.3	17.2	13.0	8.8	14.7	17.4	19.3	18.2
Investment Companies	*	*	0.2	3.3	1.6	1.4	3.9	2.9	4.6	5.3
Pension Funds	*	*	0.2	0.7	1.2	1.1	5.1	6.3	9.2	9.8
Other[d]	4.4	4.0	5.3	10.8	16.2	23.0	22.1	10.8	10.8	11.4

SOURCES: Same as for Table 18-1. Reprinted by permission of Princeton University Press.
[a]See Table 18-1, footnote a.
[b]See Table 18-1, footnote b.
[c]See Table 18-1, footnote c.
[d]In the Goldsmith data, this category includes the Federal Reserve banks, government insurance and pension plans, credit unions, finance companies, and miscellaneous institutions. There are similar categories in the Federal Reserve data except that government insurance and pension plans are excluded. Beginning with the 1968 data the Federal Reserve separated state and local government retirement funds from other assets of state and local governments. This refinement in the data arrived too late for inclusion in the tables employed in this volume.
*Less than $0.05 billion, or less than 0.05 percent.

Let us turn now to the expanding role of financial institutions. In spite of differences between Goldsmith and the Federal Reserve Board in the scope and coverage of their respective data as given in Tables 18-5 and 18-6, we can see general trends in the participation of financial institutions in major capital market instruments. We can also observe changes in the role of specific institutions as intermediaries.

As U.S. Treasury securities have grown in importance, it has been financial institutions which have accommodated the increase. However, in the area of state and local government securities, their role appears similar to what it was in the 1920s. This finding is consistent with the relative stability in the importance of these instruments in the capital markets.

The category of 1–4 family nonfarm residential mortgages is at least as important today in the portfolios of financial institutions as it was in 1929, and probably it is more so.   Corporate bonds, however, appear to be less significant.   This may be due in part to the greater variations in data coverage in this than in other areas.   But it is also the result of the decline in the importance of corporate bonds in the capital markets.

Because of the post-World War II rise in the stock market, the holdings of financial institutions seem to have surpassed their 1929 levels.   Yet, as we shall see when probing deeper into the portfolios of particular intermediaries, their role in this area is limited although potentially expandable.

As we saw in Table 18-1, bank loans, not elsewhere counted, have declined in importance among major capital market instruments.   This could be due to the decrease in the role of commercial banks, but it might also be the result of an increase in bank participation in other capital market instruments, some of which have been excluded from the table.   We shall subsequently return to this point.

The decrease in consumer credit apparent in the data on nonfinancial corporations seems largely to have been accounted for by a rise in the importance of this instrument in the portfolios of intermediaries. At the same time, the role of financial institutions in extending trade credit, always small, appears to have fallen still further.

In terms of the changing importance of financial institutions, the commercial banking system is still the single most important intermediary, although its relative position has declined over the years. Other institutions appear to have sustained a more rapid growth.   Part of this is because commercial banks have ceased to be important holders of corporate securities.   While corporate stock has never been an important part of the portfolios of commercial banks, it was significant enough in the 1920s to cause people in influential quarters to question— in light of the bank failures of the 1930s—the wisdom of carrying any corporate stock.   As a result, not only were commercial banks forbidden to underwrite corporate stocks—that is, the investment banking and commercial banking functions were separated—but the holdings of corporate stocks by commercial banks was virtually prohibited.

Changes in commercial bank holdings of major capital market instruments[19] are illustrated in Table 18-7.   While the Federal Reserve data exclude commercial bank holdings of common stock, it is apparent

[19]For a brief summary of the changes in the portfolios of commercial banks, see American Bankers Association, *The Commercial Banking Industry* (Englewood Cliffs, N.J.: Prentice-Hall, Inc., 1962), pp. 3–11.   This monograph was prepared for the Commission on Money and Credit.

TABLE 18-7:   HOLDINGS OF MAJOR CAPITAL MARKET INSTRUMENTS BY COMMERCIAL BANKS, SELECTED YEARS, 1900–1968

Security	1900	1912	1922	1929	1939	1945	1958[a]	1958[b]	1965	1968
	Absolute Magnitudes (In Billions of Dollars)									
Total[c]	5.6	13.0	28.5	35.4	35.7	115.2	174.2	172.8	276.0	355.8
U.S. Government Securities	0.5	0.8	4.6	4.7	16.3	90.6	66.2	70.2	66.9	75.1
State and Local Government Securities	0.2	0.5	1.1	2.1	3.5	4.0	16.5	16.5	38.6	59.1
1–4 Family Nonfarm Residential Mortgages	0.2	0.4	0.7	2.2	2.1	2.9	17.5	17.4	30.1	38.3
Corporate Bonds	0.7	2.0	3.4	4.7	3.4	3.0	3.5	1.3	0.8	1.9
Corporate Stock	0.1	0.3	0.5	1.2	0.6	0.2	0.2			
Bank Loans (n.e.c.)†	3.9	9.0	18.2	20.5	9.8	13.0	53.7	51.5	103.8	136.5
Consumer Credit[d]						1.5	16.6	16.0	35.8	44.9
	Percent of Total Holdings by Commercial Banks									
Total[c]	100.0	100.0	100.0	100.0	100.0	100.0	100.0	100.0	100.0	100.0
U.S. Government Securities	8.9	6.2	16.1	13.3	45.7	78.6	38.0	40.6	24.2	21.1
State and Local Government Securities	3.6	3.8	3.9	5.9	9.8	3.5	9.5	9.5	14.0	16.6
1–4 Family Nonfarm Residential Mortgages	3.6	3.1	2.5	6.2	5.9	2.5	10.0	10.1	10.9	10.8
Corporate Bonds	12.5	15.4	11.9	13.3	9.5	2.6	2.0	0.8	0.3	0.5
Corporate Stock	1.8	2.3	1.8	3.4	1.7	0.2	0.1			
Bank Loans (n.e.c.)†	69.6	69.2	63.9	57.9	27.5	11.3	30.8	29.8	37.6	38.4
Consumer Credit[d]						1.3	9.5	9.2	13.0	12.6

SOURCES: Same as for Table 18-1.   Reprinted by permission of Princeton University Press.
[a]See Table 18-1, footnote a.
[b]See Table 18-1, footnote b.
[c]See Table 18-1, footnote c.
[d]Data for 1900, 1912, 1922, 1929, and 1939 are not included in the source employed.
†N.e.c. means not elsewhere counted.

from the Goldsmith data that, because of the institutional constraints mentioned, the peak reached by common stock in 1929 has fallen to where this instrument is a negligible portion of this subsector's portfolio.

More striking, perhaps, is the decline in the role of corporate bonds. This can be explained in terms of the income tax laws. Except for special items such as deductible allocations to bad-debt reserves, commercial banks are taxed like any other nonfinancial corporation, that is, at 48 percent of income in excess of $25,000.[20] Since interest on corporate bonds is taxable income, whereas interest on state and local obligations is not, we can see why the former instruments have declined and the latter have risen in their proportion of the total value of the portfolios of commercial banks.

[20]E. Gordon Keith, "The Impact of Federal Taxation on the Flow of Personal Savings through Investment Intermediaries," in Commission on Money and Credit, *Private Financial Institutions* (Englewood Cliffs, N.J.: Prentice-Hall, Inc., 1963), pp. 383–460.

Interest on federal government securities is also fully taxable, but for commercial banks these instruments play a particular role. They act as a secondary reserve which can be easily liquidated or, if necessary, used as collateral for credit from the Federal Reserve to accomodate a temporary increase in consumer or commercial demand for money.

Commercial banks have in recent years increased their commitments on 1–4 family nonfarm residential mortgages. This is the result of the rise in the proportion of time deposits to total deposits. Since these bank liabilities, whether certificates of deposit or passbook savings accounts, are interest-bearing instruments, commercial banks must find outlets yielding a greater return on these funds than on noninterest-bearing demand deposits. Mortgages are one such outlet. Even more profitable are consumer loans. Unlike interest on mortgages, payments on consumer loans do not, as we have seen, decline with reductions in principal. Even if a bank pays 5 percent simple interest for funds, it will still earn several percentage points more than that before it pays expenses and taxes on deposits invested in consumer loans.

Suppose that we view commercial banks as attempting (within their owners' risk constraints) to maximize the long-run market value of their common stock, rather than emphasize, as is ordinarily done in economic analysis, the money-creating function they perform. We can then go a long way toward explaining the changes in the composition of the portfolio of this subsector. As we have presented them, the Goldsmith data do not show consumer credit prior to 1939. The growth in the importance of consumer credit in commercial banks' portfolios, however, is a post-World War II phenomenon resulting from an attempt to seek a more profitable outlet for funds.

Similarly, the liabilities which commercial banks market, largely demand and time deposits, are substitutes for cash and other interest-bearing securities. To the extent that other sectors choose to hold these instruments rather than bank liabilities, the commercial banking system cannot expand its assets. Consequently, while bank loans, not elsewhere counted, may have diminished in importance because of increases in instruments not included in Table 18-7, there is also the distinct possibility that they have lost ground to other financial intermediaries. If so, this is in part the result of institutional constraints, such as differential tax treatment, and restrictions placed on the composition of commercial bank portfolios.[21] Our limited data cannot give us a definitive answer to this question. But since Table 18-7 covers the major capital market instruments, and since there is no evidence of increases

---

[21]We can also argue that because of their reserve requirements, commercial banks have not been allowed to maximize the market value of their owners' equity. For a more complete discussion of this point, see Moore, *op. cit.*, pp. 153–183.

TABLE 18-8:   HOLDINGS OF MAJOR CAPITAL MARKET INSTRUMENTS BY LIFE INSURANCE COMPANIES, SELECTED YEARS, 1900–1968

Security	1900	1912	1922	1929	1939	1945	1958[a]	1958[b]	1965	1968
Absolute Magnitudes (In Billions of Dollars)										
Total[c]	0.9	2.2	4.1	7.6	17.6	35.9	80.8	80.8	108.7	120.8
U.S. Government Securities	*	*	0.9	0.3	5.4˙	20.6	7.2	7.3	5.1	4.5
State and Local Government Securities	0.1	0.2	0.4	0.6	1.8	0.7	2.7	2.7	3.5	3.0
1–4 Family Nonfarm Residential Mortgages	0.2	0.3	0.5	1.6	1.5	2.3	22.4	22.4	29.9	29.0
Corporate Bonds	0.5	1.6	2.2	4.7	8.3	11.3	44.4	44.3	61.1	71.1
Corporate Stock	0.1	0.1	0.1	0.4	0.6	1.0	4.1	4.1	9.1	13.2
Percent of Total Holdings by Life Insurance Companies										
Total[c]	100.0	100.0	100.0	100.0	100.0	100.0	100.0	100.0	100.0	100.0
U.S. Government Securities	*	*	22.0	4.0	30.7	57.4	8.9	9.0	4.7	3.7
State and Local Government Securities	11.1	9.1	9.8	7.9	10.2	1.9	3.3	3.3	3.2	2.5
1–4 Family Nonfarm Residential Mortgages	22.2	13.6	12.2	21.1	8.5	6.4	27.7	27.7	27.5	24.0
Corporate Bonds	55.5	72.7	53.7	61.8	47.2	31.5	55.0	55.0	56.2	58.9
Corporate Stock	11.1	4.5	2.4	5.3	3.4	2.8	5.1	5.1	8.4	10.9

SOURCES: Same as for Table 18-1.   Reprinted by permission of Princeton University Press.
[a]See Table 18-1, footnote a.
[b]See Table 18-1, footnote b.
[c]See Table 18-1, footnote c.
*Less than $0.05 billion, or less than 0.05 percent.

in areas not included in the table, we can infer that there has been a decline in direct participation by commercial banks. Nevertheless, given the nature of commercial bank liabilities, there is sufficient reason for concluding that these banks will continue to play a major role among financial intermediaries. What they do not undertake directly they will perform indirectly. Short-term loans to finance the trade credit of nonfinancial corporations and the consumer loans of finance companies are prime examples of their indirect participation.

While the role of commercial banks appears to have declined in importance, the role of life insurance companies has expanded. From Table 18-8 it is evident that this subsector is an important purchaser of corporate bonds and 1–4 family nonfarm residential mortgages. In fact, they dominate the corporate bond market, but, as we see in Table 18-9, they share the residential mortgage market with savings and loan associations and mutual savings banks.[22]

---

[22]For a more detailed discussion of these institutions, see Life Insurance Association of America, *Life Insurance Companies as Financial Institutions* (Englewood Cliffs, N.J.: Prentice-Hall, Inc., 1962); National Association of Mutual Savings Banks, *Mutual Savings*

TABLE 18-9: DISTRIBUTION OF MAJOR CAPITAL MARKET INSTRUMENTS AMONG SAVINGS BANKS AND SAVINGS AND LOAN ASSOCIATIONS, SELECTED YEARS, 1900–1968

Security	Absolute Magnitudes (In Billions of Dollars)									
	1900	1912	1922	1929	1939	1945	1958[a]	1958[b]	1965	1968
Total[c]	1.9	3.4	6.7	12.0	11.1	21.4	76.1	76.7	145.7	172.5
U.S. Government Securities	0.1	*	1.1	0.5	3.2	13.1	11.1	11.8	14.4	16.2
State and Local Government Securities	0.6	0.8	0.7	0.9	0.6	0.1	0.7	0.7	0.3	0.2
1–4 Family Nonfarm Residential Mortgages	0.8	1.6	3.7	8.5	5.8	7.1	58.5	58.5	124.9	145.3
Corporate Bonds	0.4	1.0	1.2	2.0	1.4	1.0	4.1	3.8	2.9	6.6
Corporate Stock	*	*	*	0.1	0.1	0.1	0.9	0.9	1.4	1.9
Consumer Credit[d]						*	0.8	1.0	1.8	2.3
Percent of Total Holdings by Savings Banks and Savings and Loan Associations										
Total[c]	100.0	100.0	100.0	100.0	100.0	100.0	100.0	100.0	100.0	100.0
U.S. Government Securities	5.3	*	16.4	4.2	28.8	61.2	14.6	15.4	9.9	9.4
State and Local Government Securities	31.6	23.5	10.4	7.5	5.4	0.5	0.9	0.9	0.2	0.1
1–4 Family Nonfarm Residential Mortgages	42.1	47.1	55.2	70.8	52.3	33.2	76.9	76.3	85.7	84.2
Corporate Bonds	21.1	29.4	17.9	16.7	12.6	4.7	5.4	5.0	2.0	3.8
Corporate Stock	*	*	*	0.8	0.9	0.5	1.2	1.2	1.0	1.1
Consumer Credit[d]						*	1.1	1.3	1.2	1.3

SOURCES: Same as for Table 18-1.   Reprinted by permission of Princeton University Press.
[a]See Table 18-1, footnote a.
[b]See Table 18-1, footnote b.
[c]See Table 18-1, footnote c.
[d]Data for 1900, 1912, 1922, 1929, and 1939 are not included in the source employed.
*Less than $0.05 billion, or less than 0.05 percent.

Life insurance companies are uniquely suited to accommodate long-term debt of households and nonfinancial corporations. Regardless of the conditions of payment, their liabilities are essentially long-term annuities[23] whose maturity is accelerated only by death of the policy-holder. Since the amount of death benefits for any given age group is subject to the law of large numbers, uncertainty as to the value of the claims filed is reduced to a probability distribution. Life insurance companies can arrange their investment portfolios so as to match the

---

Banking (Englewood Cliffs, N.J.: Prentice-Hall, Inc., 1962); Leon T. Kendall, *The Savings and Loan Business* (Englewood Cliffs, N.J.: Prentice-Hall, Inc., 1962). All volumes were prepared for the Commission on Money and Credit. For a discussion of the residential mortgage markets, see Saul B. Klaman, *The Postwar Residential Mortgage Market* (Princeton, N.J.: Princeton University Press, 1961). A study by the National Bureau of Economic Research, Inc.

[23]Some of which, such as ordinary term insurance, have zero value when the policy terminates.

expected maturity of their claims. Moreover, life insurance companies have their own income tax law, the effect of which is to lower their tax payments sufficiently to deter them from investing large sums in the issues of state and local governments. At the same time, the nature of a standard life insurance contract, that is, the fact that it is long-term and payable in a fixed sum, precludes investing substantial amounts of the policyholders' premiums in corporate stock, particularly common stock. As a result, state laws are very restrictive of the amount of common stock permitted in the portfolios of life insurance companies.[24] These restrictions are reflected in the data in Table 18-8.

Mortgage debt is even more important in the portfolios of savings and loan associations and mutual savings banks than in the portfolios of life insurance companies. Indeed, savings and loan associations are restricted almost solely to mortgages and United States government securities, although in recent years they have made modest amounts of consumer loans classified primarily as home improvement loans. Mutual savings banks, however, have a somewhat broader portfolio base which permits them to carry corporate bonds and limited amounts of corporate stock.

The greater portfolio restrictions on savings and loan associations stem from the fact that their primary purpose was "to secure funds to support home financing and home ownership in this nation."[25] On the other hand, mutual savings banks were established to promote thrift, particularly among immigrants and other small savers whose accounts in the nineteenth and early twentieth centuries were not welcomed by commercial banks.[26] Unlike commercial banks, savings and loan associations are owned mostly by their depositors, not by stockholders, while mutual savings banks by definition are not stock-issuing institutions.[27] Although they come under the corporate income tax laws, the earnings of both savings and loan associations and mutual

---

[24]For a comparison of the restrictions on the portfolios of financial institutions, see Thomas G. Gies, Thomas Mayer, and Edward C. Ettin, "Portfolio Regulations and Policies of Financial Intermediaries," in Commission on Money and Credit, *Private Financial Institutions, op. cit.*, pp. 157–263. There are some interesting ways of getting around this restriction. As we saw in an earlier chapter, nonfinancial corporations may issue and insurance companies may purchase debt, with both a fixed interest rate and contingent compensation—often warrants to purchase common stock at a specific price.

[25]Kendall, *op. cit.*, p. 2.

[26]Stanley N. Brown, "The Compound Woes of the Savings Banks," *Fortune*, vol. 75, no. 3 (March, 1967), pp. 124–126, 234 ff.

[27]Kendall, *op. cit.*, p. 11. Mutual savings banks like to stress the fact that their depositors, like those of commercial banks, are debtors whereas the depositors of savings and loan associations are owners. While it is not generally the practice, any institution can temporarily delay payment on its savings accounts. Beyond a certain period, however, perhaps 30 days, if the depositor is not fully compensated, the savings or commercial

savings banks are for the most part either paid out as interest to depositors or allocated to reserves against portfolio losses.   Since all interest
and a large part of allocations to bad-debt reserves are deductible, these
institutions pay lower taxes than commercial banks and far less than nonfinancial corporations.[28]   Consequently, although not restricted from
doing so, mutual savings banks have little incentive to hold the obligations of state and local governments.   But tax laws cannot explain the
decline in the percentage of corporate bonds in the portfolios of mutual
savings banks.   Part of the explanation apparently lies in the fact that
most of these institutions are not large enough to justify the costs of
specialized security investment officers.[29]   Like savings and loan associations that are required to do so, mutual savings banks have tended to
emphasize mortgages whose yields are generally higher than those on
corporate bonds.   For both institutions, U.S. Treasury securities provide a liquid medium through which to invest reserves for portfolio
losses.

Commercial banks, life insurance companies, savings and loan
associations, and mutual savings banks have traditionally held the bulk
of the assets of financial intermediaries.   Because of concern for the
safety of the principal or premium of the depositors or policyholders,
regulations have either restricted or seriously curtailed investments by
these institutions in corporate stock.   As a result of these restrictions,
households, not financial intermediaries, now directly finance most of
the external equity capital of nonfinancial corporations.

In fact, until recent years, only one group of financial institutions
of some consequence had appreciable investments in corporate stock.
This group is made up of non-life insurance companies, the bulk of
them being fire and casualty underwriters.   Unlike those of life insurance companies, the contracts of this group seldom run in excess of

---

bank is ordinarily "subject to seizure by the state banking supervisor."   National Association of Mutual Savings Banks, *op. cit.*, p. 63.

Presumably the assets are then liquidated and the depositors paid in full.   If funds
are insufficient, the difference is made up through deposit insurance limited to a specified
maximum, now $15,000.   Issuing institutions do not ordinarily accept passbook accounts
in excess of the insured maximum.   Although this type of insurance is available to all
depositors with respect to savings and loan associations, repayment to individual savers
may be delayed "without incurring default through partial rotating payments.   Repayment in full to the saver may be delayed indefinitely without the institution being put into
default." *Ibid.*

[28]Keith, *op. cit.*, pp. 401–412.

[29]National Association of Mutual Savings Banks, *op. cit.*, p. 177.   We should note,
however, that with interest rates reaching or exceeding historical peaks in the very tight
money markets in the late 1960s, mutual savings banks, partly attracted by narrowing
spreads between mortgages and corporate bonds," acquired more corporate bonds in
1967 than in all previous years since World War II."   See "Recent Capital Market Developments," *Federal Reserve Bulletin*, May, 1968, p. 403.

TABLE 18-10:　DISTRIBUTION OF MAJOR CAPITAL MARKET INSTRUMENTS AMONG NON-LIFE[a] INSURANCE COMPANIES, SELECTED YEARS, 1900–1968

Security	1900	1912	1922	1929	1939	1945	1958[b]	1958[c]	1965	1968
	Absolute Magnitudes (In Billions of Dollars)									
Total[d]	0.2	0.8	2.0	4.4	4.5	8.1	25.5	23.2	38.6	46.1
U.S. Government Securities	*	*	0.5	0.5	1.3	3.7	6.2	5.5	6.0	4.7
State and Local Government Securities	*	0.2	0.5	0.9	0.8	0.6	6.6	6.2	11.3	14.4
1–4 Family Nonfarm Residential Mortgages	*	*	*	0.1	0.1	*	*	*	*	*
Corporate Bonds	0.1	0.4	0.6	1.4	0.8	1.0	2.7	1.5	3.4	5.4
Corporate Stock	0.1	0.2	0.4	1.5	1.5	2.5	8.4	8.4	15.3	18.1
Trade Credit[e]						0.3	1.6	1.6	2.6	3.5
	Percent of Total Holdings by Non-life Insurance Companies									
Total[d]	100.0	100.0	100.0	100.0	100.0	100.0	100.0	100.0	100.0	100.0
U.S. Government Securities	*	*	25.0	11.4	28.9	45.7	24.3	23.7	15.5	10.2
State and Local Government Securities	*	25.0	25.0	20.5	17.8	7.4	25.9	26.7	29.3	31.2
1–4 Family Nonfarm Residential Mortgages	*	*	*	2.3	0.2	*	*	*	*	*
Corporate Bonds	50.0	50.0	30.0	31.8	17.8	12.3	10.6	6.5	8.8	11.7
Corporate Stock	50.0	25.0	20.0	34.1	33.3	30.9	32.9	36.2	39.6	39.3
Trade Credit[e]						3.7	6.3	6.9	6.7	7.6

SOURCES: Same as for Table 18-1.　Reprinted by permission of Princeton University Press.
[a]In the Goldsmith data, this category is the sum of the fire and casualty and other private insurance companies.　In the Federal Reserve data, this category is other insurance companies.
[b]See Table 18-1, footnote *a*.
[c]See Table 18-1, footnote *b*.
[d]See Table 18-1, footnote *c*.
[e]Data for 1900, 1912, 1922, 1929, and 1939 are not included in the source employed.
*Less than $0.05 billion, or less than 0.05 percent.

5 years.　Many of them are for 1 year.　Consequently, regulatory authorities allow these companies to invest more heavily in equities.[30] The results are reflected in Table 18-10.　Other than corporate stock, the primary investment media of fire and casualty companies are obligations of state and local governments.　Although tax treatment depends on whether the investor is a stock or mutual company, the rates are sufficiently high in both instances to justify substantial investments in state and local obligations.[31]　Unlike other financial institutions, non-life insurance companies assign mortgages a negligible role in their portfolios.　Instead, debt obligations of corporations, particularly public-utility bonds, are preferred.

[30]American Mutual Insurance Alliance Association of Casualty and Surety Companies and National Board of Fire Underwriters, *Property and Casualty Insurance Companies* (Englewood Cliffs, N.J.: Prentice-Hall, Inc., 1963), pp. 34–63.
[31]*Ibid.*, p. 48.

TABLE 18-11: DISTRIBUTION OF MAJOR CAPITAL MARKET INSTRUMENTS AMONG PENSION FUNDS,^{a} SELECTED YEARS 1922–1968

Security	Absolute Magnitudes (In Billions of Dollars)							
	1922	1929	1939	1945	1958^b	1958^c	1965	1968
Total^d	0.1	0.5	1.0	2.6	26.4	27.7	69.2	92.9
U.S.Treasury Securities	*	0.1	0.2	1.5	2.5	2.6	3.5	3.2
State and Local Government Securities	*	*	*	*	*	*	*	*
1–4 Family Nonfarm Residential Mortgages	*	*	*	*	0.7	0.7	3.3	3.9
Corporate Bonds	0.1	0.3	0.6	0.8	12.4	12.8	22.7	26.2
Corporate Stock	*	0.1	0.2	0.3	10.8	11.6	39.7	59.6
	Percent of Total Holdings by Pension Funds							
Total^d	100.0	100.0	100.0	100.0	100.0	100.0	100.0	100.0
U.S. Treasury Securities	*	20.0	20.0	57.7	9.4	9.4	5.1	3.4
State and Local Government Securities	*	*	*	*	*	*	*	*
1–4 Family Nonfarm Residential Mortgages	*	*	*	*	2.7	2.5	4.8	4.2
Corporate Bonds	100.0	60.0	60.0	30.8	47.0	46.2	32.8	28.2
Corporate Stock	*	20.0	20.0	11.5	40.9	41.9	57.4	64.2

SOURCES: Same as for Table 18-1.   Reprinted by permission of Princeton University Press.
   ^{a}In the Goldsmith data, this category is the same as noninsured pension plans.   The Federal Reserve Board lists data for all private pension plans.
   ^{b}See Table 18-1, footnote a.
   ^{c}See Table 18-1, footnote b.
   ^{d}See Table 18-1, footnote c.
   *Less than $0.05 billion, or less than 0.05 percent.

Since their contracts are short-term, non-life insurance companies do not allow premiums allocated to various reserves, and hence to investments, to build up to the levels held by life insurance companies. Thus non-life insurance companies represent a relatively small subsector among financial institutions.   Unless their reserves grow more rapidly than those of other intermediaries—and there is no reason to suggest that they will—we can conclude that if corporate stock is to play a more important role in the portfolio of financial intermediaries, the impetus must come from other institutions.

In the forseeable future, the candidates most likely to supply this impetus are pension funds and investment companies.   Their portfolios are shown in Tables 18-11 and 18-12.   Pension funds in particular have achieved prominence only in the post-World War II period. Statistically, we can divide pension funds into four categories: government, private, insured, and noninsured.   While the Goldsmith data for financial intermediaries include government pension funds, the Federal Reserve data do not.   Thus we have concentrated only on the private sector.   In passing, we can note that contributions to social security

TABLE 18-12:   DISTRIBUTION OF MAJOR CAPITAL MARKET INSTRUMENTS AMONG INVESTMENT COMPANIES,[a] SELECTED YEARS, 1922–1968

Security	Absolute Magnitudes (In Billions of Dollars)							
	1922	1929	1939	1945	1958[b]	1958[c]	1965	1968
Total[d]	0.1	2.3	1.4	3.4	20.0	13.0	34.3	50.6
U.S. Treasury Securities	*	*	*	0.2	0.5	0.4	0.8	1.1
State and Local Government Securities	*	*	*	*	*	*	*	*
1–4 Family Nonfarm Residential Mortgages	*	*	0.1	0.1	0.2	*	*	*
Corporate Bonds	*	0.1	0.1	0.2	1.2	0.9	2.6	3.4
Corporate Stock	0.1	2.2	1.2	2.9	18.1	11.7	30.9	46.1
	Percent of Total Holdings by Investment Companies							
Total[d]	100.0	100.0	100.0	100.0	100.0	100.0	100.0	100.0
U.S. Treasury Securities	*	*	*	5.9	2.5	3.1	2.3	2.2
State and Local Government Securities	*	*	*	*	*	*	*	*
1–4 Family Nonfarm Residential Mortgages	*	*	7.1	2.9	1.0	*	*	*
Corporate Bonds	*	4.3	7.1	5.9	6.0	6.9	7.6	6.7
Corporate Stock	100.0	95.7	85.7	85.3	90.5	10.0	90.0	91.1

SOURCES : Same as for Table 18-1.   Reprinted by permission of Princeton University Press.
[a]In the Goldsmith data, this category is investment companies.   In the Federal Reserve data, only open-end investment companies or mutual funds are included.
[b]See Table 18-1, footnote a.
[c]See Table 18-1, footnote b.
[d]See Table 18-1, footnote c.
*Less than $0.05 billion, or less than 0.05 percent.

funds, as well as payment to other federally administered programs, are invested almost exclusively in U.S. Treasury securities.   State and local governments divide most of their retirement funds among corporate bonds, Treasury securities, and their own tax-exempt obligations.   In view of the fact that the income on these funds is tax-exempt, the willingness to buy state and local obligations can be explained partly in terms of the ready market these pension funds provide for hard-pressed state and local authorities seeking outlets for their securities.[32]

Insured pension funds are simply the retirement reserves administered by life insurance companies.   All other pension plans are noninsured.   The distinction is made because of the different asset com-

[32]Gies, Mayer, and Ettin, *op. cit.*, pp. 199–200.   See also Victor L. Andrews, "Noninsured Corporate and State and Local Government Retirement Funds in the Financial Structure," in Commission on Money and Credit, *Private Capital Markets* (Englewood Cliffs, N.J.: Prentice-Hall, Inc., 1964), pp. 411–422.   See also Daniel M. Holland, *Private Pension Funds: Projected Growth* (New York: National Bureau of Economic Research, Inc., 1966), p. 6, table 5.

position of insured pension plans where heavier emphasis is placed on debt.[33]

A pension plan will be administered by an independent trustee, usually a commercial bank or life insurance company. If the plan meets certain requirements, such as "being a permanent program not just a temporary arrangement" and being established for the benefit of all employees,[34] income from the securities and capital gains from the portfolio are tax-exempt. Contributions of employers are tax-deductible by the corporation when it estimates its income taxes. The recipient of the retirement benefits must pay personal income taxes on that portion of the retirement income representing the employer's contribution. The recipient's own contributions, of course, were made from after-tax income. They are not taxed again. The employer thus avoids taxes on his contribution. By not receiving it as income today, the employee defers paying taxes on it. When it does become income, presumably he will, in retirement, be in a lower tax bracket. Although this tax advantage has prevailed since the 1920s, it is the relatively high tax rates in the post-World War II period that have provided the impetus for the growth in pension funds.

From the employer's viewpoint, there is another advantage. Unlike most financial intermediaries, the company administering a pension fund often finds little or no restrictions placed on the asset composition of its portfolio. If the benefits are fixed, and the fund can obtain its income through increases in market value, then the employer's contribution is correspondingly reduced. For this reason there has been increasing emphasis on common stocks in the portfolios of pension funds. In a growing economy where increases in income accrue to the equity owners, there is every reason to assume that pension funds will continue to expand and their participation in common stocks increase.[35]

The other expanding intermediary investing heavily in equity securities is the investment company. There are two major types of investment companies, *open-end* and *closed-end*. The difference between them lies simply in the fact that the number of shares in a closed-end

---

[33]Holland, *op. cit.*, p. 6, table 5, and p. 91. Holland goes on to argue that the distinction may not be so important. In the last several years, states have been giving insurance companies more freedom in separating pension fund reserves from life insurance reserves, allowing them to raise the equity component in the former. *Ibid.*, p. 91.

[34]Keith, *op. cit.*, p. 433.

[35]Because pension funds are still in their infancy, it is possible that their growth may slow down as more people who have paid into them reach retirement age.

At the same time, if households become more enamored of variable rather than fixed retirement annuities—and there is no reason to assume that they will not—and with Social Security as a fixed income residual, then pension funds may invest all of their contributions in equities.

company is fixed by charter. The number of shares in an open-end company is not. The latter companies—the more important of the two types—are also called *mutual funds*.

Unlike companies administering pension funds, investment companies were of some consequence in the 1920s. While they are subject to regulation under the Investment Company Act of 1940, specific securities are not regulated. Investment companies may purchase any instrument. Since most of them register under the act as diversified investment companies, the primary regulation is

> that the fund allocates 75 percent of its assets in such a way that within that 75 percent no more than 5 percent of total assets are in one issue and no more than 10 percent of voting securities in one corporation are held. These restrictions do not count for the remaining 25 percent of assets.[36]

By distributing to shareholders all or substantially all of the income and capital gains realized on their portfolios, investment companies are, for practical purposes, tax-exempt.[37] They serve merely as conduits to households that might otherwise own the securities directly. Diversification, together with a management specialized in the securities markets, provides the raison d'être of investment companies. They are a medium through which persons of modest means and/or little investment experience can easily participate in the securities markets. While the investment objectives range from income to growth, the portfolio emphasis has been on common stocks. Since most shareholders see an investment company as a substitute for income which they might directly allocate to the purchase of stocks, it seems likely that this will continue to be the type of security dominating their portfolios.

In passing, however, we should note that the statistics can understate the role that intermediaries play in equity finance. Those institutions, such as life insurance companies, whose equity purchases are restricted can and do purchase convertibles or debt instruments containing options to purchase common stock. In this way they can realize a profit from the sale of the convertibles or warrants should the price of the stock which underlies them rise in price. During the late

---

[36]Gies, Mayer, and Ettin, *op. cit.*, p. 204. For a more detailed discussion of investment companies, see Hugh Bullock, *The Story of Investment Companies* (New York: Columbia University Press, 1959); U.S. Congress, House Committee on Interstate and Foreign Commerce, *A Study of Mutual Funds*, 87th Cong., 2d Sess., 1962. This study was prepared for the Securities and Exchange Commission by the Wharton School of Finance and Commerce. See also U.S. Congress, House Committee on Interstate and Foreign Commerce, *Report of the Securities and Exchange Commission on the Public Policy Implications of Investment Company Growth*, 89th Cong., 2d Sess., 1966.

[37]Keith, *op. cit.*, p. 419.

1960s, as the price level rose at relatively high rates, insurance companies demanded that more of the debt issues they were buying carry some type of "equity sweetener" as a protection against the decline in the purchasing power of the fixed interest charge.

In conclusion, therefore, the role of financial intermediaries in the capital markets has increased in importance.   There is every reason to suspect that this trend will continue.   As income grows and specialization becomes more widespread, intermediaries will continue, within regulatory limits, to move ahead of other sectors in the holding of major capital market instruments.   In so doing they will provide services demanded by the savings sectors (households) and channel funds to the investing sectors (primarily nonfinancial corporations and government).[38]

SUMMARY

Financial intermediaries are the means through which capital can be transferred from households to nonfinancial business enterprises and government, that is, from the savings sector to the investing sectors of the economy.   While this could be done directly, in an advanced economy financial intermediaries provide a more efficient means for doing so.   Thus a corporation may wish to finance an asset out of long-term debt.   Individuals may wish to protect themselves against financial loss in the event of death of the head of the household.   An insurance company can satisfy both demands by issuing liabilities of its own, that is, insurance policies, and investing the premiums in corporate bonds.

Since capital markets provide the means for transferring funds from the savings sector to the investing sectors, the more efficient they are in performing this function, the greater their impact on the stock of real wealth.   Thus the existence of financial intermediaries may affect not only the way in which savings are channeled to the investing sectors, but the level of savings, the level of investment, and hence the aggregate stock of real wealth over time.

Using a broad definition of capital markets, we find that with respect to the historical trends in the major capital market instruments,

---

[38]In passing, we might note two of the intermediaries listed among other financial institutions in Table 18-6.   These are credit unions and finance companies.   The former obtain funds from and lend them to their own members.   In effect, they transfer funds within the household sector.   They specialize, therefore, in consumer loans.   The primary advantage is in avoiding relatively high-cost consumer loans from other intermediaries, particularly finance companies.

These latter institutions, as we have seen, specialize in installment loans, deriving their funds from the sale of common stock, subordinated debenture bonds, and finance company paper, large amounts of which are purchased by commercial banks.

the data indicate that the federal sector has grown in relative importance, since 1900, while the state and local sector has remained remarkably constant.   Among the major instruments of business finance, the relative importance of trade credit is down somewhat from earlier years. Common stock is relatively less important today than in 1929.   So are corporate bonds and bank loans, not elsewhere counted.

With respect to the historical trends in the sectors holding the major capital market instruments, only financial intermediaries show a definite rise.   The other sectors either have shown no trend or have declined in relative importance.

Households continue to be the primary purchaser of corporate stock, and nonfinancial corporations the primary purchaser of trade credit.   Financial institutions, however, have substantial holdings of nearly every major capital market instrument except trade credit.

Commercial banks are still the most important financial institution but their relative importance has declined over the years.   Perhaps the most rapidly growing intermediary has been pension funds.

Life insurance companies are the major purchasers of corporate bonds, while life insurance companies, savings and loan associations, and savings banks are the major purchasers of residential mortgages.

Non-life insurance companies, pension funds, and investment companies are major purchasers of corporate stock.   Their holdings, however, are considerably below those of households.   While some institutions, such as life insurance companies, are restricted in their acquisition of common stock, they do buy convertibles and often receive warrants to purchase the stock of the corporation whose bonds they procure.

QUESTIONS

1.   "Since households are net savers and nonfinancial business firms and government are net investors, the nation must have financial institutions to serve as conduits through which savings are channeled into investment."   Evaluate.

2.   "Like the debt issues of nonfinancial corporations, most of the equity issues will eventually be in the hands of intermediaries." Do you agree?   Explain fully.

3.   "Because of restrictions placed on their portfolios, commercial banks have declined in importance over the years when compared with other intermediaries."   Do you agree?   Explain fully.

4. "The securities of nonfinancial corporations continue to dominate the capital markets." Evaluate critically.

SELECTED REFERENCES

American Mutual Insurance Alliance Association of Casualty and Surety Companies and National Board of Fire Underwriters. *Property and Casualty Insurance Companies.* Englewood Cliffs, N.J.: Prentice-Hall, Inc., 1963. A study prepared for the Commission on Money and Credit.

American Bankers Association. *The Commercial Banking Industry.* Englewood Cliffs, N.J.: Prentice-Hall, Inc., 1962. A study prepared for the Commission on Money and Credit.

Bullock, Hugh., *The Story of Investment Companies.* New York: Columbia University Press, 1959.

Gies, Thomas G., Thomas Mayer, and Edward C. Ettin., "Portfolio Regulations and Policies of Financial Intermediaries," in Commission on Money and Credit, *Private Financial Institutions.* Englewood Cliffs, N.J.: Prentice-Hall, Inc., 1963, pp. 157–263.

Goldsmith, Raymond W., *The Flow of Capital Funds in the Postwar Economy.* New York: National Bureau of Economic Research, Inc., 1965, chap. 1.

Holland, Daniel M., *Private Pension Funds: Projected Growth.* New York: National Bureau of Economic Research, Inc., 1966.

Keith, E. Gordon. "The Impact of Federal Taxation on the Flow of Personal Savings through Investment Intermediaries," in Commission on Money and Credit, *Private Financial Institutions.* Englewood Cliffs, N.J.: Prentice-Hall, Inc., 1963, pp. 383–460.

Kendall, Leon T., *The Savings and Loan Business.* Englewood Cliffs, N.J.: Prentice-Hall, Inc., 1962. A study prepared for the Commission on Money and Credit.

Klaman, Saul B., *The Postwar Residential Mortgage Market.* Princeton, N.J.: Princeton University Press, 1961. A study by the National Bureau of Economic Research, Inc.

Life Insurance Association of America. *Life Insurance Companies as Financial Institutions.* Englewood Cliffs, N.J.: Prentice-Hall, Inc., 1962. A study prepared for the Commission on Money and Credit.

Moore, Basil J., *An Introduction to the Theory of Finance: Assetholder Behavior under Uncertainty.* New York: The Free Press, 1968.

National Association of Mutual Savings Banks. *Mutual Savings Banking.* Englewood Cliffs, N.J.: Prentice-Hall, Inc., 1962. A study prepared for the Commission on Money and Credit.

TECHNICAL APPENDIX: The Flow of Funds Matrix

Throughout this and the preceding chapter, we have used data derived from flow-of-funds matrices for various years. In Chapter 17 our concern was with sources of funds for a single sector, nonfinancial corporations. In this chapter our interest centered primarily on the role of financial intermediaries in transferring savings from households to the investing sectors, that is, to nonfinancial private enterprise and government.   In Chapter 17 we employed annual flows — or changes in assets — and liabilities; in this chapter we employed year-end levels or balance-sheet data.

In the post-World War II period, the Federal Reserve Board has been the primary source of flow-of-funds statistics. Some understanding of its approach to sectoring the data is useful in explaining the discrepancies that can arise when its results are compared with those of others.[1]

As others who use this approach have done, we shall begin with the accounting equation

$$\text{Assets} = \text{liabilities} + \text{owners' equity}$$

$$\text{Total uses} = \text{total sources}$$

To phrase it differently,

$$\text{Real uses} + \text{financial uses} = \text{internal sources} + \text{financial sources}$$

The Federal Reserve then alters the identity so that

$$\text{Real uses} + (\text{financial uses} - \text{financial sources}) = \text{internal sources} \qquad (1)$$

Furthermore, it defines the following terms:

$$\text{Private capital expenditures} = \text{real uses}$$

$$\text{Net financial investment} = \text{financial uses} - \text{financial sources}$$

$$\text{Gross investment} = \text{private capital expenditure} + \text{net financial investment}$$

$$\text{Net savings} = \text{retained earnings}$$

$$\text{Capital consumption allowances} = \text{depreciation} + \text{accidental damage to fixed assets}$$

$$\text{Net savings} + \text{capital consumption allowances} = \text{gross savings}$$

Substituting in Eq. (1), we have

$$\text{Private capital expenditures} + \text{net financial investment} = \text{internal sources} = \text{gross savings} \qquad (2)$$

Therefore

$$\text{gross savings} = \text{gross investment}$$

---

[1]While there are periodic revisions, the basic source of the details of its accounts is still Board of Governors of the Federal Reserve System, *Flow of Funds in the United States* (Washington: Board of Governors of the Federal Reserve System, 1955).

Using definitions employed in flow-of-funds accounting, the Federal Reserve can link these data with the national income accounts and reach the same equality. Realized savings must always equal realized investment.

But our purpose in using flow-of-funds data was to show the financial relationships among particular sectors of the economy. To illustrate, assume that there are three sectors: households, nonfinancial corporations, and commercial banks. We shall employ the same constraints used earlier in the chapter. Nonfinancial corporations hold both financial and real assets and issue debt and equity instruments. Households also carry financial and real assets and are indebted to banks. Commercial banks carry only financial assets, but also issue debt and stock. We can now define these various assets and obligations as follows:

A = total assets

M = money or cash

DD = demand deposits

DN = debt of nonfinancial corporations

SN = stock of nonfinancial corporations

R = reserves of commercial banks

L = commercial bank loans

MO = residential mortgages

SB = stock of commercial banks

RE = retained earnings

PE = plant and equipment, net of depreciation

Q = inventories

RC = residential construction, net of depreciation

D = capital consumption allowances

G = gross investment

I = real capital expenditure

RA = real assets

NF = net financial investment

FA = financial assets

FL = financial liabilities, including owners' equity

NS = net savings

GS = gross savings

TL = total liabilities

CI = current income

$C =$ personal consumption for households. (For nonfinancial corporations and commercial banks, is cash expenses incurred in producing the product or service)

We shall also use the following subscripts: h for households, c for nonfinancial corporations, and b for commercial banks. Where two subscripts appear, as in the case of liabilities, the first indicates the sector issuing the obligations, the second the sector owning them. Thus

Balance Sheet for Households

$$A_h = RA_h + FA_h \tag{3}$$
$$RA_h = RC_h \tag{4}$$
$$FA_h = M_h + DD_{bh} + DN_{ch} + SN_{ch} + SB_{bh} \tag{5}$$
$$TL_h = L_{hb} + MO_{hb} + RE_{hh} \tag{6}$$
$$A_h = TL_h \tag{7}$$

Balance Sheet for Nonfinancial Corporations

$$A_c = RA_c + FA_c \tag{8}$$
$$RA_c = PE_c + Q_c \tag{9}$$
$$FA_c = M_c + DD_{bc} \tag{10}$$
$$TL_c = DN_{ch} + DN_{cb} + SN_{ch} + RE_{cc} \tag{11}$$
$$A_c = TL_c \tag{12}$$

Balance Sheet for Commercial Banks

$$A_b = RA_b + FA_b \tag{13}$$
$$RA_b = \text{Zero} \tag{14}$$
$$FA_b = R_b + L_{hb} + DN_{cb} + MO_{hb} \tag{15}$$
$$TL_b = DD_{bh} + DD_{bc} + SB_{bh} + RE_{bb} \tag{16}$$
$$A_b = TL_b \tag{17}$$

Uses of Household Funds

$$G_h = I_h + NF_h \tag{18}$$
$$I_h = \Delta RC_h \tag{19}$$
$$NF_h = \Delta FA_h - \Delta FL_h \tag{20}$$
$$\Delta FA_h = \Delta M_h + \Delta DD_{bh} + \Delta DN_{ch} + \Delta SN_{ch} + \Delta SB_{bh} \tag{21}$$
$$\Delta FL_h = \Delta L_{hb} + MO_{hb} + \Delta RE_{hh} \tag{22}$$

Uses of Nonfinancial Corporation Funds

$$G_c = I_c + NF_c \tag{23}$$

$$I_c = \Delta PE_c + \Delta Q_c \tag{24}$$

$$NF_c = \Delta FA_c - \Delta FL_c \tag{25}$$

$$\Delta FA_c = \Delta M_c + \Delta DD_{bc} \tag{26}$$

$$\Delta FL_c = \Delta DN_{ch} + \Delta DN_{cb} + \Delta SN_{ch} + \Delta RE_{cc} \tag{27}$$

Uses of Commercial Bank Funds

$$G_b = NF_b \tag{28}$$

$$NF_b = \Delta FA_b - \Delta FL_b \tag{29}$$

$$\Delta FA_b = \Delta R_b + \Delta L_{hb} + \Delta DN_{cb} + \Delta MO_{hb} \tag{30}$$

$$\Delta FL_b = \Delta DD_{bh} + \Delta DD_{bc} + \Delta SB_{bh} + \Delta RE_{bb} \tag{31}$$

Sources of Household Funds

$$NS_h = CI_h - C_h - D_h \tag{32}$$

$$GS_h = NS_h + D_h \tag{33}$$

Sources of Nonfinancial Corporation Funds

$$NS_c = CI_c - C_c - D_c \tag{34}$$

$$GS_c = NS_c + D_c \tag{35}$$

Sources of Commercial Bank Funds

$$NS_b = CI_b - C_b \tag{36}$$

$$GS_b = NS_b \tag{37}$$

Returning to Eq. (2) and substituting, we get

$$(I_h + I_c) + (NFI_h + NFI_c + NFI_b) = GS_h + GS_c + GS_b$$

Private capital expenditures + net financial investment = internal sources = gross savings

Gross investment = gross savings

Similarly, we could take any specific category—in this case, net financial investment—and set up a matrix showing the relationship between the instruments employed and the issuing and holding sectors.   To do this with balance-sheet data, we would use Eq. (5), (6), (10), (11), (15), and (16). Common stock could be listed at its market rather than its book value, thereby eliminating a separate category for retained earnings.   If we choose to establish our matrix on a flow-of-funds basis, we would use Eq. (21), (22), (26), (27), (30), and (31), substituting gross savings [Eqs. (33), (35), and (37)] for changes in retained earnings.   We could also

APPENDIX TABLE 1: FLOW-OF-FUNDS SUMMARY MATRIX, (PRELIMINARY) 1965 LEVELS
(In Billions of Dollars)

	Households		Business		State and Local		Pvt. Domestic Nonfinancial, Total		U.S. Government		Finance Sectors, Total		Line
	A	L	A	L	A	L	A	L	A	L	A	L	
11 Total Financial Assets	1,437.8	...	320.0	...	83.6	...	1,841.4	...	89.4	...	953.3	...	...11
12 Total Liabilities	...	342.3	...	452.7	...	139.2	...	934.3	...	309.6	...	878.0	...12
13 Gold Stock	...	...	...	...	...	...	...	...	0.1	...	13.7	...	...13
61 Off. U.S. Fgn. Exch.	...	...	...	...	...	...	...	...	0.2	...	0.6	3.5	...61
62 IMF Position	...	...	...	...	...	...	...	...	4.4	...	...	*	...62
14 Treasury Currency	...	...	...	...	...	...	...	...	...	3.1	5.4	...	...14
15 Demand Dep. and Curr.	...	...	...	...	...	...	145.1	...	...	...	13.4	183.1	...15
37 Pvt. Domestic	87.6	...	45.4	...	12.1	...	...	...	...	...	...	173.3	...37
36 Federal	...	...	...	...	...	...	...	...	7.1	...	...	7.0	...36
56 Foreign	...	...	...	...	...	...	...	...	...	...	...	2.8	...56
16 Time and Svg. Accounts	279.4	...	...	...	...	...	310.8	...	0.7	...	0.7	319.0	...16
17 At Ccmm. Banks	108.0	...	19.2	...	12.2	...	139.5	...	0.3	...	0.2	147.2	...17
18 At Svgs. Instit.	171.4	...	...	...	...	...	171.4	...	...	...	0.5	171.8	...18
19 Life Insurance Reserves	105.9	...	...	...	...	...	105.9	...	...	7.0	...	98.9	...19
20 Pension Fund Reserves	150.0	...	...	...	...	32.8	150.0	32.8	...	19.7	...	97.5	...20
60 Consol. Bank Items	...	...	...	...	...	...	...	...	...	...	25.6	25.6	...60

430

Line	Item												
21	Credit Mkt. Instr.	796.5	327.4	47.0	274.5	57.8	103.5	901.2	705.4	52.7	272.5	856.4	81.4
22	U.S. Govt. Secur.	77.6	…	16.7	…	24.4	…	118.8	…	…	271.2	139.2	…
23	State and Local Oblig.	37.2	…	3.6	…	5.0	100.0	45.8	100.0	…	…	54.2	17.7
24	Corp. and Fgn. Bonds	4.7	…	…	97.8	25.1	…	29.8	97.8	…	…	94.0	35.2
25	Corp. Stocks	666.5	…	…	NA	…	…	666.8	NA	…	…	97.0	2.2
26	1–4 Fam. Mortgages	10.6	203.9	…	7.5	3.2	…	13.8	211.3	6.4	…	193.4	…
27	Other Mortgages	…	13.6	…	72.0	…	…	…	85.7	6.0	…	79.7	…
28	Consumer Credit	…	87.9	20.0	…	…	…	20.0	87.9	…	…	67.9	12.1
29	Bank Loans, n.e.c.	…	11.7	…	72.9	…	…	…	84.6	…	1.3	103.9	14.2
30	Other Loans	…	10.3	6.7	24.3	3.8	…	6.7	38.1	40.3	…	27.2	8.2
38	Open Mkt. Paper	…	…	6.7	1.7	…	…	6.7	1.7	…	…	17.7	6.0
39	Federal Loans	…	0.9	…	10.2	3.8	…	…	14.6	39.7	…	…	…
31	Security Credit	1.4	9.2	1.4	…	…	…	1.4	9.2	…	…	15.4	7.6
41	To Brkrs. and Dlrs.	1.4	…	1.4	…	…	…	1.4	…	…	…	6.0	7.6
42	To Others	…	9.2	…	…	…	…	…	9.2	…	…	9.3	…
57	Taxes Payable	…	…	…	20.4	1.5	…	1.5	20.4	20.6	…	…	1.8
32	Trade Credit	2.4	145.9	145.9	105.6	…	2.9	145.9	110.9	3.1	3.9	2.6	…
34	Miscellaneous Fin.	17.1	3.3	62.5	52.3	…	…	79.6	55.6	4.5	3.4	19.4	63.0

APPENDIX TABLE 1 (Continued)

		Monetary Authority		Commercial Banks		Nonbank Finance		Rest of World		All Sectors		Discrepancy	National Savings and Inventory	
		A	L	A	L	A	L	A	L	A	L			
11	Total Financial Assets	63.1	...	337.2	...	553.1	...	84.2	...	2,968.4	...	...	93.8	... 11
12	Total Liabilities	...	63.1	...	313.6	...	501.3	...	93.8	...	2,215.6	...	84.2	... 12
13	Gold Stock	13.7	...	...	...	...	...	29.5	...	43.3	...	...	...	... 13
61	Off. U.S. Fgn. Exch.	0.6	...	...	...	...	...	...	0.8	...	0.8	...	...	... 61
62	IMF Position	...	*	...	...	...	...	...	0.9	...	0.9	...	...	... 62
14	Treasury Currency	5.4	...	...	...	...	...	...	...	5.4	3.1	−2.4	...	... 14
15	Demand Dep. and Curr.	...	38.8	...	144.2	13.4	...	...	...	168.4	183.1	...	...	... 15
37	Pvt. Domestic	...	37.2	...	136.1	...	...	...	...	158.5	173.3	14.8	...	... 37
36	Federal	...	1.4	...	5.5	...	...	...	...	7.1	7.0	−0.1	...	... 36
56	Foreign	...	0.2	...	2.6	...	...	2.8	...	...	2.8	...	...	... 56
16	Time and Svg. Accounts	...	...	...	...	0.7	...	...	...	...	319.0	...	...	... 16
17	At Comm. Banks	...	...	...	147.2	0.2	...	7.3	...	...	147.2	...	...	... 17
18	At Svgs. Instit.	...	...	...	...	0.5	171.8	...	...	...	171.8	...	...	... 18
19	Life Insurance Reserves	...	...	...	...	...	98.9	...	...	...	105.9	...	...	... 19
20	Pension Fund Reserves	...	...	...	...	...	97.5	...	...	...	150.0	...	...	... 20
60	Consol. Bank Items	2.3	23.3	...	2.3	...	...	...	...	25.6	25.6	...	...	... 60

			C1	C2	C3	C4	C5	C6	C7	C8	C9	C10	C11	
21	Credit Mkt. Instr.		41.0	...	299.4	1.6	516.0	79.8	30.4	37.8	1,840.7	1,097.2	...	...21
22	U.S. Govt. Secur.		40.8	...	65.6	...	32.8	...	13.2	...	...	271.2	...	...22
23	State and Local Oblig.		...	...	38.5	...	15.8	...	...	...	...	100.0	...	...23
24	Corp. and Fgn. Bonds		...	...	0.8	1.6	93.2	16.1	0.9	9.1	...	124.7	...	...24
25	Corp. Stocks		...	...	...	NA	97.0	35.2	14.6	NA	778.0	35.2	...	...25
26	1–4 Fam. Mortgages		...	...	30.1	...	163.3	2.2	...	...	...	213.5	...	...26
27	Other Mortgages		...	...	19.2	...	60.5	...	...	...	...	85.7	...	...27
28	Consumer Credit		...	...	35.8	...	32.1	...	...	...	...	87.9	...	...28
29	Bank Loans, n.e.c.		*	...	103.8	...	...	12.1	...	7.2	...	103.9	...	...29
30	Other Loans		0.2	...	5.6	...	21.4	14.2	1.6	21.5	75.9	75.1	−0.8	...30
38	Open Mkt. Paper		0.2	...	3.3	...	0.6	8.2	1.6	2.5	...	12.4	...	...38
39	Federal Loans		...	...	...	...	...	6.0	...	19.0	...	39.7	...	...39
31	Security Credit		...	...	8.5	...	6.9	7.6	0.2	0.1	...	17.0	...	...31
41	To Brkrs. and Dlrs.		...	...	5.3	...	0.8	7.6	0.2	...	...	7.6	...	...41
42	To Others		...	...	3.2	...	6.1	...	...	0.1	...	9.3	...	...42
57	Taxes Payable		...	...	...	0.7	...	1.0	...	...	...	22.1	...	...57
32	Trade Credit		...	...	...	...	2.6	...	...	...	151.7	114.8	−36.9	...32
34	Miscellaneous Fin.		...	0.9	6.0	17.5	13.4	44.6	14.1	54.2	117.5	176.2	58.7	...34

SOURCE: Board of Governors of the Federal Reserve System, Division of Research and Statistics, *Flow of Funds, Assets and Liabilities, 1945–1965*, pp. 39–40.
*Less than $0.05 billion.

rework depreciation and net savings to account for inventory valuation adjustments and replacement cost of fixed assets.

One of the problems in devising a table of this nature, therefore, is to break down the instruments employed as well as the number of sectors holding them.   There are some 60 million economic units which must be grouped in a workable number of sectors.   In principle, each sector should be homogeneous.   Thus we should combine all units with similar behavioral characteristics.   At the same time we should not "divide assets or transactions under the control of one decision-making unit among two or more sectors."[2]   Presumably the federal government is a homogeneous sector.   Yet its behavior with respect to pension funds is more akin to that of financial institutions, and its activities in other operations resemble those of nonfinancial corporations.   In the former operation the federal government is a net saver, while in its other operations it is a net investor of funds.   Similarly, we can conclude that household and agricultural business decisions are made by separate units.   Since the choice is often arbitrary, when using overlapping data, it is not uncommon to find differences in sectors of the economy as well as in the classification of instruments.

Another problem in developing a flow-of-funds matrix is the degree of consolidation.   Within sectors, the liabilities of one unit which are assets of another are ordinarily canceled.   For instance, deposits of one commercial bank which are liabilities of another are not included in the data.   Thus, in the picture that emerges, the claims against one sector are the assets of another.

Finally, as usually presented, data are net, not gross.   Netting destroys the aggregate changes that have taken place in the holdings of one sector.   For example, if a life insurance company buys \$4,000,000 in corporate bonds and another life insurance company sells \$1,000,000 in corporate bonds, there is a net increase of \$3,000,000 in the corporate bond account of this subsector.

Bearing these points in mind, we can turn to the accompanying preliminary 1965 Federal Reserve matrix (Appendix Table 1) showing the flow of financial assets and liabilities.   There are 10 sectors listed. Each financial asset by definition is a liability of some other sector.   The sectors in this summary matrix can be subclassified as were the nonbank finance sectors.

To construct this matrix or its annual-flow-of-funds counterpart, we simply extend the equations developed earlier.   While the symbols can become tedious, the technique is mechanical and can be easily handled by a computer.

The primary problem is to explain the results.   The ultimate aim

---

[2] Goldsmith, *op. cit.*, p. 49.

is to develop a model to predict financial flows and, it is hoped, changes in aggregate savings and investment. To date no satisfactory model exists. Until one is developed, we shall have to content ourselves—as we did in this chapter—with institutional explanations of the changes that have taken place.[3]

SUMMARY TO APPENDIX

We can construct a matrix showing the interrelationships among the various sectors of the economy and the sources and uses of funds representing their contribution to savings and investment. In so doing, we face three problems.

First, we must determine the number of sectors holding instruments and the number of instruments employed. Any classification chosen will contain arbitrary elements. Second, we must determine the degree of consolidation we desire. Third, the data presented are usually net, not gross. Therefore they do not represent the total of purchases and sales but simply the differences, or net change.

However these issues are resolved, the matrix is simply a descriptive tool. It is not a model for predicting financial flows.

QUESTIONS FOR APPENDIX

1. What are the problems involved in setting up a matrix to illustrate the flow of funds? Can we predict from a matrix for any given period the flow of funds for the next period? Why or why not?

2. "If total sources equal total uses, then gross savings equal gross investment." Prove or disprove this statement.

SELECTED REFERENCES

Board of Governors of the Federal Reserve System. *Flow of Funds in the United States*. Washington: Board of Governors of the Federal Reserve System, 1955.

———. "The Federal Reserve—M.I.T. Econometric Model," *Federal Reserve Bulletin*, vol. 54, no. 1 (January, 1968), pp. 11–40.

Gurley, John G., and Edward S. Shaw. *Money in a Theory of Finance*. Washington: The Brookings Institution, 1960.

[3]One of the more promising attempts is the Federal Reserve–M.I.T. Econometric Model. See *Federal Reserve Bulletin*, vol. 54, no. 1 (January, 1968), pp. 11–40. As we might expect, its major purpose is to quantify the effects of monetary policy on the economy. Pinpointing the role of money in macrofinancial theory is a primary preoccupation of students of the subject. See John G. Gurley and Edward S. Shaw, *Money in a Theory of Finance* (Washington: The Brookings Institution, 1960).

The New Issues Market and
The Role of Investment Banking

chapter Nineteen

In this chapter we shall discuss the factors affecting the supply curve of long-term debt and external equity.   The student should read the material from the point of view of a financial manager considering the question of raising this type of capital.   What are the possible alternatives?   How have the structure, regulation, and other environmental factors altered the fluctuations in the costs of long-term debt and equity?

Introduction

From our analysis of the savings and investment relationships in the United States, we found that the rise in the importance of financial intermediaries was perhaps the most striking development in the process of channeling funds from households to the nonfinancial private enterprise and government sectors.   With respect to corporate debt and

436

stock issues, it appeared from an analysis of balance-sheet data that these securities, particularly debt, were playing an increasingly important role in the portfolios of the major intermediaries.

Tables 19-1 and 19-2 (on pages 438 and 441, respectively) show that the share of debt held by financial institutions has risen markedly when compared with the change in the share of their holdings of equity instruments. The rather slow growth in the latter share, we argued, was due in part to the restrictions placed on the equity components in the portfolios of many intermediaries. Except for non-life insurance companies, only companies administering pension funds (including those administered by life insurance companies) and investment companies are heavy or potentially heavy purchasers of equity instruments. The growth of these institutions is a relatively recent phenomenon. Thus, a major point to keep in mind in an analysis of the new issues market is that the ownership of corporate stock remains primarily in the hands of households while corporate debt is primarily in the hands of intermediaries. As we shall see, these facts may play a role in the cost of floating new securities and, therefore, in the cost of long-term debt and equity.

Although nonfinancial corporations enter the market for long-term debt and equity, they do so at irregular intervals and, as we have seen, have been doing so less frequently over the years. These sporadic sojourns into what are traditionally considered the capital markets are justified in terms of our cost-of-capital model only under two conditions. Either the rate of return on the marginal project is greater than the relatively high cost of external funds, or the net present value of the project discounted at the marginal cost of capital is positive. Since such excursions are infrequent, it is difficult for the financial manager of a nonfinancial corporation to know precisely what is currently fashionable in bond indentures and, to a lesser extent, in equity contracts. More important, he may have no more than a rough idea of the price he could anticipate, or the net proceeds the company would receive, from the sale of new securities. He must, therefore, often rely on the advice of those whose business it is to keep abreast of these developments: *investment bankers.*

Although the term investment banking can be variously defined,[1] for the present we shall limit it to those responsibilities and activities of a firm which pertain to distributing new debt or equity securities of a nonfinancial or financial corporation to the ultimate holders, that is, to financial intermediaries or households.

[1]Irwin Friend, James R. Longstreet, Morris Mendelson, Ervin Miller, and Arleigh P. Hess, Jr., *Investment Banking and the New Issues Market* (Cleveland: The World Publishing Company, 1967), pp. 80–81.

TABLE 19-1:   DISTRIBUTION OF HOLDINGS OF CORPORATE BONDS,[a] SELECTED YEARS, 1900–1968

Holder	Absolute Magnitudes (In Billions of Dollars)									
	1900	1912	1922	1929	1939	1945	1958[b]	1958[c]	1965	1968
Total[d]	5.1	14.6	23.6	38.1	32.6	27.5	88.7	80.0	124.5	158.6
Households[e]	3.3	9.5	15.9	24.1	16.8	9.3	11.1	6.9	4.6	10.7
Financial Institutions	1.8	5.1	7.7	13.5	14.8	17.7	74.2	65.5	94.2	114.7
Commercial Banks	0.7	2.0	3.4	4.7	3.4	3.0	3.5	1.3	0.8	1.9
Life Insurance Companies	0.5	1.6	2.2	4.7	8.3	11.3	44.4	44.3	61.1	71.1
Savings Banks and Savings and Loan Associations	0.4	1.0	1.2	2.0	1.4	1.0	4.1	3.8	2.9	6.6
Non-life Insurance Companies	0.1	0.4	0.6	1.4	0.8	1.0	2.7	1.5	3.4	5.4
Pension Funds	*	*	0.1	0.3	0.6	0.8	12.4	12.8	22.7	26.2
Investment Companies	*	*	*	0.1	0.1	0.2	1.2	0.9	2.6	3.4
Other Financial Institutions[f]	0.1	0.1	0.2	0.3	0.2	0.4	5.9	0.9	0.7	0.1
Other Sectors[g]	*	*	*	0.5	1.0	0.5	3.4	7.6	25.7	33.2

Holder	Percent of Total Holdings									
	1900	1912	1922	1929	1939	1945	1958[b]	1958[c]	1965	1968
Total[d]	100.0	100.0	100.0	100.0	100.0	100.0	100.0	100.0	100.0	100.0
Households[e]	63.5	65.1	67.4	63.3	51.5	33.8	12.5	8.6	3.7	6.7
Financial Institutions	34.6	34.9	32.6	35.4	45.4	64.4	83.7	81.9	75.5	72.3
Commercial Banks	13.5	13.7	14.4	12.3	10.4	10.9	3.9	1.6	0.6	1.2
Life Insurance Companies	9.6	11.0	9.3	12.3	25.5	41.1	50.0	55.4	49.1	44.8
Savings Banks and Savings and Loan Associations	7.7	6.8	5.1	5.2	4.3	3.6	4.6	4.8	2.3	4.2
Non-life Insurance Companies	1.9	2.7	2.5	3.7	2.5	3.6	3.0	1.9	2.7	3.4
Pension Funds	*	*	0.4	0.8	1.8	2.9	14.0	16.0	18.2	16.5
Investment Companies	*	*	*	0.3	0.3	0.7	13.5	1.1	2.1	2.1
Other Financial Institutions[f]	1.9	0.7	0.8	0.8	0.6	1.5	6.7	1.1	0.6	0.1
Other Sectors[g]	*	*	*	1.3	3.1	1.8	3.8	9.5	20.9	20.9

SOURCES: Raymond W. Goldsmith, Robert E. Lipsey, and Morris Mendelson, *Studies in the National Balance Sheet of the United States* (Princeton, N.J.: Princeton University Press, 1963), vol. II.   A study for the National Bureau of Economic Research, Inc.   Reprinted by permission of Princeton University Press.   For the years 1900, 1912, 1922, 1929, and 1939, see Tables IV-b-13d, 14a, 11c-2, 15a, 17b, 1-a, IV-b-6a, and 7a.   For the years 1945 and 1958, see Tables IV-b-13, 14, 11a-2, 15, 16, 17, 9, 6, and 7.   For the remaining years, except 1968, the data were taken from Board of Governors of the Federal Reserve System, Division of Research and Statistics, *Flow of Funds, Accounts, 1945–1967.* For 1968 the data are courtesy of the Federal Reserve System.

[a]In the Goldsmith data, government corporations fully guaranteed by the United States government are included in corporate bonds for the prewar years and in the Treasury securities for 1945 and 1958.   Moreover, the classifications are mixed in other ways.   The Federal Reserve data are labeled "corporate and foreign bonds";

In this context we can visualize the investment banker as the catalyst in the savings and investment process. By assuming responsibility for distribution of the securities, he or a group of similar firms constituting a syndicate of investment bankers can underwrite or guarantee the corporation a specific price for the issue. Given this commitment, the syndicate then markets the securities at a higher price. From the difference or spread, the participants hope to realize a profit. Thus, when investment bankers underwrite an issue, they relieve the nonfinancial corporation of the market risk, that is, the possibility that the security is overpriced relative to the demand for it. If the syndicate is wrong, the issue or some portion of it will not sell. The participants in the syndicate will have to lower the public offering price. As a result, members might experience not only a reduction in spread but an outright loss on the sale of the issue.

Later in the chapter we shall look more fully into the mechanics of distributing new securities. However, Figure 19-1 (page 440) gives some insight into the investment banking function by picturing these firms as intermediaries between nonfinancial corporations and households and financial institutions. It is possible for nonfinancial corporations to bypass investment bankers altogether. A typical example is a rights offering or privileged subscription to stockholders. In this case a corporation seeking to add to its outstanding equity first offers new stock, as it often must under the law, to existing shareholders, largely households. Investment banking firms do not underwrite this type of issue except insofar as they might agree to exercise any unsubscribed rights. Suppose, for example, that a corporation offers existing stockholders the rights to purchase 100,000 shares at $50 a share. Two percent of the rights are not exercised because shareholders, for one reason or another, forgot to take advantage of them during the subscription period. Investment bankers will then exercise these rights at the subscription price. Since the subscription price is usually well below the current market price, this standby commitment carries with it little market risk. Many companies whose stock is widely

---

the Goldsmith data for 1945 and 1958 are labeled "other bonds and notes," and for earlier years merely "corporate bonds."

  [b]Goldsmith, Lipsey, and Mendelson data.

  [c]Federal Reserve data.

  [d]Because of rounding, absolute magnitudes may differ slightly from the totals listed in the sources. For the same reason, the sum of the individual percentages may not equal 100.00.

  [e]The 1968 figure for corporate and foreign bonds for households is not comparable with earlier years. Hence the author added the flow for 1968 to the 1967 stock to arrive at a figure for 1968. See Board of Governors of the Federal Reserve, *op. cit.*, p. 174a, and *Federal Reserve Bulletin*, May, 1969, p. A69.3.

  [f]In the Goldsmith data, this includes government pension plans as well as other finance.

  [g]In the Goldsmith data, these are nonfinancial corporations and Government sectors. In the Federal Reserve data, these are state and local government and the rest of the world.

  [*]Less than $0.05 billion, or less than 0.05 percent.

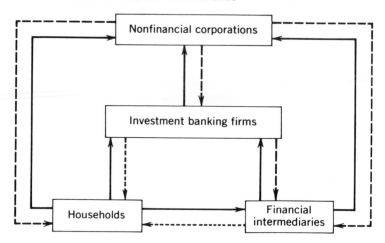

——— Savings

――― Securities of nonfinancial corporations

------ Securities of financial intermediaries

Figure 19-1 The new-issues market for securities of nonfinancial corporations and financial intermediaries.

held have found that with sufficient publicity and a subscription price well below the current market price, they can sell the entire issue without retaining an investment banker under a standby agreement.[2]

Similarly, a nonfinancial corporation may find it cheaper to let one or a few financial institutions purchase a new issue of long-term debt rather than market it publicly through an investment banking syndicate. It is possible, in this case, that an investment banking firm might receive a finder's fee for helping the corporation locate an interested investor or group of investors. But it does not participate directly in the distribution of the securities and hence assumes no underwriting risk.[3]

But even when investment bankers do help to distribute new securities, they may not make a firm commitment. For instance, the stockholders of a closely held firm may agree to market additional shares to other households. In so doing, they seek out the services of an investment banking firm. Its management in turn agrees to make available the firm's facilities for distributing new securities, that is, its sales force. Management may even form a syndicate with other banking

[2] *Ibid.*, p. 374.

[3] Unlike their role in making standby commitments in rights offerings, investment bankers have come to play an increasingly important role as agents in placing new securities privately. *Ibid.*, table 6.5, p. 347. See also pp. 345–50, 372, 378.

TABLE 19-2: DISTRIBUTION OF HOLDINGS OF CORPORATE STOCKS, SELECTED YEARS, 1900–1968

Holder	Absolute Magnitudes (In Billions of Dollars)									
	1900	1912	1922	1929	1939	1945	1958[a]	1958[b]	1965	1968
Total[c]	13.9	37.9	76.1	186.8	100.2	146.6	465.5	418.2	778.2	1035.8
Households	10.7	30.1	55.5	138.3	73.2	111.6	343.0	372.3	666.5	873.2
Financial Institutions	0.4	0.7	1.4	6.1	4.4	7.3	43.5	37.6	97.1	143.1
Commercial Banks	0.1	0.3	0.5	1.2	0.6	0.2	0.2	*	*	*
Life Insurance Companies	0.1	0.1	0.1	0.4	0.6	1.0	4.1	4.1	9.1	13.2
Savings Banks and Savings and Loan Associations	*	*	*	0.1	0.1	0.1	0.9	0.9	1.4	1.9
Non-life Insurance Companies	0.1	0.2	0.4	1.5	1.5	2.5	8.4	8.4	15.3	18.1
Pension Funds	*	*	*	0.1	0.2	0.3	10.8	11.6	39.7	59.6
Investment Companies	*	*	0.1	2.2	1.2	2.9	18.1	11.7	30.9	46.1
Other Financial Institutions[d]	0.1	0.1	0.3	0.7	0.2	0.3	1.0	0.9	0.7	4.2
Other Sectors[e]	2.8	7.1	19.2	42.3	22.6	27.7	79.0	8.3	14.6	19.5

Holder	Percent of Total Holdings									
Total[c]	100.0	100.0	100.0	100.0	100.0	100.0	100.0	100.0	100.0	100.0
Households	77.0	79.4	72.9	74.0	73.1	76.1	73.7	89.0	85.6	84.3
Financial Institutions	2.9	1.8	1.8	3.3	4.4	5.0	9.3	9.0	12.5	13.8
Comercial Banks	0.7	0.9	0.7	0.6	0.6	0.1	*	*	*	*
Life Insurance Companies	0.7	0.4	0.1	0.2	0.6	0.7	0.9	1.0	1.2	1.3
Savings Banks and Savings and Loan Associations	*	*	*	0.1	0.1	.0.1	0.2	0.2	0.2	0.2
Non-life Insurance Companies	0.7	0.5	0.5	0.8	1.5	1.7	1.8	2.0	2.0	1.7
Pension Funds	*	*	*	0.1	0.2	0.2	2.3	2.8	5.1	5.8
Investment Companies	*	*	0.1	1.2	1.2	2.0	3.9	2.8	4.0	4.5
Other Financial Institutions[d]	0.7	*	0.4	0.4	0.2	0.2	0.2	0.2	0.1	0.4
Other Sectors[e]	20.1	18.7	25.3	22.6	22.6	18.9	17.0	2.0	1.9	1.9

SOURCES: Same as for Table 19-1.
[a]See Table 19-1, footnote b.
[b]See Table 19-1, footnote c.
[c]See Table 19-1, footnote d.
[d]In the Goldsmith data, this includes government pension plans as well as other finance.
[e]In the Goldsmith data, these are government sectors and nonfinancial corporations.   In the Federal Reserve data, they are the rest of the world.
*Less than $0.05 billion, or less than 0.05 percent.

firms.   The group may even suggest specific contract features, but they will not underwrite the offering.   In short, they make available their facilities and services on a *best efforts* basis and are compensated accordingly.

The narrow definition of investment banking therefore excludes other services that could be rendered by investment bankers, as well as techniques employed in distributing new securities.   Investment banking firms might even offer advice on a new issue without participating in the underwriting syndicate.   As we shall see, this is common practice on securities marketed under competitive bidding procedures. Moreover, as a surgeon may decide not to operate, an investment banker may advise his client not to issue any securities, at least for the time being.   Many investment bankers, of course, continue to counsel their clients on financial matters which only infrequently entail a public offering of securities.

Finally, lest there be any misunderstanding, we should point out that investment banking is only one function offered by firms specializing in securities.   There are today very few financial concerns that confine their activities to underwriting or assisting in the flotation of new issues.[4]   Most financial firms are department stores of finance.   It is possible for a firm to participate in the underwriting of securities of nonfinancial corporations while selling instruments of financial intermediaries; for instance, shares in mutual funds.   In Figure 19-1 we have shown savings flowing from households to financial intermediaries. These funds may be channeled directly into the hands of nonfinancial corporations or indirectly to them through investment bankers. Savings may also flow indirectly through investment bankers engaged in other activities connected with the securities markets.   In either case, households receive directly or indirectly the securities of financial institutions.

Perhaps more widespread is the combination of investment banking and trading activities.   A firm underwriting new corporate securities may also trade in, and offer brokerage services to others trading in, outstanding issues.   In so doing it may underwrite secondary offerings. For instance, an institutional investor may wish to dispose of a large block of outstanding stocks or bonds.   In order to facilitate the sale, it may engage the services of an investment banking syndicate which, in turn, makes a firm commitment for the securities, redistributing them in much the same way as it would a primary issue.

Finally, a securities firm may not confine its activities to the private sector but may also engage in underwriting, distributing, trading in, as

---

[4]*Ibid.*, pp. 102–112.

well as offering brokerage services to others also trading in federal and state and local obligations.   While we shall continue to speak of investment banking firms, realistically we are simply discussing the investment banking function, as previously defined, of concerns engaged in various aspects of the securities business.

The New Issues Market—Historical Trends

Since its inception in 1934, the Securities and Exchange Commission has published data on the flotation of long-term corporate issues.   The figures from 1946 to the present are given in Table 19-3.   It is readily apparent that the bulk of long-term corporate issues is debt.   As presented, however, the figures tend to understate the role of equity, particularly common stock.[5]   The primary reasons for this assertion are (1) that the series on debt includes convertible bonds and (2) the series on stock excludes the issues of investment companies.   Let us look, for example, at the year 1967.   Gross sales of long-term corporate securities were approximately $24,798 million, of which $21,954 million was debt. However, $4,475 million of these securities was in convertibles and hence was really part debt and part equity.   Moreover, open-end investment companies in 1967 recorded a net increase—that is, new issues less redemptions—of $1,927 million in equity securities.   If we include this with our new issues of common stock and treat the convertibles as a hybrid, we can see from the results shown in Table 19-4 (page 445) that stock issues are far more important and debt issues far less important than the SEC figures would seem to indicate.

By excluding investment companies, particularly open-end companies, the SEC has left out what in recent years has become the most important issuer of stock.[6]   As we have seen from the data presented in an earlier chapter, there has been a secular decline in the relative importance of new stock issues in the capital structure of nonfinancial corporations.   While financial intermediaries can and do issue stock, many of them—such as companies administering pension funds and mutual savings and insurance institutions—do not.   Moreover, large numbers of them specialize in selling their own liabilities, such as insurance policies, savings accounts, and demand deposits.   As a result,

[5]If we were looking primarily at investment banker participation in the securities market, we would find that the increase in secondary offerings of common stock understates the importance of this security in issues underwritten by investment bankers. *Ibid.*, pp. 360–362.   Keep in mind that SEC statistics are for new issues and that offerings under $100,000 are excluded from the data.   See Securities and Exchange Commission, *Statistical Bulletin* (April, 1967), p. 14.

[6]Friend *et al.*, *op. cit.*, table 1.3, pp. 52–53.

TABLE 19-3: GROSS SALES OF NEW ISSUES OF LONG-TERM CORPORATE DEBT AND STOCKS, SELECTED YEARS, 1946–1968
(Absolute Magnitudes in Millions of Dollars)

Year	Total Issues[a]	Long-term Debt[a]	Percent of Total[a]	Preferred Stock[a]	Percent of Total[a]	Common Stock[a]	Percent of Total[a]
1946	6,900	4,882	70.8	1,127	16.3	891	12.9
1947	6,577	5,036	76.6	762	11.6	779	11.8
1948	7,078	5,973	84.4	492	7.0	614	8.7
1949	6,052	4,890	80.8	425	7.0	736	12.2
1950	6,362	4,920	77.3	631	9.9	811	12.7
1951	7,741	5,691	73.5	838	10.8	1,212	15.6
1952	9,534	7,601	79.7	564	5.9	1,369	14.4
1953	8,898	7,083	79.6	489	5.5	1,326	14.9
1954	9,516	7,488	78.7	816	8.6	1,213	12.7
1955	10,240	7,420	72.5	635	6.2	2,185	21.3
1956	10,939	8,002	73.2	636	5.8	2,301	21.0
1957	12,884	9,957	77.3	411	3.2	2,516	19.5
1958	11,558	9,653	83.5	571	4.9	1,334	11.5
1959	9,748	7,190	73.8	531	5.4	2,027	20.8
1960	10,154	8,081	79.6	409	4.0	1,664	16.4
1961	13,165	9,420	71.6	450	3.4	3,294	25.0
1962	10,705	8,969	83.8	422	3.9	1,314	12.3
1963	12,237	10,872	88.8	342	2.8	1,022	8.4
1964	13,957	10,865	77.8	412	3.0	2,679	19.2
1965	15,992	13,720	85.8	725	4.5	1,547	9.7
1966	18,075	15,561	86.1	574	3.2	1,939	10.7
1967	24,798	21,954	88.5	885	3.6	1,959	7.9
1968	21,966	17,383	79.1	637	2.9	3,946	18.0

SOURCES: Securities and Exchange Commission. For data on total issues and debt through 1962, see *30th Annual Report of the Securities and Exchange Commission*, table 5, p. 179. For more recent figures, see monthly issues of the *Federal Reserve Bulletin*.

[a]Because of rounding, the totals may not necessarily equal the sum of the components. For the same reason, the sum of the individual percentages may not equal 100.0.

of these intermediaries, only investment companies have a capital structure consisting substantially, indeed almost completely, of equity. Furthermore, only open-end companies or mutual funds can by definition issue an unlimited number of shares.

In Table 19-5 we have presented the SEC data for 1967 broken down into their industrial components. The securities of the two largest users of the long-term capital markets — manufacturing and electric, gas, and water utilities — constituted over 64 percent of all the securities issued during that year. Of the two groups, only one issued common stock in amounts substantially in excess of that issued by other subsectors. Were it not for public utilities, the preference shares issued would have been reduced from a small to an inconsequential amount. Regulatory commissions treat corporate income taxes as an expense

**TABLE 19-4:   MODIFICATIONS IN THE GROSS SALES OF NEW ISSUES OF
LONG-TERM CORPORATE DEBT AND STOCKS FOR THE YEAR 1967**
(Absolute Magnitudes in Millions of Dollars)

Security	Sales	Percent	Adjusted Sales	Percent
Total[a]	$24,798	100.0	$26,725	100.0
Bonds	21,954	88.5	17,479	65.4
Less Convertibles of $4,475			4,475	16.7
Preferred Stock	885	3.6	885	3.3
Common Stock, Excluding Issues of Open-end Investment Companies	1,959	7.9	1,959	7.3
Net Common Stock Issues of Open-end Investment Companies			1,927	7.2

SOURCES : Securities and Exchange Commission.   Data for all securities save for those of investment companies can be found in Securities and Exchange Commission, *Statistical Bulletin* (April, 1968), p. 12.   The figure for open-end investment companies was taken from *Federal Reserve Bulletin* (May, 1968), p. A-43.
[a]Because of rounding, the totals may not necessarily equal the sum of the components. For the same reason, the sum of the individual percentages may not equal 100.0.

**TABLE 19-5:   GROSS PROCEEDS FROM NEW CORPORATE SECURITIES BY TYPE OF
ISSUER AND TYPE OF SECURITY FOR THE YEAR 1967**
(Absolute Magnitudes in Millions of Dollars)

Issuer	Total Absolute Magnitude[a]	Percent of Total[a]	Long-term Debt Absolute Magnitude[a]	Percent of Total[a]	Preferred Stock Absolute Magnitude[a]	Percent of Total[a]	Common Stock Absolute Magnitude[a]	Percent of Total[a]
Total Corporate	24,798	100.0	21,954	100.0	885	100.0	1,959	100.0
Manufacturing	11,058	44.6	9,894	45.1	231	26.1	933	47.6
Extractive	587	2.4	406	1.8	7	0.8	175	8.9
Electric, Gas, and Water Utilities	4,935	19.9	4,217	19.2	537	60.7	181	9.2
Railroads	286	1.1	280	1.3	0	0	6	0.3
Other Transportation	1,781	7.2	1,670	7.6	10	1.1	101	5.2
Communication	1,979	8.0	1,786	8.1	70	7.9	123	6.3
Financial and Real Estate (Excluding Investment Companies)	2,433	9.8	2,247	10.2	9	1.0	177	9.0
Commercial and Others	1,738	7.0	1,453	6.6	21	2.4	263	13.4

SOURCE : Securities and Exchange Commission, *Statistical Bulletin* (April, 1968), p. 12.
[a]Because of rounding, the totals may not necessarily equal the sum of the components.   For the same reason, the sum of the individual percentages may not equal 100.0.

TABLE 19-6: GROSS SALES OF NEW ISSUES OF LONG-TERM CORPORATE DEBT AND STOCKS, SELECTED YEARS, 1901–1968
(Absolute Magnitudes in Millions of Dollars)

Short Periods	Total[c]		Long-term Debt[a]		Preferred Stock[b]		Common Stock[b]	
	Dollars	Percent	Dollars	Percent of Total	Dollars	Percent of Total	Dollars	Percent of Total
1901–1912	17,482	100.0	10,284	58.8	1,014	5.8	6,184	35.4
1923–1929	40,014	100.0	16,513	41.3	7,911	19.8	15,590	39.0
1946–1958	114,279	100.0	88.596	77.5	8,397	7.3	17,287	15.1
1959–1968	150,797	100.0	124,015	82.2	5,387	3.6	21,391	14.2

Longer Periods	Total[c]		Long-term Debt[a]		Preferred Stock[b]		Common Stock[b]	
	Dollars	Percent	Dollars	Percent of Total	Dollars	Percent of Total	Dollars	Percent of Total
1901–1922	39,576	100.0	21,651	54.7	3,979	10.1	13,946	35.2
1913–1939	84,749	100.0	43,957	51.9	12,682	15.0	28,110	33.2
1940–1958	131,068	100.0	102,803	78.4	10,110	7.7	18,155	14.0
1946–1968	265,076	100.0	212,611	80.2	13,784	5.2	38,678	14.6

SOURCES: For 1901–1939, see Raymond W. Goldsmith, *A Study of Savings in the United States* (Princeton, N.J. Princeton University Press, 1955), vol. 1, tables V-15, V-17, and V-19. Reprinted by permission of Princeton University Press. For 1940–1968, see sources of Table 19-3.
[a]In the Goldsmith data, bonds are limited to straight domestic corporate bonds and are broken down into three categories: railroads, utilities, and other industries. The SEC data are broken down into more subsectors and include convertible bonds.
[b]In the case of preferred and common stock, the Goldsmith data include investment companies, among other categories, whereas the SEC data do not.
[c]Because of rounding, the totals may not necessarily equal sum of the components. For the same reason, the sum of the individual percentages may not equal 100.0.

to be passed on to the consumer; that is, the utility earns an allowable rate of return after, rather than before, taxes. Hence it has no incentive to substitute some form of junior debt whose interest charges are tax-deductible for preferred stock whose dividends are not. Moreover, for reasons which are not altogether clear, regulatory commissions encourage public utilities to maintain a small amount of preferred stock in their capital structures. Thus this group keeps alive what has otherwise become all but an obsolete instrument of finance.

While a breakdown of data for other recent years might show slight changes in the relative importance of each group and each instrument, the results are consistent with both our cost-of-capital model and our analysis of the expanding role of financial intermediaries in the nation's capital markets. Of the three types of instruments, long-term corporate debt is the cheapest source of funds and a partial substitute for the most expensive source, preferred stock. Common stock would only be issued by new companies in expanding industries, including some areas of finance, and by companies whose demand for capital funds is sufficiently large to justify the cost of additional shares of external equity,[7] that is, by existing companies in expanding industries.

Moreover, with the exception of a few years during the 1920s (more specifically, 1928 and 1929),[8] long-term corporate debt has always been the most important of the three sources of funds while preferred stock has always been the least important. This is evident from the data in Table 19-6. To be sure, the figures for the years 1901–1939 are not totally comparable with the SEC data from 1940 to the present. If they were, they would show, without altering the above generalizations, a somewhat smaller decline in the importance of the role played by common stock, a somewhat smaller increase in the importance of long-term debt, and little change in the secular trend in preferred stock.[9] Long-term debt, therefore, has nearly always dominated the new-issues market.

The Techniques of Investment Banking

While the statistical data are not at variance with our cost-of-capital model, there has been a secular increase in the importance of long-term debt. Yet, as we saw earlier, there has also been a secular decline in the importance of the role of external sources among nonfinancial corporations. There are numerous institutional factors responsible for these trends. We have already treated at some length the effect of corporate income taxes on the cost of both debt and equity. We have also argued that personal income taxes work in favor of retaining earn-

[7]Alternatively, it is also possible for the cost of common equity capital to be relatively low because the current E/P ratio is less than the E_a/P ratio. But is management of the corporation always acting in the best interest of its common stockholders when it takes these opportunities to float new issues of common stock?

[8]Friend et al., *op. cit.*, table 1.5, p. 69.

[9]Compare, for example, the Goldsmith and the SEC data for four overlapping years, 1935–1939.

	Total		Long-term Debt		Preferred Stock		Common Stock	
	Millions of Dollars[a]	Percent of Total[a]	Millions of Dollars[a]	Percent of Total[a]	Millions of Dollars[a]	Percent of Total[a]	Millions of Dollars[a]	Percent of Total[a]
Goldsmith Data	13,429	100.0	10,508	78.2	1,037	7.7	1,884	14.0
SEC Data	13,532	100.0	11,895	87.9	947	7.0	691	5.1

SOURCES: For the Goldsmith data, see sources of Table 19-6. Reprinted by permission of Princeton University Press. The SEC data are by courtesy of the Commission, with totals and debt figures through 1962 reprinted from *30th Annual Report on the Securities and Exchange Commission*, table 5, p. 179.

[a]Because of rounding, the totals may not necessarily equal the sum of the components. For the same reason, the sum of the individual percentages may not equal 100.0.

ings.   But we have done little in analyzing the impact of other aspects of a changing environment on the new-issues market and ultimately on the composition of financing.

We have seen from earlier chapters that the importance of the corporation as a vehicle through which goods and services are produced and rendered is a relatively recent phenomenon.   Prior to the turn of the century, most industrial enterprises were partnerships and proprietorships whose capital needs could be met without a public sale of securities.   There were exceptions, the most conspicuous of which were the railroads.   But only when a national market developed did industrial and merchandising establishments find that a larger scale of enterprise organized under the corporate form was more efficient.   They were joined by public utilities whose capital requirements, like those of railroads, were sufficiently large to necessitate substantial amounts of outside financing.   It was out of industry's and business's need to tap diverse sources of funds that investment bankers rose to importance.

Although the origins of investment banking date from the early 1800s, its modern phase apparently begins with Jay Cooke's efforts to finance the Civil War and somewhat later the rapidly expanding railroad network.   While using publicity to reach a mass market, he also developed techniques which, although altered in form, are the basis for procedures employed today for distributing new issues through investment bankers to households and financial intermediaries.[10]

By the early twentieth century, it was not uncommon for corporations to sell an entire issue to a single investment banker.   The firm, or originating house, would in turn form a purchase syndicate among other firms.   To spread the risk still further, a third group, or banking syndicate, would sometimes be formed.   The originating house, or house of issue, would make a firm commitment to the company and then step up the price to the purchase syndicate, which in turn would mark up the price still further when the issue was sold to the banking syndicate.   Often the originating house would participate in the purchase syndicate.   Then, together with members of the purchase syndicate, the originating house would join in the banking syndicate.   The originating house would manage both groups.   Depending on the financial resources at its command, an investment banking firm would enter the process at some stage along the route.   During the 1920s, selling groups, usually consisting of brokerage firms, were added to the structure.[11]

[10]Merwin H. Waterman, *Investment Banking Functions: Their Evolution and Adaptation to Business Finance* (Ann Arbor: Bureau of Business Research, School of Business Administration, University of Michigan, 1958), pp. 22–26.

[11]Harold R. Medina, *Opinion: U.S. vs. Morgan, et al.* (New York: The Record Press, 1953), pp. 15–37.

Today the procedures are more simplified,[12] yet vestiges of an earlier era remain. The financial manager of a nonfinancial corporation, although he may seek out offers from various houses, usually negotiates with one house at a time. Once an agreement is reached, the originating house forms and manages the purchasing or underwriting syndicate. Since many firms are actively engaged in both investment banking and the brokerage business, there may be no need to form a selling group. Today a syndicate is more likely to consist of a group of firms with sufficient capital to underwrite, and sufficient brokerage outlets to sell, a new issue without forming several intermediate groups. The spread between the price paid to the issuer and the price paid by the investor is divided according to a predetermined formula into the management fee, the underwriting compensation, and the sales commission. Dealers not engaged in underwriting the securities, but who are able to sell some of the issue, may receive as much as 50 percent of the spread on each security sold. Some will receive both a sales commission and an underwriting compensation which together equal perhaps 90 percent of the spread. The manager is further compensated for the time spent with the issue in preliminary negotiations, preparation of statements to be filed with the Securities and Exchange Commission, clauses in the security contract, etc., by receiving perhaps 10 percent of the spread on all securities sold.

The compensation for the underwriting risk takes on significance only because the security may not be sold at the public offering price. Those agreeing to underwrite the issue agree also to maintain the price of the security during the flotation period of, say, 30 days. The purpose of instituting this temporary price support is to help distribute the securities to the ultimate purchasers. If the issue is quickly sold out, the underwriters will liquidate the syndicate and a secondary market in the issue may develop. If, however, all or some of the issue remains unsold at the end of the flotation period, the underwriting syndicate distributes the remainder in proportions previously agreed upon. Each underwriter is free to dispose of the issue as he sees fit. Some may "put it on the shelf." Others may choose to dispose of their share at a reduced price. The outcome, of course, is a reduction in spread. A

---

[12]There are three reasons why the structure of underwriting syndicates has been simplified. First, the Federal transfer tax on bonds would apply to each successive syndicate as the securities moved from the issuer to the banking syndicate and finally to the selling group. Second, with the separation of commercial from investment banking, a number of firms which had been departments of commercial banks found their sources of funds seriously curtailed. Many were unable to participate at any level in the underwriting process. Finally, under the liability provisions of the Securities Act of 1933, if the originating house bought the issue, it was fully liable for the entire amount of the issue. By having the issue bought by the syndicate, the liability was shared among the participants. See Friend et al., *op. cit.*, pp. 401–402.

sufficient number of these mistakes, given the banker's overhead, can result in substantial operating losses for the year. On the other hand, a succession of rapid sales in which the firm moves its capital from one commitment to another can be highly profitable.

Federal Regulation of Investment Banking

A factor significantly altering the market for new securities as well as the investment banking function has been the increase over time in federal regulation. There are certain features of this regulation which are relevant to the new-issues market. Prior to the Great Depression, investment banking operated in a relatively laissez faire environment. During this period, investment banking was intertwined with commercial banking. Furthermore, as there was, by today's standards, relatively little financial information on which to judge the merits of a particular issue, the public linked the quality of the security to the name of the originating house. By having a partner or chief officer of the investment banking firm on the board of directors of the corporation issuing the security, purchasers were presumably assured that their interests were represented. Unfortunately, this was not always the case. Particularly in the 1920s, unknown firms capitalizing on a securities-hungry public were able to sell issues which the purchasers might not have bought if they had had sufficient information as to the risks involved in committing their funds.

In the wake of the 1929 market debacle and the subsequent Great Depression, there were enacted a series of laws accompanied by regulations which permanently altered the investment banking industry. In 1933, the Banking Act separated commercial from investment banking, the former being forbidden to underwrite or deal in securities other than those of federal, state, and local governments. Major investment banking firms which were security affiliates of commercial banks were forced to separate. Private bankers who "had previously conducted a deposit business along with investment banking had to elect one or the other option."[13] The J. P. Morgan Company, for example, chose to remain in commercial banking while a new investment banking firm, Morgan Stanley & Company, was founded. The result was a substantial decline in bank deposits available for investment in securities. The commercial bank's role in the distribution of corporate issues was reduced to short-term loans to investment bankers floating new securities.

Of perhaps greater significance was the passage of the Securities

[13]*Ibid.*, p. 101.

Act of 1933.   Drafted to provide full and "fair disclosure of the character of securities sold," its immediate impact was to raise the cost of
public offerings of corporate issues.   Any corporation desirous of
marketing its securities through a *public offering* must file with the
Securities Exchange Commission certain financial information in a
formal *registration statement*.   Assuming it is not amended, the registration statement will become effective 20 days after it is filed.   No
public offering can take place prior to that date.   If it is amended, either
by the company or at the request of the Commission, the 20-day waiting
period can start all over again.   As a result, depending on the number
of amendments filed, it may be much longer than 20 days before the
issue can be offered.[14]

During the waiting period, a preliminary *prospectus* — an official
summary of the information contained in the registration statement —
is circulated by the underwriting syndicate through its retail outlets or
through other brokers and dealers interested in, but not participating
in, the underwriting syndicate.   While no securities may be sold prior
to the date when the registration statement is filed, during the waiting
period "offers to sell the securities are permitted but no written offer
may be made except by means of a statutory prospectus."[15]   Moreover,
during this period a dealer can "orally solicit indications of interest or
offers to buy and may discuss the securities with his customers and
advise them whether or not in his opinion the securities are desirable
or suitable for them."[16]   However, the principal purpose of the waiting
period is to enable dealers and investors to familiarize themselves with
the information contained in the registration statement and arrive at
an "unhurried decision."   Thus the Commission states that "no
contracts of sale can be made during this period, the purchase price may
not be paid or received and offers to buy may be cancelled."[17]

Those connected with a public offering not only must abide by
these formal procedures, but also can come under both civil and
criminal liabilities for any false and misleading information which
might appear in the registration statement.   The SEC is never responsible for the information contained in these statements.   But even after
the statement has become effective, if the SEC finds that it includes

[14]"The median number of calendar days from the date of the original filing to the
effective date for the 1,280 registration statements that became effective during the
1966 fiscal year was 38, compared with 36 days for the 1,097 registration statements in
fiscal 1965 and 36 days for 960 registration statements in fiscal year 1964."   Securities
and Exchange Commission, *32nd Annual Report* (Washington: Government Printing Office,
1967), p. 23.

[15]Securities and Exchange Commission, *Securities Act of 1933*, Release No. 4697, p. 1.

[16]*Ibid.*, p. 2.

[17]*Ibid.*

false and misleading information, it can issue an order stopping further sales, investigate the case more fully, and take appropriate legal steps against the parties involved.   Recourse in the courts is also open to the purchasers who suffer losses because they relied on information in the registration statement which subsequently proved to be false or misleading.

These additional risks together with the expenses incurred in preparing the registration statement and the fee charged by the Commission to register the offering all add to the flotation costs and hence to the cost of a public offering.   Indeed, if the issuer and the investment bankers were forced to agree on the price and spread when the statement is filed, the market risk involved would virtually prohibit a public offering.   Thus these facts are added as amendments to the registration statement on the day when it is to take effect.   The SEC then accelerates what would ordinarily be another 20-day waiting period and allows the securities to be marketed.

When the registration does become effective, a firm commitment among the purchasers and the underwriting and selling group can be made.   In these circumstances, the waiting period can be useful in sounding out investor interest in the offering and hence in the price at which it may be sold.   But even after the statement becomes effective, the underwriting syndicate must observe rather rigid rules as to the distribution of the issue to the purchasers.   Advertising is restricted to formal *tombstone* announcements simply listing the securities for sale and the underwriting firms from which a prospectus can be obtained. Each purchaser must receive a final prospectus summarizing the registration statement which has become effective and listing the price at which the issue is being offered to the public.

Private Placements and Public Offerings

Largely because of the costs of complying with the law, those companies seeking funds through the sale of securities have sought ways of avoiding these expenses.   The simplest means of doing so is to place the issue privately with one or a few investors rather than offering it publicly. The SEC defines securities privately placed as "issues sold to a restricted number of investors without public offering."[18]   What constitutes a restricted number of investors is decided by the SEC.   It may vary from case to case.   However, if the issuer and the purchasers deal directly with one another in setting the terms of the issue and if the number of persons to whom it is offered is "small," the issue is a *private placement.*

[18]Securities and Exchange Commission, *Statistical Bulletin* (April, 1967), p. 14.

The purchasers, of course, are usually institutional investors, although they need not be.[19]

Tables 19-7 and 19-8 (pages 454–455) give a detailed breakdown of securities privately placed and publicly offered. It has been estimated that between 1900 and 1933, $1 billion in debt, or 3.0 percent of all corporate issues, were placed privately.[20] Since the SEC was not established until 1934, it did not publish data for 1934 covering the full calendar year. But it is evident that private placement was growing in importance by the late 1930s. It continued to do so until the early 1950s, when the share of issues privately placed declined somewhat. Since that time, issues directly placed have fluctuated from year to year, often accounting for well over 30 percent of all issues and 50 percent of all debt.

Nearly all the securities placed privately are some form of corporate debt. Very few equity issues are directly placed. This should come as no surprise. As we have seen, institutional investors making heavy purchases in equities are still relatively few compared with those investing funds primarily in debt obligations.[21] Moreover, most of these institutions confine their activities to outstanding issues or new issues of well-known corporations.[22] Historically, therefore, the trends in private placement are largely the trends in the placement of corporate debt. Since life insurance companies are the primary purchaser of these instruments, the amount placed in any given year may well depend on the funds available to these companies. As the investment income of life insurance companies changes relative to the volume of corporate debt issues, private placements can be expected to change as well. For the issuing corporation, the marginal cost of a public offering is always greater than a private placement. However, the total cost to maturity need not be. It is possible for institutional investors to quote bids above

[19]Avery B. Cohan, *Private Placement and Public Offerings: Market Shares since 1935* (Chapel Hill: University of North Carolina, School of Business Administration, 1961), pp. 2–3.

[20]*Ibid.*, p. 1, and Donald L. Demmerer, "The Marketing of Securities 1930–52," *Journal of Economic History*, vol. 12, no. 4 (Fall, 1952), p. 459.

[21]Small issues, both debt and equity, are sometimes privately placed. This has been particularly true of equity issues of less than $1 million. See Friend et al., *op. cit.*, p. 345. Presumably one of the social advantages of private placement is that it allows a knowledgeable institutional investor to purchase the securities of a relatively unknown company whose real financial strength is sufficient but whose value is unappreciated by a public applying conventional ratio analysis to accounting statements rather than analyzing the pattern of probable cash flows.

[22]Beginning in 1958, small-business investment companies, established under government encouragement, were supposed to provide equity capital for small businesses. Not only have these investment companies shown only sporadic growth, but a substantial portion of their assets are invested in loans and convertibles rather than straight equity instruments. See Small Business Administration, 1966 *Annual Report*, pp. 22–27.

TABLE 19-7: CORPORATE ISSUES PUBLICLY OFFERED AND PRIVATELY PLACED, 1935–1968
(Absolute Magnitudes in Millions of Dollars)

Calender Year	Total Issues Publicly Offered and Privately Placed[a]	Public Offerings			Private Placements		
		Total[a]	Percent of All Issues[a]	Total[a]	Percent of all Issues[a]	Debt Issues[a]	Equity Issues[a]
1935	2,332	1,945	83.4	387	16.6	385	2
1936	4,572	4,199	91.8	373	8.2	369	4
1937	2,309	1,979	85.7	330	14.3	327	3
1938	2,155	1,463	67.9	692	32.1	691	1
1939	2,164	1,458	67.4	706	32.6	703	4
1940	2,677	1,912	71.4	765	28.6	758	7
1941	2,667	1,854	69.5	813	30.5	811	2
1942	1,062	642	60.5	420	39.5	411	9
1943	1,170	798	68.2	372	31.8	369	3
1944	3,202	2,415	75.4	787	24.6	778	9
1945	6,011	4,989	83.0	1,022	17.0	1,004	18
1946	6,900	4,983	72.2	1,917	27.8	1,863	54
1947	6,577	4,342	66.0	2,235	34.0	2,147	88
1948	7,078	3,991	56.4	3,087	43.6	3,008	79
1949	6,052	3,550	58.7	2,502	41.3	2,453	49
1950	6,362	3,681	57.9	2,680	42.1	2,560	120
1951	7,741	4,326	55.9	3,415	44.1	3,326	88
1952	9,534	5,533	58.0	4,002	42.0	3,957	45
1953	8,898	5,580	62.7	3,318	37.3	3,228	90
1954	9,516	5,848	61.5	3,668	38.5	3,484	185
1955	10,240	6,763	66.0	3,477	34.0	3,301	176
1956	10,939	7,053	64.5	3,886	35.5	3,777	109
1957	12,884	8,959	69.5	3,935	30.5	3,839	86
1958	11,558	8,068	69.8	3,490	30.2	3,320	169
1959	9,748	5,993	61.5	3,755	38.5	3,632	122
1960	10,154	6,657	65.6	3,497	34.4	3,275	221
1961	13,165	8,143	61.9	5,022	38.1	4,720	302
1962	10,705	6,064	56.6	4,640	43.3	4,529	111
1963	12,237	5,823	47.6	6,413	52.4	6,158	255
1964	13,957	6,453	46.2	7,504	53.8	7,243	261
1965	15,992	7,442	46.5	8,550	53.5	8,150	399
1966	18,075	10,372	57.3	7,703	42.6	7,543	159
1967	24,798	17,633	71.1	7,165	28.9	6,964	199
1968	21,966	15,003	68.3	6,963	31.7	6,651	312

SOURCES: Securities and Exchange Commission.   For the data from 1935–1962, see also *30th Annual Report of the Securities and Exchange Commission*, table 5, p. 179.

[a]Because of rounding, the totals may not necessarily equal the sum of the components.   For the same reason, the sum of the individual percentages may not equal 100.0.

the going rate of return, particularly if they wish to discourage an issuer.   They might also attach clauses to a bond indenture restricting, for example, management's prerogatives to pay dividends unless interest is covered by a particular multiple of earnings.   They may also

TABLE 19-8: PRIVATE PLACEMENT AND PUBLIC OFFERING OF CORPORATE DEBT, 1935–1968
(In Millions of Dollars)

Year	Amount[a]	Publicly Offered[a]	Percent of Total Publicly Offered[a]	Privately Placed[a]	Percent of Total Privately Placed[a]
1935	2,225	1,840	82.7	385	17.3
1936	4,029	3,660	90.8	369	9.2
1937	1,618	1,291	79.8	327	20.2
1938	2,044	1,353	66.2	691	33.8
1939	1,979	1,276	64.5	703	35.5
1940	2,386	1,628	68.3	758	31.7
1941	2,389	1,578	66.1	811	33.9
1942	917	506	55.1	411	44.8
1943	990	621	62.7	369	37.3
1944	2,670	1,892	70.9	778	29.1
1945	4,855	3,851	79.3	1,004	20.7
1946	4,882	3,019	61.8	1,863	38.2
1947	5,036	2,889	57.4	2,147	42.6
1948	5,973	2,965	49.6	3,008	50.4
1949	4,890	2,437	49.8	2,453	50.1
1950	4,920	2,360	48.0	2,560	52.0
1951	5,691	2,364	41.5	3,326	58.4
1952	7,601	3,645	48.0	3,957	52.1
1953	7,083	3,856	54.4	3,228	45.6
1954	7,488	4,003	53.5	3,484	46.5
1955	7,420	4,119	55.5	3,301	44.5
1956	8,002	4,225	52.8	3,777	47.2
1957	9,957	6,118	61.4	3,839	38.6
1958	9,653	6,332	65.6	3,320	34.4
1959	7,190	3,557	49.5	3,632	50.5
1960	8,081	4,806	59.5	3,275	40.5
1961	9,420	4,700	49.9	4,720	50.1
1962	8,969	4,440	49.5	4,529	50.5
1963	10,872	4,714	43.4	6,158	56.6
1964	10,865	3,623	33.3	7,243	66.7
1965	13,720	5,570	40.6	8,150	59.4
1966	15,561	8,018	51.5	7,543	48.5
1967	21,954	14,991	68.3	6,964	31.7
1968	17,383	10,731	61.7	6,651	38.3

SOURCES : Same as for Table 19-7.
[a]Because of rounding, the totals may not necessarily equal the sum of the components. For the same reason, the sum of the individual percentages may not equal 100.0.

insist on sinking fund provisions, a guarantee that the issue will not be called for perhaps 10 years, or a voice in management if earnings fall below a particular level.   These and similar provisions may discourage the issuer from placing the securities of the company privately.

Statistics, of course, can also fluctuate because of a change in issues not covered in the data.   The SEC series on debt, for instance, excludes notes sold exclusively to commercial banks, intercorporate transactions, and issues "which institutions had contracted to purchase but which were not taken down during the period covered by the statistics."[23] Moreover, while mortgages on business property are not excluded from the SEC series on debt, they are in practice excluded from the data.[24] Thus a decline in private placements from one year to the next might occur if nonfinancial corporations increased their mortgages at the expense of corporate bonds.

In spite of these qualifications there is sufficient evidence to conclude that the provisions of the Securities Act of 1933 were responsible for the secular decline in the public offering of corporate debt. This is not to say that the act was responsible for an increase in institutional participation. Even if the act had not been passed, financial intermediaries would probably have continued to expand their holdings of long-term corporate debt more or less in relation to the funds they receive and in light of their alternative investment opportunities.

Increased reliance on private placement, however, may help to lower the investment banker's spread. A competitive alternative appears to exist now where there was none before. We shall return to this point shortly. Before doing so, we must consider another important change brought about by government regulation — the institution of competitive bidding.

Competitive Bidding

Even if securities are publicly offered, the issuer may not be able to negotiate with investment bankers. The company may have to submit the issue to *publicly sealed bids.* Since 1928, the Interstate Commerce Commission, with control over railroad issues, has required that equipment trust certificates be submitted to *competitive bidding.*[25] Since 1944, it has required publicly sealed bids for all railroad debt issues. Similarly, since 1941, the Securities and Exchange Commission has required all interstate gas and electric companies subject to the provisions of the Public Utility Holding Company Act to submit their issues to competitive bidding. Following the SEC lead, the Federal Power Commission issued similar requirements — as did many state utility commissions — for the companies under its jurisdiction.

[23]Securities and Exchange Commission, *Statistical Bulletin* (April, 1967), p. 14.
[24]*Ibid.* See also Cohan, *op. cit.,* p. 2.
[25]Donald M. Street, *Railroad Equipment Financing* (New York: Columbia University Press, 1959), pp. 59–62, 135.

By the mid-1940s, most of the debt issues of the regulated industries were subject to competitive bidding.[26] Prior to the inauguration of these regulations, competitive bidding applied to a rather small percentage of corporate securities. Between 1935 and 1940, for instance, "this method involved less than five percent of the total underwritten offerings of corporate bonds."[27] From 1940 to 1944, competitive bidding applied to nearly 33 percent of the corporate debt floated, rising to over 54 percent by 1951. Public utilities accounted for over 24 of the 33 percent and over 52 of the 54 percent. Since that time, the percentage of debt subject to competitive biddings appears to have declined, with utilities again accounting for nearly all of it.[28]

Except among regulated industries, there seems to be little use made of competitive bidding. Since external financing by railroads has declined relative to total external finance over the years, the continued importance of competitive bidding appears to depend on the volume of public-utility financing. More specifically, it depends on the amount of debt financing, for while equity instruments of these companies may sometimes be subject to competitive bidding, in practice they are usually exempted.[29]

As for companies not required to use competitive bidding, there seems to be little disposition to choose this procedure. Probably the lack of enthusiasm comes from the fact that, under competitive bidding, members of the competing syndicates cannot help the issuer in preparing the registration statement or the terms of the securities' contract without disqualifying themselves from the bidding. This means that a financial manager must usually hire a separate investment banking firm to assist him in these matters. The total flotation costs to the issuer may not differ significantly whether the issue is subjected to publicly sealed bids by competing syndicates or marketed through a negotiated transaction with the issuing house participating from the beginning.

[26]Sidney M. Robbins, "Competitive Bidding in the Sale of Securities," *Harvard Business Review*, vol. 27, no. 5 (September, 1949), pp. 646–664.

[27]Friend et al., *op. cit.*, p. 385.

[28]*Ibid.*, table 6.23, p. 390. See also Halsey, Stuart and Company, Inc., *A Twenty-Year Record and Study of Corporate Debt Financing in the United States* (Chicago: Halsey, Stuart and Company, Inc., 1962).

[29]Friend et al., *op. cit.*, p. 387. Not all states require competitive bidding. Moreover, many operating gas and electric companies have gradually worked themselves free from the provisions of the Public Utility Holding Company Act and the jurisdiction of the SEC. See Cohan, *op. cit.*, pp. 35–36.

Competition in the Flotation of New Securities

The problem, of course, is to determine whether the leading investment bankers have monopoly power. If they do, then competitive bidding should result in a decline in the total flotation costs to the issuer. To prove conclusively whether or not monopoly power exists we would have to select a random sample from a homogeneous group of securities all issued at the same time. Some of the securities would have to be publicly offered through negotiated transactions while others would have to be subjected to competitive bidding. Moreover, we would have to make the spreads under the two procedures comparable. To do so, we could add to the competitive bid the costs incurred by the investment banker if he had helped prepare the issue from the start, or alternatively subtract these costs from the compensation in the case of the negotiated offering. If the adjusted differences in spreads were statistically significant, with the spread on the competitive bids lower, we could conclude that for the period under study the investment banking industry exercised a degree of monopoly power that resulted in a higher cost of capital to the issuer using a negotiated public offering.

As with most efforts in applied economics, the data necessary to implement the tests suggested by the model often fail to meet the standards required. We must therefore base our conclusions on imperfect information. The facts are that under competitive bidding the spread is smaller than in a negotiated transaction.[30] But how much of this reflects not only differences in services rendered but also heterogeneity in the securities offered? That is, assuming negotiated issues were submitted to publicly sealed bids or those issues bid for competitively were negotiated, would the spread on competitive bids still be lower after appropriate allowances were made for differences in services rendered?

Another problem in interpreting data is that all the statistics pertaining to spread represent gross underwriting compensation. There are no figures on net income attributable to investment banking activities and, hence, no measure of profits after expenses.[31] *Gross spread*, as we have defined it for an underwritten issue, is the difference between the anticipated offering price and the firm commitment given the issuer by the group of underwriters. If a syndicate offers a corporation a price of $992 on each of a series of 6 percent 20-year first-mortgage bonds which it plans to market at par (or $1,000), the gross spread is $8.00 per bond. Just as division of this spread varies among members of the syn-

[30]Friend et al., *op. cit.*, p. 39. See also Avery B. Cohan, *Cost of Flotation of Long-term Corporate Debt since 1935* (Chapel Hill: University of North Carolina, School of Business Administration, 1961), p. 31.

[31]Friend et al., *op. cit.*, p. 35.

dicate in accordance with the services performed (that is, management of the issue, compensation for the risk assumed, and compensation for selling the security), so too does it vary according to the services performed by the syndicate.   Not only is the gross spread lower for a publicly sealed bid than for a negotiated offering, but it is even less for a best-efforts sale than for an underwritten issue.   Fees charged for standby commitments and for acting as agents in private placement are even less.   These results logically follow from the differences in the services performed.

Moreover, for any given year, the gross spread may be a function of the type of security and the size of the issue.   Securities and Exchange Commission studies of new offerings in recent years indicate that the spread on common stock is greater than the spread on preferred stock, and the spread on preferred stock is higher than the spread on bonds.   From Figure 19-2 it is apparent that for all three types of issues, the spread as a percentage of gross proceeds falls rapidly for issues under $10 million.   In the case of common stock, the spread on issues of less than $1 million may vary between 11 and 21 percent.   For debt of the same size or less, the cost may be 7 to 8 percent, and for preferred stock it may be 8 to 9 percent.

Once the size of the issue of preferred stock and debt exceeds $10 million, the flotation costs level off at slightly under 1 percent in the case of the latter and between 2 and 3 percent in the case of the former.   The flotation costs of common stock continue to decline as the size of the

Figure 19-2   Gross spread as a percentage of gross proceeds from the sale of new issues. SOURCES:Securities and Exchange Commission, *Cost of Flotation of Corporate Securities, 1951–1955* (Washington: Government Printing office, 1957), pp. 18–19 and 21.

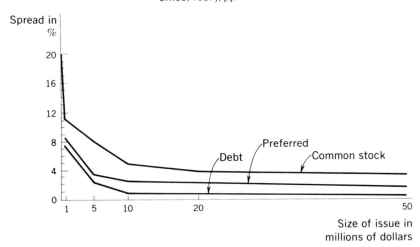

issue rises from \$10 to \$20 million, averaging in excess of 4 percent. As the size of the issue rises from \$20 to \$50 million, there may be a tendency for the spread to increase slightly.

The relative differences in flotation costs are of the order we would expect. The greatest risk lies in a common stock flotation. Not only is the issue subject to wider price fluctuations, but the market, as we have seen, is largely households. To dispose of an issue of a given size requires more selling effort than in the case of bonds. Increased selling compensation may even account for the increase in spread sometimes observed as the size of the issue expands from \$20 to \$50 million or more. Preferred stock lies somewhere in between. Unless convertible into common stock, its price will fluctuate narrowly as in the case of bonds. In addition, preferred stock may be acceptable to some institutions whose equity purchases might otherwise be restricted.

While the spread for any given year appears to vary according to type and size of the issue,[32] there is some tendency for it to decline over time.[33] The trend is more pronounced for common stock than for debt or preferred stock. This declining trend in gross spread may be due to increasing competition from private placement and competitive bidding. But it may also be the result of other factors. For example, gross spread on common stock flotation is often only part of the compensation received. In addition to cash compensation, the syndicate may be given options to purchase new shares below the offering price. This was particularly important in the early 1960s. Moreover, the data on common stock go back only to 1940, whereas bond and preferred stock series can be carried back further. Given the strong bull market in the 1950s, there was an apparent reevaluation of risk in equities. In a rising and, hence, receptive market, it is easier to float new equity issues, and the risk attached to doing so is lessened.

Interest rates, on the other hand, fell through the 1930s and were held at artificially low levels in the 1940s and early 1950s. Thereafter

[32]In making spread a function of the size of the issue, we are oversimplifying and perhaps overstating its role. The results of studies employing multiple regression analysis show that in the case of debt issues for any given year, the size of the offering is not a statistically significant variable. More important in the determination of spread is the yield on the bonds. Gross compensation varies directly with yield. Similarly, although the size of the offering and the size of the issuing corporation are statistically significant variables in determining gross spread on common stock, the price of the issue is far more important. See Cohan, *Cost of Flotation of Long-term Corporate Debt since 1935 op. cit.* and Friend et al., *op. cit.*, pp. 38–39, 419–425, 428–449. Since yield reflects the quality of the bond, investment bankers apparently gauge their underwriting risk and selling costs more on this variable than on the size of the issue. Even in the illustrations in Figure 19-2, size becomes relatively unimportant once the \$10 million figure is reached. On the other hand, while selling costs on common stock are traditionally a function of price, size of the issue retains some of its importance, with spread rising slightly for larger issues.

[33]Cohan, *ibid.*, and Friend et al., *op. cit.*, pp. 36–37 and 406–419.

the trend was upward, with prices on bonds falling accordingly. Yet the rise in the importance of institutional investors may have more than offset this pattern, substantially lowering the risks in underwriting long-term debt.

The regulations of the Securities Act of 1933 may cut both ways. Since the registration costs are the responsibility of the issuer they would not be reflected in the spread. But to the extent that investment bankers are unable to indemnify themselves against the liabilities under the Act, they increase their risk and, therefore, the costs of underwriting the issue. On the other hand, the waiting period does give them an opportunity to assess the market for the issue. Nevertheless, once the registration statement is filed, unless the issuer withdraws it, the syndicate is committed. Sudden changes in the market during this period can add to the risk in underwriting the issue.

Finally, if, on balance, the expenses incurred by underwriters have declined over time—that is, if the capital markets are more efficiently organized—then the gross spread could fall without affecting the net return on investment banking services. Indeed, in competitive markets this is what we would expect to happen with lower investment banking expenses reflected in a lower supply price of external funds to the issuer.

Since the relevant data on performance are lacking, these mixed conclusions are all that can be reasonably offered. There is, however, one other piece of evidence bearing on the competitive nature of the investment banking industry: its structure. There has been, over time, a considerable decline in the concentration in negotiated issues. For example, the largest five firms accounted for 56 percent of these flotations in the years 1935–1937, 45 percent in the years 1947–1949, and 39 percent in the years 1961–1963. In competitive bidding transactions, however, the largest five firms accounted for 73 percent of the flotations in the years 1935–1937 (when they were relatively unimportant), 75 percent in the years 1947–1949, and 73 percent in the years 1961–1963.[34] To be sure, a comparison of relatively prosperous years with those near the end of the Great Depression can overstate the apparent decline in concentration of negotiated issues. As the absolute volume of offerings increases relative to the capacity of the industry, new firms will enter. This is what happened in the 1920s. It occurred again in the late 1950s and early 1960s, particularly in issues in which offerings would ordinarily be negotiated.[35] Moreover, during this latest period, there has been little change in the rank of the top five investment banking firms that

[34]Friend et al., *ibid.*, p. 156.
[35]U.S. Congress, House Committee on Interstate and Foreign Commerce, *Report of the Special Study of the Securities Markets of the Securities and Exchange Commission*, 88th Cong., 1st Sess. part 1, pp. 553–557.

consistently manage more than 50 percent of the dollar volume of new issues.[36]

While the student may draw his own conclusions, the weight of the available evidence seems to support the assertion that competition in the new issues market has increased over time, resulting in a lower cost of external sources.   But issues publicly offered remain the most expensive source of funds.   To the extent that nonfinancial corporations can meet their needs through internal and external sources privately placed, they can be expected to continue to place less reliance on public offerings.[37]

SUMMARY

Corporations ordinarily enter the capital markets at rather infrequent intervals.   When they do, their financial managers must often rely on the services of companies specializing in financial advice, that is, securities firms offering investment banking services.

When securities specialists perform the investment banking function, they ordinarily assume responsibility for distributing new debt or equity securities of firms seeking long-term capital.   They are the catalyst between the savings and investing sectors of the economy.   Corporations, of course, can and do make direct offerings of stock to stockholders.   They often place debt privately with financial institutions.   In each instance, the role of the investment banking firm is limited.   In a rights offering to stockholders, it may be employed on a standby basis to purchase shares representing unexercised rights.   When debt is privately placed, an investment banking firm may have been instrumental in bringing the issuer and the institutional investor or investors together.

The traditional procedure, however, is for the investment banking firm to form a syndicate to underwrite the offering.   The purchase price represents a guarantee to the issuer.   The investment banking syndicate will then market the issue to the public at a higher price.   If

---

[36]Friend et al., *op. cit.*, p. 159.   In the years 1961–1963, these firms were, respectively, Morgan Stanely & Company, Halsey, Stuart and Company, First Boston Corporation, Blyth & Company, and Lehman Brothers.   The major changes were the rise of Halsey, Stuart from eighth to second between the years 1935 and 1963, and the decline of Smith, Barney & Company from fourth to twelfth.

[37]But when financial managers realize, as they did in 1966, that intermediaries, particularly commercial banks, may have to curtail their lines of credit, they will turn to long-term debt and, if necessary, to a public offering of bonds to meet their demand for fixed assets and working capital.   In so doing they are substituting a more expensive source of funds.   Depending on the rate of return, or net present value, of the marginal project and their subjective evaluation of their liquidity needs, the managers of these firms will, accordingly, alter the volume of funds they demand.

the offering is successful, the difference or spread between the price paid to the issuer and the public offering price is the compensation received by the syndicate for the risk and expenses of distributing the securities.   If the syndicate had been unwilling to make a firm commitment for the securities, it might have been willing to distribute them on an unguaranteed or best-efforts basis.

Several factors altered the importance of the traditional means of floating new securities.   Of primary importance were the disclosure provisions of the Securities Act of 1933.   Requiring the issuer to file a registration statement, to distribute a detailed summary of the registration statement as a prospectus to purchasers, to adhere to a waiting period before selling the securities, and to stand liable for false and misleading statements in the registration statement or prospectus resulted in additional risks and costs.   Since these requirements applied only to public offerings, the issuer could avoid them by placing the securities privately.   Following the passage of the Securities Act there was an accelerated increase in the private placement of corporate debt.

Requiring investment banking syndicates to bid competitively for long-term debt of the regulated industries further lowered the importance of negotiated offerings.

Although we must be careful in interpreting the evidence, there has been some decline over time in the costs of floating new securities. This could reflect the increased competition from publicly sealed bids and private placements.   But it could also be due to other factors, such as more efficiently organized capital markets and a decline in the concentration of flotations among the largest investment banking firms.

QUESTIONS

1.   "Increased competition over the years has lowered the costs of floating long-term securities."   Evaluate.

2.   Explain the role of investment banking in the process of capital formation.

3.   "Were it not for public-utility commissions, competitive bidding would cease to be an important means by which new securities would be distributed to the public."   Evaluate.

4.   "Of the three basic types of long-term securities, corporate debt has always dominated the new issues market.   This is what we would expect in light of our cost-of-capital model."   Evaluate.

5. "The provisions of the Securities Act of 1933 have increased the cost of flotation of new securities." Do you agree? Explain fully.

SELECTED REFERENCES

Cohan, Avery B. *Cost of Flotation of Long-term Corporate Debt since 1935.* Chapel Hill: University of North Carolina, School of Business Administration, 1961.

————. *Private Placement and Public Offerings: Market Shares since 1935.* Chapel Hill: University of North Carolina, School of Business Administration, 1961.

————. *Yields on Corporate Debt Directly Placed.* New York: National Bureau of Economic Research, 1967.

Friend, Irwin, James R. Longstreet, Morris Mendelson, Ervin Miller, and Arleigh P. Hess, Jr. *Investment Banking and the New Issues Market.* Cleveland: The World Publishing Company, 1967, pp. 80–81.

Halsey, Stuart and Company, Inc. *A Twenty-Year Record and Study of Corporate Debt Financing in the United States.* Chicago: Halsey, Stuart and Company, Inc., 1962.

Kemmerer, Donald L. "The Marketing of Securities 1930–52," *Journal of Economic History*, 12, no. 4 (Fall, 1952), pp. 454–468.

Medina, Harold R. *Opinion: U.S. vs. Morgan, et al.* New York: The Record Press, 1953.

Robbins, Sidney M. "Competitive Bidding in the Sale of Securities," *Harvard Business Review*, vol. 27, no. 5 (September, 1949), pp. 646–664.

Waterman, Merwin H. *Investment Banking Functions: Their Evolution and Adaptation to Business Finance.* Ann Arbor: The University of Michigan Press, 1958.

The Market for Existing Securities

chapter Twenty

In reading this chapter the student should note the rationale under-lying the existence of the secondary or trading markets. Moreover, he should take cognizance of the impact of the structure and practices of the trading markets on stock prices and the costs of portfolio transactions. Finally, he should compare the thesis that the market price of a stock is an observation on a random variable with the model developed in the chapter on the cost of capital.

Introduction

Although a well-developed market for new issues is important in trans-ferring funds from the savings to the investing sectors of the economy, in order to ensure the success of the flotations, it may also be necessary to make use of or develop a secondary or trading market in the issue.

In fact when new securities, particularly shares of common stock, are publicly offered, they are often additions to shares for which a trading market already exists. For example, management of a corporation listed on the New York Stock Exchange may use a privileged subscription to add new shares to those currently outstanding and for which an active trading market already exists.

But even if the shares were not already outstanding (that is, the company is "going public" for the first time), once the issue is sold, securities dealers, some of them participants in the original distribution, will often stand ready to make market in the stock. This may come about as a by-product of an agreement to maintain the offering price of the issue during the flotation period. Undistributed allotments taken by the participants are then sold at whatever price the market will bear.

On the other hand, perhaps the amount demanded at the offering price was greater than the available supply. Dealers may then stand ready to purchase shares from the original buyers at a higher price; hoping to mark them up still further. Alternatively, they may act as brokers between owners and prospective purchasers, charging a commission for their services.

Whatever the origin of the market for a particular issue, the economic function of the trading markets is *liquidity*. Without secondary markets, purchasers of new issues would have to hold their securities to maturity or, in the case of common stocks, indefinitely. This may be enough to discourage a large group of investors. Thus management of nonfinancial corporations invests temporarily idle funds in negotiable CDs and Treasury bills rather than in some other securities partly because there are dealers ready to make market in these instruments should management require the funds for operations sooner than anticipated.

On the other hand, the largest purchaser of corporate bonds, life insurance companies, may be more concerned with safety of principal and interest than with liquidity. Management plans to hold these bonds until maturity, using the investment income to help meet, if necessary, the fixed-income claims of policyholders. Consequently, depending on whether those purchasing securities demand liquidity as part of the services rendered when they buy the issue, trading markets may or may not develop. For instance, the last thing management of a closely held corporation may desire, at least initially, is a secondary market in the stock of the company. But the ordinary investor uninterested in managing the company may buy the shares of a publicly held corporation in hopes of reselling them at a profit. For him liquidity is a prerequisite for purchasing the stock.

With large amounts of corporate debt in the hands of institutional investors planning to hold the issues to maturity, and with much of the stock of publicly held corporations in the hands of individuals or institutions seeking capital gains, it would seem likely that the secondary market in corporate securities is primarily an equity or stock market. Available data tend to support this inference. In 1967, for example, the total market value of securities traded on stock exchanges registered with the Securities and Exchange Commission was in excess of $168 billion. Nearly $162 billion represented the trading of 4.5 billion shares of stock. The market value of bonds, exclusive of United States government obligations, was approximately $6 billion, with a principal amount in excess of $5 billion.[1] Similar results obtain for earlier years of the decade, although the total market value was substantially lower. In 1962, for example, the market value of securities traded was in excess of $56.5 billion. The market value of the stocks traded was over $54.7 billion, with nearly 1.7 billion shares exchanging hands. Both the market and the face value of the bonds traded was in excess of $1.7 billion.[2]

Although more bonds as well as stocks are traded elsewhere than on formal exchanges, the meager data available seem to be consistent with the assertion that the secondary market in stocks is quantitatively far more important than the trading market in bonds. For instance, in a 10-month study sponsored by the Securities and Exchange Commission, "it was found that broker-dealers advertised markets in approximately 14,000 domestic over the counter stocks and for a shorter period in 3,340 United States, other Government, and corporate bond issues."[3] Most of our discussion and analysis, therefore, will be in terms of a secondary market for corporate stocks rather than for stocks and debt.[4]

The Structure of the Trading Markets

Traditionally, the secondary market for corporate stocks may be divided into two subcategories, the *organized exchanges* and the *over-the-counter*

[1]Securities and Exchange Commission, *Statistical Bulletin* (March, 1968), p. 11.

[2]*Ibid.*

[3]U.S. Congress, House Committee on Interstate and Foreign Commerce, *Report of Special Study of the Securities Markets of the Securities and Exchange Commission*, 88th Cong., 1st Sess., 1963, part 2, p. 548. See also Irwin Friend, C. Wright Hoffman, and Willis J. Winn, *The Over-the-Counter Securities Markets* (New York: McGraw-Hill Book Company, 1958), table 2-3, p. 53.

[4]In one marketable instrument, commercial paper, there is no secondary market where investors can sell the paper before it matures. See Nevins D. Baxter, *The Commercial Paper Market* (Boston: The Bankers Publishing Company, 1966), p. 109. See also pp. 110–118.

markets.   The exchange is a formal organization in which orders to buy and sell the securities listed on it are centralized.   At any moment in time there is one set of quotations and one only at which the stock can be bought or sold.   While the quotations can change quickly, when offered they represent firm commitments of the person charged with organizing the market in the stock, that is, the *specialist* in the security. Thus if the specialist is quoting 100 shares of a particular stock at 55 bid and $55\frac{1}{4}$ offered, he is committed to buy 100 shares at 55 or sell an equal amount at $55\frac{1}{4}$.   When a transaction takes place (say a broker who is a member of the exchange takes advantage of the quotation to buy 100 shares for a customer at $55\frac{1}{4}$), the specialist may then change his quotation to, say, $55\frac{1}{8}$ to $55\frac{3}{8}$.   But each time he makes a quotation, he is committed to it at least until another transaction takes place.

Unlike the organized exchanges, the over-the-counter markets have no centralized location for trading.   There are no formal requirements for listing.   Any broker or dealer who is registered under the provisions of the Securities Exchange Act of 1934 and who complies with the rules adopted by the Securities and Exchange Commission under this statute can participate.   Dealers tend to divide into two groups.   The first, or wholesalers, are those making markets in stocks. They stand ready to buy and sell securities at prices quoted over the phone or through wire services to retailers.   The latter act as brokers for the public at large.   ·The dividing line is not always sharp.   Firms which are retailers might also make market in certain issues, that is, act as a wholesaler.   This may be particularly true of a firm in a small city which does a volume of retail business over the counter in nationally known stocks, but which also makes market in issues of local interest, say the shares of banks in the city.

When an individual wishes to buy, say, 100 shares of a stock listed on a registered exchange, he goes to a securities firm which is a member of the exchange.   His order is sent to the floor of the exchange and is executed by the commission broker, his partner, or a chief officer of the firm.   As we pointed out above, the broker may buy the stock from the specialist.   Alternatively, he may be able to buy the stock from another broker representing a customer desirous of selling 100 shares.   Instead of the broker with the buy order purchasing the stock at $55\frac{1}{4}$ from the specialist and the broker with the sell order selling it to the specialist at 55, the two brokers may agree to split the difference and exchange the shares at $55\frac{1}{8}$.

If the stock is not sold on an exchange but is traded over the counter, the broker will attempt to reach dealers or wholesalers in the issue in an effort either to secure or to sell the shares for his customer. Because the over-the-counter markets are not centralized, there may be more than one dealer in a stock and, hence, more than one set of quotations. To guide him in his search, the broker has available "sheets" published daily by the National Quotation Bureau. Quotations of stocks with fairly wide national markets are published daily in the financial press. Whether generally published or not, the quotations represent possible prices at which the retailer might buy the issue from or sell it to a dealer. Before buying or selling the stock for his customer, the retailer adds a markup to compensate him for the brokerage services rendered.

To illustrate the procedure, suppose that a customer is interested in buying 100 shares of a particular issue widely traded in the over-the-counter market. He noticed that the stock was quoted in the *Wall Street Journal* at 15 bid and 17 asked. His broker, however, cautions him that these quotations reflect the wholesale price. Like other brokers and dealers, all of whom are members of the National Association of Security Dealers, he will add a commission for his services, say 2 percent of the price at which he purchases the stock. Moreover, he also warns his customer that the quotations are yesterday's. They may not reflect the bid and asked prices today. He could pay more or less than 15.

Suppose that in an effort to obtain the best possible price the broker is able to find a dealer willing to sell at $15\frac{1}{4}$. Adding a 2 percent commission, or $0.305 per share, the price is $15.555, or $1,555.50 per 100 shares. If the customer agrees, the transaction will take place.

Even with a network of wire and phone services connecting wholesalers and retailers of a stock, it is possible for the quotation to change before the transaction is completed. A broker checking the market for his customer may try to get firm quotations from various wholesalers only to find that in the interim required to secure them all, some have changed. In fact, traders have been accused on occasion of backing away from firm commitments, making it more difficult to secure the highest bid or lowest offer for a customer.[5] Nevertheless, trading in the over-the-counter markets is important. In recent years the dollar volume has been as high as 60 percent of market value of stock traded on organized exchanges, although 30 to 50 percent may be a more normal range of percentages.[6]

In fact, for many issues, wholesalers trading in the over-the-counter markets provide the only means whereby securities can be traded. Organized exchanges often have stringent listing requirements which cannot be met by many companies. The New York Stock

[5]U.S. Congress, House Committee on Interstate and Foreign Commerce, *op. cit.*, part 2, p. 573.
[6]*Ibid.*, p. 547.

TABLE 20-1:   DOLLAR VOLUME AND NUMBER OF SHARES TRADED ON EXCHANGES REGISTERED WITH THE SECURITIES AND EXCHANGE COMMISSION DURING 1967
(Absolute Magnitudes in Millions of Dollars)

	Market Value[a]	Percent of Total[a]	Number of Shares[a]	Percent of Total[a]
All Registered Exchanges	$161,752	100.0	4,504	100.0
American Stock Exchange	23,111	14.3	1,290	28.6
Boston Stock Exchange	1,086	0.7	20	0.4
Chicago Board of Trade	0	0	0	0
Cincinnati Stock Exchange	62	*	1	*
Detroit Stock Exchange	716	0.4	15	0.3
Midwest Stock Exchange	4,996	3.1	109	2.4
National Stock Exchange	22	*	3	0.1
New York Stock Exchange	125,329	77.5	2,886	64.1
Pacific Coast Stock Exchange	4,530	2.8	113	2.5
Philadelphia-Baltimore-Washington Stock Exchange	1,830	1.1	38	0.8
Pittsburgh Stock Exchange	52	*	1	*
Salt Lake Stock Exchange	8	*	12	0.3
San Francisco Mining Exchange[b]	1	*	4	0.1
Spokane Stock Exchange	8	*	10	0.2

SOURCE: Securities and Exchange Commission, *Statistical Bulletin* (March, 1968), p. 11.
[a]Because of rounding, absolute magnitudes may differ slightly from the totals listed in the source.   For the same reason, the sum of individual percentages may not equal 100.0.
[b]Exchange was dissolved on August 15, 1967.
*Less than 0.1 of 1 percent.

Exchange, for example, requires that a company desiring to list its stock for trading on the exchange must have demonstrated earning power of $2.5 million before taxes for the most recent year and $2 million before taxes for the two preceding years.   Among other requirements the company must have 1,000,000 shares outstanding of which at least 800,000 common shares are publicly held among not less than 1,800 out of a total of 2,000 shareholders.[7]   While requirements for listing on the American and so-called regional exchanges are less stringent, most of the dollar and share volume of exchange-traded securities, as we can see from Table 20-1, is accounted for by the New York Stock Exchange.   The dollar proportion accounted for by the New York Stock Exchange may have declined slightly in recent years. For example, in 1961 its portion was in excess of 82 percent.   Its proportion of the share volume for that year was about the same as in 1967, that

[7]New York Stock Exchange, *1968 Fact Book of the New York Stock Exchange*, p. 22.

is, approximately 64 percent.[8]   There are reasons for the decline in the share volume, and we shall return to this point later in the discussion.

Unlike the over-the-counter markets, however, the organized exchanges are solely trading markets.   New issues, even new shares of stocks already listed on an exchange, are distributed initially over the counter through the underwriting syndicate.   Thus, besides providing the mechanism for trading in securities which cannot meet the listing requirements of an organized exchange, securities firms engaged in over-the-counter transactions also use the widespread telephone and wire services connecting them to the markets for new issues of stocks.   Moreover, as we shall subsequently learn, the over-the-counter markets in recent years have also become increasingly important in the trading of securities, largely stocks, already listed on the organized exchanges, particularly the New York Stock Exchange.

The Market Price of the Stock as a Random Variable

When we developed the principles underlying the investment value of a stock, we noted that the current price of a share might depart from the value suggested by discounting the future stream of earnings or dividends.   Indeed, even if in a growing economy there is a long-term upward trend in the market value of the shares,[9] reflecting growth in both earnings and dividends, it is highly unlikely that the market price at any moment in time reflects the investment value of the security.

This may be so partly because the values for E_a (or D_a), g, and r are not known; that is, the market price of a stock is a composite of the beliefs of various investors as to the value of these variables.   More important perhaps is their evaluation of the impact of current events on these values.   What will happen if Congress passes or fails to pass a tax bill or if the military budget is lowered or raised?   Will the assassination of a President or other national leader raise r at least temporarily and, hence, lower the market price of the issues traded?   In short, are the events so numerous and the reaction to them by investors so varied that changes in the market price of a share from one time period to the next appear to follow no predictable pattern?   Can we, in other words, assume that the current market price is an observation on a *random variable*?

[8]Calculated from data in Securities and Exchange Commission, *Statistical Bulletin* (February, 1962), p. 10.

[9]Assuming reinvestment of dividends, two writers have demonstrated that between 1926 and 1960 rates of return (or capital appreciation) on investments in common stocks have shown—depending on the investor's tax status—an annual increase of between 6.8 and 9.0 percent.   See L. Fisher and J. H. Lorie, "Rates of Return on Investments in Common Stocks," *Journal of Business*, vol. 37, no. 1 (January, 1964), p. 9.   See also pp. 1–21.

This thesis has gained increasing acceptance among students of stock market behavior.[10]   To illustrate its effects using a crude example,[11] suppose that the current equilibrium price for a stock listed on the New York Stock Exchange is 40, that is, the quantity demanded equals the quantity supplied at this price.   When transactions are consummated, they take place at eighth-of-a-point intervals, that is, at $39\frac{7}{8}$ or $40\frac{1}{8}$, etc.   Now suppose that there is a random sequence of bids and asks on the stock.   In other words, there is just as much chance of a price below 40 as there is of a price above 40.   We can generate this sequence by using a table of random numbers, such as the table in Appendix C of this volume.   In employing the table we can select the numbers in any orderly sequence.   We shall start in the upper left-hand corner with the first two-digit number and work downward.

Let us assume that the first digit tells us whether the order is a bid (an even number, including zero) or an ask (an odd number).   The second digit tells us the price at which the buyer or seller wants the order transacted; that is, 0 is $39\frac{3}{8}$, 1 is $39\frac{1}{2}$, 2 is $39\frac{3}{4}$, etc.   With 9 representing the upper limit, or $40\frac{1}{2}$, the range of values over which the price can fluctuate is $39\frac{3}{8}$ through $40\frac{1}{2}$.

For the time being, let us assume that there is no specialist making market in the stock and that each order represents 100 shares.   An exchange official records the buy and sell orders as they are received, with the lowest offer and the highest bid taking precedent.   When bids and asks are the same, the first received is the first executed.   If a bid exceeds the lowest offer, the transaction takes place at the bid price.   Using the first 20 two-digit numbers from the table in Appendix C, we can generate the sequence of bids, asks, and transactions illustrated in Table 20-2.

Under the assumptions employed, there were 10 bids and 10 offers and 9 transactions.   An unfilled bid of $39\frac{3}{8}$ and an unfilled ask of $40\frac{1}{2}$ remain on the books of the exchange official processing buy and sell orders in this security.   Presumably they will remain until executed or until canceled by those placing them.

Since the sequence of bids and asks is random, the pattern of price changes is unpredictable.   If we had used the table of random numbers in an alternative sequence, perhaps going by rows rather than columns, we would have generated an entirely different set of prices.   Yet, while the sequence of bids and offers and therefore of transactions is random, it represents, as we have pictured it, fluctuations about a stable equi-

---

[10]See, for example, the articles in Paul H. Cootner (ed.), *The Random Character of Stock Market Prices*, rev. ed. (Cambridge, Mass.: The M.I.T. Press, 1964).

[11]For a similar analysis, see George J. Stigler, "Public Regulation of the Securities Markets," *Journal of Business*, vol. 37, no. 2 (April, 1964), pp. 126–129.

TABLE 20-2: RANDOM SEQUENCE OF BIDS, ASKS, AND TRANSACTIONS PRICES AROUND AN EQUILIBRIUM PRICE OF 40

Random Number	Bid	Ask	Transaction Price	Ask Eliminated by Transaction
10		$39\frac{3}{8}$		
37		$40\frac{1}{4}$		
08	$40\frac{3}{8}$		$40\frac{3}{8}$	$39\frac{3}{8}$
99		$40\frac{1}{2}$		
12		$39\frac{5}{8}$		
66	$40\frac{1}{8}$		$40\frac{1}{8}$	$39\frac{5}{8}$
31		$39\frac{1}{2}$		
85	40		40	$39\frac{1}{2}$
63	$39\frac{3}{4}$			
73		$39\frac{3}{4}$	$39\frac{3}{4}$	$39\frac{3}{4}$
98		$40\frac{3}{8}$		
11		$39\frac{1}{2}$		
83	$39\frac{3}{4}$		$39\frac{3}{4}$	$39\frac{1}{2}$
88	$40\frac{3}{8}$		$40\frac{3}{8}$	$40\frac{1}{4}$
99		$40\frac{1}{2}$		
65	40			
80	$39\frac{3}{8}$			
74		$39\frac{7}{8}$	40	$39\frac{7}{8}$
69	$40\frac{1}{2}$		$40\frac{1}{2}$	$40\frac{3}{8}$
09	$40\frac{1}{2}$		$40\frac{1}{2}$	$40\frac{1}{2}$

librium. The more substantive question, therefore, is how the equilibrium is determined. In terms of the analysis presented in this volume, our answer must be $P = E_a/(r-g)$ or $P = D_a/(r-g)$.

We noted earlier, however, that the values of these variables are, at best, educated guesses and are themselves subject to probability distributions. Since the variables are constantly being reassessed in the light of the multitude of factors affecting them, we can expect the equilibrium to be changing, and sometimes changing rapidly. Consequently, what appears to be a series of random price fluctuations may just as easily be interpreted as a changing equilibrium showing no tendency toward stability.

If we carry this reasoning to its logical conclusion, we must drop the assumption that there is a stable equilibrium price—that is, in our example, 40. Moreover, we would have no reason to suspect that prices would fluctuate narrowly within that range. They could, but they need not. There might be a bid of 50 followed by an offer of 35, which in turn is followed by two bids at 44, etc.

But will such wide fluctuations be the case? The chances are they will not. First, in perfectly competitive markets, the investment value P is the equilibrium price. To the extent that E_a, D_a, r, and g are certain, P is also known. If a value of a variable changes, say g rises, then $r - g$ declines. In this instance, given E_a and D_a, P must rise. Behind the mathematics lies the fact that investors learning of the increase in g now, in the light of the alternatives available, increase their demand for the available supply of the stock, thereby causing the price to rise.

Second, while E_a, D_a, and g are subject to a probability distribution, this will be accounted for in the discount rate, or opportunity cost, r. Thus, even in a world of uncertainty, we can expect an equilibrium price. How often this equilibrium changes will depend on the forces affecting E_a, D_a, and g. If demand for the products or services produced by the firm in question shows little change and if costs remain reasonably stable, there will be very little change in E_a and D_a. Therefore, g will approach zero. On the other hand, if demand fluctuates widely or continues to accelerate rapidly while costs remain relatively stable, E_a, D_a, and g and the equilibrium price will vary accordingly.

Finally, whether the equilibrium price changes frequently or infrequently, there will continue to be random fluctuations about the equilibrium. A bid may come in because the prospective purchaser is anticipating a change in the value of the security. But another bid may also be entered because the purchaser just received an inheritance check. Similarly, an order to sell shares may be placed in anticipation of a fall in the price of the stock. But it may also be made because the seller has been pressed by his bank to repay a loan, or because of an unexpected increase in property taxes, or in his son's college tuition.

There are, therefore, reasons to suspect that stock prices, while displaying a random pattern, do so about a trend representing the investment value or values of the stock during the time period under study. Consider, for example, the hypothetical pattern of prices for a stock over a 3-month period illustrated in Figure 20-1. It is quite possible that the forces affecting the investment value of the stock were suddenly altered at B. Perhaps new information suggesting that E_a had been underestimated was released at the end of the month, causing an increase in demand and a new equilibrium price at C. There was a reevaluation at the end of, say, the second month. This time management disclosed the information that their estimate of E_a for the year had to be revised downward but not as far as the earlier estimate. Price fell accordingly, this time to E.

The changes between B and C and between D and E represent transactions that move the price toward a new equilibrium. Some of these transactions can be random, as can some of the transactions

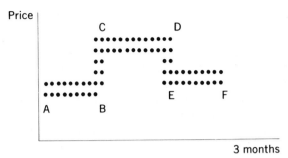

Figure 20–1

between A and B, between C and D, and between E and F. Price, in other words, does not have to jump immediately to the new equilibrium but can rise, fall back somewhat as it moves from B to C, or fall and rally for a period as it moves from D to E.

Yet the speed with which these changes in the equilibrium take place is an indication of the efficiency of the secondary market. For example, had the pattern appeared as in Figure 20-2 rather than as in Figure 20-1, it might reflect the fact that the communication of information relevant to changes in E_a had been slow. Those receiving the information first, that is, insiders, will adjust their position by buying at B and selling at D. If the information is available to all interested parties at once—that is, there are no insiders—the change in the equilibrium price will be sudden.[12] The more rapid the change to a new equilibrium price, the more efficient are the markets in reflecting the change in the investment value of the stock.

[12]Henry G. Manne, *Insider Trading and the Stock Market* (New York: The Free Press, 1966), pp. 77–91.

Figure 20–2

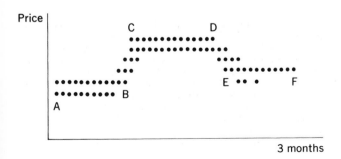

The Specialist and the Market Price of the Stock

If there are both an equilibrium price and random fluctuations about that price, an additional sign of efficient secondary markets would be the degree to which these random fluctuations could be reduced.   In other words, is there a way of bringing each transaction closer to the equilibrium price?   If so, what is the cost of doing it?

Any trader anticipating the equilibrium price can reduce random fluctuations by selling shares when he believes the current price is above the equilibrium and buying shares when he believes it is below.   But only the stock exchange specialist appears to have this task as a primary reason for his existence.[13]

We noted earlier that, on an organized exchange, specialists have the responsibility for centralizing the bids and asks in particular stocks. In organizing the market for the stocks in which he is responsible, the specialist often buys and sells shares for his own account; that is, he deals in the stocks in which he specializes.   Under the provisions of Section 11(b) of the Securities Exchange Act of 1934, the Securities and Exchange Commission has the power to regulate or even prevent a specialist's activities as a dealer in the stocks for which he is responsible.   To the extent that SEC regulations permit the specialist to trade for his own account, they "shall restrict his dealings so far as practicable to those reasonably necessary to maintain a fair and orderly market."   Since 1937, as a result of the so-called "Saperstein interpretation" of this section of the statute, the general position of the SEC has been that a specialist could trade for his own account when his dealings were "reasonably calculated to contribute to the maintenance of price continuity and to minimize the effects of temporary disparity between supply and demand."[14]   In implementing this interpretation, the New York Stock Exchange expects the specialist to buy and sell for his own account at prices close to the price of the previous transaction.   In minimizing the temporary disparity between supply and demand, the specialist is

---

[13]The discussion which follows is based in part on Ward S. Curran, "Some Thoughts on the Stock Exchange Specialist," *Quarterly Review of Economics and Business*, vol. 5, no. 1 (Spring, 1965), pp. 55–62.   Reprinted by permission of the editor.   See also Stigler, *op. cit.*, pp. 124–133; U.S. Congress, House Committee on Interstate and Foreign Commerce, *op. cit.*, part 2, pp. 57–171; William J. Baumol, *The Stock Market and Economic Efficiency* (New York: Fordham University Press, 1965), chap. 2; Ralph and Estelle James, "Disputed Role of the Stock Exchange Specialist," *Harvard Business Review*, vol. 40, no. 3 (May-June, 1962), pp. 133–146; and G. Keith Funston, "Letter of Comment: Re 'Disputed Role of the Stock Exchange Specialist'," *Harvard Business Review*, vol. 40, no. 5 (September-October, 1962), pp. 7–8, 10, 12.

[14]U.S. Congress, House Committe on Interatage and Foreign Commerce, *op. cit.*, part 2, p. 81.

expected to buy at a price lower or sell at a price higher than the price of the previous transaction.

To illustrate, let us use a hypothetical example with the specialist organizing the bids and asks, that is, acting as a broker while at the same time carrying out his responsibilities as a dealer. Most of the orders he receives are from the general public and have been brought to him by partners or officers of brokerage firms which are members of the exchange. When the specialist executes these orders he does so in the name of the brokerage firm, not the firm's customers who are ultimately buying or selling the stock.

The bids and asks he receives fall into three general categories. One type is a limited price order which states specifically the lowest price which the customer expects to receive for his stock or the highest price he expects to pay. If a limited order to sell 100 shares is placed at 40, the stock must be sold at least at that price. Of course, it could be sold at $40\frac{1}{8}$ or higher. Similarly, if a limited order to buy 100 shares is placed at 40, the order cannot be executed at a higher price. The shares can, of course, be purchased at $39\frac{7}{8}$ or some lower figure.

A second type of bid or ask is a market order. There is no minimum or maximum price that must be received or paid. The order is executed at whatever the market will bear.

A third type of tender is confined largely to the New York Stock Exchange. It is a stop order. A stop order cannot be executed until the market price reaches the stop price. If a transaction takes place at 40, a stop order to sell becomes a market order to sell at the best possible price. This could be 40 or a price higher or lower than 40. There is no limit on how far above or below 40 the stock might sell.[15] Similarly, a stop order to buy becomes a market order to buy when the stop price is reached.

While a specialist may execute all three types of orders, he will probably handle all stop and limited price orders. The reason for his doing so is that both types will be "away" from the current market price. Assume, for example, that 100 shares of the common stock of the XYZ Corporation changed hands at $55\frac{1}{2}$. At the same time the specialist receives two orders. The first is a limited order to buy 100 shares at $52\frac{1}{2}$ and the second is a stop order to sell 100 shares at 52.

The person placing the first order may be anticipating a decline in the market price. The person placing the second order may have

---

[15] A customer could conceivably place a limit of, say, $39\frac{1}{2}$ or less on a stop order to sell at 40. If this is done, the stock must be offered at $39\frac{1}{2}$ or better and not sold at whatever the market will bring. This is the only type of stop order allowed on the American Exchange. See Sidney M. Robbins, *The Securities Markets: Operations and Issues* (New York: The Free Press, 1966), pp. 147–148.

bought the stock under the assumption that the price would rise. In so doing he may have borrowed part of the purchase price; that is, he purchased the stock on margin. To protect himself from severe losses should the price drop unexpectedly, he has chosen to place a stop order to sell below the current market price.

Because the orders are, respectively, 3 and $3\frac{1}{2}$ points below the last transaction price, they are unlikely (particularly if the stock is actively traded) to be executed in the next few minutes. The representative of the commission brokerage house with which the orders were placed could stay at the post where the stock is traded and wait for other brokers to trade with one another or with the specialist until the market price falls first to $52\frac{1}{2}$ and then to 52. Not only might the market price rise rather than fall, but the broker is likely to have orders in other stocks traded at different posts on the floor to which he must also attend. He therefore leaves the orders with the specialist, who in turn makes a record of them by entering the stocks in his book.

The specialist's book contains part of the potential demand for and supply of the stock should the limited or stop prices of these bids and asks be reached. The range of the potential market in the stock is given by the price and volume of the highest bid and the lowest offer. In our example, suppose that the highest bid was 100 shares at $54\frac{1}{2}$ and the lowest offer was 100 shares at $56\frac{1}{2}$. Since the last transaction was at $55\frac{1}{2}$, if the specialist did nothing, a transaction would take place only if one or two events occurred. A limited order to sell at the market (or $54\frac{1}{2}$ or less) or to buy at the market (or $56\frac{1}{2}$ or more) is entered. Alternatively, simultaneous orders to buy and sell at the market or at limited prices — the purchase price being higher than the sales price — are entered.

Since the specialist is expected to buy and sell for his own account in order to maintain price continuity and minimize the effects of temporary disparity between supply and demand, what should he do to carry out this function? Clearly he cannot sell stock at $54\frac{1}{2}$ or buy it at $56\frac{1}{2}$. Not only would he be putting himself in front of a customer's order, which is illegal, but he would be doing nothing more than engaging in a transaction which might have been brought about by chance.

He could, however, offer to buy 100 shares of the stock at $55\frac{1}{4}$ or sell 100 shares at $55\frac{3}{4}$. To make a firm commitment, he quotes the market at $55\frac{1}{4}$ to $55\frac{3}{4}$ for 100 shares. Suppose that a broker with a market order to sell 100 shares comes to the specialist and receives this quote. Seeing no other broker with an order to buy, he makes a firm commitment with a specialist and a transaction takes place at $55\frac{1}{4}$. The specialist now quotes the market at 55 to $55\frac{1}{2}$, again straddling the last market price. This time, as chance would have it, a broker with a market order to buy 100 shares comes to the specialist.   Again seeing no other broker with an order to sell, he buys 100 shares from the specialist at $55\frac{1}{2}$.   On these transactions the specialist has made 25 cents per share or $25 per 100 shares simply by being an intermediary between two brokers with complementary orders but who did not receive them simultaneously.

If he held in his book a limited price order to buy 100 shares at $55\frac{1}{4}$, the specialist would have bought for the book at $55\frac{1}{4}$ and sold for his own account at $55\frac{1}{2}$.   For the first transaction, he would have received a portion of the commission paid by the customer to his broker for seeing that his limited buy order is executed.   In the second transaction, the specialist would have sold the stock from his own account at $55\frac{1}{2}$.

In either case, in the eyes of exchange officials, he would at least be maintaining price continuity; that is, successive transactions were within a quarter of a point of one another.   They could have been closer; that is, the specialist might have quoted the market at $55\frac{3}{8}$ and $55\frac{5}{8}$, buying 100 shares for his own account at the former price, then quoted the stock at $55\frac{1}{4}$ and $55\frac{1}{2}$, this time selling 100 shares at the higher figure. His profit for the "jobber's turn" will be $12.50 rather than $25, but there would have been a closer sequence of prices.   Exchange officials would have considered either eighth- or quarter-of-a-point differences as evidence of price continuity.   Moreover, if there had been a limited order to buy at $55\frac{1}{4}$, the specialist, rather than undercut the book by an eighth (unless he felt the need to increase his inventory in anticipation of future sales), would probably buy from the book at this price instead of for his own account at $55\frac{3}{8}$.

Whether these transactions minimize the effects of temporary disparity between supply and demand is another question.   Unlike price continuity, this objective is more difficult to interpret.   Stock exchange officials have used, among other measures, the following criteria as a standard of performance.   If the specialist sells on an "uptick" in the market (that is, at a figure higher than the previous price) or buys on a "downtick" (that is, at a figure below the previous price), his dealings are said to be "stabilizing."   To accomplish this, all a specialist need do is to straddle the previous sales price with a bid below and an offer above it, as we did in our example.

To the extent that bids and asks representing demand and supply are random, these "stabilizing" transactions can indeed minimize the effects of temporary disparity between supply and demand by reducing the variability in fluctuations about the equilibrium price.   But what service does a specialist render if he sells on an uptick in what is otherwise a rapidly falling market or buys on an uptick in a rapidly rising

market?   The answer is that if the rapid change does not represent a
shift in the investment value of the stock, the specialist is adding to
rather than countering the effects of a temporary disparity between
supply and demand.

On the other hand, if the change does represent a fundamental
shift in the investment value of the stock, by adding to the trend the
specialist is hastening the transfer to a new equilibrium.   In reality,
of course, the problem is to know whether a rapid change reflects a
shift in the investment value or is simply the result of an unusual
occurrence.   Sometimes the answer would appear obvious.   The
market break following the assassination of President Kennedy might
be written off as an irrational response.   The losses incurred were
erased in a relatively short period.   Yet we could also argue that prices
of stocks, until the exchanges were closed, were seeking a new equilibrium in the light of the uncertainty following the initial upheaval.
Would the new government be able to maintain order or would there be
an extended period of confusion threatening trade and commerce and
ultimately profits and dividends?   In the light of hindsight, the probabilities were remote, but to many at the time these fears may have been
real.

But whether the change is temporary or represents a fundamental
shift in investment value, the greatest risk a specialist incurs is having to
sell far more shares in a rising market than he will buy or having to buy
more shares in a falling market than he will sell.   Whatever the reason,
once there is a movement toward a higher price, by implication, bids
will exceed offers.   The specialist is under pressure to supply the stock
in an effort to maintain price continuity from transaction to transaction.
Similarly, as price moves lower he will increase his inventory of stock
since offers exceed purchases.

As compensation for assuming this risk, the specialist receives risk-
free brokerage income on any orders executed from his book and an
opportunity to realize a profit from a jobber's turn, that is, buying
100 shares at $55\frac{1}{4}$ and then selling 100 at $55\frac{1}{2}$.   Moreover, within the
limits imposed by the orders on his book and his responsibilities as a
dealer, he can anticipate changes in the equilibrium price and position
himself accordingly.   Since he alone among those trading in the market
has access to the book, the specialist can make use of it in determining
his position in a stock.   For example, if he finds brokers submitting a
growing number of limited orders to sell well above the current market
price, the specialist may interpret this as a sign that the equilibrium price
will soon rise.   He can then anticipate a large number of buy orders
and can begin to increase his inventory in anticipation of liquidating it
as the market rises.   If he is wrong and the equilibrium price falls, the

specialist will find himself with a still larger inventory of shares which he may be able to liquidate only at a loss.

Within the framework of the specialist's operations, individual abuses or questionable practices have been brought to light.[16] Undercutting the book by an eighth of a point may in some cases be considered improper. Suppose, for example, that a specialist uses a stop order to sell placed considerably below yesterday's close to open the market in a stock for which the number of bids that have accumulated overnight equals the number of offers. This can be viewed as taking unfair advantage of the customer who placed the stop order. He used a stop order to protect himself from loss if the market price were to fall. He did not anticipate the specialist using the order to cause the price to fall.

Yet, on balance, whether the services performed by specialists are justified can be answered only in terms of the rate of return on the capital employed in making market in these stocks. Is the return in line with the return on alternatives to which these funds can be put, or do specialists earn monopoly profits?

Following their lengthy investigation of the securities markets in the early 1960s, the Securities and Exchange Commission in its Special Study gave limited coverage to this question. In the two years for which data were presented, 1959 and 1960, the average incomes earned from trading by firms of specialists on the New York Stock Exchange were approximately 59 and 45 percent, respectively, of the capital available for this purpose. There was, however, considerable dispersion about the averages. In 1959, one out of the 110 groups of specialists lost money. In 1960, two out of the 110 units incurred losses.[17]

In presenting the data, however, no consideration was given to the expenses of maintaining a firm of specialists, that is, clerks, space rentals, etc. This was done on the grounds that such expenses are small relative to those incurred in other areas of the securities industry. As a result, we cannot calculate a net return. Morevoer, the data for two years are hardly adequate for making a judgement on the existence of monopoly profits.

We can level a more substantive criticism at the definition of trading capital — or, in the parlance of the SEC's Special Study, "liquid capital" — employed. "This figure did not include other assets that specialists had available but did not employ in their specialist business."[18] Would it not be fruitful to compare the returns from using these funds in the business with the income the funds could be earning elsewhere?

---

[16]U.S. Congress, House Committee on Interstate and Foreign Commerce, *op. cit.*, part 2, pp. 57–171, *passim*.
[17]*Ibid.*, pp. 67–71 and 371–374. Percentages were calculated from the data.
[18]*Ibid.*, p. 70.

It would give us some indication of the risk differential which specialists might demand for committing their funds to trading rather than to alternative investments.

Without sufficient evidence we can conclude this section only by pointing out that an institution for minimizing random fluctuations is available and is frequently employed, at least in that portion of the secondary markets served by the exchanges. But the costs of the service are virtually unknown. Until we have more information, we cannot say whether the price paid by the public — that is, the profit earned by the specialist — is in excess of that required to maintain the service.

Margin Requirements

While the specialist can affect the current market price of the stock by trading for his own account, the Federal Reserve may have an impact on the price of stocks in at least two ways. First, it can take steps to increase or decrease the reserves of commercial banks. As a result, the money supply may expand or contract as banks make new loans or fail to renew outstanding loans. Many of these loans represent credit extended to customers buying stocks.

Second, under the provisions of Section 7 of the Securities Exchange Act of 1934, the Federal Reserve can regulate the supply of credit granted for the purpose of buying securities or selling them short, that is, selling borrowed securities in hopes of repurchasing them at a lower price.

The first power, creation and destruction of bank reserves, is general. If the money supply changes, stock prices will usually follow in the same direction. A decline in the money supply is accompanied by a fall in the average level of stock prices; an increase in the money supply is accompanied by a rise in the average level of stock prices.[19]

The second power, the regulation of security credit, is specific or selective. In spite of statements to the contrary, there is some question as to whether these controls have an impact on stock prices.[20] To the extent that they do not, part of the explanation lies in the fact that until recently there were a considerable number of loopholes either in the regulations of the Federal Reserve or in the law itself.[21]

---

[19]Beryl W. Sprinkel, *Money and Stock Prices* (Homewood, Ill.: Richard D. Irwin, Inc., 1964), pp. 1–13, 115–142.

[20]Thomas Gale Moore, "Stock Market Margin Requirements," *Journals of Political Economy*, vol. 74, no. 2 (April, 1966), pp. 158–167.

[21]Jules I. Bogen and Herman E. Kroos, *Security Credit: Its Economic Role and Regulation* (Englewood Cliffs, N.J.: Prentice-Hall, Inc., 1960). For an updating in the requirements, see *Federal Reserve Bulletin* (February, 1968), pp. 167–220, and "Margin Account Credit," *Federal Reserve Bulletin* (June, 1968), pp. 470–481.

As a general rule, the Federal Reserve can specify, within wide limits, the loan value of securities purchased. The difference between the loan value and the market price represents the margin or down payment which the purchaser must make on the securities. For example, if the stock of the XYZ Corporation is selling at $100 a share, the cost of 100 shares exclusive of brokerage commissions is $10,000. If the loan value of the securities is 30 percent, the margin requirement is 70 percent, or $7,000. The purchaser may use cash or its equivalent in securities owned by him as a means of meeting the margin requirements. A broker, for instance, extending credit to the customer could accept United States government securities in lieu of cash. He may also use shares of stock which he owns and which are listed on an exchange.[22] The loan value of the shares, however, is in this case only 30 percent. Consequently, the market value of the securities used must be $23,333 ($7,000 ÷ .30).

What is true of purchases on margin is also true of short sales. If a customer sells stock which he does not own, he must borrow the shares, usually from the broker extending credit. If the Federal Reserve stipulates a margin requirement of 70 percent on short sales, the customer must also deposit cash, or its equivalent in securities, equal to 70 percent of the market value of the securities at the time they are sold short.

Once the margin payment has been made, the Federal Reserve could require that it be maintained at 70 percent or at some other figure. In practice, it confines its regulation to the initial requirements. The stock exchanges, however, do prescribe conditions for maintenance of margin. Under these regulations member firms must compute margin daily. The margin for purchases can be computed by the following formula.[23]

$$\text{Margin} = \frac{\text{value of collateral} - \text{debit balance}}{\text{value of collateral}}$$

The debit balance is the amount lent; the value of collateral is the value of securities purchased on margin. If the initial purchase price was $10,000 and the margin requirements were 70 percent, then

$$70\% = \frac{\$10,000 - \$3,000}{\$10,000}$$

---

[22]A broker can always demand more than the law or the regulations of the Federal Reserve require. For instance, while there are no margin requirements on United States government securities, the major exchanges require 5 percent margin on all credit accounts of customers of member firms borrowing to finance these instruments.

[23]George L. Leffler and Loring C. Farwell, *The Stock Market*, 3d ed. (New York: The Ronald Press Company, 1963), p. 370.

The figure for margin moves in the same direction as the value of the collateral. Thus, if the value of the collateral falls to $6,000, the margin declines to

$$50\% = \frac{\$6,000 - \$3,000}{\$6,000}$$

If the value of the collateral rises to $12,000, the margin increases to

$$75\% = \frac{\$12,000 - \$3,000}{\$12,000}$$

On short sales the margin requirements can be calculated as follows:[24]

$$\text{Margin} = \frac{\text{net proceeds of sale plus initial margin}}{\text{market value of stock}} - 1.00 \times 100$$

Using the same margin requirements and sales value, the initial margin is

$$70\% = \frac{\$17,000}{\$10,000} - 1.00 \times 100$$

This time, however, the margin moves inversely with the market value of the collateral. Thus, if the value of the stock falls to $6,000, the margin is

$$116.67\% = \frac{\$13,000}{\$\ 6,000} - 1.00 \times 100$$

If the value of the collateral rose to $12,000, the margin would decline to

$$58.33\% = \frac{\$19,000}{\$12,000} - 1.00 \times 100$$

Since a person selling short does so in anticipation of a decline in the price of the securities, he can cover his short sale by buying more cheaply when the price of the securities falls. In these circumstances, his margin must rise. Similarly, it must fall as the market value of the securities sold short rises.

Exchanges may have different maintenance-of-margin requirements for different securities, some of which are higher than the Federal Reserve requirements. As a general rule, however, the New York Stock Exchange requires that margin never fall below 25 percent on stock purchases and 30 percent on short sales.[25] When stocks fall

---

[24]*Ibid.*, p. 371.

[25]Minimum amount of cash or its equivalent in securities must be maintained at all times in margin accounts. For a full discussion, see *ibid.*, chap. 21, and Bogen and Kroos, *op. cit., passim.*

below the minimum requirements, the customer must either increase his margin, have his securities sold, or have his short sale covered.[26]

The Loopholes The loopholes in the margin requirements are numerous. To detail them would necessitate a separate volume.[27] Many have been or are in the process of being closed. Most of these loopholes may be divided into two classifications. For our purpose we may classify the exceptions first according to the security on which credit is extended and second according to the lending institution.[28]

Under the law certain securities are exempt, all government securities, for example. Until recently, corporate bonds convertible into stock were not covered by the margin requirements. Purchases under a privileged subscription of additional shares of stocks already outstanding and subject to margin requirements could be financed, until recently, with 25 percent margin. Margin purchases of convertibles and stocks in subscription accounts were taking place at a time when the Federal Reserve was requiring 70 percent margin on purchases of stocks registered on a national securities exchange. There are now separate margin requirements for convertibles, and stocks in a subscription account are subject to the regular margin requirements.[29]

Perhaps more important have been the recent changes in the requirements as they pertain to lenders.[30] The Federal Reserve for years confined its margin requirements to banks and brokers and dealers. Although there was ample authority under the law, nonbank lenders other than brokers and dealers were not subject to margin requirements. They could and did make loans on small margin and at relatively high rates of interest. Under Regulation G adopted in March, 1968, margin requirements applicable to brokers, dealers, and banks are applicable to other lenders.[31]

But even banks have had fewer restrictions placed on them than have brokers and dealers. Under the Securities Exchange Act, brokers

---

[26]When the margin falls below the initial requirements but is still above the minimum maintenance requirements, the account is restricted. Securities can be sold only under certain conditions. See Leffler and Farwell, *op. cit.*, pp. 378–381. From these restricted margin purchase accounts may come some of the shares used in short sales.

[27]This was the intention of Bogen and Kroos, *op. cit.*, *passim*.

[28]For a broader classification, see U.S. Congress, House Committee on Interstate and Foreign Commerce, *op. cit.*, part 4, pp. 1–39.

[29]*Federal Reserve Bulletin* (February, 1968), p. 168.

[30]In passing, we might note that as an aid to specialists in carrying out their dealer obligations under the law, the margin requirements have been limited to the exchanges' requirements for maintenance of margin. When buying for their own account, specialists can borrow up to 75 percent on purchases in the stocks in which they specialize. Similarly, on short sales they need only maintain a 30 percent margin.

[31]*Federal Reserve Bulletin* (February, 1968), pp. 205–215.

and dealers are prohibited altogether from lending on unlisted securities where the purpose is to purchase or carry securities. Hence, Regulation T, prescribing the margin requirements for loans made by brokers and dealers, pertains only to margin purchases and short sales of listed securities.

Under Regulation U, similar limitations are placed on banks, limiting them to the amount lent on stocks to purchase or to carry stocks listed on an exchange. But prior to July 30, 1968, banks could not be restricted in loans to carry other listed or unlisted securities. Thus, among other possibilities, a person could have gone to a commercial bank and negotiated a loan to buy stock using corporate bonds as collateral. The loan value of these bonds would have been determined by the bank, not by the current margin requirements of the Federal Reserve. However, a bill to extend Federal Reserve margin requirements on unlisted securities to banks and to allow brokers and dealers to extend credit on unlisted securities was enacted in 1968.[32]

Finally, the loan value of securities under the margin rules is relevant only if the purpose is to purchase securities. Nonpurpose loans, whether made by brokers and dealers or banks, are not subject to the margin requirements. Suppose that the margin requirements were 70 percent and the reader wished to purchase $6,000 in stock listed on the New York Stock Exchange. He does not have $4,200 in cash available but he does own $20,000 in listed stocks. A bank can lend him 30 percent of their market value, or $6,000, thus allowing him to buy the securities. If he had wanted to borrow funds for some purpose other than the purchase of stocks, say home improvements, the bank might have lent him 50 or 60 percent of the market value should he have desired it. The bank must take the customer's word that the funds are not for the purpose of carrying securities subject to the margin requirements. Nothing can prevent him from using some of the proceeds for home improvements and the remainder — if not the entire amount — for the purchase of stocks.

Since many of the loopholes in the regulations or in the law are gradually being closed, the impact of margin requirements on the amount of credit extended (and, hence, on the price of the securities) may be greater in the future than it has been in the past.

However, the impetus for legislation on margin requirements came from the pyramiding of credit which helped to precipitate the crash of 1929. When prices first weakened, lenders making loans to carry stocks on 10 to 20 percent margin became apprehensive. When

---

[32] *Wall Street Journal*, July 30, 1968, p. 2.

their calls for more margin could not be met, they sold out their customers, thereby adding to the decline.

Presumably the higher margin requirements of today and the closing of loopholes will prevent such a pyramiding of credit from raising prices. They cannot, however, prevent individuals from bidding up the price of stocks by buying without borrowing. In other words, margin could be 100 percent and prices of individual stocks or the average level of stocks could continue to rise. Moreover, they could rise well beyond what might be considered by many as their investment value. Assuming that this happens, prices will not long remain at these levels. When they decline, individuals having purchased them at relatively high prices can liquidate them only at a loss.

At best, margin requirements can have only a limited impact on the price of securities. If individuals are desirous of bidding up the prices of stocks, they cannot be prevented from doing so simply by curtailing credit purchases.[33]

The Third Market

Earlier in the chapter we noted that stocks listed on an exchange, particularly the New York Stock Exchange, are also traded over the counter. The dollar volume in this so-called third market has in recent years approximated 3 to 5 percent of all the transactions in listed securities on the New York Stock Exchange.[34]

The figure itself is not so important as the implications of the fact that the third market exists. In an efficient market the "price of a security will almost invariably be 'made' in one exchange."[35] The function of an exchange is to organize the market in a security. The more transactions there are taking place on the exchange, the smaller the price variations from random bids and offers. In some cases the market "makes itself." The volume of trading is so heavy that the sequence

[33]Similarly, they could not be prevented from bidding securities down simply by curtailing margin requirements on short sales. However, short selling by the public is today very limited. In 1967, 7.2 percent of sales on the New York Stock Exchange were short sales. Well over half of them were the result of specialists carrying out their dealer function. Another one-fifth were made by nonspecialist members and the rest by the general public. Some of these sales may have been to protect paper profits in a stock, carrying the transaction over into the next tax year. See New York Stock Exchange, *1968 Fact Book of the New York Stock Exchange*, p. 39.

[34]M. E. Polakoff and A. W. Sametz, "The Third Market—The Nature of Competition in the Market for Listed Securities Traded Off-Board," *Antitrust Bulletin*, vol. 11, nos. 1 and 2 (January-April, 1966), pp. 200–203, and New York Stock Exchange, *op. cit.*, p. 14.

[35]Stigler, *op. cit.*, p. 129.

of bids and asks are, with little or no help from the specialist, an eighth to a quarter of a point from the preceding transaction.   To the extent that the exchange loses volume to a third market, the greater will be the disparity in bids and offers, and the more costly it then becomes to smooth random fluctuations or to facilitate an orderly change to a new equilibrium.   The specialist, in other words, must, in order to carry out his responsibilities, assume greater responsibility for making the market.

We do not have to look far to discover why there is a third market.[36] Foremost among the reasons is the fact that until recently the structure of brokerage commissions makes no allowance for volume discounts. Those trading in odd lots—that is, in most cases, those buying or selling less than 100 shares—are aware of the fact that they must pay (depending on the price of the security) an eighth to a quarter of a point more. Thus, if an individual bought 25 shares of stock at 20 per share, he really paid $19\frac{7}{8}$ for the stock, with an eighth of a point going to the odd-lot dealer.   Moreover, he knows he must pay a minimum brokerage fee regardless of the size of the order.

At the other end of the scale, however, it costs a person ten times as much to buy or sell 1,000 shares of a stock as to buy or sell 100 shares.[37] Unless by chance he finds another individual interested in buying the number of shares he wishes to sell or in selling the number of shares he wishes to buy, the small trader has little recourse except to place his bid or offer through a brokerage firm and ultimately through the exchange.

Those trading in large lots, however, do have an alternative. Brokerage firms which do a large over-the-counter business but are not members of the New York Stock Exchange have contacts with institutional investors willing to buy and sell shares listed on an exchange. Many of these investors are directors of mutual funds whose shares are sold over the counter by brokerage firms.   While these brokerage firms receive commissions for selling its shares, management of a mutual fund

---

[36]We should point out that we are explicitly excluding from our discussion secondary distributions of stocks listed on an exchange.   These offerings—often holdings of institutions amounting to several million dollars—are distributed over the counter through investment bankers in much the same way as if they were new securities.   This is done with exchange approval and at a price below the current market price of the stock.   The rationale for this concession is the financial insufficiency of most specialists—that is, they lack sufficient capital to take a position in very large blocks of stock and then attempt to distribute them piecemeal on the floor of the exchange.   While the New York Stock Exchange has been improving its techniques for distributing large blocks, some of the practices discussed in the text may have added to the number of secondary distributions. See New York Stock Exchange, *op. cit.*, pp. 12–13.

[37]Leffler and Farwell, *op. cit.*, pp. 382–386, and New York Stock Exchange, *1967 Fact Book of the New York Stock Exchange*, p. 45.   On stocks selling below $55, the odd-lot differential is an eighth of a point.   It is a quarter of a point on odd lots selling above $55.   The minimum brokerage commission is $6.00.

is always anxious to find additional incentives to encourage further sales. One way of doing this is to offer these brokerage firms a share of the commission business inherent in turning over the portfolio of the fund. Failing this, another alternative is to insist that the brokerage fee be split between the firm executing a sell or buy order for the fund and another brokerage firm which management of the fund designates.

For years, the rules of the New York Stock Exchange prohibited volume discounts. While fee sharing was permitted among firms which were members of the exchange, fees earned by a member firm could not be split with nonmember firms, many of whom not only concentrated in the over-the-counter markets but were also prime sellers of mutual fund shares.[38] Indeed, until 1966, members of the New York Stock Exchange were forbidden to execute orders except on the floor of the exchange. Under SEC pressures, this was modified to allow member firms to seek out the best bid or offer over the counter, and to give the specialist in the stock a chance to match it before executing it off the floor.

But the Securities and Exchange Commission had looked with disfavor on fee splitting on the grounds that it unnecessarily raised the cost of portfolio transactions to shareholders in mutual funds.[39] For similar reasons it had favored the introduction of volume discounts.[40]

Not only was there pressure from the SEC, which could itself have forced the changes, but the New York Stock Exchange was also under increased market pressure to initiate these reforms. In the first place, institutional investors who in 1949 held over 12 percent of the market value of all stocks listed on the exchange had by the end of 1966 increased their share to 21 percent. It is estimated that their share will reach 30 percent by the year 1980.[41]

Second, volume discounts and fee splitting existed not only on over-the-counter transactions, but they also helped to explain the increased volume on regional stock exchanges. Under the law, once a stock is listed on a regional exchange, it can be traded on any exchange registered with the SEC without being registered on that exchange.

The regional stock exchanges have long served as markets for stocks listed on the New York Stock Exchange. Some brokerage firms not members of the New York Stock Exchange have seats on, say, the Midwest or Pacific Coast Exchange. While the price of the stock may be

[38]U.S. Congress, House Committee on Interstate and Foreign Commerce, *Report of the Securities and Exchange Commission on the Public Policy Implications of Investment Company Growth*, 89th Cong., 2d Sess., 1966, p. 170.

[39]*Ibid.*, p. 175.

[40]"Taking Stock of Stock Exchanges," *Wall Street Journal*, June 13, 1968, p. 18.

[41]New York Stock Exchange, *Institutional Activity on the New York Stock Exchange, Week of October 24–28, 1966*, pp. 2–4.

made in New York, regional exchanges are often willing to allow their members to grant volume discounts and fee splitting.[42]   Thus, if a firm is a member of the New York Stock Exchange and a regional exchange, it may choose to use the facilities of the latter to execute an order for a large block of stock held by an institutional investor seeking a lower commission or demanding that a portion of the fee be given to an over-the-counter firm.

Capitulating at last to these several forces, member firms of the New York Stock Exchange agreed late in 1968 to volume discounts and to end customer-directed fee splitting.[43]   Whether the fees now charged will reflect competitive pricing is a moot point.   In terms of structure, the secondary market for corporate stocks is an oligopoly.   When the SEC forced the New York Stock Exchange to allow member firms to seek prices from dealers over the counter, it promulgated a rule requiring that those firms making market must themselves meet specific capital requirements.[44]   The effect of this rule was to eliminate the competition among brokers vying for the business of the institutional investor.

Moreover, the cost of odd lots will probably not decline significantly. Indeed, it may rise over time.   Assuming that the demand for brokerage services is relatively inelastic (that is, there is no available alternative),[45] brokers can raise prices in this area of the market — subject to SEC approval, of course — while lowering their commissions on large lots.[46]

However, it seems to the author that instead of charging higher brokerage fees for odd lots, there should be a fee for services rendered other than those connected directly with the execution of an order — that is, research reports, keeping track of margin accounts, etc.   For in effect what institutional investors want is an intermediary to make market for the securities they wish to buy and sell.   For the most part they do their own research on securities.   To the extent that they use the facilities of brokerage firms for this purpose, they should pay for it.

[42]U.S. Congress, House Committee on Interstate and Foreign Commerce, *Report of Special Study of the Securities Markets*, part 2, pp. 911–952; *ibid.*, *Report of the Securities and Exchange Commission on the Public Policy Implications of Investment Company Growth*, pp. 171–172.

[43]*Wall Street Journal*, Oct. 25, 1968, p. 2.

[44]"A market maker must maintain a net worth of $1.5 million or a minimum net capital of $250,000 for each security in which he is qualified to make market."   See *Wall Street Journal*, Oct. 21, 1966, p. 7.

[45]We noted earlier that individuals by chance might engage in transactions directly with one another.   While this so-called "fourth market" does indeed exist, it is apparently confined to institutions and large individual stockholders, not those we would ordinarily expect to be engaging in odd-lot transactions.   See Robbins, *op. cit.*, pp. 257–261.

[46]This was indeed the essence of a proposal which died for lack of enthusiasm from the SEC.   See *Wall Street Journal*, Nov. 17, 1966, p. 32.

Thus, instead of packaging a series of services and marketing them at one price, most stockholders would be better served if securities firms priced their services individually, letting the investor choose the combination which suited his particular needs.[47]

SUMMARY

The primary function of the secondary or trading markets is to promote liquidity. Since most bonds are held to maturity, the public demand for liquidity is largely a demand for trading markets in stocks.

Stocks are traded on organized exchanges and over the counter, The former group consists of centralized trading markets, notably the New York Stock Exchange. The latter group consists of a number of dealers in various stocks who are connected by wire service, quotation sheets, and membership in the National Association of Securities Dealers. As a result, the prices of successive transactions on trades over the counter will probably vary more widely than will prices of successive transactions on an organized exchange.

The structure of the trading markets is such that the forces affecting the market price at any moment may vary consiserably. This has given rise to the thesis that the current market price of a stock is an observation on a random variable. However, to the extent that this is the case, these observations may reflect random fluctuations about the underlying or fundamental trend suggested by the model developed earlier in this volume. Since Ea, Da, r, and g can change, so can the market price of the stock.

There can, however, be random fluctuations about the new equilibrium. It is the function of the stock exchange specialist to smooth out these fluctuations. In so doing, he has the opportunity to earn a jobber's turn from buying and selling for his own account. He may, for example, buy 100 shares at $88\frac{1}{8}$ and a few moments later sell 100 shares at $88\frac{1}{4}$. His profits are a measure of the costs of minimizing random fluctuations about the changing equilibrium.

While the specialist does have an impact on the pattern of stock

---

[47]We should note in passing that the American Stock Exchange does not have the same difficulties with the third market as the New York Stock Exchange has. In the first place, mutual fund trading is concentrated heavily in the stocks listed on the latter exchange. Second, through the use of associate memberships, broker and dealer firms can receive reductions in rates on transactions which they initiate but which are carried out by members of the New York Stock Exchange. See U.S. Congress, House Committee on Interstate and Foreign Commerce, *Report of the Securities and Exchange Commission on the Public Policy Implications of Investment Company Growth*, p. 157, and Robbins, *op. cit.*, p. 182. Nevertheless, members of the American Stock Exchange have also adopted a program of volume discounts and the elimination of fee splitting.

prices, there is some doubt about the effect of the margin requirements. By raising the initial margin requirements, the Federal Reserve can presumably control the volume of credit going into the securities markets. But until recently, when many of the loopholes in the regulations were closed, there were numerous ways of avoiding the margin requirements. Even with these loopholes closed, the margin requirements cannot prevent purchasers from bidding up the prices of stock by using 100 percent equity.

Finally, we should note that the structure of the securities markets has been altered by the rise of institutional investors. Managers of mutual funds, for example, have sought to lower the costs of portfolio transactions or to reward those who sell their shares by seeking volume discounts and encouraging fee splitting. The result has been the development of a third market in exchange-listed stocks. With volume discounts now available but with fee splitting curtailed, there is more price competition in brokerage services than previously existed.

QUESTIONS AND PROBLEMS

1.   "Without a secondary market for corporate securities, capital formation would be seriously handicapped." Evaluate critically.

2.   Using the table of random numbers in Appendix C of this volume, establish a sequence of 30 bids, asks, and transactions prices assuming each bid and ask represents 100 shares. Plot this sequence on a graph. Explain how a specialist charged with maintaining a fair and orderly market in the security would alter the sequence.

3.   Explain what is meant by margin. Who sets the initial margin requirements? Who sets maintenance-of-margin requirements? If no one were allowed to purchase or sell shares short on margin, would this prohibition have a major impact on the market price of shares? Why or why not?

4.   "If it were not for the lack of competition in the setting of brokerage fees by the New York Stock Exchange, there would be no third market." Do you agree? Explain fully.

5.   "The theory that the market price of a stock at any point in time is a random variable is inconsistent with the theory that bases the value of shares on expected earnings or dividends." Evaluate critically.

SELECTED REFERENCES

Baumol, William J. *The Stock Market and Economic Efficiency.* New York: Fordham University Press, 1965.

Bogen, Jules I., and Herman E. Kroos. *Security Credit: Its Economic Role and Regulation.* Englewood Cliffs, N.J.: Prentice-Hall, Inc., 1960.

Curran, Ward S. "Some Thoughts on the Stock Exchange Specialist," *Quarterly Review of Economics and Business,* vol. 5, no. 1 (Spring, 1965), pp. 55–62. *Federal Reserve Bulletin* (February, 1968), pp. 167–220.

James, Ralph, and Estelle James. "Disputed Role of the Stock Exchange Specialist," *Harvard Business Review,* vol. 40, no. 3 (May-June, 1962), pp. 133–146.

Leffler, George L., and Loring C. Farwell. *The Stock Market,* 3d ed. New York: The Ronald Press Company, 1963.

Manne, Henry G. *Insider Trading and the Stock Market.* New York: The Free Press, 1966, pp. 77–91.

"Margin Account Credit," *Federal Reserve Bulletin* (June, 1968), pp. 470–481.

Polakoff, M. E., and A. W. Sametz. "The Third Market: The Nature of Competition in the Market for Listed Securities Traded Off-Board," *Antitrust Bulletin,* vol. 11, nos. 1 and 2 (January-April, 1966), pp. 191–207.

Robbins, Sidney M. *The Securities Markets: Operations and Issues.* New York: The Free Press, 1966.

Stigler, George J. "Public Regulation of the Securities Markets," *Journal of Business,* vol. 37, no. 2 (April, 1964), pp. 117–142.

U.S. Congress, House Committee on Interstate and Foreign Commerce, *Report of Special Study of the Securities Markets of the Securities and Exchange Commission,* 88th Cong., 1st Sess., 1963, part 2 and part 4, chap. 10.

Regulation of the Securities Markets

chapter Twenty-one

In reading this chapter, the student should analyze the role of regulation in terms of the goal of financial management. Is regulation of the securities markets consistent with this goal or does regulation serve other objectives?

Introduction

Throughout the two preceding chapters we have had occasion to mention in specific circumstances the role of the law, or of the regulatory agencies in administering the law, as it applies to both new issues and the market for outstanding securities. In this chapter we shall outline the primary functions and selected provisions of the law pertaining to these markets and the role of the Securities and Exchange Commission in administering the law. This discussion will, in turn, be followed by an economic analysis of federal regulation of the securities markets in which we shall pay particular attention to the impact such

494

regulation may have on the market value of the ownership interests and on the supply of capital. In the last part of this chapter we shall consider the equity aspects of securities regulation.

The Legal Background

Prior to the Great Depression, regulation both of new securities and of trading in outstanding issues was confined to the states. These so-called "blue sky" laws varied considerably. Yet nearly every state in the Union had some laws pertaining to the purchase and sale of securities.[1]

The regulations—as carried forward to the present time—can be broken down into three types.

First, most states have provisions in their laws to prevent the sale of fraudulent securities and to prohibit the dispensing of false and misleading statements concerning the quality of securities offered.

Second, brokers and dealers must be registered in most states.

Finally, most states require the registration of securities sold within their borders.[2]

But the regulation of transactions taking place between states is ordinarily outside the jurisdiction of each state. There had been attempts at federal regulation of traffic in securities beginning early in the century.[3] But it was the aftermath of the crash of 1929—that is, the Great Depression and the New Deal—which prompted Congress to invoke the Commerce clause and imbue the securities markets "with the public interest," thereby placing them constitutionally within the domain of federal regulation.

The result was the passage of the Securities Act of 1933 and the Securities Exchange Act of 1934. Both have been amended from time to time. Portions of the latter were altered considerably as a result of the congressionally sponsored investigation of the securities markets in the early 1960s.

The philosophy of the Securities Act of 1933, stated clearly in the preamble, is

> to provide full and fair disclosure of the character of securities sold in interstate commerce and through the mails, and to prevent frauds in the sale thereof.

[1] Investment Bankers Association of America, *A Primer on State Securities Regulation* (Washington: Investment Bankers Association of America, 1961), p. 3.
[2] *Ibid.*
[3] Sidney M. Robbins, *The Securities Markets: Operations and Issues* (New York: The Free Press, 1966), p. 86.

The emphasis on disclosure is crucial.   The Securities and Exchange Commission, established under the Securities Exchange Act of 1934 to administer both statutes, never approves of the securities to be sold in interstate commerce.   It simply makes certain that the information contained in the registration statement and prospectus adequately describes the company's financial history, present financial position, and future prospects, including in the latter category the role which the proceeds of the proposed issue are to play.   If the information is adequate, the investor or his advisor can evaluate the risks involved. Securities in ventures with high probabilities of failure are not barred from being distributed to the public as long as the purchasers are aware of the slim chance of success.   Some states take a more paternalistic attitude.   Officials may actually bar the sale of securities whose registration statement has been accepted by the SEC, but which in the eyes of the officials are too risky, thus preventing distribution of the securities within the state.

Besides concerning itself with "full disclosure" in a public offering of securities, Congress in framing the statute devoted several sections to the prevention and punishment of fraud and misrepresentation in the sale of securities, whether they be registered or exempted from registration under the provisions of the act.

Not only does the SEC fail to approve the securities at the time when the registration statement becomes effective, but there is always the possibility that false or misleading statements may come to light after the issue is offered.   The SEC can, if it subsequently discovers statements which are false or statements which it considers misleading, issue an order stopping further sales of the securities.   Of course, what is false or misleading varies with the circumstances.   When the proceeds from the sale of shares in a mining concern are to be used to finance operations in a new locale, the SEC may consider it misleading if management fails to include geologists' estimates of the low probabilities of discovering ore in the area.   A statement of earnings which grossly underestimates expenses or treats items in a manner which is not in accordance with generally accepted accounting procedures may also be considered false or misleading.

Moreover, those persons associated with the registration statement— including not merely the underwriters and the issuer but also independent accountants, engineers, etc., certifying the accuracy of portions of the statement — are responsible for their contribution, as indeed is any person who has a hand in preparing it.   Anyone, save the issuer, may demonstrate that he took appropriate steps to ensure the accuracy of the registration statement or those portions he prepared or certified and thereby escape civil liabilities under the act.   But the burden of proof is his. Persons buying securities in which the registration statement is shown to be defective can sue those responsible for the deception. While the amount recoverable depends on the losses sustained as a result of purchasing the issue whose registration statement has proved to be defective, the amount recovered can be as much as the purchase price of the security.[4]

Besides being liable to civil action under the law, willful violations of the provisions of the statute are punishable by fines, imprisonment, or both.

In contrast to the objectives of the Securities Act of 1933, those of the Securities Exchange Act of 1934 as amended are not as easily summarized. The preamble of the statute states that the intent of Congress is

> to provide for the regulation of securities exchanges and of over-the-counter markets operating in interstate and foreign commerce and through the mails, [and] to prevent inequitable and unfair practices on such exchanges and markets.

But the interrelationship between the SEC and the trading markets is more complex. "It is not only a regulator but a supervisor of 'self' regulators."[5] For example, exchanges must be either registered with the SEC or, because of the limited volume of the securities traded, exempted from registration. Yet the exchange has its own disciplinary procedures. But the law proclaims that no registration can be granted or remain in force

> unless the rules of the exchange include provision for the expulsion, suspension, or disciplining of a member for conduct or proceeding inconsistent with just and equitable principles of trade, and declare that the willful violation of any provisions under this title or any rule or regulation thereunder shall be considered conduct or proceeding inconsistent with just and equitable principles of trade.

---

[4]Information contained in the registration statement, in the light of hindsight, can prove to be wrong. For example, projected earnings did not materialize or the company ran into financial difficulties because of factors which no one could reasonably foresee at the time. To prevent people from taking advantage of these situations several months or years after the registration statement has been filed, the law makes it more difficult to sue those responsible for the statement. If a company makes an annual report generally available 12 months after the effective date of the registration statement, then in order to recover the losses sustained the plaintiff must show that he relied on the untrue statements in the registration statement.

[5]U.S. Congress, House Committee on Interstate and Foreign Commerce, *Report of Special Study of the Securities Markets of the Securities and Exchange Commission*, 88th Cong., 1st Sess., 1963, part 4, p. 501.

Clearly, the purpose is to force an exchange to regulate itself within the context of the law. Yet under Section 19 of the statute, the SEC can force an exchange to adopt rules or make changes in rules "to insure the protection of investors or to insure fair dealing in securities traded. . . ." The areas in which the SEC can force adoption include everything from the financial responsibility of members to the fixing of commission rates and fees for listing, interest on loans by member firms, and other charges.

Similarly, under Section 15A of the act, the so-called Maloney amendment, there are provisions for the registration of associations to self-regulate the over-the-counter markets. It was for this purpose that the National Association of Securities Dealers was formed.

But the authority of the SEC goes beyond the supervision of self-regulation of the facilities through which trading takes place. Those brokers and dealers engaged in an over-the-counter business must be registered with the SEC. If they are also members of a registered exchange, they must meet the requirements, both financial and otherwise, for membership in the exchange. Directly or indirectly, the SEC has control over the trading activities of brokers and dealers. The Commission can either revoke their registrations as broker-dealers or, if they are members of an exchange, have them suspended for a period of up to 12 months for violating the provisions of the act.

The SEC also has control over the registration of securities traded. When a security is listed on a registered exchange, it meets the listing requirements of the exchange including a requirement for presenting periodic financial information to security holders, particularly annual reports to stockholders. Somewhat similar information must also be filed with the SEC. Until the 1964 amendments to the act, the SEC had no authority to register securities traded over the counter. Now, with some exceptions,[6] every issuer with assets whose book value is $1,000,000 or more and with 500 or more stockholders must register the stock of the company directly with the SEC. Moreover, issuers of securities registered with the SEC must file periodic financial information with the Commission.

While there are securities exempted from the SEC requirements (for example, government bonds), the Commission's control over corporate issues is now widespread. So too is the SEC's control over the trading facilities as well as the personnel of the finance industry. Historically, this authority began with regulation of the exchanges, their members, and the securities traded on the exchanges. Under sub-

---

[6]The most prominent exception is the stock of insurance companies. They must comply with the provisions of the act through the insurance commissioner of the state in which the company is domiciled.

sequent amendments to the laws, including the most recent major changes in 1964, control which was at first spotty in the over-the-counter markets was gradually extended.   Today, therefore, regulations applying to listed securities and to practices forbidden on exchanges often apply to securities traded over the counter.

The periodic filing of financial information just cited is a case in point.   Another example concerns the responsibilities of all officers and directors and all stockholders who own or have beneficial interest in 10 percent or more of the shares of the company.   At the end of the calendar month, each individual must file with the Commission a statement of his holdings at the close of the month and the changes that have occurred in them during the month.   Moreover, any profits earned on the sale of the company's stock within a period of less than 6 months can be recovered by the company.   Finally, officers, directors, and major stockholders cannot engage in short sales in the company's stock.   These prohibitions originally applied to equities listed on an exchange.   Since 1964 they have also applied to stocks registered with the SEC but traded over the counter.[7]

The recovery of profits and the prohibition of short sales were designed to discourage insiders from taking advantage of knowledge not generally available to the public but which could reasonably be expected to have at least a short-run impact on the market price of the stock.   Favorable or unfavorable earnings reports coupled with dividend increases or decreases are prime examples.

But what is to prevent officers, directors, or owners of 10 percent of the stock in one company from trading inside information with those in a similar position in another company?   Moreover, what is to prevent those who are not officers, directors, or 10 percent beneficial owners in a company from making use of inside information?

The answer, according to one authority,[8] lies in the powers granted the SEC under Section 10b of the Securities Exchange Act of 1934. The regulation states that it is illegal for any person

> to use or employ in connection with the purchase or sale of any security registered on a national securities exchange or any security not so registered, any manipulative or deceptive device or contrivance in contravention of such rules and regulations as the Commission may prescribe as necessary or appropriate in the public interest or for the protection of investors.

[7]Prior to 1964, some firms which could meet the listing requirements of the New York Stock Exchange probably did not list their stock because they wanted to avoid these requirements.

[8]Henry G. Manne, *Insider Trading and the Stock Market* (New York: The Free Press, 1966), pp. 33–34.   See also pp. 17–31 and 35–46.

Using this section together with authority to prevent fraud in the sale of securities granted it under the Securities Act of 1933, the SEC promulgated a rule which in the light of court decisions defines an insider "to include any person who has direct or indirect access to corporate information not available to those with whom he is dealing,"[9] A broker-dealer, for example, has access to inside information, say a dividend cut just voted by the board of directors in response to a decline in earnings. The information has not yet been made available to the general public through the wire services. Before it is, he liquidates his holdings in the security, selling them to individuals who are unaware of the impending earnings report and dividend cut.

In such circumstances the broker-dealer could be sued by the individuals purchasing the stock for the losses sustained by them. In addition he could be subject to criminal penalties under the act for willful violation of its provisions. As in the case of the Securities Act of 1933, the criminal penalties consist of fines, imprisonment or both.

Although there are other provisions of the law applicable to securities traded both over the counter and on national securities exchanges,[10] as well as rules promulgated under the act, to engage in a lengthy discussion of them would carry us far afield.[11] From what has been said in this chapter and the two preceding ones, we have a feel for the direction which regulation has taken under the provisions of the law. We can turn now to a more substantive analysis, using additional details or elaborating further on previous examples to help explain the economic impact of regulation.

The Economic Effects of Regulating the Securities Markets

Let us begin our analysis with the full and fair disclosure theme underlying the Securities Act of 1933. What are the results of making pro-

---

[9]Robbins, *op. cit.*, pp. 99–100. See also Manne, *op. cit.*, p. 34.

[10]Since 1964, over-the-counter securities have come under the SEC's proxy rules, which have always been applicable to exchange-listed securities. Not only do issuers of both have to solicit proxies in a manner prescribed by the SEC, but if proxies are not solicited, then prior to any annual or other meeting of the holders of these securities, the issuer under the provisions of the act shall,

> in accordance with rules and regulations prescribed by the Commission, file with the Commission and transmit to all holders ... of such security information substantially equivalent to the information which would be required to be transmitted if a solicitation were made ....

[11]Robbins, *op. cit.*, 59–123.

visions for registration of new issues and of instituting a waiting period before the securities can be marketed?   One well-known economist, George J. Stigler, questioned whether disclosure requirements had any significant impact on the market price of the stock.[12]

To test the effects of the disclosure requirements in this area, he chose two periods.   The first was a period prior to the formation of the SEC, that is, the years 1923–1928.   The second was a period after the formation of the SEC, that is, the years 1949–1955.   Both were periods of rising stock prices.   From a sample of new stocks issued each year, he calculated the relative price at the time of issue with the price 1, 2, 3, 4, and 5 years after the issue.   Thus, if a stock is floated in 1949 at $10 a share and rises to $16 a share in 1952, the price ratio for this period is 16/10, or the price index is 160.   This can be interpreted to mean that the price of the stock rose by 60 percent over the 3-year period.

However, to eliminate the effects of the general market conditions on these ratios, Stigler divided them by an average of stock prices for the same period.   Consequently, if stocks in general rose 60 percent over the same period—that is, the index is 160—then 160/160 is 1, or the index is 100.   The market price of the new issue would have risen in proportion to the average of market prices as a whole.

Using this procedure, Stigler found first that in both the pre- and post-SEC periods the price of new issues of common stocks purchased fell relative to the market.   Second, in both periods the average performance of new issues for each of the first two years after flotation was not significantly different.   In other words, variations in the average performance of new issues could be explained as the result of chance. In the third and fourth years after flotation, the performance was significantly better in the post-SEC period.   In the fifth year, however, the differences were again found to be due to chance.[13]   In all but the first year, however, whether statistically significant or not, the average of new common stock prices relative to the market average was better in the post- than in the pre-SEC period.   In order that the student may compare the averages, we have reproduced them in Table 21-1.

---

[12]George J. Stigler, "Public Regulation of the Securities Markets," *Journal of Business*, vol. 37, no. 2 (April, 1964), pp. 117–142, particularly pp. 120–124.   For a debate concerning Stigler's analysis, see Irwin Friend and Edward S. Herman, "The SEC through a Glass Darkly"; Sidney M. Robbins and Walter Werner, "Professor Stigler Revisited"; J. Stigler, "Comment," all in *Journal of Business*, vol. 37, no. 4 (October, 1964), pp. 382–422. See also Irwin Friend and Edward S. Herman, "Professor Stigler on Securities Regulation: A Further Comment," *Journal of Business*, vol. 38, no. 1 (January, 1965), pp. 106–110.

[13]Stigler, "Public Regulation of the Securities Markets," pp. 120–121.

TABLE 21-1: AVERAGE OF NEW COMMON STOCK PRICES RELATIVE TO THE MARKET AVERAGES

	Year after Issue				
	First	Second	Third	Fourth	Fifth
Pre-SEC Average	81.9	65.1	56.2	52.8	58.5
Post-SEC Average	81.6	73.3	72.6	71.9	69.6

SOURCE : George J. Stigler, "Public Regulation of the Securities Markets," *Journal of Business*, vol. 37, no. 2 (April, 1964), table 1, p. 121. Reprinted by permission of the author.

As in any empirical investigation, matters of judgment are involved in interpreting the results.[14] The period following the 1920s, that is, the Great Depression, could have had a more disastrous impact on the profits and market price of the shares of new companies than on the profits and market price of the shares of established companies represented by the market averages. By contrast, the mid-1950s was followed by a period of recession and some increase in unemployment, but it was not like the catastrophe of the early 1930s. New firms could have survived more easily. If this was indeed so, it might account for the significant differences in performance of new issues as between the pre- and post-SEC periods for the third and fourth years after issue.[15] But it does not explain the lack of statistical significance in the fifth year after issue.

On the other hand, to eliminate the effects of general market conditions simply by dividing the change in price by the market average for the same period — even though this is a necessary adjustment — implicitly assumes that the market for outstanding issues is not affected by the presence or absence of the SEC. Furthermore, can we assume that the differences that do exist as between the two periods are due primarily to the influence of the SEC?[16]

Finally, there is the agonizing question as to how long we can reasonably expect the disclosure requirements to have an impact on the market price of a new issue. As time passes, the price of the security varies more on the basis of events which take place after the

[14]In this particular instance, two students of the securities markets discovered errors in Stigler's calculations. When reworking the data, they found that the averages for the post-SEC period were greater than shown in each of the 5 years after issue. See Friend and Herman, "The SEC through a Glass Darkly," p. 397 and appendix 1, p. 403. Not to be outdone, Stigler discovered further errors and in his corrected version showed that for each of the 5 years following the issue of the stock, there was for the two periods no significant difference in the average of common stocks relative to the market average. The differences that did exist, however, favored the post-SEC period in all but the first year after issue. See Stigler, "Comment," table 2, p. 418.

[15]Stigler, "Public Regulation of the Securities Markets," p. 121.

[16]Friend and Herman, "The SEC through a Glass Darkly," p. 387.

issue. The information in the registration statement and prospectus becomes dated and its influence on the price in the trading markets is lessened. Consequently, will the disclosure requirements be influential for at most 1 or 2 years after the flotation period or will their influence be felt 3, 4, 5, or more years later? As Stigler points out, the answer given is largely intuitive.[17]

To go beyond the intuitive argument is in practice quite difficult. To do so we would have to separate information provided simply because SEC regulations require it from information obtained through private sources at the time of the issue.[18] Is the quality and distribution of the information improved because of the SEC requirements or would private channels prove just as effective?

As long as the choice of the appropriate time period over which to test the effects of disclosure requirements is intuitive, there will always be disagreement as to the appropriate length of this period. While we might be inclined to favor shorter periods on the grounds that the information required eventually becomes obsolete, some have argued that a longer time span is a more important test of performance. Professional traders and speculators are more likely to be concerned with results in the short run, perhaps a year, while investors are desirous of knowing the influence the disclosure requirements might have on the price of the stock for several years into the future, if not indefinitely.[19] If it can be shown not only that the market results in the post-SEC period were better than the performance in the pre-SEC period but that the information requirements of the SEC were the cause of the improvement, then the SEC can be said to have contributed to making the capital markets more perfect.

Besides showing the difficulties involved in interpreting the differences in the average performance of new issues in the pre- and post-SEC periods, Stigler's data show clearly that in each subsequent year after issue there was greater variation in the performance of individual stocks during the 1920s than during the late 1940s and early 1950s.[20]

Graphically, this result can be shown as in Figure 21-1 on the next page. If OM and OM' represent the average market price of all stocks relative to their issue price,[21] the variation above and below the average is greater in the pre-SEC period than in the post-SEC period.

Stigler's tests show that the differences in variation are too great to

---

[17]Stigler, "Comment," p. 416.
[18]*Ibid.*
[19]Friend and Herman, "The SEC through a Glass Darkly," p. 392.
[20]Stigler, "Public Regulation of the Securities Markets," table 1, p. 121, and p. 122.
[21]We shall simplify by assuming that the distributions are symmetrical. The average, an arithmetic mean, could just as easily have been the median or mode.

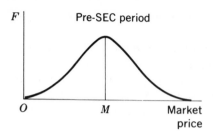
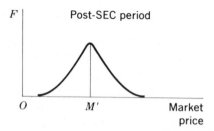

Figure 21-1

be attributed to chance. Moreover, with less dispersion about the average, there is less chance that an individual issue will be very much above or very much below the average.

How do we interpret this result? For some analysts a reduction in variance can be interpreted as proof that the disclosure requirements are effective. Investors in the post-SEC period had a better idea of the degree of risk involved. As a result, investors might be more reluctant to buy shares which could rise rapidly or decline severely in price in the secondary, trading, or aftermarket.[22]

However, we might also interpret the decline in variance to mean that the SEC had eliminated both the very poor and the very successful issues. As Stigler points out, it is not likely that the SEC had planned to do both.[23] But as we argued in an earlier chapter, registration of issues for public offering adds to the cost of flotation. Not only does the SEC charge a fee for the service, but the corporation must meet the costs of preparing the registration statement. If the waiting period gives the investment banking syndicate an opportunity to assess the market and the price at which the issue can be sold, its risk may be lowered. As a result, the syndicate may accept a lower spread for marketing the securities, thereby offsetting, in part at least, the cost of registering the issue.

Suppose, however, that on balance the information required by the SEC raises the cost of flotations. Two outcomes are possible. First, there may be fewer firms entering the capital markets. New firms, in

---

[22]Friend and Herman, "The SEC through a Glass Darkly," p. 391. Stigler implies that these authors forgot that variations could just as easily be above as below the average. See Stigler, "Comment," p. 419. Given our earlier analysis of the subjective attitude of management and presumably of owners toward risk, potential investors with "complete" information might not buy shares of stock in which there is a good chance for the market value to vary substantially on either side of the offering price. The subjective evaluation of the probability of a gain is more than offset by the evaluation of the probability of a loss. As a result, the expected utility of the outcome is negative.

[23]Stigler, "Public Regulation of the Securities Markets," p. 122.

504

particular, may be less likely to float stock issues. If the size of the issue is small, the flotation costs per share, as we have seen, are relatively high. As it gains experience and as the firm builds an earnings record, management finds that proceeds from a larger issue of stock could be profitably invested. By this time, there may be less doubt as to the probabilities of success and less reason for suspecting that the market value would fluctuate as greatly on either side of the offering price.

Second, if new firms have been excluded from the capital markets,[24] what has been the impact on the supply curve of capital? From our earlier analysis we should expect the supply curve to rise, intersecting the demand curve at a higher cost-of-capital, or net present value, figure. As a result, there should be a decline in the amount of capital employed. In short, an increase in the supply price of capital should result in a decrease in the quantity demanded. The decrease however, is probably marginal. In terms of dollars, depending on the elasticity of demand, the decrease may be very small.

Moreover, we can never be sure that the decrease in public offerings has not been offset by an increase through some other channel. In the case of bonds, of course, private placement provides an alternative. For new issues of stock, private placement is still relatively rare. The alternative to new stock issues is to place greater reliance on retained earnings. Since this can be accomplished only at the expense of dividends, we are back to our old problem of the impact that lowering dividends (or at least not raising them as rapidly as might otherwise be the case) will have on the market price of the shares.

Ultimately, we must conclude that for the post-SEC period the significant reduction in variability could very well be due to the exclusion of new firms. But even if we accept this as a possibility, the impact of the disclosure requirements on the supply price of capital and on the amount of capital employed could be small. If substitute channels for acquiring the funds are available, the impact may be negligible. But even if there are lasting effects on capital formation, it may reflect the fact that the price investors are willing to pay for relative stability in the market value of stocks they purchase.

While we have concentrated thus far on the effects the disclosure requirements might have on the market value of the stock and on the variability about the offering price, we should note that other provisions of the law, and regulations by the SEC under the law, might also affect the results. For the period under study, keeping financial information up to date and in the hands of the SEC and investors would be applicable

---

[24]Stigler points out that in his sample of 26 firms during the post-SEC period, only six were companies less than 3 years old. For the pre-SEC period, 38 out of 53 issues were of companies less than 3 years old. *Ibid.*, footnote 7.

only if the issues were subsequently listed on a registered exchange.

But there are numerous other practices, common in the 1920s but prohibited under the Securities Act of 1933 and Securities Exchange Act of 1934, which could affect the statistical results.[25]   In particular, portions of the latter act were directed against "inequities and unfair practices" both on exchanges and over the counter.

In the 1920s, for instance, it was not uncommon for interested parties to form a pool or cartel to support the market price of a stock. During the flotation period, of course, this practice is still legal, for it is designed to let the investment banking syndicate distribute the issue to the ultimate investors.   But these pools were quite common in the trading markets.   It is possible that the price of a new issue was artificially pegged while the cartel stimulated interest from other less knowledgeable individuals.   As it liquidated its holdings, the cartel also terminated its price-support program.   As a result, the value of the issue would decline.   If these cartels operated in the first year after issue and were then liquidated, they might be a factor in explaining the relatively poor performance of stocks in the second, third, and subsequent years following their issue during the pre-SEC period.

On the other hand, it is also possible for a cartel to be formed to drive the price of the stock downward through the use of short sales. The purpose of this so-called "bear raiding" tactic was to force the price low enough that when the cartel decided to cover its short sales, it would be able to do so at a substantial profit.   While this method may have been more commonly employed in exchange-listed securities, it could take place in securities actively traded over the counter, and certainly in issues initially floated over the counter but subsequently listed on an exchange.   To discourage attempts at driving the price of the stock downward, short sales on exchange-listed securities are permitted to take place only at a price above the previous market price, that is, on an uptick in the market.

Besides cartels and pools designed to manipulate the price of a security, the spreading of misinformation, particularly rumors, to drive up the price of an issue was quite common in the 1920s.   Creating the impression of activity in a stock, especially listed securities, through false transactions between parties was a technique that also abounded. Shares would be sold at a price, but the individual selling them would not deliver the securities and the person buying them would not pay for the shares.   By creating an impression of market activity it was hoped that others would submit orders, thereby bidding up the price while allowing those who initiated the activity to liquidate their holdings.

[25]Friend and Herman, "The SEC through a Glass Darkly," pp. 388–389.

These and similar techniques could, of course, account in part for the higher variability in share prices during the pre-SEC period. By forbidding or at least seriously curtailing such practices, the law and regulations by the SEC under the law may have helped to prevent price variations due to market manipulations.

We cannot, however, press the argument too far. The law forbids particular practices. It is always possible to devise new schemes or to participate inadvertently in practices which differ in form from those previously prohibited but whose impact on the market price is the same. As an example, consider the "hot issues" market of 1959–1961.[26] According to those investigating the securities markets in the early 1960s, the climate of speculation in this period "may rank with [the] excesses of previous eras,"[27] presumably including the 1920s. Stocks sold at prices which in the light of hindsight were in excess of their investment value. Within this climate, stockholders of companies which were closely held found a rare opportunity to float issues at exceptionally low E_a/P ratios. This was particularly true of firms in the electronics or other glamour industries.

Sensing a profitable opportunity, members of the securities industry who had little or no investment banking experience formed syndicates to market these issues. While some would offer the issues at whatever they felt the market would bring, others deliberately set a relatively low offering price, reasonably certain from the information gathered during the waiting period that investor interest at that price was substantially in excess of the number of shares being offered.

When the registration statement became effective, the syndicate would use various devices to delay distribution or to channel the securities sold into accounts controlled by them. The issue was very quickly sold out, the syndicate was dissolved, and a trading market was allowed to develop. As expected, the price would rise and the members of the syndicate would begin to liquidate holdings from the accounts which they controlled. Not only did they earn an investment banker's spread but they also profited from the speculative demand in the trading markets.

Even when most of the stock was allocated to customers and not placed in accounts controlled by the syndicate, the aftermarket would develop at prices in excess of the offering price. Accordingly, "stocks were being quoted at premium prices in the aftermarket before all customers knew of their allotments, before the closing at which the managing underwriter remitted proceeds of the offering to the issuer,

---

[26]U.S. Congress, House Committee on Interstate and Foreign Commerce, *op. cit.*, part 1, pp. 514–559.
    [27]*Ibid.*, p. 553.

and before customers received their stock certificates."[28] Broker-dealers, many of them part of the underwriting syndicate connected with the original distribution, were taking—and in some cases actively soliciting—orders in the aftermarket. These bids were competing against a supply of stock whose distribution was as yet undetermined and whose potential owners had not yet been able to make it available for resale. Sometimes underwriters did not deliver these certificates for days or weeks after the syndicate had been closed, thereby discouraging the owners of these securities from selling.

Clearly, under these conditions, it is possible for the market price to rise well above the offering price, and then decline as the supply of stock is forthcoming. The statistical results tend to support this analysis. Of the issues which were floated in the 1959–1961 period and for which quotations were available at the end of September, 1962, only 22 percent were selling above the offering price. By contrast, 85 percent had sold at a premium immediately after offering.[29] The results do reflect in part the general market decline in May, 1962; but this in turn was a reaction to the speculative fever which sent these and other issues to levels substantially in excess of their investment value.

To the extent that investment bankers capitalized on market conditions by withholding securities, the effect on the market price would be similar to what would be expected under a cartel designed specifically to influence the market price of the issue rather than distribute it to the ultimate investors. The outcome may also be accidental. Given the volume of business relative to the capacity to serve it, there are numerous delays in the issuance of securities which affect supply in the secondary market. Nevertheless, there would also result a rapid rise in the market price although this was not the intention of the syndicate.

Consequently, whether accidental or intentional, the causes of wide variations in the price of securities in the trading markets have not necessarily been eliminated by the law or by regulations under it. In the 1949–1955 period, the pools, cartels, and other arrangements which had contributed to market instability in the 1920s may have been effectively curtailed. The arrangements or market imperfections prevalent in 1959–1961 period may not have been present in the early 1950s. While their absence may help to account for the relative price stability during the period, the presence of regulation does not ensure that this characteristic of the post-SEC period will continue.

[28]*Ibid.*, p. 555.
[29]*Ibid.*, p. 517.

Equity in the Regulation of the Securities Markets

While the principles of financial management are concerned with the market price of the ownership interests and principles of economics with efficiency in the allocation of resources, the law is primarily concerned with what is fair or equitable in the process of issuing or transferring securities from one individual to the next.

But what is fair and equitable transcends both the principles of economics and the principles of financial management. In perfect markets, shares change hands at their investment value. By recognizing that the market price of a stock can depart from its investment value, we are admitting to the imperfections in real world markets. Whether we call these imperfections random fluctuations, view them as speculation based on inadequate knowledge, or classify them in some other manner, the fact that they exist may be all that interests the majority of people. In recognizing these imperfections, we are tacitly assuming that they can lead to a redistribution of wealth and income contrary to what might be considered "fair and equitable."

Consider, for example, the "hot issues" market just discussed. Suppose that management and, in this instance, the owners of a closely held concern approach an investment banking firm hoping to market stock in their company at $50 a share. After studying the relevant information, including the projected sales and income figures, management of the underwriting firm agrees that it could probably sell the stock at $50 a share even though it is reasonably certain that should the "hot issues" market subside, the price could easily decline to $35 or $40, a figure more nearly in line with projected earnings. Should the investment banking firm agree to form a syndicate to underwrite the issue? The problem may not be the risk incurred by the underwriter, particularly if management of the company offering the stock is willing to accept a best-efforts offering.

For management of the investment banking concern the essential problem is whether it owes its allegiance to those wanting to market the stock or to the potential purchasers. In terms of the underlying goal of this volume, we would have to conclude that the interests of the firm lie with neither. Management of the underwriting firm should be concerned with the market value of its owners' equity. If the proposition presented is profitable and within the risk constraints of the firm's owners, it will add to the total value of the equity in the investment banking company.

Even though we have noted before that it is in the tradition of the law for the decisions of management to reflect primarily the interests of its owners, when the industry in which a firm operates becomes "affected with the public interest," the goal of maximizing the market value of the owners' equity is severely compromised. Such is the case in the securities industry. The SEC as well as many students of the securities markets would probably applaud the action of management of an underwriting concern which refused to market the issue. If the firm chose to underwrite the offering, priced the stock near its investment value, saw to it that the prospectus and the shares were distributed to purchasers as soon as possible, and refrained from attempts to encourage speculative bidding in the aftermarket, there would be fewer plaudits but probably few signs of disapproval. After all, the firm would be acting within the spirit of the law. If they distribute a prospectus to each purchaser and even go to the trouble of giving one to people who show interest in purchasing the shares in the trading market, management of the underwriting concern and the firms participating in the syndicate cannot be expected to do more. If prospective purchasers do not care to make use of the information available — or even to read it or to have it interpreted when such a service is offered — there is nothing that can be done under the law.

In an effort to comply with the letter as well as the spirit of the law, many investment banking firms, particularly the more experienced and more heavily capitalized concerns, refused to underwrite (or at least refused to encourage) speculation in the "hot issues" market. The void was filled by broker-dealers who had little investment banking experience and were often thinly capitalized firms. This was one of the reasons why minimum net capital requirements were recommended for all broker-dealers.[30]

The economics of this requirement is straightforward. It is designed as a barrier to entry into the securities industry. Presumably, "a minimum net capital requirement is of high importance as one of several different approaches to assuring a broker-dealer community of principals and firms reasonably qualified in terms of responsibility and commitment."[31] Freedom of entry, a necessary condition for competitive capital markets, is to be sacrificed in favor of responsibility on the part of broker-dealers, whether they are acting as underwriters, making market in the stock after it has been distributed, or acting as brokers for the public at large. In other words, if the public, against its own long-run interests, insists on speculating in securities, those firms which constitute the industry should not be parties to the speculation nor make any attempts to encourage it.

This concern with equity is manifested in several ways. We shall deal with but one more: insider trading. Since the original hearings

[30]*Ibid.*, pp. 557 and 161–162.
[31]*Ibid.*, p. 161.

which eventuated in the Securities Act of 1933 and the Securities Exchange Act of 1934, nearly everyone interested in the subject has "castigated insider trading as being costly to shareholders and giving unfair and undeserved gains to insiders."[32]

To illustrate this point of view, suppose that the stock of a company is selling at $30 a share. Assume that this price represents the investment value of the stock. Information becomes available which indicates that E_a will increase well above the amount originally anticipated. The board of directors decides in the light of this knowledge to raise the dividend. As we noted in the previous chapter, if the information becomes generally available, then, random fluctuations aside, the market price of the stock will move instantly toward a new equilibrium. In an efficient market, we would expect news of this nature to be distributed swiftly. To the extent that it is not—that is, some people are aware of it before others and act on it by buying shares—these insiders profit from having made purchases prior to a general advance in the market price.

For this activity to be "costly to stockholders," however, we have to assume that those who sold shares would have refrained from doing so at least until the price rose to an equilibrium reflecting the enhanced investment value of the stock. For purchases to result in "unfair and undeserved gains to insiders," we must assume that the sole claim to profits by those exercising inside information is the fact that they possess this information.

In any given transaction, both of these conditions could be met. A shareholder planning to liquidate his holdings to make a down payment on a house might have chosen to wait a few days or weeks had he known of the change in earnings and dividends. Similarly, the one who bought the stock may have no more than a remote connection with the company and, more important, was in no way responsible for the factors causing the rise in earnings.

On the other hand, the stockholder might have sold his shares whether the information was available or not. Furthermore, suppose the person selling the shares had been a trader anticipating (in this case wrongly) the trend in the price of the stock rather than an investor who had held the stock for years. Would we be as sympathetic to the income loss resulting from selling to an insider?

The individual purchasing the shares may have been instrumental in causing the favorable trend in earnings. If he was an officer, presumably he was compensated for his efforts with stock options, a bonus,

---

[32]Henry G. Manne, "In Defense of Insider Trading," *Harvard Business Review*, vol. 44, no. 6 (November-December, 1966), p. 113. For a complete discussion, see Manne, *Insider Trading and the Stock Market, passim.*

or a similar plan with fixed compensation attached to it. But he may also have been a promoter, or in the classical economic sense an entrepreneur or innovator.[33] While he will probably be compensated for his innovation, he considers a fixed compensation inadequate. Consequently, management agrees to keep the promoter informed of developments affecting earnings and dividends, making the information available to him before it is made available to the general public. This allows the promoter to take a position in the company's stock, thereby trading on inside information.

Since transactions in the securities markets are anonymous, we never know in any given situation whether it is a trader or investor selling the shares and whether the one buying them is an insider who was instrumental in causing the increase rather than one who was not. On closer analysis, therefore, we might conclude that some insider transactions need not reflect what many might consider an unfair redistribution of wealth or income from the stockholder to the insider. It follows that the more complete the prohibition against insider trading, the more likely, in the light of these normative standards, that transactions which might be allowed to take place are in effect prohibited.

To set up standards for "justifiable or unjustifiable" purchases or sales involving inside information necessitates—as do any decisions affecting the distribution of wealth and income—interpersonal comparisons of who is or who is not deserving.[34] Moreover, the policies designed to implement these standards may sometimes conflict with both the economic goal of optimum resource allocation through efficient capital markets and the financial goal of maximizing the market value of the ownership interests. When this conflict occurs, all our analysis can do is clarify the issues. The choice is based on value judgments.

If insider trading is an efficient way of rewarding innovators, then to prohibit it will have some effect, however small, on resource allocation and perhaps economic growth. On the other hand, if there are substitute forms of compensation just as effective, a general prohibition against insider trading may have little economic impact, save, providing for a more efficient transition from an old to a new equilibrium price. At the same time, the prohibition, by preventing an investor from selling to an "undeserving" insider, may be consistent with society's normative standards for justice in the distribution of income.

[33]For a full discussion of this point, see Manne, *Insider Trading and the Stock Market*, pp. 111–158.

[34]Kenneth W. Boulding, *Principles of Economic Policy* (Englewood Cliffs, N.J.: Prentice-Hall, Inc., 1958), chap. 4, particularly pp. 105–108.

SUMMARY

The offering of and trading in corporate securities was first regulated by the states under "blue sky" laws and subsequently by the federal government primarily under the Securities Act of 1933 and the Securities Exchange Act of 1934.   The purpose of the Securities Act of 1933 was to provide for full and fair disclosure of the character of new issues offered publicly.   The Securities Exchange Act of 1934 set up the mechanism for supervised self-regulation of the trading markets, first for the organized exchanges, then in subsequent amendments for the over-the-counter markets.

The extent of the impact of this regulation on stock prices is debatable.   There is some evidence that the disclosure requirements may have resulted in better performance in the average market price of new issues relative to the market as a whole.   There is considerable evidence that the dispersion about the average is less in the post-SEC period than in the pre-SEC period.   But the results are subject to different interpretations.

Moreover, empirical tests based on the economic goal of efficiency in the allocation of resources or on the financial goal of maximization of the market value of the owners' equity may not be the primary objective of securities market regulation.   Indeed, much of regulatory practice is directed toward the redistribution of income and wealth resulting from trading in securities.   In a phrase, regulation is equity-oriented.   For example, suppose that there is evidence that fraud and deception in public offerings are more widespread among small, relatively low-capitalized investment banking firms than among relatively large, well-established firms.   Regulatory authorities could argue that raising the capital requirements would help eliminate these practices. This in turn would lower price competition in the flotation of new securities, raising the supply price of capital.

QUESTIONS

1.   "Disclosure requirements of the SEC have had no appreciable impact on the market price of the stock."   Evaluate critically.

2.   "To judge the effectiveness of the Securities Act of 1933 and the Securities Exchange Act of 1934 on the basis of their economic impact is to miss the central reason for their existence."   Do you agree? Explain fully why or why not.

3.   The SEC is said to be a supervisor of self-regulators.   Explain what is meant by this expression.   Does the supervisor determine regulatory policy?   If so, how?

4.   "Financial management cannot control the factors determining the supply of capital but it can react to these forces in a way that will maximize the market value of the ownership interests."   Do you agree?   Explain fully.

SELECTED REFERENCES

Friend, Irwin, and Edward S. Herman.   "The SEC through a Glass Darkly," *Journal of Business*, vol. 37, no. 4 (October, 1964), pp. 382–405.

—— and ——.   "Professor Stigler on Securities Regulation: A Further Comment," *Journal of Business*, vol. 38, no. 1 (January, 1965), pp. 106–110.

Hazard, John W., and Milton Christie.   *The Investment Business: A Condensation of the SEC Report*.   New York: Harper and Row, Publishers, Incorporated, 1964.

Manne, Henry G.   "In Defense of Insider Trading," *Harvard Business Review*, vol. 44, no. 6 (November-December, 1966), pp. 113–122.

——.   *Insider Trading and the Stock Market*.   New York: The Free Press, 1966.

Murray, Roger F. "Urgent Questions about the Stock Market," *Harvard Business Review*, vol. 42, no. 5 (September-October, 1964), pp. 53–59.

Robbins, Sidney M.   *The Securities Markets: Operations and Issues*.   New York: The Free Press, 1966, chaps. 3–5.

—— and Walter, Werner.   "Professor Stigler Revisited," *Journal of Business*, vol. 37, no. 4 (October, 1964), pp. 406–413.

Robinson, Roland I., and H. Robert Bartell, Jr. "Uneasy Partnership: SEC/ NYSE," *Harvard Business Review*, vol. 43, no. 1 (January-February, 1965), pp. 76–88.

Silberman, Lee.   "Critical Examination of SEC Proposals," *Harvard Business Review*, vol. 42, no. 6 (November-December, 1964), pp. 121–132.

Stigler, George J.   "Public Regulation of the Securities Markets," *Journal of Business*, vol. 37, no. 2 (April, 1964), pp. 117–142.

——.   "Comment," *Journal of Business*, vol. 37, no. 4 (October, 1964), pp. 414–422.

U.S. Congress, House Committee on Interstate and Foreign Commerce, *Report of Special Study of the Securities Markets of the Securities and Exchange Commission*, 88th Cong., 1st Sess., 1963, parts 1 and 2, and part 4, chap. 12.

Mergers and Reorganizations

PART
FIVE

Mergers

chapter Twenty-two

In reading this chapter, the student should relate the material presented to the principles of fixed-asset management, noting the modifications which must be made when applying the analysis to mergers. He should view the case study as an illustration of the complexities which management must face in consummating a merger.

Introduction

Having developed the principles by which financial management can maximize the market value of the owners' equity, we shall focus our attention in this and the next chapter on two topics to which these principles are applicable: mergers and reorganizations in bankruptcy. Traditionally, these areas have been viewed as special topics outside the mainstream of financial management. In one sense they are. Unless the firm is a holding company whose primary function is to acquire the ownership interests of various operating companies, its management will rarely face the need to familiarize itself with the details involved in combining business firms. Similarly, if financial management is successful in its day-to-day concern with liquidity, it will not face bankruptcy or the details involved in reorganizing the firm or liquidating its assets.

But mergers can also be viewed as in the mainstream of the principles of business finance, particularly as an aspect of the capital budgeting techniques developed earlier. Seen in this perspective, one concern may acquire the facilities of another in lieu of building its own. Similarly, it may enter the market for a product through merger rather than by developing a substitute. A paper company may purchase the plant of another firm instead of building one of its own. A soap manufacturer may attempt to enter the bleach industry through purchase of an existing producer rather than by manufacturing its own brand.[1] Although the details will differ, these decisions should be evaluated on the basis of discounted cash flows.[2] In both instances the firms are dealing with mutually exclusive investment opportunities. The one firm will not build its own capacity if it can purchase existing facilities. The other firm will not produce a new bleach if it can buy a firm already manufacturing the product.

More generally, if two firms combine assets, the economic basis for doing so is additional profits. The merger must have *synergistic* effects. In other words, the profits resulting from the merger must be greater than the sum of the profits of the separate concerns.[3] The present value of these gains represents the additional increment of wealth accruing to the owners and is consistent with the goal of maximizing the market value of their equity.[4]

---

[1]Scott Paper Company was first attracted to a merger with the Hollingsworth and Whitney Company because the latter owned an integrated mill in Mobile, Alabama. Because of increased demand, Scott was faced with the decision of building its own new capacity or acquiring through merger the facilities of another company and adapting it to its own needs. Hollingsworth owned facilities in a location suitable to Scott. See Robert L. Masson, Pearson Hunt, and Robert Anthony, *Cases in Financial Management* (Homewood, Ill.: Richard D. Irwin, Inc., 1960), pp. 549–564.

Similarly, Proctor and Gamble tried to enter the bleach market through purchase of Clorox. In this instance the merger was struck down by the Supreme Court as a violation of the antitrust laws. See Robert A. Bork, "The Supreme Court versus Corporate Efficiency," *Fortune*, Vol. 76, no. 2 (August, 1967), pp. 92ff.

[2]Samuel Schwartz, "Merger Analysis as a Capital Budgeting Problem," in William W. Alberts and Joel E. Segall (eds.), *The Corporate Merger* (Chicago: The University of Chicago Press, 1966), pp. 139–150.

[3]J. Fred Weston, "The Determination of Share Exchange Ratios in Mergers," in Alberts and Segall, *op. cit.*, pp. 117–138, particularly pp. 130–131.

[4]The division of this wealth among the owners should in principle be based on the net contribution each firm is expected to make to the increase. However, as the chapter develops, the reader will see that the price to be paid for an acquisition is usually not a single estimate but a range based on the value of the merger as seen by the management of

Although mergers can be used to implement the ultimate goal of the enterprise, bankruptcy is related superficially at least to the lack of sufficient working capital and ultimately to the objective of maintaining liquidity.   The underlying cause may be inadequate consideration given to circumstances affecting the variability in revenues.   This often manifests itself in an overlevered capital structure with revenues insufficient to pay interest when due.   If a company is to be reorganized under the provisions of the bankruptcy laws, projections of revenues must be made and discounted to arrive at a valuation for the firm.   The total amount of new securities issued should equal this valuation.   But the capital structure must be rearranged to eliminate many of the fixed-interest-charge securities.   If the reorganization is successful, the result will be a satisfactory level of net working capital to meet the seasonal and cyclical conditions under which the firm operates.   While the details again differ, the principles developed in the preceding chapters are applicable to bankruptcy reorganizations.   Indeed, if properly applied, these principles will indicate whether reorganization is feasible or liquidation advisable.

The analysis which follows, therefore, is merely an extension of the techniques already developed.   It will be applied in this chapter to mergers and in the next to reorganizations.   Although for each topic the institutional aspects discussed apply to the corporation, the analysis is relevant to any form of business organization.

Historical Background

As a means of implementing policy objectives, the merger has played an important role at different periods in the nation's history.   Students of industrial organization have singled out three distinct merger movements in the United States.   The first wave occurred about the turn of the century.   During the period 1897–1903 over 2,800 mergers took place.[5]   The second movement followed World War I, with nearly 4,700 mergers recorded during the 6-year period 1925–1930.[6]

---

each participant. Through bargaining, the net gains are divided among the shareholders of the respective concerns.   When the stockholders of each company are asked to vote on the terms agreed upon by management, little or no attention is given to quantifying the gains anticipated from the merger.   Every effort is made to convince the owners that they stand to gain from the merger.

[5]Ralph L. Nelson, *Merger Movements in American Industry, 1895–1956* (Princeton, N. J.: Princeton University Press, 1959), table 14, p. 37.   A study by the National Bureau of Economic Research, Inc.

[6]Willard F. Mueller, "Merger Movements in American Industry," in U.S. Congress, Senate Subcommittee on Antitrust and Monopoly of the Committee on the Juditiary, *Hearings: Economic Concentration*, 1965, part 2, p. 502.

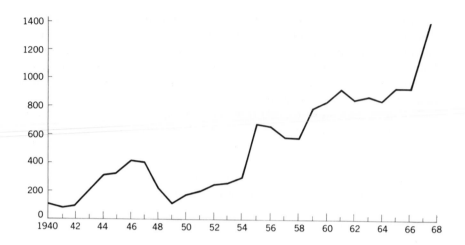

Figure 22-1

The third wave of mergers began during World War II. It slackened in the late 1940s and since that time has followed, with some interruptions, an upward trend. The general pattern of this latest movement can be seen in the data for mergers in manufacturing and mining presented in Figure 22-1. By the late 1960s this movement had shown no signs of abating.

There has also been considerable speculation as to the cause or causes of each of the movements.[7] The hypotheses range the gamut from economies of scale and consolidation of monopoly power in the first wave to diversification and tax considerations to the seller in the post-World War II movement. These and other explanations, however, for purposes of this volume, may be viewed simply as a means of enhancing the objective of profitability and maximizing the long-run market value of the owners' equity.

If economies of scale do result from a merger, costs decline and profits rise. In seeking monopoly power, the firms merging are attempting to raise their profits over and above what they would be in a more competitive environment. This may run counter to the social philosophy expressed in our antitrust laws, but it is consistent with the goal to which the enterprise is assumed to aspire.

Similarly, the seller of a family-owned company may seek out a merger with a firm whose stock has a ready market value. In so doing,

[7]*Ibid.*, pp. 507–508; Nelson, *op. cit., passim*: J. Keith Butters, John Lintner, and William L. Cary, *Effects of Taxation: Corporate Mergers* (Boston: Harvard Graduate School of Business Administration, 1951), *passim*.

his motive may be to prevent the Internal Revenue Service from placing a valuation on his shares for estate tax purposes. He believes, rightly or wrongly, that the net value of his estate after taxes will be greater if he exchanges his stock for the stock of a firm whose securities are publicly held. Again the owner's purpose is to maximize — in this case for his heirs — the market value of his equity.

Even diversification, to the extent that it affects fluctuations in the earnings of combined companies, can alter (depending on how investors value relative stability in earnings) the market price of the surviving concern. Suppose, for example, that a company manufacturing winter sports equipment merges with a concern producing lawn furniture. There may, of course, be some economies in working capital as a result of the combination. If each firm had $1,000,000 in working capital seasonally invested in marketable securities, the combination may result in as much as $1,000,000 being released for investment in long-lived assets. It is at least possible to assume that the $1,000,000 will now be used in operations for the entire year while the additional $1,000,000 can be allocated among cash or risk-free marketable securities held for precautionary motives, long-lived assets, and extra dividends. As a result of allocating these funds more profitably, the market value of the shares of the combination should be greater than the sum of the market values of shares of the separate firms.

Suppose, however, that the variation in the earnings of the combined concerns was less than the variation in the earnings of either enterprise. This could happen if the forces affecting profitability (both positive and negative) of one company were offset by opposite forces affecting profitability (positive and negative) of the other company. For the market area served, say, there is a tendency for a cold, snowy winter to be followed by a wet, mild summer or for a hot, dry summer to be followed by a mild winter. Thus fluctuations in demand for lawn furniture and for winter sports equipment would be compensating, as would fluctuations in the respective profits of the enterprises. For this reduction in variability, investors might value shares of the combination at a higher figure than the sum of the shares of the components.

This is not to say that all mergers have synergistic effects. Promoters have at times arranged combinations in which there was little basis for anticipating net gains, or they have painted an overly optimistic picture of the prospects and expropriated what gains there were in the shares of the newly formed concern. This payment for their services dilutes the equity component of the capital structure. The per share earnings of the combination may then be equal to or less than the sum of the per share earnings of the separate concerns.

Moreover, even if there are economies to be realized from a merger, the costs of assimilation may more than offset these gains.[8] Inadequate attention to the details of the source and the amount of the increase, together with the cost of implementing the merger, may lead to a decrease rather than an increase in the market value of the shares of the combined concerns.

In the illustration of the merger between the manufacturer of winter sports equipment and the producer of lawn furniture, management of the combined concerns will probably include individuals from both enterprises.   In order to effect economies in sales and manufacturing, responsible personnel in each business will have to familiarize themselves with the details of the other business.   During the assimilation period, costs, when added together, may exceed what they would have been, had the firms remained as separate entities.   Economies may eventually materialize, but the further removed they are the less their present value.

Firms in the same industry involved in horizontal mergers may not be as difficult to assimilate since management is familiar with the products produced or services rendered by each of the firms.   With vertical mergers, management may be less familiar with the products or services of the company it is planning to purchase.   But since the primary purpose is to acquire ownership in a source of supply or in an outlet for a product, the unknowns involved will be less than in the case of a diversified combination.

In the final analysis, there is no substitute for a careful study of the potential gains and costs expected from a combination.   Since management may be under pressure to point to growth in sales and profits in order to convince stockholders that it is earning its compensation, the merger appears to provide a convenient vehicle for achieving this growth.   But as we saw in our chapter on measuring business income, to raise the rate of return on assets and hence on invested capital, management must raise the sales-asset ratio, the ratio of earnings to sales, or both.   By turning assets over more rapidly, earnings on invested capital will rise.   This can be accomplished by eliminating redundant assets.   Parallel tracks owned by merging railroad companies is a good example.   Earnings as a percentage of sales can also rise.   Since total revenues less total costs equals total earnings, increases in total earnings can be accomplished by raising sales revenues or lowering operating costs.   Whether management can achieve these gains successfully through merger without encountering forces which

---

[8]Eamon M. Kelly, *The Profitability of Growth through Mergers* (University Park: Center for Research of the College of Business Administration, The Pennsylvania State University, 1967), p. 60.

tend to lower the sales-asset ratio or the ratio of earnings to sales is a question which the following careful analysis of a hypothetical illustration is designed to answer.

The Valuation Problem

In principle, the capital budgeting techniques developed earlier are as applicable to the purchase of another company as to the building of new assets. A cigarette firm, for example, may have a large sales organization, but a competitor with a smaller sales force has developed a new filter tip which promises to reduce the harmful effects of smoking. By saving research outlays (in the case of the first company) and expenditures for training a larger sales force (in the case of the second company), net gains from the merger are possible.   In the eyes of the purchaser, if the present value of these net gains is greater than the sum of the outlay and costs of consummating the merger, or if the rate of return on the merger investment is greater than the cost of capital, then the combination is worth undertaking.

In practice, however, the details of a merger are sufficiently complex to make the valuation problem a highly sophisticated exercise in capital budgeting. In the first place, the firms may have combined because of synergistic effects in one area.   But suppose that one or both of the cigarette producers also manufactured candy and gum.   Would there be additional net gains from the merger or does the firm which possesses the filter have a relatively low rate of return on capital invested in its other operations?   In short, an accurate evaluation of a potential merger may entail a separate analysis of the profitability of the additional products produced by the firm to be acquired.   If the chief asset in an otherwise relatively unsuccessful operation is the filter, the acquiring firm may wish to purchase only the rights to produce this filter.   The firm to be acquired may be interested only in a merger, not in the sale of its patent or in the issuance of license to produce the filter-tip cigarette. It often happens that the acquiring firm must take into account not only the asset or assets giving impetus to the merger but also the outlays and benefits, positive or negative, that will result from buying the concern.   Realistically, therefore, the merger may entail not one but a sequence of capital budgeting decisions requiring additional outlays after the combination is completed.   If the company possessing the filter does have other operations that are unprofitable, then the purchasing firm must consider the outlays necessary to raise the profitability in these areas and the benefits derived from so doing.   It may prove even more profitable to liquidate these operations than to continue them.

Second, the acquiring firm inherits not only the assets but also the capital structure of the acquired firm. Its management must therefore ask itself what effect, if any, the assumption of the seller's debt will have on the marginal cost of capital and ultimately on the market value of the shares of the combined enterprise. For example, suppose that the ratio of debt to total capital of the firm to be acquired was 40 percent, while the debt ratio of the acquiring firm was 30 percent. If the market value of the shares of the combination does not change (that is, it equals the sum of the market values of the shares of the component firms), the debt ratio of the new enterprise will be between 30 and 40 percent. The stockholders of the firm to be acquired will receive shares in an enterprise with lower leverage while stockholders of the acquiring firm will now have shares in a combination with a higher debt ratio.

It is possible that the differences in debt ratios reflect differences in the sizes of the firms. The larger of the two firms may have a higher debt ratio. Assuming that this is so, these differences could be compensating. In other words, the larger the firm, the greater the leverage possible without an adverse effect on the market price of the shares of each firm. But suppose that the debt ratios are not compensating. Then the market value of the shares of the combined enterprise will not rise as much as the economies effected by the merger indicated it would. To illustrate, assume that if the debt ratios of the two cigarette firms had been equal prior to the merger, the market value of the combination would have increased by $2,000,000 over the sum of the market values of the shares of the two firms. With differences in debt ratios, the market value of the combination rises by only $1,500,000.

To management of the acquiring firm, therefore, assumption of the debt of the firm to be acquired will result in lowering the potential gain from the combination by $500,000. It must, therefore, convince management and owners of the other firm that since their firm's higher debt ratio is responsible for a loss of potential value in the shares of the combination, they and not the owners of the acquiring firm should bear the risk in terms of a proportionately lower participation in the merger.

This conclusion leads to a third problem. Stockholders of the company to be acquired may feel that the compensation offered by the purchaser is inadequate. Similarly, owners of the acquiring firm may feel that compensation offered by management of the other firm overstates the contribution to be made by this firm.

To continue with the illustration of the cigarette firms, the concern with the superior sales organization estimates that the present value of the net gain resulting from marketing the new filter-tip cigarette is $3,000,000. Management is uncertain of the profitability of the separate divisions of the other company but the current market value of that company's shares is $10,000,000. The debt ratios of both companies are approximately the same. For want of a better estimate, this figure can serve as a proxy for the minimum amount the acquiring firm can hope to pay for the shares of the firm to be acquired. Presumably, the aggregate market value of the stock reflects the value of the filter to the present owners. Let us assume, therefore, that the synergistic effects accrue solely from merging a superior sales staff with a superior product. Thus the maximum price the acquiring firm is willing to pay is $13,000,000. Consequently, for the prospective purchaser the bargaining terms lie within a $10,000,000-to-$13,000,000 range.

In the eyes of the prospective seller, however, the net gains from being acquired may be something other than $3,000,000. Assume that from its point of view, all the purchasing firm has to offer is its superior sales force. Suppose, for the prospective seller, that the net present value of an outlay to train an expanded sales force is lower than the net present value, for the prospective purchaser, of the research expenditures necessary to develop the filter. Assume that the former is $1,000,000. If the firm to be acquired made the outlay to train an expanded sales force, presumably the market value of its shares would rise by $1,000,000 and would be $11,000,000. The range for effective bargaining is therefore $11,000,000 to $13,000,000. Thus, below $11,000,000 the prospective seller will not sell and above $13,000,000 the prospective purchaser will not buy.[9] Moreover, if the net gain to the seller from expanding its sales force had exceeded the net gain to the purchaser from developing its own filter, there would be no basis for a merger. The amount demanded would be in excess of what the prospective purchaser would be willing to pay, that is, in excess of $13,000,000.

Finally, even if the maximum offer of the purchaser is equal to or greater than the minimum offer acceptable to the seller, successful consummation of the merger may depend on the form in which the combination takes place and the nature of the compensation.

While we have used the term merger to include any combination, the law states that a merger takes place when one of the two concerns is eliminated or a third concern is formed. The latter arrangement is often called a consolidation. But whatever the resulting organization is called, the combining corporations would carry out the procedure in accordance with the laws of incorporation of the state or states of both

[9]Implied in the above analysis, of course, is the assumption that either the mode of financing the outlays has no effect on the market value of the shares or any effects on the cost of capital are accounted for in the discounting process. Moreover, each firm uses its own marginal cost of capital to determine the value of the acquisition or of being acquired.

the acquiring and the acquired companies. In the case of a merger, the surviving company would acquire the assets and assume the liabilities of the firm to be liquidated. If a consolidation results, the new corporation acquires the assets and assumes the liabilities of each of the combined firms. In the case of a statutory merger, stockholders of the firm to be liquidated may receive cash or securities of the surviving concern. For reasons which will subsequently become clear, they will probably receive voting stock—common in exchange for common, preferred in exchange for preferred—in the surviving company. When a consolidation takes place, the stockholders of both firms receive shares in the new enterprise.

Thus, if the firm producing the filter and the firm with the superior sales force agreed to a statutory merger, they would make arrangements whereby the assets and liabilities of the one would be transferred to the other in exchange for stock of the survivor. The stock would then be distributed to the shareholders of the acquired concern, which would then be liquidated.

If the two firms agreed to form a third or new corporation, each would transfer its assets and liabilities to the new company in exchange for its stock. The stock would then be distributed to all the shareholders and both concerns would be liquidated.

While the procedure appears neat and in many cases is satisfactory, it has a major drawback. To effect a statutory merger or consolidation, state laws ordinarily require that a specified percentage of those holding voting stock—usually two-thirds of each class outstanding—must approve the combination.[10] Even if the requisite percentage is obtained, dissenters must ordinarily be compensated in cash for the full value of their claims. Since negative votes are usually the result of dissatisfaction over the terms of the merger and therefore over the compensation received, subsequent litigation to establish the value of these claims is necessary. Not only does this involve additional expenses, but it may delay final approval of the combination. The synergistic effects of the combination may be partly dissipated by lengthy delays; that is, the acquiring firm may be developing its own filter, the company to be acquired its own sales force.

Moreover, if compensation is to be in stock, then substantial cash

---

[10]Realistically, if ownership is divorced from control in the selling corporation, top management of this corporation will be concerned over its future in the combined enterprise. Since these managers have a vested interest in their jobs, unless satisfactory arrangements are made for them in the combined enterprise, they may see to it that the proposed merger never comes to the stockholders for their approval. If it does, it is probably because management of the prospective purchaser has appealed directly to the stockholders of the seller.

outlays to dissenting stockholders may entail flotation of additional securities to finance these payments.   For these and similar reasons, management of both companies may condition the merger on a majority vote substantially in excess of the statutory requirements, perhaps 80 to 90 percent or more of the voting stock of both companies.

But if the management of each company is acting in the interests of its respective stockholders, why should there be any dissent?   The answer is implied in the previous analysis.   The maximum price the purchaser was willing to pay was in excess of the minimum price the seller was willing to accept.   The sale price could be anywhere between $11,000,000 and $13,000,000.   The $2,000,000 differential is subject to bargaining.

While the simplest solution would appear to be a compromise at $12,000,000, there is no reason to assume that the merger will take place at that price.   The respective managements know their minimum sale and maximum purchase prices.   But the seller does not know the purchaser's maximum nor the purchaser the seller's minimum price. To be sure, each can make an educated guess based on its own cost experience with outlays and expenditures for sales training and research on filter tips.   Yet neither is completely certain of the other's estimate.

Even if both managements were relatively confident of their estimates of the bargaining range and settled at $12,000,000, there may be shareholders in both companies voting against the merger.   Stockholders of the purchasing concern may feel that management has overvalued the filter and is paying too dearly for the other firm.   Stockholders of the firm being sold may feel that management has undervalued the filter or overvalued the benefits to be derived from selling out to the purchasing firm.   Since estimates are imperfect, differences of opinion and therefore dissenting votes are bound to appear.   Furthermore, stockholders of the firm being sold, particularly a minority interest, may feel that if they hold out now, while the majority goes along with the merger, they may later receive higher compensation from the purchasing firm before arriving at the point of seeking adjudication of their claims in court.

The firms can, of course, use other techniques to implement the combination.   Management of the prospective buying firm can negotiate a purchase of assets rather than a statutory merger.   In this case, the selling company gives up title to its assets, usually in exchange for voting stock of the purchasing firm.   The selling firm then becomes a holding company which can be subsequently liquidated, at which point the stock of the purchasing firm will be distributed to the stockholders of the selling firm.

Thus, suppose that the firm with the filter has sold its assets in exchange for shares of the company with the superior sales force. The only asset of the selling firm is the stock of the purchasing firm. Its stockholders' sole source of income is in the form of dividends paid on the stock of the purchasing firm. The market value of its shares vary with the market value of the shares of the purchasing firm. Under this technique, the stockholders of the selling corporation must approve the sale, with cash compensation going to dissenters. But ordinarily under the law management of the buying firm does not have to ask its stockholders to approve the purchase.

A technique widely used by purchasing concerns is to appeal, with or without the blessing of the selling firm's management, directly to the stockholders of the company in which the purchaser is interested. Through the use of tenders, management of the purchasing firm may offer to buy the other company's stock at a premium over the current market value, thereby paying a portion of the net gain to these stockholders. To illustrate, assume that the purchasing firm does agree to pay $12,000,000 for the firm with the filter. Assume further that the firm being sold has 200,000 shares of common stock outstanding. There is no preferred stock in its capital structure. Since the aggregate market value of its common stock is $10,000,000, the per share price is therefore $50 while the tender price is $60. Assume now that the current per share market price of the buying corporation's stock is $30. If the offer is to be made in terms of the buyer's stock each shareholder of the firm being sold will receive two shares of the purchasing firm's stock for every one share given up. In order to ensure that the results of the tender do not leave a substantial minority of the stock outstanding, management may make its offer on the condition that holders of, say, 95 percent of the stock accept it. Again, stockholders of the purchasing corporation do not ordinarily have to approve of the acquisition. Although, if the shares required exceed the authorization limits, the stockholders of the purchasing corporation may have to vote to increase the number authorized. The stockholders of the firm being sold indicate their preferences by accepting or rejecting the offer.

If the purchasing corporation's conditions are met and the terms accepted, the 95 or more percent of the selling corporation's stock is held by the buying corporation. The selling corporation becomes a subsidiary while the minority interest remains outstanding. Even though a direct purchase of the selling corporation's stock is legally less complicated than a statutory merger or sale of assets, as long as minority interests remain outstanding, they have a nuisance value. Minority stockholders can institute suits against the purchasing corporation to prevent management from carrying out policies that are adverse to their interests.   For example, these stockholders can try to prevent management from using certain accounting techniques which reduce the reported earnings of the subsidiary even if the income of the consolidated enterprise is unaffected.

Thus, regardless of the form in which the merger takes place, minority interests can prove troublesome.   To eliminate them at a higher price adds to the cost of the merger.   Yet to insist that a specified majority of the stockholders accept the terms of the combination may forestall it completely.

Finally, the means of compensation can also affect the outcome. We indicated earlier that most combinations are paid for with voting stock — common in exchange for common and preferred in exchange for preferred.   If voting stock is used as payment, it usually qualifies as a tax-free exchange.   To illustrate, continuing with the example of the cigarette producers, the selling company's shareholders receive $60 in exchange for $50, or receive a net gain of $10 per share.   If under a statutory merger or sale of stock the stockholders receive common stock of the purchasing company,[11] there is no personal income tax paid on the capital gains.   If the stock is subsequently sold, the basis for taxation is the difference between the price paid at the time of purchase and the price received at the time of sale.   Suppose that a shareholder of the selling company bought one share of stock a year earlier at $40.   When the merger took place he relinquished it for two shares of the purchasing company's stock at $60.   This qualifies as a tax-free exchange.   A year later he sells both shares for a total of $70.   Before the end of that tax year he must pay a capital gains tax on $30.   The rates will vary in accordance with the tax on his other sources of income, but because he held the shares for a period of 6 months or more, he will pay a capital gains tax on $30 at a maximum rate of 25 percent, or a total of $7.50.

On the other hand, if compensation has been given in cash or in other securities,[12] the increase (for the stockholder in question, $60 − $40, or $20) is ordinarily subject immediately to a capital gains

---

[11]In the case of a sale of assets, the stock of the purchasing company becomes an asset of the selling company.   The company can be subsequently liquidated and the stock of the purchasing company distributed to the stockholders of the selling company. If the selling company is not liquidated, it may avoid a capital gains tax on the sale of its assets by listing the stock received at the book value of the assets exchanged.

[12]When and under what conditions preferred stock can be given in exchange for common stock is subject to considerable qualifications.   The Internal Revenue Service argues that it is usually not a tax-free exchange.   See U.S. Treasury Department, Internal Revenue Service, *Tax Credit for Small Business* (Washington: Government Printing Office, 1968), pp. 74–75.   Yet in the case study presented in the next section, convertible preferred stock was given in exchange for common stock on the assumption that it was a tax-free exchange.   The fact that the stock was convertible into common stock probably played a role in this opinion.

tax. Shareholders, therefore, would ordinarily prefer compensation in stock.

However, when the purchasing company does pay in cash, it can use for corporate income tax purposes the actual purchase price as the basis for depreciating the assets acquired. But if the combination was the result of a tax-free exchange of shares, the purchasing company must accept for tax purposes the value of the assets on the tax books of the selling company.

For example, if the book value of the selling company's assets had been $9,000,000 for corporate income tax purposes and the combination resulted in a tax-free exchange of shares at $12,000,000, the buying company would have to continue to value the assets of the acquired company at $9,000,000. If compensation had been in cash or its equivalent in securities that did not qualify as a tax-free exchange, then the purchase price would be the basis on which the buying company could value the selling company's assets. The higher the valuation, the greater the annual depreciation allowances, and the lower the taxable income. Thus the buying company may be willing to pass on some of these tax savings in the form of a higher purchase price if the stockholders of the selling company agree to accept cash or securities other than common stock.

Consummating a Merger — A Case Study[13]

Ideally, in order to analyze a merger, we need an estimate of the synergistic effects expected from the combination as well as of the anticipated distribution of gains among the participants. Realistically, what interested parties (and certainly those who are stockholders of publicly held corporations are interested parties) receive from those negotiating a merger are vague statements pertaining to the economies anticipated and specific information on the terms of the agreement. As an example let us look at the merger between the Sun Oil Company and the Sunray DX Oil Company finally approved by stockholders of the latter on June 20, 1968.[14]

The Sun Oil Company was incorporated May 2, 1901 under the laws of the State of New Jersey. It is presently engaged in all aspects of the industry. This includes the acquisition and development of

---

[13]Unless otherwise noted, the material on which this section is based, including the tables, is drawn from the proxy statement of March 20, 1968, to the stockholders of Sunray DX Oil Company.

[14]*Wall Street Journal*, June 21, 1968, p. 19. The stockholders of the Sun Oil Company had given their approval earlier.

lands, foreign and domestic, with proven reserves of oil and gas, production and distribution of crude oil and its derivatives, and both the wholesale and retail marketing of crude oil and its products in the eastern United States and Canada.

The Sunray DX Oil Company was incorporated in Delaware in 1929 and at the time of the merger was also engaged in nearly all phases of the oil business. In addition, it had in recent years expanded its activities to include manufacturing and marketing of agricultural chemicals. Its domestic marketing of oil and gasoline covered 18 states constituting the center of the nation.

Thus, for practical purposes, the merger can be termed a horizontal combination between two fully integrated oil producers whose domestic market now extends from the East Coast to the Rocky Mountains and includes portions of southern Canada. As of December 31, 1967, the book value of the assets (and therefore the liabilities and stockholders' equity) of the Sun Oil Company and its subsidiaries was $1,598,513,000. For the Sunray DX Oil Company and its subsidiaries, a comparable figure was $748,997,000. Over 64 percent of the book value of the capital structure of Sun Oil was in equity, as compared with nearly 69 percent for Sunray DX.

The long-term debt of Sun Oil was $318,327,000. The major item was a series of $4\frac{5}{8}$ percent sinking fund debentures due November 15, 1990 with annual payments of $4,000,000 between 1970 and 1989 and a payment of $20,000,000 in 1990. The principal amount outstanding on December 31, 1967 was $100,000,000. There were also term loans in excess of $42,800,00 evidenced by notes payable to banks. The interest rate was $4\frac{1}{2}$ percent with the notes maturing between March 31, 1969 and December 31, 1974. The remainder of the long-term liabilities consisted of various types of notes of the company or its subsidiaries, including over $11,500,000 of 6 percent convertible debentures of the latter maturing May 15, 1975.

The long-term debt of Sunray DX was $92,477,000. Of this amount, $75,000,000 represented $4\frac{1}{4}$ percent sinking fund debentures due in 1987 with the sinking fund requirements beginning in May, 1971. The remainder consisted of notes, including a $2\frac{7}{8}$ percent note due July 1, 1970. Its value as of December 31, 1967 was in excess of $6,600,000. Payments of $1,667,000 had to be made on the note semiannually. The terms of the loan agreement restricted cash dividends. But as of December 31, 1967, there was still $180,000,000 in retained earnings free of such restrictions.

Consequently, in terms of book value, the capital structure of the Sunray DX Oil Company was somewhat more conservative than the capital structure of the Sun Oil Company. However, the latter company was nearly twice as large as the former. As we pointed out earlier, the ability of a firm to employ leverage without affecting the market price of the shares—the Modigliani and Miller hypothesis notwithstanding—may be positively correlated with the size of the firm. If we assume that this is the case in this instance, then the differences in debt ratios could be compensating. Perhaps one of the economies from the merger is an even larger debt capacity.

When we turn to the income statements for the 5 years preceding the merger, we find that Sun Oil shows an upward trend in revenues, earnings, and dividends for all 5 years but Sunray DX for only the last 3 years. The figures are illustrated in Tables 22-1 and 22-2.

TABLE 22-1: REVENUE AND INCOME STATISTICS FOR SUN OIL COMPANY

	1963	1964	1965	1966	1967
Total Revenue[a]	$855,150	$850,097	$942,721	$1,071,341	$1,173,250
Net Income	61,216	68,507	85,520	100,574	108,576
Net Income per Share[b]	2.44	2.73	3.40	4.00	4.32
Cash Dividend per Share[b]	$0.57	$0.60	$0.63	$0.78	$0.95

SOURCE : Proxy statement to stockholders of the Sunray DX Oil Company dated March 20, 1968, p. 9.
[a]Includes operating and nonoperating income.
[b]Adjusted for annual stock dividends and for a four-for-three stock split in 1966. The figures are accordingly retrospectively based on the shares outstanding on December 31, 1967.

TABLE 22-2: REVENUE AND INCOME STATISTICS FOR SUNRAY DX OIL COMPANY

	1963	1964	1965	1966	1967
Total Revenue[a]	$486,968	$473,300	$491,406	$535,645	$592,084
Net Income	42,528	35,793	38,868	62,873[b]	54,464
Net Income per Share	2.29	1.93	2.09	3.41[b]	2.95
Cash Dividend per Share	$1.40	$1.40	$1.40	$1.40	$1.42½

SOURCE : Proxy statement to stockholders of the Sunray DX Oil Company dated March 20, 1968, p. 10.
[a]Includes operating and nonoperating income.
[b]The net amount of $17,280,000, or $0.94 per share, reflects extraordinary or nonrecurring income.

The common stock of Sun Oil and the common stock of Sunray DX are both listed on the New York Stock Exchange. The range in the market price of each stock over the 5 year period is shown in Table 22-3.

MERGERS 533

TABLE 22-3: FLUCTUATIONS IN THE MARKET PRICE OF THE COMMON STOCK OF SUN OIL COMPANY AND SUNRAY DX OIL COMPANY, 1963–1967

Period	Sun Oil Common[a] High	Low	Sunray DX Common High	Low
1963	$33\frac{3}{4}$	$25\frac{3}{4}$	$39\frac{3}{8}$	$25\frac{1}{4}$
1964	$44\frac{1}{8}$	$30\frac{3}{8}$	$37\frac{1}{4}$	29
1965	$43\frac{1}{8}$	36	$35\frac{1}{4}$	$28\frac{1}{8}$
1966	$50\frac{3}{4}$	$40\frac{7}{8}$	34	$26\frac{3}{8}$
1967				
First Quarter	56	$46\frac{7}{8}$	$32\frac{1}{8}$	$28\frac{7}{8}$
Second Quarter	$68\frac{5}{8}$	$54\frac{3}{8}$	36	$31\frac{1}{8}$
Third Quarter	$75\frac{1}{8}$	$64\frac{3}{8}$	$38\frac{1}{2}$	$34\frac{1}{8}$
Fourth Quarter	$72\frac{3}{8}$	60	$40\frac{3}{8}$	$31\frac{5}{8}$
1968				
January 1 to July 2	$72\frac{1}{2}$	$60\frac{1}{8}$	$48\frac{3}{8}$	$37\frac{1}{8}$

SOURCE : data for 1963, 1964, and 1965 are from Moody's 1967 *Industrial Manual*, p. 9105, and are adjusted for stock dividends and splits. Data for 1968 are from the *Wall Street Journal*, July 3, 1968. Data for 1966 and 1967 are from the proxy statement to stockholders of the Sunray DX Oil Company, March 20, 1968, p. 15.
[a]Figures are adjusted for annual stock dividends and for a four-for-three stock split in 1966.

As the directors of Sun Oil have declared stock dividends each year and split the stock four-for-three in 1966, the market price of the shares has been retrospectively adjusted. In other words, the market price for each year or quarter reflects the value of the shares under the assumption that the number of shares outstanding in the years preceding 1968 was the same as the number outstanding in 1968.

It is evident from the figures that the price of the shares of each company corresponded through 1967 to the general trend in reported earnings. The shares of the Sun Oil Company showed a consistent upward trend, as did earnings. The shares of the Sunray DX Oil Company followed the general pattern of reported earnings which for 1964 and 1965 were below those of 1963. Not until 1966 and 1967 did earnings show an upward trend, after an allowance of 94 cents per share in 1966 for nonrecurring income.

Finally, as of December 31, 1967, the per share book value of the stockholders' equity of the Sun Oil Company was $40.87. The comparable figure for the Sunray DX Oil Company was $27.98. The stocks of both companies were selling in excess of their book value, reflecting, of course, the limitations of the accounting approach to valuation. After allowances for debt, the market in both cases placed a higher value on the stockholders' share of assets than did accountants. The latter used generally accepted principles of accounting to arrive at a value for assets less liabilities, that is, for stockholders' equity.

As we have argued, the market price, random fluctuations aside, reflects investors' estimates of $E_a/(r-g)$ or $D_a/(r-g)$ for each company, with emphasis in this volume placed on the former. Although we can never be certain of the values for D_a, E_a, r, and g, and in spite of the difficulties inherent in the accounting valuation, let us use the reported earnings for 1967 as an estimate of E_a for that year. We shall assume that P is the average of the range of market prices for the year. Thus

$$\text{Sun Oil Company} \qquad \text{Sunray DX Oil Company}$$

$$r - g = \frac{\$4.32}{\dfrac{(72\frac{5}{8} + 46\frac{7}{8})}{2}} \qquad r - g = \frac{\$2.95}{\dfrac{(40\frac{3}{8} + 28\frac{7}{8})}{2}}$$

$$r - g = \frac{\$4.32}{\$59.75} \qquad r - g = \frac{\$2.95}{\$34.625}$$

$$r - g = 7.2\% \qquad r - g = 8.5\%$$

From the information presented earlier, there is probably no reason to assume that the business or financial risk of the two companies differs markedly. Thus the rate of discount was higher in 1967 for Sunray DX probably because investors anticipated a slower growth in earnings than in the case of Sun Oil.

Given this background, we have a basis on which to evaluate the terms of the merger from the viewpoint of the stockholders of both companies. However, we have no way of knowing the source of the economies expected from the merger. Moreover, to find these economies, the stockholder must read between the lines of the information given to him. For example, in urging owners to approve the merger, the chief executive officer of Sunray DX noted the following in the proxy statement.

> Your Board of Directors has carefully considered the proposed merger and has unanimously concluded it is in the best interests of the stock-holders. This conclusion is supported by many sound reasons. The combined companies will be active in oil exploration and production in most of the prominent petroleum extractive regions of this country and of the world. It will have an efficient network of crude oil and product pipelines and ocean-going tankers for effective raw material and finished goods movement. It will have manufacturing facilities located in key strategic positions surrounding its market territories, able to process a variety of raw materials. Its markets will extend from the east coast to the Rocky Mountain states and into southern Canada. Its growth areas will include the rapidly expanding fields of synthetic crude oil, petro-

chemicals, agricultural chemicals and minerals.   It will have an expanded capacity in research and development.

At the time, apparently, management anticipated economies in the production and distribution of oil products with an enhanced ability to develop and exploit markets for new products.   If we interpret this statement in this way, the directors of Sunray DX and presumably those of Sun Oil anticipate a rise in total earnings due primarily to a more efficient utilization of existing capacity.   In addition, the sale of new products, perhaps at a higher profit margin, may also add to the return on invested capital.

If assets are to be used more efficiently, we would expect the sales-asset ratio of the combined firms to rise.   If the rate of return on sales is to rise, then costs per unit of sales must decline.   Stockholders were given no estimate of the synergistic effects from the merger.   On the contrary, they were warned that the optimism expressed by the chief executive officer of Sunray DX had to be tempered by the fact that many factors could affect the earnings of the surviving corporation.   In the proxy statement, the following appears.

COMPETITION AND REGULATION

The oil industry is highly competitive.   There is competition not only among companies in the industry, but also from products of other industries.   Occasional price wars have had a material adverse effect on industry profits.   The business of the Surviving Corporation may be affected by future competition; by taxes, including taxes on the sale of gasoline; by developments in government regulation involving production, imports, transportation, materials or prices; by labor conditions; or by developments in the general economic or international situation which may affect the Surviving Corporation or the oil industry as a whole.

Crude oil production of Sun and Sunray, and consequently of the Surviving Corporation, in most areas, is subject to production schedules, drilling and other regulations which have been prescribed from time to time under the laws of certain states and provinces for the purpose of conserving resources through more orderly and efficient production.   In addition, sales of natural gas to interstate pipe lines for resale are subject to price regulation by the Federal Power Commission under the Natural Gas Act of 1938.

Particular restraints on foreign developments will be felt by the Surviving Corporation as a result of the restrictions placed on direct foreign investments under the Balance of Payments Regulations promulgated by the United States Department of Commerce.

The merger will result in a reduction in the combined oil import quotas of Sun and Sunray.   The extent of such reduction cannot presently be ascertained.

All these factors, of course, affect the companies whether separately or as a combination. The relevant question is whether the adverse effects will be greater on the surviving concern. Only in the case of its ability to import oil is there definite agreement that the combination will be affected adversely. Here it is admitted that the extent of the reduction cannot be ascertained.

On the synergistic effects of the merger, therefore, there is a tendency to be vague. Management does not, and perhaps the SEC will not let it, speculate as to the value which should be placed on the merger. From the information presented in the proxy statement and from the terms of the merger, stockholders are expected to make up their minds as to whether or not the combination is to their advantage.

When offered to the stockholders and ultimately approved by what was in this instance holders of at least two-thirds of the number of shares outstanding, the terms of the merger called for Sun Oil to be the surviving corporation. It acquired the rights, properties, and assets of Sunray DX and assumed its liabilities. In exchange, the stockholders of Sunray DX received one share of $2.25 cumulative convertible preferred stock of Sun Oil with a stated value of $5.00 for each share of common stock of Sunray DX owned. The convertible preferred stock was created for the purpose of consummating the merger. While the shares exchanged were not identical—that is, preferred was exchanged for common—the convertible preferred stock could be exchanged for common stock.

Moreover, management argued that the stockholders of Sunray DX would recognize no gain from the merger if they exchanged their shares.[15] Sun Oil would assume the assets of Sunray DX at their book value.

In order to effect the merger, Sun Oil also created a class of common stock with a par value of $1. Existing shares of Sun Oil common stock with no par value were converted into $1-par-value stock on a share-for-share basis. The preferred stock issued to the stockholders of Sunray DX was also made convertible into the same class of common stock. The conversion ratio was 0.65 of a share of Sun Oil $1-par-value common stock, adjusted for stock dividends and splits, for each share of preferred stock.

The shareholders of Sunray DX can convert their stock at any time into the common stock of Sun Oil. Moreover, the stock is not redeemable until June 1, 1975. Thereafter it is redeemable at prices decreasing from $60 per share to $57 per share. In the event of voluntary liquida-

---

[15]The assets and liabilities of the companies having been combined, if the shareholders of Sunray DX converted their preferred stock into common stock, the per share book value of their holdings would decline from $27.98 to $24.88.

tion, shareholders are entitled to $55 per share.   Should liquidation take place as a result of bankruptcy proceedings, shareholders are entitled to $52 per share.   While outstanding, each share of preferred stock is entitled to one-quarter of one vote, while the common stock into which it is convertible is entitled to one full vote.

In terms of per share book value at the end of 1967, the stockholders of Sunray DX, under the terms of the conversion ratio, were receiving somewhat less in common stock in Sun Oil than they were giving up.   The ratio was

$$\frac{\$27.98}{\$40.87} = 0.685$$

They were, however, receiving an immediate increase in income of about 58 percent, that is, $2.25 rather than 1.42\frac{1}{2}$ per share.

To arrive at the investment value of the preferred stock in late 1967 and early 1968, when the negotiations were taking place, we might have discounted the dividend at 5 percent, so that

$$\frac{\$2.25}{0.05} = \$45$$

This would be a liberal estimate.   Given the tight money conditions and the high level of interest rates prevailing at the time, a 6 or 7 percent discount rate would not have been unreasonable.   Consequently, when the merger was presented for stockholder approval, a person anticipating that the stock would sell in excess of $45 was probably basing his analysis on the assumption that the conversion value of the shares exceeded or would soon exceed their investment value.

The price of Sunray DX common immediately after the merger did tend to correspond closely to the conversion value, sometimes falling below and sometimes rising above this liberal estimate of its investment value.   On June 20, 1968, the day the merger was approved, the shares of Sunray DX were trading between 44$\frac{5}{8}$ and 45$\frac{3}{4}$ while those of Sun Oil varied between 69 and 70.   The highs and lows of both stocks, together with the ultimate conversion value of Sunray DX common into Sun Oil common, are given in Table 22-4.

There are, of course, differences between the market price of Sunray DX and its theoretical value.   We can account for these discrepancies partly on the basis of random factors.   But a more substantive rationalization of the differences lies in the attempt by the market to place a value on the increased dividend that shareholders would receive from exchanging their shares of Sunray DX common for Sun Oil preferred, while at the same time anticipating the trend in the price of Sun Oil common.

TABLE 22-4: FLUCTUATIONS IN THE MARKET PRICE OF THE SHARES OF SUN OIL AND SUNRAY DX AND THE CONVERSION VALUE TO THE STOCKHOLDERS OF SUNRAY DX
June 21 to July 22, 1968

	Sun Oil Common		Conversion Factor		Conversion Value		Sunray DX Common	
	High	Low	X		High	Low	High	Low
June 21	68 3/8	67 1/8	.65	=	44.44	43.63	45 1/2	44 1/2
June 24	67 3/8	67	.65	=	43.79	43.55	44	42 5/8
June 25	67 1/4	67	.65	=	43.71	43.55	44 1/2	42 1/2
June 27	68 1/2	67 1/4	.65	=	44.53	43.71	46 1/4	44 3/4
June 28	71 1/2	68 3/4	.65	=	46.48	44.69	48	47
July 1	72 1/2	70 3/4	.65	=	47.13	45.99	48 3/8	47 3/4
July 2	70 3/4	70	.65	=	45.99	45.50	48 5/8	47 7/8

SOURCE: *Wall Street Journal*, June 22 to July 3, 1968. The stock exchanges were closed on June 26, 1968.

At the time, two factors complicated the analysis. The first was the possibility, however small, that the merger might be blocked, perhaps by antitrust action, before it was consummated or shortly thereafter, thus forestalling the dividend increase indefinitely. The second was the signing into law of a 10 percent surtax on federal income taxes. This latter factor would be expected to have an impact on interest rates. Presumably, a tax increase would tend to lower the interest rates by lowering the profitability of investments and hence the demand for capital.[16] It would, therefore, cause the investment value of fixed-income securities, including the Sun Oil convertible preferred stock, to rise. This is why we tended toward a liberal estimate of the discount rate, placing the investment value at $45. As for the delay in consummating the merger, management anticipated settling the remaining details by August, 1968. The companies were finally merged in November, 1968.

However individual investors in the shares of Sunray DX common may have valued the terms of the merger, on the day the merger was approved by the shareholders, the market price of the stock was at or near its high for those years for which data have been presented. It slipped shortly thereafter but rose again to a new high, perhaps indicating that investors felt that, on balance, they were receiving something of value from the merger.

But what were the gains to the holders of Sun Oil stock? From

[16]The analysis, of course, proved to be incorrect. The Federal Reserve, following enactment of the surtax, at first relaxed and then tightened credit. Inflation did not subside and interest rates continued to rise into 1969.

their viewpoint they received a company whose reported earnings after taxes in 1967 more than covered the dividend requirement on the new issue of preferred stock. To the extent that reported earnings were not overstated, the residual accrued to the holders of Sun Oil stock. To be sure, the holders of Sunray DX stock could share in this residual. To do so, they could convert their Sunray DX preferred into Sun Oil common, giving up their \$2.25 dividend in exchange for a dividend of \$0.6175 per share (0.65 × \$.95) at the 1967 rate. On the other hand, they might hold their shares at least until the Sun Oil Company was able to exercise the option to redeem them, that is, until June 1, 1975. Earnings and hence the market price of Sun Oil common could continue to rise. In such circumstances Sun Oil preferred would rise in proportion to its conversion value.

Consequently, at the time the merger was consummated, it would appear that under its terms the primary risk to the stockholders of the Sun Oil Company was that the acquisition would fail to generate earnings after taxes and replacement cost of plant, equipment, and inventory sufficient to cover the dividends on the convertible preferred stock. In return for this risk, they would gain if the earnings exceeded the dividend requirements. The stockholders of the Sunray DX Oil Company, on the other hand, gained current income by agreeing to the merger. Moreover, they could also enjoy at least for a few years the possibility of a rising market value for the preferred stock they received should the price of Sun Oil common continue to rise.

The stockholders of both companies thus were making some sacrifice. If there were no synergistic effects from the merger or if diseconomies resulted, the primary burden would fall on the holders of Sun Oil common stock as management would try to meet the cumulative dividend payment on the preferred stock rather than eliminate payments altogether on the common stock. If, however, the gains did materialize the holders of Sun Oil stock would participate more proportionately than the holders of Sunray DX stock.[17]

When management of each company submitted the terms of the merger to its respective owners, the stockholders of the Sun Oil Company had to decide whether the risks they were assuming were more than offset by the potential gains to them. Those of the Sunray DX Oil Company had to decide whether the relative certainty of a higher but unchanging dividend was worth the sacrifice of some of the potential earnings which, of course, might never be realized.

---

[17]The student should remember that in terms of book value at least the conversion ratio was .6, whereas the ratio of the book value of Sunray DX common to Sun Oil common was .685. Thus the stockholders of the Sunray DX Oil Company were giving up some of their share in the anticipated gains from the merger in exchange for current income.

In the final outcome, the shareholders of both companies approved the merger, those of the Sun Oil Company when it was first presented to them. A large stockholder of the Sunray DX Oil Company tried unsuccessfully to block the merger. He argued in part that

> ... Sunray DX alone earns substantially more than Sun will have to pay out in this preferred dividend. In addition to those present earnings, Sun stockholders will benefit from any savings that develop from combining these two large organizations and any future increases in the years to come . . . .
>
> We believe that Sunray DX management made a poor deal for stockholders. We believe if they intend to sell that a more attractive deal is available. On the other hand, should we sell at all?
>
> After years of insignificant exploration we now have some exciting foreign opportunities to discover oil and gas . . . .
>
> We will vote our 616,000 shares "AGAINST" the merger because we feel the stockholders deserve a better offer.[18]

To argue that the Sunray DX management sold too cheaply may, in the light of our analysis, be valid. But to assert that the stockholders of the Sun Oil Company will share in the savings, while also correct, is not to imply that the gain is improper. For the charge of impropriety to be valid, we would have to assume that any synergistic effects from the merger are due solely to the Sunray DX Oil Company. This is highly unlikely. For example, if, as we mentioned earlier, the optimum capital structure is a function of the size of the firm, the economies realized are the result of the combination and cannot be attributed solely to one or the other of the two firms.

Apparently the vast majority of shareholders of the Sunray DX Oil Company agreed with the opinion expressed by another large stockholder, an investment banking firm which was asked to express its views on the terms of the merger. In evaluating the combination, the firm stated,

> we have considered the relative earnings, market values and dividends of each company as well as the book values and our estimate of the appraised values of their respective assets. In making our studies, we have relied on reports and documents made available to the public by the respective companies along with certain more detailed information furnished to us by them. We have assumed the accuracy of all the data examined by us but have not independently verified such data. . . .
>
> Based on the foregoing, it is our opinion that the terms of the proposed merger are fair and equitable to the Sunray DX stockholders.[19]

[18] Letter of April 11, 1968 to Sunray DX stockholders from W. H. Helmerich, III, president of Helmerich & Payne, Inc., Tulsa, Oklahoma.

[19] Letter of February 28, 1968 to the chairman of the board of Sunray DX Oil Company from Eastman, Dillon, Union Securities & Company, New York, N.Y.

In the final analysis, therefore, shareholders of both companies must make a subjective evaluation of the terms offered them. Since there is usually disagreement over the economies expected from a merger, charges that the combination is unfair to the stockholders of one or the other company, or in some cases both companies, must be anticipated. In order to obtain approval from a satisfactory number of shareholders of both companies, management must convince enough of them that on balance they will receive something of value from the combination.

SUMMARY

Corporate mergers often represent mutually exclusive investment opportunities. Rather than build its own facilities, management acquires facilities of another firm. In principle, management can compare the present value of the cash flows from the merger with the present value of the cash flows from building its own facilities.

More generally, the economic basis for a merger is either an increase in expected profits, a reduction in profit variability, or both. When expected earnings rise or the variability in expected earnings falls, the market value of the equity in the combined concerns rises. The additional profits, or the synergistic effects of a merger, may come from cost reduction or economies of scale. The reduction in variability in total profits may be the result of diversification.

While the impetus for a merger may be the substitute investment opportunity it offers, in practice there are additional details which must be considered. The acquiring company may be interested in only a portion of the facilities of the other company, yet to consummate the merger it must acquire the entire company. It may take over other assets which are of little value. Moreover, it will assume the financial liabilities of the company acquired. As a result, the debt ratio of the combined concerns may be higher than the debt ratio of the acquiring firm. Furthermore, stockholders of the concern acquired may feel that they are receiving inadequate compensation for their assets. On the other hand, stockholders of the acquiring company may feel that they are paying too much. This conflict stems from the different perspectives in which the stockholders of each company view the merger. The value of the merger to each concern will ordinarily differ. Thus, if the maximum value of Company A to Company B is $13,000,000, but the minimum value to Company B of being acquired by Company A is $11,000,000, there is a $2,000,000 differential which is subject to bargaining.

Finally, there are the problems of the form in which the merger is to take place and the type of compensation to be employed. For example, the companies can combine under the merger statutes of the state or states of incorporation. In lieu of a statutory merger, one company may acquire the assets of another; or alternatively, it can purchase the stock of the company to be acquired. The form of compensation can be cash or securities, usually voting stock of the acquiring company. Which procedure is employed may depend on the particular circumstances. In most cases, however, the form of compensation is voting stock or securities convertible into voting stock of the acquiring company. In our case study, the acquiring company used convertible preferred stock. Its reason for this was that the stock represented a tax-free exchange to the shareholders of the company acquired. Cash would not. However, when cash compensation is employed, the acquiring company can list the assets at their purchase price. When the combination employs a tax-free exchange of shares, for tax purposes it must depreciate the assets on the basis of the book value at the time of acquisition. If the purchase price is higher than the book value at the time of purchase, the basis for depreciation is correspondingly higher.

When the factors underlying a merger are viewed as in our case study, it is evident that the outcome, based as it is on imperfect information, will elicit complaints from stockholders of the participating companies. It is, therefore, the function of the management of each company to convince a sufficient number of stockholders that they will receive something of value from the merger.

QUESTIONS AND PROBLEMS

1. As a class project, plot the trend in earnings of the Sun Oil Company since its merger with the Sunray DX Oil Company. Do you have a basis for judging which set of stockholders gained more from the merger? Why or why not?

2. "The economies from a merger are no easier to isolate than the diseconomies that might result." Evaluate.

3. Two firms of the same size, producing the same products, and with the same capital structure, are contemplating a merger. The current E/P ratio of one company is 12%; the current E/P ratio of the other is 10%. The dividends paid by the second are $1.75 a year; those of the first are $1.50 a year. The per share market price of the stock of the company with the lower E/P is $50. The per share market price

of the other company is $40.   In the case of the first company, earnings have been growing at 2 percent a year.   Earnings of the company with the lower E/P ratio have shown no growth.   Assuming that the companies plan to form a new concern, what do you think should be the distribution of shares among the stockholders of the two concerns?

4.   "If there are synergistic effects from a merger, their distribution between stockholders of the combining companies can be resolved only through bargaining."   Do you agree?   Explain fully.

5.   "The provisions of the corporate income tax laws ensure that combinations will take place through the exchange of securities rather than through the scale of securities or assets for cash." Evaluate.

SELECTED REFERENCES

Alberts, William W., and Joel E. Segall (eds.).   *The Corporate Merger.*   Chicago: The University of Chicago Press, 1966.

Butters, J. Keith., John Lintner, and William L. Cary.   *Effects of Taxation: Corporate Mergers.*   Boston: Harvard Graduate School of Business Administration, 1951.

Kelly, Eamon M.   *The Profitability of Growth through Mergers.*   University Park: The Pennsylvania State University Center for Research of the College of Business Administration, 1967.

Nelson, Ralph L.   *Merger Movements in American Industry, 1895–1956.*   Princeton, N.J.: Princeton University Press, 1959.   A study by the National Bureau of Economic Research, Inc.

Wyatt, Arthur R., and Donald E. Kieso.   *Business combinations: Planning and Action.*   Scranton, Pa.: International Textbook Company, 1969.

Reorganizations

chapter Twenty-three

Failure to meet obligations as they come due usually results in bankruptcy and reorganization or perhaps liquidation of the firm. Since a major objective of working capital management is to prevent financial failure, the student can relate the material in this chapter to the principles of working capital management. Moreover, he can employ the analysis underlying the management of fixed assets in developing principles of reorganization consistent with the statutory requirements of the federal Bankruptcy Act.

Introduction

In financial parlance the term reorganization has taken on various meanings. For example, the word is commonly used to mean a voluntary readjustment of the terms of a bond or stock contract, including a stock split. Our concern, however, is with reorganization as it applies

544

to formal changes in the capital structure through application of the provisions of the federal Bankruptcy Act. More generally, the purpose of this chapter is to discuss the causes and consequences of inadequate provision for the maintenance of liquidity. As in the analysis of mergers, the institutional material employed is relevant to the corporation, but the principles discussed are applicable to any business enterprise.[1]

Conceptually, there are two conditions which can precipitate failure. The first occurs when the value of a firm's assets is less than the aggregate value of the claims held against these assets. The enterprise, in other words, is *technically insolvent*. The second occurs when the firm is unable to meet its debts as they come due.

Although both of these conditions may be in effect simultaneously, it is the second which usually precipitates bankruptcy proceedings. Often a concern may be technically solvent yet unable to meet its obligations as they mature. When a company fails to pay either principal or interest on most forms of debt when due, the holders of these contracts can theoretically seize the assets of the concern to satisfy their claims. As a practical matter, the concern forestalls the seizure of its assets by seeking protection under the Bankruptcy Act. If it is subsequently found that the value of the assets does exceed the aggregate indebtedness, the firm may be liquidated and the claims against it settled out of the assets of the enterprise.

Even if the assets of the firm cannot satisfy the value of the claims against them, the firm may still be reorganized. If continuance of the services of a railroad or other public utility, for instance, is deemed essential to the public interest, the company will be reorganized rather than liquidated. Similarly, if the value of the assets of any firm does exceed its aggregate indebtedness, the firm will probably also be reorganized rather than liquidated. Thus, while liquidation is a possible outcome of any bankruptcy proceeding, it is more likely that the enterprise, unless it is technically insolvent and unaffected "with the public interest," will be reorganized.[2]

But how likely is it that management will find itself in a situation in which the firm faces bankruptcy? Based on empirical evidence, the odds appear to be small. In recent years they have been lower than in the 1920s and certainly lower than in most of the 1930s. From Table 23-1, on the next page, it is evident that in the post-World War II period the failure rate, while fluctuating, has been one-half to one-third what it

[1]Recall from Chapter 2 that if the firm is unincorporated—a general partnership, for example—then to the extent that each partner has assets that are unencumbered by personal liabilities or are exempt from seizure, these assets may be used to liquidate the unsatisfied claims of the firm's creditors.

[2]We should point out that any firm can be liquidated voluntarily for reasons totally unrelated to its inability to meets its obligations as they come due.

TABLE 23-1: TOTAL INDUSTRIAL AND COM-MERCIAL FAILURES IN THE UNITED STATES FOR SELECTED YEARS, 1925–1939, AND FOR THE YEARS 1946–1968

Year	Number of Failures per 10,000 Concerns[a]	Year	Number of Failures per 10,000 Concerns[a]
1925	100.0	1955	41.6
1928	109.0	1956	48.0
1932	154.0	1957	51.7
1937	46.0	1958	55.9
1939	70.0	1959	51.8
1946	5.2	1960	57.0
1947	14.3	1961	64.4
1948	20.4	1962	60.8
1949	34.4	1963	56.3
1950	34.3	1964	53.2
1951	30.7	1965	53.3
1952	28.7	1966	51.6
1953	33.2	1967	49.0
1954	42.0	1968	38.6

SOURCES: For the years 1925–1929, see, *Annual Report of the Small Business Administration*, 1966, p. 5. For the years 1946–1966, see U.S. Department of Commerce, Office of Business Economics, *1967 Business Statistics: A Biennial Supplement to the Survey of Current Business*, p. 36. For 1967 and 1968, see *Survey of Current Business* August 1969, p. S–7.

[a]Data are presented as given in sources. For the years 1925–1939, they have been rounded to the nearest whole number. For the years 1946–1968, they have been rounded to the nearest tenth.

was in 1925, 1928, and 1932. Even in the depths of the Great Depression, in 1932, when the failure rate reached an all-time high of 154 bankruptcies per 10,000 concerns, these bankrupt firms represented only 1.54 percent of the industrial and commercial business community.

Yet the impact of failure on the value of the owners' equity can be serious. Indeed, as we shall see, the outcome of bankruptcy proceedings, even if the company is reorganized, can be a disaster for the owners. Under certain conditions they can forfeit their entire claims to the equity of the reorganized enterprise.

Inadequate Working Capital

If inability to pay principal or interest when due is the factor which usually precipitates bankruptcy, it follows that the apparent cause of failure is inadequate working capital. We must emphasize the word apparent, for the more basic question is: Why was working capital inadequate?

Recall from our discussion of the principles of working capital analysis that given the capital structure, management will determine the firm's permanent level of working capital on the basis of cyclical and secular changes in demand and costs. Moreover, it will subsequently consider the consequences of being caught short because of loss in profits from investing in current rather than in long-lived assets. The optimum level of permanent working capital is the amount with the highest expected utility. As management is willing to accept the costs of inventory stockouts, that is, losses in sales, so it is willing at some point to accept the ultimate penalty for cash stockouts, that is, bankruptcy.

Since the consequences of bankruptcy are severe, we must assume that management will maintain a level of net working capital at which the probabilities of a cash stockout are relatively small. Yet it cannot completely eliminate the possibility without severely curtailing the profitability of the firm. Thus, there is usually some chance, even a small one, that bankruptcy will occur.[3] However, while there is always this chance of failure, it is likely to take place because management neglected to make appropriate calculations or because lacking the necessary data, it could not accurately forecast the possibilities that failure would occur. A less likely reason for failure is that management has consciously accepted a relatively high probability of bankruptcy.

The Institutional Framework

Whatever the apparent cause of failure, it is highly improbable that the conditions giving rise to it will materialize overnight. Most likely, management will receive some advance warning. Profits may begin to decline as a result of a secular decrease in demand or increase in costs. This will have a tendency to lower current assets. These assets in turn may be replenished by reducing or eliminating dividends. The capital structure may be altered by using cash to reduce debt and hence interest on the debt.

But if these and similar measures fail to compensate for the decline in profits and the day eventually comes when management is unable to meet its obligations as they come due, the firm faces the alternatives of letting the creditors seize its assets or of seeking relief under the provisions of the bankruptcy laws.

[3]If the capital structure contains 100 percent equity, the firm will never face bankruptcy. But the enterprise can still be a failure financially if the return on capital is, given the business risk, greater than the rate that can be earned elsewhere.

Management may, of course, seek an extension on the obligations due. Creditors, particularly unsecured creditors, may grant an extension rather than risk a settlement under the bankruptcy laws. Not only would this be a costly and perhaps involved procedure, but if the firm is liquidated and the assets sold, the creditors may not receive the face amount of their debts. Secured creditors having prior claims to assets will be satisfied first. To risk bankruptcy, therefore, may not be in the interests of many creditors. Thus, if it appears that management may be able to correct its imbalance in working capital and continue to meet prior claims as they come due, unsecured creditors could well find it in their interest to agree to an extension.

Even if there are no prior claims, such as a secured bank loan, unsecured creditors may still find it useful to extend terms of credit. Indeed, they may value the relationship with their customer so much that they are willing to accept only a percentage of what is owed. Suppose, for example, that the manager of a retail outlet is unable to meet his obligation to a supplier for merchandise delivered to him. As it is not uncommon to grant an extension on trade credit, let us assume that this is done. The debtor is still unable to pay the full amount of the claim. The supplier, valuing his retail outlet, formally agrees to accept 75 percent of the face value of the debt due him, foregoing any claim to the remainder. If other suppliers are also involved, they may agree to the same conditions. The contracts between the suppliers and the debtor are legally binding.

Such an arrangement—a composition, as it is called—is not widely employed. Ordinarily, if a creditor does not agree to an extension, he is prepared to force the firm into bankruptcy where, under certain conditions, a compromise similar to a composition will be worked out under the guidance of the court. The procedure for doing so comes under Chapter XI of the Bankruptcy Act.[4]

The provisions of this section of the law are available to any individuals or corporations unable to meet obligations as they come due. To qualify, however, the debtor must have no secured debt or publicly held securities outstanding. Moreover, the provisions do not apply to railroads.

When a qualified debtor seeks relief under Chapter XI, he petitions the court to consider a particular plan providing for the extension of debts or for a composition. The court will then call the interested parties and verify their claims. In the interim, management of the debtor firm ordinarily continues to operate the enterprise. The court will ask the creditors to agree to the settlement, making some modifica-

---

[4]Under the Constitution, Congress can enact legislation pertaining to bankruptcy.

tions in the proposal if necessary. If the court is satisfied that the composition conforms to the requirements of the law and is in the best interests of all parties, it will probably approve it. In so doing it will want approval of at least a majority of the creditors and preferably all of them.

Once the plan has been approved by the court, the debtor is discharged from all debts save those included in the composition. Thus, if a firm owed $1,000,000 in accounts payable and creditors agreed to accept $700,000 in payment under a Chapter XI reorganization, the debtor would be relieved from paying the remaining $300,000.

A Chapter XI reorganization is a relatively simple procedure which usually results in the debtor being relieved of a portion of his debts and allowed to continue in business. But if a nonrailroad corporation has secured debt or publicly held securities and management is unable to meet a portion or all of the company's debts as they come due, then the bankruptcy proceedings must take place under Chapter X of the Federal Bankruptcy Act.

Under the provisions of this section of the law, if liabilities of the debtor total $250,000 or more, the court must appoint one or more "disinterested" trustees to conduct the business during the period the company is in bankruptcy. Under Chapter XI, third parties are not ordinarily called in to administer the affairs of the company. They can be called at the discretion of the court, but the procedure is usually to allow the present management to retain control over the corporation.

Under the provisions of Chapter X it is the responsibility of the trustee or trustees to present a plan of reorganization or to explain why reorganization is not feasible. Thus, representatives of various security holders, that is, creditors' committees and stockholders committees, must convince the trustees and ultimately the court of the validity and value of their claims.

Moreover, the Securities and Exchange Commission can act as an advisor in the proceedings under a Chapter X reorganization. Accordingly, the Commission

> participates in proceedings under Chapter X in order to provide independent, expert assistance to the courts, the participants and investors in a highly complex area of corporate law and finance. It pays special attention to the interests of public security holders who may not otherwise be represented effectively.[5]

---

[5]*33rd Annual Report of the Securities and Exchange Commission* (Washington: Government Printing Office, 1968), p. 128. The SEC will on occasion ask that the proceedings of a firm to be reorganized under Chapter XI be transferred to proceedings under Chapter X. The petition is made and sometimes granted by the court for various reasons. As an example, management of a firm with secured debt in the capital structure attempts

When the aggregate indebtedness of the company exceeds \$3,000,000, the court, before giving its approval, must submit the plan of reorganization to the SEC for a report.   If the indebtedness does not exceed \$3,000,000, the judge, if he deems it advisable, may submit the plan of reorganization to the SEC before approving it.   The SEC is under no obligation to comment on the reorganization plan.   Indeed, it usually seeks to participate "principally in those proceedings in which a substantial public investor interest is involved."[6]   But even if the SEC does submit a critique of the plan of reorganization and substitutes one of its own, the court is under no obligation to adhere to it.   The SEC can only advise.   It has no authority over the final reorganization.

Once a plan of reorganization is approved by the court, if two-thirds of the creditors and—if they are allowed to participate—a majority of stockholders accept it, the plan is put into effect and the company emerges from bankruptcy.   If it is decided that the firm should be liquidated, this will be carried out under the jurisdiction of the court and proceeds from the sale of the assets will be used to satisfy the claims of the creditors, with the residual, if any, distributed to the owners.

If the corporation in bankruptcy is a railroad, it comes under the provisions of Section 77 of the Bankruptcy Act.   A key difference is that the Interstate Commerce Commission replaces the Securities and Exchange Commission, but not as an advisor.   The ICC must approve the reorganization while the court sees to it that the plan conforms to the law.   If the court finds that the plan does conform to the law but has not been approved by two-thirds of the creditors, it can force the creditors to accept it.[7]

But whether the reorganization is under Chapter X, Chapter XI, or Section 77 of the Bankruptcy Act, the court is charged with the responsibility of seeing that the plan of reorganization conforms with the law.   Conformity with the law, of course, includes technicalities which need not detain us.   But it also includes the requirement that the reorganization plan be "fair and equitable and feasible."   "Fair and

---

a composition under Chapter XI whereby the secured debt is left undisturbed.   The SEC feels that a more thorough reorganization is required, including an adjustment of the claims of secured creditors, if the company is to survive in the future.   See *ibid.*, p. 140.

[6]*Ibid.*, p. 128.   The SEC may also participate "because an unfair plan has been or is about to be proposed, public security holders are not represented adequately, the reorganization proceedings are being conducted in violation of important provisions of the Act, the facts indicate that the Commission can perform a useful service, or the judge requests the Commission's participation." *Ibid.*

[7]Under the provisions of the Mahaffie Act, the Interstate Commerce Commission can approve alterations in the contract of any class of railroad securities as long as the holders of 75 percent of each class affected agree.   The plan then becomes binding on all without further adjudication.

equitable" implies that the security holders be treated in accordance with the provisions of their contracts. "Feasible" implies that once the firm is reorganized, it is not likely to find itself in bankruptcy in the foreseeable future. The standards of fairness and equitability are legal. The standards of feasibility are economic and financial. We shall deal first with feasibility.

The Valuation Problem

Before a firm can be reorganized, there must be a valuation placed on it. There are two reasons for this. First, if the firm is technically insolvent, that is, the value of the claims against it exceed the value of its assets, there may be general agreement that the company be liquidated rather than reorganized.

Second, if it is to be reorganized, the valuation is necessary in order to establish the total amount of securities to be issued. In other words, the total capitalization of the firm should reflect the value of its assets. Consequently, until the court has a valuation figure, it has no basis for determining whether the capital structure proposed in a plan of reorganization is feasible. Similarly, no plan of reorganization can be deemed feasible unless it is cast within a valuation framework.

The appropriate techniques for arriving at a value of a firm are primarily modifications of principles of capital budgeting developed earlier in this volume. But the modifications are numerous. In the first place, we are now concerned with finding the total value of the firm, not just increments to total value from adding to the stock of assets.

Second, in order to determine total value we must use the present value approach. Thus we need a figure for the cost of capital. The figure we use will represent the average and not the marginal cost of capital. The cost of capital may vary with the capital structure; indeed, it will vary when differences in tax treatment of various capital instruments are taken into account. Consequently, we cannot divorce the capital structure from the valuation problem.

Furthermore, we are determining the value of the firm in order to have a basis for satisfying the claims against it. Consequently, the amount discounted is the sum of the interest, preferred dividends, and earnings (or, if the reader prefers, dividends) on common stock. In other words, the income stream to be capitalized is composed of earnings before payment of interest and preferred dividends but after payment of taxes. Since taxes paid are a function of the level of debt in the capital structure, the figure to be capitalized will vary accordingly.

Thus we are faced with the very real and seemingly intractable problem of determining simultaneously the average cost of capital and the income stream to be capitalized. To solve the dilemma we must rely on the concept of opportunity cost. We can ask ourselves: What is the after-tax rate of return earned on the market value of the securities of a company facing similar business risks? What are the capitalization ratios of this firm?

Discovering a firm facing a comparable set of business risks is always difficult. No two concerns are exactly alike. Moreover, even when they are similar in this respect their capital structures may differ because of differences in size. To have found a close approximation, however, will give interested parties to a reorganization at least a basis for estimating the cost of capital as well as for proposing the capital structure if the debtor is to be reorganized.

To illustrate, suppose that a trustee for a firm in bankruptcy discovers that other companies in the industry earn approximately 10 percent on the market value of their securities. In other words, each company's earnings before payment of interest and preferred dividends but after payment of taxes, when capitalized at 10 percent, will equal the aggregate market value of that company's securities. Applying this capital structure to the debtor, the trustee finds that the most likely outcome is $5,000,000. The probability of its occurrence is .5. There are also equal probabilities of .25 that the outcome will be $2,000,000 or $8,000,000.

Unlike capital budgeting, however, the present problem requires an objective valuation. Management's or the owners' subjective risk preferences are not an issue in determining the value of the firm. But what valuation figure do we use? The most likely outcome? A weighted average? Should we make use of the range of probable values? We shall try to answer this valuation question more fully later in the chapter. In this instance, if we relied on the most likely outcome it would be $5,000,000. If we used a weighted average it would also be $5,000,000, or $(.25 \times \$2,000,000) + (.5 + \$5,000,000) + (.25 \times \$8,000,000)$. Let us, therefore, use $5,000,000 as a measure of the income stream to be capitalized.

If the $5,000,000 was expected to continue indefinitely, the total value of the firm and thus the total value of the securities to be issued is

$$\text{Total value} = \frac{\$5,000,000}{.10}$$

$$= \$50,000,000$$

It is, of course, quite likely that any estimate of earnings before payment of interest and preferred dividends but after payment of taxes will be viewed as finite rather than infinite.   In either case, the procedure remains the same.   It is the outcome which differs.   For example, if it is assumed that the income stream will continue to be $5,000,000 for 20 years, the total value of the firm is

$$\text{Total value} = \$5,000,000\left[\frac{1-(1+.10)^{-20}}{.10}\right]$$

$$= \$42,567,800$$

There is no reason why we cannot anticipate a pattern of risk-adjusted earnings which varies over a period of years as well as an average cost of capital which changes over time.   Either factor can be incorporated into the analysis.   Whether such changes are justified depends on the circumstances surrounding the case under consideration.

But even if the trustee of the firm in bankruptcy is able to find an appropriate capitalization rate and capital structure from a going concern facing similar risks, he may still recommend that the debt in the capital structure be kept at a level lower than that of the firm used for comparison.   He can assume that both demand and costs and hence current assets and liabilities are subject to probability distributions. Therefore, to enhance the feasibility of the reorganization (that is, lower the chances that the firm, in the foreseeable future, will be unable to meet its debts as they come due), the capital structure which he recommends for the reorganized company may be conservative when compared with the capital structure of similar firms.   As a result, the chances that net working capital will be less than zero will be relatively small, if not negligible.

Ideally, then, in terms of feasibility, the reorganized concern, when it emerges from bankruptcy, will have a capital structure with a debt ratio lower than the debt ratio of the capital structure of its predecessor and perhaps lower (and certainly not higher) than the debt ratios of the capital structures of firms facing comparable risks.   The total value of the securities issued will equal the capitalized value of the stream of earnings before payment of interest and preferred dividends but after payment of taxes.

There is, of course, the possibility that because of management's tendency to be overly conservative, those receiving the common stock may find that the value of their shares is below what it would have been if the reorganized concern had a higher debt ratio.   If this is the case, then management of the new company can usually take steps to raise the proportion of debt in the capital structure.

Distributing the New Securities

Once the total value of the firm and the new capital structure have been determined, there still remains the problem of distributing the new securities to the old security holders. Unlike the problem of valuation, the distribution of new securities involves principles that are not derived from economic or financial analysis, but from legal doctrine as codified in case law. In general, the security holders in a reorganization are to be treated as though the firm is to be liquidated and its assets sold.[8] To apply this so-called doctrine of *absolute priority*, the claims of secured creditors must be satisfied in full before those of the unsecured creditors are given consideration. The claims of the unsecured creditors must be satisfied before those of the preferred stockholders are adjudicated. The claims of the preferred stockholders must be satisfied before the common stockholders can participate.

Moreover, there may be specific claims which are ranked ahead of those of all security holders. For example, unpaid wages and taxes usually have prior claims. So do court-authorized debts incurred during reorganization proceedings. Furthermore, leased property may have considerable value to the concern. Without it, perhaps the firm's operations will cease. If this is the case, then the claims of the lease-holder to unpaid rentals will command a high priority. Equipment obligations sold under the Philadelphia Plan fall into this category. Since a railroad or other transport agency does not take title to the equipment until the obligations have been redeemed, it is leasing these assets. Since the equipment is indispensable to operations, the holders of these equipment obligations will be accorded a high priority in the reorganization. Their claims are likely to be left undisturbed. On the other hand, if the lease is not considered of importance to the survival of the firm, the lessor's claim against unpaid rent will receive the same treatment as the claims of unsecured creditors.

Contractual obligations of some security holders may alter the normal pattern of distribution in the event of liquidation. We have noted earlier that it is possible for preferred stockholders to participate equally with common stockholders in a reorganization. Indeed, this is usually the case unless the preferred stock contract specifies preference in, as well as the extent of, participation in the event of liquidation. Similarly, the chief feature of subordinated debentures is the fact that in the event of liquidation they are subordinated to all debt, secured as

---

[8] The leading decision in which the "absolute priority" doctrine was established is *Case v. Los Angeles Lumber Products Company*, 308 U.S. 106 (1939).

well as unsecured.   Straight debentures, on the other hand, are treated like the claims of unsecured creditors.[9]

Claims with high priorities, such as back wages, taxes, and rentals on important leases, will be liquidated as soon as possible from cash generated through operations.   Claims of other creditors, however, particularly the claims of holders of long-term bonds, will be satisfied out of new securities.

As we have seen, the debt ratio must be lowered.   In consequence, creditors must accept securities junior to those they presently hold. For example, the claims of mortgage bondholders might be satisfied in full.   But 50 percent of their contractual claims may represent new mortgage bonds and 50 percent junior securities, perhaps income bonds or preferred stock.

Finally, stockholders, preferred or common, will participate only to the extent that the aggregate amount of indebtedness does not exceed the total value of the firm.   To use a simple illustration, suppose that a firm in bankruptcy has a capital structure whose book value is as shown below.

Short-term Debt	
Loans Incurred during Bankruptcy	$ 900,000
Interest on Long-term Debt	100,000
Long-term Debt	
6 Percent 1st-mortgate Bonds	4,000,000
7 Percent Debentures	1,000,000
Preferred Stock	
Par Value $100	1,000,000
Common Stock	
Par Value $10	2,000,000
Paid-in Surplus	900,000
Earned Surplus	100,000
Total Capitalization	**$10,000,000**

There are no back wages, taxes, or important leases.   Failure to pay interest on the mortgage bonds precipitated bankruptcy.   The most probable value of the firm, estimated on the basis of discounting future earnings, is $6,500,000.   Preferred stock has preference over

---

[9]There are times when debt which is secured by a specific lien on property will not participate ahead of unsecured debt.   In railroad reorganizations, for instance, separation-of-earnings tests have rendered branch lines (and therefore the liens on branch lines) of railroads valueless.   Debt secured by these liens is then treated as unsecured debt.   If the reorganization is drastic and the unsecured creditors do not participate, neither will these secured bondholders.   For an interesting case in which this point appears, see Arthur Stone Dewing, *The Financial Policy of Corporations*, 5th ed. (New York: The Ronald Press Company, 1953), vol. II, pp. 1472–1474.   See also pp. 1462–1481.

common stock in the event of liquidation, with a value equal to its par value of $100 per share. On the basis of comparisons with firms facing similar business risks, it has been decided that the long-term debt ratio should be about 30 percent of the market value of the firm, or $1,950,000 (30 percent of $6,500,000).

Since the aggregate claims of the creditors and the preferred stockholders on the books of the corporation exceed $6,500,000, common stockholders are excluded from the reorganization. Moreover, only $500,000, or 50 percent, of the claims of preferred stockholders can be satisfied. The short-term debt will be left undisturbed for it represents loans made during the reorganization by approval of the court and unpaid interest on the long-term debt.

By rounding the total amount of new debt outstanding to $2,000,000, the new capital structure of the firm might appear as follows:

Short-term Debt	
Loans Incurred during Bankruptcy	$ 900,000
Interest on Long-term Debt	100,000
Long-term Debt	
6 Percent 1st-mortgage Bonds	1,000,000
7 Percent Debentures	1,000,000
Preferred Stock	
Par Value $ 100	1,000,000
Common Stock	
Par Value $ 10	2,500,000
Paid-in Surplus	
Earned Surplus	
Total Capitalization	$6,500,000

In the distribution of the new securities, the mortgage bondholders received $4,000,000; that is, 25 percent of their claims in mortgage bonds, 25 percent in debentures, 25 percent in preferred stock, and 25 percent in common stock. The debenture holders, whose claims were unsecured, received $1,000,000 in common stock. The remainder, or $500,000, of the common stock went to the preferred stockholders.

Other combinations are, of course, possible, but the legal theory, if taken literally, implies that the claims will be satisfied on the basis of priority rights in the event of liquidation. To satisfy these claims by using securities different from those presently outstanding is a practical compromise with the need for lower debt ratios in the capital structure. Where possible, of course, important claims will be either liquidated out of cash or left undisturbed. Where doing so would raise some doubts as to the feasibility of the reorganization, security holders whose contractual claims have value will be satisfied out of junior securities, a portion of which will be equity.   In this manner the court can adhere to the statutory requirement of feasibility as well as accommodate the legal doctrine of absolute priority necessary to render the reorganization "fair and equitable."

Reconciling Imperfect Standards

While the economic, financial, and legal principles presented in this chapter should serve as a basis for a reorganization in bankruptcy, there is some question as to whether in practice they are strictly followed. The doctrine of absolute priority is of sufficient clarity that confusion as to its meaning is at a minimum.   But if a valuation figure representing the most likely outcome is the basis on which the doctrine is applied, the reorganization might prove unfair to the junior security holders.

Suppose, for example, that the valuation figure, in the light of hindsight, proves to be too low. Junior security holders who might otherwise have participated turn out to be unjustly excluded from the reorganization. This is a severe penalty. In applying the doctrine of absolute priority, the court should be certain of the valuation figure. But this certainty simply does not exist. The question then arises as to whether the principle of absolute priority is modified or perhaps even ignored in practice.

On analytical grounds there is certainly a basis for modification. Reorganization is legally a substitute for liquidation. Liquidation, in turn, implies that there is a valuation figure on which everyone can agree—the amount received from the sale of the assets.[10]   In the case of reorganization, the valuation figure is admittedly an estimate.   Consequently, parties to a reorganization might legitimately question whether the contractual rights of the security holders can be enforced if the basis for doing so requires not an estimate but a certainty which can be obtained only by actual sale of the assets. The Supreme Court, almost from the time that it espoused the doctrine of absolute priority, recognized the dilemma.   In an early opinion it stated that since the determination of earning power "requires a prediction as to what will occur in the future, an estimate, as distinguished from mathematical certitude, is all that can be made."[11]   Hence, in implementing the doctrine, "practical adjustments rather than a rigid formula are necessary."[12]

[10]There may have been disagreement on the value of the assets before they were sold.   But once the sale is made and the proceeds realized, there is no longer any uncertainty.

[11]*Consolidated Rock Products Company et al. v. DuBois*, 312 U.S. 526 (1940).

[12]*Ibid.*, p. 529.

In one case involving a railroad, the Court went so far as to state:

> A requirement that dollar values be placed on what each security holder surrenders and on what he receives would create an illusion of certainty where none exists and would place an impractical burden on the whole reorganization process.... It is sufficient that each security holder in the order of his priority receives from that which is available for the satisfaction of his claim the equitable equivalent of the rights surrendered.[13]

In practice, therefore, the doctrine of absolute priority, originally adopted to avoid compromising the claims of senior security holders, is apparently itself subject to compromise. Often the facts of the case dictate the degree of adherence to it,[14] so that few generalizations can be made. When modifications are brought about, each set of security holders is expected to make a relative sacrifice. For example, instead of some senior debt being left undisturbed, the stockholders eliminated, and the junior debtors given common stock, all senior security holders may be asked to accept, say, 95 percent of their claims in mortgage income bonds with interest contingent on earnings.

The original stockholders may be given the right to fractional participation in the reorganization (say, one share for each ten shares owned) and issued warrants for the remaining nine shares. The warrants will allow them to purchase additional shares. The junior debtors may be given a combination of subordinated income debentures and common stock equal to 60 percent of the value of their claims.

Each group, depending on the priority of its claims, makes a larger sacrifice than the holders of securities senior to it. In this way, if the valuation figure turns out to be too low and the firm prospers, junior security holders, particularly the former stockholders, will not have been excluded from the reorganization. At the same time, the feasibility of the reorganization is maintained by using less debt, making much of the interest subject to earnings.

As a means of mitigating the effects of the imprecision of the valuation estimate, the doctrine of *relative priority*[15] has a practical appeal.

---

[13]*Group of Institutional Investors et al. v. Chicago, Milwaukee, St. Paul & Pacific Railroad Company*, 318 U.S. 565 (1942).

[14]For an excellent case study illustrating the complexities of a reorganization, see Jacob J. Kaplan, Daniel J. Lyne, and C. Keefe Hurley, "The Reorganization of the Waltham Watch Company: A Clinical Study," *Harvard Law Review*, vol. 64, no. 8 (June, 1951), pp. 1262–1286.

[15]The controversy over whether there should be relative sacrifices made by all security holders is long-standing. The absolute and relative priority theories were best articulated by James C. Bonbright and Milton C. Bergerman, "Two Rival Theories of Priority Rights of Security Holders in a Corporate Reorganization," *Columbia Law*

But technically it is not the law of the land. Moreover, we might question whether it should be. To call for relative sacrifices on the part of all security holders so that all of them may participate in reorganization is to compromise the provisions of contracts which were freely entered into by the parties involved. Unless the contract is a violation of the law, such as a contract in restraint of trade under the Sherman Act, the courts are obliged to enforce its provisions. This is ordinarily not the case in a bankruptcy reorganization.

Consequently, rather than compromise a fundamental right of security holders—that is, the right to enforcement of contracts freely entered into—it would be better to recognize the imperfections of using the most likely outcome as an estimate of the value of the firm, and employ a range of values encompassing the probability distribution of anticipated earnings before payment of interest and preferred dividends but after payment of taxes.

As in the case of capital budgeting, parties to a reorganization might estimate both an optimistic and a pessimistic outcome as well as the most probable outcome, with the courts making use of the range of values thus obtained in applying the doctrine of absolute priority. If the value of the firm under the most optimistic assumptions about earnings, is less than the aggregate amount of the claims of its creditors, then there are grounds for excluding stockholders from the reorganization.

If, however, the range of probable outcomes indicates that there is some finite probability that the firm is not insolvent, then participation of equity holders should be based on these probabilities. Similarly, under the most pessimistic assumptions, if there is still sufficient value in the firm to satisfy the entire claims of the mortgage bondholders, then they should be satisfied in full.

As an illustration, consider our earlier example. The most probable value of the firm is $6,500,000. The book value of the capitalization is $10,000,000. Suppose that under the most optimistic assumptions the market value of the firm is $8,000,000. Under the most pessimistic assumptions it is $5,000,000. The probabilities of occurrence of the two extremes are each .25. Thus the probability attached to the most likely outcome is .5.

Under the most optimistic assumptions the aggregate value of the common stockholders' claims would be $1,000,000. In the most probable outcome and under the most pessimistic assumptions the aggregate

---

Review, vol. 28, no. 2 (February, 1928), pp. 127–165. This article played a role in the landmark Supreme Court case establishing the absolute priority theory as the law of the land. See *Case v. Los Angeles Lumber Products Company*, 308, U.S. 116 (1939). See also Arthur Stone Dewing, *op. cit.*, vol. II, pp. 1300–1310, particularly p. 1306, ftnt. i.

value of the stockholders' claim would be zero. Thus the expected value of the claims of the common stockholders is

$$
\begin{aligned}
\$0 \times .25 &= \$0 \\
\$0 \times .5 &= \$0 \\
\$1,000,000 \times .25 &= \underline{\$250,000} \\
\text{Expected Value} &= \$250,000
\end{aligned}
$$

For the preferred stockholders, if the most optimistic outcome materialized, they would have all their claims satisfied. If the most probable outcome occurred, they would have half of their claims satisfied. If the most pessimistic outcome came about, their claims would have no value. Thus the expected value of their claims is

$$
\begin{aligned}
\$0 \times .25 &= \$0 \\
\$500,000 \times .5 &= \$250,000 \\
\$1,000,000 \times .25 &= \underline{\$250,000} \\
\text{Expected Value} &= \$500,000
\end{aligned}
$$

For the debenture holders, if the most optimistic outcome materialized, their claims would be paid in full. If the most pessimistic outcome materialized, their claims would not be satisfied. If the most probable outcome occurred, their claims would also be satisfied in full. The expected value of their claims is

$$
\begin{aligned}
\$0 \times .25 &= \$0 \\
\$1,000,000 \times .5 &= \$500,000 \\
\$1,000,000 \times .25 &= \underline{\$250,000} \\
\text{Expected Value} &= \$750,000
\end{aligned}
$$

The remainder of the debt would be satisfied in full even if the most pessimistic outcome occurred. The expected value of the claims of all security holders is

Short-term Debt	
Loans Incurred during Bankruptcy	$ 900,000
Interest on Long-term Debt	100,000
Long-term Debt	
6 Percent 1st-mortgage Bonds	4,000,000
7 Percent Debentures	750,000
Preferred Stock	
Par Value $100	500,000
Common Stock	
Par Value $10	250,000
Total Capitalization	$6,500,000

The expected value of all the securities is equal to the expected value of the three outcomes. Because the probability distribution is symmetrical, the expected value of all outcomes equals the value of the most likely outcome.

The distribution of new securities, however, would be altered. The common stockholders would be allowed to participate at the expense of the debenture holders. The latter would make a greater sacrifice because, in view of the best estimates available, there are relatively high odds that an outcome might materialize which would not satisfy the full value of their claims. Similarly, there is a probable outcome which, if it occurred, would penalize the common stockholders unnecessarily.

Again basing our capital structure on approximately a 30 percent debt ratio, the distribution of new securities to mortgage bondholders would remain the same. On the basis of expected value, there would be no change in the common stock going to preferred stockholders. Debenture holders, however, would receive $750,000 rather than $1,000,000 in common stock, with the remainder going to the common stockholders.

In employing expected values to determine the distribution of securities, we have taken into consideration the range of valuations of probable outcomes. In so doing we are not modifying the doctrine of absolute priority as it was meant to be applied. In terms of the value received in exchange for the value of the claims given up, holders of senior debt have, in principle, made no sacrifices. In practice, some of them—in this case the mortgage bondholders—have had the composition of their holdings altered. If the most pessimistic outcome materialized, the market value of the securities of mortgage bondholders would decline to a figure below the book value of their forgone claims.

To illustrate, given the most pessimistic conditions (that is, the market value of the securities is $5,000,000), suppose that earnings cover interest and preferred dividends but there is nothing left for holders of common stock. Assume further that this leads to a decline in the market value of the shares and that this in turn accounts for the difference between the valuation under the most pessimistic assumptions and the valuation of $6,500,000 in the most probable outcome. The market value of the common stock is $1,000,000 rather than $2,500,000. But the bondholders would have received $1,000,000 in common stock based on the assumption that the market value of the stock would be $2,500,000. Thus they would realize only

$$\frac{\$1,000,000}{\$2,500,000} \times \$1,000,000 = \$400,000$$

Since the rest of their claims would be in securities whose market value has not declined, as a result of the reorganization the bondholders would receive only $3,400,000 for $4,000,000 in claims given up.

On the other hand, if the most optimistic outcome materialized, the market value of the securities would have risen to $8,000,000. Again assuming that the difference between this figure and $6,500,000 is due solely to changes in the market value of the common stock, the mortgage bondholders would have received

$$\frac{\$4,000,000}{\$2,500,000} \times \$1,000,000 = \$1,600,000$$

In this case they would have given up $4,000,000 in claims for $4,600,000 worth of securities.

Thus, in distributing new securities to holders of old securities on the basis of value received, it is virtually impossible to give them claims equal dollar-for-dollar to those given up and still meet the statutory requirements of feasibility. But to compromise with the requirement of feasibility is not the same thing as compromising with the doctrine of absolute priority. In our example, even under the most pessimistic assumptions, there is sufficient value to satisfy 100 percent of the bondholders' claims. Thus, if a court is to adhere to the doctrine of absolute priority, these claims should be satisfied in full before those of unsecured creditors are considered. But because of the need to reduce the debt ratio in order to lower the risk of another failure, a portion of the bondholders' claims must be satisfied in securities, the total value of which may just as likely exceed as be exceeded by the book value of its claims.

In reality, however, it is not the habit of the courts, in rendering decisions on bankruptcy reorganizations, to explain the conflict between fairness and feasibility in terms of simple probability analysis. Yet those who take the position "that fairness requires only that the paper awarded in reorganization be equal in quality to that given up"[16] implicitly recognize the conflict. But they do not offer a solution which could be termed equitable. Allowing bondholders as well as other security holders to participate on the basis of the weighted averages of their valuations of probable outcomes is at least a step in the right direction. In so doing we are implicitly assuming that the courts will ignore the subjective risk preferences of the security holders. Thus, in the

---

[16]Walter J. Blum, "Full Priority and Full Compensation in Corporate Reorganizations: A Reappraisal," in John L. O'Donnell and Milton S. Goldberg (eds.), *Elements of Financial Administration* (Columbus, Ohio: Charles E. Merrill Books, Inc., 1962), p. 665. The article is reprinted from *The University of Chicago Law Review*, vol. 25, no. 3 (Spring, 1958), pp. 417–444.

example given, the bondholders are just as likely to lose $600,000 from the reorganization as to gain $600,000. For this group, however, the expected utility of the loss of $600,000 may be greater than the expected utility of the gain. Perhaps the same may be said of the other participants.

If the court does give consideration to the subjective risk preferences of security holders, these preferences should be treated on the basis of absolute priority, the secured debt receiving first consideration and the common stockholders last consideration. Again we run up against the requirement that the reorganization be feasible. We would anticipate that bondholders will prefer to have their claims settled in debt. Since this may not be feasible, their preferences will be compromised.

The complexities which underlie bankruptcy reorganizations are therefore explicable in terms of the analysis developed in this volume. This does not make the decision in any given instance easier, but it does help us to understand why it is difficult for a reorganization to be fair and equitable as well as feasible. In optimizing among these objectives, the courts will be influenced by the circumstances surrounding the case. For example, if the local economy of the community or the national defense is assumed to be dependent on a technically insolvent firm's continuing in business, every effort will be made to preserve it.[17] The arguments of creditors' committees, stressing absolute priority, may be compromised to such an extent that some of the expected value of their claims will be sacrificed in the interest of continuing the enterprise. In such circumstances, both the legal and the financial standards discussed here implicitly give way to other objectives deemed by the court to be more important.

SUMMARY

Bankruptcy is the ultimate consequence of a cash stockout. Since the consequences of bankruptcy are severe, management will likely keep net working capital at a level where the probabilities of a cash stockout are relatively small. Yet it cannot completely eliminate the possibility without severely curtailing the profitability of the firm.

Since inability to meet cash obligations as they come due is the factor precipitating bankruptcy, the company's only recourse to seizure of its assets is court protection under the relevant provisions of the federal Bankruptcy Act. If the firm is to be recognized rather than

[17]Kaplan, Lyne, and Hurley, *op. cit.*, pp. 1262–1286.

liquidated, the reorganization must be "feasible." Feasibility implies that the company will not face bankruptcy in the foreseeable future. If the court finds that the company should be reorganized, then the distribution of new securities must be "fair and equitable." Fairness and equitability imply that the claims of holders of senior securities should be satisfied in full before the claims of holders of junior securities are considered. Their treatment, in other words, is the same as if the firm had been liquidated rather than reorganized.

In principle, to carry out a reorganization, the total earnings before payment of interest and preferred dividends but after payment of taxes are capitalized at a rate reflecting the average cost of capital of firms facing comparable business and financial risk. New securities equal in value to the claims surrendered are then distributed on the basis of the priority of the claims of each class of securities. To help ensure feasibility, the debt component of the capital structure will be reduced. Thus, senior debtors may receive some or all of their claims in junior securities and junior debtors some or all of their claims in stock. Stockholders will participate only if the firm's value is greater than the value of its liabilities.

In practice, a reorganization often reflects the fact that the valuation figure on which the claims are based is at best the most likely or most probable outcome. However, rather than base participation on a probability distribution of expected claims, the courts are influenced by the circumstances surrounding the reorganization. Indeed, if the social or economic pressures for a firm's survival are sufficiently strong, the courts will make every effort to preserve the firm. The legal doctrine that the reorganization be "fair and equitable and feasible" will be fashioned to serve this end.

QUESTIONS AND PROBLEMS

1. What is the difference between the absolute and the relative priority theories of corporate reorganization? Is the latter a substitute for the lack of precision in estimating the value of the enterprise? Explain.

2. Discuss the differences in procedures between a Chapter X and a Chapter XI reorganization. What is the role of the SEC in the former?

3. The capital structure of the ABC Corporation is as follows:

Short-term Debt		
	Loans Incurred during Bankruptcy	$ 1,000,000
	Interest on Debt	50,000
	Unpaid Wages	100,000
Long-term Debt		
	6 Percent Equipment Obligations	4,000,000
	8 Percent Subordinated Debentures	6,000,000
Common Stock		
	Par Value $1	2,000,000
	Paid-in Surplus	150,000
	Earned Surplus	
		$13,300,000

There is a .3 probability that the aggregate market value of the firm will be $5,000,000 and a .3 probability that this value will be $9,000,000. The most probable outcome is $7,000,000. Develop a plan of reorganization which meets the statutory requirements of "fair and equitable and feasible."

4. "The primary cause of failure is inadequate working capital." Evaluate.

5. "It is impossible to ensure that a firm emerging from bankruptcy will never fail again."   Evaluate.

6. "Basing the participation of security holders in a reorganization on the weighted average of their valuations of probable outcomes reconciles the conflict inherent in the judicial standards of 'fair and equitable and feasible'."   Evaluate.

SELECTED REFERENCES

Blum, Walter J. "Full Priority and Full Compensation in Corporate Reorganizations: A Reappraisal" *The University of Chicago Law Review*, vol. 25, no. 3 (Spring, 1958), pp. 417–444.

Bogen, Jules. *Financial Handbook*, 4th ed. New York: The Ronald Press Company, 1964 sec. 22.

Dewing, Arthur Stone. *The Financial Policy of Corporations*, 5th ed. New York: The Ronald Press Company, 1953, vol. II, chaps. 38–43.

Kaplan, Jacob J., Daniel J. Lyne, and C. Keefe Hurley.   "The Reorganization of Waltham Watch Company: A Clinical Study," *Harvard Law Review*, vol. 64, no. 8 (June, 1951), pp. 1262–1286.

The Goal of Financial Management—
A Reconsideration

Alternative Goals of Financial Management

chapter Twenty-four

In reading this chapter, the student should note the limitation of the goal toward which the principles presented in this volume have been directed. What are the alternatives? What are the implications of pursuing them?

Introduction

Throughout this volume we have consistently taken the position that the primary goal of financial management is to maximize the market value of the owners' equity. In this concluding chapter we shall first look more critically at this assumption. Then we shall consider some of the alternative objectives open to management and the implications of pursuing them.

We have waited until the end of the book to pursue this discussion on the assumption that the reader, having absorbed the principles of financial management and gained a feel for the institutional environment in which financial decisions must take place, will now be ready to assess critically the foundations on which these principles rest.

The Conflict between Maximizing Owners' Wealth and Maximizing the Market Value of the Owners' Equity

In postulating that management will maximize the market value of the owners' equity, we implicitly assumed that this is the same as maximizing the total wealth of the owners. But the two goals do not necessarily coincide. To illustrate, let us reconsider the Modigliani and Miller hypothesis. Recall that in perfectly competitive markets and in the absence of the corporate income tax,

$$x = rd + r'(1-d)$$

where x is the average cost of capital, d is the market value of senior securities divided by the market value of all securities, r is the interest on senior securities, and r' is the return on equity securities.

Under this hypothesis, the cost of capital is independent of the capital structure. As management substitutes debt for equity, the increased financial risk raises r' by lowering the market price of the stock. This offsets the cheaper cost r of debt, resulting in a constant average cost of capital.

Since the total value of the firm is gross earnings of the firm capitalized at x, then

$$V \equiv S + D = \frac{E}{x}$$

where V is the market value of the securities, S is the market value of the equity, and E is earnings before payment of interest. To keep x and therefore V constant as debt is substituted for equity, the value of S must fall.[1] If the conditions on which the Modigliani and Miller hypothesis depend were in fact realized, and assuming for the moment that there is adequate evidence supporting their hypothesis, the market value of the owners' equity is at a maximum when there is no leverage in the capital structure.

Now let us introduce the corporate income tax. As we have seen, the cost of debt capital is now $r(1 - \text{tax rate})$. If the tax rate is 48

---

[1] Per share earnings rise, of course, but total earnings before interest remain constant. Why?

percent and the yield to maturity on debt is 6 percent, the effective interest cost is $0.06(1-0.48)$, or 3.12 percent. Looked at differently, in the absence of corporate income taxes the market value of 6 percent bonds is D. The market value of 3.12 percent bonds is D', which, because of differences in yield, is 0.52 of D. In order to raise the same amount of capital as it will with a 6 percent issue, management must float a series of bonds at 2.88 percent. The market value of these bonds is D'', or 0.48 of D. In other words, because of the income tax laws management can float D dollars of debt at an effective cost of 3.12 percent. If interest were not tax-deductible, the firm would have realized only $0.52D$ in net proceeds. It has therefore saved $0.48D$ in debt issues.

Let us now generalize the reasoning by letting T equal the percentage of debt saved, that is, the tax rate times D, or TD. Suppose that we let V_e equal the market value of the firm under the assumption that there is no debt in the capital structure. It follows that

$$V_e = S$$

In the absence of tax considerations,

$$V = S + D$$

When taxes are considered,

$$V = S + TD$$

Substituting and simplifying,[2]

$$
\begin{aligned}
V &= V_e + TD \\
S &= V - D \\
&= V_e - D + TD \\
&= V_e + TD - D \\
&= V_e - (1-T)D
\end{aligned}
$$

Therefore, as the final equation tells us, given the tax deductibility of interest, the market value of the shares in an all-equity capital structure is lowered by the factor $(1-T)D$. Consequently, in order to maximize the owners' wealth we would have to maximize V, the total value of all securities, by substituting debt for equity. Thus, in the light of tax considerations, a firm with an unlevered capital structure is not maximizing the total wealth of its owners.

To illustrate, consider what would happen to the owners' or stockholders' wealth if debt is substituted for equity. Suppose that a firm has a capital structure whose market value is $20,000,000. The capital

[2]A similar proof can be found in John Bosson's discussion of an article by Eugene M. Lerner and Willard T. Carleton entitled "Financing Decisions of the Firm," *Journal of Finance*, vol. 21, no. 2 (May, 1966), pp. 202–214. The proof is in *ibid.*, p. 245, footnote 2.

structure consists entirely of equity. In other words, V_e is $20,000,000. Now let us assume that management floats a bond issue for $1,000,000. The market value of the debt is D, or $1,000,000. To the firm, however, it is $(1-T)D$, or

$$(1-0.48)\$1,000,000 = \$520,000$$

Presumably, management might distribute up to $480,000 as dividends without affecting the market price of the stock. Although the dividends would be taxed, the marginal rate of taxation is never 100 percent. Consequently, the aggregate wealth of the stockholders would appear to be maximized by substituting debt for equity and distributing the tax savings as dividends. Similarly, if the firm expands its structure of assets, it will employ debt as well as equity in the capital structure.

What we have returned to, of course, is the problem of determining an optimum capital structure. Moreover, the validity of the above analysis depends on the validity of the Modigliani and Miller hypothesis. If the average cost of capital in the absence of tax savings rises with leverage, then it would not be in the stockholders' interests to use debt. The market value of the firm would be at a maximum with an unlevered capital structure. Thus, if the cost of capital is 10 percent, earnings are $2,000,000 a year indefinitely, and g is 0, then

$$V_e = \frac{\$2,000,000}{0.10}$$

$$= \$20,000,000$$

If the substitution of debt for equity raises the average cost of capital to, say, 12 percent for a debt ratio of 5 percent, then, letting V_d equal the market value of the firm with leverage, we get

$$V_d = \frac{\$2,000,000}{0.12}$$

$$= \$16,666,667$$

The tax savings from using debt will prevent the average cost of capital from rising as rapidly as it would otherwise. But the fact that debt is in the capital structure will, under the above assumption, cause the market value of S and the market value of the firm to fall. Whether, as a general proposition, management should seek to maximize the market value of the owners' equity rather than maximize the owners' wealth, therefore, depends ultimately on the empirical evidence supporting the Modigliani and Miller hypothesis. While there is a growing body of evidence helping to substantiate the hypothesis,[3] there will probably never be unanimous agreement that, in the absence of tax savings and other factors such as the size of the firm, the average cost of capital is independent of the capital structure.   Moreover, if it turns out that the traditional belief holds—that is, the average cost of capital declines with modest amounts of leverage—then the tax savings on debt simply accelerate the trend toward higher debt ratios.   Tax savings or not, a capital structure consisting entirely of equity would fail to maximize the wealth of all the owners.

The conflict between maximizing the owners' wealth and maximizing market value of the owners' equity can also be explained on a more prosaic level.   We noted earlier that tax treatment of dividends also affects the wealth of owners.   Suppose, for example, that management foregoes an increase in dividends of $1.00 per share in order to plow the funds back into the firm.   Assume that as a result the market price rises by the amount of the present value of the increase in earnings expected from not having increased the dividends.   Suppose that a stockholder, had he received the dividends, would have been able to exclude them from taxes under the $100 exemption provision of the federal income tax laws.   In order to realize the cash equivalent of the foregone dividend, he must sell some of his shares and pay a capital gains tax.   His wealth is reduced accordingly.   Similarly, if management reinvests earnings at a rate which is lower than

$$\frac{E_a}{P}\left(1-\text{tax rate}\right)$$

the individual shareholder's total wealth will be reduced.   He would have been better off if he had received the funds as dividends.

In emphasizing the difference that may exist between maximizing the market value of the owners' equity and maximizing the owners' wealth, we are simply taking cognizance of the conflict that exists in the literature of finance.   In our initial illustration, if the average cost of capital is independent of the capital structure or declines as the debt ratio increases, the total wealth of the owners will be greater if some debt is employed.   In the first instance (cost of capital is independent of capital structure), it is the tax treatment of debt which makes this true. In the second instance (cost of capital declines as debt ratio increases), the tax factor simply raises the optimum debt ratio.

In each instance, however, management is placed in the awk-

[3]Merton H. Miller and Franco Modigliani, "Some Estimates of the Cost of Capital to the Electric Utility Industry, 1954–57," *American Economic Review*, vol. 56, no. 3 (June, 1966), pp. 333–391.

ward position of enhancing the wealth of some owners at the expense of others. Those in relatively high income tax brackets will find that their wealth has risen because of the decision to plow back earnings at relatively low rates of return. Management has simultaneously reduced the wealth of those in relatively low income tax brackets.

Moreover, suppose that the average cost of capital increases with leverage, the tax savings serving to slow down the rise in cost but not completely offsetting it. Then, depending on each individual's personal income tax bracket, a substitution of debt for equity with the tax savings distributed as dividends could raise or lower the value of each individual's wealth. To illustrate, suppose that the dividends to a stockholder resulting from substituting debt for equity amount to $10 and the market value of his shares declines by $5. He pays only $2 in personal income taxes on the dividends. In this instance the shareholder gained $3. Had the personal income tax been more than $5, his wealth would have been reduced by the substitution of debt for equity.

Dilemmas which arise out of differences in personal income tax rates may be arbitrated by using (as suggested earlier) the average of marginal tax rates, hoping, on balance, to maximize the aggregate wealth of stockholders. Alternatively, management can take a position with respect to dividend policy—for example, it can decide on a low pay-out ratio—and let owners adjust accordingly. Those in relatively high income tax brackets will purchase shares of this firm while those in relatively low income tax brackets will seek shares of firms with higher payout ratios.

Maximizing Total Revenues

It is not impossible to conceive of management attempting to maximize some variable other than the market value of the owners' equity or the wealth of shareholders. Suppose, for example, that management opinion is heavily weighted in favor of individuals whose business background is marketing. There may be a tendency for the firm to emphasize sales. The success of the concern, in management's eyes, is measured by the rate of increase in the level of sales over time. Management may, therefore, direct its efforts toward maximizing the sales volume.

From what has been said earlier, it should be clear that sales could possibly increase at the expense of profits and ultimately at the expense of the market value of the owners' equity as well as the value of the owners' wealth.

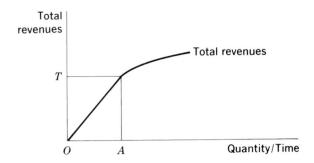

Figure 24–1

To maximize sales is the same as to maximize total revenues. Thus, as long as management can keep selling additional output, total revenues will expand. In a perfectly competitive market the firm can sell all it desires at a going price. But if sales keep expanding, management will soon find that it is acquiring a large enough share of the total market that its output decisions will affect the market price of the product. The firm is no longer in a perfectly competitive market. Management can sell more only at a lower price. Total revenues begin to rise at a decreasing rate.

In Figure 24-1, total revenues increase at a constant rate up to output OA, from which point they increase at a decreasing rate. The addition to total revenues—that is, the marginal revenue—is at first constant and then declines.[4] To maximize sales, management would have to increase output up to the point where total revenues are at a maximum, that is, up to the point where additions to total revenues equal zero.

[4]The demand curve, in other words, is infinitely elastic and then falls as shown below.

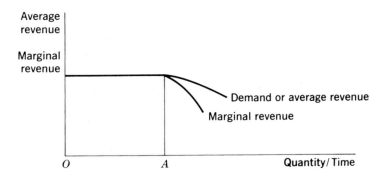

Long before this point is reached, of course, management will have realized the absurdity of setting this goal. As we have seen, given the firm's capacity to produce, total costs may rise at an increasing rate, perhaps even before total revenues begin to rise at a decreasing rate. As additions to total costs exceed additions to total revenues, profits suffer. If the expansion process is carried to an extreme, the working capital and hence the liquidity position of the firm is threatened.

As a compromise, management might set a figure on what it considers to be an adequate level of profit. It will not expand sales to the point where profits will fall below this figure. Such a compromise is quite realistic. But in so doing, management not only fails to maximize the owners' wealth or equity, but also fails to maximize total revenues. Instead of recognizing one goal, management now recognizes two. Accordingly, it can no longer maximize either but must give consideration to both. Now management must take into account the impact of marginal increases in sales on the value of the shareholders' equity or wealth, as well as the impact on sales of trying to add to the owners' equity or wealth. Maximizing one goal now gives way to optimizing between two.

"Satisficing" versus Maximizing

According to one student of decision making, "in most psychological theories the motive to act stems from drives, and action terminates when the drive is satisfied."[5] Thus when management strives to optimize between conflcting goals, it will try to "satisfice" rather than maximize each of its objectives. To continue with the conflict between sales and profits, management might set as a target an after-tax rate of return on invested capital of, say, 10 percent. As long as the return does not fall below this amount, management is free to expand capacity in the interest of a maximum increase in sales. The capital budget in that case is not based on the present value of projects discounted at the marginal cost of capital. At best, the rate of discount is 10 percent. At worst, it is less than 10 percent if the firm is already earning more than 10 percent on its outstanding investment. Management will be satisfied if the rate of return on total capital does not fall below this level.

But suppose that the firm sets a goal for sales as well as for the rate of return. Assume that the goal is an average annual increase of 8 percent. In pursuing both of these objectives, management discovers

[5]Herbert A. Simon, "Theories of Decision-making in Economics and Behavioral Science," *American Economic Review*, vol. 49, no. 3 (June, 1959), pp. 262–263.

that the expected growth in market demand is only 3 percent a year. It can maintain the firm's proportional share by letting output expand to encompass this increase.   To acquire the other 4 percent, however, management must increase the firm's share of the market.   To do this, it may have to engage in an extensive advertising campaign.   The advertising costs add to the costs of producing and selling the additional output.   The result may be to lower the net profits and hence the return on investment.   The additional costs, in other words, exceed the additional revenues gained from adding 7 rather than 3 percent to total sales.

The decline in profits will lower the return on total investment. It could cause it to fall below the 10 percent minimum which management is trying to maintain.   Suppose that this is what happens.   Then management must readjust its objective to encompass what is feasible. It may find that an annual sales increase of 4 percent is consistent with a minimum return of 10 percent on invested capital.   The desire to "satisfice" various objectives then must be amended in the light of the realities which the firm faces.   Management must alter one of its standards.   It can either lower the acceptable rate of return or decrease its sales target.

The trade-off between sales and return on investment — and ultimately on the owners' wealth, or market value of the owners' equity — is only one of a number of objectives which management may be trying to optimize.   Targets may be set for minimum levels of cash or working capital and minimum debt ratios.   Any or all of these targets may be established without regard to their impact on the market value of the shares (that is, the wealth of the owners).   Observe a small manufacturing firm whose current ratio is never below 7 or 8 to 1 and whose capital structure consists almost entirely of equity and you will probably have found a firm whose management is so adverse to risk that it is satisfied with a rate of return just sufficient to prevent a stockholder revolt and the subsequent loss of its position.[6]   If management is maximizing anything in this case, it is job security.

Models have been developed[7] under the assumption that manage-

---

[6]If the firm is individually owned and operated, then management is carrying out the desires of the firm's owner to trade wealth for security.   However if management owns a controlling interest in the enterprise, its decision will still stand, but it may not reflect the desires of the minority interests. All they can do is acquiesce in the decision or liquidate their holdings.   While students in certain sections of the country might believe that the high current ratios and negligible debt ratios suggested are unrealistic, we hasten to assure them that there are examples of this phenomenon among small New England manufacturing firms.

[7]Richard M. Cyert and James G. March, *A Behavioral Theory of the Firm* (Englewood Cliffs, N.J.: Prentice-Hall, Inc., 1963).

ment has a set of objectives in mind, only one of which is rate of return on investment. It is assumed that management is interested in "satis-ficing" instead of maximizing. Models of this nature are designed to explain how management actually behaves. This so-called behavioral approach to decision making contrasts sharply with the maximizing approach we have employed. While the models based on target values for key variables such as sales growth, rate of return, and markup over costs can be useful in predicting company decisions, they fail to provide a rationale for the outcome. Why should management opti-mize among a series of objectives rather than direct its efforts toward maximizing the owners' wealth, or the market value of the owners' equity?

Ownership versus Control

Any rationale for optimizing rather than maximizing probably flows from the fact that much of the output of American industry is produced by corporations wherein ownership is effectively divorced from control. The perspective of management in such enterprises may differ sub-stantially from that of the owners. The management team has a vested interest in the survival of the firm. Jobs are at stake. Although he may enjoy stock options, a manager's primary source of income is usually his salary. He would like to see the market value of his holdings rise over time. But a manager or management team is less likely than an absentee owner to sacrifice the liquidity of the firm in favor of increased profits.

The owner views an investment in the stock of a company as a portfolio decision. If the company goes into bankruptcy and is sub-sequently liquidated, he may lose all or part of his investment, but the manager loses his stock options, his pension, and his job. He will doubtless be able to find another job, but with perhaps less income. Even if the company is reorganized, particularly under Chapter X of the Bankruptcy Act, the stockholders might still maintain at least a portion of their former interests in the company, whereas management will probably be replaced. Consequently, where ownership is effectively divorced from control and those managing the enterprise are com-pensated largely through salary, we can expect management and the owners to have different evaluations of the goals of the firm. The manager with more to lose is less likely than the stockholder to be inclined toward profitability at the expense of liquidity.

It is possible, of course, to find situations in which owners are more timid than management. Moreover, where ownership and control are vested in the same individual or group, liquidity may be more important than maximizing the market value of the shares, or the wealth of the owners. For example, as in the case of the candy concern with which we began this volume, an owner-manager of a firm may have a reasonably successful business. He has in effect satisfied his desires. Now, at sixty and with no opportunity to find a new job, he becomes more cautious of his investment and sole source of income. He does not take the risks involved in modernizing his firm which a younger manager might be ready to assume. The latter, if the venture fails, has alternative employment opportunities. If the modernization program succeeds, profits will grow and the value of the firm will rise.

While it is relatively easy to conjure up exceptions to our generalization, it is hard to overlook the fact that when ownership is divorced from control, financial failure can be more of a burden to management than to owners. As a result, management identifies with the corporation, whereas the owners are concerned with performance in terms of earnings, dividends, and share prices.

As one author noted, the different identifications lead to differences in priorities.[8] For example, to control the firm, that is, to make policy decisions, management must have control over the company's resources. It must have financial flexibility in order to alter production, acquire a subsidiary, enter a new field, etc. To have this flexibility, it must have cash or liquid assets readily available. The level of current assets and the cash flow generated from operations not only are of prime importance to the survival of the firm, they are crucial to the decision-making process. In the area of capital budgeting, therefore, the payback period may take precedence over such alternatives as the rate of return or net present value of investment. Profitability is sacrificed for cash flow and liquidity.

In acquiring subsidiaries, since a cash transaction will curtail its flexibility, management will almost always prefer the use of common stock or securities convertible into common stock. Moreover, enthusiasm for accelerated depreciation may stem as much from saving cash as from saving taxes. We can even view stock options as attempts to curb the cash flows of the firm.[9]

Any or all of these measures may adversely affect the market value of the shares in the firm and ultimately the owners' wealth. So much stock may be issued to pay for the acquisition that there is a dilution in per share earnings of the combined enterprises. The market value of

---

[8]Gordon Donaldson, "Financial Goals: Management vs. Stockholders," *Harvard Business Review*, vol. 41, no. 3 (May-June, 1963), pp. 116–129, particularly pp. 120–128.

[9]*Ibid.*, p. 120–123.

the shares falls and the stockholders of the buying company suffer a loss as a result of the merger.

Similarly, to the extent that the market price reflects accounting rather than economic profits (and accelerated depreciation understates the latter), the market value of the shares will be below their maximum.

If management offers itself options at a price sufficiently below the going market price of the stock, once these options are exercised, the number of shares outstanding will increase and the total market value could decrease. Suppose, for instance, that management can purchase stock at $50 per share with the market price of the stock at $75 per share. While it has the incentive to take steps to enhance the value of its options, again the choice is relative. At the margin, does it trade profitability for cash flow or liquidity? Let us assume that it takes steps to see that profits grow to such an extent that the market value rises to $100.

Now suppose that members of the management team begin to exercise their options. For each share purchased, a manager pays $50 to the company and sells his stock at $100. Since options represent stock which is not outstanding, the total number of shares increases. To the owners of the corporation the net effect is the acquisition of equity funds at a cost of

$$\frac{E_a}{P_{A'}} + g$$

where $P_{A'}$ is the option price. Assuming that P_A, or the cost of new shares floated through an investment banking syndicate or a privileged subscription, is less than $P_{A'}$, the cost of equity capital is correspondingly higher. If the funds are invested in projects whose net present value when discounted at $(E_a/P_{A'}) + g$ is negative, the market value of the shares will fall.

We could argue, of course, that there is a greater incentive to maximize the market value of the owners' equity with stock options than without them. We have no reason for denying this possibility. All we are doing is pointing out that a stock option can be an expensive source of funds when compared with conventional equity instruments.

There are other areas where the priorities may differ.[10]   Management will view the return on new investment in the light of past performance. This may reflect a target rate of return. But it is independent of the marginal, and hence the opportunity, cost of capital. From the stockholders' viewpoint, it is the latter factor which is important. Suppose, for example, that the acceptable rate of return is 15 percent,

[10]*Ibid.*, pp. 123–125.

but the marginal cost of capital is 10 percent. By failing to accept investment projects which have a positive net present value when discounted at the marginal cost of capital, management is failing to maximize the market value of the owners' shares. In other words, to show a high return on capital invested in operations is not the same thing as showing a high growth in earnings and a maximum market value for the firm's shares.

To use another illustration, suppose that management insists on an after-tax return of 50 percent and a 27-year payback period. It may find that it earns this amount on a few projects meeting these criteria. But in cutting off its investment opportunities at such a high rate, management will discover that the firm's current assets will probably rise over the years relative to its long-lived assets. Since the return on current assets is relatively low, the growth in total earnings will also be relatively low. As a result, the market price of the shares will grow very little compared with their anticipated growth under a more dynamic investment policy.

Finally, there may be differences in priorities as to sources of funds.[11] For our purposes, these differences reflect the fact that owners are willing to accept a greater degree of financial risk than is management. The primary source of disagreement is over the debt ratio. Management will always prefer retained earnings over all other sources. Not only are retained earnings safer in terms of liquidity, but they give management more flexibility than debt and, to a lesser extent, preferred stock. The proceeds from the sale of bonds may be restricted to employment in particular assets. The bond indenture may restrict dividends. The preferred stock contract may be cumulative. The tax laws, of course, help to make management's interest in retained earnings as a major source of funds coincide with that of the owners. The fact that interest is tax-deductible will probably encourage management— theories of the optimum capital structure aside—to employ a modest amount of debt. But because of the liquidity factor, management may resort to the use of common stock at a debt ratio which is lower than that preferred by the owners.

While we could multiply the examples, enough has been said to show how differences in risk evaluation on the part of management and the owners can arise. As a result, the structure of assets may be weighted more heavily in favor of current assets, and the composition of financing less heavily in favor of debt than the owners would seem to desire. If this occurs, the market value of the owners' equity is not as high as it might otherwise be.

[11]*Ibid.*, pp. 125–127.

To be sure, American industry consists of firms in which management's attitude toward risk may reflect that of the owners. As we observed earlier, the two should coincide over time. Stockholders will adjust their holdings accordingly. Those seeking relative security of investment will purchase shares in industries so managed. Those seeking growth at the expense of liquidity will buy stock in firms in which management is more profit-oriented.

But suppose that, on balance, the dichotomy between owners and management persists; that is, because they view the firm in a different light, the managers are willing to increase the business and financial risk to a lesser extent than the owners. Then the only alternative is for owners to adjust their own personal portfolios so as to lower the debt component and raise the equity component. Perhaps one of the reasons why households have foresaken corporate bonds over the years is that they are more desirous of increasing their proportion of higher-risk instruments. The same might be said for the increase in the preference for variable annuities rather than fixed incomes as pensions, and for the increased interest in the shares of mutual funds.[12] In this manner, owners are able to offset, partially if not completely, the divergence in objectives which probably accompanies the separation of ownership from control.

Social Responsibility as a Goal of Management

The legal framework within which the business unit functions presumes that management operates the enterprise for the benefit of the owners. Moreover, according to one authority, "management responsibility to stockholders has been legally enforced in suits brought by individual stockholders."[13] Perhaps the most famous is the minority stockholder suit against Henry Ford for refusing to declare dividends on the company's stock.[14] While the court did not question the right of the

---

[12]The standard argument that stocks are a hedge against inflation is usually employed to explain their popularity. But not all stocks rise in price. Some fall, and at times (even in the post-World War II period) the drop has been considerable. An investor is clearly taking a greater risk of loss by investing in stocks, though at the same time he hopes to realize a larger gain over time than would be true if he had purchased debt. Offsetting some of this risk through diversification, that is, by purchasing shares in some mutual funds, has the effect of slowing down the rate of growth in market value by increasing the chances of both high- and low-growth performers.

[13]Wilbur G. Katz, "Responsibility and the Modern Corporation," *Journal of Law and Economics*, vol. 3 (October, 1960), p. 75.

[14]Arthur Stone Dewing, *The Financial Policy of Corporations* (New York: The Ronald Press Company, 1953), vol. I, pp. 102–103, ftnt. yy.

directors (in this case, Henry Ford) to pass the dividend, it took exception to one of the reasons given for so doing. In the brief filed by his attorneys, Ford contended that he was plowing back profits not merely to expand production in a profitable enterprise but "to employ still more men, to spread the benefits of this industrial system to the greatest possible number, to help them build up their lives and their homes."[15]

But the court found that the primary obligation of the directors is to the stockholders. To have a social goal of the type Ford described as a statement of general policy was ruled outside the scope of the company's activities. It was in legal parlance ultra vires. Consequently, although the law has never precluded a company from making eleemosynary decisions—gifts of corporate funds to colleges and universities, for example—there is no legal basis for stating that corporations have the same responsibilities to labor, to the public, or to the community in general as they have to the owners.[16]

Yet where management is divorced from control, there is, as we have seen, a probable dichotomy in goals. Those who own the firm have the law on their side. Those who manage it have the authority to make the decisions. What is needed, in the eyes of some observers, is a rationale for departing from the traditional legal position so that management will be allowed as much freedom as possible in determining the goals of the firm. The doctrine of *social responsibility* provides a convenient rationale.

Some years ago two eminent scholars argued to the effect that when ownership is divorced from control, the stockholders "have surrendered the right that the corporation should be operated in their sole interest."[17] Nor should it be operated in the interest of those who control it. Rather, the "modern corporation [should] serve not alone the owners or [those who] . . . control [it] but all society."[18]

Others have argued that there are economic grounds for not conducting the enterprise exclusively for the benefit of the owners.[19] Much of the business activity of corporations in which ownership is divorced from control is carried on in imperfectly competitive markets. If management maximized the market value of the owners' equity, the level of profits accruing to the owners might reflect monopoly gains. To protect consumers and the public, it is argued, business should exercise a socially responsible attitude by seeking "adequate"

---

[15]Quoted from *ibid.*

[16]Katz, *op. cit.*, p. 82.

[17]Adolf A. Berle, Jr., and Gardiner C. Means, *The Modern Corporation and Private Property* (New York: The Macmillan Company, 1932), p. 355.

[18]*Ibid.*, p. 356.

[19]Katz, *op. cit.*, p. 76.

profits at a "just" price. Similarly, management should pay a "fair" wage to its employees while contributing a portion of its time and energies to community projects. In general, management is the trustee of the properties of the enterprise and should conduct the affairs of the business in such a way as to serve employees, customers, stockholders, and the general public.[20]

But whether the grounds be legal or economic, when management compromises the interests of the owners in favor of those of other groups, it is sacrificing a relatively specific goal, which it can attempt to maximize, for a vague doctrine which can be molded to suit its own purposes. Almost any decision management might make can be rationalized in terms of social responsibility. To contribute corporate funds as well as management's time and energy to building a community center may create good will for the company. But if the product or products produced are sold nationally, this outlay may do little to raise sales and therefore, it is hoped, profits for the firm. Nor is the good will created likely to result in increased productivity from the labor force which in part benefits from the community center. Yet management may argue that it must carry out its responsibilities to the community. This includes something other than providing jobs for workers at pay rates which reflect the value of their productivity.

As we might expect, the advocates of social responsibility are numerous. Indeed, some are vehemently opposed to the economic goal of profit maximization and, by implication, the financial goal of maximization of the market value of the owners' equity. One commentator[21] argues in effect that the information necessary to implement this goal is difficult to acquire. In the extreme case, management does not know where its orders are coming from or how much its costs will vary from expectations. This information is simply unavailable in some instances, rendering useless the capital budgeting techniques developed earlier. Of course, as we have argued, there is uncertainty in the estimates. Management takes this into account as best it can in selecting from among alternative projects. But to admit that implementing the goal is difficult does not destroy the case for adhering to it. If the goal is to be jettisoned, it must be on other grounds. The basis for doing so is apparently ethical.

> A businessman is a human being, and it is completely unrealistic to assume that he should act in an ethical vacuum. As a human being he is deeply concerned with how his actions jibe with his own conscience. . . . Moral

---

[20]*Ibid.*, p. 77.

[21]Robert N. Anthony, "The Trouble with Profit Maximization," *Harvard Business Review*, vol. 38, no. 6 (November–December, 1960), pp. 126–134.

standards change ... today society clearly expects the businessman to act responsibly. He cannot do this and at the same time seek to maximize the share of income going to just one of the several parties that have a stake in the business.[22]

In a phrase, to maximize profits, to maximize the wealth or equity of the owners' is not only difficult, "it is immoral."[23]

On the other hand, there are articulate opponents of the doctrine of social responsibility. One noted economist has stated:

This view shows a fundamental misconception of the character and nature of a free economy. In such an economy there is one and only one social responsibility of business—to ... engage in activities designed to increase its profits so long as it stays within the rules of the game which is to say engages in open and free competition, without deception or fraud.[24]

One legal scholar has even gone so far as to suggest that "clear acceptance of profit maximization as a legal principle might well do something, perhaps a good deal to order the pattern of corporate policy."[25] Thus counsel is divided, and deeply so.

The Conflict in Goals—An Evaluation

When we began this volume, we asked the reader to imagine himself as manager of a candy factory. We showed him the decisions he would have to make in order to operate this firm and promised to develop a framework within which these decisions could be made. In subsequent chapters, we carried out this promise by suggesting a goal toward which management might strive and by developing the principles underlying it. To complete the framework, we discussed the institutional environment within which financial decisions must be made and its effect on these decisions. Now that we have reached the end of our survey, must we conclude that the goal itself is open to serious doubt?

To be sure, polemics can be hurled against maximizing the market value of the owners' equity (or maximizing their wealth) or against its counterpart in economics, maximization of total profits. Nevertheless, we feel that the case for maximizing is on stronger grounds than the

[22]*Ibid.*, pp. 132–133. Reprinted by permission of the author.

[23]*Ibid.*, p. 134.

[24]Milton Friedman, *Capitalism and Freedom* (Chicago: The University of Chicago Press, 1962), p. 133. Reprinted by permission of the publisher.

[25]Eugene V. Rostow, "To Whom and for What Ends Is Corporate Management Responsible?," in Edward S. Mason, *The Corporation in Modern Society* (Cambridge, Mass.: Harvard University Press, 1959), p. 71.

case for abandoning it in favor of social responsibility and optimization of several objectives. It is not simply that social responsibility is vague, (obviously it is) or that wealth or equity maximization is easily implemented (clearly it is not). Rather, our objection lies first in the fact that failure to maximize can lead to a misallocation of resources. Second, the doctrine of social responsibility places in the hands of management a power over the distribution of income which properly belongs to the citizenry as a whole and which can best be implemented through its representatives in state legislatures and Congress.

Let us look at the first objection. Whatever the slight differences in outcome, the goal of maximization of profits, equity, or wealth is designed to allocate scarce resources efficiently in terms of the alternative goods and services people desire. If the earnings of companies in some industries are at a relatively high level when compared with those of companies in other industries, resources should enter the first category of industries so that output here will expand until the market price of the product falls to the point where further expansion is no longer advantageous.

The capital budget is a means by which management not only maximizes the market value of the owners' equity but also allocates capital resources efficiently. If the net present value of a project discounted by the marginal cost of capital is negative, the resources have a higher value elsewhere. It is the "responsibility" of management to let them be employed where the net present value is positive. Consequently, many who criticize the maximization hypothesis on ethical grounds sometimes forget, or at least deemphasize, the fact that there are ethical considerations underlying the goal.

If maximization is to be challenged at all, it should be on the grounds that scarcity is no longer a problem. This position has been eloquently defended.[26] But to the extent that it is true, those who follow it see the role of government expanding and that or private enterprise contracting. In other words, in an affluent society, people's desires for goods and services basic to their survival have nearly been satiated. As income rises, demand for food, clothing, and shelter increases, but slowly. Other wants may arise, but they may also be created through advertising. In the meantime, goods which cannot be easily produced in the market place are ignored.

Clean air is a good example. As producers' strive to maximize the wealth of their owners, they do so as cheaply as possible. Wastes

---

[26]John Kenneth Galbraith, *The Affluent Society*, college ed. (Boston: Houghton Mifflin Company, 1958); *The New Industrial State* (Boston: Houghton Mifflin Company, 1967).

are released into the atmosphere, polluting the air. If the atmosphere could be parceled out to those who want it, then, in principle, business firms could clean the air and market it at a price to cover costs. Since this is impossible, business firms have the alternative of using more costly methods of manufacturing goods whose production has been partly responsible for the air pollution or allowing government to step in and, through taxation and expenditures, take measures to clean the air. If business firms elect the first alternative, either consumers buying the goods or stockholders of the firms producing them or both will pay through higher prices and lower profits for the cost of preventing air pollution. If the government takes measures to clean the air, society as a whole will pay for it through taxes.[27]

Clean air, of course, is but one of numerous examples of products, ranging from war and defense materials to public education, which either cannot be or traditionally have not been produced and sold through private markets. Government, in one way or another becomes involved in the production, or the product is not produced at all. The air is allowed to stay dirty because business firms producing products which help to contaminate it cannot or will not take steps to clean it, and certainly they cannot market it in the same way as they would market automobiles, television sets, or some other line of merchandise. Because it is unmarketable in the traditional sense, we can call air a *social good* which must be shared in common. Because it is free to all, those using it as a disposal area for their wastes do so in order to lower their costs of production. The cost of the resources necessary to rid the air of pollution or to prevent it from becoming polluted reflects the social cost of the product.

From the viewpoint of management of a firm which might be contributing to air pollution, the firm would be making a socially responsible decision by adding to its production costs the costs of disposing of its wastes so as not to pollute the atmosphere. Let us assume that management takes this step. Whether the wealth of the owners will decline is dependent, in part at least, on the nature of the competition the producer faces. In a highly competitive market, it will be difficult to pass on these costs as a price increase unless the remaining firms do likewise.[28] While other costs can be reduced, this is not likely in a highly competitive market. Profits, and hence the market value of the owners' equity, will suffer. In an imperfectly competitive market, some if not all of the increase in price may be passed on to consumers.

---

[27]The Government could also force producers to adopt higher cost techniques of waste disposal. The results would then be the same as if firms elected to do so themselves.

[28]In order that all the increases in costs might be passed on to consumers, the market demand curve would have to have a price elasticity of zero.

Other costs may be cut, but there is a good chance that the owners will bear at least some of the burden. Let us assume that this is the case. If management volunteers to do what it can to prevent air pollution, it must sacrifice maximization of wealth, equity, or profits in favor of its responsibilities to the community.

But suppose that management chose not to make this decision. The alternatives, as we have seen, are either more air pollution or government action to abate it. When air pollution becomes a serious health problem, as it has in many cities, pressures will become sufficiently strong that government action becomes inevitable. Suppose now that government subsidizes or underwrites the costs of preventing further air pollution. In the case of the firm under discussion, government pays the differences between what it would cost the firm to dispose of the wastes in the atmosphere and the cost of disposing them in the next least expensive but socially acceptable manner. In other words, if the next least expensive way of disposing of waste is to let it flow into rivers, this would not be a socially desirable alternative. Government would have to help underwrite a still more expensive means of waste disposal. To pay for the subsidy, suppose that a general income tax is levied on all citizens. Consequently, the decision not to sacrifice the wealth of the owners not only will affect the handling of the problem, it could have an impact on who pays for it, that is, on the distribution of income.

Moreover, assuming that the air pollution problem is acute, individual members of the managerial community, acting as private citizens, could just as easily support their government in its efforts to combat the problem through a taxation and subsidy program as they could support action through voluntary programs entered into individually or collectively.

Furthermore, if society, through its government, should insist that consumers bear the costs of air pollution to the extent possible, then manufacturers can attempt to pass their own costs on as price increases. The result would be the same as if management had taken the initiative; that is, owners and consumers would probably share the costs. But the decision would reflect the will of the citizenry as to how it wants to allocate resources between social and private benefits (goods and services) and how it wants these benefits paid for, that is, how income is to be redistributed.

It is quite probable, therefore, that those among management who prefer to optimize among a series of objectives, including an adequate level of profits, do so with the full intention of using the resources of the enterprise for purposes for which it was not originally intended. These activities can sometimes be couched in terms of social responsibility. Moreover, in many cases, the "adequate level of profits" may be about what would be earned in competitive industries. The rest, a monopoly gain, may be distributed in various ways, that is, to labor, to the community through charitable contributions, etc. In exercising social responsibility, management may be hoping to avoid prosecution under the antitrust laws.

It is not that we object to corporate participation in these socially responsible activities. On the contrary, the modern privately owned corporation may be a convenient vehicle through which social goods can be produced and nonmarket activities such as higher education subsidized. But we frankly see little evidence, the affluent society notwithstanding, that scarcity is no longer a problem. Resources should continue to be allocated efficiently and their distribution among the sectors of the economy producing social and private goods should be determined by Congress and state legislatures. Management may use its position of power to influence the relative share of resources going to the production of social goods as well as the means of paying for these goods. In this way, the business community is like any other political pressure group. Its influence will depend on a number of factors, not the least being the unanimity of its members and the views of other groups. But to go beyond this and depart from the maximizing goal in favor of social responsibility is to forsake a more basic duty, that of allocating resources efficiently.

SUMMARY

In the literature on financial management, there is a conflict between two goals. Should management maximize the market value of the owners' equity or maximize the owners' wealth? It is not altogether clear which of the two is the more appropriate goal. Either of them, however, assumes that management will maximize a single variable. In fact, it may optimize between two or more objectives. If so, the appropriate model for explaining firm behavior is one which assumes that management will try to "satisfice" rather than maximize each of its objectives.

Moreover, there is some evidence that where ownership is divorced from control, the objectives of management may differ from those of the stockholders. The latter, because they view their investment simply as a portfolio decision, may be willing to assume more business and financial risk than is management.

Management, on the other hand, may be more willing to use the resources of the firm to promote social objectives. It may view the business firm as an entity responsible to the interests of labor and the community as well as to the interests of stockholders. The doctrine of social responsibility has its advocates. To carry it in practice to its logical conclusion, however, could impair the more basic economic goal of efficiency in the allocation of resources.

QUESTIONS

1. "The discrepancies between maximization of the market value of the owners' equity and maximization of the owners' wealth hinge on the validity of the Modigliani and Miller hypothesis." Evaluate.

2. "A firm cannot maximize total sales and the total wealth of its owners at the same time." Do you agree? Explain fully.

3. "If the value of an unlevered capital structure is $10,000,000, the issuance of $1,000,000 in bonds would raise the total value of the firm." Do you agree? Explain fully.

4. "Social responsibility is a rationalization for the independence which management enjoys in determining the composition of a firm's assets and its capital structure." Do you agree? Explain fully.

5. "The stock option is perhaps the most expensive way for a firm to acquire equity capital." Evaluate.

SELECTED REFERENCES

Anthony, Robert N. "The Trouble with Profit Maximization," *Harvard Business Review*, vol. 38, no. 6 (November-December, 1960), pp. 126–134.
Cyert, Richard M., and James G. March. *A Behavioral Theory of the Firm.* Englewood Cliffs, N.J.: Prentice-Hall, Inc., 1963.
Donaldson, Gordon. "Financial Goals: Management vs. Stockholders," *Harvard Business Review*, vol. 41, no. 3 (May-June, 1963), pp. 116–129.
Friedman, Milton. *Capitalism and Freedom.* Chicago: The University of Chicago Press, 1962, chap. 8.
Katz, Wilbur G. "Responsibility and the Modern Corporation," *Journal of Law and Economics*, vol. 3, (October, 1960), pp. 75–85.
Mason, Edward S. *The Corporation in Modern Society.* Cambridge, Mass.: Harvard University Press, 1959.
Simon, Herbert A. "Theories of Decision-making in Economics and Behavioral Science," *American Economic Review*, vol. 49, no. 3 (June, 1959), pp. 253–283.

APPENDIX: On Tax Reform

President Nixon signed the 1969 Tax Reform and Reduction Act into law on December 30 of that year. Unfortunately, its enactment came too late to allow us to include the relevant material in the appropriate places in this volume. We can, however, briefly summarize the features pertinent to the discussion we have developed.

Of perhaps primary importance are the changes in the capital gains tax. The 25 percent rate on individual capital gains applies only to the first $50,000 realized during the tax year. By 1972 larger gains can be taxed at rates up to 35 percent. Furthermore, only 50 percent rather than 100 percent of an individual's long-term capital losses can be charged against ordinary income. Thus an individual now needs $2,000 in long-term losses to offset the maximum of $1,000 in ordinary income allowed under the law. Finally, the long-term capital gains rate for corporations was raised from 25 percent to 30 percent.

In other areas a surtax of 5 percent rather than 10 percent was extended to June 30, 1970. The rates for single individuals were lowered and the 7 percent investment tax credit was repealed.

The student may wish to compare this information with the material presented earlier, particularly with the discussion on pages 25–29 and with footnote 6 on page 92.

Appendix A:

Present Value of a Dollar Received at the End of the Year

$$P = \frac{1}{(1+r)^n}$$

Year	Present Value at 1%	Present Value at 2%	Present Value at 3%	Present Value at 4%	Present Value at 5%
1	0.990099	0.980392	0.970874	0.961538	0.952381
2	0.980297	0.961169	0.942596	0.924556	0.907030
3	0.970591	0.942322	0.915143	0.888997	0.863838
4	0.960981	0.923846	0.888488	0.854804	0.822703
5	0.951467	0.905731	0.862610	0.821927	0.783527
6	0.942047	0.887972	0.837486	0.790314	0.746216
7	0.932720	0.870560	0.813093	0.759917	0.710682
8	0.923485	0.853491	0.789411	0.730690	0.676841
9	0.914342	0.836755	0.766418	0.702587	0.644610
10	0.905289	0.820348	0.744096	0.675564	0.613914
11	0.896326	0.804263	0.722423	0.649581	0.584680
12	0.887452	0.788493	0.701382	0.624597	0.556838
13	0.878666	0.773033	0.680953	0.600574	0.530322
14	0.869966	0.757875	0.661120	0.577474	0.505069
15	0.861353	0.743015	0.641864	0.555264	0.481019
16	0.852825	0.728446	0.623169	0.533908	0.458113
17	0.844381	0.714163	0.605019	0.513373	0.436299
18	0.836021	0.700160	0.587397	0.493629	0.415523
19	0.827744	0.686431	0.570289	0.474643	0.395736
20	0.819549	0.672971	0.553678	0.456387	0.376891
21	0.811434	0.659776	0.537552	0.438834	0.358944
22	0.803401	0.646839	0.521895	0.421956	0.341851
23	0.795446	0.634156	0.506694	0.405727	0.325573
24	0.787571	0.621722	0.491937	0.390122	0.310070
25	0.779773	0.609531	0.477609	0.375117	0.295304

Year	Present Value at 6%	Present Value at 7%	Present Value at 8%	Present Value at 9%	Present Value at 10%
1	0.943396	0.934580	0.925926	0.917431	0.909090
2	0.889996	0.873439	0.857339	0.841680	0.826446
3	0.839619	0.816298	0.793832	0.772184	0.751314
4	0.792093	0.762896	0.735029	0.708425	0.683013
5	0.747258	0.712987	0.680583	0.649931	0.620921
6	0.704960	0.666343	0.630169	0.596268	0.564473
7	0.665057	0.622750	0.583490	0.547034	0.513158
8	0.627412	0.582010	0.540268	0.501866	0.466507
9	0.591898	0.543934	0.500249	0.460429	0.424098
10	0.558394	0.508350	0.463194	0.422412	0.385543
11	0.526787	0.475094	0.428883	0.387534	0.350494
12	0.496969	0.444013	0.397114	0.355535	0.318631
13	0.468839	0.414965	0.367698	0.326179	0.289664
14	0.442301	0.387818	0.340461	0.299247	0.263331
15	0.417265	0.362447	0.315241	0.274539	0.239392
16	0.393646	0.338735	0.291890	0.251870	0.217629
17	0.371364	0.316576	0.270269	0.231074	0.197845
18	0.350344	0.295865	0.250249	0.211995	0.179859
19	0.330513	0.276509	0.231712	0.194490	0.163508
20	0.311805	0.258420	0.214548	0.178432	0.148643
21	0.294155	0.241514	0.198656	0.163699	0.135130
22	0.277505	0.225714	0.183940	0.150182	0.122846
23	0.261797	0.210948	0.170315	0.137782	0.111678
24	0.246979	0.197148	0.157699	0.126405	0.101525
25	0.232999	0.184250	0.146018	0.115968	0.092296

Year	Present Value at 11%	Present Value at 12%	Present Value at 13%	Present Value at 14%	Present Value at 15%
1	0.900901	0.892857	0.884956	0.877193	0.869565
2	0.811623	0.797194	0.783147	0.769468	0.756144
3	0.731191	0.711780	0.693050	0.674971	0.657516
4	0.658731	0.635518	0.613319	0.592080	0.571753
5	0.593451	0.567426	0.542760	0.519368	0.497178
6	0.534641	0.506631	0.480319	0.455587	0.432328
7	0.481659	0.452349	0.425061	0.399638	0.375938
8	0.433927	0.403883	0.376160	0.350559	0.326902
9	0.390926	0.360610	0.332885	0.307508	0.284263
10	0.352185	0.321973	0.294589	0.269744	0.247185
11	0.317284	0.287476	0.260698	0.236618	0.214944
12	0.285841	0.256675	0.230707	0.207559	0.186908
13	0.257515	0.229174	0.204165	0.182070	0.162528
14	0.231996	0.204620	0.180677	0.159710	0.141329
15	0.209005	0.182696	0.159891	0.140096	0.122895
16	0.188293	0.163121	0.141496	0.122892	0.106865
17	0.169633	0.145644	0.125218	0.107800	0.092926
18	0.152823	0.130039	0.110813	0.094561	0.080805
19	0.137678	0.116107	0.098064	0.082948	0.070265
20	0.124034	0.103667	0.086782	0.072762	0.061100
21	0.111743	0.092560	0.076799	0.063826	0.053131
22	0.100669	0.082643	0.067963	0.055988	0.046201
23	0.090693	0.073788	0.060145	0.049112	0.040174
24	0.081705	0.065882	0.053225	0.043081	0.034934
25	0.073608	0.058823	0.047102	0.037790	0.030377

Year	Present Value at 16%	Present Value at 17%	Present Value at 18%	Present Value at 19%	Present Value at 20%
1	0.862069	0.854701	0.847458	0.840336	0.833333
2	0.743163	0.730514	0.718184	0.706165	0.694444
3	0.640658	0.624371	0.608631	0.593416	0.578704
4	0.552291	0.533650	0.515788	0.498669	0.482254
5	0.476113	0.456112	0.437109	0.419050	0.401878
6	0.410442	0.389839	0.370431	0.352143	0.334898
7	0.353830	0.333196	0.313925	0.295918	0.279082
8	0.305026	0.284783	0.266038	0.248671	0.232568
9	0.262953	0.243404	0.225456	0.208967	0.193807
10	0.226684	0.208038	0.191065	0.175603	0.161506
11	0.195417	0.177810	0.161919	0.147565	0.134588
12	0.168463	0.151974	0.137219	0.124005	0.112157
13	0.145227	0.129893	0.116288	0.104205	0.093464
14	0.125195	0.111019	0.098549	0.087567	0.077886
15	0.107927	0.094888	0.083516	0.073586	0.064905
16	0.093040	0.081101	0.070776	0.061837	0.054088
17	0.080207	0.069317	0.059980	0.051964	0.045073
18	0.069144	0.059245	0.050830	0.043667	0.037561
19	0.059607	0.050637	0.043076	0.036695	0.031301
20	0.051385	0.043279	0.036505	0.030836	0.026084
21	0.044298	0.036991	0.030937	0.025913	0.021736
22	0.038188	0.031616	0.026217	0.021775	0.018114
23	0.032920	0.027022	0.022218	0.018298	0.015095
24	0.028379	0.023096	0.018829	0.015377	0.012579
25	0.024465	0.019740	0.015957	0.012922	0.010482

Year	Present Value at 21%	Present Value at 22%	Present Value at 23%	Present Value at 24%	Present Value at 25%
1	0.826447	0.819672	0.813008	0.806451	0.800000
2	0.683013	0.671862	0.660982	0.650364	0.639999
3	0.564474	0.550706	0.537384	0.524487	0.511999
4	0.466508	0.451399	0.436898	0.422974	0.409600
5	0.385544	0.369999	0.355201	0.341108	0.327680
6	0.318631	0.303278	0.288782	0.275087	0.262143
7	0.263331	0.248589	0.234782	0.221844	0.209715
8	0.217629	0.203761	0.190880	0.178907	0.167772
9	0.179859	0.167017	0.155187	0.144280	0.134217
10	0.148644	0.136899	0.126168	0.116354	0.107374
11	0.122846	0.112213	0.102576	0.093834	0.085899
12	0.101526	0.091977	0.083395	0.075673	0.068719
13	0.083905	0.075391	0.067800	0.061026	0.054975
14	0.069343	0.061796	0.055122	0.049215	0.043980
15	0.057308	0.050652	0.044815	0.039689	0.035184
16	0.047362	0.041518	0.036435	0.032007	0.028147
17	0.039142	0.034031	0.029622	0.025812	0.022518
18	0.032349	0.027894	0.024083	0.020816	0.018014
19	0.026735	0.022864	0.019579	0.016787	0.014411
20	0.022095	0.018741	0.015918	0.013538	0.011529
21	0.018260	0.015361	0.012941	0.010918	0.009223
22	0.015091	0.012591	0.010521	0.008804	0.007378
23	0.012472	0.010321	0.008554	0.007100	0.005902
24	0.010307	0.008459	0.006954	0.005726	0.004722
25	0.008518	0.006934	0.005654	0.004618	0.003777

APPENDIXES

Year	Present Value at 26%	Present Value at 27%	Present Value at 28%	Present Value at 29%	Present Value at 30%
1	0.793651	0.787401	0.781250	0.775193	0.769321
2	0.629881	0.620001	0.610351	0.600925	0.591716
3	0.499907	0.488190	0.476837	0.465834	0.455166
4	0.396751	0.384402	0.372529	0.361111	0.350128
5	0.314882	0.302678	0.291038	0.279931	0.269329
6	0.249906	0.238330	0.227374	0.217001	0.207176
7	0.198338	0.187661	0.177636	0.168218	0.159366
8	0.157411	0.147764	0.138778	0.130401	0.122589
9	0.124930	0.116350	0.108420	0.101086	0.094299
10	0.099150	0.091614	0.084703	0.078361	0.072538
11	0.078691	0.072137	0.066174	0.060745	0.055798
12	0.062453	0.056801	0.051699	0.047089	0.042922
13	0.049566	0.044725	0.040389	0.036503	0.033017
14	0.039338	0.035216	0.031554	0.028297	0.025397
15	0.031220	0.027729	0.024652	0.021935	0.019536
16	0.024778	0.021834	0.019259	0.017004	0.015028
17	0.019665	0.017192	0.015046	0.013181	0.011560
18	0.015607	0.013537	0.011755	0.010218	0.008892
19	0.012386	0.010659	0.009183	0.007921	0.006840
20	0.009830	0.008393	0.007174	0.006140	0.005261
21	0.007802	0.006608	0.005605	0.004760	0.004047
22	0.006192	0.005203	0.004379	0.003690	0.003113
23	0.004914	0.004097	0.003421	0.002860	0.002395
24	0.003900	0.003226	0.002672	0.002217	0.001842
25	0.003095	0.002540	0.002088	0.001718	0.001417

Year	Present Value at 31%	Present Value at 32%	Present Value at 33%	Present Value at 34%	Present Value at 35%
1	0.763358	0.757575	0.751879	0.746268	0.740740
2	0.582716	0.573920	0.565322	0.556916	0.548696
3	0.444822	0.434789	0.425055	0.415610	0.406442
4	0.339558	0.329385	0.319590	0.310156	0.301068
5	0.259205	0.249535	0.240293	0.231460	0.223013
6	0.197866	0.189041	0.180672	0.172731	0.165195
7	0.151043	0.143213	0.135843	0.128904	0.122367
8	0.115300	0.108495	0.102138	0.096197	0.090642
9	0.088015	0.082193	0.076795	0.071788	0.067142
10	0.067187	0.062267	0.057741	0.053573	0.049735
11	0.051288	0.047172	0.043414	0.039980	0.036840
12	0.039151	0.035736	0.032642	0.029836	0.027289
13	0.029886	0.027073	0.024543	0.022265	0.020214
14	0.022814	0.020510	0.018453	0.016616	0.014973
15	0.017415	0.015537	0.013874	0.012400	0.011091
16	0.013294	0.011771	0.010432	0.009253	0.008216
17	0.010148	0.008917	0.007843	0.006905	0.006085
18	0.007746	0.006755	0.005897	0.005153	0.004508
19	0.005913	0.005117	0.004434	0.003846	0.003339
20	0.004514	0.003877	0.003334	0.002870	0.002473
21	0.003445	0.002937	0.002506	0.002141	0.001832
22	0.002630	0.002225	0.001884	0.001598	0.001357
23	0.002007	0.001685	0.001417	0.001192	0.001005
24	0.001532	0.001277	0.001065	0.000890	0.000744
25	0.001170	0.000967	0.000801	0.000664	0.000551

Year	Present Value at 36%	Present Value at 37%	Present Value at 38%	Present Value at 39%	Present Value at 40%
1	0.735294	0.729927	0.724638	0.719424	0.714285
2	0.540657	0.532792	0.525099	0.517571	0.510203
3	0.397542	0.388900	0.380507	0.372353	0.364431
4	0.292310	0.283869	0.275730	0.267880	0.260308
5	0.214934	0.207204	0.199804	0.192719	0.185935
6	0.158040	0.151243	0.144786	0.138647	0.132810
7	0.116206	0.110396	0.104917	0.099746	0.094864
8	0.085445	0.080581	0.076027	0.071759	0.067760
9	0.062827	0.058818	0.055092	0.051625	0.048400
10	0.046196	0.042933	0.039921	0.037140	0.034571
11	0.033968	0.031338	0.028928	0.026720	0.024694
12	0.024976	0.022874	0.020963	0.019223	0.017638
13	0.018365	0.016696	0.015190	0.013829	0.012599
14	0.013503	0.012187	0.011007	0.009949	0.008999
15	0.009929	0.008895	0.007976	0.007157	0.006428
16	0.007300	0.006493	0.005780	0.005149	0.004591
17	0.005368	0.004739	0.004188	0.003704	0.003279
18	0.003947	0.003459	0.003035	0.002665	0.002342
19	0.002902	0.002525	0.002199	0.001917	0.001673
20	0.002134	0.001843	0.001593	0.001379	0.001195
21	0.001569	0.001345	0.001154	0.000992	0.000853
22	0.001153	0.000982	0.000836	0.000713	0.000609
23	0.000848	0.000716	0.000606	0.000513	0.000435
24	0.000623	0.000523	0.000439	0.000369	0.000311
25	0.000458	0.000381	0.000318	0.000265	0.000222

SOURCE: Values for $P = 1/(1+r)^n$ were computer-generated. As a result, the values for the first year need not correspond to the values for the first year in the table in Appendix B.

Appendix B:

Present Value of a Dollar Received Each Year for Twenty-five Years

$$P = \frac{1-(1+r)^{-n}}{r}$$

Year	Present Value at 1%	Present Value at 2%	Present Value at 3%	Present Value at 4%	Present Value at 5%
1	0.990057	0.980401	0.970872	0.961542	0.952377
2	1.97029	1.94153	1.91345	1.88609	1.85939
3	2.94089	2.88386	2.82858	2.77508	2.72323
4	3.90186	3.80771	3.71705	3.62990	3.54593
5	4.85330	4.71346	4.57965	4.45182	4.32946
6	5.79529	5.60140	5.41714	5.24213	5.07567
7	6.72798	6.47199	6.23024	6.00205	5.78635
8	7.65147	7.32546	7.01963	6.73274	6.46318
9	8.56576	8.16221	7.78605	7.43533	7.10780
10	9.47104	8.98259	8.53014	8.11089	7.72171
11	10.3673	9.78684	9.25255	8.76048	8.30639
12	11.2547	10.5753	9.95393	9.38508	8.86323
13	12.1334	11.3483	10.6348	9.98565	9.39355
14	13.0034	12.1062	11.2960	10.5631	9.89861
15	13.8647	12.8492	11.9378	11.1183	10.3796
16	14.7174	13.5776	12.5610	11.6523	10.8377
17	15.5618	14.2918	13.1660	12.1656	11.2740
18	16.3978	14.9920	13.7534	12.6592	11.6895
19	17.2256	15.6784	14.3237	13.1339	12.0852
20	18.0451	16.3514	14.8773	13.5903	12.4621
21	18.8565	17.0112	15.4149	14.0291	12.8211
22	19.6599	17.6580	15.9368	14.4510	13.1629
23	20.4553	18.2921	16.4435	14.8568	13.4885
24	21.2429	18.9139	16.9354	15.2469	13.7986
25	22.0226	19.5234	17.4130	15.6220	14.0939

Year	Present Value at 6%	Present Value at 7%	Present Value at 8%	Present Value at 9%	Present Value at 10%
1	0.943398	0.934574	0.925922	0.917429	0.909090
2	1.83339	1.80801	1.78326	1.75910	1.73554
3	2.67301	2.62430	2.57709	2.53129	2.48685
4	3.46510	3.38720	3.31212	3.23972	3.16987
5	4.21236	4.10018	3.99270	3.88965	3.79078
6	4.91733	4.76652	4.62288	4.48591	4.35526
7	5.58238	5.38928	5.20637	5.03295	4.86842
8	6.20979	5.97129	5.74664	5.53482	5.33492
9	6.80170	6.51522	6.24689	5.99523	5.75901
10	7.36010	7.02357	6.71007	6.41764	6.14456
11	7.88688	7.49864	7.13896	6.80518	6.49505
12	8.38384	7.94266	7.53607	7.16071	6.81369
13	8.85267	8.35763	7.90377	7.48689	7.10335
14	9.29497	8.74545	8.24424	7.78614	7.36668
15	9.71224	9.10789	8.55948	8.06068	7.60607
16	10.1058	9.44663	8.85137	8.31255	7.82370
17	10.4772	9.76320	9.12164	8.54362	8.02155
18	10.8276	10.0590	9.37189	8.75561	8.20141
19	11.1581	10.3355	9.60359	8.95010	8.36492
20	11.4699	10.5939	9.81814	9.12853	8.51356
21	11.7640	10.8354	10.0167	9.29224	8.64869
22	12.0415	11.0612	10.2007	9.44242	8.77153
23	12.3033	11.2721	10.3710	9.58020	8.88321
24	12.5503	11.4693	10.5287	9.70661	8.98474
25	12.7833	11.6535	10.6747	9.82257	9.07703

Year	Present Value at 11%	Present Value at 12%	Present Value at 13%	Present Value at 14%	Present Value at 15%
1	0.900897	0.892858	0.884955	0.877193	0.869563
2	1.71252	1.69005	1.66810	1.64665	1.62570
3	2.44371	2.40183	2.36115	2.32163	2.28322
4	3.10244	3.03735	2.97447	2.91371	2.85498
5	3.69589	3.60477	3.51723	3.43308	3.35214
6	4.23054	4.11141	3.99754	3.88866	3.78447
7	4.71218	4.56375	4.42260	4.28830	4.16041
8	5.14611	4.96763	4.79876	4.63886	4.48732
9	5.53704	5.32824	5.13164	4.94637	4.77158
10	5.88922	5.65022	5.42623	5.21611	5.01876
11	6.20651	5.93770	5.68693	5.45272	5.23370
12	6.49235	6.19437	5.91763	5.66028	5.42061
13	6.74986	6.42354	6.12180	5.84235	5.58314
14	6.98185	6.62816	6.30248	6.00207	5.72447
15	7.19085	6.81086	6.46237	6.14216	5.84736
16	7.37915	6.97398	6.60387	6.26505	5.95423
17	7.54878	7.11963	6.72909	6.37285	6.04716
18	7.70161	7.24966	6.83990	6.46741	6.12796
19	7.83928	7.36577	6.93796	6.55036	6.19822
20	7.96332	7.46944	7.02475	6.62313	6.25933
21	8.07506	7.56200	7.10154	6.68695	6.31245
22	8.17574	7.64464	7.16950	6.74294	6.35866
23	8.26642	7.71843	7.22965	6.79205	6.39883
24	8.34813	7.78431	7.28287	6.83513	6.43377
25	8.42174	7.84313	7.32998	6.87292	6.46414

Year	Present Value at 16%	Present Value at 17%	Present Value at 18%	Present Value at 19%	Present Value at 20%
1	0.862068	0.854700	0.847456	0.840335	0.833333
2	1.60523	1.58521	1.56564	1.54650	1.52777
3	2.24588	2.20958	2.17427	2.13991	2.10648
4	2.79818	2.74323	2.69006	2.63857	2.58873
5	3.27429	3.19934	3.12716	3.05763	2.99060
6	3.68473	3.58918	3.49760	3.40977	3.32550
7	4.03856	3.92237	3.81152	3.70569	3.60459
8	4.34359	4.20716	4.07756	3.95435	3.83715
9	4.60654	4.45056	4.30302	4.16332	4.03096
10	4.83322	4.65860	4.49408	4.33893	4.19247
11	5.02864	4.83641	4.65600	4.48649	4.32705
12	5.19710	4.98838	4.79322	4.61050	4.43921
13	5.34233	5.11827	4.90951	4.71470	4.53268
14	5.46753	5.22929	5.00806	4.80227	4.61056
15	5.57545	5.32418	5.09157	4.87586	4.67547
16	5.66849	5.40528	5.16235	4.93769	4.72955
17	5.74870	5.47460	5.22233	4.98966	4.77463
18	5.81784	5.53385	5.27316	5.03332	4.81219
19	5.87745	5.58448	5.31624	5.07002	4.84349
20	5.92884	5.62776	5.35274	5.10086	4.86958
21	5.97313	5.66475	5.38368	5.12677	4.89131
22	6.01132	5.69637	5.40990	5.14855	4.90943
23	6.04424	5.72340	5.43212	5.16684	4.92452
24	6.07262	5.74649	5.45095	5.18222	4.93710
25	6.09709	5.76623	5.46690	5.19514	4.94758

Year	Present Value at 21%	Present Value at 22%	Present Value at 23%	Present Value at 24%	Present Value at 25%
1	0.826445	0.819672	0.813007	0.806453	0.800000
2	1.50946	1.49153	1.47399	1.45681	1.44000
3	2.07393	2.04224	2.01137	1.98130	1.95200
4	2.54043	2.49363	2.44827	2.40427	2.36160
5	2.92598	2.86363	2.80347	2.74538	2.68928
6	3.24461	3.16691	3.09225	3.02047	2.95142
7	3.50794	3.41550	3.32703	3.24231	3.16113
8	3.72557	3.61926	3.51791	3.42122	3.32891
9	3.90543	3.78628	3.67310	3.56550	3.46313
10	4.05407	3.92318	3.79926	3.68185	3.57050
11	4.17692	4.03539	3.90184	3.77568	3.65640
12	4.27845	4.12737	3.98523	3.85136	3.72512
13	4.36235	4.20276	4.05304	3.91238	3.78009
14	4.43169	4.26456	4.10816	3.96160	3.82407
15	4.48900	4.31521	4.15297	4.00129	3.85926
16	4.53637	4.35673	4.18941	4.03330	3.88741
17	4.57551	4.39076	4.21903	4.05911	3.90992
18	4.60786	4.41866	4.24312	4.07993	3.92794
19	4.63459	4.44152	4.26270	4.09672	3.94235
20	4.65669	4.46026	4.27861	4.11025	3.95388
21	4.67495	4.47562	4.29155	4.12117	3.96310
22	4.69004	4.48822	4.30208	4.12998	3.97048
23	4.70251	4.49854	4.31063	4.13708	3.97638
24	4.71282	4.50700	4.31758	4.14280	3.98111
25	4.72134	4.51393	4.32324	4.14742	3.98488

Year	Present Value at 26%	Present Value at 27%	Present Value at 28%	Present Value at 29%	Present Value at 30%
1	0.793650	0.787403	0.781250	0.775194	0.769231
2	1.42353	1.40740	1.39160	1.37612	1.36094
3	1.92343	1.89559	1.86843	1.84195	1.81611
4	2.32018	2.27999	2.24096	2.20306	2.16624
5	2.63507	2.58267	2.53200	2.48299	2.43556
6	2.88497	2.82099	2.75937	2.69999	2.64274
7	3.08331	3.00866	2.93701	2.86821	2.80211
8	3.24072	3.15642	3.07579	2.99861	2.92470
9	3.36565	3.27277	3.18421	3.09970	3.01900
10	3.46480	3.36439	3.26891	3.17806	3.09153
11	3.54349	3.43652	3.33509	3.23880	3.14733
12	3.60594	3.49333	3.38679	3.28589	3.19025
13	3.65551	3.53805	3.42718	3.32240	3.22327
14	3.69485	3.57327	3.45873	3.35070	3.24867
15	3.72607	3.60100	3.48338	3.37263	3.26821
16	3.75085	3.62283	3.50264	3.38963	3.28324
17	3.77051	3.64002	3.51769	3.40282	3.29480
18	3.78612	3.65356	3.52944	3.41304	3.30369
19	3.79851	3.66422	3.53863	3.42096	3.31053
20	3.80834	3.67261	3.54580	3.42710	3.31579
21	3.81614	3.67922	3.55140	3.43186	3.31984
22	3.82233	3.68443	3.55579	3.43555	3.32295
23	3.82725	3.68852	3.55921	3.43841	3.32535
24	3.83115	3.69175	3.56188	3.44063	3.32719
25	3.83424	3.69429	3.56397	3.44234	3.32860

Year	Present Value at 31%	Present Value at 32%	Present Value at 33%	Present Value at 34%	Present Value at 35%
1	0.763359	0.757577	0.751880	0.746270	0.740742
2	1.34607	1.33149	1.31720	1.30318	1.28944
3	1.79089	1.76628	1.74225	1.71879	1.69587
4	2.13045	2.09567	2.06184	2.02895	1.99694
5	2.38966	2.34520	2.30214	2.26041	2.21996
6	2.58752	2.53424	2.48281	2.43314	2.38515
7	2.73857	2.67745	2.61865	2.56204	2.50752
8	2.85387	2.78595	2.72079	2.65824	2.59816
9	2.94188	2.86814	2.79759	2.73003	2.66530
10	3.00907	2.93041	2.85533	2.78360	2.71504
11	3.06036	2.97758	2.89874	2.82358	2.75188
12	3.09951	3.01332	2.93138	2.85342	2.77917
13	3.12939	3.04039	2.95593	2.87569	2.79938
14	3.15221	3.06090	2.97438	2.89230	2.81436
15	3.16962	3.07644	2.98825	2.90470	2.82545
16	3.18292	3.08821	2.99869	2.91396	2.83366
17	3.19307	3.09713	3.00653	2.92086	2.83975
18	3.20081	3.10389	3.01243	2.92601	2.84426
19	3.20673	3.10900	3.01686	2.92986	2.84760
20	3.21124	3.11288	3.02020	2.93273	2.85007
21	3.21469	3.11582	3.02270	2.93487	2.85190
22	3.21732	3.11804	3.02459	2.93647	2.85326
23	3.21932	3.11973	3.02601	2.93766	2.85427
24	3.22086	3.12101	3.02707	2.93856	2.85501
25	3.22203	3.12197	3.02787	2.93922	2.85556

Year	Present Value at 36%	Present Value at 37%	Present Value at 38%	Present Value at 39%	Present Value at 40%
1	0.735295	0.729928	0.724637	0.719425	0.714287
2	1.27595	1.26272	1.24973	1.23699	1.22449
3	1.67349	1.65162	1.63024	1.60935	1.58892
4	1.96580	1.93549	1.90597	1.87723	1.84922
5	2.18073	2.14269	2.10577	2.06995	2.03516
6	2.33877	2.29393	2.25056	2.20859	2.16797
7	2.45498	2.40433	2.35548	2.30834	2.26283
8	2.54042	2.48491	2.43150	2.38010	2.33059
9	2.60325	2.54373	2.48660	2.43172	2.37899
10	2.64945	2.58666	2.52652	2.46886	2.41357
11	2.68342	2.61800	2.55545	2.49558	2.43826
12	2.70839	2.64088	2.57641	2.51481	2.45590
13	2.72676	2.65757	2.59160	2.52864	2.46850
14	2.74026	2.66976	2.60261	2.53859	2.47750
15	2.75019	2.67866	2.61058	2.54575	2.48393
16	2.75749	2.68515	2.61636	2.55089	2.48852
17	2.76286	2.68989	2.62055	2.55460	2.49180
18	2.76681	2.69335	2.62359	2.55726	2.49414
19	2.76971	2.69587	2.62579	2.55918	2.49581
20	2.77185	2.69772	2.62738	2.56056	2.49701
21	2.77342	2.69906	2.62854	2.56155	2.49786
22	2.77457	2.70004	2.62937	2.56227	2.49847
23	2.77542	2.70076	2.62998	2.56278	2.49891
24	2.77604	2.70128	2.63042	2.56315	2.49922
25	2.77650	2.70167	2.63074	2.56342	2.49944

SOURCE: Values for $P = [1-(1+r)^{-n}]/r$ were computer-generated. As a result, the values for the first year need not correspond to the values for the first year in the table in Appendix A.

Appendix C:
Random Numbers

```
10 09 73 25 33    76 52 01 35 86    34 67 35 48 76    80 95 90 91 17    39 29 27 49 45
37 54 20 48 05    64 89 47 42 96    24 80 52 40 37    20 63 61 04 02    00 82 29 16 65
08 42 26 89 53    19 64 50 93 03    23 20 90 25 60    15 95 33 47 64    35 08 03 36 06
99 01 90 25 29    09 37 67 07 15    38 31 13 11 65    88 67 67 43 97    04 43 62 76 59
12 80 79 99 70    80 15 73 61 47    64 03 23 66 53    98 95 11 68 77    12 17 17 68 33

66 06 57 47 17    34 07 27 68 50    36 69 73 61 70    65 81 33 98 85    11 19 92 91 70
31 06 01 08 05    45 57 18 24 06    35 30 34 26 14    86 79 90 74 39    23 40 30 97 32
85 26 97 76 02    02 05 16 56 92    68 66 57 48 18    73 05 38 52 47    18 62 38 85 79
63 57 33 21 35    05 32 54 70 48    90 55 35 75 48    28 46 82 87 09    83 49 12 56 24
73 79 64 57 53    03 52 96 47 78    35 80 83 42 82    60 93 52 03 44    35 27 38 84 35

98 52 01 77 67    14 90 56 86 07    22 10 94 05 58    60 97 09 34 33    50 50 07 39 98
11 80 50 54 31    39 80 82 77 32    50 72 56 82 48    29 40 52 42 01    52 77 56 78 51
83 45 29 96 34    06 28 89 80 83    13 74 67 00 78    18 47 54 06 10    68 71 17 78 17
88 68 54 02 00    86 50 75 84 01    36 76 66 79 51    90 36 47 64 93    29 60 91 10 62
99 59 46 73 48    87 51 76 49 69    91 82 60 89 28    93 78 56 13 68    23 47 83 41 13

65 48 11 76 74    17 46 85 09 50    58 04 77 69 74    73 03 95 71 86    40 21 81 65 44
80 12 43 56 35    17 72 70 80 15    45 31 82 23 74    21 11 57 82 53    14 38 55 37 63
74 35 09 98 17    77 40 27 72 14    43 23 60 02 10    45 52 16 42 37    96 28 60 26 55
69 91 62 68 03    66 25 22 91 48    36 93 68 72 03    76 62 11 39 90    94 40 05 64 18
09 89 32 05 05    14 22 56 85 14    46 42 75 67 88    96 29 77 88 22    54 38 21 45 98

91 49 91 45 23    68 47 92 76 86    46 16 28 35 54    94 75 08 99 23    37 08 92 00 48
80 33 69 45 98    26 94 03 68 58    70 29 73 41 35    53 14 03 33 40    42 05 08 23 41
44 10 48 19 49    85 15 74 79 54    32 97 92 65 75    57 60 04 08 81    22 22 20 64 13
12 55 07 37 42    11 10 00 20 40    12 86 07 46 97    96 64 48 94 39    28 70 72 58 15
63 60 64 93 29    16 50 53 44 84    40 21 95 25 63    43 65 17 70 82    07 20 73 17 90

61 19 69 04 46    26 45 74 77 74    51 92 43 37 29    65 39 45 95 93    42 58 26 05 27
15 47 44 52 66    95 27 07 99 53    59 36 78 38 48    82 39 61 01 18    33 21 15 94 66
94 55 72 85 73    67 89 75 43 87    54 62 24 44 31    91 19 04 25 92    92 92 74 59 73
42 48 11 62 13    97 34 40 87 21    16 86 84 87 67    03 07 11 20 59    25 70 14 66 70
23 52 37 83 17    73 20 88 98 37    68 93 59 14 16    26 25 22 96 63    05 52 28 25 62

04 49 35 24 94    75 24 63 38 24    45 86 25 10 25    61 96 27 93 35    65 33 71 24 72
00 54 99 76 54    64 05 18 81 59    96 11 96 38 96    54 69 28 23 91    23 28 72 95 29
35 96 31 53 07    26 89 80 93 54    33 35 13 54 62    77 97 45 00 24    90 10 33 93 33
59 80 80 83 91    45 42 72 68 42    83 60 94 97 00    13 02 12 48 92    78 56 52 01 06
46 05 88 52 36    01 39 09 22 86    77 28 14 40 77    93 91 08 36 47    70 61 74 29 41

32 17 90 05 97    87 37 92 52 41    05 56 70 70 07    86 74 31 71 57    85 39 41 18 38
69 23 46 14 06    20 11 74 52 04    15 95 66 00 00    18 74 39 24 23    97 11 89 63 38
19 56 54 14 30    01 75 87 53 79    40 41 92 15 85    66 67 43 68 06    84 96 28 52 07
45 15 51 49 38    19 47 60 72 46    43 66 79 45 43    59 04 79 00 33    20 82 66 95 41
94 86 43 19 94    36 16 81 08 51    34 88 88 15 53    01 54 03 54 56    05 01 45 11 76

98 08 62 48 26    45 24 02 84 04    44 99 90 88 96    39 09 47 34 07    35 44 13 18 80
33 18 51 62 32    41 94 15 09 49    89 43 54 85 81    88 69 54 19 94    37 54 87 30 43
80 95 10 04 06    96 38 27 07 74    20 15 12 33 87    25 01 62 52 98    94 62 46 11 71
79 75 24 91 40    71 96 12 82 96    69 86 10 25 91    74 85 22 05 39    00 38 75 95 79
18 63 33 25 37    98 14 50 65 71    31 01 02 46 74    05 45 56 14 27    77 93 89 19 36

74 02 94 39 02    77 55 73 22 70    97 79 01 71 19    52 52 75 80 21    80 81 45 17 48
54 17 84 56 11    80 99 33 71 43    05 33 51 29 69    56 12 71 92 55    36 04 09 03 24
11 66 44 98 83    52 07 98 48 27    59 38 17 15 39    09 97 33 34 40    88 46 12 33 56
48 32 47 79 28    31 24 96 47 10    02 29 53 68 70    32 30 75 75 46    15 02 00 99 94
69 07 49 41 38    87 63 79 19 76    35 58 40 44 01    10 51 82 16 15    01 84 87 69 38
```

SOURCE: This table is reprinted by permission of the RAND Corporation. From Edwin B. Cox (ed.), *Basic Tables in Business and Economics* (New York: McGraw-Hill Book Company, 1967), p. 200.

Index